History of the U.S. Fertilizer Industry

Lewis B. Nelson

Retired Manager
National Fertilizer Development Center
Tennessee Valley Authority
Muscle Shoals, Alabama

Cover by Martha Lott

J. Harold Parker
Editor

Published by the
Tennessee Valley Authority
Muscle Shoals, Alabama 35660

Copyright © 1990
Tennessee Valley Authority

ISBN 0-87077-004-7

TVA is an equal opportunity employer, and is committed to ensuring that the benefits of programs receiving TVA financial assistance are available to all eligible persons regardless of race, color, national origin, handicap, or age.

FOREWORD

The quality of man's life is directly dependent upon that thin layer of the earth's crust we call "soil." The soil supports our food and fiber production, and thus the welfare of all. Man's management of the soil determines its productivity over the long term. Management has many facets, but few are more important than maintaining an adequate supply of plant nutrients for use by growing crops.

Many individuals and organizations are involved in the nutrient supply scenario. Researchers develop principles and identify specific needs. Educators, fertilizer dealers and others interpret and make recommendations. The industry converts raw materials into fertilizers and delivers them and related services to farmers. Growers then make final decisions on which inputs to use and in what quantities.

Few have a better grasp of the entire scenario than Dr. Lewis B. Nelson. He started out on an Idaho farm and spent the first half of his professional career in agronomic and soils research and administration. In the Agricultural Research Service of the U.S. Department of Agriculture, he focused on protecting and managing the soil resource. Then, he moved to TVA to manage a unique research program centered on the chemistry and engineering of fertilizers and transfer of the resulting technology to the private sector for the benefit of all consumers.

From this broad perspective, Dr. Nelson in the decade following his retirement has compiled an impressive description of the origins, growing pains, major transformations, maturing process, and key impacts of the fertilizer industry in the United States. It is a worthy reference for teachers and students of agriculture and for others who have special interests in the area, including those whose concerns focus heavily on resource use or environmental issues.

We are indebted to the author for his insights and documentations of a vital and dynamic industry.

J. Harold Parker
Editor

PREFACE

Volumes have been written about fertilizers. Information is available in thousands of scientific and trade journals, data surveys, farm magazines, reports of land-grant universities, symposia proceedings, patents, and books detailing various aspects of fertilizer chemistry, manufacture, and use. However, a general history of the American fertilizer industry has not existed.

My interest in fertilizer history was triggered by reading K. D. Jacob's account of more than 100 years of superphosphate-making, a book published jointly in 1964 by the U.S. Department of Agriculture and the Tennessee Valley Authority (TVA). My interest was further stimulated through my twenty years with the National Fertilizer Development Center (NFDC), operated by the TVA at Muscle Shoals, Alabama.

For three decades, I have lived and worked at the birthplace of TVA, which itself evolved out of a national controversy over public versus private use of the hydropower produced from what began as a wartime project. I often felt I became a part of that history. From my office window I could view buildings and facilities dating from the World War I era. Although focused primarily on fertilizer technology and agriculture, these facilities had to be ready for conversion to national defense priorities when the need arose. Finally, I daily crossed the historic but now submerged shoals that until well into the twentieth century was a major barrier to development of the Tennessee Valley region.

My associations at TVA with some of the world's best fertilizer technologists gave me a new awareness of what man can do and has done to make more effective and more economical use of nature's resources to provide for our daily food and fiber needs.

Today's and tomorrow's generations should be acutely aware that growing plants require a total of 16 chemical elements or plant nutrients, to complete their life cycle. Most of these elements are found in the soil, but the soil's supply can be depleted with year-after-year cropping. Also, some nutrients are lost by natural processes. Growers use chemical fertilizers to supplement those nutrients that exist in the soil in less than adequate amounts for optimum crop production.

Plant nutrients usually are grouped in three categories: primary, secondary, and micronutrients. The primary nutrients are nitrogen, phosphorus, and potassium. Secondary nutrients are calcium, magnesium, and sulfur. Micronutrients are boron, chlorine, copper, iron, manganese, molybdenum, and zinc; they are needed in much smaller amounts than other nutrients. Carbon, hydrogen, and oxygen round out the 16; it is not necessary, however, to supply them in fertilizer products.

Nitrogen surrounds us; it comprises 78 percent of the air we breathe. But major energy and technological resources are required to convert this nitrogen into compounds that crops can use. Phosphorus, potassium, and sulfur are mined from natural deposits and processed into fertilizers. Calcium and magnesium usually are supplied as liming agents. Micronutrients are mined; they also are retrieved as byproducts of various manufacturing operations.

As I approached retirement, I became increasingly interested in documenting the forces and institutional and corporate structures that have comprised and/or guided the U.S. fertilizer industry. In short, fertilizer history became a hobby. Thus, I undertook in 1980 the task of filling the fertilizer history void. I felt the job could be accomplished in three or four years; it took eight years of hard but absorbing work.

Such an investigation requires considerable research and access to special library facilities. I was aided immensely in my research by the ready access to the substantial collections of the NFDC library and by the helpfulness of its staff in accessing the resources of others. In addition, I am grateful for the constructive reviews of TVA's Dr. Gary Akin and Dr. Orvis Engelstad. I am particularly appreciative of the thorough and insightful review of Travis P. Hignett, whose fertilizer research predates TVA and who at TVA became a world authority on fertilizer technology. Finally, I appreciate TVA's support and publication of the book.

The book generally is organized by time and subject matter. The first chapter reviews major scientific developments of past centuries that laid the foundations for a fertilizer industry. The history of fertilizers in the United States then is examined in five general time periods:

- 1840-1870—The beginnings with a new spirit to improve agriculture and correct problems carried over from Colonial times.
- 1870-1920—Fertilizer use climbs, especially in the South. Major mineral discoveries. Ammonia synthesis achieved.
- 1920-1939—Hard times. Fertilizer use slumps. Farm overproduction. U.S. moves into potash and ammonia production.
- 1940-1960—Time of change and transition. Strong food demand. Revolutionary changes in making and marketing fertilizers–granulation, fluids, bulk blends. Crop yields double and triple.
- 1960-1980—Nutrient use continues upward, then levels and turns down. Nation again imports most of its potash. Resource use and environmental concerns get increased attention.

Finally, I would emphasize that my review basically ends with 1980. Change has continued in the industry. Changes in the 1980's, however, reflected business trends and heightened environmental sensitivity more than major developments in technology and use.

April 1990   Lewis B. Nelson

Contents

Foreword   v
Preface   vii

1. Antecedents of the U.S. Fertilizer Industry: 1000 B.C.–1860 A.D.   1
  1   The Greek Period
  2   The Romans and Practical Farming
  3   The Arabic Revival of Farming and Science
  4   The Middle Ages: 12th to 16th Century
  5   The Forerunners of Chemistry
  7   Precursors to Understanding Plant Growth
 10   The First Fertilizers
 12   The Coming of Chemical Fertilizers
 18   Field Experiments with Chemical Fertilizers
 20   Other Discoveries Affecting Soil Fertility

2. Beginning of Fertilizers in the United States: 1840's–1870's   23
 23   The Colonial Period—Agricultural Practices of the Indians • Early Colonists as Farmers • The Search for Adapted Crops • Colonial Farming Practices
 26   Agriculture and the New Nation—Worn-out Soils • The Search for Ways to Improve Agriculture • Agricultural Training Makes Its Appearance
 34   The Introduction of Commercial Fertilizers—Seabird Droppings; Leading Fertilizer for Nearly a Half Century • Superphosphate and Mixed Fertilizers • Fish Scrap as a Fertilizer • Slaughterhouse Wastes • Use of Bones • Wood Ashes • Sodium Nitrate • Ammonium Sulfate • Cottonseed Meal • Poudrette
 45   Fertilizer Industry Expansion—Fertilizers Move South • Fertilizer Frauds and S. W. Johnson • Fertilizer Inspection and Control Laws • Field Experiments with Commercial Fertilizers • Early Textbooks

3. Discovery and Development of Phosphate Rock and Sulfur Deposits: 1867–1920   55
 55   South Carolina Phosphate—Discovery • The First Miners • Early Land Rock Prospecting and Mining • Land Rock Processing • River Rock Mining and Processing • Production and Companies • Decline of the South Carolina Deposits

- 63 Florida Phosphates—Types of Florida Phosphate Deposits • The Phosphates of North Florida • The Phosphates of Central Florida • World War I and Exports Tumble
- 72 Tennessee Phosphates—Discovery • Initiation of Mining • White Rock Phosphate • Early Mining Methods for Blue Rock • Discovery of the Brown Rock Field • Mining Brown Rock • Marketing of Tennessee Rock • The Mining Companies
- 79 Western Phosphates—Discovery • Mining Becomes a Reality • Phosphate Surveys • Withdrawl of Phosphate Lands • Status of Mining: 1910-1920
- 84 Other Phosphate Deposits
- 85 Sulfur—Early Sulfur Imports • Pyrites Come of Age • Sulfur from Smelter Gases • Recovery of Elemental Sulfur • Gulf Coast Sulfur Deposits • Herman Frasch Enters the Scene • Expansion of Gulf Coast Mining • Frasch Goes International • Elemental Sulfur Takes Over

4. The Fertilizer Industry: 1870–1920   97

- 97 Fertilizer Consumption and Industry Expansion
- 99 Geographic Shifts in Use and Production
- 102 The Consolidated Fertilizer Companies
- 107 Fertilizer Materials by the Dozens—Inorganic Nitrogen Materials • Organic Nitrogen Materials • Phosphatic Materials • Potash Materials
- 123 Mixed Fertilizers—Commercial Mixed Fertilizers • Home Mixed Fertilizers
- 126 Sulfuric Acid—Processes for Manufacture
- 128 Fertilizer Control Laws—Formulation of the Laws • The AOAC and Improvement of Analytical Methods
- 130 The Agricultural Institutions—State Agricultural Colleges • State Agricultural Experiment Stations • The State Extension Services • The U.S. Department of Agriculture
- 136 Fertilizer Field Experiments—Planning the First Stations • "Soil Test" Experiments • Coping with Soil Variability • Practical Information Gained
- 140 Other Progress in Soil Fertility—Microorganisms and Soil Fertility • Fate of Added Plant Nutrients in Soils • Nutrient Composition of Crops • Total Chemical Analysis of Soils • Methods for Determining Soil Fertility • The Whitney-Cameron Soil Fertility Theories and Reverbations

145 Fertilizer Trade Associations—The Fertilizer Exchanges • Birth of the Fertilizer Associations • The Soil Improvement Committees • C. G. Hopkins Fights Committees
148 Fertilizer Journals

5. The Great Potash Search: 1910–1935   153
153 The German Potash Hassle
155 The Potash Search, 1910-1914—Activities of the U.S. Government Agencies • Activities of the Private Sector • Activities of the University of Texas
167 Potash Famine and Wartime Exploitation—Producers from Natural Brines: 1915-1920 • Other Operations
180 The Potash Search, Related Activities: 1915-1920—Activities of the Geological Survey • Activities of the Bureau of Soils
182 Post-War Collapse of the Industry—Imports from Europe Resumed • Decline of Domestic Potash
185 Renewal of the Potash Search—Discovery of Carlsbad, N.M. Deposits • Successful Mining and Production

6. Launching of the U.S. Fixed-Nitrogen Industry: 1890's–1930's   193
193 Sir William Crookes' Plea to World Scientists
194 Nitrogen-Fixation Processes—The Arc Process • The Cyanamide Process • The Cyanide Process • Ammonia Synthesis
202 Oxidation of Ammonia to Nitrogen Oxide
204 Initiating a Wartime Fixed-Nitrogen Program—Three Years of Delay and Debate • The Final Decision
208 The Government Nitrate Plants—U.S. Nitrate Plant No. 1 • Differences: Sheffield and Oppau Plants • U.S. Nitrate Plant No. 2 • U.S. Nitrate Plants 3 and 4 • The Bucher-Cyanide Plant
215 The Fixed-Nitrogen Research Laboratory—Ammonia Synthesis Research • Research on Cyanamide and New Fertilizers • Arc Process
218 The Muscle Shoals Controversy—The Problem of Nitrate Plants 1 and 2 • Henry Ford Becomes a Bidder • Enter the Power Companies and George Norris • The Tennessee Valley Authority Act
226 Domestic Production of Synthetic Ammonia, 1921-1932

7. Production of Phosphate Rock, Sulfur, and Sulfuric Acid: 1920–1980   233

235 Phosphate Rock Production by States—Phosphate Rock Reserves • Exports • Uses

238 Advances in Mining and Beneficiation—Phosphate Mining with Draglines • Beneficiation by Flotation

241 Florida Phosphate Rock—Hard Rock • Soft Rock • Florida Pebble • The Phosphate Rock Export Associations • The North Florida Field • Overcoming Environmental Problems

249 North Carolina Phosphate

250 Tennessee Phosphate Rock—Mining Brown Rock • Waning Brown Rock and Attempts at Beneficiation • Electric Phosphorus Furnaces Become Important • Companies Operating in the Brown Rock Field

255 Western Phosphate Rock—Status of Mining Prior to 1920 • Mining Activities: 1920-1950 • Mining Activities: 1950-1980

260 Sulfur and Sulfuric Acid Production—Advances in Sulfuric Acid Manufacture • Sources of Sulfur

8. Potash Production and Sources: 1935–1980   281

281 The Ever Changing U.S. Potash Situation

283 The Expanding Domestic Industry: 1935-1966—The Producing U.S. Companies • World War II Potash Situation • New Companies: 1950-1966 • Status of Mining and Beneficiation by the Mid-1960's

295 Emergence of the Canadian Potash Industry—Discovery and Exploration • Commercial Development • Saskatchewan Government Involvement

304 Canadian Potash in Perspective

304 Decline of U.S. Potash Production: 1966-1980—U.S. Becomes Leading Potash Importer • Declining Quality of Carlsbad Ores • Changing U.S. Potash Producers: 1966-1980 • Court Suits

314 Potash Particle Size Grades—Processes for Granulating Potash

317 Domestic Potash Outlook: 1980

9. Ammonia Synthesis: 1932–1980 — 323
- 324 The Formative Years: 1932-1950—Status of the Industry in 1932 • Wartime Expansion • Major Technological Advances Prior to 1950 • The 1950's, Beginning of a New Era
- 333 Big Single-Train, Centrifugal Compressor Plants
- 336 Reshaping Ammonia Storage and Transport—Storage Tanks • Jumbo Tank Cars • Barge Transport • Ocean Shipment • Long-Distance Ammonia Pipelines
- 339 The 1960's: New Companies, New Problems
- 342 Highs and Lows of the Uncertain '70's—Here One Year and Gone the Next

10. A New Generation of Primary Nutrient Fertilizer Materials: 1920–1980 — 351
- 351 Nitrogen Materials—Natural Organics • Sodium Nitrate • Ammonium Sulfate • Calcium Cyanamide • Improvements in Nitric Acid Production • Ammonium Nitrate • Anhydrous Ammonia • Urea • Nitrogen Solutions • Slow-Release Nitrogen Fertilizer Materials
- 371 Phosphatic Materials—Wet-Process Phosphoric Acid • Furnace-Grade Phosphoric Acid • Superphosphoric Acid and Polyphosphates • Superphosphates • Ammonium Phosphates • Phosphate Rock for Direct Application • Basic Slag • Calcium Metaphosphate • Fused Phosphate Materials • Nitric Phosphates
- 392 Potash Materials—Sources: 1920-1938 • Sources: 1939-1960 • Potassium Chloride • Potassium Magnesium Sulfate • Potassium Sulfate • Potassium Nitrate
- 399 Plant Environmental Problems

11. Secondary and Micronutrient Fertilizer Materials: 1850's–1980 — 407
- 407 Secondary Nutrients—Calcium • Magnesium • Sulfur
- 413 Discovery of the Essential Micronutrients— Identification of Field Deficiencies, 1920-1950 • The Changing Micronutrient Situation: 1955-1980
- 422 Micronutrient Sources and Materials—Inorganic Salts • Frits • Synthetic Chelates • Natural Organic Complexes

12. Mixed Fertilizers: 1920–1980   431
   432 Mixed Fertilizers: 1920-1950—Nutrient Content • Materials Used in Manufacture • Mixed Fertilizers Grades • Attempts to Introduce High Analyses Mixes • Types of Mix Plants in 1938 • Granulation of Mixed Fertilizers • Introduction of Pesticides into Fertilizers
   438 Mixed Fertilizers: 1950-1980—Primary Nutrient Contents • Changing Marketing Systems • Granular, Homogeneous, Mixed Fertilizers • The Pipe-Cross Reactor • Bulk Blending • Fluid Mixed Fertilizers • Suspension Fertilizers
   455 Status of Clear and Suspendion Mixtures
   456 Fertilizer Application Methods and Machinery—Methods and Machinery Prior to 1950 • Methods and Machinery: 1950-1980

13. Fertilizer Consumption, Role, And Impacts: 1920–1980   469
   469 Primary Nutrient Consumption: 1920-1980
   471 Nutrient Consumption by Regions: 1934-1980—The Northeastern States • South Atlantic • East and West North Central • East South Central • West South Central • Mountain • Pacific • Hawaii, Puerto Rico, Alaska
   480 Highest Fertilizer-Using States
   481 Crop Yield Breakthroughs
   486 International Assistance
   488 Changes in Farm Production and Efficiency
   491 Environmental Impacts

14. Fertilizer Trade Associations   495
   496 The National Fertilizer Association and the Southern Fertilizer Association: 1920-1925—National Fertilizer, Inc.
   498 American Plant Food Council
   498 National Plant Food Institute
   498 American Potash Institute and Successors 1935-80
   500 Agricultural Ammonia Institute
   502 The National Fertilizer Solutions Association
   506 The Fertilizer Institute
   507 The Sulphur Institute

Selected Readings   511

Index   513

Tables

2.1.	Comparative analysis of early fertilizers	39
4.1.	Trends in U.S. consumption of fertilizers	100
4.2.	Superphosphate and dry mixing plants	100
4.3.	Fertilizer consumption by regions and states	104
4.4.	U.S. consumption of natural organic nitrogen materials	113
4.5.	Nutrient contents of nitrogenous organics	114
4.6.	U.S. consumption of phosphatic materials	116
4.7.	U.S. consumption of potash containing materials	123
5.1.	U.S. potash imports and prices	168
5.2.	U.S. potash production by sources	169
7.1.	Production of phosphate rock	234
7.2.	U.S. phosphate rock reserves	236
7.3.	U.S. sulfur production, exports, imports and consumption	263
8.1.	Potash developments in Saskatchewan, Canada	300
8.2.	U.S. potash producers and production capacities	308
9.1.	Growth of U.S. synthetic ammonia industry	324
9.2.	Government-owned synthetic ammonia plants constructed during World War II	326
9.3.	Use of 600–1,500-ton-per-day centrifugal compressor ammonia plants in U.S.	335
9.4.	Annual capacities of five leading ammonia producers	341
9.5.	Leading ammonia producing states	341
11.1.	Micronutrients sold for fertilizers in U.S.	420
11.2.	Number of firms marketing micronutrients	422
11.3.	Micronutrient sources and their nutrient contents	424
12.1.	Consumption and nutrient content of mixed fertilizers	433
12.2.	Seven mixed fertilizer grades used in largest tonnages	434
12.3.	Average grades of mixed fertilizers consumed in U.S.	436
12.4.	Consumption of fertilizers by classes	440
12.5.	Primary nutrient content of mixed fertilizers	440
12.6.	Growth in fluid-mix (liquid and suspension) industry	455
13.1.	Consumption of primary nutrients for selected years	470
13.2.	Primary nutrient consumption by regions	474
13.3.	Share of U.S. nutrients used by seven leading states	481
13.4.	Changes in farm population and number of farms	489

Figures

8.1.	U.S. potash production, imports, exports and consumption	282
9.1.	Ammonia pipeline system of mid-1970's	338
9.2.	Nitrogen fertilizer trade	344
10.1.	Production of phosphate fertilizer materials	372
13.1.	Major geographic subdivisions of the United States	472

Plus more than 100 unnumbered photographs and other graphics.

1

Antecedents of the U.S. Fertilizer Industry 1000 B.C.–1860 A.D.

The roots of the U.S. fertilizer industry trace to the earliest agriculture as man struggled to improve quality of life by increasing food production. He learned not only to cultivate different crops and to use irrigation in dry regions, but also to increase the soil's productivity through application of manures, composts, ashes, and other amendments. The latter practices laid the groundwork for the future discovery and use of chemical fertilizers.

Agriculture appears to have started in Mesopotamia (now Iraq) in the river basins of the Euphrates and the Tigris, and in the Nile Valley (7, 21). Independent developments, however, may have occurred in the Orient and elsewhere. By Graeco-Roman times, the art of farming had reached a comparatively high state. Most important to the future, the Greeks and Romans documented their observations and thinking, both good and bad. Much of this survived to influence agricultural practices and philosophies well into the eighteenth century A.D. (6, 23).

The Greek Period

From about 1000 B.C. until shortly before the birth of Rome in 234 B.C., the Greeks laid the foundations of literature, art, philosophy and science, including geometry, astronomy, mathematics, medicine, zoology, and botany, for the western world. Their writings include many references to farming and the use of various soil amendments, along with ideas on plant nutrition and soils. Plato (428-348 B.C.), Aristotle (384-322 B.C.), Theophrastus (372-287 B.C.), and others dealt with farming, although they were not explicit as to the actual practices of the time. They tried to explain plant nutrition and natural phenomena through reasoning and speculation. Considerable nonsense resulted, such as notions that plants have souls, change their species, and absorb earth through their roots. Explaining plant nutrition, of course, was clearly impossible without an adequate plant science base backed up by chemistry, both of which did not start to develop until late in the eighteenth century (6, 17, 21, 23).

Many Greek theories and ideas, plausible or not, became established and led to wasted effort for many centuries. Aristotle, for example, believed that organic matter was the source of all nourishment for plants. His organic matter theory, much later subscribed to in the humus hypothesis, prejudiced thinking until disproved by Liebig in 1840. Empedocles (490-430 B.C.) thought that everything, organic and inorganic, was composed of four elements–earth, air, fire, and water. Plato adopted the idea, but with a few modifications. The four-element theory was widely accepted until finally laid to rest by Robert Boyle in 1661 (6, 17).

Theophrastus, the last of the Greek philosophers, was interested in practical farming. He recommended abundant manuring on poor lands and the use of bedding in stalls to absorb urine and further stretch manures. He classified various manures as to richness, recognized that saltpeter (potassium nitrate) was of value to plants, recommended the use of sewage from Athens on nearby truck gardens and olive groves, and made references to the relation between soils and plants (6, 19).

The Romans and Practical Farming

The Romans, including Cato the Censor (234-140 B.C.), Varro (116-27 B.C.), Pliny the Elder (23-79 A.D.), Virgil (70-19 B.C.), Columella (1st century A.D.), and Palladius, were more practical than the Greeks in their approach to agriculture, and this was reflected in their writings. They were not inclined to philosophize, although they were aware of and apparently accepted many of the Greek theories. It also appears likely that practices used by Roman farmers were similar to many of those used by Greek farmers (6, 19).

Cato, Columella, and Palladius authored textbooks on Roman farming, and Pliny's *Natural History* was widely reproduced and used through the Middle Ages. Besides dealing with crops and their cultivation, these writers recommended ways to increase soil productivity. The value of manures and composts was strongly emphasized. They urged that pits be dug near farm buildings and that all animal, fowl, and human excreta be thrown in along with leaves, vegetable refuse, and other wastes. Soil could be added and the mass stirred from time to time. Pigeon manure was highly prized, and was to be sown separately on the land like seed and at about the same rate. Wastes from olive presses and dregs from wine making were to be returned to the land, preferably to olive orchards and vineyards. Some of the writers recommended that stubble, weeds, prunings, and brush be burned in place to improve the soil. Lime from lime kilns was considered excellent for olive groves, and the spreading of ashes or lime on lowland soils was recommended. The value of marl was known, partly from observations made by Pliny and Varro while in Gaul. Pliny also mentioned the usefulness of saltpeter to crops. Legumes were known to increase soil fertility, and several writers recommended the plowing under of green manures, especially lupines and vetch (6, 15, 17, 19).

The Romans gave considerable thought to classifying soils according to suitability for crop production. Black soils were generally rated more productive than light-colored, although Columella disagreed. Soil structure was given attention and those with a crumb structure, as found under meadows, were considered the best. A "test" was devised for soil density. It involved digging a hole, placing the soil back in the hole and stamping it down; if it more than filled the hole, the soil was good. Good plowing was considered the essence of good farming; on sloping lands, the furrow was to be drawn across the slope to prevent erosion and reduce the strain on oxen and plowmen. Heavy and poorly drained soils were to be plowed later in the season after they had dried out (6,15).

The decline of the Roman Empire halted Roman contributions to agriculture. As Western Europe headed into the six centuries of the Dark Ages scholars and leaders were interested largely in religious and theological matters, war, and, later, the Crusades. Economic organization was destroyed and only slowly rebuilt. Farming persisted through serfdom on large feudal land holdings and on the many holdings that were in the hands of the Church. Some copies of Graeco-Roman treatises survived in monastic establishments, the most widely read apparently being Pliny's *Natural History*. The extent of use of practices described in these documents is not known except that certain of the monasteries apparently adopted some for use on their lands (5, 6, 19).

The Arabic Revival of Farming and Science

The situation was almost the reverse in the East where the rise of Islamic civilization and its Arabic followers occurred at about the time that Rome crumbled. Here, interest in scholarship, education, literature, and the sciences thrived. The caliphs recognized the backwardness of the Arabs in science and philosophy and sought information, especially that of the Greeks. They searched for and collected manuscripts from many sources, particularly from Syria, where a wealth of Greek culture persisted. A school of translation was set up, and massive translations were made into Arabic, which became the language of the scholastic world until Latin began to dominate in the twelfth century. It was due to these translations that much of the Greek knowledge survived. They also served as a base from which the Moslems developed many of their own contributions that continued into the twelfth century (6,19).

Unfortunately, even in this favorable environment, apparently little progress was made in advancing the basic knowledge of soil improvement and plant nutrition. Only one Islamic agricultural publication is known to survive, although many others were written. This publication, *The Book of Agriculture*, was written by a Spanish Moor, Ibn al Awam (or Ibn-alawam). It had been translated into French. Recently it was translated into English from the original twelfth century Arabic for the U.S. Department of Agriculture and the National Science Foundation. Inasmuch as Ibn al Awam reviewed in detail a number of other Arabic treatises on agriculture, the book appears to reflect the thinking and farm practices that were prevalent during the Islamic period. These are very similar to those of the Greeks and the Romans. Little new appears to have been added on soil improvement, although considerable effort was devoted to adapting and refining the older practices and ideas to specific crops and conditions. Ibn al Awam dealt in detail with different manures, their relative value, and their application and use on specific crops. Like the Romans, he favored the questionable practice of composting manures up to four years before application (6, 10).

The Middle Ages: 12th to the 16th Century

Political and economic order was being restored in Europe by the eleventh and twelfth centuries. Serfdom on farms slowly gave way to a predominately peasant proprietorship. Interest gradually revived in the classical learning of the past, which was to influence European agriculture throughout the Middle Ages. Arabic translations, primarily of Greek classics, were translated into Latin and remained important until original documents emerged and were translated. As indicated earlier, Pliny's *Natural History* was widely used. Pietro de Crescenzi of Italy in 1304 wrote his *Opus ruralium commodorum*. This not only influenced agriculture in Italy, but when variously translated was used throughout much of Europe (16). It had the distinction of being the first agricultural book to be printed following the invention of the printing press in the fifteenth century. Crescenzi leaned heavily on the early Roman writers, on personal observations of Italian agriculture, and upon advice from the Dominican monastery at Bologna which also engaged in farming (6, 16, 19, 23).

After Crescenzi, nothing material was added to agricultural knowledge for many years, although numerous new books on farming appeared in the late seventeenth and early eighteenth centuries. As a result, soil fertility and soil amendment practices remained much as those of the Greeks and the Romans. The mainstays were animal manures; composts; sewage and other waste products; seasand, seaweed, and fish along coastal areas; bones; and liming materials, particularly marl. Manure applications often were scanty because of low livestock populations. Crop yields remained low; wheat, for example, sown at 2 to 2-1/2 bushels per acre returned seed-yield ratios of 1:3 or slightly higher, with 1:6 occurring only under the most favorable

The discovery of phosphorus by Brandt of Germany was an early contribution to systematic chemistry from the era of the alchemists. *(Fisher Scientific Company)*

conditions. There still were no scientific guidelines that could be applied to farms, although a few farmers late in the period started evaluating various materials in field trials (6).

The Forerunners of Chemistry

As had been the case in the past, lack of knowledge in two areas was holding back real progress in development of fertilizers; these were chemistry and how plants grow.

The development of chemistry followed a slow and tortuous path (4). Nevertheless, by the start of the nineteenth century, the groundwork had been laid for chemistry to be recognized as a distinct science, and enough knowledge gained to permit some application in agriculture. The earliest chemical discoveries made by the ancients related largely to metallurgy and the medical arts. Gold, silver, copper, tin, iron, and lead, and some of the simpler alloys and metallic salts were known in Graeco-Roman times. From then until well into the sixteenth century, chemistry was dominated by the alchemists, whose main object was to transmute lower value base metals, particularly lead, into gold. Many, however, changed direction under the influence of Phillippus Theophrastus Paracelsus (1490-1541), a German physician, who told the alchemists that their main purpose was not to make gold, but to devise new medicines (4,6).

The alchemists were not without accomplishments which were to prove of some importance to the future fertilizer industry. Potash (crude potassium carbonate) had long been known, but was used primarily in glassmaking and soaps. It was obtained by leaching wood ashes in wooden tubs and evaporating the resulting solution to dryness in iron pots, hence the name "potash." Saltpeter, of course, was known but not its composition. Johann Glauber (1604-1670), working with a number of salts, discovered ammonium sulfate, which eventually became a major fertilizer. Hennig Brand of Germany discovered phosphorus in 1669 by preparing it in elemental form from urine (4, 19).

Aristotle's theory of four elements–earth, air, fire, and water–which chemists accepted for 2000 years, was demolished by Robert Boyle in 1661 with publication of his famous book, *The Sceptical Chymist*. This should have cleared the way for progressive thinking, but the chemists became involved almost immediately with the "phlogiston" theory. This theory, which seemed logical at the time, was accepted too dogmatically for too long and proved to be a stumbling block for another century. In this theory, developed largely by John Joachim Becher (1625-1682) of Germany, phlogiston was not fire, but the material of fire which left a body that was burning or rusting. When a metal was converted to its calx, or oxide, it lost phlogiston, and when it was converted to the metal, it regained phlogiston. Joseph Priestley, the discoverer of oxygen, surprisingly remained its staunch defender. The theory was gradually disproved, with Lavoisier dealing the death blow when he arrived at the correct interpretation of chemical oxidation about 1775 (4).

Rapidly increasing productivity of chemistry in the latter part of the eighteenth century is indicated by the numbers of elements and compounds discovered. Daniel Rutherford of England is credited with discovering nitrogen in the early 1770's, although he had some close contenders. Priestley, of England, discovered oxygen in 1774 and described its properties. He called it dephlogisted air, later to be given the name of oxygen by Lavoisier. Henry Cavendish, also of England, discovered hydrogen in 1776; J. G. Gahn of Sweden discovered manganese in 1774; and molybdenum was discovered by Carl Scheele, also of Sweden, in 1782. Sulfur, known since prehistoric times, was first classified as an element by Lavoisier in 1777.

Although ammonia, easily recognized by its smell, and the salt sal ammoniac (ammonium chloride) had long been known, Priestley in 1774 first prepared ammonia gas by heating sal ammoniac with lime. In 1777, Scheele showed that ammonia gas contained nitrogen; in 1785, C. L.

Exhibit of equipment used by Lavoisier. He discovered sulfur and disproved earlier theories about oxygen. *(Fisher Scientific Company)*

Berthollet ascertained its exact composition. Glauber in the seventeenth century accidentally discovered a process for making sulfuric acid by producing sulfur trioxide and dissolving it in water. Nitric acid, known earlier, was first made chemically by Glauber from reacting nitre with sulfuric acid. By 1771, it was being produced commercially. In 1778, I. Milner of England discovered that nitric acid could be made by passing ammonia over heated manganese dioxide.

Urea was identified in 1773 when it was first crystallized from urine. In 1775, Scheele, while looking for an easier method for preparing elemental phosphorus, found that bones contained large amounts of calcium phosphate. Cavendish in 1784 made the far-reaching discovery that water was composed of two volumes of hydrogen and one of oxygen. Also during this period analytical methods were improved slowly (4, 6).

Precursors to Understanding Plant Growth

Progress in understanding plant processes by using experimental procedures began slowly and then accelerated at about the time that chemistry was gaining new life. Francis Bacon (1561-1624) of England tried to back up some of his numerous theories on plant growth by observing simple experiments, but nothing much came of them (20). The first true experiment with a living plant appears to have been conducted by Jan Baptiste van Helmont (1577-1644), a Flemish physician and chemist, in his often-quoted "willow" experiment (6, 19, 23). Although he drew the wrong conclusion, the directness, simplicity, and use of quantitative measurement in the experiment played an important role in launching the experimental approach of the future.

> I took an earthen vessel in which I put 200 lb. of soil dried in an oven, then I moistened it with rain water and pressed hard into it a shoot of willow weighing 5 lb. After exactly five years the tree that had grown up weighed 169 lb. and about 3 oz. But the tree had never received anything but rain water or distilled water to moisten the soil (when this was necessary) and the vessel remained full of soil which was still tightly packed; lest dust from outside should have got into the soil it was covered with a sheet of iron coated with tin but perforated with many holes. I did not take the weight of the leaves that fell in the autumn. In the end I dried the soil once more and got the same 200 lb. that I started with, less about 2 oz. Therefore the 164 lb. of wood, bark and root arose from the water alone (20, pp. 18-19).

Van Helmont's conclusion that the plant is made out of water was wrong, because he didn't know that carbon dioxide from the air supplied carbon to the plant or that the soil provided essential mineral elements to the plant besides serving as a storage for water.

Robert Boyle (1627-1691) in England repeated van Helmont's experiments using a squash, with the same results. He concluded that water was transmuted to plant substances and insisted that salts from the soil served no useful purpose. Boyle did, however, end the long-held fallacy that earth, air, fire and water were the basic components of all substances (6, 20, 23).

Johann Glauber (1604-1670), the German chemist, working with various salts, also made some contributions in the plant nutrition field. He collected saltpeter (potassium nitrate) from the soil under pens of cattle, established that it came from the droppings, and argued that it must have originated from the plants the animals ate. He applied the saltpeter to plants and observed large increases in growth. He concluded that saltpeter was essential to plant growth, and he was not far wrong in that he was dealing with two of the major nutrient elements (6,23).

John Woodward (1665-1728) of England made another important advance when he conclusively disproved the idea that water alone was the essential plant food. In a classical experiment, Woodward grew sprigs of mint in distilled water and in other waters containing varying amounts of impurities, including water to which some soil had been added. He determined the gain in weight of the sprigs, the weight of the water transpired by the plant into the atmosphere, and the water transpired per unit of gain. The experiment showed that most of the water taken up by the plant was transpired, and that the plant grew in proportion to the amount of matter contained in the water. Woodward inferred that earth, not water, was the matter that constituted vegetation, which, of course, was not entirely correct (20).

Jethro Tull (1674-1741), an Oxford-educated Englishman, who made commendable improvements in farm machinery, nevertheless was not

Joseph Priestly's work with gases helped lay the foundation for an understanding of photosynthesis. *(Fisher Scientific Company)*

caught up in the new spirit of experimentation. He held, as had some Greeks, that plant roots forced fine soil particles into their "lacteal mouths." The smaller the soil particle, the easier it was to absorb, and fine division of soil particles could be attained by repeated hoeing. He believed that the value of manure and saltpeter was due to their ability to help break up the soil particles. Manure, however, was not to be applied where vegetables were grown because it spoiled their taste. After roots took up the soil particles, the stalks and leaves received them and discharged into the atmosphere those parts not needed by the plant. Tull's works were widely read in England and a version reached the Continent (6, 20).

The first real breakthrough in understanding the physiology of plants came through work with gases, which led to an understanding of photosynthesis. It was generally known that some gaseous elements existed, but they were not identified because air was considered an element itself. For example, it was known that the so-called "fixed air" (carbon dioxide) would extinguish flame and was destructive to animal life, and that "pure phlogiston in isolation" (hydrogen) was flammable. Joseph Priestley was the first to make a definite contribution by relating gas to plants. He made his first experiments in 1767 on the fixed air found in the fermenting vats of a brewery. Later he found that mint placed in a vessel poisoned by breathing of mice restored the air so that a candle would burn again, even though the flame had been extinguished before. Priestley was interested solely in the effect of plants on the air and not in the reciprocal influence of air upon the plants. Even though he discovered oxygen, he failed to tie it to plants, possibly because of his attachment to the phlogiston theory (6,19). (Priestley, a radical on religion and politics, fled to Pennsylvania to escape mobs. Here he spent the rest of his life defending the phlogiston theory.)

Carl Scheele (1742-1786) of Sweden conducted a number of experiments on the respiration of plants and further verified Priestley's work. However, it was left to Jan Ingen-housz (1730-1799), a Dutch physician, to make the next advance. He established that plants could not take up carbon dioxide or release oxygen except when exposed to sunlight. He also found that oxygen would not be released except when carbon dioxide was available. He concluded that atmospheric air was essential for plant growth (6).

Theodore de Saussure (1767-1845), a native of Geneva, made major strides in developing an understanding of the nutrition of plants. He built upon the knowledge gained by others, employed quantitative experimentation, and drew logical conclusions from his data. He showed that hydrogen and oxygen from water and carbon dioxide from the air contributed to the dry matter of plants, and that these were more important sources than humus. De Saussure also showed that plants must take up nitrates and mineral matter from the soil for normal nutrition, and that whatever was absorbed by the roots was in dilute solution. He concluded that while the salts found in plants were affected by selective absorption, plants absorbed some that were of no use to them or were actually harmful. De Saussure published his findings in 1804, but most investigators of the day either did not know of or ignored his findings (19).

Sir Humphrey Davy popularized chemistry to the progress of agriculture in a series of lectures given before the English Board of Agriculture between 1802 and 1812. His lectures were published in 1813 in his book, *Elements of Agricultural Chemistry*. His definition of agricultural chemistry, upon which he directed his lectures, included the arrangement of matter connected with the growth and nourishment of plants. Davy consulted more than 100 works and gave order and coherence to the body of knowledge, including many theories that would be disproved later. He believed that most of the carbon in plants was taken up by the roots, and he even went so far as to suggest oil as a fertilizer because of its carbon content. By 1839, his book had been through six English and two American editions and had been translated into French, German, and Italian. It remained a standard text for 50 years. Davy, using electrolysis, also discovered the elements potassium, sodium, calcium, and chlorine in rapid succession between 1807 and 1810. In addition, he was a codiscoverer of boron in 1808 (8, 20).

The First Fertilizers

The demand for bones grew rapidly in England, starting about the beginning of the nineteenth century. The value of bone was now being correctly attributed to its calcium phosphate content rather than to organic matter as believed earlier. Farmers also were able to buy an improved bone product. Earlier, bones had been broken up on the farm by axes and hammers. This resulted in large pieces which only slowly became effective when applied to the land. By 1800, this practice had been displaced by use of power mills in the hands of commercial establishments, which produced a finer, higher quality material. Application rates ranged up to a ton or more per acre, but this was expected to last for a number of years. Domestic sources of bone soon became inadequate as demand increased. By 1815, bones began to be imported from the Continent in rapidly increasing quantities until a maximum of about 30,000 tons per year was reached (8,11). This brought an outburst from Liebig:

> England is robbing all other countries of their fertility. Already in her eagerness for bones, she has turned up the battlefields of Leipsic, and Waterloo, and of Crimea; already from the catacombs of Sicily she has carried away skeletons of many successive generations. Annually she removes from the shores of other countries to her own the manurial equivalent of three million and a half of men.... Like a vampire she hangs from the neck of Europe... (8, p. 108).

With the rising demand for bone phosphate, searches also were initiated for apatites and phosphorites in which phosphorus had been identified by earlier investigators.

Guano or bird excrement which had accumulated in large deposits on low-rainfall islands off the coast of Peru and which the Incas may have used as early as the twelfth century, became an important fertilizer material in the first half of the nineteenth century. European interest in guano arose when Alexander von Humboldt, a German naturalist, brought back samples from a visit in Peru in 1804 and urged its importation. Analyses of these samples, which were the first to be made on guano, showed high contents of nitrogen and phosphate. By the 1840's, experiments had been conducted in England with favorable results, and guano was introduced in both England and the United States. Although its use increased rapidly, it was years before it became an important product on the Continent. Searches for guano extended, and deposits were found and mined in many parts of the world. Hundreds of vessels were eventually involved in its transport. Some guanos contained up to 16 percent each of N and P_2O_5 but quality varied greatly. Also, inasmuch as guano brought high prices, all sorts of ways were found to adulterate the material, and considerable analyses, both physical and chemical, were conducted to prevent fraud. Widespread use of guano, could not be sustained since deposits were soon depleted. Although there are no overall statistics on how much guano was used and when, imports peaked in 1860 in the United States at about 58,000 tons annually (8, 11).

Of great importance to the future fertilizer industry was the discovery and development of natural deposits of nitrate of soda in what is now northern Chile (2, 3, 9). The importance of these deposits as a fertilizer material was first recognized and promoted in 1809 by Taddeo Haenke, a German living in Bolivia. Enormous deposits occur in the provinces of Tarapaca' and Antofagasta in the center of the Atacama Desert, which lies between the slopes and foothills of the Andes and the coastal plains bordering the Pacific Ocean at elevations of 3,000 to 7,000 feet. These deposits, which proved to be the only commercially mineable natural deposits in the world, would eventually supply a major share of the fertilizer nitrogen for Europe and the United States.

Some efforts to develop the deposits apparently were made in 1813 by the Spaniards, who at that time still controlled this part of South America. Production and export began on a continuing basis in 1830 when 860 tons was shipped by Peru from the Tarapaca' province. Exports climbed to 10,000 tons in 1840; 22,000 in 1850; and 100,000 in 1870. Expansion occurred rapidly after 1880 when Chile, as a result of the War of the Pacific, acquired the Antofagasta province from Bolivia and the Tarapaca' province from Peru. Exports exceeded 2 million tons annually from 1910 through 1930 (2,3,9).

The deposits containing the nitrate usually occur 3 to 10 feet below the surface in a caliche layer varying in thickness from a few inches to about 10 feet in a cemented matrix of sand and gravel with nitrates, sodium chloride, and other soluble salts. The sodium nitrate content of the caliche ranges up to about 70 percent, but usually falls within a range of 12 to 25 percent. Earliest mining involved selecting materials containing not less than 50 percent. The caliche was broken up and boiled in water in pans over an open fire. The boiling liquid was ladled into settling tanks where insolubles and chlorides were deposited. It was then ladled into other pans where the sodium nitrate crystallized. In 1856, steam replaced open fires and other process improvements followed. In the Shanks Process, crushed ore was progressively extracted in a series of tanks with boiling nitrate liquor until saturated, after which the solids were removed (2, 3, 9).

Following the arrival of nitrate of soda in Europe in the 1830's, numerous experiments were made which proved the value of the product as a fertilizer material. The first shipment to England was 100 tons in 1831; about 2,000 tons were sold in 1839. The early material contained numerous impurities, and its nitrogen content declined in later years (9).

The Coming of Chemical Fertilizers

A third important fertilizer material made its appearance along with guano and nitrate of soda. This was sulfate of ammonia, a by-product of the destructive distillation of coal to make coal gas for use in illumination. The first practical coal gas plant apparently was an experimental facility built in 1795 to illuminate an English factory.

Essentially the apparatus consisted of a retort containing coal, which was heated out of contact with air by a fire on a grate below. To make the product usable, the gas had to be cleansed of unwanted impurities, including carbon oxides, various hydrocarbons, and ammonia; ammonia was produced at the rate of 20 to 30 pounds of ammonium sulfate equivalent per ton of coal decomposed. The ammonia was recovered initially by cooling the gas and bubbling it through water to produce an ammonia liquor. This was soon found to have some value as a fertilizer. Also, experiments were made on bubbling the gas through dilute sulfuric acid to produce ammonium sulfate and through hydrochloric acid to produce ammonium chloride. Both products were recovered in solid form by crystallization. In 1812, the Gas Light and Coke Company was incorporated in London to illuminate the city and in 1815 started producing sulfate of ammonia. Although the initial product was unsatisfactory, respectable amounts were being produced and farmers were realizing its value by the 1830's. First publication of the results of field experiments with the product was in Scotland in 1841, and more extensive experiments followed. Lawes conducted field experiments with both sulfate of ammonia and nitrate of soda in 1841 at Rothamsted, England, obtaining excellent crop responses to both. Later, improvements were made worldwide in the coal gas process, including the recovery of sulfate of ammonia. With expanded use of coal gas, sulfate of ammonia gained wide usage, at times rivaling nitrate of soda in importance. By-product ammonium sulfate from various sources has survived. Synthetic ammonium sulfate was produced and marketed in the United States (18, 22).

The start of the superphosphate industry resulted from frequent observations that bones were not equally effective in increasing crop yields on all soils, and from the need to find a source of phosphate more plentiful than the limited bone supply. Acidulation of bones with an acid, usually sulfuric, started sometime in the early 1800's as a means for making phosphate in bones more soluble. Indications are that James Murray of Ireland, a medical doctor and physician, may have acidulated bones prior to 1810, but no records are available to substantiate this. Murray did, however, refer to acidulating mineral phosphates and used the term "superphosphate of lime" in a series of lectures before the Royal Exchange in 1835 at Dublin. In 1841, he started selling a liquid fertilizer that was made by pouring sulfuric acid over crushed bones. Also, he was granted patents in Ireland, England, and Scotland in 1842 covering acidulation of bones and apatite. Heinrich Köhler, in 1831, acidulated bones with sulfuric acid in his bone-charcoal factory near Pilsen, Bohemia, and obtained an Austrian patent the same year. Gotthold Escher of Brünn, Moravia, suggested moistening bones with acid in 1835 (12).

Justus von Liebig in his 1840 and subsequent editions of *Organic Chemistry in Its Application to Agriculture and Physiology* recommended:

Sir John Lawes in 1836 began experiments on his Rothamsted estate, which an ancestor had acquired in 1611, on the manuring of agricultural plants. A pioneer of the fertilizer industry, he was granted a patent in 1842 for the manufacture of phosphate fertilizers. Shown below is Lawes' advertisement in the *Gardener's Chronicle*. (Rothamsted Experiment Station)

Gardener's Chronicle July 1st, 1843

GUANO ON SALE, as Imported, of first quality, and in any quantity, direct from the bonded stores, either in Liverpool or London. Also, NITRATE of SODA. Apply to H. ROUNTHWAITE & Co., Merchants, 6 Cable-street, Liverpool.

J. B. LAWES'S PATENT MANURES, composed of Super Phosphate of Lime, Phosphate of Ammonia, Silicate of Potass, &c., are now for sale at his Factory, Deptford-creek, London, price 4s. 6d. per bushel. These substances can be had separately; the Super Phosphate of Lime alone is recommended for fixing the Ammonia of Dung-heaps, Cesspools, Gas Liquor, &c. Price 4s. 6d. per bushel.

M'Intosh's New Edition of the
PRACTICAL GARDENER, in ONE VOLUME, containing the latest and most approved modes of Management of KITCHEN, FRUIT, and FLOWER-GARDENS, GREEN-HOUSE, HOTHOUSE, CONSERVATORY, &c.; comprising numerous explana-

... Pour over the bones, in a state of fine powder, half their weight of sulfuric acid diluted with three or four parts of water, and after they have digested for some time, to add one hundred parts of water, and sprinkle this mixture over the field before the plow ... Experiments ... have distinctly shown that neither corn, nor kitchen-garden plants, suffer injurious effects in consequence, but that on the contrary they thrive with much more vigour (13, pp. 184-195).

Liebig, who had many other interests, attached little importance to acidulation of bone and made no attempt to establish a patent. Whether he arrived at the idea of acidulation independently is not known. However, because of his vast reputation and influence, Liebig's short statement on bone acidulation focused a great deal of attention on the sulfuric acid treatment (12).

John Bennet Lawes used considerable quantities of bone dust on his estate near Harpenden, England, as a fertilizer for turnips during the period 1836-1838, but the bone dust was not effective on his farm. This led him to start a series of experiments in 1839 with bones and mineral phosphates treated with sulfuric and other acids. The resulting materials initially were tested, in pot experiments and with a few plants in the field, and proved effective in increasing plant growth. In 1840, he fertilized a half acre of turnips and in 1841 applied 20 tons of superphosphate which he had prepared in a cattle feed trough (8).

In 1842, Lawes was granted his famous superphosphate patent. Key statements in the patent, according to A. D. Hall, are:

> Whereas bones, bone ash, and bone dust and other phosphoric substances have been heretofore employed as manures, but always to the best of my knowledge, in a chemically undecomposed state, whereby their action on the soils to which they have been applied has been tardy and imperfect. And whereas it is in particular well known that in the case of a large proportion of the soils of this country, the application of bone dust is of no utility in producing crops of turnips on account of the slow decomposition of the bone dust in the soil, and the consequent exposure of the young plant for a long period to the ravages of the turnip fly. Now, the first of my improvements consists in decomposing, in manner following, the said bones, bone ash, bone dust, and other phosphoritic substances. Previous to using them for purposes of manure, I mix with the bones, bone ash, or bone dust, or with apatite or phosphorite, or any other substance containing phosphoric acid, a quantity of sulphuric acid just sufficient to set free as much phosphoric acid as will hold in solution the undecomposed phosphate of lime (8, p. 121).

Lawes amended his patent in 1848 by disclaiming all references to bone and bone products and confining it to "apatite and phosphorite, and other substances containing phosphoric acid." He claimed he had not known of Liebig's 1840 publication until after the date of the patent. In 1846, Lawes purchased Murray's patent, which had been issued in 1842 on almost the same date as the Lawes patent. His stated reason for doing this was to avoid any question of priority that might arise (8).

Lawes began manufacturing and selling superphosphate by 1842, using bone and coprolites obtained in England and a shipment of apatite from Spain. He also produced mixed fertilizers from superphosphate, guano, animal substances, and ammoniacal salts. His factory, which was near London, was operated until 1855, when he built a larger plant near Barking. Regardless of the often raised question as to whether or not Lawes developed superphosphate independently, he did launch the superphosphate industry through his manufacturing activities. Also, as will be discussed later, he initiated the Rothamsted Experimental Station as a result of his interest in fertilizers and the money he received from their sales (12).

Manufacture of superphosphate spread rapidly in England with 14 plants operating by 1853. A number of countries, including the United States, were producing it in the 1850's, although mostly from bone (12).

Full development of the industry, however, occurred only after the discovery and development of some of the large world deposits of phosphate rock. Even then, discovery of the fertilizing value of basic slag, a by-product of the steel industry, in about 1880 held back wide scale use of superphosphate in Germany and several other European countries.

In addition to suggesting that bones be treated with acid, Liebig (1803-1873), greatly influenced thinking on plant nutrition and fertilizers (1, 20). Although he performed no real experiments in these areas, many of his theories stimulated research by others. Liebig was an organic chemist of note and made many substantive advances in this field. From 1824 to 1843, he was professor of chemistry at the University of Giessen where he did most of his organic research and much of the thinking that made him famous. After 1843, he held a similar post at the University of Munich. His interest in agriculture and plant nutrition developed unexpectedly in the late 1830's. He had thoroughly studied the research of de Saussure, Boussingault, and others, from which he made his own deductions, which were often quite revolutionary and frequently erroneous. All of these were laid out in his 1840 book, *Organic Chemistry in Its Application to Agriculture and Physiology*; interestingly it was dedicated to the British Association for the Advancement of Science before which he had given a lecture on organic chemistry in 1837 (13). The book was an instant success and eventually almost equaled Davy's in overall influence. Within eight years it had gone through 17 editions and translations during which Liebig sometimes modified his opinions and stands. After 1842, he dropped "organic" from the title. In 1863, he came out with another book, *Natural Laws of Husbandry*, in which he gave a final update of his thinking, reargued some of his earlier theories, and commented, sometimes sarcastically, on recent advances and experiments (14).

Liebig successfully rejected the old idea that plants get their nourishment from humus by pointing out that plants obtained most of their carbon from carbon dioxide in the air. He believed that plants got their nitrogen from ammonia in the air which was brought down in precipitation, and that this source was sufficient to meet most plant needs. Liebig held that ammonia in the air came from decomposition of animal and vegetable matter which released ammonia as a gas. This was erroneous, of course, and it resulted in bitter controversies even though it was dispelled by others through careful experimentation.

Liebig correctly conceived that plants obtained their inorganic constituents from the soil. He believed that chemical analysis of the ash of normal plants showed their need for the constituents in the amounts present in the ash. He also thought that the value of manure lay in the mineral content of its ash and that it had no other merits except supplying some ammonia to the atmosphere during decomposition. Both of the latter immediately led to controversies. He strongly believed that the fertility of the soil could be maintained by addition of mineral elements alone. This belief, while disregarding nitrogen, did focus a great deal of attention on the need for mineral fertilizers. Liebig also set forth his "Law of Minimum," which stated that if one nutritive element is deficient, plant growth will be poor even though all other elements are present in abundance. Plant growth will be increased to the extent the deficient element is supplied up to the point where it is no longer limiting. This concept greatly influenced soil fertility thinking, although it is known today that improving plant growth is usually much more complex than strictly considering the single most limiting factor. Liebig also patented a mineral fertilizer based on his ideas. But he made one critical mistake–he assumed that if he used soluble materials, they would be washed away by rain. As a result, he used only insoluble materials that were of no value to plants (8).

Liebig has been variously described as having a commanding personality, as being undiplomatic, and as having an innate ability to stir controversies. He was overpowering in his arguments and was extremely critical of anyone who disagreed with him. At the same time, he had an unusual knack for isolating a key problem and then fitting together information to develop a solution in a way overlooked by others. Liebig and his writings had amazing impact upon scientists, both those who accepted his ideas and those who strove to disprove them. As stated by A. D. Hall, " . . . he was the man who drove home to the minds, both of scientific men and of farmers, the true theory of plant nutrition" (8, p. 7).

J. B. Lawes (1816-1900), in addition to launching the superphosphate industry, established the Rothamsted Experimental Station on his estate in Harpenden in 1843. Lawes was educated at Oxford but had no formal training in chemistry or other sciences, although he apparently attended lectures of C. G. Daubeny, a highly respected English chemist and botanist. Lawes' earlier work with fertilizer materials led him to want to continue experimentation. His first step was to hire Joseph Henry Gilbert (1817-1901) whose primary interest was chemistry. Gilbert had attended Glasgow University and University College, London, and had studied briefly under Liebig. Lawes and Gilbert remained together for nearly 60 years. The two men had almost exactly opposite characteristics, according to E. John Russell, later a director of Rothamsted. Lawes was a shrewd, far-seeing, practical man of affairs, laying down broad outlines, and very able in business. Gilbert, on the other hand, was a born student, much devoted to detail, meticulously accurate, but loath to change. He also was characterized as a martinet of jealous disposition, who did not like younger scientists working with him for fear they would take credit he felt he was due. As a result, few scientists would work at Rothamsted during his reign, and, with one exception, those who did remained only short periods. Instead, Gilbert hired boys from the village school, trained them to do a specific job, and retained the more successful. Lawes supported Rothamsted entirely from his own funds and left an endowment after his death (20).

Sir Henry Gilbert joined Lawes in 1843, and the two had a long and productive scientific partnership at what soon was known as the Rothamsted Experiment Station. At the right is an 1880's harvesting scene on the Broadbalk field, a experiment devoted to winter wheat since the 1840's. *(Rothamsted Experiment Station)*

Field Experiments with Chemical Fertilizers

The work at Rothamsted fell into long-term field experiments and laboratory support investigations. The first experiments were with wheat and turnips, comparing applications of farmyard manure, no manure, and ammonium salts of sulfate or chloride. In 1852, the classical field experiments were laid out in their final form on continuously cropped wheat, barley, roots, clover, and, a few years later, grass for hay. The treatments included nitrogen only; minerals only, including superphosphate and sulfates of potassium, sodium, and magnesium; nitrogen plus minerals; farmyard manure; and no manure. Each experiment continued year after year, with few changes, and some are still operating. Careful records were kept on weather, crop, and soil conditions, and crop and soil samples were analyzed. At times, shorter term experiments were initiated. Feeding experiments with farm animals were conducted between 1848 and 1862. Studies also were made with use of fertilizers in crop rotations. Lawes and Gilbert found time to attack some of Liebig's theories, as did many others. They showed conclusively that atmospheric ammonia brought down in rainwater was insufficient to meet crop needs, and that the ash content of a crop plant was not a reliable indicator of its needs for mineral elements.

There is little question that the long-term experiments at Rothamsted produced valuable information on the effects of different fertilizer materials on the soil and the crop, much of which we accept today. Lawes in 1876 invited Robert Warington to conduct microbiological research at Rothamsted. Warington's work on nitrification of ammonia produced a classic breakthrough and will be discussed later. Major quarrels broke out between Gilbert and Warington, and Warington, too, was forced to leave, but not until 1890. It remained for A. D. Hall, the next director after Gilbert's death, and his successors to inject new blood, new funds, and new directions into the Rothamsted program. The contributions from Rothamsted have been monumental in this century, and many of its scientists became world leaders in their respective fields (20).

Field experiments, of course, were not unique to Rothamsted. Lavoisier (1743-1794), the great French chemist, in 1778 began laying out quantitative experiments and demonstrations on his estate at Freschines (6). He demonstrated great yield increases in an area of France where soils were unproductive and urged the establishment of experimental farms across the country. His activities, which might have moved agriculture ahead by several decades, were terminated abruptly by the French Revolution in which he was guillotined because of his activities in governmental affairs. J. B. Boussingault (1802-1882), another famous French chemist also interested in plant nutrition, established a farm at Alsace where he conducted quantitative field plot experiments from 1834 to 1871 (19, 20). He weighed and analyzed the manures, fertilizers, and other materials he added and also the crops he harvested. About 1818, the Highland and Agricultural Society of Scotland initiated experiments that were conducted by farmers on the fertilizer value of salt. Farmyard manures, bone, and a fish compost were included in 1823, and nitrate of soda was introduced into the comparisons in 1831. In 1841, comparisons included nitrate of soda, sulfate of ammonia, muriate of ammonia, ammoniacal liquor, guano, urine, gypsum, and other materials (20). Georges Ville (1824-1897), of Vincennes, France, conducted numerous well-thought-out field experiments from 1848 to 1863, greatly advancing the practical understanding and use of chemical fertilizers (24).

Field experiments of the nineteenth century were subject to inaccuracies which easily led to erroneous conclusions. Plots usually were very large, there was no replication, and they were laid out systematically, which did not permit adequate separation of differences due to treatment from those due to natural soil variability. Furthermore, results often were extrapolated to soils and conditions where they might not apply. This point was not lost on Liebig, who stated in 1863, "... the facts which Lawes found to be true on a very small piece of land at Rothamsted became axioms for all England" (14, p. 10).

Other Discoveries Affecting Soil Fertility

J. Thomas Way of England made an important discovery in 1855 that evolved into a basic principle of soil fertility and soil acidity (20). He showed that when ammonium sulfate was added to the soil, the soil released calcium equivalent to the amount of ammonia retained, thus indicating that a chemical reaction had occurred. He also discovered that this occurred only in the clay fraction of the soil and demonstrated that the clay fraction lost this capability upon ignition. What he had demonstrated was cation exchange, where positively charged ions are attracted to negatively charged soil colloids. This important reaction was not understood until years later. Way made another important contribution in 1865 when he analyzed drainage water from soil fertilized with ammonium sulfate. He found, as he expected, not ammonia, but large amounts of nitrate. The explanation of this had to await the discovery of the role of microorganisms in the nitrification of ammonia.

Pasteur's work on fermentation in the late 1850's that established the science of bacteriology was of tremendous importance to the advancement of fertilizers and soil fertility. Two early advances resulting from the new science were the unraveling of the mysteries of nitrification and determining the mechanism by which legumes obtained nitrogen from the atmosphere.

Schlosing and Muntz of France in 1877 determined that nitrification was not 'a chemical phenomenon, as previously thought, but was instead biological, when they found that diluted sewage trickled through tubes of soil lost its ammonia and gained an equivalent amount of nitrate. The formation of the nitrate could be stopped by sterilization with chloroform vapor and started again by adding some garden soil. At Rothamsted, Warington followed up on the this discovery, showing that two groups of organisms were involved in the nitrification process. The first produced nitrites from ammonia, and the second produced nitrates from the nitrites. Warington was unable to isolate the organisms, but S. N. Winogradsky, who had similar work underway, announced in Paris in 1891 that he had isolated two separate organisms–the nitrite-formers, *Nitrosomonas,* and the nitrate-formers, *Nitrobacter.* Understanding the nitrification process was of great practical importance in soil fertility investigations, since the work of Boussingault and Ville had made it apparent that most of the nitrogen taken up by crops was in the nitrate form (19, 20).

Legumes had been an enigma since Graeco-Roman times, inasmuch as they flourished on soils where nonleguminous plants often performed poorly, and nonlegumes grew better when they followed a legume crop. The idea gradually developed, starting with Boussingault in 1838, that legumes in some way obtained their nitrogen from the atmosphere, whereas nonlegumes could not. The first hint of the true situation came when Woronin, a Russian, demonstrated in 1866 that the nodules on legume roots contained bacteria. The answer came when Hellriegel and Wilfarth of Germany in 1886 proved that gaseous nitrogen from the air was definitely fixed during the growth of leguminous plants, not by the plants themselves, but by the micro-organisms living in the nodules. They grew peas in pots of calcined soil, but to some pots added leachings from a fertile soil. The peas on soil receiving the leachings turned green, made thrifty growth, and developed root nodules replete with micro-organisms. Beijerinck in 1888 isolated the responsible bacteria, which was later named *Rhizobia*. Still later, it was found there were different strains of *Rhizobia*; each was specific to a given legume and would not invade the roots of other legumes (19, 20).

Chemical analyses during the nineteenth century were cumbersome and laborious. Nevertheless, chemists devoted great effort to analyses of crops, crop products, and various fertilizing materials. Some productive efforts were made to follow uptake of nutrients at various stages of plant growth and the extent of translocation between plant parts during growth. Real progress was made in determining elements essential to plant growth, although it was difficult to separate the essential from the nonessential since all were taken up by the growing plant at least in some quantity. Essential micronutrients were the last to be identified.

The discovery of the German potash deposits near Stassfurt and initiation of production in 1860 had a major impact on the U.S. and world fertilizer industry. For the first time, agriculture was freed from dependence on wood ashes and other organic sources for needed potash.

Summary

This chapter traces man's early efforts in the western world to increase the productivity of his soils and explain the mysteries of plant nutrition and plant growth. These have direct bearing on fertilizer development and use in the United States, since our fertilizer heritage was through Europe. Although the first real burst of progress in the development of fertilizers as we know them today occurred in Europe in the first half of the nineteenth century, the groundwork was laid over a period of some 2,600 years, starting with the Greeks, reinforced by the Romans, and surviving, but remaining essentially static, until the period of enlightenment began about 1750. It was during the latter half of the eighteenth century that experimentation, chemistry, and plant physiology set the stage for nineteenth century breakthroughs.

REFERENCES

1. Anon. 1940. The Liebig Symposium. *Amer. Fert.* 93:6, 5-7, 26.
2. ____. 1976. Nitrates. *Indust. Minerals.* 102:15-19, 21-22.
3. Cottrell, A. 1923. The manufacture of nitric acid and nitrates. Gurney and Jacobs, London.
4. Farber, E. 1952. *The Evolution of Chemistry: A History of Its Ideas, Methods, and Materials.* Ronald Press Co., New York.
5. Fussell, G. E. 1965. *Farming Technique from Prehistoric to Modern Times.* Pergamon Press Ltd., London.
6. ____. 1971. *Crop Nutrition: Science and Practice before Liebig.* Coronado Press, Lawrence, Kansas.
7. Gruber, J. W. 1948. Irrigation and land use in ancient Mesopotamia. *Agr. Hist.* 22:69-77.
8. Hall, A. D. 1915. *Fertilizers and Manure.* E. F. Dutton Co., New York.
9. Hoksbawn, I. B. 1917. Nitrate industry in Chile. *Comm. Fert.* 15(3): 27-30, 32,34.
10. Ibn-alAwam. 1975. *Book of agriculture.* Translation from Arabic of twelfth century. U.S. Dept. of Agr. No. TT 74-58045.
11. Jacob, K. D. 1964. Predecessors of superphosphate. In *Superphosphate: Its History, Chemistry, and Manufacture.* pp. 8-18. U.S. Dept. of Agr. and Tenn. Valley Authority, U.S. Gov't Printing Office, Washington, D.C.
12. ____. 1964. History and status of the superphosphate industry. In *Superphosphate: Its History, Chemistry, and Manufacture.* pp. 19-94.
13. Liebig, J. 1840. *Organic Chemistry and its Application to Agriculture and Physiology.* Edited by L. Playfair. Taylor and Walton, London.
14. ____. 1863. *The Natural Laws of Husbandry.* Edited by J. Blyth. D. Appleton and Co., New York.
15. Olson, L. 1943. Columella and the beginning of soil science. *Agr. Hist.* 17: 65-72.
16. ____. 1944. Pietro de Crescenzi: The founder of modern agronomy. *Agr. Hist.* 18: 35-40.
17. ____. 1945. Cato's views on the farmer's obligation to the land. *Agr. Hist.* 19: 129-132.
18. Paddington, J. R. and L. H. Parker. 1922. *The Nitrogen Industry.* Constable and Co., Ltd. London.
19. Reed, H. S. 1942. *A Short History of Plant Sciences.* Chronica Botanica Co., Waltham, Massachusetts.
20. Russell, Sir E. John. 1966. *A history of Agricultural Science in Great Britain, 1620-1954.* George Allen and Unwin, Ltd. London.
21. Semple, E. C. 1928. Ancient Mediterranean agriculture. *Agr. Hist.* 2: 61- 98.
22. *The Encyclopedia Britannica.* 1929. 14th ed. 10:41-52. The Encyclopedia Britannica Co., Ltd. London.
23. Tisdale, S. L. and W. L. Nelson. 1975. In *Soil and Fertilizers.* p. 5-20. Macmillan Publishing Co., Inc. New York and Collier Macmillan Publishers, London.
24. Ville, G. 1871. *Chemical Manures.* 3rd ed. Translated by E. L. Howard.

2

Beginning of Fertilizers in the United States 1840's-1870's

Use of commercial fertilizers in the United States was underway by the early 1840's with the introduction of Peruvian guano, followed in the 1850's by superphosphate and mixed fertilizers. Fertilizers arrived at a time when the new Nation was struggling to overcome the ravages of nearly two centuries of soil exploitation and of the unbelievably mismanaged farming that was practiced during Colonial times and which, to a considerable degree, still persisted. The country was, however, responding with a new spirit to improve its agriculture, to build agricultural institutions, to train people, and to encourage farmers and planters to adopt better farming practices.

Although the climate was favorable to the adoption of fertilizers, when they appeared, they created problems that were not easily or immediately solved. It was not until the early 1870's that the stage had been set for major advances in fertilizer production and use in the decades ahead. This chapter documents the beginnings of fertilizers in this country, recounts some of the events and situations that preceded and followed their introduction, and describes some of the more important institutional developments which were to prove indispensable to sound fertilizer development and use.

The Colonial Period

Agricultural Practices of the Indians

By the time the early colonists arrived, the American Indians along the Atlantic Coast had developed an effective agriculture. They lived in fixed habitations, grew crops, and used wildlife and food products from the forest. The Indians had made amazing progress in adapting and improving native American plants for their use, including corn (maize), edible beans, squash, pumpkins, melons, sunflowers, and tobacco. Small acreages of land were cleared by girdling the larger trees and burning the trunk, roots, smaller trees, and brush. Corn was planted with a digging stick at three or four kernels in hills spaced four to six feet apart. After the corn emerged, beans were frequently planted in the hills so that the corn would serve as a prop. Often the land between the hills was planted to squash or pumpkins. As the corn grew, loose earth was scraped around the hills, with the same hills used season after season—often becoming small mounds. Weeds were controlled using mattocks or clamshell hoes (19).

Indians along certain streams in New York and New England improved the fertility of their fields by catching fish that came up the streams in the spring to spawn and placing two or three at each hill of corn. Little intentional effort apparently was made outside of New York or New England to improve the soil. When fields were cropped to the point where they were no longer worth working, they were abandoned; new land was cleared or previously abandoned fields were brought back into production after a long rest period (19).

Early Colonists as Farmers

The early colonists were, for the most part, poor agriculturists. Those who settled at Jamestown, Virginia, in 1607, and Plymouth, Massachusetts, in 1620, were in deep trouble immediately as they attempted to grow English crops under conditions of climate and soil that were far different from those of the mother country. Only by trading with the Indians, taking over previously cleared Indian fields, and adopting Indian crops and cultural methods were they able to stave off starvation and survive during the first years. The Plymouth colonists, under the direction of the much appreciated Indian, Squanto, even applied fish to the corn hills.

Not only did many of the seventeenth century colonists have no farm experience whatsoever, but those from England who had lived on farms also were acquainted with an agriculture that had changed little since the Middle Ages. Most were ill-suited to establish a sound agriculture under the best of conditions, much less in the strange surroundings in which they found themselves. There were some exceptions, notably the Dutch, who came to New Amsterdam (New York) about 1645 and settled along the Hudson River, and the Germans, who settled in Pennsylvania about 1700. These were experienced farmers who knew how to till the soil and keep it productive. In general the middle colonies, especially Pennsylvania, New Jersey, and Delaware, developed the best agriculture (15, 19, 24).

The Search for Adapted Crops

The colonists, regardless of their shortcomings, did attain agricultural achievements of lasting importance. They introduced livestock of all types; adopted Indian crops, especially corn; and introduced and adapted crops grown in Europe and some from tropical and semi-tropical countries. Crops introduced from Europe included wheat, rye, barley, oats, buckwheat, peas, clover, timothy, bluegrass, apples, cherries, peaches, and common garden crops. In the southern colonies, a great search was made for profitable export crops. Different plants were collected from all over the world, including the West Indies and South and Central America. These were propagated first in botanic or test gardens.

About the only permanent crops that survived the early testing were some good tobacco varieties, cotton, rice, indigo, and sugarcane. Numerous attempts were made to develop a silk industry, since mulberry trees grew well, but none was successful. It is interesting that the Jamestown colony imported a good tobacco variety at almost the first try in 1612, and, from it, was able to launch the highly profitable tobacco crop in Virginia and Maryland (19,24).

Two markedly different systems of agriculture developed. The northern colonies, where large land grants to individuals were seldom made, were dominated by the small farmer whose aim in life was to wrest a living for himself and his family. He had little opportunity or motivation to make a profit from the crops he grew since they could not compete with similar crops already being grown in northern Europe. In contrast, the colonies of Maryland, Virginia, and those to the south made large land grants to individuals, who launched the profit-motivated, labor-intensive plantation system. The warm climate permitted growing such crops as tobacco, indigo, rice, and cotton that could not be grown successfully in Europe, and as a result offered a ready cash market. Although the small-farm system predominated in the North, there were a few large land holdings; and in the South, besides plantations, there also were small farms (15).

Colonial Farming Practices

An unlimited supply of land available at low cost was characteristic of all 13 colonies. Farm tools used during colonial times were the axe, the hoe, the scythe, and unwieldy wooden plows. Harvesting and threshing were done by hand labor. So much land so easy to acquire, however, led to an exploitative agriculture which encouraged land abandonment and inefficient use, rather than enticing farmers to put forth the labor required to keep the soil productive. A common practice, paralleling that of the Indians, was to plant corn or grains on the same fields year after year until yields declined to an unprofitable level and then move to a new field. The old land was left in fallow for a number of years until it was deemed suitable for cropping again. This cycle was repeated until low yields over the entire farm dictated abandoning the entire operation and seeking a new farm elsewhere (19, 24).

Farmers seldom hauled manure to the fields even when they had a sufficient livestock population to sustain the productivity of the soil. Numerous observers reported that farmers in the Northeast would let manure accumulate for years in the barnyard, even to the point of damaging farm buildings. Eventually the farmer had to either haul out the manure or build another barn. Crop rotations were seldom practiced and clovers were seldom used. Tillage of the soil was usually a mere scratching of the soil surface. Nevertheless, a few farmers took better care of their land. Some along northern coastal areas applied seaweed, fish, and fish offal to their fields (15, 38).

It was not until about 1750 that any interest developed in the application of liming materials or gypsum, and this was minimal. Farmers in Pennsylvania began using lime produced in lime kilns by heating limestone, but the extent of its use was small. The New Jersey marl deposits were recognized but seldom used. Spent ashes from potash manufacture, where they were available, apparently were applied to the soil. Oyster shells were collected along coastal areas and applied to the land, although unground. Gypsum (called "plaster of Paris") shipped from Europe appeared about 1770; although creating a lot of interest, it was not used extensively (15,19).

The colonists by 1763 had settled and farmed a strip of land averaging approximately 100 miles wide stretching along the east coast from northern New England to southern Georgia. This essentially was the land heritage of the United States of America. More land would have been settled by the colonists except for the difficulties with the French and the Indians in the North, and the obstacles posed by the mountains in the South (15,19).

Agriculture and the New Nation

The young United States was immediately faced with the problem of improving agriculture and making it more productive. Farming was by far the foremost occupation of the Nation's people; 85 percent of a total population of about 4 million made their living on farms. The sad state of the country's agriculture presented a situation that no leader or thinking citizen could ignore. Yet, there was no base upon which to build. The country had no trained agriculturists, no chemists, and no scientists. The educational institutions that existed were not interested in agriculture or science, and had no capability for training people who were. An agricultural press was practically nonexistent; nor where there other institutions that could help the farmer or the planter. The hard fact was that the great numbers of people on the land were entirely on their own when it came to improving farming operations. As a result, most followed the destructive farming practices of those who had farmed before them. So great was the need to improve the existing agriculture, however, that an agricultural awakening occurred which stimulated many people to strike out on various fronts in an attempt to bring about change.

Worn-out Soils

Widespread recognition of the problem of "worn-out" or "exhausted" soils was a key factor leading to the nationwide move to improve farming. Decreasing land values, abandonment of farms, and low crop yields presented a serious economic problem in all 13 states, especially to the individual landowner. The problem was not a simple one to solve in light of the knowledge available at the time. Depletion of plant nutrients, especially nitrogen, was probably the most frequent cause. In addition, soil acidity, poor drainage, inadequate tillage, and accelerated soil erosion on sloping lands all apparently played a role. As a result, practices that worked well in one situation were often of little value in others. Although some soils, such as bottomlands and other alluvial soils, were slower to exhaust than others, the overall magnitude of the problem undoubtedly was great. The problem of worn-out soils, without question, helped lead to the establishment of many of our agricultural institutions, and were a leading factor in the widespread development and use of commercial fertilizers (15, 24, 38).

The Search for Ways to Improve Agriculture

Nation's Leaders Become Experimenters—Many national leaders and landowners began experimenting on their own to find ways to improve agriculture. They attacked a range of problems, usually dealing with culture of various crops, although studies with gypsum seemed to have wide appeal. Benjamin Franklin was interested in gypsum and reportedly applied it on a hillside pasture to spell out the words, "This land has been plastered."

As early as 1760, George Washington began to study agricultural problems and to conduct experiments on how best to farm his lands at Mount Vernon. This interest continued throughout his life. He obtained books on agriculture from England and carried on an extensive correspondence with similarly minded people at home and abroad. He tried many of the ideas he gathered; for example, he was probably the first person in the upper South to grow alfalfa. His main interest, however, was in soil improvement, and his first experiment was in this area. In this experiment he built a box of 10 compartments, each with a capacity of three pecks, in which he grew a few plants each of wheat, barley, and oats on treatments composed of an untreated field soil, and the untreated soil plus separate incorporations of horse, cow, and sheep manure, two kinds of marl, a mixture of the untreated soil with sand, mud taken out of the creek, clay, and black mould. Washington made many field experiments with manures, marl, gypsum, a variety of green manures, and salt. (Marl is a mixture of clays, calcium and magnesium carbonates, and remnants of shells.) In addition, he experimented with mud from the Potomac River, deep plowing, and different crop rotations (47).

At Monticello, Thomas Jefferson also was intensely interested in improving agriculture. His interest ranged from crop rotations through collection of different kinds of plants and crops, improvements in machinery, pest control, and improvements in livestock. He apparently was less interested than Washington in experimenting with manures, liming materials, and gypsum. He did become keenly interested in the soil erosion problem of his area where farmers were plowing up and down the hills. He and his son-in-law, Thomas Randolph, developed a side hill plow which permitted easier contour tillage (51).

The Agricultural Societies—Soon after the Revolution, groups of educated people started getting together to discuss ways to improve agriculture. This led almost immediately to the formation of agricultural societies similar to those that had already taken hold in Europe. The first agricultural societies in this country were the Philadelphia Society for Promoting Agriculture and the South Carolina Society for Promoting and Improving Agriculture and Other Rural Concerns. Both were organized in 1785. Similar societies were soon organized in Maine, New York City, Boston, New Haven, Middlesex County, Massachusetts, and elsewhere. Membership consisted largely of practical men of all professions: doctors, lawyers, merchants, ministers, and people who had become prominent in political life. Agriculture was only one of their many interests and only a few actually were engaged in farming.

Most of the societies were involved in obtaining and publishing information on improvements in agriculture in other countries and highlighting good farming practices observed in this country. They offered substantial premiums for experimentation, development, and description of practices that would improve agriculture, including soil improvement. The Connecticut Society for Promoting Agriculture, for example, recorded experiments with gypsum, ashes, creek and harbor mud, farm and green manures, and fish as fertilizers. Unfortunately many of the premiums went uncollected. The farmers themselves were opposed to "book farming" and the good practices that were published and recommended by the societies were largely ignored. These early societies did amass a considerable agricultural literature in their memoirs, transactions, and pamphlets. Many of the early societies disbanded in the 1820's; new societies that came later were more successful in promoting agriculture and in wielding significant political influence (15, 47).

Agricultural Fairs—As an outgrowth of the failure of the early agricultural societies to influence the practicing farmer, Elkanah Watson of

Massachusetts came up with the idea of county agricultural societies which would sponsor agricultural fairs. The fairs, where livestock and farm produce were exhibited, were intended to imbue farmers with a spirit of competition and personal ambition. They were spiced with entertainment for the entire farm family and were interspersed with educational programs aimed at improving farming practices. The membership of the societies included farmers. The idea caught on rapidly, particularly after the states began supplying part of the funds needed. By 1819, about 100 such societies were operating; by 1852, some 300 were active in 31 states and 5 territories (15, 46).

Agricultural Journals—What proved to be a major step toward education of farmers and consequent improvement in agriculture was the launching of the agricultural journals. These were devoted almost entirely to agricultural matters and were aimed specifically at farmer readership. Although passing attention had been given to farm matters in newspapers, the first substantial and successful effort to develop an agricultural press was the publication of *The American Farmer*. This journal was established in Baltimore by John S. Skinner in April 1819. It was a weekly of about eight pages and was continued until 1862. *The Plough Boy* appeared in Albany, New York, in June 1819; *The New England Farmer* at Boston in 1822; *The New York Farmer*, in New York City in 1827; and *The Southern Agriculturist*, at Charleston, South Carolina, in 1828. Others followed and by 1845 there were 26 such journals, mostly published on a weekly or monthly basis. *The Cultivator*, probably the most popular, had 18,000 subscriptions by 1837. Although the journals contained much trivia, they also dealt with matters of substance. European agricultural progress was described and discussed, including the ideas of Davy, Liebig, and others. Fertilizers became a favorite topic. *The Southern Cultivator* and other journals in the South particularly played a major role in convincing farmers to use fertilizers (15,46).

The Profit Incentive—Most early efforts to coax farmers into improving agriculture overlooked the importance of a strong profit incentive. This became clear as a manufacturing base developed in the larger cities of the Northeast and the population began to climb. The nonfarm population in these centers needed farm products and was willing to pay a good price. By 1790, Boston had a population of 18,000; New York, 33,000; and Philadelphia, 55,000.

The population of these and many smaller cities continued to grow. By 1840, Boston's population had reached 93,000; New York's, 313,000; and Philadelphia's, 258,000. The demand and good prices encouraged farmers close to the markets to give up subsistence farming, turn to a more intensive agriculture, and improve their soils. They adopted practices that they had mostly ignored before, such as using gypsum and lime, preserving and using manure, and growing clover. Manure also was gleaned from the streets of the cities and offal was hauled from the slaughterhouses. Those near New York City sent vessels up the Hudson River and loaded them with spent ashes from potash works; Long Island farmers covered their land with fish at rates up to 10,000 per acre. Very intensive market gardening or truck farming was introduced by immigrants from Europe (15).

Farmers Show Progress—Outside the heavily populated areas most farmers continued their old ways, but some improvements were becoming apparent. By the early 1800's, farmers In the Northeast were using more manure as livestock populations increased. Use of gypsum, which previously had been imported, increased with the opening of quarries in about 1815 in western New York and along the Hudson River. Farmers close to the quarries used considerable amounts, and large amounts were shipped down the Susquehanna River to eastern Pennsylvania. Lime also came into general use in the Susquehanna Valley. By 1820, New Jersey greensand marl, which in addition to calcium carbonate contained about 2 percent phosphate and 4.5 percent potash, came into general use in that State (15).

Ruffin Awakens Southern Agriculture—Agriculture also was undergoing an awakening in the upper South, in large measure due to the efforts and contributions of one man, Edmund Ruffin. His accomplishments, both in experimentation and in convincing others to improve their soils, justify more than passing comment.

Ruffin initially was a young, obscure plantation owner at Coggins Point on the James River in Prince George County, Virginia. His father had died and he was placed in full control of the family estate in 1813 at the age of 19. Ruffin, who read widely, decided almost immediately to improve his unproductive farmlands. He put into practice the recommendations of another Virginia planter, John Taylor, who preached crop rotation; use of clover, composts and manures; and resting the soil frequently without grazing. Taylor had directed a lot of attention to these practices in a recently published book, *Arator*. Unfortunately, the practices produced no yield increases on Ruffin's land, and after four or five years he considered giving up his estate and moving westward to new lands.

About this time Ruffin read Davy's *Elements of Agricultural Chemistry* and was taken with a statement that some soils were sterile because of high soil acidity which could be corrected by applying quicklime. Davy indicated that presence of iron sulfate in the soil was an indicator of the acid condition. Ruffin could find no iron sulfate in his soils, but still concluded acidity was the problem largely because sheep sorrel, an acid-loving plant, and pine trees grew well where crops would not. Marl was available on his farm, so he set up an experiment where he applied the marl at the rate of 200 bushels per acre. Corn yields were increased about 40 percent. Over the next few years he conducted a large number of additional experiments and also marled most of his fields. Clover grew amazingly well and wheat and corn benefited. However, when he increased the rate to 600 bushels per acre on some of his fields yields were depressed, except for clover. The situation Ruffin described precisely with crops grown on the over-marled lands indicates to us today that he had created deficiencies of a micronutrient, probably zinc. From then on, Ruffin recommended lower rates (18, 41, 42).

Ruffin published his observations and the results of his experiments in *The American Farmer* in 1821, stressing the importance of correcting soil acidity before employing other practices to increase yields. His conclusions at the time were so dramatic that the magazine republished the edition and sent it free to farmers. Ruffin enlarged this article into a full size book, *An Essay on Calcareous Manures*, in 1832. His book was widely read in the South and had profound influence on agricultural practices, especially in areas where marl was available. The success of the book encouraged Ruffin to begin publishing a monthly farm journal, the *Farmer's Register*, in 1833. This stimulated further transformation of agriculture in the upper South by the 1850's (18,42).

Ruffin, who held very strong views–political and otherwise–attacked supposed frauds and abuses by banking interests in 1837 and was so adamant that he lost most of the *Register's* readers and had to stop publication in 1843. He was also a strong supporter of slavery and worked to promote secession. With his time devoted to these interests, his effectiveness in agricultural reform declined; however, he did establish a new plantation, Marlbourne, and greatly increased its productivity and profitability (18,42).

Agricultural Training Makes Its Appearance

The Old Line Colleges—The existing higher education institutions of the country in the early years had only limited capability to train and develop chemists, scientists, and people interested in agriculture. Most colleges were church-connected, and the curricula consisted largely of philosophy, theology, the "dead" languages, and mathematics. Changes, however, slowly began to take place. Columbia University in 1792 established a professorship of natural history, chemistry, and agriculture. A number of others began giving lectures in some branch of natural science by 1820. Princeton had a chemical laboratory of sorts about 1800; Williams College, in 1812; and Harvard, by 1820 (22, 46).

Pressures for trained agriculturists and those with special skills in chemistry and science continued to mount. In the early 1840's, the works of Liebig, Lawes, J. F. W. Johnston of Scotland, and others attracted a great deal of attention in the farm journals and the agricultural societies. As a result, young men began going to Europe for study, especially to the University of Giessen in Germany where Liebig was a

Edmund Ruffin of Virgnina was a leader in improving southern agriculture, but lost much of his influence after he focused his energies on other issues. *(Virginia State Library and Archives)*

professor. From 1841 through 1852, no less than 14 American students had trained under Liebig; later, others followed him to the University of Munich (40).

Yale College at New Haven responded to agricultural pressures by setting up the Yale Scientific School in 1846. John P. Norton, who had worked under J. F. W. Johnston, was hired as professor of agricultural chemistry and vegetable and animal physiology, and Benjamin Silliman, Jr., was appointed professor of chemistry. A regular course in agricultural chemistry opened in 1848 with the aim of training teachers for the new agricultural colleges. S. W. Johnson, who was destined to play an important role in fertilizers and agricultural research, was one of the first students. Norton was enthusiastic about total soil analysis and, with the help of his students, analyzed hundreds of soils. However, enthusiasm for soil analysis, which was in vogue in this country at the time, was short lived. It soon became apparent that the analysis, which required a tremendous amount of work, could not distinguish highly fertile from worn-out soils, much less indicate their needs for fertilizers or soil amendments. In 1856, S. W. Johnson became head of Yale's agricultural program, which was to become the endowed Sheffield Scientific School about 1860 (40, 47).

Harvard College, also in 1846, decided to strengthen its program in science. Eben N. Horsford was chosen to head the program. Horsford had spent three years in Liebig's laboratory and was enthusiastic about agricultural chemistry, Liebig style. He decided to create at Harvard a Liebig Laboratory of America. Recently endowed funds for the Lawrence Scientific School permitted him to proceed, but not on the scale he had visualized; however, he did build and equip the best analytical laboratory in the country. Unfortunately, his attention and that of his colleagues was soon diverted to problems of public health and mineral chemistry, and agricultural chemistry received little attention at Harvard until 1870 when the Bussey Institution was established (40,45).

The New Agricultural Colleges—A great step forward in agricultural education and training came with the establishment of four state agricultural colleges in the 1850's specifically for this purpose. These should not be confused with eight already established state universities and colleges (Georgia, Tennessee, Delaware, Missouri, Wisconsin, Minnesota, Florida, and Louisiana) which were not based on agriculture, although some had added agricultural courses. The first was Michigan State Agricultural College founded in 1855 on a 676-acre farm three and a half miles from Lansing. Its president was Joseph R. Williams, and it opened in 1857 with five professors and 61 students. The second was the Farmers' High School of Pennsylvania (now Pennsylvania State University) authorized in 1854 and opened to students in 1859. Its first president was Evan Pugh who had studied in Germany and worked briefly at Rothamsted with Lawes and Gilbert. Maryland Agriculture College (now University of Maryland) was incorporated in 1856 and opened in 1859 on a 428-acre farm in Prince Georges County. Iowa appropriated funds for the Iowa State Agriculture College and Farm (now Iowa State University) in 1858, but it did not open until after further assistance came through the Morrill Act discussed below (22,45).

Vocational Schools—Interest also developed in vocational schools, or academies, aimed at education of farmers' sons in agriculture. The first practical school of this nature was the Gardiner Lyceum established by Robert H. Gardiner, a prominent citizen of Maine, at Gardiner, Maine, in 1821. He located the school on his model farm with "the purpose of teaching mathematics, mechanics, navigation, and those branches of natural philosophy and chemistry which are calculated to make scientific farmers and skillful mechanics." The school closed in 1832, but several of the staff occupied important positions later, including John H. Lathrop who became president of the Universities of Missouri, Maryland, and Wisconsin. Other schools of similar type developed but all were premature because there was not a body of knowledge or textbooks that could be used. Most failed within very short periods, but they did demonstrate the need for agricultural colleges (46).

The Morrill Act—The Morrill Act of 1862, signed by President Lincoln, proved to be the stimulus needed to establish agricultural colleges across the Nation. This Act was introduced by Justin S. Morrill, a member of the House of Representatives from Vermont, who for years had championed the idea of using grants of public lands for partial support of agricultural colleges. These colleges were "to teach such branches of learning as are related to agriculture and mechanic arts." The Morrill land grant amounted to over 17 million acres, and each participating state was to select its own lands from the public domain, prorated according to the number of members that state had in Congress. In 1862, grants went to the four already established agricultural colleges, to five private colleges, and to the eight state supported nonagricultural universities or colleges. The numbers gradually increased, including land-grant colleges for blacks. Success of these institutions was not achieved at once, but eventually the United States developed the top college level agricultural educational system in the world (22,46).

The Patent Office and Agriculture—Various proposals were made through the years that the Federal Government itself become involved in agricultural improvement. The first Federal agency to do so was the Patent Office. It received a small appropriation in 1839 for promotion of agriculture in response to a request by Henry L. Ellsworth, Commissioner of Patents, who was actively interested in farming. The Patent Office concerned itself largely with collection and dissemination of seeds and plants, usually from foreign sources. At its peak it was distributing over two million packets of seeds annually, and was making some major importations of wheat from Europe, sugarcane from South America, and sorghum from China. It also published information on a wide variety of agricultural subjects, although it conducted few investigations of its own. Included were reports on soils, manures, and fertilizers. The Patent Office activities in agriculture continued until the formation of the Department of Agriculture (47).

U.S. Department of Agriculture—The U.S. Department of Agriculture was established in 1862 to be devoted principally to the interests of the Nation's agriculture. Owen Lovejoy of Illinois introduced a bill into the House of Representatives in January 1862, and after some amendments it was passed by Congress and signed by President Lincoln on May 15. Isaac Newton, Chief of the Agricultural Section of the Patent Office, was appointed the first Commissioner of Agriculture. Besides continuing the agricultural activities of the Patent Office, the new department was expanded initially to include a chemist, a horticulturist, and a statistician. An entomologist was added soon after. Land in the city of Washington between the Smithsonian Institution and the Washington Monument was set aside for an experimental farm. Fertilizers were seldom mentioned in the early Department reports except for a review of European work which appeared in the 1870 report of the Commissioner and an occasional chemical analysis of different fertilizer brands (45).

The Introduction of Commercial Fertilizers

First sales of a commercial material for the purpose of adding nutrients to the soil began with the importation of Peruvian guano, the first shipments of any size being in the 1840's. Previously, sales of materials to improve the soil had been limited largely to liming materials, gypsum, unprocessed fish, and untreated slaughterhouse wastes. Even the use of these materials was not widespread. By the time guano arrived, however, the need for soil improvement was becoming widely recognized as a result of educational processes being set in place. The early introduction of guano was followed in the 1850's by acidulated phosphates and mixed fertilizers, and soon after by fish scrap and processed slaughterhouse wastes.

Seabird Droppings: Leading Fertilizer for Nearly a Half Century

Guano, which was the principal fertilizer material used in this country between about 1840 and 1870, first arrived in 1824 when a consignment of two casks from Peru was shipped to John S. Skinner, editor of *The American Farmer*, at Baltimore. Some was tested by Governor Lloyd of Maryland on his farm, who claimed it was the most powerful manure he had ever applied to Indian corn. The first commercial shipment reportedly arrived in 1832, although there are other indications that shipments did not start until 1841. There is no question, however, that shipments were arriving regularly in Baltimore and New York by 1843. First use was on Long Island and along the coasts of New Jersey, Maryland, and Virginia. South Carolina was using guano in 1845, and the practice spread into North Carolina and Georgia. U. S. imports climbed from about 1,000 tons in 1848 to 174,000 tons in 1855, but never again exceeded 100,000 tons in a single year. For the 10-year period ending in 1860, about 841,000 tons entered the country; however, due to the Civil War, only 310,000 tons came in during the 10-year period ending in 1870 (13, 27).

The first guanos were from the arid Chincha Islands off the southern coast of Peru and had a high content of both nitrogen and phosphate; the better products contained from 12 to 14 percent nitrogen and 10 to 12 percent phosphate (P_2O_5). Later, guanos contained less nitrogen. Phospho-guanos, which were low in nitrogen and high in phosphate as a result of more humid climatic situations, were discovered on islands in the Caribbean Sea, the Gulf of Mexico, and the Pacific Ocean. Their composition usually ranged from 5 to 8 percent nitrogen and 20 to 25 percent phosphate), although some from the West Indies and the Pacific contained as much as 40 percent phosphate. The phospho-guanos were used extensively in the early fertilizer plants for acidulation with sulfuric acid to produce a soluble phosphate product (2, 4, 27).

Fraud and misrepresentation of guanos were common since they sold at high prices ($60 to $65 per ton at port of entry) and were easily adulterated. Rough empirical methods were soon developed to indicate quality, such as heating the guano with lime to detect ammonia, and ashing to get an idea of unwanted residues. Maryland passed a guano inspection law in 1848 and hired a state chemist. As a result, some shipments were refused because of poor quality and had to be diverted to ports in other states which did not protect shippers (13, 49).

Congress and the U.S. Government became deeply concerned with the guano monopoly of various countries and the high prices they levied. In the early 1850's, guano became the subject of diplomatic correspondence between the United States and Peru and also Venezuela in an attempt to secure a desired reduction in prices, but the negotiations failed. American firms sought guano elsewhere, and in 1854 the deposits of Aves Islands were taken over by a Boston firm. In 1855, the American Guano Company of New York was organized to develop deposits in the South Pacific. The U.S. Congress in 1856 authorized protection for citizens of the United States who discovered guano. Any uncharted island containing guano became the property of the U.S. citizen discovering it. Eventually, claims were filed for 75 islands, mostly in the West Indies and South Pacific (4,13).

An interesting claim was made by a Captain Edward Cooper of Baltimore who accidentally discovered an uncharted guano island off the west coast of Haiti in 1856 when he went ashore to bury a crew member. He named the island Navasso and claimed it and several smaller adjoining islands for himself based on the right of discovery. Congress allowed him possession, but this was challenged by Haiti which also took possession. U.S. forces, with the approval of President Buchanan, were ordered to clear the islands of Haitian forces and this order was executed promptly. Cooper, again in possession, was faced with no labor to mine and load the guano and negotiated with the State of Maryland to provide prisoners for this purpose. Cooper, in 1864, sold his islands to New York interests; they continued the operation for many years, but without the unfortunate Maryland prisoners (13).

Superphosphate and Mixed Fertilizers

Commercial production of superphosphate and mixed fertilizers in the United States began shortly after the opening of Lawes' first fertilizer plant in England in 1842. Exactly who first made superphosphate and when is not certain, but it was produced and sold in 1852 and 1853. The earliest producers, however, likely were James J. Mapes, C. D. DeBurg, and possibly P. Stockton Chappell. Both Mapes and De Burg made what today would be considered a mixed fertilizer.

Early U.S. Producers, 1852-1960—Mapes was a New York City merchant who developed an intense interest in chemistry and made some worthy improvements in extracting and refining of cane sugar. He also edited *The Working Farmer*, a monthly journal which he had founded in 1849. As a result of this journal, Mapes' activities in the fertilizer field were fully documented and his fertilizer and claims well advertised, much to the chagrin of some of his competitors. Mapes professed knowledge of acidulation of bones as early as 1832, and by 1848 or 1849 he was preparing acidulated bones for use on his own land. From 1849 to 1852, he recommended in his journal that farmers do the same (28). In March 1852, he announced the formation of a company made up of himself and a group of capitalists for superphosphate manufacture. His announcement read:

> We are happy to announce that parties are now engaged erecting buildings for the manufacture of super-phosphate of lime (bone dust dissolved in sulphuric acid) and on such a scale as to be able to furnish it to the farmers at a cost less than that which it can be prepared by individuals in a small way. With 45 cents per bushel for bone turnings, sawings, or dust, and 2-1/2 cents per pound of sulphuric acid, the farmer cannot make true superphosphate of lime for less than 3 cents per pound, as part of the weight of bone-dust, as usually sold, is water. The proposed establishment will be conducted by respectable and dependable parties, who propose to improve the quality of their product by the addition of Peruvian guano, and sulphate of ammonia, selling the result in pure state at 2-1/2 cents per pound. This can only be done by manufacturing largely, so as to enable them to make the sulphuric acid where used, and purchasing the bones in large quantities in such sections of the country as furnish them. Many tons of bones are daily sent from Cincinnati and other places where cattle are slaughtered (28, pp. 38-39).

Mapes appointed Fred'k. McCready, the publisher of *The Working Farmer*, with offices in New York City, as general sales agent. The plant was located in Newark, New Jersey, and Mapes initially supervised production himself. The first advertisement of Mapes' Improved Superphosphate of Lime was in the May 1, 1852 issue of *The Working Farmer*. His fertilizer was soon being used in New England and the Middle Atlantic states. His company was taken over by his son in 1877 and organized as the Mapes Formula and Peruvian Guano Company (28).

C. D. De Burg also made and sold superphosphate products from his Long Island factory as early as 1852, and continued at least through 1857. Little is known about De Burg except that he had experience in fertilizer manufacture in Europe. He named his first product "C. D. De Burg's No. 1 Superphosphate of Lime." The product was described in an advertisement in *The Country Gentleman*, as follows: "It is made of bone and coal dissolved in sulphuric acid, after which a large quantity of Peruvian guano is added, likewise the residue of ammoniacal chambers, which of itself is an extraordinary fertilizer" (28, p. 41). Thus, it was similar to Mapes' fertilizer except for the coal. Comparison of the analyses of samples of Mapes' and De Burg's fertilizers in 1852 by S. W. Johnson at Yale College is shown in Table 2.1 (29).

In addition to Mapes and De Burg, several others started acidulating phosphate in the 1850's. P. S. Chappell's fertilizer was listed in the Baltimore city directory in 1853 under the name of Chappell's Chemical Works. Coe's Superphosphate was being manufactured at Middletown, Connecticut, by the brothers Russell and Elmer Coe by 1854. They also

HORNER'S
MARYLAND SUPER PHOSPHATE
CONTAINS:

Peruvian Guano	700 lbs.
Bone Dust and Concentrated Animal Matter,	1150 "
Muriate of Potash	150 "
	2000 "

Liberal Discount to Dealers.

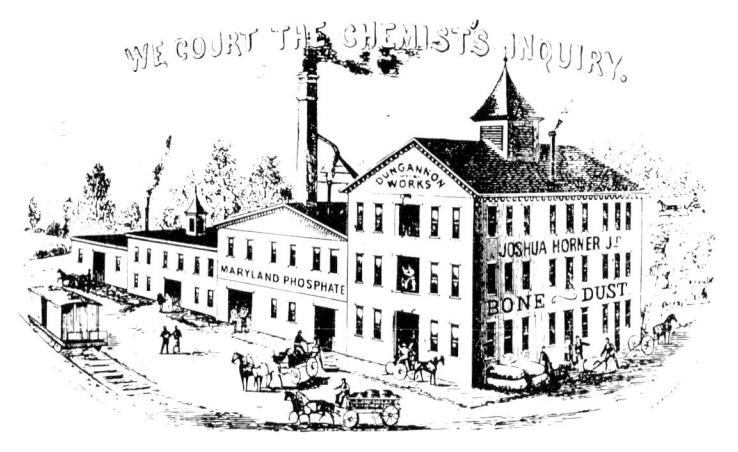

BONE DUST Ammonia, 3.
Bone Phosphate, - 59.63
Soluble Phosphoric Acid, 29.16

Maryland Super Phosphate	$50 per ton.
Bone Meal	50 " "
Tobacco Sustain (extra quantity) Potash	50 " "
Bone Dust	45 " "
Dissolved Bone	48 " "
Ground Plaster	$1.75 per bbl.

Peruvian Guano, Oil Vitriol, Potash, and other Chemicals for Fertilizing.

New Bags and no charge for delivery.

JOSHUA HORNER, jr.
54 S. GAY STREET.

A nineteenth century fertilizer advertisement by a Maryland producer.
(Baltimore Museum of Industry)

Table 2.1. Comparative Analysis of Early Fertilizers (29)

Components	Mapes	De Burg
	%	%
Water, organic, and volatile matters	27.50	27.65
Sand and matters insoluble in acids	1.48	8.45
Phosphoric acid soluble in water	10.65	5.96
Phosphoric acid insoluble in water	10.17	14.37
Ammonia	2.78	1.38
Phosphate of lime (equivalent to phosphoric acid)	45.11	45.5

opened a plant at Roxbury, Massachusetts, in 1857. Baugh and Sons Company commenced manufacture of superphosphate in Chester County, Pennsylvania, in 1855. Several others produced superphosphates and mixed fertilizers in Baltimore in this period. B. M. Rhodes was marketing fertilizers, presumably of his own manufacture, by 1857. Also in 1857, Gustavus Ober, John Kettlewell, and others built and operated the city's first plant devoted strictly to the manufacture of fertilizer. It was located next to the Davison and Kettlewell sulfuric acid plant which had been erected in 1832. John Reese and Company started fertilizer production in 1858 (13, 28).

Many others also produced and marketed acidulated phosphates in the 1860's and early 1870's. William L. Bradley by 1866 had plants at Pine Island, Roxbury, and North Weymouth, Massachusetts. The Pacific Guano Company in 1865 was marketing acidulated guano from a plant at Woods Hole, Massachusetts. Cincinnati, Ohio, had two plants in 1865, one operated by George E. Currie and the second by Amor Smith and Company. In Maryland, besides those at Baltimore, T. R. Hubbard and Son in 1866 was producing superphosphate at Chestertown. The early acidulators of phosphate appear to have confined themselves largely to acidulation of bone or bone products and phospho-guanos. These remained the major phosphate sources until the opening of the South Carolina phosphate deposits (28, 37). The first manufacture of acidulated phosphates at Charleston, South Carolina, was by the Lewis M. Hatch family in 1860. The opening of the South Carolina phosphate rock deposits in 1867 resulted in the establishment of several companies who used the rock as a raw material. The Wando Mining and Manufacturing Company was the first to use the rock, and by 1873 others were the Sulphuric Acid and Superphosphate Company, the Pacific Guano Company, Stone Company, Wappoo Mills, and the Atlantic Company (28). The earliest census data on production of superphosphate was for the year 1870, when 102,800 tons was reported. This had increased to 320,000 tons in 1880 (32).

Some of these early companies and names remained associated with fertilizers for long periods. The Mapes company functioned until the 1920's. The Ober name, later Ober and Sons, persisted until 1935. The Davison, Kettlewell & Company eventually became the Davison Chemical Company which remained an independent fertilizer producer until about 1956, then retained its identity for a few more years as a part of W. R. Grace & Company. Baugh and Sons remained under the original name until 1960 (13, 28).

Early Methods of Manufacture—Early manufacture of superphosphate and mixed fertilizers was quite crude. The first method used by the Davison, Kettlewell & Company in Baltimore in the early 1850's to make superphosphate was to grind bones into a powder and transfer it into a large pit in the ground. Sulfuric acid was poured on and the mass stirred vigorously with large wooden paddles. The product was shoveled out (presumably after curing) and sifted through a screen. In the late 1850's, Ober and Kettlewell ground bones in a burr mill and then dumped them onto the floor. Acid was poured on, water added from a hose, and the mass stirred with a hoe. It was then hauled to storage to cure.

From about 1866, the firm, now Ober and Sons, used iron pots in which the raw phosphate and the sulfuric acid were mixed. The acid was poured from a carboy and the mass stirred with wooden paddles. Production was about 8 tons per day per pot. Ober and Sons' mixed fertilizer product consisted of Peruvian guano as the main nitrogen source, Navasso phospho-guano as the raw phosphate, gypsum from Nova Scotia, and salt. None of the materials going into the mixture was weighed, but measured by putting the same volume into each batch. The final product was shipped in barrels (12,28,37).

The early manufacture of superphosphate was a hard and unpleasant task for the workers. Everything was done by hand labor in a disagreeable atmosphere of steam and gases. A first step in this country to improve this situation was the building by Potts and Klett of Philadelphia in 1864 of a power mixer to incorporate the acid with the raw phosphate. It was made of stone and was stationary with a center shaft with arms to which teeth were attached. The acid was delivered through a perforated pipe connected to revolving arms. When mixing was complete, the machine was stopped and the product removed by shovels (37).

An improved plant that overcame many of the earlier shortcomings was designed and built by the Wando Mining and Manufacturing Company at Charleston in 1870. In this plant, South Carolina phosphate rock was received at the wharf, dried, loaded into railroad cars and hauled to a new four-story building where it was crushed and pulverized. The prepared rock and other materials going into the fertilizer were elevated to the fourth floor and emptied into bins. A revolving mixer received definite amounts of the rock, sulfuric acid, and other materials which were mixed thoroughly. After mixing, the material was deposited on the third floor where it was allowed to cool and set. It was then broken up by picks and crushed by passing between rollers until it was a powder. From here it passed by means of spouts into bags resting on scales and weighed until the desired amount was reached. The bags were trucked to the warehouse and sewed. A suction blower removed fumes during processing (28).

Although major emphasis of the early U.S. fertilizer industry revolved primarily around guano and acidulated phosphate, organic by-products were making their appearance, mostly as a source of nitrogen. Fish scrap became one of the more important materials.

Fish Scrap as a Fertilizer

Unprocessed fish was used as a fertilizer by Indians and farmers alike along the rivers and coastal areas of the Northeast. As a fish oil industry developed and fish scrap became available as a by-product, fish assumed an important role as a fertilizer. However, as farmers piled more and more whole fish on their land, it became apparent that fish oil was accumulating in the soil and reducing its productivity. Farmers eventually discovered that when they placed the fish in barrels with water and allowed them to putrefy, the oil separated and rose to the surface. Once the oil was skimmed off, the fish residue could be spread on the land without deleterious effect.

Later it was found that cooking the fish in water accomplished the same thing, only less offensively. A high demand for the oil developed. This led to its commercial production in which steam cookers and presses were used to extract the oil. The remaining scrap was dried, bagged, and sold to fertilizer plants. The first fish oil factory was built near Portsmouth, Rhode Island, about 1841; it was followed by one in New York in 1850, and one near Groton, Connecticut, in 1853. In 1866, eleven were built in Maine. Production of these early factories is not known, but by 1900 there were 30 factories were producing 60,000 tons of scrap and 35,000 barrels of oil (9, 11, 25).

The fish most used was menhaden (*Brevoota tyrannus*) which, full grown, weighed about a pound and measured 9 to 15 inches in length. The fish traveled in immense schools along the Atlantic coast, usually starting in March or April and continuing into November or December. They swam close to the surface, packed side by side and tier on tier. The fish were taken with boats using seine nets, often 75 to 100 feet wide and 750 to 1,000 feet long, and arranged in such a way that two nets could be drawn together as soon as a school was surrounded. The nets were then fastened to the side of the mother ship and the fish bailed into the hold using a large dip net operated by a donkey engine. At the height of the industry over 100 steamers were engaged in the harvest. The menhaden were not considered edible and their sole value rested in the oil which was used in paints, lubricants, and chemicals, and the scrap which was sold only for fertilizers (35). The scrap contained 7 to 8 percent nitrogen and nearly the same amount of phosphate. Consumption of fish scrap from all sources was about 10,000 tons in 1850; 21,500 in 1860; 43,500 in 1870; and 52,000 tons in 1880 (32).

Odors from decaying fish and fish scrap were overwhelming. Observers traveling on Long Island where whole fish had been applied on the fields by the farmers noted that the stench of Long Island was intolerable. Men were often overcome by the fumes when loading and unloading fish scrap. One sea captain stated "Should I haul fish scrap, it would be impossible for me to mingle with shoremen or call on my friends in the city. The odor of fish scrap is obnoxious and it clings to a person with bulldog tenacity" (10). Farmers, however, associated fertilizer quality with the intensity and the disagreeableness of the odor.

Slaughterhouse Wastes

Soon after slaughterhouses were established in east coast cities, the wastes began to be used by nearby farmers as fertilizer. Dressed animals represent only about half of the live weight of the animal which, even without the moisture, leaves a considerable weight in bone, offal, blood, hoofs, tallow, and greases. These, along with carcasses unfit for human consumption, have to be disposed of as profitably as possible. Up until about 1850 the bones were picked out since there was a ready market for use in making bone black, buttons, and the like, and the remainder lumped together and sold to nearby farmers. As slaughterhouses (soon given the more esthetic name of "packing houses") grew in size, especially in the Midwest where vast numbers of livestock were available, great effort was made to recover and process all marketable by-products. Several of these were to be of importance to the fertilizer industry. Besides bone, blood was recovered and dried since it contained 12 to 14 percent nitrogen. "Tankage," because of its quantity and relatively high nitrogen content, was the packing house waste, other than bones, of greatest importance to the fertilizer industry. It contained otherwise unusable animal parts such as intestines, heart, liver, heads, and the like. These were dumped together in tanks and rendered to remove fats. The residue, or tankage, was drawn off, pressed to remove most of the water, and dried and ground. The better grades contained about 10 percent nitrogen, but the phosphate content was highly variable. Hoof meal and other wastes sometimes were sold as fertilizers, but apparently their volume was small (5, 33, 52). No data are available on early tonnages of dried blood or tankage used for fertilizers. In 1870, however, Chicago packing plants shipped 6,000 tons of fertilizer materials to the south and east (2). By 1880, output of all plants was 5,000 tons of dried blood and 20,000 tons of tankage (32).

Early American settlers made "pot ash" from wood ashes. *(Potash & Phosphate Institute)*

Use of Bones

Bones apparently were not used as a fertilizer in the United States until about 1830, even though they were popular in England by 1800 (Chapter 1). Early American writers paid scant attention to their use, and then only in relation to European experiences. The first known interest was in 1825 when Junius Brutus Booth, the tragedian, advertised for a supply of bones for use on his farm near Bel Air, Maryland. He also introduced a mechanical device for breaking them into small pieces. William Trego in 1836 was crushing and selling bones to farmers in Harford and Montgomery Counties, Maryland. Philip T. Tyson, who later became one of Maryland's state chemists, applied bones to his fields in Harford County at the rate of 35 to 40 bushels per acre. In the 1850's, pulverized bones and bone refuse were being used in the manufacture of superphosphate. Bonemeal for direct application to the soil became available as the meat packing industry grew and became more sophisticated. The recovered bones were stripped of flesh, dried, ground, and marketed as raw bone meal (27, 33). The product contained about 2 percent nitrogen and 22 to 25 percent phosphate. The best bonemeal market was in the Northeast. National consumption of bonemeal was 5,000 tons in 1850; 10,000 in 1860; and 30,000 in 1870 (32).

Wood Ashes

Wood ashes, although often in plentiful supply, had little use as a fertilizer material. The main uses were in soapmaking, glassmaking, wool scouring, and dyeing cloth. Since Colonial times the potash was extracted and used both domestically and for export. During the earlier periods as farmers cleared fields and burned the timber, the ashes were collected and brought to a central "potash house" where they were leached, the leachate boiled to dryness, and the potash that was in the leachate packed for shipment. A higher grade product, called "pearl ash," was made by calcining the leachate residue in a kiln (15). (The first patent issued in the United States and signed by George Washington was a process to extract potash from wood ashes.) The period of greatest production of wood ashes was from the end of the Revolutionary War to about 1870. In 1850, about 600 plants were producing potash from wood ashes, much of which was exported. Ashes were in very short supply in the Northeast from 1850 to 1870, and some were shipped into New England from Canada. The chemical composition of ashes varied considerably depending on the type of tree, ranging from 3 to 8 percent potash and from 1 to 2.5 percent phosphate. Nutrient contents are lowest in soft woods and highest in hard woods (44).

Sodium Nitrate

Sodium nitrate (Chapter 1), shipped from what was then Peru, first arrived at Norfolk, Virginia, in 1830. According to one account this shipment found no purchasers and was sent on to Liverpool, England, and, finding no purchasers there, was returned to Norfolk (17). A second account indicates that only a small assignment arrived first, its fertilizing value recognized, and that 100 tons was ordered for the following year (6). Its high price reportedly discouraged its use, and it was used very sparingly in the United States as a fertilizer until after the Civil War, and then primarily in the South. (England used almost all of the limited Peruvian output until 1860. Total exports that year from Peru were only 22,000 tons, and during the next decade England shared the total output about equally with the Continent (20, 34).

Ammonium Sulfate

Ammonium sulfate, much like sodium nitrate, was being used in England by about 1840 (Chapter 1), but was not used appreciably in the United States until almost the turn of the century (8). The United States, however, had coal gas plants that produced sufficient ammonia to support a sizable ammonium sulfate market. The Gas Light Company of Baltimore constructed an illuminating gas plant in Boston in 1822. Other plants followed: New York City a year later; Brooklyn and Bristol, R.I. in 1825; and Louisville and New Orleans in 1837. Several others were operating in 1850 when the national consumption of illuminating gas exceeded 5 million cubic feet annually. Very little of the ammonia was recovered. Mapes and De Burg, however, both used ammonia in fertilizer manufacture (28). In 1858, the Henry Bower Chemical Manufacturing Company erected a plant to produce ammonium sulfate and mixed fertilizer using ammonia recovered from the Philadelphia Gas Works. Total consumption of ammonium sulfate from all sources was estimated at 500 tons in 1860 and 2,000 tons in 1870 (26).

Cottonseed Meal

Farmers in the South began using cottonseed meal as a fertilizer soon after the Civil War, and the practice gained prominence in subsequent years. The meal was made from material left over after the oil was extracted from cottonseed. It contained 6 to 7 percent nitrogen, about 3 percent phosphate, and 2 percent potash. Although the first cottonseed oil mill began operation about 1830, the meal remained a waste product looked upon with suspicion by farmers as a livestock feed, and no one had thought about using it as a fertilizer. First to try the product as a fertilizer was G. W. Scott of the Scott Manufacturing Company in Atlanta who procured a ton of cottonseed cake from New Orleans in 1867. He ground this and mixed it with wood ashes. It performed so well that he bought 300 tons the following year. Also, in 1868, the Wando Mining and Manufacturing Company of Charleston introduced cottonseed meal in fertilizers with good results. Although its use grew, the state inspector of fertilizers in Georgia refused in 1876 to certify any fertilizer containing cottonseed meal (7, 16).

Poudrette

Poudrette or human excrement was sold as a fertilizer from about 1850 to 1890. It was collected in the cities and larger towns from privies and vaults, frequently mixed with peat or swamp muck, air-dried, and bagged or placed in barrels for marketing. Extravagant claims were made of its value as a fertilizer, and it frequently brought unrealistic prices. S. W. Johnson at Yale investigated poudrette, including that sold by two American companies, the Liebig Manufacturing Company of East Hartford, Connecticut, and the Lodi Manufacturing Company of New York City. His analyses showed that the product as sold was of no greater value than dried barnyard manure. Nevertheless, he concluded that poudrette properly processed could be a useful material that otherwise would continue to accumulate in the cities and present nuisance and health problems (29). Sizable tonnages were marketed: 5,000 tons in 1850; 10,000 in 1860; 25,000 in 1870; and 70,000 in 1880 (32).

Fertilizer Industry Expansion

The new fertilizer industry expanded rapidly. Bureau of Census data show that in 1859 there were 47 superphosphate and dry-mixing plants; they were operated by 308 employees and produced an estimated 32,000 tons of product. By 1869 there were 126 plants employing 2,500 people and producing 153,000 tons of fertilizer. Nutrient content of the fertilizer over this period averaged about 14.5 percent, made up of about 5 percent N, 8 percent P_2O_5 and 1.5 percent K_2O (17, 32).

David Dickson of Sparta, Georgia, was promoting the use of fertilizer on cotton before 1850. He also developed and marketed his own fertilizer, "Dickson's Compound." *(Ina Dillard Russell Library, Georgia College)*

Fertilizers Move South

Baltimore soon became the fertilizer producing center of the Nation; in the 1860's and 1870's it produced about half of all manufactured fertilizers used. The states to the south had begun to absorb Baltimore's production in the 1850's at about the time that local markets became saturated.

Several factors favored the city's early supremacy in fertilizers. These included its being a major seaport, having good rail connections, the presence of sulfuric acid plants, and its proximity to the first fertilizer-using areas. The Civil War (1861-1865) brought southern fertilizer shipments, in fact use of all fertilizers in the South, to an abrupt halt. But after the war, Baltimore soon regained its southern market and retained it until the industry itself shifted south to better utilize the South Carolina phosphate rock deposits, and later the Florida and Tennessee phosphate deposits (13, 28).

In the South worn-out lands were everywhere, and awareness of the problem and that something could be done about it had been highlighted by Edmund Ruffin and others. The livestock population was low and could provide little manure. The cash crop system, especially cotton and tobacco, placed further pressure on the soil. The need for fertilizers initially was greatest in the long-farmed areas along the coasts of Virginia, the Carolinas, and Georgia (17).

One of the earliest and most effective leaders in the South in promoting fertilizers was David Dickson of Georgia. As early as 1846, Dickson, owner of a plantation near Sparta, started using guano on cotton. He was an excellent farmer who believed in and practiced good tillage, used manure and increased its production by stocking his plantation with hundreds of animals, and practiced crop rotation. Within a few years he had developed his own fertilizer, "Dickson's Compound." It was made by mixing 240 pounds of acidulated bones, 160 pounds of guano, 160 pounds of gypsum, and 100 pounds of salt. The benefits from using his fertilizer in combination with his other good farming practices were amazing.

Dickson preached his findings and attacked the prevailing southern practices. By 1860 he had farmers and plantation owners listening, and his plantation became the mecca for hundreds of visitors each year. *The Southern Cultivator* touted Dickson and his system in almost every issue, and started a crusade for soil improvement. Others began reporting favorable results from fertilizers, agents for guano and the new fertilizers made their appearance, and some shipments of fertilizer came in from the North, all of which halted with the advent of the Civil War (1, 36, 48).

Soon after the war, southern interest in fertilizer accelerated with renewed vigor. Several factors were responsible. The farmlands during the war had been badly neglected and suffered a further decline in productivity. There was neither labor or capital available for clearing new land, so farmers worked their old fields in hope of making them pay. And, in order to secure credit, farmers had to become even more dependent upon cash crops, especially cotton, which in turn made it easier to finance fertilizers (48). Fish scrap, tankage, and other by-products were becoming available in increasing amounts; sodium nitrate from Chile and the local cottonseed meal were making their appearance; the opening of the South Carolina phosphate deposits assured a plentiful supply of phosphate for superphosphate; and imports of guano were still continuing at a fairly high level.

Interest in fertilizers in the South after the Civil War grew into what has been variously described as a fertilizer craze. *The Southern Cultivator* and other farm journals continued to publish letters of Dickson and other agricultural leaders. Interest became so intense that the *Cultivator*'s circulation jumped from 3,000 to 14,000 during 1869. Newspapers and journals were cluttered with fertilizer advertisements. The promise of quick action appealed to farmers as they were told repeatedly that they could obtain immediate returns and easily recoup their investment in the year the fertilizers were applied, whereas the older practices for soil improvement promised no such quick results. Further, most southern farmers did not have large amounts of manure and weren't much inclined to scrape together what they did have. Many farmers came to believe that use of fertilizers did away with the need to follow other good soil management practices. Unfortunately, too many of the products on the market were either misrepresented or were outright frauds that were difficult to detect (36, 48).

States and territories to the west had not yet felt the impact of commercial fertilizers, but indications of soil exhaustion were already being noticed, especially in the more eastern areas. For example, C. C.

Clay, in a speech before Congress just prior to the Civil War, referred to soil exhaustion in Madison County in northern Alabama as follows:

> In traversing that county one . . . observes fields, once fertile, now unfenced, abandoned and covered with those evil harbingers, fox-tail and broomsedge, ... Indeed, a country in its infancy, where, fifty years ago, scarce a forest tree had been felled by axe of the pioneer, is already exhibiting the painful signs of senility and decay, apparent in Virginia and the Carolinas (24, p. 446).

In contrast, most soils of the vast farming areas of the Midwest were still highly fertile. Soil improvement practices were almost totally ignored, the attitude being ". . . we have the soils to begin with which these Atlantic Shore and English farmers would like to make with manures" (15, p. 273).

Fertilizer Frauds and S. W. Johnson

The advent of commercial fertilizers brought immediate concern over fraud, which was first evidenced in the case of guano. Farmers had no way open to them to determine the nutrient content or the value of the fertilizers they were purchasing. All they had to go on was the brand name and the claims of the producer or his agent. Appearance, texture, color, or smell had little to do with true quality, and many producers and sellers took advantage of this to make false claims or to foist upon the farmer inferior or worthless products. State fertilizer control and inspection laws were slow to be developed and enacted, so great illicit profits were made at the farmers' expense.

S. W. Johnson, probably more than anyone else, focused attention on fertilizer frauds. In fact, much of his early career seemed devoted to proving that most commercial fertilizers were indeed subject to deceit. While a Yale student in 1853 he had analyzed Mapes' and De Burg's fertilizers and found them satisfactory, although he was suspicious of Mapes' integrity.

Johnson published a series of papers in *The Connecticut Homestead* whose editor, Mason C. Weld, had been his roommate in Germany; gave speeches on frauds in commercial fertilizers; and also published a special report detailing the results of his investigations. All of this created considerable excitement and because of his capability as an analyst and his concern over fraud, he was appointed chemist of the Connecticut Agricultural Society after returning from a period of study in Europe. He also was soon appointed professor of analytical and agricultural chemistry at Yale College. In a relatively short period in 1856 he had analyzed 43 additional fertilizer samples. He concluded that superphosphate-based fertilizers varied considerably in composition, and also that these fertilizers sold at double or more the prices that were justified by their nutrient content (29).

Fertilizer Inspection and Control Laws

It is generally accepted that the first workable fertilizer inspection and control law in the United States was enacted in Massachusetts in 1873. Even though others, including Massachusetts, had passed earlier laws they all had limitations of one kind or another. The Massachusetts Fertilizer Control Act of May 26, 1873, required that all commercial fertilizers sold in the state be identified with the manufacturer or seller, along with ". . . a true analyses or specification of the chemical elements and their several amounts contained therein, and also the quantity contained therein. . . ." A penalty was provided for not meeting the requirements of the law, or for claiming 5 percent more of any fertilizer ingredient than was actually contained in the package. It also authorized Massachusetts to procure an analysis of any fertilizer offered for sale in the state.

Earlier fertilizer laws had been enacted but these were generally considered ineffective, mostly because no provisions were made to carry out their requirements. Connecticut, Massachusetts, and Maine had enacted laws in 1869, an older guano law had been amended in Maryland to include fertilizers at about the same time, and Alabama and Delaware had laws in 1871. As a result, the 1873 Massachusetts law became the pattern for most of the new laws in the years ahead. New Jersey and Georgia passed legislation in 1874, and Virginia and North Carolina in 1877 (3, 23, 39).

Various early laws had been enacted to allow for inspection of plaster of Paris (gypsum), lime, and guano. Massachusetts had a lime inspection law as early as 1785, and Maryland had both lime and plaster of Paris laws in 1833. Also, a guano inspection law in effect for Baltimore in 1847 was extended statewide in 1848. Virginia had a lime and guano inspection law in 1852, and Pennsylvania adopted one in 1860. Just how effective these laws were is not known; however, Maryland appointed a state chemist in 1848 who conducted inspections of guano and plaster of Paris and made chemical analysis of the guano to determine ammonia and phosphate contents. These analyses were rated A, B, C, or D, according to a quality scale, and the ratings displayed on the container. Also, the inspection and analysis information was published in the farm journals and in Baltimore's daily newspapers. The state chemist had authority to impose fines for failure to have the guano inspected or could prohibit its sale (49).

Field Experiments with Commercial Fertilizers

Numerous field experiments were conducted with the new fertilizers to evaluate their effectiveness in increasing crop yield. Most of the experiments were of doubtful value. Those conducting the experiments usually did not have the know-how or recognize the need for a systematic and quantitative approach. Too often the experiments were aimed at comparing different brands rather than on its plant nutrient content even if it was available. Only a few trained people like S. W. Johnson, J. P. Norton, E. N. Horsford, and Evan Pugh had the necessary knowledge, but they were so involved in institution building or unrelated jobs that they had no time or funds to devote to experimentation.

The early state agricultural colleges began field experiments soon after they were founded, although, as indicated, many of these added little to the advance of knowledge. The Farmers' High School of Pennsylvania made a number of simple fertilizer experiments during its first 10 years, but even with Evan Pugh, who had studied in Europe and worked at Rothamsted, as its president, none was very satisfactory. Maryland Agricultural College in 1858, immediately after the land was acquired but before buildings were constructed, carried out field experiments using corn, oats, and potatoes to test the relative value of different fertilizers being offered for sale in the Baltimore and Washington area; however, the work had to be discontinued in two or three years because of financial stress. In 1865, soon after Rutgers College in New Jersey was designated as a land-grant institution, fertilizer experiments were started on the newly purchased farm. Other newly instituted land-grant colleges that began fertilizer experiments were Massachusetts Agricultural College at Amherst in 1867, and Maine State College of Agriculture and Mechanic Arts at Orono in 1868 (47).

The first real attempt to advance fertilizer knowledge and science appears to have been that of Levi Stockbridge at Massachusetts Agricultural College beginning about 1869. Stockbridge was a nearby farmer who had taken natural science and chemistry courses at Amherst College, had built a small laboratory on his farm, and had studied the works of Liebig, Lawes and Gilbert. After receiving a staff appointment at the new agricultural college, he began a systematic investigation to study the theory that the plant, rather than the soil, should be fed and that the needs of the plant should be determined by its chemical composition. He collected soils from the college farm and neighboring farms which were placed in pots, later in large boxes, and sown with seeds of various crops. The plants ". . . were fed from time to time with the chemical elements which they were known to contain, and in absolutely soluble condition. The elements were occasionally varied and sometimes compounded in such proportions as they had been found to exhibit in the several varieties" (43).

Stockbridge concluded after several years of work that ". . . the only substances the farmer must supply were nitrogen, potash, and phosphoric acid; and second, that there was a marked relation between the quantity of the crop produced and the elements applied, if the elements were mixed in such proportion as they exhibit in the entire plant being fed" (43). Later, Charles A. Goessman, who was professor of chemistry

S.W. Johnson was noted for fighting misrepresentation of fertilizers and for publishing textbooks in agricultural chemistry and plant nutrition.

at the college, joined Stockbridge in further experiments. Goessman, who was born in Naumburg, Germany, and attended the University of Gottingen, needs additional mention since it was he who worked out the principles and details of the highly respected Massachusetts Fertilizer Control Act of May 26, 1873. At Amherst he analyzed commercial fertilizers and studied problems of their manufacture and use. After passage of the Act, he became the state inspector of fertilizers (39, 47).

Early Textbooks

S. W. Johnson met the rapidly growing need for comprehensive textbooks in the fields of agricultural chemistry and plant nutrition in his two books, *How Crops Grow*, published in 1868 (30), and *How Crops Feed*, in 1870 (31). These resulted from his lectures at Yale's Sheffield Scientific School and elsewhere, and from his keeping abreast of scientific advances in Europe since Davy's and Liebig's first books. Sufficient time had elapsed since the latter were published to allow researchers time to correct the mistakes and inadequacies and, in so doing, greatly enhance scientific knowledge. Johnson's books were immediate successes and became standard textbooks in the agricultural colleges for the next 40 years. They also attracted attention in other countries and were translated into at least five other languages. Both went through numerous reprintings but apparently only *How Crops Grow* was revised, and that in 1890 (40, 50).

How Crops Grow dealt with the chemical composition of plants and their structure and physiology. Liebig's book had stirred a great effort among chemists to analyze plants, even though the procedures were slow and laborious and required considerable skill. By the time Johnson wrote his book, hundreds of chemical analyses were available, many of which had never been summarized or interpreted. He was able to include the ash analysis, involving both metals and nonmetals, for a large number of crops, as well as the composition of certain crops at successive stages of growth. The data also made it possible to determine variability within certain species. Johnson's second book, *How Crops Feed*, dealt with the atmosphere and the soil as related to plant nutrition (30). This subject area had been investigated in great depth since 1840. The original simple chemical concepts had been replaced by more complex and comprehensive views, particularly in the area of the relationships between the soil and the plant. Chemical analysis as a means of understanding organic processes in the soil had about reached its limits; however, the important role of bacteria had not surfaced when Johnson wrote the book. Johnson, at the end of *How Crops Feed* (31, 50), arrived at two surprising conclusions. First, the large amounts of inert nitrogen in soils could be converted chemically into nitrates, hence there was no danger of nitrogen deficiency in most soils. Second, there were enough minerals in soils that would break down into forms available to the crop to eliminate any danger of soil exhaustion. Coming from Johnson, who had been so involved in documenting scientific evidence of the day related to fertilizers, these conclusions were amazing (40).

Summary

As this chapter closes, commercial fertilizers had become rooted in the Nation's agriculture, at least in the older farming areas. More and more, farmers were becoming aware of the value of fertilizers for improving the productivity of previously abused and impoverished soils, although many still expected them to be a cure-all. Agricultural institutions of various sorts, in place or being established, would be the key to sound fertilizer development, use, and promotion. Many of the early growing pains of the new fertilizers were over, and a number of lessons had been learned the hard way. A host of fertilizer materials was present or on the horizon. All in all, a promising future for fertilizers seemed assured.

REFERENCES

1. Anon. 1868. Southern agriculture. In *Report of the Commissioner of Agriculture for the year 1867.* pp. 412-428. U.S. Govt. Printing Office, Washington, D.C.
2. _____ 1871. Report of the Commissioner of Agriculture for the year 1870.
3. _____ 1897. Agricultural facts of the year 1869. *Am. Fert.* 7(3):113-115.
4. _____ 1900. Guano deposits. *Am. Fert.* 18(2):75-78.
5. _____ 1903. Derivation of animal ammoniates. *Am. Fert.* 19(3):5-23.
6. _____ 1904. History of the fertilizer industry. *Am. Fert.* 21(4):30-33.
7. _____ 1904. Cottonseed meal industry. *Am. Fert.* 21(5):12-16.
8. _____ 1905. Sulphate of ammonia. *Am. Fert.* 22(2):5-9.
9. _____ 1911. Menhaden industry. *Comm. Fert.* 2(6):20.

10. ____ 1911. First fertilizer ship at Charleston. *Comm. Fert.* 3(2):10, 35.
11. ____ 1914. The fish scrap industry of the Atlantic Coast. *Comm. Fert.* 8(1):16-17.
12. ____ 1917. The beginning of the industry. *Am. Fert.* 46(2):30-31.
13. ____ 1950. Baltimore. The birthplace of the industry in America. *Comm. Fert.* 81(4):32-33, 35. 81(5):35-36, 56, 58. 81(6):62, 64-70.
14. Barnett, L. 1975. Buffalo bones in Detroit. *Detroit Perspective*, a journal of regional history. 2(2):89-96.
15. Bidwell, P. W. and J. L. Falconer. 1925. *History of Agriculture in the Northern United States, 1620-1860.* Carnegie Inst., Washington, D.C.
16. Blair, A. W. 1940. An expanding fertilizer industry. *Am. Fert.* 93(6):8-9, 22, 24. 93(7):22.
17. Brand, C. J. 1940. A century of plant food progress. *Am. Fert.* 93(3): 5-9, 22, 24, 26.
18. Bruce, K. 1932. Virginia agricultural decline: A fallacy. *Agr. Hist.* 6(1):3-13.
19. Carrier, L. 1923. *The Beginnings of Agriculture in America.* McGraw-Hill Book Co., Inc., New York.
20. Cottrell, A. 1923. *The Manufacture of Nitric Acid and Nitrates.* Gurney and Jacobs, London.
21. Curtis, H. A. 1925. By-product ammonia in the United States. *Am. Fert.* 63(9):33-36.
22. Eddy, E. D., Jr. 1956. *Colleges for Our Land and Time.* Harper and Brothers, New York.
23. Fisher, H. J. 1950. 75 years of real service to agriculture. *Comm. Fert.* 80(4):32-33, 35-36, 38.
24. Gray, L. C. 1933. *History of Agriculture in the Southern United States to 1860.* Carnegie Inst., Washington, D.C.
25. Haskin, F. J. 1913. Our growing menhaden industry. *Comm. Fert.* 5(6):36-38.
26. Haynes, W. 1945. The by-products of coal. In *American Chemical Industries.* pp. 124-180. D. Van Nostrand Co., Inc., New York.
27. Jacob, K. D. 1964. Predecessors of superphosphate. In *Superphosphate: Its History, Chemistry and Manufacture.* pp. 8-18. U.S. Dept. of Agr. and Tenn. Valley Authority. Washington, D.C.
28. ____ 1964. History and status of the superphosphate industry. In *Superphosphate: Its History, Chemistry and Manufacture.* pp. 37-94.
29. Johnson, S. W. 1859. *Essays on Peat, Muck, and Commercial Manures.* Brown and Gross, Hartford, Conn.
30. ____ 1868. *How Crops Grow: A treatise on the chemical composition, structure, and life of the plant.* Orange Judd & Co., New York.
31. ____ 1870. *How Crops Feed: A treatise on the atmosphere and the soil as related to the nutrition of agricultural plants.* Orange Judd & Co., New York.
32. Mehring, A. L., J. R. Adams, and K. D. Jacob. 1957. *Statistics on fertilizer and liming materials in the United States.* U.S. Dept. of Agr. Stat. Bull. No. 191, U.S. Gov't. Printing Office, Washington, D.C.
33. Paget, E. M. 1904. The packing-house industry. *Am. Fert.* 21(3):22-28.
34. Partington, J. R. and L. H. Parker. 1922. *The Nitrogen Industry.* Constable and Co., London, Bombay, and Sydney.
35. Peacock, F. S. 1894. Menhaden fish manure. *Am. Fert.* 1(4):213-218.
36. Range, W. 1954. *A Century of Georgia Agriculture, 1850-1950.* Univ. of Georgia Press, Athens.
37. Rasin, R. W. L. 1894. Growth of the fertilizer industry. *Am. Fert.* 1(1): 5-8.

38. Rasmussen, W. D. 1975. *Agriculture in the United States; A Documentary History. Vol. I.* Random House, New York.
39. Ross, B. R. 1926. The chemist as detective and policeman, or fertilizer, feed, and insecticide control. In *Chemistry of Agriculture*, pp. 358-374. The Chemical Foundation, Inc., New York.
40. Rossiter, M. W. 1975. *The Emergence of Agricultural Science: Justus Liebig and the Americans, 1840-1880.* Yale Univ. Press, New Haven and London.
41. Ruffin, E. 1832. *An Essay on Calcareous Manures.* Published by J. W. Campbell, Petersburg, Va.
42. Sitterson, J. C. 1961. Edmund Ruffin, agricultural reformer and southern radical. In *An Essay on Calcareous Manures.* Ed. by J. C. Sitterson. pp. vii-xxxiii. The Belknap Press of Harvard Univ. Press, Cambridge, Mass.
43. Stockbridge, L. 1875. *Report of Agricultural Experiments.* Mass. Agr. College Ann. Rpt. 12:56-63.
44. Storer, F. H. 1897. *Agriculture in Some of its Relation to Chemistry. Vol. II,* 7th ed. Charles Scribner's and Sons, New York.
45. True, A. C. 1894. *Education and Research in Agriculture in the United States.* U.S. Dept. of Agr. Yearbook, pp. 81-116, U.S. Gov't. Printing Office, Washington, D.C.
46. ____ 1929. *A History of Agricultural Education in the United States 1785-1925.* U.S. Dept. of Agr. Misc. Publ. No. 36, U.S. Gov't. Printing Office, Washington, D.C.
47. ____ 1937. *A History of Agricultural Experimentation and Research in the United States 1607-1925.* U.S. Dept. of Agr. Misc. Publ. No. 251. U.S. Gov't. Printing Office, Washington, D.C.
48. Taylor, R. H. 1947. The sale and application of commercial fertilizers in the South Atlantic States to 1900. *Agr. Hist.* 21:46-52.
49. Veitch, F. P. 1934. Maryland's early fertilizer laws and her first state agricultural chemist. *J. Assoc. Official Agr. Chemists* 17:474-483.
50. Vickery, H. B. 1969. Samuel W. Johnson and *How Crops Grow.* In *How Crops Grow, A Century Later.* Conn. Agr. Expt. Sta. Bull. 708, pp. 7- 24, New Haven, Conn.
51. Ward, J. E. 1945. Monticello: an experimental farm. *Agr. Hist.* 19: 183-185.
52. Wendler, R. L. 1894. Dried blood and other ammoniates. *Am. Fert.* 1(2):80-82.

3

Discovery and Development of Phosphate Rock and Sulfur Deposits 1867-1920

The discovery and development of domestic phosphate rock and sulfur-bearing deposits marked a major turning point for the U.S. fertilizer industry and assured the use of low-cost phosphate fertilizers by the American farmer. They freed the United States from dependence on scarce phosphate sources, opened the world's great phosphate fields for fertilizer development, and eventually provided an unlimited and low-cost supply of sulfuric acid. In fact, the events relating to phosphate raw materials from about 1867 to 1920 helped mold the U.S. phosphate industry into its present form.

Phosphate ores were first mined in relatively small amounts in England, France, and Spain in the mid-1840's and in Norway and Germany in the 1860's. Until the South Carolina deposits were discovered, the only phosphate mining in North America was in the provinces of Ontario and Quebec. Production began there in 1863 and continued to about 1895. Most of that ore was shipped to England and had no influence upon the U.S. industry (20).

South Carolina Phosphate

Phosphate rock was identified in South Carolina in 1837. However, its value as a source of phosphorus was not discovered until 1859. Mining began in South Carolina in 1867. The opening of these deposits came at a time when the growing U.S. fertilizer industry was desperately in need of a good domestic phosphate source. The field was large and easily mined, and it was in an area readily accessible to both water and land transportation.

The South Carolina deposits occur in a band about 70 miles long and 30 miles wide paralleling the coast from the mouth of the Wando River in Charleston County and extending in a southwesterly direction to the Broad River in Beaufort County. Charleston is a major city and port in the northern portion of the area and Beaufort in the southern. The deposits are of sedimentary origin with the phosphate occurring as nodules varying in size from sand grains to large boulders embedded in clay and calcareous mud overlying marl. The phosphate beds are shallow, ranging from a few inches to 3 feet in thickness but averaging about 1 foot. The beds are covered with an unconsolidated, sandy overburden ranging from a few inches to well over 12 feet in depth.

The phosphate rock exists both on the uplands, which are only a few feet above tide level, and in the bottoms of the numerous rivers, creeks, and arms of the ocean. The upland phosphate was designated as "land rock" and that in water as "river rock." Both are of the same material, the river rock merely being land rock washed down and concentrated in beds by the moving water. The river rock contained less objectionable impurities. The mined rock, after washing and drying, averaged about 61 percent bone phosphate of lime (BPL) (69). (The term "bone phosphate of lime," or BPL, is used in the phosphate rock industry to express the phosphate content of the rock as tricalcium phosphate [$Ca_3(PO_4)_2$] equivalent. The term is a carry-over from the early days when bones were a common source of phosphate. One pound of tricalcium phosphate is equivalent to 0.4576 pounds of P_2O_5.)

Discovery

Originally, the phosphate area was known as the "fish bed" because of the presence of numerous teeth and bones of marine animals in the sedimentary deposits. Edmund Ruffin, of Virginia marl fame, first examined and described the phosphate-bearing nodules while making an agricultural survey for the South Carolina legislature in 1842. He noted their low content of lime carbonates but failed to recognize their value as a phosphate source.

First to note or suspect the nodules as a valuable phosphate source was Dr. C. U. Shepard, a professor at Yale and a mineralogist of high standing. When he examined the marls of the area he observed that some of the samples contained phosphate of lime. In a lecture before the Medical Association of South Carolina in 1859, he referred vaguely to the "phosphate stone" near Charleston. Later, he compared the analysis of his samples with that of a sample of phospho-guano and noted the similarity. Shepard also suggested to Lewis M. Hatch, the builder and operator of South Carolina's first superphosphate plant in Charleston in 1860, and who was having difficulty obtaining enough bones to keep his plant running, that he look to the Ashley River deposits as a source of phosphate. Hatch hauled some of the rock to his plant, but with the onset of the Civil War he never used the material and did not reopen the plant after the war (15, 45, 56).

In the summer of 1867, Dr. St. Julien Ravenal, a chemist at the Medical College of South Carolina who had associated himself with a company planning to build a superphosphate plant near Charleston, collected and analyzed some rock samples and found they contained considerable phosphate. Ravenal also gave some of his samples to Dr. N. A. Pratt of Georgia, a chemist who had been connected with the niter bureau of the Confederacy. Pratt reported that the samples contained 55 to 60 percent BPL. There no longer was any question of the value of the material as a phosphate source (15, 45).

The First Miners

Dr. Pratt teamed up with Dr. F. S. Holmes, who had been a professor of geology and natural history at Charleston College and who, many years before, had collected nodule samples but never had them analyzed. They attempted to raise money in Charleston to start a mining company but failed. They turned north for capital and interested George T. Lewis and Frederick Klett of Philadelphia, who raised $800,000. The Charleston Mining and Manufacturing Company was formed in November 1867, initially with Holmes as president and Pratt as chemist and superintendent. The company bought a large area of land on both sides of the Ashley River and, in December 1867, shipped 16 barrels of the ore to Philadelphia where it was converted into superphosphate by Potts and Klett (15, 31).

Meanwhile, Ravenal and some associates in Charleston had organized the Wando Fertilizer Company in November 1866 and bought property at Bee's Ferry. They shipped a sample lot of nodules to New York in December 1867, and a 100-ton cargo to Baltimore in April 1868. In April, the Charleston Mining and Manufacturing Company shipped two 300-ton cargoes to Philadelphia. The shipments of the two companies created a great deal of excitement in northern fertilizer circles as chemists confirmed the quality of the rock, and it became known that the ore was found within the continental United States in great abundance and at an easily accessible location. Samples were sent to Coates and Company in London who distributed them to other European chemists (15, 31).

Charleston Mining shipped a total of 4,400 tons of rock to Philadelphia in 1868 and installed its first washer in 1869. The Wando Company immediately began to use its rock in superphosphate manufacture. The Sulphuric Acid and Superphosphate Company was formed in May 1868 solely to produce sulfuric acid for fertilizer manufacture. Known as the "Etiwan Works," and using imported Sicilian sulfur, it became the first acid producer south of Baltimore. The Pacific Guano Company began operating in 1869, mining its own rock, producing its own acid, and making superphosphate (15).

The first mining was confined to land rock, but the entrepreneurs quickly learned that valuable deposits lay in the stream beds. The state,

Artist's rendition of phosphate operations of Charleston Mining and Manufacturing Company. The oldest U.S. phosphate mining company, it began operations in 1866 and was acquired by Virginia-Carolina Chemical Company in 1900. *(Mobil Mining and Minerals Company)*

however, controlled all navigable streams and waters within its jurisdiction and thus had control over any mining done in them. Through some maneuvering on the part of the Marine River Phosphate Mining and Manufacturing Company, the state legislature in 1870 gave this company exclusive mining rights on all navigable waters of the area for a 21-year period for the payment of one dollar for each ton of river rock mined. The Marine River company started mining but also transferred some of its rights to the Coosaw Mining Company and the Oak Point Mines Company, a British corporation. The state then started granting additional licenses on its own to independent miners and other companies. All of this caused no great confusion and river rock mining prospered (15, 31).

Early Land Rock Prospecting and Mining

Early mining and prospecting methods left much to be desired since no one had experience or other sound information. It took several years of hit-and-miss operations before workable systems began to emerge. Land mining at first consisted of digging a number of pits in an unsystematic manner and then mining those that seemed to have enough phosphate close enough to the surface to justify the effort. As experience accumulated, potential mining areas were located by pounding long steel sounding rods or auguring through the overburden to determine the depth at which the cemented matrix occurred. If it was within 6 or 8 feet of the surface, exploratory pits were dug to determine the thickness of the phosphate deposit and to obtain samples for chemical analysis. A general rule of thumb was not to mine unless the bed was a foot thick and the overburden less than 7 feet deep. Such beds would average about 850 tons of rock per acre (56).

The method which soon evolved for mining the land rock was to lay out an area about 600 feet wide and of varying length depending on the deposit and the topography. The area was surrounded by a drainage trench and a roadway run down the middle. Six-foot-wide parallel lines were then laid out at right angles to the roadway and ending at the drainage trench. One man was assigned to each of the parallel strips, starting near the drainage trench where he would remove the overburden by shovel for a distance of about 12 feet. He would then loosen the uncovered phosphate matrix and shovel it onto the unstripped area in front where a helper would shovel it into a wheelbarrow and cart it to the roadway. After the first 6- by 12-foot pit was mined, the overburden from the next pit was shoveled into the one behind. When trees were encountered they were undercut with mattocks and any phosphate adhering to the roots picked out.

Water from the drainage trenches, when it could not be removed by gravity, was pumped out by steam pumps. The land rock that accumulated at the central roadway was loaded on rail cars and pulled by horse or steam to a washer located at the nearest deep stream. Most of the mining was done by contract, with the payment based upon the tonnage of rock delivered to the washer. Steam shovels were introduced about 1895 to remove all but the shallowest overburden, but the thinness of the phosphate strata continued to require hand mining, although eventually a hoist was used to lift the material directly into rail cars (45, 69).

Land Rock Processing

When land rock was first mined it either was left unwashed or was handwashed using brushes to free the sand and clay. Even with the coming of mechanical washers, much of the ore was imperfectly cleaned. As a result, land rock as marketed was of poor quality and gained a bad reputation, especially in Europe. The early washers, called log washers, were crude affairs. They did a poor job of washing and lost much of the valuable phosphate in the process.

The matrix containing the rock, as received from the mines, was either hauled up an incline in rail cars or hoisted up by a donkey engine and dumped into steel crushers. The crushers broke the matrix into chunks four inches or less in diameter and discharged them directly into a log washer. This consisted of a pair of half-circular troughs about 25 feet long and elevated about 2 feet at one end. The troughs contained a revolving center shaft or log to which metal spikes or paddles were attached to form a screw which would move the rock upward. The shaft was revolved by a small steam engine and clean water flowed in from the top.

The churning effect in the trough separated the fine materials which ran out at the bottom into the adjacent stream or were dumped on land nearby. The rock discharged at the top passed over a series of screens and was sprayed with additional water. Considerable hand-picking was still required to remove clay balls, marl, and other unwanted waste material. The finer material carried away in the wash often contained 60 to 65 percent of the phosphate that was in the unwashed material. The process yielded about 4 or 5 tons of cleaned rock per hour (25, 45, 69).

Drying of the washed rock was desirable before shipping, but for a number of years the land rock was air dried only. Drying with hot air was introduced in 1879. The most common method was to draw air through a wood-burning furnace; the heated air along with combustion products was carried by brick flues into drying sheds where it was distributed by pipes to bins containing the wet rock.

This method was largely abandoned after 1882 when "kiln drying" was introduced. This consisted simply of spreading about a two-foot layer of wet rock on the floor in an open shed, crisscrossing logs over the layer, and then piling about 8 more feet of rock on top of the logs. The logs were fired and after several days the rock was dry and partially calcined. Thus, kiln drying raised the grade of the rock by burning the organic matter and driving off carbon dioxide. In the process the organic matter contributed energy for drying. About six cords of wood would dry about 100 tons of rock (45, 56).

River Rock Mining and Processing

River mining began in 1870 and was done by hand. The process in shallow water consisted of loosening the nodules by pick and crowbar and throwing them into flatboats to be carried ashore. In somewhat deeper water, oyster tongs were used to bring up the material. Diving was sometimes practiced in summer months in water 6 to 10 feet deep. Large amounts of phosphate were originally recovered by hand and the shallower deposits were soon exhausted. Steam "dipper" dredges, floated on barges, were introduced to work in water up to about 20 feet in depth. Clamshell or "grappler" dredges were used in deeper water.

All washing was done before the rock was taken ashore. The dredge emptied the rock directly into a conical washer where it was cleaned with heavy streams of water. After leaving the conical washer, the rock was either sent ashore for drying or entered a crusher and then passed through some type of cylindrical washer for final cleaning. Drying was done on shore, mostly using the kiln dryer as previously described. The dried rock was then transferred to ships, usually three- or four-masted schooners (45, 56).

Labor demands for the mining operations were high, ranging up to around 3,500 people. Blacks did most of the work since they were available, accustomed to working in the hot summer, and less subject to malaria. Convicts were provided through contracts with the state. Also, Italian immigrants who had settled in New York City were enlisted during the winter months when work was not available elsewhere and the working conditions at the mines were less severe. Pay was $1-2 per day (25, 45).

Production and Companies

Production of South Carolina rock increased almost every year until 1889 when it peaked at 329,000 long tons (one long ton equals 2,240 pounds) of land rock and 212,000 tons of river rock. Production of river rock exceeded that of land rock in the late 1870's, but soon fell behind. Florida production started to cut into South Carolina's markets by 1890, but for years South Carolina was the world's chief producer of phosphate rock (32, 38).

Twenty-two companies and individuals were actively mining land rock and 12 were mining river rock in 1885. Charleston was a center for manufacture of superphosphate with 16 companies in production, some of which did their own mining. Closeness to the deposits and the rapidly growing southern fertilizer market made superphosphate production in the Charleston area highly desirable. Local companies preferred the land rock over the river rock because it was softer and easier to grind. Production of fertilizers by the local companies by the mid-80's reached about 140,000 short tons annually (19, 38).

Decline of the South Carolina Deposits

The first half of the 1890's was the period of greatest prosperity for the mining companies. Shortly thereafter, overproduction occurred and prices fell from the usual $6.00 per ton of rock to $4.50. This was particularly hard on the river companies who had to pay a $1.00 royalty to the state. Also, freight rates to Europe were rising. The land companies with their high labor requirements were having increasing difficulties in obtaining cheap labor and the deposits easiest to mine were becoming exhausted (15, 38).

To make matters worse, the major river rock producer, the Coosaw Company, ran into serious trouble when the state decided not to renew the exclusive rights grant made to the Marine and River Company 21 years earlier and which were due to expire in 1891. Soon after the original grant had been made, the Marine and River Company signed over part of its rights to the Coosaw Company and the Oaks Point Company. The Marine and River Company had gone out of business in 1882 and the Oaks Point Company had recently merged with the Coosaw Company under the Coosaw name. Thus Coosaw was the only mining company affected by the state decision. In deciding not to renew the rights, the state appointed a board of phosphate commissioners to take charge of the Coosaw territory, issue new mining licenses, and enjoin all parties from interfering with them or attempting to mine without a license. Interfering companies or those who mined rock without a license were to come under ownership of the state, have all of their property confiscated, and the officers of a company were to be fined or imprisoned. Litigation resulted, but the courts upheld the state's position. This, and Coosaw's inability to apply for a license on enough of its old territory, forced the company to abandon operations in March 1891. The state promptly licensed other companies to move in (15, 56).

The state's action against the major exporter of river rock triggered a decline of the river industry. Once the European consumers switched to Florida rock they found the higher grade Florida product, which was also low in iron and aluminum, very satisfactory and were no longer interested in the South Carolina river rock. The Coosaw Company, however, tried a comeback by resuming operations on a non-navigable stream and finally by obtaining a license to mine some of its original territory. By that time, most of its market was lost and the company ceased operations in 1897.

The final blow to the limping river companies came from mother nature. A disastrous hurricane that struck the area on August 31, 1903, destroyed the expensive floating equipment of practically all of the river companies. Production stopped, but the companies were able to get the state to halve its royalty in order to help them rebuild. Some of the industry rebuilt, but by the time they were back in production even more of the remaining market had been lost to Florida. With ever-increasing Florida competition, river rock production declined steadily and more companies folded. Mining ceased in 1909 (15, 49, 56).

Land rock production, which had started to decline after 1890, fell rapidly after about 1904 and ceased in 1920, except for one last gasp in 1925 when someone produced 2,100 tons. There was no foreign market; the domestic market of the coastal states was easily met by Florida; and Tennessee was well situated to supply the inland states. Local fertilizer manufacturers in the Charleston area bolstered the land rock industry for a period, but as mining costs continued to increase, they too turned to Florida rock. Also, many of the local manufacturers had been taken over by the Virginia-Carolina Chemical Company which, ironically, mined its own rock in Florida through a subsidiary, the old Charleston Mining and Manufacturing Company.

Total production of South Carolina phosphate rock was about 13 million long tons (38).

Florida Phosphates

The discovery of the vast Florida phosphate rock fields in the 1880's came at an opportune time. South Carolina could not for long continue to meet the needs of the rapidly growing American fertilizer industry, and mining costs were increasing rapidly. Florida, on the other hand, had almost unlimited deposits, especially in its great land pebble field where the phosphate beds were capable of producing 20 to 40 times more phosphate per acre than was possible from the South Carolina deposits. Furthermore, the pebble deposits were of a higher phosphate content, easier to mine, and subject to mechanization on a huge scale. Nevertheless, even though the various Florida deposits were much different from those encountered in South Carolina, the Florida industry profited from South Carolina's pioneering efforts. Markets had been nurtured and developed; considerable knowledge had been developed about phosphates; and certain of the rock mining, processing, and handling methods that had evolved in the Palmetto State could be applied in Florida.

Types of Florida Phosphate Deposits

Florida's phosphate deposits are of four types: land pebble, river pebble, hard rock, and soft rock, with land pebble dominating production after only a few years. The land pebble is found in Polk, Hillsborough, Manatee, and Hardee Counties, and in scattered locations northward to the Georgia line. Most of the mined rock came from a circular area roughly 30 miles in diameter in Polk and Hillsborough Counties. The land surface in this area is a flat upland having an elevation of 100 to 150 feet. The pebble occurs in nearly horizontal beds as part of the Bone Valley Formation, ranging in thickness from about 10 to 30 feet. The matrix consists of clay, silica sand, and phosphate pebbles ranging from clay-size particles to nodules of 1-1/2 to 2 inches in diameter. The overburden, consisting of sand, sandy clay and conglomerate rock, averages 15 to 20 feet in depth. The mined pebble ranges from 55 to 85 percent BPL, but averages about 65 percent (1, 36, 67, 68).

The river pebble, which was mined only for a short time, was concentrated in the bars of rivers, streams, and lakes of the area, with the greatest production coming from the Peace River. The river pebble was similar to the adjacent land pebble, but was lower in phosphate content than the land pebble in the major land pebble area. The BPL content of the mined river pebble ranged from 58 to 68 percent.

The hard rock field is on the west side of the Florida peninsula and north of the pebble field. It extends in a belt about 100 miles long and

Mining pebble phosphate with hydraulic gun at Coronet Phosphate Company's Hopewell mine near Plant City, 1923. *(G.R. Mansfield-- U.S. Geological Survey)*

Prospector removing Polk County phosphate matric from augur, 1924. *(G.R. Mansfield--USGS)*

5 to 30 miles wide in a north-south direction from Suwanee and Columbia Counties to Citrus and Hernando Counties, although some unminable deposits have been found as far north as Tallahassee. The phosphate rock occurs as nodules ranging in size from fine clays to boulders, sometimes weighing hundreds of tons, embedded in a matrix of sand, clay, or soft phosphate resting on limestone.

Deposits range in thickness from a few feet to as much as 70 feet, and are found in irregular pockets which vary in size from a few square yards to several acres. An overburden of sand and clay, varying in depth from a few inches to 30 feet, covers the deposits. Unlike the pebble deposits, which are of sedimentary origin, the hard rock is of secondary origin in which the phosphate minerals were dissolved in acid ground waters and precipitated on the underlying limestone (13). The average grade of the rock after washing and drying is 77 percent BPL with less than 3 percent iron and aluminum oxides.

The soft rock, which occurs either in combination with the hard rock or as separate deposits, is fine-textured, averages only about 55 percent BPL and has a high iron and aluminum content.

The Phosphates of North Florida

Early Discoveries—The first discovery of phosphate in north Florida was purely accidental, and occurred in the hard rock region in Alachua County at Hawthorne, near Gainesville. C. A. Simmons, who had a rock quarry to provide building stone, sent some samples to Washington, D.C. in 1879 for analysis. Results showed the presence of phosphate and Simmons mined some of his rock for use as a fertilizer in 1883, but abandoned the project a year later due to lack of funds.

In 1884 and 1885, as part of a building stone survey, Dr. Lawrence C. Johnson of the U.S. Geological Survey made explorations in several northern and north central Florida counties. He noted widespread presence of phosphate, particularly in the area from Live Oak in Suwanee County to Ocala in Marion County. Also in 1884, John A. Preston found phosphate in a sink on his land near Waldo in Alachua County and observed that it was valuable as a fertilizer. Judge James Bell of Gainesville discovered phosphate in a sink known as the Devil's Millhopper, and W. T. Duvall found phosphate near Tallahassee. Thus, by the mid-1880's, the presence of phosphate in the hard rock region was well established; still it caused no wave of excitement (9, 19).

Florida's phosphate boom was triggered by activities of Albertus D. Vogt, a real estate speculator in the new town of Dunnellon. Vogt first became involved in phosphates when he became interested in local rocks containing fossils. He had analyses made of samples taken while sinking a well on 10 acres of property he owned and found they contained phosphate. He gave some of his samples to John C. Dunn,

Stripping overburden from soft phosphate near Ocala, 1919. *(R.W. Stone--USGS)*

president of the Merchants' National Bank at Ocala, and tried to impress upon him the importance of the discovery and of the advantages of financing a mining company. Dunn, who knew Vogt as an optimist, was slow in taking any action, but finally took the samples to a local chemist and druggist, Dr. R. R. Snowden, who found they contained 76 percent BPL. Other samples, which Dunn had sent to a St. Louis chemical firm, confirmed the local analysis. Furthermore, the St. Louis chemist attached a footnote to his report stressing the unusually high phosphate content.

The conservative Dunn then had Vogt obtain more samples, not only from the well but also other properties, and these were sent to other chemists. The results, for the most part, were very positive and Dunn was convinced. He bought up half of Vogt's 10 acres for $10,000 and set Vogt and his brother to prospecting and buying up land of which the Vogts received a part interest. The Dunnellon Phosphate Company was organized in 1889 and soon controlled 70,000 acres of land. The company started mining in February 1890, but the Marion Phosphate Company had already started hard rock production in 1889 (6, 9).

News of a fabulous phosphate field was spread by newspapers everywhere. The great Florida phosphate boom was on. Thousands of prospectors and speculators flooded the area. Few of the prospectors knew what they were looking for, but this didn't bother the speculators. Tracts changed hands time and again. Ocala became the focal point for the boom which was restricted largely to the hard rock region. Only a small spillover affected the pebble field and this was centered at Bartow. Vogt made a fortune but spent lavishly and, just like the boom, in a few years it was gone (6, 9).

First Hard Rock Mining—The hard rock field was first mined at sites of outcrops, and many disappointments resulted. Because of the spotty nature of the deposits, no one could predict whether or not the phosphate was extensive enough to justify setting up a mining operation. A post hole type of digger, called a "cup digger," was soon introduced to penetrate the overburden and obtain some idea of the amount of phosphate underneath, but it could be used only to a depth of about 30 feet. It wasn't until about 1903 that more sophisticated drilling equipment was developed that could penetrate deeper.

Initially, overburden was removed by horse-drawn scrapers which were replaced, in turn, by steam shovels. By 1905, the larger companies began using hydraulic methods, since these had proven well suited to the type of overburden encountered in the hard rock field. Hand mining of the matrix, was standard procedure for some time; however in mines where water levels were high, dredges equipped with dipper shovels were used. After it was dug and the large boulders either broken by sledge hammers or dynamited, the matrix was loaded into carts or small rail cars and hauled up an incline to a washer. Large deposits justified the use of cable-hoisting machinery, equipped with buckets of about one-half ton capacity, to raise the rock to the land surface. After crushing, log washers were used to clean the rock. Kiln drying by burning with logs was used initially, but was later replaced, in part, by rotary dryers. About two-thirds of the phosphate mined was lost in wastes (9, 67, 68).

Most of the hard rock was shipped abroad. It largely dominated the export market as South Carolina river rock declined until export of Florida pebble became a factor. Much of the rock was sold under a guarantee of 77 percent BPL and a maximum of 3 percent iron and aluminum oxides. Only the very lowest grades were used in domestic fertilizer manufacture. All of the product for export was transported by rail to ports at Jacksonville, Fernandina, or Fort Inglas (9, 67).

Soft Rock—The soft rock, which had a much lower phosphate content and was high in iron and aluminum, was in very small demand, being used only for direct application to the soil. A small tonnage was mined up to 1897, after which production ceased until 1918. It was not until the 1930's that it was produced on a continuing basis (1, 9, 68).

Major Mining Companies—A great many companies were organized during the early boom days and presumably most mined some hard rock. By 1894, only 30 companies remained in operation, including a few that were foreign-owned. The largest company, Dunnellon Phosphate, operated 12 mines. The number shrank to 20 companies in 1909 and to six by 1913. Of these, J. Buttgenbach and Company, C and J Camp Phosphate Company, and Dunnellon Phosphate Company operated in the field almost to its closure in 1965. Production peaked in 1907 and dropped to practically nothing from 1915 through 1918 as World War I cut off most overseas shipments. Production costs were much higher for hard rock than for land pebble, although the higher grade hard rock brought premium prices on the foreign market (9).

The Phosphates of Central Florida

Early Discoveries of the River Pebble Field—As discoveries were made to the north, attention also was being directed independently to the river pebble deposits to the south. While surveying for a canal in 1881, Captain J. L. LeBaron, the chief engineer of a detachment of U.S. Army Engineering Corps, discovered river pebble in the Peace River south of Fort Meade. Samples sent to S. W. Baird of the Smithsonian Institution for analysis confirmed the presence of phosphate. Baird urged a geological survey, but LeBaron was unable to obtain approval from his commanding officer to pursue the matter further. LeBaron, who was transferred out of the area, took leave in 1882 and 1883 during which time he tried unsuccessfully to interest northern capitalists in his discovery. Also in 1883, some rock fragments collected from a channel improvement operation in Hillsborough Bay (Tampa) were sent to the Ashley Phosphate Company in South Carolina for analysis. That company sent representatives to look for other deposits and bought some land, but apparently nothing materialized (9).

A project that did materialize resulted when John C. Jones and W. R. McKee of Orlando, while on a hunting trip in 1886, discovered phosphate between Fort Meade and Charlotte Harbor. The next year the Peace River Phosphate Company was formed by Jones, McKee, Messrs. Hill and Hunt of Birmingham, and George W. Scott, who owned a fertilizer company in Atlanta. The company hired M. T. Singter, an Alabama geologist, and a Mr. Pratt from Georgia (presumably Dr. N. A. Pratt of South Carolina fame) to examine the phosphate beds of the Peace River. Pratt analyzed samples in his tent as they moved along, and these showed an average of 61 percent BPL. As a result, the company bought extensive mileages of property on both sides of the Peace River (9).

River Pebble Mining—River pebble mining was beset with problems from the outset. The Peace River, on which most of the mining was done, was fast-moving and, at times, either too shallow or too deep to accommodate the dredges. Mining machinery was costly, and the state, like South Carolina, soon levied $1.00 per ton royalty. Hand methods were employed at first. This was succeeded by dipper dredges, and finally by dredges equipped with centrifugal pumps which could recover up to 45 tons of pebble per day. The rock was washed and screened on a barge and conveyed down-river by scows to land-based dryers. Various methods of drying were used, but rotary dryers were most popular. The rotary dryer consisted of a brick furnace at one end of a rotating iron cylinder through which the gases and flames from the furnace were passed. Phosphate rock was fed in at the far end, and flanges in the cylinder served as a screw to carry the phosphate toward the furnace. Just before it reached the furnace, the phosphate was dropped out.

Peace River rock was loaded on steamers at Punta Gordo or farther down in Charlotte Harbor. Rock from the Alafia River was loaded at Tampa Harbor (9).

Seventeen companies were mining river rock in 1892, mostly from the Peace and Alafia Rivers. The number of companies declined to four by 1894, at which time all were combined into the Peace River Phosphate Mining Company. The Peace River Company was purchased by the American Agricultural Chemical Company in 1899. River rock mining ceased in 1908. Even though the state had long since stopped collecting royalty payments, river pebble could not compete with land pebble, which was less costly to produce and of higher grade. Peak production

Hard rock phosphate mine of Buttgenbach & Company, 1919. *(R.W. Stone--USGS)*

View of Buttengenbach's phosphate washing plant, 1923. *(G.R. Mansfield--USGS)*

of 123,000 tons occurred in 1893. Total production over the life of the river industry was only about 1.2 million tons, practically all of which was supplied to the domestic market (9).

Pioneer Land Pebble Miners—The Peace River Company, however, was not the first to mine. LeBaron, who had maintained his interest in the deposits, induced one of his former employees, T. S. Moorhead of Pennsylvania, to purchase some sand bars on the Peace River near Arcadia. Moorhead formed a small company, the Arcadian Phosphate Company, and in May 1888, about a year ahead of the Peace River Company, sent 10 boxcars of the pebble to Scott's Fertilizer Company in Atlanta. This was the first commercially mined phosphate in Florida (9).

The first mining companies, the Pharr Phosphate Company and Florida Phosphate Company, were organized in 1890; both began mining in Polk County in 1891. The Pharr Company, after stripping the overburden, used hand methods for digging the phosphate which was loaded on railcars and pulled by a small locomotive to a site where it was washed and dried. The Florida Company mined with a dipper dredge, bringing water in ditches from ponds and streams. Crushing and washing was done on barges, much as in river mining. After washing, the rock was conveyed in buckets by a hoist to a dryer. This method proved highly successful and was used by a number of pebble companies thereafter, although the water usually was obtained from artesian wells (1, 9).

Land Pebble Mining—The first mining of the pebble field used dipper dredges to work the large deposits below the water level. Usually a pit was dug in the deposit and filled with water brought in by ditches. Hydraulic mining of the phosphate matrix began in 1902. This was followed by hydraulic removal of overburden. The first hydraulic mining involved the use of dredges. The overburden was removed by steam shovel, and dredges were fitted with steam engines and boilers to operate hydraulic pressure pumps and centrifugal pumps. Streams of water under pressure easily disintegrated the matrix, which was carried along with the return water to a sump from which it was pumped onto a barge for screening and further washing. The mined-out pits served not only as the dump area for the washings, but also as a waterway for barges to transport the washed pebble to a dryer (25).

In contrast to the phosphate in the hard rock field, the pebble was ideally suited to hydraulic mining since the nodules were small and of more or less uniform size that could be easily handled with the centrifugal pumps. The deposits were thick and continuous, and lay in a horizontal position. Hydraulic mining had an additional advantage in that the pebble was partially washed in the mining operation, although a final washing was still required with a log washer. Rotary dryers were used exclusively. Hydraulic removal of the overburden, although preferred, was not always practical due to the presence of boulders in the overburden at some locations. Where hydraulic removal of overburden was used the washed-down material was carried to sumps and pumped to mined-out areas (44).

The introduction of electricity into the pebble field came on the heels of the first hydraulic mining. This permitted abandonment of steam power and eliminated the need for dredges. With the coming of electric power, the pebble in the sump was lifted by centrifugal pumps and forced through pipes directly to a central mill area where the material was screened, further washed, and dried. Electricity powered not only all of the mining equipment, but also the washers. Central generating stations were installed at all of the larger mines and at the central mills. Wood and coal were the most common sources of fuel, although some of the mines used diesel-driven generators (9, 25).

Production of land pebble increased rapidly from 58,000 tons in 1891 to 221,000 in 1900, a million tons in 1908, and almost two million in 1911. The product was sold under guarantees ranging from 60 to 75 percent BPL, and a maximum of 3 percent iron and aluminum oxides.

Practically all rock having a BPL content of least 70 percent was marketed abroad. This amounted to about half of the total production until 1906; the share dropped to 33 percent in 1910. The foreign market was lost in 1914 as a result of World War I. This led to a decline in total production inasmuch as growth in domestic use was not sufficient to make up the difference (44, 68).

Large Companies Take Over—Operations in the pebble field expanded from two companies in 1891 to 20 in 1894, but consolidations reduced the number to 14 by 1909. The large domestic fertilizer companies moved into land pebble mining in a big way, starting with the International Agricultural Corporation (now International Minerals and Chemical Corporation) in 1900. By 1912, the mining was largely controlled by the domestic fertilizer companies; three giants, International, American Agricultural Chemical Company, and Virginia-Carolina Chemical Company, controlled nearly half of the production.

The extent of the control of U.S. fertilizer companies in the pebble field is indicated by the ownerships of the 16 companies that were mining in 1913. The American Agricultural Chemical Company operated through two subsidiaries, the Pierce Phosphate Company and the Palmetto Phosphate Company. Virginia-Carolina mined through the Charleston Mining and Manufacturing Company, United Phosphate Company, and a half interest in the Amalgamated Phosphate Company, the other half being shared by Baugh and Sons and a couple of other fertilizer companies.

The International Agricultural Corporation controlled the Florida Mining Company and the Peoria Pebble Phosphate Company. F. S. Royster Guano Company owned the Florida Phosphate Mining Company. Armour was producing phosphate under its own name, and Swift owned the State Phosphate Company. Peters, White, and Company, New York fertilizer brokers, owned the Phosphate Mining Company. This left three French-owned companies, the Coronet Phosphate Company, the International Phosphate Company, and the Interstate Chemical Company (29, 44).

Labor Problems—Obtaining labor to operate Florida's phosphate mines was a problem almost from the outset. Although no data seem to be available during the early years, the average number of wage earners increased from 2,800 in 1902 to 4,900 in 1909, then decreased to about 2,300 in 1919 (25). Local labor was scarce and Blacks were hired from Alabama and Georgia for $1.00 per day and board. Convicts were enlisted from the state which had no penitentiary system and leased them out to reduce expenses. As mechanization progressed, especially with the introduction of hydraulic mining and use of electricity, much of the handwork was eliminated, and the number of workers declined sharply. Skilled workers, however, were required in greater numbers (9).

World War I and Exports Tumble

The bottom fell out of the Florida phosphate rock export market with the outbreak of World War I in 1914, and the subsequent British blockade and German embargo. Many companies went out of business. Hardest hit was the hard rock field because most of its product was exported. The total U.S. phosphate rock sold or used by producers fell from 2.9 million tons in 1913 to 1.5 million in 1915. In 1916, however, domestic consumption began increasing (9, 39, 64).

Tennessee Phosphates

Development of Tennessee phosphate came on the heels of the Florida phosphate discoveries and early production. Tennessee production increased from 42,000 tons in 1894 to 510,000 in 1900. The State surpassed South Carolina in 1889. Tennessee's inland location assured a ready market not only in Tennessee, but also in surrounding states and the Midwest. Tennessee phosphate was never a major factor in the export market, although some was shipped abroad in the earlier days.

Tennessee's deposits occur in the western part of the Nashville Basin and the western portion of the surrounding Highland Rim. Nashville is the major city, and the main streams are the Cumberland, Duck, and Tennessee Rivers, with the Duck playing the major role in phosphate operations. Three kinds of phosphate rock have been mined in the region, the brown, the blue, and the white. Another kind, nodular, the so-called "kidney rock," played an important role in the discovery of the Tennessee phosphates, but was never of economic importance (14).

Brown rock and blue rock phosphates are of sedimentary origin and derived from phosphatic limestones that have been weathered. White rock deposits are of secondary origin in that phosphate was leached from overlying rocks and precipitated upon contact with underlying limestones in the same manner that the Florida hard rock originated (13). Of the three, brown rock has dominated production and is the only one that has proved of lasting importance.

The mineable brown rock lies mostly in Maury, Giles, and Williamson Counties with the most important deposits covering wide areas and usually lying near the surface of the hills. The rock occurs in beds ranging in thickness from a few inches to 20 to 30 feet, with an average of 6 to 8 feet, consisting of phosphatic sand and hard, close-grained phosphate rocks. The deposits sometimes outcrop but most are covered with an overburden varying in depth to a point when the ratio of overburden to phosphate exceeds about five to one. Collars of brown rock also are found around the sides of steep hills where the phosphatic limestone outcropped and weathered. The higher grades of brown rock contained 78 percent BPL, with the lower grades running about 60 percent. Most of the higher grade brown rock had about 4 percent iron and aluminum oxides (14).

The blue rock is found in the hills along the edge of the Highland Rim on the southwest side of the Nashville Basin, mostly in Hickman and Lewis Counties and the western part of Maury County. The rock is a part of a sandstone member of the Chattanooga Shale formation and occurs only where it overlies phosphatic limestones. The phosphate beds outcrop on the sides of steep hills and are continuous through the hills, but erratic. Seams from a few inches to 3 or 4 feet in thickness contain massive, close-grained phosphatic rock. Also, nodular phosphate, when present, was picked out during mining from the shale immediately overlying the sandstone seam. The BPL content of the blue rock varies greatly; the more dense rock ranges up to 75 percent, with an average of about 65 percent (14).

White rock is found in Perry and Decatur Counties in the hills on both sides of the Tennessee River, but it was never mined extensively. This material closely resembles the hard rock of Florida and occurs in irregular pockets and as large boulders along with clay and chert. It ranges from 72 to 78 percent BPL (14).

Discovery

The discovery of phosphate in Tennessee occurred in the Highland Rim, presumably in the Swan Creek area of Hickman and Lewis Counties. Geologists for many years had observed the dark colored seams of the Chattanooga Shale formation, and local residents believed these were related to the presence of coal. No one suspected that they might contain phosphate. The first known discovery of phosphate in Tennessee was of the nodular variety which originated in the shale outcrops and lay exposed along the streams. As early as 1887, Dr. Safford, a geologist at Vanderbilt University, collected some nodules and found that they contained 64 percent BPL, but this awakened no interest (42).

In 1893, more nodules, ranging from 1 to 6 inches in diameter, were collected by two men, Crake and Arnold, from the Swan Creek area. Upon analysis at Vanderbilt, these were found to contain an average of 65 percent BPL. This brought a flurry of leases on land where the nodules lay exposed. No one had identified the high phosphate content of the blue rock seams (42). This apparently occurred late in 1893, purely by accident, and was in no way related to the discovery of the nodules. Several versions of this discovery exist, but in all cases the blue rock was mistaken for coal.

Meadows and Brown ascribe the discovery to R. W. Childs. He had his samples analyzed by J. C. Wharton who found they averaged 75 percent BPL (42). Ruhm stated that the version most accepted locally was that two cattle buyers sampled an outcrop on the bluffs of Swan Creek in

Hickman County in December 1893 (57). Still another version identifies a local resident, George W. Harder, with making the discovery on Swan Creek (8). At any rate, the discovery in 1893 set off a rush of prospecting in the Swan Creek area, and many acres were optioned, leased, or bought. Companies seriously interested in mining concentrated their efforts in the Swan Creek area of Hickman and Lewis Counties where the display of high-grade mineable phosphate was greatest.

Enough rock was garnered for a test by the Nashville Fertilizer Company, a manufacturer of superphosphate. The test was very satisfactory, both with nodules and blue rock. A sample of blue rock also was sent to Dr. N. A. Pratt for laboratory testing. His report stated: "From the small amount sent us, we made here in the lab a small quantity of acid phosphate, which quickly set and dried out, leaving a friable beautiful acid phosphate, fully up in appearance and working qualities to any we have seen" (42, p. 583).

Initiation of Mining

By the spring of 1894, three companies were chartered to begin operations in Hickman and Lewis Counties: the Tennessee Phosphate Company with headquarters in Baltimore, the Southwest Phosphate Company officed in Nashville, and the Duck River Phosphate Company, also quartered in Nashville. The first shipment of blue rock was made by Southwest Phosphate about May 1, 1894, from a mine on Swan Creek near the mouth of Fall Branch in Hickman County. The company installed a crusher and hauled the product by wagons over a rough road to the nearest railroad at Aetna. Forty or 50 laborers were employed and some 5,000 tons was shipped by the end of the year (40, 41).

The Duck River Company also began shipments in 1894. It erected a crusher and mined at Totty's Bend on the Duck River, also in Hickman County, and hauled 4,000 tons of ore to Centerville, a distance of nine miles. Because of the distance and the bad roads, the company developed a plan to barge the rock down the Duck River to Centerville. The Tennessee Company, the third to start operations during the year, mined at the head of Swan Creek in Lewis County four miles from Aetna. At the same time, it started building a spur line to connect with the L & N Railroad (40, 41). Four additional companies were operating by December 1895 (57).

White Rock Phosphate

White rock deposits were found in Perry and Decatur counties soon after the Swan Creek operation in Hickman county got underway. Prospectors familiar with the north Florida white phosphate came to the region. Among these was E. Slattery, at Linden, who had brought along some white rock samples. He gave one sample to C. C. Sutton, who found

Mining of phosphate bank near Mt. Pleasant, Tennessee. *(C.W. Hayes--USGS)*

Kiln burning to dry phosphate near Mt. Pleasant. *(W.C. Phalen--USGS)*

Phosphate washing plant of Federal Chemical Company, Maury County, Tennessee, 1914. *(W.C. Phalen--USGS)*

a deposit on Town Creek which resembled his sample. Another sample was given to P. L. Smothers who discovered a similar deposit near Red Bank Creek. Samples submitted to Nashville were erratic and showed both low and high BPL values. The deposits were exposed on the sides of valleys and on the sides of hills and were removed using both open pits and tunneling. Perry Phosphate Company mined and shipped a few thousand tons in 1898 and 1899. However, distance from transportation, rough topography, and erroneous analyses of the phosphate contents caused the project to be abandoned (26, 42, 57).

Early Mining Methods for Blue Rock

The early phosphate mining in Tennessee, as in South Carolina and Florida, was of the simplest form possible. As the industry stabilized and expanded, more sophisticated methods were adopted either from those used in Florida or through innovations designed to meet the specific needs and conditions encountered in Tennessee (23).

The earliest blue rock mining was through stripping operations on the exposed hillside outcrops. Underground mining, however, was soon required, and this involved the conventional room-and-pillar method employed in coal mining. Tunnels were driven into the stratum, often several hundred feet long. Rooms about 25 feet wide were excavated at regular intervals and at right angles to the tunnel. The overlying roof of slate or shale required little in the way of timber supports. The rock was cut by drills and loosened by blasting, loaded on tram cars, and pulled out of the mine by human or mule power. Prior to abandoning a tunnel, the pillars were drawn, leaving the roof to collapse. The rock was crushed before shipping; washing was unnecessary, but dryers were eventually used. Starting about 1904, drills were operated by compressed air, and exhaust fans were installed in most mines (14, 57).

Discovery of the Brown Rock Field

Just as the blue rock companies were settling down, building spur lines, and improving their facilities, the higher grade, more easily mined brown rock field in the vicinity of Mount Pleasant was discovered. This brought about an almost complete suspension of blue rock mining for a time (57).

H. D. Ruhm, who lived at Mount Pleasant and had formed his own mining company, described the discovery as follows:

> In January 1896, Judge S. Q. Weatherly, who had been active in the discovery and development of the Hickman County deposits, found on the farm of W. S. Jennings, a little way out from the town of Mount Pleasant, in Maury County, a rock which, on analysis, ran high in bone phosphate of lime, and further investigation disclosed large bodies of it in the neighborhood, especially in and around the town of Mount Pleasant. The high grade of this rock, and the

apparent cheapness in getting it out, assisted by the fact the deposits lay near the L. and N. R.R. [sic] (Louisville and Nashville railroad), attracted attention, and in July, 1896, mining began. At the time, labor being cheap and the rock being mined from the outcrop, it could be loaded on cars at ridiculously low prices (57, p. 8).

Mining Brown Rock

Many miners, including some from the blue rock field, flocked to Mount Pleasant, obtaining rock at first by paying small royalties to the landowners. Farmers themselves began digging, hauling to town, and selling the rock as they would their farm products. In 1897, the following companies and individuals were mining: Tennessee Phosphate Company, T. C. Meadows and Company, Blue Grass Phosphate Company, Columbian Phosphate Company, Hardy and Bryon, John Carpenter, C. H. Harder and Company, H. H. Graves, J. R. Ingram, Robin Jones, C. W. Barrett, H. D. Ruhm, and others (57).

Virtually every landowner in middle Tennessee hunted for phosphate during the years 1897 through 1900, the period of brown rock discovery. Hillsides were dotted with prospect holes. Local newspapers were caught up in the excitement, each trying to outdo the others by proclaiming ever more wondrous discoveries, facts notwithstanding. For example, the *Nashville American* announced in glaring headlines on its front page the following "discovery" near Lawrenceburg, an area containing little if any mineable phosphate:

> A very valuable phosphate bed has been discovered about two miles north of here (Lawrenceburg) on the lands of W. H. Bradner. An analysis of some of the rock showed it to contain 28 percent moisture, 11 percent phosphoric acid and 111 percent bone phosphate. The bed is very large and contains thousands of tons (57, p. 9).

Maury County was transformed by the mining. Mount Pleasant grew from a quiet little town of 300 to thousands almost overnight. Fields outside the town had row upon row of white tents and barren shacks to accommodate the hundreds of Black workers. Agriculture practically stopped, and land originally worth $5 to $10 per acre sold as high as $1,000 (17). By 1904, most of the Tennessee rock still came from Maury County, with only one mine each in Giles and Sumner Counties, and only two or three in Hickman County (57).

In the brown rock field, the first mining was limited to outcrops. Operations merely involved loosening and shoveling the rock into wagons and hand-carrying the larger pieces. Removal of overburden, which soon became necessary, was done with mule-drawn scrapers. Initially the rock was air dried by spreading it out on the ground and turning it over occasionally with a shovel. Rock mined in wet weather or destined for export was kiln dried by burning with cordwood as was done in both South Carolina and Florida. Dried rock was crushed by hand or with machinery, screened, and stored in sheds awaiting shipment. Washing, using the conventional log washers, was soon introduced by the larger companies in order to save rock that had formerly been thrown away because of its "dirt" content, and also to increase the grade of the final product. Steam shovels were introduced about 1904 to remove overburden. By 1910, coal-fired rotary dryers had come into use, and draglines were introduced to remove the deeper overburden. Hand mining of the ore appears to have continued at least up to 1920 (3, 17, 57).

Marketing of Tennessee Rock

Tennessee production grew rapidly from around 19,000 tons in 1894 to 129,000 tons in 1897, 450,000 in 1900, and about 700,000 tons in 1907, a tonnage not exceeded until after 1920. By 1902, Tennessee was producing 28 percent of the phosphate mined in the United States; South Carolina 21 percent, and Florida the remaining 51 percent. Tennessee's share declined after 1907 as Florida's output increased (25, 30, 43).

Brown rock dominated production. Production of blue rock, which had suffered a short setback upon the discovery of brown rock, resumed and increased with production peaking at about 90,000 tons in 1908 and continuing at this level till 1920. White rock was mined sporadically by the Perry Phosphate Company starting about 1900, but contributed only about 10,000 tons by 1908 when mining stopped (14).

Practically all of the Tennessee rock up until 1920 was sold or used by the producers for domestic fertilizer production in Tennessee, the surrounding states, and the Midwest, although some found markets in the eastern states. Surprisingly, in view of its inland location, fairly substantial tonnages of brown rock from the Mount Pleasant area moved into the export trade over a period of about 10 years starting in 1897. Foreign sales peaked in 1899 at 162,000 tons, but decreased materially thereafter because of the long haul to ports and the higher than desired iron and aluminum oxide content of the rock. Marketing was done through brokers, and shipments were made at several ports although most went through Pensacola or New Orleans (3, 5, 30, 44, 57).

The Mining Companies

Ownership of mining companies in Tennessee, as in Florida, at first was in the hands of small independents. This was followed by consolidation into large companies, many of which were owned by major fertilizer manufacturers. By 1905, in addition to the smaller independents, the Charleston Mining and Manufacturing Company (Virginia-Carolina), International Agricultural Chemical, and the French-owned Central Phosphate Company were operating in Maury County, and the

Swift Fertilizer Company in Hickman County (3,57). In 1913, the American Agricultural Chemical, International Agricultural Chemical, and Virginia-Carolina produced 55 percent of the phosphate mined in Tennessee. Armour and Swift were both operating, as well as the Federal Chemical Company owned by fertilizer manufacturers in Louisville, and the Standard Phosphate and Chemical Company. Still, eight independents kept their small operations going (29).

Quality of the brown rock was declining by the start of World War I, but events stimulated by the war extended the life of the brown rock field. These involved sudden increases in demand for electric furnace phosphorus (elemental phosphorus) for military uses and for by-product ferro-phosphorus. Furnace plants were built and research on electric furnaces was initiated (29).

Western Phosphates

The western phosphate deposits are among the largest in the world. Hundreds of millions of tons are mineable under today's conditions, and billions of tons make up a resource that might be mined sometime in the future (12, 13).

The western deposits cover more than 100,000 square miles in portions of Idaho, Utah, Wyoming, and Montana. The deposits are of sedimentary origin and occur in the Phosphoria Formation, which was laid down in the floor of the sea. Those in the eastern part of the area lie more or less horizontally, while those to the west are variously tilted, folded, and faulted due the earth's movements. The formation consists of dark-colored chert, black shale, and phosphate. The phosphate occurs in two horizons, one near the base of the formation, and the second, by far the more extensive, near the top. The beds of phosphate rock are found in the shale, and the rock itself is dense and characteristically oolitic (partly nodular) in nature. Most beds are 3 to 9 feet in thickness, but some vary from a few inches to over 12 feet. Phosphate content varies greatly, with the better deposits containing about 70 percent BPL (13, 16, 46).

Discovery

Discovery of the western phosphate is claimed by Albert Richter of Salt Lake City who, according to his report, first recognized the true character of the deposits in the vicinity of La Plata, Cache County, Utah, in 1889. He traced the deposits as far as Bear Lake, Idaho. In 1901, he submitted samples of the phosphate rock, which analyzed as much as 70 percent BPL, to leading fertilizer manufacturers of Chicago, but the firms showed no interest in developing the deposits (24, 34, 35, 55).

Regardless of the validity of Richter's claim, phosphate was discovered independently in a roundabout manner through R. A. Pidcock, a mail carrier of Ogden, Utah. While on a prospecting trip in the summer of 1897, Pidcock camped on Twelve Mile Branch of Woodruff Creek in Rich County, Utah, and noted some old mine workings in a black shale formation nearby. Believing he saw signs of gold, he and some friends took up a number of claims. As hopes for a profitable individual development dwindled, the claims were incorporated into the Alice Mining Company. Various ore samples were sent to the U.S. Geological Survey for analysis, but no returns were ever received. Finally, in 1899, a large sample was sent to Thomas Price and Sons of San Francisco. It showed no gold or silver but a large amount of phosphate, equivalent to 70 percent BPL. Even so, all of the individual stockholders dropped out, leaving the Alice Mining Company to one man, Frank Howe (24, 34, 35).

In 1903, Charles C. Jones, a mining engineer for the British-owned Mountain Copper Company, Ltd., of Keswick, California, was sent to the Woodruff Creek site to explore the phosphate deposit. He examined the deposit with Frank Howe, and studied the surrounding area. He found that the phosphate in the deposit was oolitic in structure and continued for about two and one half miles, but dipped sharply.

Jones also studied the Hayden Report of 1871, which was a reconnaissance-type geological survey, and the Survey of the 40th Parallel. These led him to extend his exploration to other areas, including the Ogden and Echo Canyon area, and a canyon near Logan, Utah. In August 1903, he learned of a coal mine being opened near Montpelier, Idaho, and examined the shaft which had been sunk 250 feet on an incline. This revealed a phosphate deposit at the lower level. He found that the phosphate seam was exposed in Montpelier Canyon for a distance of three miles–a discovery which was to lead to the first phosphate mining in the western field. He also traced the formation in the immediate area. Jones wrote his company regarding his investigations, stating "This may be one of the world's great deposits of phosphate." A little later he wrote them that he believed the Carboniferous Formation would prove "one of the greatest store houses of phosphoric acid in the world." His company promptly bought up the Alice Mining Company, but never developed the holdings (24, 34, 35).

Jones corresponded with the U.S. Geological Survey in 1903 and 1904, sending numerous samples in an attempt to gain a better understanding of the Carboniferous Formation. During 1904 and 1905, he expanded his studies throughout much of the immediate area of southeastern Idaho, eastern Utah, and southwestern Wyoming, which confirmed the widespread occurrence of the phosphate (34, 35). Jones thus became a pioneer in the development of the western phosphate field, and to him is due much credit for the systematic, scientific way in which his field investigations were conducted. Furthermore, he published papers giving full accounts of his findings and of the methods he followed (24).

Mining Becomes a Reality

Mining began in the western field at Montpelier in 1906 by the San Francisco Chemical Company which was the operating department of Mountains Copper Company, Ltd., the firm that originally employed Jones. The mine, known as the "Waterloo," was located on the outcrop in Montpelier Canyon, the strata dipping at an angle toward the stream bottom. Mining at first merely required blasting which caused the ore to roll down the hill in a chute to a storage house from which it was loaded on wagons and hauled to the Oregon Short Line of the Union Pacific Railroad at nearby Montpelier. It required no washing or drying. By late 1906, an average of two carloads of phosphate rock per day were being shipped to San Francisco. Shipments continued to March 1907, then were suspended briefly until the company could assess its position. Even with the low cost of the mining and nearness to the railroad, the margin of profit after paying for the freight was far too small (71, 72).

Two other companies were operating in 1907. P. B. and R. S. Bradley Company of Boston, mined in Utah about eight miles from Sage, Wyoming, to which the rock was shipped. Union Phosphate Company of Los Angeles was mining near Cokeville, Wyoming. Both shipped on the Union Pacific Railroad to the west coast. Due to the distance from the market, both encountered the same high freight rate problems as did the San Francisco Company. Subsequently, the Brown and Perkins Company of Montpelier and Nashville, Tennessee, and Messrs. Duffield and Jeff of Salt Lake City entered the field; these were the only companies operating in 1912 (11, 34, 71, 72).

Phosphate Surveys

The U.S. Geological Survey first became seriously interested in the western phosphate field in 1906, and started detailed surveys in 1909. First attention was directed to southeastern Idaho and the adjacent areas in Utah and Wyoming which had been explored by Jones. Three geologists, H. S. Gale, R. W. Richards, and Eliot Blackwelder, were in charge of the investigations. Work was limited to the summer months because of the deep snows and cold conditions that existed over much of the rest of the year. The surveys involved description of the deposits, estimation of the thickness and extent of each deposit and the likely tonnages that could be derived from it, taking ore samples for analysis, and classifying the land into either phosphate or nonphosphate categories. The surveys continued until about 1920, by which time the phosphate in Idaho, Utah, Wyoming and Montana, had been surveyed fairly completely. There was no longer any question of the enormity of the western field (16, 24, 54, 62, 63, 71).

Upper part of phosphoria formation, Uintah County, Utah.
(C.R. Thomas--USGS)

Mine and buildings of Western Phosphate Company, Bear Lake County, Idaho, 1920.
(G.R. Mansfield--USGS)

Mountainside phosphate mining in Lincoln County, Wyoming, 1907.
(F.B. Weeks--USGS)

Phosphate was discovered in western Montana in 1911 by J. T. Pardee of the U.S. Geological Survey who was examining Northern Pacific Railway land grants near Garrison, Phillipsburg, and Elliston. Detailed phosphate surveys began in 1913, and mining got under way in 1924 (65).

Withdrawal of Phosphate Lands

The U.S. Government withdrew huge acreages of the western phosphate lands, along with a small amount in Florida, as a national reserve as a result of concern that the Florida and Tennessee deposits would soon be depleted. Since most of the western deposits were in the public domain, the Secretary of Interior decided in 1908 to set aside 4,541,000 acres in Wyoming, Idaho, and Utah (24). This action preceded the start of the detailed surveys by the Geological Survey, and there was no way to separate phosphate from nonphosphate lands.

Land placed in the phosphate reserve also took with it any rights to agricultural use. This caused an immediate uproar among livestock and other agricultural interests since there was no law on the books that distinguished surface from mineral rights. This led to a hastening of the phosphate surveys to ensure that only valuable phosphate deposits were included. As rapidly as the surveys could be made, the government began restoring lands that contained little or no phosphate; by 1912 more than half of the withdrawn acreage had been released (7). Additions and subtractions continued to be made as the surveys progressed, but the area withdrawn remained around 2 million acres. Congress in 1914 finally passed a law opening the land to agricultural uses while retaining the mineral rights (7, 18, 37).

Another legal problem arose in the early period of western phosphate prospecting and mining. Claimants could file for a phosphate deposit on the public domain either as a placer right at the site of an outcrop, or as a lode right on the seam itself, but not both. The placer right was by far the more restrictive, while a lode right gave the claimant the right to follow a seam for an indefinite distance. Most early applicants opted for the placer right. Numerous lawsuits resulted, since a holder of a placer grant would suddenly find a holder of a lode grant many miles away also claiming what he thought was his property; the conflict existed even when the lode grant had been made later than the original placer grant. Most courts upheld the lode rights and, in 1912, the Department of Interior also decided that a western phosphate deposit was a lode. This was far from a desirable solution, but it wasn't until 1920 that a phosphate leasing law was put into effect on the public domain which limited a lease to a maximum of 2,560 acres, with the remainder of the deposit being retained by the United States (37, 71).

Status of Mining: 1910-1920

Mining in the western field remained confined to a relatively small radius in the Idaho, Utah, Wyoming area until 1920. Few companies participated, and the tonnages mined were insignificant. Total production in 1910 was 9,500 long tons. This declined to about 5,000 tons annually in 1913 and 1914, and plummeted to 1,700 tons in 1916. In 1917, as a result of the war, shipments jumped to 15,000 tons from the four companies then mining. They were San Francisco Chemical Company, Western Phosphate Mining and Manufacturing Company, P. B. and R. S. Bradley, and Union Phosphate Company. All mined by underground tunneling. Union Phosphate discontinued operations in 1918. The remaining three curtailed mining sharply in 1919 as wartime needs vanished, but continued to ship from stockpiles. By the end of the year Western Phosphate Company went into receivership, leaving only the San Francisco Company and the Bradley's still operating (29, 62, 63, 64).

Even though demand surged unexpectedly in 1920, western phosphates still faced a rough road.

Other Phosphate Deposits

In addition to deposits discussed in earlier sections (in Florida, Idaho, South Carolina, Tennessee, Utah, and Wyoming), phosphate rock was found in 14 other states prior to 1920. These states are Alabama, Arkansas, Georgia, Illinois, Kentucky, Massachusetts, New Jersey, New York, Mississippi, Nevada, North Carolina, Oklahoma, Pennsylvania, and Virginia. Several of these deposits were mined for short periods, but none produced significant amounts of ore or competed with the major phosphate mining centers. Low grades, high mining costs, poor yields, isolated locations, deep overburden, and long distances from markets worked against their exploitation (70). Mining in Alabama, Arkansas, Kentucky, New Jersey, New York, North Carolina, and Pennsylvania during this period is briefly discussed here (35).

Mining of a deposit near Batesville, Arkansas, started in 1900. The rock was of sedimentary origin and contained from 55 to 60 percent BPL. It was mined and used by the Arkansas Fertilizer Company at Little Rock. Underground mining was used and the rock was kiln dried. Operations ceased in 1912, after a total production of about 31,000 tons (70).

The presence of phosphate in Kentucky was first noted in 1877 by Dr. Robert Peter of the Kentucky Geological Survey. The agency conducted surveys from 1912 to 1915. The major deposit, brown rock which is related geologically to the similar deposit in Tennessee, was found in several counties in the Lexington area, but proved spotty. Only in Woodford County, west of Lexington, was the deposit mined. The United

Phosphate and Chemical Company mined there from late 1919 through 1926. The beds were 3 to 5 feet thick and the phosphate content averaged well under 70 percent BPL. The phosphate was dried and screened but no washing was done. About 93,000 tons was produced over the seven-year period (70).

Apatite was mined in small amounts prior to 1882 at Hurdstown (Sussex County), New Jersey and in Sussex County, New York, at Crown Point (35).

North Carolina was known before 1920 to have extensive deposits of phosphate rock. They were in a belt 15 to 20 miles wide extending from the South Carolina line northeastward along the coast to the Neuse River with its southeastern boundary 20 to 25 miles from the coast line. Some mining was done, but production was limited, totaling about 25,000 tons between 1896 and 1899. The exact locations of the mining remains uncertain. No mining was done after 1903 due to the scattered nature of the deposits and the high mining costs (19, 33, 35).

Operations were initiated in 1899 in Juniata County, Pennsylvania, not far from Port Royal, on a sedimentary deposit where the mining was done by tunneling. Most of the material was low grade, ranging from 43 to 54 percent BPL. Tuscarora Fertilizer Company built a fertilizer plant at one of the mines. Apparently the operation was short lived since no rock production is indicated after 1904, at which time only 5,000 tons had been produced (4, 33).

Sulfur

Sulfur is a key plant nutrient. In addition, sulfur goes hand in hand with phosphate rock. It is the second essential raw material for the manufacture of superphosphate. The history of sulfur in this country, particularly as it relates to the fertilizer industry, is as exciting as that of phosphate rock. The story begins when the nation was totally dependent on foreign sources and goes to the era in which the United States became the world's largest producer and exporter of elemental sulfur. This section covers events up until 1920.

Early Sulfur Imports

Prior to the 1880's the United States relied entirely on imports of elemental sulfur from Sicily for manufacture of sulfuric acid. Significant mining of the huge Sicilian deposits, which cover about 1,600 square miles in the center of the island, began in 1787. Sicily dominated the elemental sulfur market until the advent of U.S. Gulf Coast sulfur production. Underground mining was required in Sicily, and the sulfur had to be separated from gypsum, limestone, and other impurities before shipment. Purification was accomplished by placing the mined material in pits with sloping bottoms, igniting the sulfur, and using its own heat of combustion to convert the remainder to molten form which was then run off and solidified in pure state. As demand increased worldwide, cartels and interests that controlled the marketing of the Sicilian sulfur capitalized on their monopoly by manipulating prices and output (27, 28).

Drastic price increases and unexpected shortages by 1825 stimulated importing countries to search for alternatives. A French chemist, Michael Perret, in 1833 developed a practical method to obtain sulfur dioxide by roasting pyrites. Roasting involved heating pyrites to about 1650°F using energy from burning of sulfur. (Pyrites is the term used for the iron sulfide minerals, pyrite and marcasite (FeS_2) and pyrrhotite (Fe_7S_8), containing in pure state 53 percent sulfur for the first two, and 40 percent for the third.) Nearly all European countries had turned to pyrites as a source of sulfur for sulfuric acid production by 1860. U.S. industries, however, did not adopt pyrites until the 1880's. They resisted gearing up and learning to use pyrites, relying on lower quality domestic pyrites, and paying a duty tax on the iron in imported pyrites inasmuch as they had no need to obtain iron as an expensive by-product. As late as 1885, Sicilian sulfur still accounted for 85 percent of the Nation's sulfuric acid production. From 1900 through 1917, pyrites supplied 80 percent or more of the sulfuric acid used in the United States (27, 28).

Pyrites Come of Age

Domestic and imported pyrites were used in about equal tonnages in the United States until the duty tax on iron was repealed in 1890, after which imports shot ahead. The duty-free status of imported pyrites meant that pyrites from Spain could be laid down in East Coast ports, where most acid plants were located, more economically than U.S. pyrites could be mined and transported to the place of use. As a result, imports increasingly exceeded the tonnages of domestic pyrites. Even in 1916, when domestic production reached an all-time mark of 440,000 tons, imports totaled more than 1 million tons. Spain, the major exporter, was in a very favorable position to compete with U.S. pyrites. Huge deposits in the Huelva Province were of high quality, easy to mine, and labor costs were much lower than in the U.S. (27, 47, 50, 51, 52, 59, 60).

Pyrites occur extensively in the United States, but only a few deposits are of commercial importance. States in which the ore was mined prior to 1920 included New York, Massachusetts, New Jersey, Pennsylvania, Virginia, North Carolina, Georgia, Alabama, Missouri, and Wisconsin. Some was recovered as a by-product of coal mining in Ohio, Illinois and Indiana; in the West, mining was limited largely to California and Colorado. The pyrites, usually a mixture of pyrite and pyrrhotite, were found as veins or lenses in igneous rocks. Sulfur content varied, as did the size of the deposit and the depth and angle at which the pyrites were found. These factors, along with the location of the deposit with respect to transportation and markets, determined the output of the mine and its profitableness. As a result, few mines remained in production for long. Only in two states, Virginia and California, were pyrites mined consistently over a long period of time (47, 51, 53, 59, 66).

Virginia, with large favorably located deposits, for years mined more than half of all pyrites produced in the country. The deposits occur in a belt running northeastward through Buckingham, Fluvanna, Louisa, Spotssylvania, Stafford, and Prince William Counties. The pyrites were found in lenses, some measuring 700 feet long and 80 feet thick, and were removed through shafts which followed the dip of the deposits. The deposits were known as early as 1850, when some were mined for their copper content. Exploitation to recover the sulfur in the ore began in the 1880's, and production peaked at about 150,000 tons of ore annually. Companies mining the Virginia deposits in 1917 were Armenius Chemical Company, Sulphur Mining and Railroad Company, E. I. duPont de Nemours and Company, Old Dominion Sulphur Company, and General Chemical Company (48, 50, 53, 59).

Pyrite production started slowly in California due to an inadequate market (66). The first mines apparently were in Sierra, Nevada, and Pumas Counties (59). Production by 1911 was 30,000 tons, at which time in ranked second to Virginia. In 1919, with 128,000 tons, California became the country's major producer (60). Producing companies listed in 1916 were Mountain Copper Company which mined near Keswick in Shasta County; Leona Chemical Company and the Stauffer Chemical Company, operating in Alameda County; and Vantrent Mining Company, in Placer County (58).

Sulfur from Smelter Gases

U.S. companies began recovering sulfur dioxide from smelter stack gases as sulfuric acid about the same time that pyrites came into use. The smelting of zinc and copper releases large amounts of sulfur dioxide from pyrites and other sulfides in the ore. Release of the sulfur dioxide in stack gases devastated vegetation for miles around. Germany was recovering the sulfur dioxide from zinc smelters as early as 1855, and from copper smelters by 1872. The first by-product sulfuric acid plant in this country was placed in operation in 1881 by the Mathiesson and Hegler Zinc Company at LaSalle, Illinois. This plant was so successful that other recovery plants were built in the Missouri and Illinois zinc fields, and by the New Jersey Zinc Company at Palmerton, New Jersey. By 1911, zinc smelters accounted for 10 percent of the sulfuric acid produced in the United States (28).

The first domestic by-product sulfuric acid from copper smelting was produced by the Ducktown Sulphur, Copper and Iron Company, Ltd., a British corporation, at Ducktown, Tennessee, in 1908. This came about

Pollution reduction was a driving force leading to byproduct sulfuric acid production at smelting operations such as this one at Copperhill, Tennessee. The acid was used largely by the fertilizer industry. *(Tennessee Chemical Company)*

as the result of a lawsuit by the State of Georgia against the Ducktown Company and the Tennessee Copper Company to cease spewing stack gases into nearby Georgia and killing vegetation. The case was appealed to the U.S. Supreme Court which ruled in favor of Georgia. The Ducktown Company, as a result, built the largest sulfuric acid plant in the world. To sell the huge amount of acid produced, it formed the Tennessee Chemical and Fertilizer Company, which sold the entire output in a 10-year contract to the International Agricultural Corporation (22,28).

By 1919, six copper companies and 11 zinc companies were producing the equivalent of more than 800,000 short tons of sulfuric acid of 60° Be' strength (60).

Recovery of Elemental Sulfur

Elemental sulfur was mined domestically as early as 1880 in the western states from small, widely scattered deposits of volcanic origin and deposits from sulfur springs. Producing states included Nevada, Utah, Wyoming, Colorado, and California. Production was small, usually only a few hundred tons per year but sometimes rising to a few thousand. Mining costs were high and the sulfur had to be extracted from rocks and other unwanted material by melting. Uses were local in nature, such as in making sheep dips and for controlling diseases and insects in California vineyards (2, 48, 53, 66).

U.S. production of elemental sulfur changed dramatically with discovery of the first Gulf Coast sulfur deposit in Calcasieu Parish, Louisiana, in 1867, and its first successful extraction by Herman Frasch in 1894. Production from Sulphur Mine in Calcasieu Parish and later from two other sulfur domes in Texas took the United States from the role of a major importer to that of a major exporter. Further, the early production laid the groundwork for elemental sulfur to become again the major sulfur source for domestic sulfuric acid production.

Mining sulfur deposited by volcanic action, Humboldt County, Nevada.
(F.L. Ransome--USGS)

Gulf Coast Sulfur Deposits

All of the great Gulf Coast sulfur deposits are similar geologically. They occur as sulfur domes, varying in size from a few up to several hundred acres. The domes resulted from the upward intrusion of rock salt from an underlying bed as a result of earth pressures. The effect of the intrusion is often apparent on the land surface as elevated mounds. Immediately overlying the salt bed is a deep bed of anhydrite ($CaSO_4$), which, in turn, is overlain with a cavernous limestone. Covering this is a dense caprock of limestone overlain at varying depth with unconsolidated materials, sometimes containing quicksand impregnated with sulfurous water.

All of the overlying strata drape the intruded salt as a mantle. The sulfur occurs in the cavernous limestone which overlies the anhydrite, and underneath the dome formed by the dense limestone. Current theory is that hydrogen sulfide formed as a result of the action of anaerobic bacteria on the anhydrite, with the hydrogen sulfide rising into the cavernous limestone where it was trapped by the caprock and oxidized to sulfur. Petroleum, which is always present in the strata to some extent, supplied the carbon source needed by the bacteria. Some 30 sulfur domes exist in the Gulf Coast area, many of them mined out (10, 27, 59).

The Calcasieu Parish discovery traces back to observations shortly before the Civil War of oil seepage into the marshes surrounding the 50-acre mound. In 1867, General Jules Brady of New Orleans organized an oil company and made an exploratory drilling on the mound. Traces of oil were found, but when he drilled through the limestone caprock at 450 feet his borings brought up the cavernous limestone loaded with sulfur. In 1870, Brady reviewed his core samples with Professor Eugene W. Hilgard, then on the staff at the University of Mississippi, who was

Steaming and pumping wells of Freeport Sulphur Company at eastern edge of sulfur dome at Bryan Heights, Texas, 1917. *(USGS)*

Bank of sulfur that has been solidified from the molten state in which it was pumped from underground deposits at Louisiana mine. *(C. W. Hayes--USGS)*

making an oil and mineral survey for Louisiana. Hilgard convinced Brady of the value of the sulfur and suggested that a shaft should be sunk to mine it. As a result, the Calcasieu Sulphur and Mining Company was organized in New Orleans, largely with the backing of French capital. Antoine Granet, a leading French engineer, was sent over to study the deposit and determine how best to mine it. With more drillings, he confirmed the value of the deposit, and proposed to sink a shaft through the quicksand into the caprock by lining it with cast iron rings, each five feet high and 10 feet in diameter. The shaft was to be filled with water to keep the sand from flowing in; after reaching the caprock, the water was to be pumped out. The company had the rings built in Belgium, but even with the rings they were unable to penetrate the quicksand and the project failed. Several other companies followed, but none was successful. Finally, the American Sulphur Company took over and again tried to use Granet's rings, but with modifications. The project was abruptly terminated when several men were killed from exposure to hydrogen sulfide gas (27).

Herman Frasch Enters the Scene

Herman Frasch, who had studied the various company pamphlets along with reports in mining and geological journals, was challenged by the problem and began thinking about ways to remove the sulfur. Frasch, then chief of research and development for the Standard Oil Company, was a brilliant and innovative engineer, a good chemist, and an astute businessman. Before joining Standard Oil, he had engaged in petroleum desulfurization, salt mining, and other endeavors and was financially independent. Without visiting the mound, he conceived the idea of using heated water to melt the sulfur and then pumping it to the surface in liquid form. His first patent on this idea was issued in 1890 (21, 27).

Frasch, who had two free months a year to pursue his own interests, enlisted two fellow executives at Standard Oil, Frank Rockefeller and F. B. Squires, to join him in a project to mine the Calcasieu sulfur. The first move was to sink some exploratory wells near the mound, since Frasch had reasoned that the sulfur bed, like those in Sicily, covered a wide area. After drilling four wells in 1891 and 1892, Frasch had to conclude that he was in error and that the sulfur existed only under the mound. He and his partners then approached the American Sulphur Company, who still owned the mound, and with them formed a new corporation, the Union Sulphur Company.

Frasch bought a number of small boilers to superheat the water, drilled a 10-inch well to accommodate the injection of the water, and installed an oil well pump to raise the molten sulfur. In late December 1894, the first attempt to operate the process was made. Frasch's described what happened as follows:

... the man at the throttle (of the pump) sang out at the top of his voice 'She's pumping.' . . . Within five minutes the receptacles under pressure were opened and a beautiful stream of golden fluid shot into the barrels we had ready to receive the product. After pumping about fifteen minutes, the forty barrels we had supplied were seen to be inadequate. Quickly we threw up embankments and lined them with boards to receive the sulphur that was gushing forth; . . . When the sun went down we stopped the pump . . . . I mounted the sulphur pile and seated myself on the very top . . . proof that my object had been accomplished (21, pp. 137-138).

Thus, the soundness of the process was demonstrated, but it was far from perfected. The oil pumps never worked satisfactorily and had to be replaced with compressed air to force the liquid sulfur to the surface. Wells were lost for various reasons, larger boilers were required, and numerous other problems, including financial, had to be solved. It was not until 1896 that the process could be called a success, and only in the early 1900's did the operation start yielding a profit.

Fuel for the boilers was a problem since 14 tons of water heated to 335°F was required to recover one ton of sulfur. Wood from the surrounding area was burned initially, but this supply was soon exhausted, and coal had to be shipped in from Alabama at considerable cost. An unexpected stroke of luck resulted with the discovery of oil at Spindletop 60 miles away; it provided fuel at a fraction of the earlier cost. Sulphur Mine proved to be a huge success and continued in operation until 1924 with a total production of over 9 million tons of 99.5 percent pure sulfur (27).

Expansion of Gulf Coast Mining

Exploratory drilling for oil soon indicated presence of sulfur at similar mounds in Texas. Expiration of the Frasch patents encouraged the formation of new sulfur companies. Sulfur was noted at Bryanmound, Texas, near Freeport, in 1906. This eventually led to the formation of the Freeport Sulphur Company, which first produced sulfur in 1912. This mine continued in production until 1935, producing over 5 million tons. The next mine to come into operation was at Big Hill in Matagardo County, Texas. It was owned by the Texas Gulf Sulphur Company. Overproduction of sulfur delayed building a plant at Big Hill, and it wasn't until 1919 that operations began. Big Hill operated until 1936, producing about 12 million tons. Many other mines would be opened in the years ahead (27, 48, 50, 60).

As a result of the opening of the Gulf Coast deposits, U.S. production of elemental sulfur climbed from around 3,100 long tons in 1900 to over a million tons per year from 1917 through 1920. In the same period, U.S. imports of elemental sulfur fell from 168,000 tons in 1900 to less than 1,000 tons by 1917. Sicilian imports disappeared by 1912, and the small Japanese imports which supplied the West Coast ceased in 1916.

Frasch made his first export shipment in 1904 of 3,000 tons, and this increased to about 36,000 tons in 1907. Exports increased to about 90,000 tons in 1913 after Freeport Sulphur opened its mine, and reached 480,000 tons in 1920 after Texas Gulf started production (47, 61).

Frasch Goes International

The Sicilians at first did not believe that Gulf Coast sulfur was a threat. Frasch held meetings with the Anglo-Sicilian Company, which from 1896 to 1906 controlled two-thirds of the Sicilian export market, in an attempt to work out some arrangement that would stop the dumping of Sicilian sulfur at unrealistic prices at U.S. ports. He was told to go his way and they would go theirs, advice he promptly followed. Union Sulphur had mined 218,000 tons in 1905, which was about one-fourth of the total world production, a fact that could not be long ignored. Nevertheless, the new Sicilian-controlled Sulphur Consortium, which took over from the Anglo-Sicilian Company, also underrated the rising U.S. competition and told Frasch it wanted one-third of the U.S. market and all of the European market. As U.S. production continued to increase, an agreement was reached that the Union Sulphur Company would receive one-third of the world market, but no stipulations were made as to the U.S. market. The United States continued to be an increasingly important factor on the world market since it was producing nearly half of the world's output by 1914, and about 80 percent by 1920 (27).

Elemental Sulfur Takes Over

The shift back to elemental sulfur for U.S. sulfuric acid production was underway by 1913, when 16,000 long tons were used for this purpose. The tonnage climbed to 52,000 in 1915 and reached 197,000 in 1919 (61). At this point, 48 percent of the Nation's acid was made from elemental sulfur, 15 percent from domestic pyrites, 21 percent from imported pyrites, and 16 percent from sulfur dioxide recovered from zinc and copper smelters. This was in sharp contrast to the situation in 1909 when only two percent came from elemental sulfur, while domestic pyrites accounted for 20 percent, imported pyrites 64 percent, and smelter gases 12 percent (27, p. 327). In 1920, 204 sulfuric acid plants were operating in 32 states with about one-third of their output going into fertilizer manufacture (61).

REFERENCES

1. Anon. 1889-1890. Fertilizers. *Min. Res. of the U.S.* pp. 449-455.
2. ____. 1889-1890. Sulphur. *Min. Res.of the U.S.* pp. 515-570.
3. ____. 1899. Tennessee phosphates in 1898. *Am. Fert.* 10(1):8-10.
4. ____. 1899. The Tuscarora Fertilizer Company. *Am. Fert.* 10(3): 104-107.
5. ____. 1904. Tennessee phosphate rock. *Am. Fert.* 21(1):5-7.
6. ____. 1908. The phosphates of Florida. *Am. Fert.* 29(4):5-9.
7. ____. 1912. Great western phosphate fields. *Am. Fert.* 37(7):51
8. ____. 1914. Tennessee phosphates used extensively. *Comm. Fert.* 8(5):27.
9. Blakey, A. F. 1973. *The Florida Phosphate Industry: A History of Development and Use of a Vital Mineral.* Harvard Univ. Press, Cambridge, Mass.
10. Bondenlos, A. J. 1973. Sulfur. In *U.S. Mineral Resources.* U.S. Geol. Sur. prof. paper 820, pp. 605-618.
11. Brown, L. P. 1912. Phosphate deposits in the Rocky Mountain States. *Am. Fert.* 37(5):37-41.
12. Cathcart, J. B. 1980. World phosphate reserves and resources. In *The Role of Phosphorus in Agriculture.* pp. 1-18. Publ. by American Society of Agronomy, Madison, Wisc.
13. ____. 1980. The phosphate industry of the United States. In *The Role of Phosphorus in Agriculture.* pp. 19-42. Publ. by American Society of Agronomy, Madison, Wisc.
14. Chapman, O. C. 1952. The phosphates of Tennessee. In *Phosphoric Acid, Phosphates and Phosphatic Fertilizers* by W. C. Waggaman. pp. 72-83. Hafner Publishing Co., Inc., New York.
15. Chazal, P. E. 1904. *The Century in Phosphates and Fertilizers–A Sketch of the South Carolina Phosphate Industry.* Lucas- Richardson, Charleston, S.C.
16. Condit, D. D., E. H. Finch, and J. T. Pardee. 1928. *Phosphate Rock in Three Forks-Yellowstone Park Region, Montana.* U.S. Geol. Sur. Bull. 795-G.
17. Cooke, D. S. 1905. Phosphate mining in Tennessee, *Am. Fert.* 23(5): 5-10.
18. Curtis, H. A. 1941. *The problem of utilizing phosphates from the deposits in the western states.* Tenn. Valley Auth., Dept. of Chem. Eng. Rpt. No. 14.
19. Day, D. T. 1885. Phosphate rock. *Min. Res. of U.S.* pp. 445-458.
20. ____. 1885. Apatite. *Min. Res. of U.S.* pp. 455-458.
21. Frasch, H. J. 1912. Perkin Medal address of acceptance. *Ind. Eng. Chem.* 4:134-140.
22. Freeland, W. H. and C. W. Renwick. 1911. Smeltery smoke as a source of sulphuric acid. *Am. Fert.* 34(5):42-46.
23. Fuller, R. B. 1951. The history and development of phosphate rock mining. *Min. Eng.* 3(8):708-712.
24. Gale, H. S. 1914. *Geology of phosphate deposits northeast of Georgetown, Idaho.* U.S. Geol. Sur. Bull. 577.
25. Haskill, A. P., Jr. and O. E. Kiessling. 1938. *Technology, employment, and output per man in phosphate rock mining, 1880-1937.* Works Progress Administration, National Research Project Rpt. No. E-7.
26. Hayes, C. W. 1895. *The Tennessee phosphates.* U.S. Geol. Sur. Ann. Rpt. Part 4. pp. 610-630.

27. Haynes, W. 1942. *The Stone That Burns*. D. Van Nostrand Co., Inc., N.Y.
28. ____. 1954. Revolutions in sulfuric acid. In *American Chemical Industry, a History. Vol. I, 1609-1911.* pp. 253-268. D. Van Nostrand Co., Inc., New York.
29. ____. 1945. Phosphate rock and elemental phosphorus. In *American Chemical Industry, a History. Vol. II, 1912-1922.* pp. 182-194. D. Van Nostrand Co., Inc., New York.
30. Hillebrew, J. B. 1899. Phosphate industry in Tennessee. Am. Fert. 11(2):63-64.
31. Holmes, F. S. 1870. *Phosphate Rocks in South Carolina and the Great Carolina Marl Bed.* Holmes Book House, Charleston, S.C.
32. Hovey, E. O. 1903. Phosphate rock. Min. Res. of the U.S. pp. 1047-1058.
33. ____. 1904. Phosphate rock. Min. Res. of the U.S. pp. 1053-1061.
34. Jones, C. C. 1907. Phosphate rock in Utah, Idaho, and Wyoming. Eng. Min. 83:953-955.
35. ____. 1913. *The discovery and opening of a new phosphate field in the United States.* Am. Inst. Min. Eng. Bull. 82. pp. 2411-2435.
36. LeBaron, M. 1969. Florida pebble phosphate. In *Phosphoric Acid, Phosphates, and Phosphatic Fertilizers*, by W. H. Waggaman. pp. 50-71. Hafner Publishing Co., Inc., New York.
37. Mansfield, G. R. 1922. Phosphate rock. Min. Res. of the U.S., Part II. pp. 109-121.
38. Mappus, H. F. 1935. *The phosphate industry of South Carolina.* Master of Science thesis. Dept. of Chem., Univ. of South Carolina.
39. McCaskey, H. D. 1915. Phosphate rock. Min. Res. of the U.S., Part II. pp. 227-244.
40. Meadows, T. C. 1894. Tennessee phosphates. Am. Fert. 1(4):209-212.
41. ____. 1895. Tennessee phosphates in 1894. Am. Fert. 2(1):24-25.
42. ____ and L. Brown. 1895. The phosphates of Tennessee. Trans. Am. Inst. Min. Eng. 24 (Feb. 1894 to Oct. 1894):582-594.
43. Mehring, A. L., J. R. Adams, and K. D. Jacob. 1957. *Statistics on fertilizers and liming materials in the United States.* USDA Stat. Bull. No. 191.
44. Menninger, C. G. 1912. Phosphate mining in relation to the fertilizer industry. Comm. Fert. 4(2):24,26,30,32.
45. Moses, O. A. 1882-1883. The phosphate deposits of South Carolina. Min. Res. of the U.S. pp. 504-521.
46. Norris, E. M. 1969. Western phosphates. In *Phosphoric Acid, Phosphates, and Phosphatic Fertilizers*, by W. H. Waggaman. pp. 84-89. Hafner Publishing Co., New York.
47. Phalen, W. C. 1910. Sulphur and pyrite. Min. Res. of the U.S., Part II. pp. 783-798.
48. ____. 1912. Sulphur, pyrite, and sulphuric acid. Min. Res. of the U.S., Part II. pp. 931-953.
49. ____. 1912. Phosphate rock. Min. Res. of the U.S., Part II. pp. 855-876.
50. ____. 1913. Sulphur, pyrite, and sulphuric acid. Min. Res. of the U.S., Part II. pp. 23-47.
51. ____. 1915. Sulphur, pyrites, and sulphuric acid. Min. Res. of the U.S., Part II. pp. 291-306.
52. Pratt, J. H. 1903. Sulphur and pyrite. Min. Res. of the U.S. pp. 1073-1087.
53. ____. 1904. Sulphur and pyrite. Min. Res. of the U.S. pp. 1079-1094.

54. Richards, R. W. and G. R. Mansfield. 1914. *Geology of the phosphate deposits northeast of Georgetown, Idaho.* U.S. Geol. Sur. Bull, 577.
55. Richter, A. 1911. Western phosphate discovery. *Mines and Methods* 2(9):207.
56. Rogers, G. S. 1913. The phosphate deposits of South Carolina. In *Contributions to Economic Geology. Part I.* U.S. Geol. Sur. Bull. 580. pp. 183-184, 209-220.
57. Ruhm, H. D. 1904. History of the fertilizer industry. *Am. Fert.* 21(5):5-11.
58. Smith, P. S. 1916. Sulphur, pyrite, and sulphuric acid. *Min. Res. of the U.S., Part II.* pp. 403-431.
59. _____. 1917. Sulphur, pyrites, and sulphuric acid. *Min. Res. of the U.S., Part II.* pp. 19-62.
60. _____. 1919. Sulphur and pyrites. *Min. Res. of the U.S., Part II.* pp. 535-546.
61. _____. 1920. Sulphur, pyrites, and sulphuric acid. *Min. Res. of the U.S., Part II.* pp. 301-308.
62. Stone, R. W. 1916. Phosphate rock. *Min. Res. of the U.S., Part II.* pp. 29-41.
63. _____. 1918. Phosphate rock. *Min. Res. of the U.S., Part II.* pp. 199-222.
64. _____. 1919. Phosphate rock. *Min. Res. of the U.S., Part II.* pp. 211-225.
65. _____. and C. A. Bonine. 1914. *Elliston phosphate field, Montana.* U.S. Geol. Sur. Bull. 580-N. pp. 373-383.
66. Struthers, J. 1902. Sulphur and pyrite. *Min. Res. of the U.S.* pp. 933-943.
67. Van Horn, F. B. 1911. The production of phosphate rock in 1910. *Am. Fert.* 35(5):21-28.
68. Waggaman, W. H. 1911. A review of the phosphate fields of Florida. *Am. Fert.* 35(1):33-43.
69. _____. 1913. A report on the phosphate fields of South Carolina. *Comm. Fert.* 7(3):32,34,36,38,40.
70. _____. 1952. Phosphates of South Carolina, Kentucky, Arkansas, and Virginia. In *Phosphoric Acid, Phosphates, and Phosphatic Fertilizers.* pp. 100-110. Hafner Publishing Co., New York.
71. Weeks, F. B. 1908. Phosphate deposits in the western United States. *Am. Fert.* 28(4):24-27.
72. _____ and W. F. Ferrier. 1907. *Phosphates in the western United States.* U.S. Geol. Sur. Bull. 315. pp. 449-462.

4

The Fertilizer Industry 1870-1920

The fledgling U.S. fertilizer industry, which had been based almost entirely on guanos, bones, and, too often, frauds, came of age during the 1870 to 1920 period. There was a great shift in raw materials used in the manufacture of superphosphates, from organic sources to domestic phosphate rock. Potash, for the first time, became an important nutrient in fertilizers. Nitrogen sources, other than the high-nitrogen guanos that by 1870 were in short supply, came to the forefront. Use of other natural organics, both old and new, grew rapidly. The inorganics, sodium nitrate and ammonium sulfate, which were important nitrogen sources in other countries, were adopted widely. Also, fertilizer materials based upon nitrogen synthesized from the atmosphere made their appearance.

The 50-year period saw the use of plant nutrients increase 23-fold, break out of the confines of the Atlantic seaboard, and advance into the states to the west. Fertilizer-using states enacted strong fertilizer inspection and control laws, established fertilizer control laboratories, and improved and standardized analytical methods. This period also saw the establishment of practical fertilizer trade associations and the initiation of journals devoted entirely to fertilizer production, distribution, and use.

Finally, after many difficulties and growing pains, the agricultural colleges and experiment stations accomplished many of the goals envisioned for them affecting agriculture, farmers and the fertilizer industry alike. Extension services were set up to carry the results of the research to the users. Also, the U.S. Department of Agriculture developed research and other programs in soils and fertilizers.

In summary, foundation was laid that the fertilizer industry and public sector institutions could build upon for many years.

Fertilizer Consumption and Industry Expansion

Tables 4.1 and 4.2 show the increases in U.S. fertilizer consumption and industry expansion from the 1850's to 1920. The data, compiled by

Nineteenth century plant of Atlantic and Virginia Fertilizer Works at Richmond. (*Virginia State Library and Archives*)

the Bureau of Census, show consistent and rapid growth throughout the period. Not shown in the tables, however, are the short breaks in the growth pattern which occurred during the Civil War and World War I.

Several factors, operating together, were responsible for the rapid increases in fertilizer consumption after 1870. Key among these were the discovery and development of our domestic sources of phosphate rock, the imports of German potash and Chilean nitrate, the scavenging of natural organics by the industry, and the domestic production of by-product ammonium sulfate. The availability of adequate supplies of fertilizer materials plus the growing awareness by farmers of the value of fertilizers assured an ever-increasing market.

In order to meet the demand, the number and size of fertilizer plants were increased, more and more people were employed in the production and distribution of fertilizers and, for the times, large amounts of capital were spent. The fertilizer industry became one of the very largest in the country, by 1919 employing about 38,000 people in manufacturing and mixing, and producing products valued at nearly $300 million annually.

Geographic Shifts in Use and Production

Before 1870, fertilizer use was greatest in the Middle Atlantic and the New England States, but a strong shift toward Virginia, the Carolinas, and Georgia had begun. Production was largely in or close to the harbor cities of Baltimore, Philadelphia, New York, and Boston, with Baltimore emerging as the number one producer. Following the Civil War, use further intensified in the South Atlantic States. With development of the South Carolina phosphate deposits, manufacturing also began to intensify in the Charleston area.

The future of the Charleston area as a fertilizer manufacturing center apparently was first recognized by the Sulphuric and Superphosphate Manufacturing Company, which initiated construction of a sulfuric acid plant in 1868, and by the Wando Fertilizer Company which began in 1869 to manufacture superphosphate from South Carolina phosphate rock. More than 20,000 tons of fertilizer was shipped from Charleston in 1871, and the 100,000-ton mark was reached 10 years later. By 1884, eleven companies were manufacturing fertilizers in the area, and by 1902, Charleston had replaced Baltimore as the top fertilizer-producing city of the Nation (34, 62).

Fertilizer use increased rapidly in the older fertilizer-using states between 1880 and 1920. Fertilizers also began to make their mark in states where use previously had been inconsequential or nonexistent. These changes are apparent from the data in Table 4.3, which shows the fertilizer consumption by regions, states, and territories at 10-year intervals. Overall, the Nation's use of fertilizers increased 10-fold during the 1880-1920 period, from about 753,000 tons of material to 7 million tons. Greatest use throughout the period was in the South Atlantic

Table 4.1. Trends in U.S. Consumption of Fertilizers (67).

Year	All fertilizers	Nitrogen	P_2O_5	K_2O	Total
		1,000 tons			
1850	53	3	4	1	8
1860	164	10	1	3	25
1870	321	14	31	4	49
1880	753	19	70	13	102
1890	1,390	38	132	31	201
1900	2,730	62	246	86	394
1910	5,547	146	499	211	856
1920	7,296	228	660	257	1,145

Table 4.2. Superphosphate and Dry Mixing Plants (67).

Year	Plants	Production	Wage earners	Salaried employees	Cost of materials	Value of products
	No.	1,000 T.	No.	No.	$1,000	$1,000
1859	47	32	308	-	591	891
1869	126	153	2,501	-	3,808	5,815
1879	364	727	8,598	-	15,595	23,651
1889	390	1,899	9,026	-	25,114	39,181
1899	422	2,887	11,581	1,712	8,958	44,657
1909	550	5,618	18,310	3,317	69,522	103,960
1919	600	8,237	26,296	6,007	107,955	281,144

States, which used about 50 percent of all fertilizers consumed in the United States, with the percentage increasing somewhat in the last two 10-year periods. Of the five states in the region, North Carolina, South Carolina, and Georgia were the big users, together consuming more than 40 percent of the Nation's total. The second largest consuming region, the Middle Atlantic States, registered a fourfold increase during the period, from about 255,000 tons to slightly over a million, but the region's share in the total U.S. consumption declined steadily from about 34 percent in 1880 to about 14 percent in 1920.

Use in the New England States increased about 8-fold during the period, from around 41,000 to 341,000 tons enabling the region to retain its 5-percent share throughout the period. This was due almost entirely to rapid increases in fertilizer use in Maine, which by 1910 had become the largest fertilizer-using state in the region.

The East South Central States showed a 14-fold increase over the period, from 49,000 to 692,000 tons. This region averaged about 11 percent of the U.S. total. Alabama was consistently the largest fertilizer-using state of the region, accounting for 71 percent of that used in 1880 and 54 percent in 1920. Alabama used about 6 percent of the U.S. total during the period, or more than the New England region.

Use in the East North Central region was mostly in Ohio, Michigan, and Indiana. The regions use increased nearly 20-fold, from 35,000 tons in 1880 to 682,000 tons in 1920, at which time consumption was 9 percent of the U.S. total.

Little fertilizer was used in the other states and territories. In 1880, the remaining states used only 12,000 tons; by 1920, however, use had climbed to 761,000 tons or about 10 percent of the Nation's total. In the West South Central States use in Louisiana, Arkansas, and Texas achieved significance only in the latter half of the period. Oklahoma used practically no fertilizer as late as 1920. In the West North Central region, only Missouri used appreciable tonnages and then not until about 1910. Fertilizer use in the Mountain States remained nil. California was the only Pacific State using much fertilizer, and that not until about 1910. Hawaii and Puerto Rico also began using fertilizer after the turn of the century.

Several factors accounted for the slow spread of fertilizers into the two north central regions. First, prairies brought into cultivation originally were high in fertility and slow to deplete. This led many farmers to believe their nutrient supplies were inexhaustible. Second, land was cheap, labor scarce, and capital expensive. Also, the advent of farm mechanization encouraged farmers to cultivate larger acreages rather than intensify operations on smaller acreages. Finally, in most of the states, rotation farming that included legumes was widely practiced, and a heavy livestock population provided relatively large amounts of manure. All of this caused many of the land-grant colleges and experiment stations to be cautious in recommending fertilizer use (36, 68, 77).

The situation was much different in the South Central regions where the westward spread of fertilizers was much faster. Most of the soils were already worn out or easily exhausted, there were few livestock to provide manure, and a cash crop system of farming predominated, with fields devoted to the same crop year after year. Low-cost labor was available, and the leaders and the colleges generally favored fertilizer use (45, 80).

Although fertilizer plants initially were located at or near East Coast harbor cities, plants built after about 1900 usually were positioned near use areas. Exact locations of fertilizer mixing plants have not been summarized. However, the locations of superphosphate plants suggest wide dispersal of the fertilizer industry. Most of these not only manufactured their own mixed fertilizers but also sold superphosphate to other mixers in the vicinity. A 1914 listing shows 257 superphosphate plants in 25 states and Hawaii. The number of plants in a state usually was related to the amount of fertilizer consumed in that state or in adjacent states. Georgia had 54 superphosphate plants, South Carolina 25, North Carolina 16, Alabama 20, Maryland 18, Pennsylvania 15, Virginia 14, Ohio 16, California 11, New Jersey 9, Florida 9, Mississippi 8, and Illinois and Louisiana each 7. Most of the other fertilizer-using states had one to six plants each. By regions, the South Atlantic States had 118 superphosphate plants, the Middle Atlantic 45, New England 7, East South Central 35, East North Central 28, West South Central 9, West North Central 2 (both in Missouri), Pacific 11 (all in California), Mountain 0, and Hawaii, 1. Plants equipped to manufacture superphosphate accounted for about 40 percent of all fertilizer plants from 1914 to 1920 (56).

The Consolidated Fertilizer Companies

Fertilizer companies continued to increase in size and numbers from 1870 into the 1890's. They typically manufactured both superphosphate and mixed fertilizers or produced only mixed fertilizers. Both groups bought their nitrogen and potash individually, with the

Fertilizer use was slow to develop in the Midwest, whose soils were inherently quite fertile and which was settled later than the South and the Atlantic states.
(U.S. Department of Agriculture)

mixers usually buying superphosphate from the first group. Those manufacturing superphosphate and mixed fertilizers and the larger mixers marketed largely through dealers, while the smaller mixers sold direct to farmers. Most of the larger companies required outside financial backing, and either the dealers or the companies usually provided or arranged for credit until the crops were harvested and sold. Most of the early companies were independents, owning only the plant they operated.

A trend toward consolidation began in the mid-1890's. Large parent companies acquired independent manufacturers, either as subsidiaries or affiliates, and also moved into phosphate rock mining. They not only produced their own superphosphate from their own rock, but also acquired or built their own sulfuric acid plants. Their main product, mixed fertilizers, was marketed through dealerships which the parent company sometimes owned or controlled. They also marketed superphosphate and phosphate rock in excess of their needs. The companies dealt directly with the German potash syndicate, and one company owned shares in a German potash mine. Two companies, owned by large Chicago meat packers, produced their own animal organics.

The first of the consolidated companies to emerge was the Virginia-Carolina Chemical Company in 1895. Five consolidated companies were operating by 1913. They and two independents largely dominated the U.S. fertilizer market. This "Big Seven" (sometimes called the"Big Six" when the independent Baugh & Sons Company was not included) sold almost 4 million tons of mixed fertilizers in 1913, or about 50 percent of all the fertilizer consumed in the country. The two giants of the Big Seven, Virginia-Carolina and the American Agricultural Chemical Company, each sold more than a million tons of mixed fertilizer per year. Five others sold more than 200,000 tons each. These were the International Agricultural Corporation, Armour Fertilizer Works, Swift and Company, and the two independents, F. S. Royster Guano Company and Baugh & Sons Company (50).

In 1916, Virginia-Carolina controlled or owned 34 companies that mined phosphate rock, manufactured and sold fertilizers, or sold fertilizers only. American Agricultural Chemical had 32 companies involved with fertilizers and 16 operating in other fields. The International Agricultural Corporation controlled 48 fertilizer companies; Swift, 16; Armour, 11; and F. S. Royster, 7 (50).

These companies, as a part of their fertilizer manufacturing operations, also were major superphosphate producers; in 1920, the companies operated 101 of the country's 232 superphosphate plants. Virginia-Carolina had 37 plants; American Agricultural Chemical, 22; International, 14; Armour, 14; Swift, 9; and F. S. Royster, 5. More than half of these plants were also equipped to produce sulfuric acid (56).

The large companies moved into fertilizers in different ways. Virginia-Carolina was organized in 1895 in Richmond, Virginia, by two leaders

Table 4.3. Fertilizer Consumption by Regions and States (67).

	1880	1890	1900	1910	1920
			Tons Material		
			South Atlantic		
Virginia	55,000	100,000	220,000	344,900	465,200
N. Carolina	65,000	140,000	276,200	630,900	1,170,400
S Carolina	86,500	126,000	292,200	975,000	1,098,500
Georgia	152,500	288,000	412,800	1,022,000	1,003,050
Florida	1,200	31,000	33,200	172,600	262,000
Total	360,100	685,200	1,234,400	3,145,600	3,999,300
			Middle Atlantic		
New York	39,000	85,000	247,000	229,600	250,000
New Jersey	30,000	39,500	66,000	125,000	164,800
Pennsylvania	90,000	110,000	213,000	287,000	319,700
Delaware	6,000	8,000	12,000	23,000	36,200
Maryland	84,000	100,000	151,000	148,000	172,400
District of Columbia	500	700	1,000	1,000	1,000
West Virginia	5,000	15,000	25,000	27,300	35,400
Total	254,500	358,216	715,000	840,900	1,018,300
			New England		
Maine	5,000	17,000	40,000	95,700	168,000
New Hampshire	3,000	7,500	12,270	12,800	17,000
Vermont	4,000	8,500	15,500	18,000	20,000
Massachusetts	22,000	40,000	75,100	41,600	61,400
Rhode Island	2,000	5,000	6,000	6,500	10,000
Connecticut	5,000	15,000	35,000	42,000	65,000
Total	41,000	93,000	183,900	216,600	341,400
			East South Central		
Kentucky	4,500	7,300	24,000	58,000	88,000
Tennessee	4,000	8,600	36,400	58,600	98,500
Alabama	35,000	99,900	150,000	425,000	374,900
Mississippi	6,000	28,000	98,000	132,800	131,100
Total	49,500	143,731	308,448	674,389	692,479
			East North Central		
Ohio	15,000	40,000	89,000	130,000	280,000
Indiana	7,000	29,000	58,000	151,900	231,800
Illinois	4,000	8,000	11,000	15,000	45,000
Michigan	5,000	6,000	15,000	38,400	112,600
Wisconsin	4,000	3,000	2,500	2,000	12,000
Total	35,000	86,000	175,500	337,300	681,400

Table 4.3 (continued)

	1880	1890	1900	1910	1920
	\multicolumn{5}{c}{Tons Material}
	\multicolumn{5}{c}{West South Central}
Arkansas	50	300	3,000	30,000	77,550
Louisiana	5,000	11,120	31,813	88,396	110,765
Oklahoma	-	-	-	1,000	4,000
Texas	1,000	2,000	10,000	34,000	55,405
Total	6,050	13,420	44,913	153,396	247,720
	\multicolumn{5}{c}{West North Central}
Minnesota	1,000	1,000	1,000	2,000	5,000
Iowa	1,000	1,000	1,000	1,200	3,500
Missouri	1,000	1,500	3,300	31,585	92,737
North Dakota	-	-	-	-	200
South Dakota	-	-	-	-	200
Nebraska	-	-	-	100	500
Kansas	1,000	700	700	1,200	12,700
Total	4,000	4,200	6,000	36,100	114,800
	\multicolumn{5}{c}{Mountain}
Montana	-	-	-	-	-
Idaho	-	-	-	-	300
Wyoming	-	-	-	-	-
Colorado	100	300	500	500	250
New Mexico	100	100	200	300	700
Arizona	-	-	-	-	500
Utah	100	200	200	200	200
Nevada	-	-	-	-	30
Total	300	600	900	1,000	2,000
	\multicolumn{5}{c}{Pacific}
Washington	-	100	400	1,000	6,000
Oregon	100	200	500	2,500	6,000
California	2,000	2,500	8,000	44,900	66,400
Total	2,100	2,800	8,900	48,400	78,400
Hawaii	-	3,000	50,000	70,000	70,000
Puerto Rico	-	-	2,000	23,000	50,000
Alaska	-	-	-	10	10
Total	-	3,000	52,000	93,000	120,000

in the fertilizer industry, S. T. Morgan and S. A. Crenshaw. Gaining a foothold in the rapidly growing southern fertilizer industry was a major objective, and it soon acquired eight firms. One move involved gaining control of most of the fertilizer companies clustered around Charleston, South Carolina. At least one of these companies, the Charleston Mining and Manufacturing Company, was a major miner of phosphate rock. This acquisition placed Virginia-Carolina in the mining business, which it expanded by moving into the Florida pebble field, using Charleston Mining and Manufacturing as one of its major subsidiaries in this field (49, 62).

American Agricultural Chemical (later Agrico) was organized in 1889 to acquire and operate fertilizer plants in the northern and eastern states. Within a short time it controlled several well-established companies. In 1902, it acquired the Peace River Phosphate Mining Company, and in 1905 moved into the Florida land pebble field. By 1912, American Agricultural Chemical and Virginia-Carolina were the major Florida pebble producers. They and the International Agricultural Corporation, accounted for more than half the phosphate rock mined in Tennessee (49, 51).

The International Agricultural Corporation (now International Minerals and Chemical Corporation) got its start in the Tennessee phosphate fields about 1899 as the U. S. Agricultural Corporation founded by T. C. Meadows and O. L. Dortch to produce superphosphate from the rock. "International" was added to its name in 1901 when it sold part of its shares to the German firm of Kaliwerke Sollstedt Gewerkschaft for an interest in that company's Sollstedt potash mine. International had phosphate rock nines in the Tennessee brown rock field and purchased several superphosphate and mixed fertilizer plants. In 1908, it contracted for the entire output of sulfuric acid from the Ducktown, Tennessee, copper smelters. Also, it obtained two mining subsidiaries in the Florida pebble field (51).

Two companies, Armour and Swift, moved into the fertilizer business initially to market animal by-products-tankage, dried blood, bonemeal, and other meat packing house wastes. In the early 1900's, they expanded by obtaining phosphate rock mines and superphosphate and mixed fertilizer plants. The F. S. Royster Guano Company, got its start when Royster, a store clerk, built a fertilizer plant in Tarboro, North Carolina in 1885. The company soon had 24 plants. Royster labeled each bag prominently with "FSR" and he became known as "Fish Scrap Royster." In 1900, he added "guano" to the company name (50). Baugh & Sons, the other family-owned operation, was one of the earliest manufacturers of superphosphate, starting in Pennsylvania in 1855. Unlike other companies, Baugh did not acquire subsidiaries, but built and owned plants in Pennsylvania and Baltimore (56).

Although the Big Seven were the largest fertilizer producers, three others in 1913 were marketing 75,000 to 100,000 tons of mixed fertilizers each, and 10 were in the 50,000-ton range. None of the other 780 firms in the industry sold more than 50,000 tons annually; the average was about 4,700 tons (50, 67).

The small mixers found size less of a disadvantage then one might expect. Even the large companies had to purchase most of their fertilizer materials, except for superphosphate, on the open market; at most the small mixers paid only slightly more. The small mixers usually had no problem in obtaining superphosphate at reasonable prices since the highly competitive producers of superphosphate often had difficulty in disposing of surplus stocks and sometimes sold at cut-rate prices. In some areas, small mixers made inroads into the sales of their larger competitors; in Georgia, for example, they often drove manufacturers' dealers out of business (50).

Fertilizer Materials by the Dozens

The number of fertilizer materials profilerated between 1870 to 1920. Inorganic nitrogen forms, sodium nitrate and ammonium sulfate, came into general use, and calcium cyanamide made its appearance. So many natural organic nitrogen sources were searched out that the industry was often characterized as being a scavenger. Superphosphate manufactured from phosphate rock appeared and became the prime phosphate source. Use of ground rock started, and concentrated superphosphate and ammonium phosphates appeared in the marketplace. Natural potash salts became major fertilizer materials, and potash from almost every conceivable domestic source was sought out and used during the World War I years.

Inorganic Nitrogen Materials

Sodium nitrate use in the United States increased slowly, due largely to the farmers' preference for organic nitrogen materials. Although some was used shortly after the Civil War, consumption was only 10,000 tons by 1880, and only 37,000 tons was used as late as 1900. By 1910, however, some 244,000 tons was consumed and, in 1920, the figure reached 483,000 tons (67).

Chilean Nitrate—The Chilean nitrate industry underwent major changes to enable production to keep abreast of growing U.S. and world demand. Perhaps the most important change was the development and introduction around 1880 of the Shank's process for extracting and refining the product. Also, the larger producers mechanized mining of the caliche containing the nitrates and its transportation to processing plants (38).

After the Chilean Government possession of the nitrate deposits in 1880 following the War of the Pacific, it soon adopted a policy of permitting private owners to work the deposits. It also imposed an export duty on all nitrates they shipped, a tax that eventually became the government's greatest source of revenue. Although some Chilean companies apparently mined and processed nitrates, foreign companies were very active. At first, British companies dominated foreign interests but, as German imports grew, German companies appeared in considerable numbers. U.S. interests in the field were inconsequential by comparison. The DuPont Nitrate Company began operations in 1913, controlling one company,"Oficiano Delaware," and further increased its holdings in 1917. W. R. Grace and Company, a major shipper and seller of nitrates in the United States, bought out a British company in 1916, and produced about 4,000 tons of nitrate monthly (49).

Production of Chilean nitrate increased tremendously, approaching 3 million tons in 1913; its use, however, no longer was limited to fertilizers. For example, in 1913 an estimated 40 to 55 percent of nitrate imports into the United States were used as fertilizers, 10 to 12 percent went into general chemicals, and 35 to 40 percent went into explosives, mainly industrial. In 1918, as a result of the war, 61 percent went into munitions manufacture and only 17 percent into fertilizers (49).

For years, W. R. Grace and Company imported and sold to distributors most of the sodium nitrate used in this country. Grace carried on a large trading business in South American countries using its own freight-carrying steamers, and trade in Chilean nitrate fit well into its overall business. In 1913, H. J. Baker & Bro. of New York, a leading broker in fertilizer materials, made a favorable sales-agency agreement with a London firm and, through price-cutting, was able to establish a foothold. At times both American Agricultural Chemical and Armour imported nitrates on a small scale (49).

As it became increasingly evident that the United States would become involved in World War I, imports of sodium nitrate climbed to around 2 million tons per year and continued at this level until hostilities ceased. Chilean nitrate was the Nation's leading source of inorganic nitrogen, far exceeding that from by-product coke oven plants, cyanamide, and the one arc plant. It was used to meet most military and industrial needs, and to furnish much of the nitrogen required by agriculture. Prices soared as a result of the large demand, wartime conditions, and the activities of speculators. This, plus the need for assuring an adequate supply, caused the War Industries Board to take over as centralized purchasing agent, distributing the nitrogen on a nonprofit basis. Some of the nitrogen was released for farm use when Congress authorized $10 million under the Food Control Act to the U.S. Department of Agriculture to provide sodium nitrate to farmers. Allocations were made to individual farmers through the county agricultural agents with the farmer paying $80 per ton at port of entry plus additional handling and freight costs. Even so, supplies of sodium nitrate for fertilizer use were tight as were all nitrogen sources. Other inorganics had largely been diverted for

Old sodium nitrate production facilities in Chile. *(Chilean Nitrate Corporation)*

munitions; high-grade organics were by this time being used increasingly in livestock feeds, and the fish scrap industry was crippled by the diversion of its steamers to other uses. Nevertheless, consumption of nitrogen in fertilizers held at about 200,000 tons of N annually, largely as a result of the sodium nitrate allocations plus increased use of the lower grade organics. The abrupt ending of the war in November 1918 left the War Department with a surplus of sodium nitrate. Some was released immediately to farmers at cost plus freight, but it was quickly used in the 1919 spring planting season (33, 50).

Natural nitrates occur in many parts of the United States. In the West and Southwest they are found in caliche deposits, and throughout most of the country they accumulated on the walls and floors of bat-infested caves. The growing market and high prices for Chilean nitrate brought a flurry of prospecting by private individuals and companies starting about 1912. During the World War I period, when supplies from Chile were thought to be endangered, the Ordnance Department and the U.S. Geological Survey also entered the search. A great many high-quality specimens and small deposits of both sodium nitrate and potassium nitrate were discovered, with the most promising being the caliche deposits of the Amargosa region in southeastern California. Although some attempts were made by private companies to bring various deposits into commercial production, none contained sufficient quantities of nitrates to justify development (29, 60, 71).

Ammonium Sulfate—Ammonium sulfate became a major fertilizer material in this country only after by-product coke ovens made their appearance shortly before the turn of the century. Before the coming of the by-product ovens, ammonium sulfate was produced exclusively from city gas works built to supply illuminating gas; however, most of these did not bother to recover the ammonia released in the gasification process. Although a great deal of coke from coal was made in "beehive ovens," no byproducts were recovered since all of the gases produced in the coking process were burned to provide heat for the carbonization. Largely as a result, in 1870 only about 2,000 tons of ammonium sulfate was used as fertilizer, and, even by 1900, use did not exceed 5,000 tons. As more by-product ovens came into use, tonnage climbed to 135,000 in 1910 and reached 273,000 in 1920 (67).

The first by-product coke oven plant in the United States was constructed in 1892 by the Solvay Process Company in Syracuse, New York. It used 12 Semet-Solvay ovens developed by an associate company in Belgium. The Solvay Process Company had been formed in 1881 to manufacture soda ash by the ammonia-soda process. The Company located at Syracuse to take advantage of large limestone and salt deposits in the area, and to tap city gas works in central New York for ammonia. It immediately ran into the problem of an insufficient supply of ammonia and tried unsuccessfully to encourage the gas works to increase their recovery of ammonia. Solvay, as a result, built by-product ovens which proved to be a huge success (13, 51).

The Semet-Solvay Company was formed in 1895 to promote, construct, and operate, if necessary, by-product coking plants in this country. The first plant built in 1896 for the Dunbar Furnace Company at Dunbar, Pennsylvania, had a battery of 50 ovens. Other types of by-product ovens soon came into operation; by 1902, about 1700 ovens of all types were operating at 10 locations. By 1912, 4,624 ovens in 13 states produced a total of 155,000 tons of ammonium sulfate. Their numbers continued to increase, with a great surge of new ovens coming into operation during the war years of 1917 and 1918 (49, 86).

As used during the period, the by-product ovens essentially heated crushed coal in chambers by burning a part of the cleaned gas produced in the overall process. The heat generated by the burning of the gas was transferred to the chambers by vertical flues placed around the walls. The gases evolved from the coal carbonization were drawn through air- and water-cooled condensers in which the first set of condensers removed the crude tars and a second set, ammoniacal liquor. The ammoniacal liquor was then distilled, with either the ammonia being concentrated for industrial uses or reacted with sulfuric acid to form ammonium sulfate. The crude tars were distilled, at first to produce benzene and toluene, and later a host of other chemicals. The purified gas not used for heating the chambers was sold for heating or illumination purposes, and the coke produced captured the markets previously held by the beehive oven producers and the gas works.

The advent of the by-product ovens gave a great boost to ammonium sulfate production, since recovery of byproducts was an important and profitable part of the whole operation. In the old gas works it was never highly profitable to recover the ammonia as the only chemical, and few did. Most were content to sell the purified gas and the coke, salvage the crude tars which were in demand for roofing and a few other purposes, and dump the ammonia liquor into a sewer or the closest stream (49).

Calcium Cyanamide—Calcium cyanamide was first used in the United States as a nitrogen fertilizer material in 1909. It was produced by the American Cyanamid Company at Niagara Falls, Ontario, Canada. The initial output of the plant was only 5,000 tons annually, nearly all of which was marketed in the United States. Production increased slowly to 28,000 tons in 1913, and eventually reached about 120,000 tons. Use as a fertilizer also was severely crippled during the war years as cyanamide was diverted to munitions manufacture. Nevertheless, the introduction of calcium cyanamide as a fertilizer represented a major step toward the successful use of atmospheric nitrogen as a fertilizer source in this country (21, 43, 49, 58, 94). A second cyanamide plant was completed in 1918 at Muscle Shoals, Alabama, as a munitions plant for the U.S. Government, but the war ended before it could come into production. Except for a short test run, the plant was never operated to produce cyanamide (25).

The founding of the American Cyanamid Company and the location of the plant at Niagara Falls, Ontario, resulted from the activities of Frank S. Washburn. Washburn, a civil engineer and official of the Alabama Power Company, was deeply interested and involved in hydropower development in the southeastern Appalachian region and in the selection of key power sites. Also, having worked at one time as an engineer in the Chilean nitrate fields, he was enthralled with the idea of using hydropower as a source of energy for fixing atmospheric nitrogen to use in fertilizers. He had two sites in mind as possible locations for an air nitrogen plant, one at an existing hydroplant on the Coosa River owned by Alabama Power, and the second at an undeveloped location on the Tennessee River at Muscle Shoals, Alabama (49).

Washburn originally thought that the electric arc process should be used and traveled to Norway to gain further information on the process. He was soon convinced that the power demands of the arc process were too great, and turned to the more energy-efficient cyanamide process. Before leaving Europe, he bought American patent rights to the cyanamide process from the Italian patent holder. Upon returning home, he and some of his associates at Alabama Power founded American Cyanamid in 1907, with Washburn as president. They soon found that the Coosa River hydroplant did not have sufficient uncommitted power to accommodate a cyanamide plant; the idea of building a dam at Muscle Shoals was thwarted by the Federal Government which wanted a dam that would accommodate navigation as well.

Washburn and his group then decided to locate the plant at Niagara Falls, New York, but again found that the power had been allocated for other uses. On the Canadian side, however, large blocks of power were still available, and the plant finally found a home in Niagara Falls, Ontario (49).

Organic Nitrogen Materials

Natural organics constituted the Nation's sole source of nitrogen in fertilizers until sodium nitrate and ammonium sulfate came into use. Even in 1900, organics accounted for nearly 90 percent of the nitrogen in fertilizers; thereafter, their share declined, reaching 57 percent in 1909 and 34 percent in 1919 (67). The organics, although providing less of the total nitrogen, continued to increase in total tonnage from about 140,000 tons in 1870 to around 1 million by 1920. Table 4.4 gives the consumption of the more important organics at 10-year intervals from 1870 to 1920.

Many of the organics listed in the table appeared before 1870 and were described in Chapter 2. Acidulated fish was produced by adding sulfuric acid to make the bones more soluble and to reduce the odor of the final product. Bat guano, collected from caves, came mostly from Carlsbad Caverns in New Mexico, which produced over 100,000 tons from about 1900 to 1920. Linseed meal was the residue left over after extracting oil from flaxseed. Castor pomace was the by-product from production of castor oil from castor beans, and was sold only for fertilizer use since it was poisonous to animals (37, 67).

Animal Tankage—Animal tankage, produced by the meat packing industry, was an important material. It was made up of offal of animal carcasses, some bones not processed separately, and carcasses of whole animals rejected as unfit for human consumption. These were dumped into tanks and subjected to boiling and steaming under pressure not only to make a better tankage product but also to reclaim fats which had many uses. The tankage was dried, ground, and sold as a fertilizer material. Blood from slaughter operations was drained into kettles and dried by evaporation, using steam coils. Garbage tankage was the garbage collected in the cities and consisting of household wastes, dead animals, and other refuse. At first the waste was dried and ground before selling as a fertilizer. Later, it was digested in a manner similar to that used for animal tankage, with fats reclaimed and the residue dried, ground, and sold as a low-grade tankage. The purpose of the cities in processing the garbage was to defray collection costs (10, 37, 70).

Table 4.4. U.S. Consumption of Natural Organic Nitrogen Materials (64).

	1870	1880	1890	1900	1910	1920
			Tons			
Cottonseed meal	15,000	35,000	200,000	434,000	447,000	450,000
Linseed meal	5,000	8,000	22,000	10,000	4,000	1,000
Castor pomace	500	2,000	3,000	5,000	17,000	23,000
Garbage tankage	-	-	10,000	80,000	120,000	140,000
Animal tankage	-	20,000	155,000	185,000	228,000	210,000
Dried blood	-	5,000	19,800	32,600	19,000	33,000
Fish scrap	40,000	43,800	38,000	36,000	60,000	61,000
Acidulated fish	1,000	5,000	16,000	28,000	30,000	49,600
Peruvian guano	49,400	500	-	1,300	13,200	-
Bat guano	-	-	1,200	1,000	4,500	5,500
Poudrette	25,000	70,000	60,000	5,000	2,000	-
All other[1]	3,800	14,500	10,500	12,600	40,500	96,500
Total	139,700	203,800	573,500	886,500	985,200	1,069,600

[1]Includes other seed meals; cocoa byproducts; shrimp scrap; crab and lobster scrap; whale byproducts; hoof and horn meal; leather scraps; and hair, wool, and felt scraps.

Other Organics—Cottonseed meal was the leading organic material after 1890 because of its popularity in the South where fertilizers were being used in large quantities. It accounted for about 35 percent of the organics used in the country in 1890. Its share climbed to nearly 50 percent in 1900, and then declined gradually to 42 percent by 1920. Animal tankages ran second, making up 27 percent in 1890 and holding around 20 percent for the rest of the period. Peruvian guano had practically disappeared by 1880 due to exhaustion of the deposits. Poudrette remained popular until around 1890, but declined rapidly thereafter, apparently due to the spread of sanitary sewers in the cities. Use of garbage tankage grew constantly in tonnage after 1890 in spite of its low nutrient content.

Shortly before 1910, the higher grade organics–cottonseed meal, dried blood, animal tankage, and fish scraps–began to be diverted to the more profitable animal feed market (56). The diversion from fertilizer uses is apparent in Table 4.4 which shows a definite plateauing or tapering off in consumption for the years 1910 and 1920. To offset this, particularly in the Southeastern States where organics were in high demand, manufacturers used more of such low-grade, inert organics as hair, feathers, leather scraps, wool and fur wastes, and garbage tankage. To

Table 4.5. Nutrient Contents of Nitrogenous Organics (37, others).

Material	N	P_2O_5	K_2O
		percent	
Cottonseed meal	6-9	2-3	1.5-2.0
Linseed meal	5.5	1.7	1.3
Castor pomace	5-6	2	1
Garbage tankage	2-3	1-3	0.5-1.5
Animal tankage	9-11	0.1-3.5	-
Dried blood	8-14	0.3-1.5	0.5-0.8
Fish scrap	7-10	4-8	-
Acidulated fish	6	6	-
Peruvian guano	12	11	2
Bat guano	2-12	1-14	2
Poudrette	1-2	1-2	1-2

make the relatively inert nitrogen more available to crops, these materials increasingly were used in the manufacture of wet-base goods; this involved their acidulation along with phosphate rock in superphosphate plants, a process that hydrolyzed the inert proteins to more easily decomposed forms. As a result, production of wet-base goods expanded markedly from about 100,000 tons in 1900 to 380,000 tons in 1920 (35, 56).

Nutrient contents of the organics, shown in Table 4.5, varied greatly. Nitrogen contents ranged from 12 percent or slightly higher for the best grade organics, to as low as 2 percent for poorer materials. Phosphate contents averaged about 2 to 3 percent for most of the materials, but were considerably higher for fish products and some of the guanos. Potash was very low in all of the materials. Nitrogen, even in the higher grade organics, was not immediately available for plant uptake, requiring decomposition in the soil by micro-organisms. The better materials–including cottonseed meal, animal tankage, fish scrap, and dried blood–were about 80 percent as effective as sodium nitrate, while the more inert materials were only about 10 percent as effective (37).

Farmers, especially in the Southeast, had a deep-rooted respect for the organics and usually preferred them over the inorganics. Most evaluated a fertilizer more on its smell, taste, and color than on the nutrient content indicated on the tag.

Phosphatic Materials

The period from 1870 to 1920 was a golden age for normal superphosphate. ("Normal" superphosphate is a term commonly used to designate superphosphate made by acidulating phosphate rock with sulfuric acid. "Normal" actually wasn't used over most of the period. Instead, the product was variously referred to as "regular," "standard," "ordinary," or "single.") Its success was assured with the plentiful and low-cost phosphate rock available, first from the South Carolina field and subsequently from the Florida and Tennessee fields. And it was relatively simple to manufacture, with the plants located close to the use areas. As a result, normal superphosphate soon completely dominated all other phosphate sources combined. Organic sources of phosphate (bones and guanos) had supplied all of the phosphate in fertilizers previous to 1868, but the importance of organics as phosphate carriers faded rapidly. In 1870, organics supplied 78 percent of all phosphate consumed; the share declined to 28 percent in 1900, and to 14 percent in 1920 (67).

Consumption of the various phosphate materials, excluding organics used primarily for their nitrogen content, is given by 10-year intervals from 1870 to 1920 in Table 4.6. Tonnages of normal superphosphate skyrocketed during the 50-year period. On the other hand most of the earlier products had almost disappeared, and several new products had come on the market. Of the older products, only bone meal gained in tonnage over the years, but its gains were insignificant compared to those recorded for normal superphosphate.

Normal Superphosphate—The normal superphosphate was much lower in available P_2O_5 than the 20 percent product eventually achieved. Average phosphate content was 11.01 percent in 1880, 13.80 in 1890, 13.98 in 1900, 15.68 in 1910, and 16.66 in 1920. The increases resulted from the introduction of higher grade rocks from Florida and Tennessee, and improvements in manufacturing which reduced the moisture contents and the citrate-insoluble levels of the final products (56).

Methods used in the manufacture of superphosphate improved greatly during the period, although acidulation by the old batch method remained unchallenged. The methods used around 1914 are described below.

The phosphate rock was crushed into small pieces and pulverized in a roll mill in which steel rollers revolved within a steel ring. The pulverized material was discharged continuously and passed through revolving or vibrating screens to assure the desired degree of fineness. Capacity of the mill was usually 10 or 12 tons per hour. Several types of mixers were used to mix the sulfuric acid with the pulverized rock, the most common consisting of a cast-iron revolving pan, 4 to 8 feet in diameter and 1 to 2 feet deep, driven by pinions. The pan was equipped

Table 4.6. U.S. Consumption of Phosphatic Materials (64, 65, 67).

	1870	1880	1890	1900	1910	1920
	\multicolumn{6}{c}{1,000 tons}
Normal super- phosphate	80	320	690	1,446	2,565	3,533
Bone mea	130	82	121	104	139	170
Dissolved bones	15	25	40	5	1	2
Dissolved bone black	6	12	18	7	10	7
Wet-base goods	-	-	10	100	300	380
Phospho-guano	20	16	21	2	-	-
Concentrated superphosphate	-	-	1	6	10	15
Basic slag	-	2	5	25	10	
Ground rock	-	-	2	9	22	81
Ammonium phosphate	-	-	-	-	-	20

with one or two agitators or stirring devices which consisted of heavy cast-iron spiders having four arms fitted with steel plows driven by bevel gears. The pan revolved in one direction and the stirring devices in the opposite direction. Charges of 50 to 52–Be' (Baume') sulfuric acid and pulverized rock were run into the pans and mixed for 2 or 3 minutes (92).

The mixture was discharged through a hole in the center of the pan equipped with a plug operated by a lever. Once the plug was raised, a scraping device was lowered, and the contents ejected directly into a curing bin below or into in a dump cart for hauling to a curing shed where it was dumped on an open pile. Dens usually were brick-lined chambers of sufficient size to hold a number of charges. The superphosphate cured in about 24 hours in the den, after which it was dug out with some type of mechanical device. The dens were equipped with flues at the top through which gases were drawn off and washed by a continuous water spray to control the fume problem. Where open piles were used, curing required several days and the escaped gases caused problems both for the workers and people living in the surrounding area. The gases, high in fluorine, also were disastrous to vegetation over fairly large areas downwind (92).

Mechanical dens, although popular in Europe, did not come into use in this country until 1911, and then only to a limited extent. Armour installed a Svenska system that year at its Carteret, New Jersey, plant. This system discharged the den by using a moving wall as a piston. The material was sheared and crumbled by a mechanical cutting device as it moved out of the den. The superphosphate then fell onto a moving belt

Agricultural colleges were a key in promoting sound fertilizer use. This county agent in Anderson County, South Carolina, is consulting with a farmer about nutrient needs of his peanut crop. *(U.S. Department of Agriculture)*

for transport to storage. Armour installed the system into seven more of its plants, but no other companies adopted the equipment during this period (55, 93).

Concentrated Superphosphate—Concentrated superphosphate, made by reacting phosphoric acid with phosphate rock and initially produced in Germany in 1872, was first manufactured in the United States in 1890, but not on a sustained basis. United States production was only 1,800 tons in 1907; 6,100 in 1910; 9,000 in 1915; and 15,200 in 1920. The domestic product contained 40 to 44 percent available P_2O_5 (65).

American Phosphate and Chemical Company was the first U.S. company to produce concentrated superphosphate. It made a product containing about 40 percent available P_2O_5 in a small Baltimore plant that operated for only a few years. The second plant, which went into production in 1898 at Pensacola, Florida, was owned by the Goulding Fertilizer Company, a subsidiary of Goulding Ltd. of Ireland. All of its product was exported. This plant ceased operations in 1901 (56, 65).

Virginia-Carolina was the first company to go into sustained production of concentrated superphosphate. It opened a plant at Charleston, South Carolina, in 1907. The plant initially used South Carolina rock to make a product containing 44 percent P_2O_5 but later switched to Florida pebble which increased the grade somewhat. Two other attempts to enter the concentrated superphosphate market before 1920 were short-lived. The Mountain Copper Company began operations at Martinez, California, in 1910 but was closed in 1912 for lack of an adequate West Coast market. Piedmont Electro-Chemical Company began production at Mount Holly, North Carolina, in 1914 using phosphoric acid produced by the electric-furnace method. The plant closed in 1916 after producing about 10,000 tons of concentrated superphosphate (56, 65).

Phosphoric Acid—The first phosphoric acid plant was built in Germany about 1870 to recover phosphate from a low-grade phosphorite ore that could not be made into a satisfactory superphosphate by direct reaction with sulfuric acid. The first U.S. phosphoric acid plant was built in Baltimore in 1890 by the American Phosphate and Chemical Company. It produced acid for manufacture of concentrated superphosphate, but operated for only a few years. Several other domestic plants were built between 1900 and 1920, with most operated by fertilizer companies (92, 93).

Up until about 1915 the phosphoric acid was manufactured by digesting finely ground phosphate rock with dilute sulfuric acid (about 16 percent H_2SO_4) in batches of one or two tons in a wooden vat. The resulting muddy slurry was filtered using lead-lined filtering pans. This separated the gypsum and other sediment from the dilute phosphoric acid, yielding a maximum of 10 to 15 percent P_2O_5 equivalent. The filtrate was concentrated in open, lead-lined pans to which bottom heat was applied. Most of the acid was used to acidulate phosphate rock to make concentrated superphosphate. Some minor changes and improvements were made in the process during the period (92, 93).

Significant changes were made in 1915 when the Dorr Company developed with a continuous process. Digestion of the phosphate rock-sulfuric acid mixture took place in a series of acid-resistant agitator tanks. Agitation was provided by paddle arms revolving on a horizontal plane. The slurry from the last agitator tank discharged into thickener tanks arranged in series for countercurrent washing. The calcium sulfate dihydrate which settles in the primary thickener is washed in the remaining thickeners to free it from entrained acid. The recovered acid contained 22 to 23 percent P_2O_5. As a result, some of the Dorr plant thickeners were replaced with the new system (92, 93).

Basic Slag—Basic slag, used extensively as a phosphate fertilizer in Europe, saw little use in the United States. The slag became popular in Europe following development of a process by Thomas and Gilchrist of England in 1878 to convert high phosphorus cast iron to a low phosphorus, nonbrittle steel. Europe's iron ores were high in phosphorus and the slag produced in Bessemer furnaces contained about 20 percent P_2O_5. In contrast, most U.S. iron ores were low in phosphorus and the slag was of little value as a fertilizer, an exception being the slag produced from ore mined in the Birmingham area of Alabama. Basic slag was first imported into this country in small amounts starting about 1890. However, in 1915 the Tennessee Coal, Iron, and Railroad Company began producing and marketing basic slag from Birmingham. The slag produced from open-hearth furnaces contained 8 to 10 percent

P_2O_5. Only small tonnages were marketed, not exceeding about 10,000 per year prior to 1920. Most of the slag was used in Alabama and Mississippi (37, 64, 93).

Phosphate Rock for Direct Application—Finely ground phosphate rock for direct application to the soil as a fertilizer was offered by several Charleston, South Carolina, mining companies as early as 1870. Soft rock from north Florida was sold for direct application from about 1890 until about 1907 after which other kinds of finely ground rock took its place. Consumption of phosphate rock for direct application during the period, however, never was substantial, amounting to only 81,000 tons in 1920 (67). Much of the rock used after 1910 was in the Corn Belt, especially in Illinois. This resulted largely from the promotional work of C. G. Hopkins of the University of Illinois. Hopkins believed strongly in a system of farming involving crop rotations with legumes, and the use of phosphate rock and lime. He was convinced that phosphate rock gave better returns per acre than superphosphate applied directly or in mixed fertilizers, since the rock cost less than half as much per ton as superphosphate and when applied on an equal nutrient basis, overall economic returns were superior (53). Unfortunately for ground rock, this was not the case in most other areas of the country.

Ammonium Phosphate—Ammonium phosphates, which eventually would become major fertilizer materials were first produced commercially in the United States in 1916 by a subsidiary of the American Cyanamid Company at Warners, New Jersey. Although production and use during World War I were limited because of diversion of the facilities to war purposes, 20,000 tons were consumed in 1920 (27, 64).

The process consisted of acidulating phosphate rock with sulfuric acid to produce phosphoric acid, and bubbling ammonia into the acid. The ammonia was obtained by steaming crude calcium cyanamide in an autoclave under several atmospheres pressure. The solution was then evaporated to dryness and marketed under the trade name of "Ammo-Phos" (27).

The key to the conversion of cyanamide to ammonia, which could be used for manufacture of either explosives or fertilizers, was a special autoclave developed in Germany shortly before the war. Walter T. Landis, chief technologist for American Cyanamid, had ordered one of the German autoclaves for experimental purposes before the war broke out, but it hadn't arrived. A week after war was declared, Landis sailed to Germany to try to expedite matters. Through scientific friends in Germany he acquired a couple of the autoclaves and got them out of Germany just before exports of chemical apparatus were stopped. Once home, Landis began experiments with the autoclaves and on converting ammonia to nitrates. This permitted Cyanamid to build and operate two small plants at sites of DuPont explosives factories (49).

The location of the ammonium phosphate plant at Warners resulted from a meeting between Washburn of American Cyanamid and James B. Duke of the Duke tobacco interests. Duke, who also had interests in the Virginia-Carolina Company and had backed an effort at Nitrolee, South Carolina, to use the arc process to produce nitric acid, suggested that an ammonium phosphate plant be built based on cyanamide from Niagara Falls and phosphate rock from Florida. As a result, the site was selected at Warners which was roughly midway between the two. Amalgamated Phosphate Company, a subsidiary of Virginia-Carolina, provided the rock and apparently initially produced the phosphoric acid at Warners. American Cyanamid formed the Ammo-Phos Corporation, shipped the cyanamide from Niagara Falls, and converted it to ammonia at Warners. American Cyanamid also eventually took over the Amalgamated Phosphate Company (49, 51).

Bone Meal—Bone meal, the most important of the bone products used as fertilizers during the period, was marketed in two forms, raw bone meal and steamed bone meal. Raw bone meal was produced by crushing and grinding untreated bones, but contained fats which reduced its effectiveness in crop production. The raw bones were the only source of bone meal until the 1880's when the meat packing companies found it was highly profitable to remove the fats and gelatinous materials from the bones and market them separately. Separation was achieved by boiling the green bones in large tanks under pressure. After fats and gelatinous materials were skimmed from the surface the bones were dried, crushed, ground, and marketed as steamed bone meal. The meal contained from 22 to 30 percent P_2O_5, somewhat higher than the phosphate content of raw bone meal. Farmers strongly resisted the steamed product initially, but eventually accepted it as a superior material. Production of steamed bone meal increased steadily from about 11,000 tons in 1890 to 70,000 tons in 1920. Raw bone meal, on the other hand, peaked in 1890 at 110,000 tons and then declined. At no time during the period did the steamed product equal raw bone meal in tonnage. Bone meal consumption was greatest in the Midwest and Northeast (10, 37, 64, 70).

Use of bones for fertilizer and other products, soon exceeded the capabilities of the meat packing industry. Other sources had to be developed. Starting in the 1870's and continuing into the 1890's, trainloads of buffalo bones were collected on the western plains, where they were found in great abundance following the great slaughter of buffalo. In addition, bones were imported from Canada and South America (70).

Dissolved bones and boneblack, the bone superphosphates which were once an important source of superphosphate, were of little importance during the period. Their use peaked around 1890 and declined sharply after 1900.

Potash Materials

Potash became an important component of U.S. fertilizers in the period 1870-1920. In 1870, the only sources were tobacco stems, wood ashes, and cotton hulls and boll ashes, and these only in small amounts. The turning point came about 1875 with the introduction of the German potash salts, which by 1890 dominated all other sources. Their domination continued until 1914, when imports ceased abruptly and the United States had to tap every conceivable domestic source. Even then, production was small and fell far short of meeting needs. High production costs caused most of the domestic sources to disappear once German potash returned to the market after the war. Except for the war years, potash consumption climbed steadily from 4,000 tons of K_2O in 1870 to 257,000 tons in 1920.

Discovery of Underground Potash in Germany—The discovery of buried deposits of water-soluble potash salts laid down in an old seabed near Stassfurt, Germany, provided the first commercial source of potash in huge quantities anyplace in the world. Saline waters from springs in the Stassfurt area had for centuries been a source of common salt. Georgus Agricola, a German mineralogist, suggested as early as 1545 that the springs must originate from an underground salt deposit. In 1839, a shaft was sunk to reach the suspected salt and, although salt was found, it was so contaminated with "bitterns" as to render it unfit for human consumption. Two new shafts started in 1856 apparently reached a usable salt deposit. It was overlain with beds of potassium and magnesium salts mixed with sodium chloride. Mined material was thrown in a dump. Upon analysis, the discarded salts were found to be a double salt of potassium and magnesium chlorides which was named "carnallite." By this time Liebig had already established the need for potash by plants, and as a result the carnallite product, which contained only 9 percent K_2O, was tested as a fertilizer and the results published in 1860. A process was developed by Dr. Adolph Frank for separating the crude carnallite from the sodium chloride present in the deposits, and also for recovering potassium chloride from the carnallite. This resulted in two plants being established in 1861 for refining the mined ore. Within two years a number of new shafts had been sunk, 14 plants were refining potash, and total production reached about 100,000 tons. Most of the early potash was used for purposes other than fertilizers since the fertilizer market was slow to develop (14, 87).

The deposits extended from Harz Mountain and the Stassfurt area to Hannover/Göttingen in the west, to Erfurt in the south, and Magdeburg in the north. The deposits contained a range of potash salts averaging from 10 to 16 percent K_2O, variously overlain with shales, sandstones and clays under which were layers of salt and anhydrite. The potash minerals mined were carnallite ($KCl \bullet MgCl_2 \bullet 6H_2O$), kainite

(KCl • MgSO$_4$ • 3H$_2$O), and sylvite (KCl). Another deposit in the North Germany lowlands produced KCl, K$_2$SO$_4$ and potassium magnesium sulfate. Sylvite deposits were discovered in Alsace, Germany, in 1904 and production began in 1910 (24, 69).

Potash Salts Marketed in the United States—The German potash salts marketed in the United States were potassium chloride, potassium sulfate, the double salt of potassium magnesium sulfate, kainite, and manure salts. The potassium chloride contained 48 to 50 percent K$_2$O plus about 15 to 20 percent by weight of sodium and magnesium chlorides that were present as impurities. The potassium sulfate contained 47 to 48.5 percent K$_2$O, and the double salt, 20 to 27 percent K$_2$O. The kainite contained 12 to 14 percent K$_2$O and was a mixture consisting of about 21 percent potassium sulfate, 2 percent potassium chloride, and the rest as sodium chloride and magnesium salts. Manure salts, which came on the U.S. market about 1900, contained about 20 percent K$_2$O; it is a mixture primarily of KCl and NaCl, plus small amounts of potassium and various impurities (95).

The early mines were initially under the control of the states (duchies), but in 1865 were thrown open to private ownership. As the number of private mines grew, problems of overproduction resulted which led to formation of the German Potash Syndicate in 1879. Its primary purpose was to regulate production and prevent price erosion, but it also conducted campaigns to increase the use of potash in fertilizers. The syndicate had great difficulty in controlling production and pricing in the early 1900's. When the syndicate came up for a five-year renewal in 1909, it ceased to exist for a short period (15, 16, 79).

U.S. Potash Consumption—Consumption of different potash materials in the United States by 10-year intervals is given in Table 4.7. Besides the potash salts and wood ashes, tobacco stems and cotton hull and boll ashes provided potash throughout the 1870-1920 period. Tobacco stems, a by-product of the tobacco industry, contained from 4 to 10 percent K$_2$O, and 2 to 3 percent N. Hull and boll ashes, a by-product of the cotton industry, contained about 22 percent K$_2$O (37).

The halting of German potash imports with the advent of the first world war had a devastating impact on U.S. fertilizer production and consumption, and brought about an intensified effort to find and produce domestic potash materials. Consumption of potash, which had totaled 244,000 tons of K$_2$O in 1913, began falling in 1914, amounted to only 81,000 tons in 1915, and bottomed out at 16,000 tons in 1916, after which it rose slightly as domestic materials began to appear in greater quantities. The German imports, which had been falling rapidly, reached zero in 1917 when the United States entered the war. Potash use did not recover fully until adequate imports became available in 1920 (67).

Table 4.7. U.S. Consumption of Potash Containing Materials (67, 64).

	1870	1880	1890	1900	1910	1920
			Tons			
Potassium chloride (50%)	-	12,000	30,000	60,000	130,000	130,000
Potassium sulfate and potassium magnesium sulfate	-	1,000	1,000	22,000	55,000	20,000
Manure salts			-	48,000	132,000	350,000
Kainite		12,000	29,000	55,000	150,000	416,000
Tobacco stems	5,000	24,000	37,000	45,000	56,000	70,000
Wood ashes	12,000	15,000	10,000	12,000	8,000	5,000
Cotton hull and boll ashes	1,000	2,000	3,000	5,000	2,000	1,000

Domestic potash sources tapped during the war period included the brines from Searles Lake, California, alunite (a potassium aluminum sulfate mineral) from Utah, brines from the lakes in western Nebraska, salty waters from the Great Salt Lake, dust from cement kilns, wastes from distilleries and sugar refineries, and kelp harvested off the shores of California, and many lesser sources. By the end of the war the combined yield from all of these sources was only 55,000 tons of K_2O, or less than a fourth of prewar annual consumption. Of the domestic sources, the native brines were responsible for 73 percent of the potash produced, with the Nebraska lakes being the largest brine source. Kelp, the second largest potash source, provided 9 percent; distillery wastes 6 percent, alunite 5 percent, and all others 7 percent (26, 49).

Potash prices increased fantastically during the war period, ranging from $400 to $600 per ton. It was only because of these prices that most of the wartime domestic supplies could be exploited. With the reappearance of German imports, prices returned to normal, and practically all of the 128 domestic plants failed. The only immediate survivors were a handful of those that produced potash as a by-product (49, 61).

Mixed Fertilizers

Mixed fertilizers were important from the beginning of the U.S. commercial fertilizer industry. Peruvian guano introduced in the 1840's, was a good quality mixed fertilizer. Early mixed fertilizers which appeared in the 1850's were acidulated mixtures of guanos, other organ-

organics, and bones or bone products. One characteristic of all of these early mixtures was that none contained significant amounts of potash. Several important changes in mixed fertilizers occurred in the 1870-1920 period. These included the addition of potash to form complete mixtures, the use of domestic phosphate rock to produce superphosphate, and the wide use of sodium nitrate and ammonium sulfate late in the period.

Commercial Mixed Fertilizers

The estimated consumption of factory mixed fertilizers in 1880 was 350,000 tons, or 46 percent of all fertilizers used (earlier data on fertilizers did not separate mixed fertilizers from the total). Consumption increased to 800,000 tons in 1890 and continued to grow to around 4 million tons in 1920 (67). Factory mixtures accounted for about 60 percent of all fertilizers in this period, although unofficial surveys in 1913 and later years indicate their share was as high as 70 percent. The primary nutrient content of mixed fertilizers in 1880 averaged 2.4 percent N, 9.1 percent available P_2O_5, and 2.0 percent K_2O, totaling 13.5 percent. Forty years later, it was up only fractionally to 13.9 percent–2.3 percent N, 9.2 percent P_2O_5, and 2.4 percent K_2O.

The nutrient content of many of the materials going into the mixes had increased over the years. However, instead of increasing the grade of the mix the manufacturers added inert fillers such as sand, earth, cinders, sawdust, and other materials to keep the average grade fairly constant. Use of fillers started about 1890 when some 50,000 tons was added. This grew to 140,000 tons in 1900, and a million tons in 1917. The avowed reason for adding the fillers was to hold the price of fertilizer per bag at a more or less constant level on the theory that the farmers would balk at higher prices. The industry, however, profited from the maneuver since the fillers cost them relatively little. The effect of fillers on the nutrient content of the mixtures has been variously calculated. For example, in 1900 the average grade without fillers would have been 16.1 percent but, with fillers, it was 14.1 percent. That year alone, when the average retail price per ton of mixed fertilizer was $25, the farmers paid over $3 million for the filler they purchased (63, 66, 67).

The order of reporting nutrients in fertilizer mixtures was usually available P_2O_5, NH_3, and K_2O, with some states reporting the nitrogen content as N. Georgia, for example, in 1902 passed a law requiring that nitrogen be reported as N rather than NH_3 based on the reasoning that popular nitrogen materials in that state, cottonseed meal, dried blood, tankage, and sodium nitrate, contained no ammonia (9).

Complete NPK mixtures dominated mixed fertilizers after the German potash salts appeared in the U.S. market, and it wasn't until about 1900 that PK mixtures started to appear. Large quantities of NP mixtures appeared during the potash shortage of World War I, at which time they comprised 64 percent of the mixed fertilizer market (63, 66, 67).

Materials going into mixed fertilizers changed over the years. Natural organics supplied about 91 percent of the total nitrogen in 1900, with 7 percent of the remainder coming from sodium nitrate, and 2 percent from ammonium sulfate. By 1909 the contribution from organics had dropped to 67.7 percent while nitrates increased to 16.2 percent and ammonium sulfate to 16.1 percent. By 1917 the percentages were 46.5, 30.2, and 18.7, respectively, with the remaining 4.6 percent coming from cyanamide (63, 66).

Of the phosphate materials used in mixed fertilizers, normal superphosphate made from domestic phosphate rock dominated. The old standbys–bonemeal, dissolved bones and boneblack, and phosphoguano–maintained their importance in mixed fertilizers through 1890, but lost ground thereafter as use of normal superphosphate skyrocketed. From 1900 through 1920, about 80 percent of the available P_2O_5 was provided by normal super, and 5 to 10 percent more came from wet-base goods made by acidulating natural organics and phosphate rock. The remainder was supplied by small amounts of bonemeal, dissolved boneblack, natural organics, concentrated superphosphate, and ammonium phosphate. Use of wet-base goods in mixtures peaked at around 518,000 tons in 1917 (63, 66).

Until German potash appeared on the U.S. fertilizer market, any potash that got into the mixtures came largely from wood ashes and tobacco stems. Of the German potash salts, kainite was initially preferred for use in mixtures. By 1900, however the higher grade potassium chloride and potassium sulfates were supplying 71 percent of the K_2O, kainite 12 percent, and manure salts 7.5 percent, with the remainder coming from domestic organic sources. Kainite gained new momentum and by 1913 provided 20.1 percent of the K_2O, while manure salts had moved up to 19.4 percent (63, 66, 67).

Home Mixed Fertilizers

Home mixing of fertilizers by farmers was strongly advocated by a number of agricultural colleges, experiment stations, and state boards of agriculture, starting in the 1890's and continuing unabated into the 1920's. These organizations provided farmers with pamphlets on home mixing, suggested the formation of community cooperatives to buy fertilizer materials in wholesale lots, and otherwise advised farmers in home mixing. Arguments put forward favoring home mixing were that the farmer could get exactly what he wanted in the way of fertilizer materials, adjust the grade of the mixture to meet his own specific soil and crop needs, produce grades of higher total nutrient content than were available from commercial mixers, avoid paying for useless filler, use his own labor, and generally save money. Big points were made that farmers had no difficulty in buying materials at reasonable prices, that

Many institutions promoted on-the-farm mixing of fertilizer ingredients earlier this century, as in this 1935 east Tennessee operation. *(TVA)*

the mixing could be done easily on barn or earthen floors, and the only equipment needed was a platform scale, a shovel, and a hoe or hand rake (1, 28).

Home mixing caused great concern in the fertilizer industry because of its potential effect on the commercial mixers. The industry countered the arguments for home mixing on the basis that farmers didn't have the skill or equipment to make mixes of good quality. They argued further that concoctions recommended to home mixers were unrealistic, that factory mixers were not overcharging, and the farmers really were losing money rather than saving it. Although there are no data or estimates on the extent that home mixing was practiced, there is no question but that it did make substantial inroads on the sale of factory mixes in certain localities (7, 28, 48, 81).

Sulfuric Acid

The Nation's sulfuric acid industry, without which production of superphosphate would have been impossible, began in 1797 when John Harrison established a plant in Philadelphia. It was based on the lead chamber process developed in England by Joshua Ward in 1736. Acid production expanded in the Philadelphia area with Farr and Kunze building a plant in 1812, Powers Weightman in 1815, and Charles Lennig in 1829 (42). Plants were established in Baltimore in 1829 by the Maryland Chemical Works and the Baltimore Chemical Manufactory, followed by William Davison in 1832 and Phillip S. Chappel in 1836, both of which were involved in superphosphate manufacture in the 1850's (56). By 1850, Cincinnati, Pittsburgh, Boston, St. Louis, and New Orleans also had acid plants (42). All of these early plants apparently used sulfur imported from Sicily. The main users of the acid prior to superphosphates were manufacturers of pharmaceuticals, textiles, and metallurgical and chemical products.

The number of sulfuric acid plants increased dramatically after 1870 as a result of the increase in superphosphate manufacture and the refining of petroleum. In 1880, 264,000 tons (100% H_2SO_4 equivalent) was produced in 49 establishments; in 1889, 963,000 tons was produced in 105 plants; and in 1899, 963,000 tons was produced by 127 plants. Production almost doubled by 1909 when 183 plants produced 1.7 million tons, and this was further doubled by 1919 when 216 plants produced 3.4 million tons (42). Production from 1870 on closely paralleled production of superphosphate.

Sulfuric acid production initially was concentrated in seaport cities of the Northeast. Major markets existed in this area. Also, seaport locations were necessary to receive sulfur from Sicily, the only source of sulfur at the time. However as phosphate rock deposits were developed and fertilizer use increased in the southern states, many new acid plants located in the South. By 1890, the South had more acid plants than the rest of the country. Another shift in acid plant locations occurred around the turn of the century when numerous plants were built in Ohio, Illinois, and other inland locations. Several factors, besides the expanding superphosphate market area, were responsible. Domestic pyrites were available in several states, SO_2 increasingly was being recovered from zinc and copper smelters, and the rapidly growing petroleum industry was demanding more acid at refinery sites. Additional plants were being built in California to use California pyrites and sulfur imported from Japan. The mining of the pure Frasch sulfur on the Gulf Coast also favored acid plant dispersal since water shipment provided economical transportation for the sulfur (Chapter 3) (42).

Processes for Manufacture

Sulfuric acid was produced in this country up through 1920 by the lead chamber process, or some modification of it, and the contact process. Sulfur dioxide, essential to both processes, was obtained from elemental sulfur, iron pyrites, and copper or zinc smelter gases. The SO_2 was oxidized to SO_3, which was combined with water to produce H_2SO_4.

In the lead chamber process, discovered by Ward, nitrogen oxide was used as a catalyst to bring about the reaction $SO_2 + NO_2 \leftrightarrow SO_3 + NO$. This reaction and the combination of the SO_3 with water occurred in a lead chamber, hence the name. The chamber process first involved burning potassium nitrate to produce NO_2. The nitric oxide (NO) formed by the reaction was not recovered for reuse until Gay Lussac in 1827 developed a tower that permitted its recovery. Another tower, invented by John Glover in 1859, accomplished denitrification and concentration of the acid. After about 1860, both towers were usually installed in the same chamber plant in Europe. U.S. acid manufacturers started to use the improved processes in the early 1870's. All U.S. sulfuric acid was made by the improved chamber plants until the contact process made its appeared around 1900. Even then the chamber process, which used sodium nitrate as the major nitrogen oxide source, dominated acid production through 1920 (40, 48, 74).

The contact process for making sulfuric acid was first patented in 1831 by Peregrine Phillips in England. He proposed the union of SO_2 and oxygen to form SO_3 by use of a heated catalyst consisting of platinum, porcelain, or some other material not attacked by the hot gases. Various studies of catalysts and conditions favoring the oxidation followed. The Badische Analin -und Soda Fabrik (BASF) of Germany in the 1890's apparently was the first company to bring the process into successful operation. The first contact plant in the United States was built for the New Jersey Zinc Company in Wisconsin in 1899. It used SO_2 recovered from smelter gas. The General Chemical Company in 1901 erected the first contact plant which used Gulf Coast sulfur. Production of Gulf Coast sulfur and the advent of the war encouraged construction of contact plants, all of which used platinum or iron catalysts. Contact plants offered major advantages over the chamber plants. They offered direct production of strong acid or acid of any desired strength and a high degree of purity of the acid. Also, contact plants were less costly to build and simpler to operate (40, 48).

Fertilizer Control Laws

Formulation of the Laws

The first workable fertilizer inspection and control law in this country was the Massachusetts Fertilizer Control Act of May 26, 1873. It required that all commercial fertilizers sold in the state be identified with the manufacturer or seller and that there be ". . . a true analysis or specification of the chemical elements and their several amounts contained therein, and also the quantity contained therein. . ." A penalty was provided for not meeting the requirements of the law or for claiming 5 percent more of any fertilizer ingredient than was actually contained in the package. It also authorized Massachusetts to procure an analysis of any fertilizer offered for sale in the state.

Fertilizer laws had been enacted earlier in Connecticut, Massachusetts, and Maine. An older guano law had been amended in Maryland to include other fertilizers at about the same time. Alabama and Delaware passed laws in 1871. These earlier laws were not very effective, however, since they contained no enforcement provisions. As a result, the 1873 Massachusetts law became a pattern for most subsequently enacted laws. New Jersey and Georgia passed legislation in 1874, and Virginia and North Carolina in 1877 (5, 44, 75).

Twenty-nine states had fertilizer laws and control laboratories by 1902. Most required such information on the bags as the brand name or trademark, the name and address of the manufacturer or shipper, place of manufacture, and number of pounds in the bag. The analysis of the fertilizer was to be given as to the percentage of nitrogen or its equivalent in ammonia, the percentage of P_2O_5 in available form, and the percentage of potash (K_2O) soluble in water. Samples of the fertilizer being sold in the state were required to be submitted, and a certificate filed. In addition, state officials had the authority to select a sample from any package of fertilizer exposed for sale. Severe penalties for violations usually were levied. Most states also collected inspection or tag fees on the tonnages sold, with the amounts levied varying greatly from state to state (6, 8).

The control system worked fairly well and intentional frauds were largely eliminated. Usually when a state adopted an enforceable law, the number of brands being sold dropped dramatically, but the effect upon the overall tonnage sold was minimal. Some problems occurred when a manufacturer or seller marketed his product in more than one state, since control laws differed from one state to another.

The AOAC and Improvement of Analytical Methods

One problem of common concern to the industry, the states, and all chemical laboratories analyzing fertilizers was that chemical analyses reported by different laboratories varied considerably, even though the same chemical method might have been used. The first positive attempt to remedy this situation was taken by R. D. Redding and Commissioner J. T. Henderson of the Georgia Department of Agriculture. They called a meeting of state, industrial, and private chemists analyzing fertilizers in Washington, D.C. in 1880 to work out a solution. More meetings were held in which some methods of analysis were agreed upon, but there was no way to harmonize differences and no organizational authority to assure adoption. As a result the Association of Official Agricultural Chemists (AOAC) was formed in 1884 (98).

AOAC's first constitution stated "Its object shall be to secure, as far as possible, uniformity of legislation with regard to the regulation of commercial fertilizers in the different states and accuracy in the methods and results of fertilizer analysis." The constitution was amended in 1886 to include cattle feeds, dairy products, soils, and other materials connected with agricultural industry. The first president was S. W. Johnson of Connecticut, followed by H. W. Wiley of the U.S. Department of Agriculture. Once formed, the AOAC operated effectively. Methods for sampling and analysis were agreed upon, adopted as official, and became binding upon the members. Control samples were circulated among laboratories so that chemists could check the accuracy of their own analyses. AOAC-approved methods were adopted in all state control laboratories and in most industry and private laboratories. The official methods and procedures were upheld by the U.S. courts (85, 98).

The Agricultural Institutions

The continued development of the Nation's agricultural institutions from 1870 through 1920 gradually led to better soil fertility practices, the demonstration and improved use of fertilizers on farms, the transfer of information to farmers, and the establishment of a trained and qualified manpower pool expert in the various branches of agriculture. Establishment and perfection of the institutions however, did not happen overnight. Prior to 1900, the institutions struggled and fumbled as they strove to develop their true roles. Most of the building blocks were in place by 1920; productivity and effectiveness of the institutions were increasing, and important national benefits to agriculture were being realized.

State Agricultural Colleges

Thirty-three state agricultural colleges had been established by 1890 under the Morrill Act of 1862, with strong backing of farmers and farm organizations. Most of the colleges had sold their land-grant script rapidly and at a low price with the result that the states had to supplement the Morrill funds materially. To improve the federal support, a second Morrill Act was passed in 1890. It provided the land-grant institutions with a portion of the proceeds from the sales of public lands and, at the same time, provided financing for the establishment of land-grant colleges to serve black students. Another boon to the colleges was the passing of the Hatch Act of 1887, which provided for the financing of agricultural experiment stations at each of the land-grant institutions. Even so, many difficulties awaited (84).

The lack of students enrolling in agriculture was a great disappointment. For example, in 1894, 17 of the colleges had 25 students or fewer enrolled in agricultural courses; only 7 had 150 or more. Few of the students who did enroll bothered to graduate; in fact, 14 of the colleges had no agricultural graduates. Part of the problem was the low incentive to return to farming due to overproduction and low returns to the farmer. The students much preferred to study the mechanic arts (engineering) which also had been provided for in the Morrill Act, since there was a large demand for engineers in railroad construction and in the rapidly expanding industrial section of the Nation (84).

Teaching and teachers also presented a serious problem in agriculture, since there were few trained teachers and few good textbooks. Many of the land-grant colleges, particularly those attached to the older universities, believed that agriculture could be taught by one or two instructors in two or three courses. This led to dissatisfaction among farm groups, which caused several state legislatures to establish their land-grant institutions at locations away from the universities. By 1900, however, the land-grant colleges were showing marked improvements. Many had developed specialized faculties, teaching subjects such as agronomy, agricultural chemistry, and animal husbandry. Also, most of the colleges had separate experiment station and extension departments, and states had increased their financial support materially. Farming had become more profitable and enrollments in agriculture increased dramatically (84).

The rapid increase in the number of agronomists graduating from the land-grant colleges was of particular value to the future growth of the U.S. fertilizer industry and to improved use of fertilizers on farms. In 1900, only three agronomists graduated as such; in 1905, there were 50, and in 1908, 99. Enough agronomists had appeared by 1907 that the American Society of Agronomy could be organized. The graduating agronomists were about equally divided between the fields of crops and soils. A number of good textbooks dealing with soils, soil fertility, and fertilizers by this time had appeared (84). These included S. W. Johnson's *How Plants Grow* (1868) and *How Plants Feed* (1870), F. H. Storer's *Agriculture and Some of Its Relations to Chemistry* (1887), E. B. Vorhees' *Fertilizers* (1898), F. H. King's *The Soil* (1895), E. W. Hilgard's *Soils* (1906), Lyon's and Fippin's *Soils* (1909), and C. G. Hopkins' *Soil Fertility and Permanent Agriculture* (1910). Several of these went through revised editions.

From the days of Davy and Liebig, agricultural chemistry had encompassed soils, plants, fertilizers, manures and life processes. By 1900 and shortly thereafter, agricultural chemistry, which at one time had covered the fields of plant nutrition and fertilizers, made a complete turnaround, narrowing its scope and dealing heavily in analytical procedures for fertilizers, feed stuffs, and farm products. Most agricultural chemistry students were trained primarily to become chemical analysts in the field of agriculture (84).

State Agricultural Experiment Stations

A major event in the latter quarter of the 19th century was the establishment of the state agricultural experiment stations. The success of agricultural experiment stations in Europe had been duly noted by Americans who had traveled and studied abroad. But conservatism and lack of appreciation of the value of agricultural science had held back their establishment in this country. One of those who had studied and visited in Europe was S. W. Johnson, who was first to sell the value of research and overcome the inertia. It was Johnson who, almost single-handedly, was responsible for the establishment of the Nation's first agricultural experiment station in Connecticut in 1875 (41, 85).

Role of S. W. Johnson—Johnson, who has been cited in Chapter 2 and several places in this chapter, was one of the nation's most influential agricultural leaders for nearly 50 years. His greatest agricultural contributions were in the fields of fertilizers and plant nutrition, although he did little research himself in these areas.

Johnson was born in Kingsboro, New York, in 1830 and raised on a farm near Lowville. While attending a local academy he decided to prepare himself for a career in chemistry. He started his chemical studies under J. P. Norton at Yale and became involved in fertilizer analysis while still a student. Johnson soon decided he needed further training and in 1853 spent a year at the University of Leipzig, then moved to Munich where Liebig was located. He also visited other laboratories and experiment stations in Europe, and submitted numerous articles to the *Country Gentleman*, mostly about fertilizer and agricultural practices he had observed. He returned to Yale in 1855 and was soon made professor of analytical chemistry. Johnson's work at Yale centered on spectral analysis, for which he was elected to the National Academy of Sciences at the age of 36 (54, 76, 91).

Johnson was ambitious and had long dreamed of establishing agricultural science in this country, including an agricultural experiment station. He soon found that he needed a rallying point that would appeal to farmers and farm groups if he were to accomplish his goals and at the same time keep up Yale's frequently flagging interest in science. Remembering his early experiences analyzing fertilizers and the stir his reports created, he launched a campaign to expose fertilizer frauds. This campaign caught on with farmers and legislatures alike, and he was able to marshal strong support, which he used to its fullest to achieve his ambitions. Interestingly, Johnson's ambitions did not include collection of college degrees–he just didn't bother. The only degree he possessed was a master's which was awarded automatically when he became a Yale professor (54, 76, 91).

Johnson began his campaign for a public-supported experiment station in Connecticut in 1872. He got the State Board of Agriculture to adopt a resolution favoring the idea and along with W. O. Atwater, a former student who had recently been a professor of chemistry at the University of Tennessee and then was at Wesleyan University, traveled throughout the state meeting with leading farmers and farm groups. Orange Judd, an influential figure in Connecticut and editor of the *American Agriculturist*, formed a group to present a bill before the state legislature. Judd was so sure of the outcome that he independently funded the start of the station at Middletown, the home of Wesleyan University of which he was a trustee, with Wesleyan providing free space and facilities. Atwater was made director. The legislature also appropriated a small amount of money for each of two years (85).

In 1877, the legislature passed an act making the station a permanent state institution, but located it at New Haven. Johnson was made director and remained in that capacity until 1900. The station was initially located in two rooms at Yale's Sheffield Scientific School until special land was purchased and a laboratory built in 1882. The first job of the station, both at Middletown and New Haven, was to analyze fertilizers, which took up most of its time, money, and effort for the first 10 years. Atwater, no longer with the station, organized and set up an extensive series of fertilizer field experiments in a number of states, and became the first director of the USDA Office of Experiment Stations (85).

Other Early Stations—California was the next state to organize its early experimentation into a station-type program. E. W. Hilgard, who had moved to the University of California in 1874, operated a small laboratory and had conducted a field experiment in 1875. This was done with a small amount of funds set aside by the university regents, with the state legislature beginning direct support of the work in 1877. Just when, during these early years, the program became designated as a true experiment station is not clear (41, 85).

The North Carolina Agricultural Experiment Station was established in 1877 by the state legislature. It was located at the University of North Carolina at Chapel Hill, which was then the land-grant college. K. C. Kettle, the president of the university, like Johnson, promoted the station largely as a way to control fertilizer frauds. The station was under the direction of the state department of agriculture and was supported by a license tax on fertilizers. Its principal work up until 1888 was analyzing fertilizers (85).

A number of other experiment stations were organized in 1879 and the early 1880's and were justified at least in part by the need for fertilizer analysis. In New Jersey, the largest item in the station's program for the first eight years was fertilizer analysis. The Maine station, called the Maine Fertilizer Control and Agricultural Experiment Station, gave considerable attention to fertilizers as did the stations in Vermont, Kentucky, and Alabama. In fact, most of these stations found themselves so deeply involved in analyzing fertilizers, feedstuffs, foods, and seeds that they could accomplish little else. By 1887, fifteen stations were operating; eight were connected with land-grant colleges, and seven were set up independently from the colleges by the state legislatures. All suffered from lack of funds (85).

The Hatch Act—About 1882, considerable agitation began in the U.S. Congress to secure passage of an experiment station act that would strengthen and help fund agricultural research. This culminated in passage of a bill introduced in the House by William H. Hatch of Missouri and in the Senate by J. Z. George of Mississippi. The bill, known as the Hatch Act, became effective in March 1887. The act provided for an experiment station at each land-grant college, with each receiving $15,000 annually. The U.S. Commissioner of Agriculture was authorized to supervise the program and to indicate those lines of inquiry that he deemed most important. An annual report from each of the stations was required, and there was a provision for disseminating the results of the research, The Commissioner set up an Office of Experiment Stations to represent him in carrying out his relations with the stations. W. O. Atwater was named the first director. To help collect and diffuse the information the office established the *Experiment Station Record* in 1889 (85).

Passage of the Hatch Act immediately resulted in the independent stations becoming part of the land-grant system, in older stations expanding their work, and in additional stations being established where none existed before. Most of the research, however, remained relatively simple, largely on pressing problems in the state or the region in which they were located. By the turn of the century the stations were well established.

Unfortunately, the type of research needed to advance agricultural science remained largely ignored. This inadequacy led to the passage in 1906 of the Adams Act, a bill introduced by Representative Henry C. Adams of Wisconsin. It provided funds for conducting original or fundamental research on problems bearing directly on U.S. agriculture. It also gave the U.S. Department of Agriculture authority over how the funds were to be spent, which led to many disagreements between the state stations and the USDA. The increased emphasis on original research indirectly resulted in graduate student training, but the big payoff in research was not realized until the 1930's (85).

The State Extension Services

Successful dissemination of information to farmers, long a dream of agricultural leaders of the country, became a reality by 1920. The establishment of the land-grant colleges and state agricultural experiment stations increasingly focused on the need for getting information to the practicing farmer, and the land-grant college system proved an ideal vehicle for accomplishing this. Agricultural extension developed as a result and became a major factor affecting, directly or indirectly, practically every farmer in the Nation.

The Grange movement, which started following the Civil War, had grown to huge proportions by the 1880's, other national farm organizations developed, and farmers' clubs became numerous in some states. Their frequent meetings presented the college and experiment station workers a natural forum for dissemination of information directly to the users. Lecture sessions at these meetings soon became known as "farmers' institutes." These first got underway in Kansas, Nebraska, and Illinois in the 1870's. State legislatures, starting with Wisconsin in 1885, began appropriating funds for the conduct of the institutes. The 1880's saw their rapid spread to some 26 states and, by 1912, practically all states had institute programs, with a total of about 7,500 "institutes" held (41, 84).

In the early 1900's the colleges began developing extension programs along different subject matter lines and coordinating the overall program through an extension department or division. More and more full-time extension staff members were employed to conduct the programs and prepare publications. In 1912, some 330 staff members were devoting full time to extension work; they were reaching about two million farmers through their meetings and publications. Even with this effort, farmers' needs were not being met satisfactorily (41, 84).

Demand by farm organizations for a greater extension effort led Asbury S. Lever, House member from South Carolina, and Hoke Smith, Senator from Georgia, to introduce the Smith-Lever Act to establish and support extension departments in all of the land-grant colleges. The act became law in 1914. The act specified that the colleges and the U.S. Department of Agriculture were to cooperate to diffuse useful and practical information on subjects relating to agriculture and home economics. The appropriation was large, reaching about $4.5 million annually within eight years, and was distributed to the states according to the rural population and on a fund-matching basis. The act also led to the permanent system of county agricultural agents. By 1917, 4100 people were employed in extension, and 1434 counties had agricultural agents (41, 84).

The U.S. Department of Agriculture

The U.S. Department of Agriculture by the 1870's had developed strong staffs in practically every area of agriculture except fertilizers, soil fertility, and plant nutrition which apparently were considered as being within the domain of the state institutions. The Hatch Act in 1887, however, involved the USDA for the first time in these areas, although its role even then was more as a fund watcher and coordinator.

A Division of Agricultural Soils was organized in USDA's Weather Bureau to investigate the effects of soil texture and other physical properties of soils on crop production; Milton Whitney was chief. This was made an independent division in 1895, and was advanced to the status of Bureau of Soils in 1901, still with Whitney as its head. The soils activities mainly involved soil surveys (eventually to become of major importance in soil fertility investigations), reclamation of alkali soils, soil laboratory investigations (headed by Frank K. Cameron), and soil fertility investigations (headed by Oswald Schreiner). The first attempts of the Bureau to conduct soil fertility research of a basic nature, however, resulted in considerable controversy (85).

About 1911, the Bureau embarked on several important lines of investigation which were eventually to have great impact upon the U.S. fertilizer industry. They include the search for sources of domestic potash, fixation of atmospheric nitrogen, and the use of electric furnaces to produce phosphoric acid (39, 78). Details are discussed in later chapters.

Fertilizer Field Experiments

Field experiments with fertilizers in the United States began with the establishment of the first agricultural colleges, but they were few in number and generally poorly planned. As a result, not much useful information was derived from them. Among the first carefully planned and thought-out field experiments were those started by W. O. Atwater in 1878 when he designed and superintended the installation of a number of uniform experiments in the northeastern states. Passage of the Hatch Act in 1887 gave field experiments an immediate boost, at least in the fertilizer-using states. Not only was Atwater–the first director of the USDA Office of Experiment Stations–an old hand at designing and conducting field experiments, but fertilizers also were a matter of interest at most of the stations. As a result, fertilizer field experiments blossomed forth not only on experiment station lands but on farmers' fields as well. Many of the experiment stations became junior Rothamsteds, embarking on long-term fertilizer experiments that were continued unchanged year after year. Those conducted by farmers on their own fields were simply tests to determine nutrient needs. Considerable information was gained from both types of studies, but at great cost in money and effort.

Planning the First Stations

The exact plans of Atwater's first uniform experiments in 1878 did not appear in the literature reviewed. However, a summary of the uniform experiments conducted in New England indicates that the comparisons involved no treatment; N, P, and K applied separately; combinations of NP, NK, and PK; and all three nutrients used together. In the New England experiments, sodium nitrate was the source of nitrogen, dissolved bone black the source of phosphate, and potassium chloride the source of potash. Gypsum was included as a separate treatment. Crops used were mostly corn and potatoes (72).

An elaborate version of Atwater's uniform experiment initiated at State College, Pennsylvania, in 1882 was destined to run for many years. Dried blood, however, was substituted for sodium nitrate as the basic nitrogen comparison material. The experiment also compared dried blood, sodium nitrate, and ammonium sulfate, using plots which also received a basic application of P and K. Other treatments included plots with barnyard manure, gypsum, and liming materials, bringing the total number of comparisons to 36, including three untreated plots. The set of 36 plots was repeated on each of four fields representing a rotation of corn, oats, wheat, and hay (clover and timothy), with each crop appearing each year as the rotation progressed. Individual plot size was one-eighth of an acre and the plots were laid out parallel to each other with permanent grass strips between plots (53).

USDA's Office of Experiment Stations invited state experiment station personnel interested in fertilizers to attend a conference in Washington in March 1889 to develop and adopt guidelines to be followed in conducting fertilizer field experiments in the various states (2). Apparently copies of these guidelines (Office of Experiment Stations Circ. No. 7) no longer exist, but the contents are apparent from numerous experiment station reports (88, 89, 90). The basic experiment and also the one to be used on farmers' fields, followed the earlier plan of no treatment; N, P, and K alone; two-by-two combinations; and the complete NPK treatment. Plots were to be laid out parallel to each other. The NPK materials suggested for the basic comparisons were sodium nitrate at 160 pounds per acre, dissolved bone black (apparently selected because it was a uniform source of highly available phosphate) at 320 pounds per acre, and potassium chloride at 160 pounds per acre.

Another part of the agreed-upon plan dealt with the comparison of the different fertilizer materials. Each major nutrient material was to be evaluated only when adequate quantities of the other two major nutrients were present. Nitrogen materials included were sodium nitrate, ammonium sulfate, dried blood, fish scrap, and cottonseed meal. Phosphate materials evaluated against the dissolved bone black were superphosphate from phosphate rock, ground phosphate rock, basic slag, bone meal, and phospho-guanos. Potash materials included potassium chloride, potassium sulfate, tobacco stems, and kainite.

Most experiment stations and agricultural colleges adhered to the agreed-upon plans, although the materials tested varied considerably from state to state depending upon the materials most used by farmers in a state. Illinois, for example, used bone meal as the basic phosphate material since it was readily available from the Chicago meat packing industry and was being used by the farmers. Some states of the South much preferred cottonseed meal as the basic material to make their nitrogen comparisons (84, 88, 89, 90).

Most experiment stations in fertilizer-using states conducted long-term experiments on their own station lands using cropping systems prevalent in their own areas. States still conducting such experiments in 1920 included Pennsylvania, Ohio, Rhode Island, New Jersey, Georgia, and Illinois. Gradually, more and more of the experiments were laid out on substations representative of farming and soil conditions occurring in different parts of the state. Overall design of the experiments changed very little over the period. New materials, such as cyanamide, made their appearance, and usually were tested in shorter term experiments.

"Soil Test" Experiments

Vast numbers of the simpler "soil test" experiments were introduced on farms to give the farmers some idea of their need for the individual nutrients and the best combinations of these. By 1906, several thousand had been conducted in states east of the Mississippi River. Test crops apparently were seldom harvested, but the plots were closely observed by the farmers. They also served as demonstrations for neighboring farmers (84).

Coping with Soil Variability

Researchers soon recognized soil variability as a major problem in evaluating fertilizer responses in field experiments. Yield differences between untreated check plots were often as great as between the untreated plots and those receiving fertilizer. As a result, many experiments had to be abandoned. The Ohio station went so far in one of its long-term experiments as to leave every third plot untreated in order to obtain more meaningful comparisons between the treated and untreated. Also, at one time the Ohio station seriously considered giving up field experiments entirely and replacing them with box experiments in which the soil had been premixed, and then measuring responses with a test crop such as a small grain (82).

Another great handicap during the period was the lack of an adequate soil science base. Without this it was virtually impossible to understand or explain many of the observations made and the data collected from the field experiments. There was no way to predetermine the levels of available P and K in a soil, or to judge the applicability of results obtained at one location to another without conducting another experiment.

Practical Information Gained

Nonetheless, a great mass of information was collected on the behavior and effectiveness of different fertilizer materials and on the need for fertilizers and fertilizer nutrients under different soil, crop and farming conditions (84). Several examples follow.
- Superphosphates usually gave much higher yields than phosphate rock.
- Crop response to small applications of superphosphate was greatest during the year of application and declined sharply thereafter.
- Phosphate rock for direct application had to be finely ground.
- Continued use of nitrogen on mixed legume-grass stands depressed legumes and favored the grasses.
- Sodium nitrate was subject to leaching.
- Prolonged use of ammonium sulfate increased soil acidity to the point that lime was required to establish legumes in a rotation.

Fertility experiments have been conducted on the famous Morrill plots on the University of Illinois campus for more than a century. *(University of Illinois)*

- Nitrogen in many of the natural organics was only slowly available to crops.
- Potash responses did not occur uniformly, being greatest in areas farmed for long periods and/or those under intensive cultivation.
- The needs for individual nutrients could vary greatly from farm to farm.

The accumulation of practical knowledge about fertilizers and their use from the field experiments resulted in a number of advantages to U.S. agriculture. Firsthand information was gained on the nutrient needs of soils and crops over a wide range of conditions, and short- and long-term effects of different nutrient carriers were evaluated. Findings from field experiments in Europe could be evaluated under U.S. soil and crop conditions prior to being recommended to farmers. A large corps of agricultural specialists having insight into the use of fertilizers was developed. Meaningful fertilizer recommendations could be made to farmers, specific to the areas in which they farmed. Large numbers of farmers were exposed to fertilizer tests conducted on their own or neighboring farms. Furthermore, the field experiments paved the way for fertilizer introduction and use in states where fertilizers had been used sparingly or not at all.

Other Progress in Soil Fertility

In addition to field experiments, progress was made in gaining a sounder and more basic knowledge of soil fertility. Also, the first serious attempts were launched to find a valid chemical means that would explain the fertility status of soils and predetermine the specific need of a specific soil for individual nutrients and lime.

Microorganisms and Soil Fertility

A great deal of information became available on the microbiological aspects of soils and soil fertility during the period. Most of this originated in Europe, although some work was beginning in the United States. For the first time scientists recognized that the soil was home for vast numbers of microorganisms and that some of these greatly influenced the supply and availability of nitrogen upon which plant life depended. Some understanding of the nitrogen cycle began to emerge, including the decomposition of soil organic matter, fixation of nitrogen from the atmosphere by certain organisms, release of ammonia from organic sources, nitrification of the ammonia to nitrates, denitrification of nitrates and the possible loss of nitrogen back into the atmosphere, the losses of nitrates into drainage waters, and the beneficial effects of liming acid soils upon nitrate formation (47, 53, 73, 99).

The importance of *Rhizobia* (symbiotic or root nodule bacteria) in nitrogen fixation for legumes was well established and the knowledge was put to use. Soils from well inoculated fields where a host legume grew luxuriantly were transferred to fields where the legume grew poorly. Artificial cultures were being used to inoculate legume seeds in this country by 1914 with the USDA providing liquid inoculants for use by farmers and Cornell University providing solid inoculants. Others also produced inoculants, although some apparently were not very effective. In Europe, information also was developing on nonsymbiotic bacteria in soils that were capable of fixing nitrogen (59, 73).

Fate of Added Plant Nutrients in Soils

Scientists knew that soluble phosphate added to the soil was fixed in highly insoluble forms due to reaction with iron, aluminum, and calcium carbonate and that, once applied, the phosphate was retained in the plow layer of most soils. It was known that potassium was adsorbed and retained in clay and loam soils, and that it was largely exchangeable with other bases such as calcium and ammonium. Information on the soil's ability to exchange bases resulted from noting the effects of different fertilizer treatments on the nutrient content of drainage waters, the leaching of soil columns with various nutrient solutions and analyzing the filtrates, and through experiments using lysimeters. Also, it was found that different bases were not adsorbed in equal proportions by all soils (52, 59, 73).

Liming of acid soils was much better understood, not only from the standpoint of the needs of different crops, but also as to the amounts of calcium and magnesium lost in drainage waters and from the removal by crops. Qualitative soil tests began to be used to determine the level of soil acidity and to give a rough indication of the amount of lime needed to correct the acid condition. Blue litmus paper was used initially as an indicator. This merely involved wetting the soils and observing the degree of redness of the paper. Later, Emil Truog of the University of Wisconsin developed a method using lead acetate paper placed over the mouth of a flask containing measured amounts of soil, calcium chloride, zinc sulfide, and water. The acids in the soil reacted with the sulfide to form hydrogen sulfide, and when boiled the sulfide gas reacted with lead in the paper. The more acid the soil, the blacker became the paper (59). S. P. L. Sorenson of Denmark in 1909 developed the hydrogen ion activity concept and the pH scale based on the negative logarithm of hydrogen ion concentration, but this did not come into general use in the United States until much later (73).

Nutrient Composition of Crops

Vast amounts of data were collected on nutrient composition of various crops, both of tops and roots, and some effort was made to trace the effects of nitrogen from legumes grown in rotations on the nitrogen contents of subsequent crops. Numerous calculations were made on the pounds per acre of nutrients removed by different crops, and a few attempts were made to develop balance sheets relating the recovery of nutrients by the crops to that applied in fertilizers and manures (53, 73, 83). Several studies followed the uptake and translocation of nutrients in corn, potatoes, barley, and wheat at various stages of growth, the most detailed being that of Jones and Huston of Purdue University with corn in 1914 (57).

Total Chemical Analysis of Soils

Some state experiment stations emphasized total chemical analysis of soils. As in the past, however, it was concluded that total analysis gave little indication of the nutrient-supplying ability of the soil and was of little or no value in predicting fertilizer needs. C. G. Hopkins of Illinois surveyed the total nutrient contents of the state's soils and the nutrient requirements of the crops growing on them. He then reduced the soil fertility needs to a bookkeeping procedure, with credit columns for the nutrients in the soil and in any manure, legumes, liming materials, and fertilizers that were applied, and debit columns for nutrients removed by the harvested crops or lost in drainage waters. This led Hopkins to conclude that most of the soils of the state required only phosphate and lime. This was based on the thesis that nitrogen could be maintained by legumes and manures, and potassium maintained by the solvent action of decaying organic matter on potassium-bearing minerals in the soil. He preferred ground phosphate rock to supply the phosphorus and coarsely ground limestone to supply calcium and magnesium (30, 53).

Methods for Determining Soil Fertility

The desirability of determining the amount of mineral nutrients in soils that were available for uptake by plants had been on the minds of chemists for years. At one time it was thought that mineral nutrients in soils existed in two distinct forms—undecomposed primary minerals that were highly unavailable, and secondary minerals, called zeolites, which contained the available nutrients. Digestion of the soil with strong acids (sulfuric, nitric, and hydrochloric) was proposed as a way to extract and measure the available nutrients. Hydrochloric acid at a specific gravity of 1.115 (the concentration of the acid after prolonged boiling) became the accepted acid largely as the result of its promotion by H. W. Hilgard of California. Although a great many analyses were made using the Hilgard strong acid method, it proved to be of little or no value and use of it and other strong acids was discontinued (52, 59).

Weak or dilute acids also were used to extract soils. These were citric, acetic, oxalic, and tartaric acids; one-fifth normal nitric and hydrochloric acids, and one-two-hundredth normal hydrochloric acid. The theory at the time was that roots excreted plant juices which were acid and exerted a solvent action upon the secondary minerals in the soil. About 1890, Bernard Dyer of the Rothamsted Experiment Station extracted juices from a large number of plants and calculated that their average acidity was equivalent to about a 1.0 percent solution of citric acid. He then used this solution to extract soils from field plots that had received continued application of phosphate and potash over long periods, and obtained good correlations between the amounts of P and K extracted and the amounts of P and K added as well as the productivity of the plots. The citric acid method, as a result, was used extensively in England. U.S. researchers, however, preferred the one-fifth normal nitric acid method, but it did not prove to be an infallible guide. G. S. Fraps of the Texas station found that the nitric acid would extract all of the calcium phosphates in soils, but dissolved only a fraction of the iron and aluminum phosphates. Some potash minerals were fairly soluble in the solution and other were not. Interest in the use of dilute organic and mineral acids waned as it became obvious that plant roots did not excrete acid plant juices (30, 47, 59).

Ulbricht and Schultze began using distilled water to extract soils as a means for determining soil productivity levels in Germany in 1863 and 1864. By continual leaching they were able to distinguish between nutrient contents of rich and poor soils. In 1904, F. H. King of Wisconsin compared two high producing soils with two low producing soils by shaking soil samples in distilled water, collecting and filtering the leachate, and then drying the soil again and repeating the operation until 11 extractions were made. These showed that the high producing soils released several times more nutrients than the poor soils (52).

Whitney-Cameron Soil Fertility Theories and Reverbations

Milton Whitney and F. K. Cameron of the USDA Bureau of Soils made a massive effort using distilled water as an extractant. They published a bulletin in 1903 with their results and conclusions. They extracted some 600 samples from productive and unproductive soils occurring on neighboring farms, found no real differences between them upon analysis of the extractants, and concluded that all soils were plentifully supplied with plant nutrients. Their interpretations led to an immediate uproar among scientists in this country and abroad, a bitter debate that lasted for several years. Adding fuel to the fire, Whitney came out with another bulletin in 1906, setting forth a theory that crops excreted poisonous organic substances from their roots, which was the cause of low yields.

Whitney and Cameron felt strongly that the differences in productive capacities of soils and farms could be explained through chemical analysis of natural soil solutions and not through the use of chemical solvents of one kind or another. However, difficulties in removing the soil solution intact and in sufficient quantity for analysis led them to abandon this approach. Instead, they settled on adding distilled water to the soil to dilute and permit extraction of the solution, which was in effect merely a water extraction. The procedure was to place 100 grams of soil in 500 cubic centimeters of distilled water, shake it vigorously for 3 minutes, allow it to settle for 20 minutes, decant the liquid, and filter it under pressure through an unglazed porcelain filter to produce a clear solution. The solution was then analyzed for bicarbonates, chlorides, sulfates, nitrates, phosphate, silica, calcium, magnesium, and potassium (97).

Soil samples were specially collected from different types of soil under various conditions of cultivation and cropping in areas varying widely in yield levels. The conclusions were:

> The exhaustive investigation of many types of soil by very accurate methods of analysis under many conditions of cultivation and cropping, in areas yielding large crops and in adjoining areas yielding small crops, has shown there is no obvious relation between the amount of several nutritive elements in the soil and the yield of crops; that is to say that no essential chemical difference has been

found between the solution produced in a soil yielding a large crop of wheat and that in a soil of the same character in adjoining fields of giving much smaller yields. The conclusion logically follows that on the average farm the great controlling factor in the yield of crops is not the amount of plant food in the soil, but is a physical factor the exact nature of which is yet to be determined. . . . It appears that practically all soils contain sufficient plant food for good crop yield, that this supply will be indefinitely maintained, . . . (97, p. 64).

They also concluded that when fertilizers gave a bona fide yield increase, this was probably not due to the plant food they contained, but to an early stimulation of the plant to get its roots out into a sufficient volume of soil, or to some other physiological or physical effect (97).

Whitney's toxic substance theory was the result of isolation by Bureau chemists of a wide range of organic compounds such as stearic acid, pyridin derivatives, and tyrosin from soils. Some of these, when introduced into water cultures, were toxic to plant seedlings. Whitney, with support from Cameron, assumed that these compounds were excreted by plant roots, and that a given crop excreted specific toxins which accumulated in the soil and lowered the yields of that crop when it appeared again on the same land. This they believed was the real reason that soils became worn out when farmed for long periods. The solution to restoring the fertility to worn-out soils was simple: use a rotation in which no crop followed itself. Then, when the time came around in the rotation to grow the crop again, the soil had had ample time to dispose of the "sewage" left from that crop when it was previously grown. Whitney explained away any observed responses to fertilizers with the statement: "Apparently these small amounts of fertilizer we add to the soil have their effect upon these toxic substances and render the soil sweet and more healthful for growing plants. We believe that it is through this means that our fertilizers act rather than supplying plant food to the plant" (96).

The two bulletins, Bureau of Soils Bull. 22 reporting the water extraction studies (97) and Farmers Bull. 257 reporting the toxic substances theory (96), were widely disseminated in the United States and in other countries, and immediately caused a wave of dissent. Not only did scientists question the water extraction method used in the first study and the assumption made in the second that plant roots excreted toxic substances, but they also disagreed with the sweeping conclusions of the authors, branding them as unrealistic and unwarranted. C. G. Hopkins of Illinois was undoubtedly the leading and most vociferous critic in the United States, but he had many close contenders in other states. A. D. Hall, director of the Rothamsted station in England, was a leading critic in Europe. A "Committee of Seven" was formed by the American Association of Agricultural Chemists to weigh the evidence presented by Whitney and Cameron. The agricultural committees in the U.S. Congress held hearings, and the Fertilizer Manufacturers

Association was deeply concerned. All in all, the theories were thoroughly refuted, without great difficulty. Nevertheless, Whitney and Cameron were adamant that their theories were correct; they published rebuttals and claimed that their ideas were widely accepted and taught in agricultural colleges. The latter provoked a survey by the Kentucky Agricultural Experiment Station that showed otherwise (11, 30, 46, 53).

Although the Whitney and Cameron theories were discredited, they did create a lot of excitement and diversion, and focused attention of younger and better trained scientists on soil fertility and plant nutrition (30). And, through it all, farmers kept right on using fertilizers.

Fertilizer Trade Associations

The Fertilizer Exchanges

Fertilizer trade associations in this country originated as "fertilizer exchanges" in the 1860's and 1870's. These were local organizations designed to unite various representatives of the trade in matters of common concern, including price stabilization. The exchanges were located mainly in the port cities where shipments of guano and sodium nitrate entered the U.S. market (32).

Certain benefits were thought to have been derived from the exchanges, which resulted in some of the leading manufacturers forming the first national association in Baltimore in 1876. This bore the ungainly name "The National Fertilizer Association of Chemical Fertilizer Manufacturers." Its purpose was to exchange opinions, overcome antagonisms among the various companies, and unite on matters of common industry concerns, mainly tariffs and trade regulations. The association functioned in a haphazard and discontinuous manner; as a result, more local exchanges were formed (3, 4, 18, 32).

Formation of the National Fertilizer Association in 1883 was a second attempt to create a strong national organization. Its first annual meeting was held in Baltimore in August 1883 with Charles Richardson of Philadelphia as its first president. Stated objectives were to bring the large and growing number of firms and corporations of the fertilizer trade into friendly contact, to facilitate the exchange of opinions upon topics of mutual interest, and to act concertedly upon matters affecting the industry. Committees were appointed on transportation, trade rules, state laws, agricultural chemistry, etc. The association issued yearly reports on fertilizer movement and trade, and on methods for fertilizer analysis. However, it fell apart in 1887 "due to two seasons of bad harvest and other drawbacks" (3, 4, 18, 32). No national trade organizations existed from 1887 until 1894.

Birth of the Fertilizer Associations

The next organization was The Association of Fertilizer Manufacturers of the West, formed by 12 manufacturers in Columbus, Ohio, in March 1894. Its first annual convention was held in Buffalo, New York, in November of that year with William T. Wuichet of Dayton, Ohio, as president. The name was changed to The Fertilizer Manufacturers Association at a meeting in Buffalo in 1901, with George Braden of Louisville as president (12, 32). The name was changed again in 1907, this time to The National Fertilizer Association, which had first been used in 1883. This decision was made at an annual meeting at Norfolk with C. A. Alling of Chicago as president (32). The association operated under this name for a great number of years.

In the meantime, the Southern Fertilizer Association had been organized at Old Point Comfort, Virginia, in June 1906, with C. G. Wilson of Atlanta as president. Thus, two strong fertilizer associations had come into existence, but with considerable duplication of membership and with more or less parallel interests and activities. In fact, both held annual meetings at the same place and the same time. Finally, in 1925, the two merged using the National Fertilizer Association name but adding "incorporated" (2, 3, 18).

Early problems in forming stable trade associations were due largely to the tumult in the industry. Some members wanted to improve the industry's image, weed out unscrupulous practices and irresponsible agents and dealers, and act concertedly and without jealousies. Others were obsessed with their own specific interests and were more concerned about state or regional problems than those of national interest. Also, some were doubtful about national associations for fear of subjecting the industry to trust-building charges by the Federal Government (3, 4).

The Soil Improvement Committees

One of the major activities of the trade associations was the work of the soil improvement committees aimed at increasing fertilizer consumption on farms in a way that would assure farmers good returns from their investment. The first to be formed was the Middle West Soil Improvement Committee of the National Fertilizer Association which was set up in 1911. This resulted from a meeting in Chicago of some of the leading fertilizer manufacturers to establish an organization "which would carry on educational work with farmers to create larger yields of better grain and crops generally." The activities of the committee were to be funded through subscriptions of manufacturers doing business in the middle western states of Ohio, Indiana, Kentucky, Illinois, Michigan, Wisconsin, and Missouri (31).

Headquarters for the committee was in Chicago. Henry G. Bell, a professor of agronomy at the University of Maine who had also worked on the agronomy staff at Iowa State College, was hired to direct the program. Activities envisaged for the committee included general publicity, conduct of practical field tests on farms, maintaining cooperation with all other agricultural and commercial interests, and working closely with the state land-grant colleges and experiment stations. The end objective, as stated by Bell, was to encourage better methods to build up and maintain soil fertility by rotation of crops, use of manure and legumes supplemented with fertilizer containing nitrogen, available phosphoric acid, and potassium, and by drainage and scientific use of lime as required (31).

Under Bell's direction, numerous publications were issued on culture of various crops along with recommended fertilizer practices, articles were prepared for use by leading agricultural newspapers, and speeches were made before farm groups of all kinds. Numerous visits were made to the colleges and experiment stations, and an attempt was made to train salesmen in sound fertilizer use (31).

C. G. Hopkins Fights Committees

The program apparently was well accepted in all of the states except Illinois, where it immediately ran afoul of C. G. Hopkins and his followers; they believed in applying phosphate rock and stood firm against use of manufactured fertilizers. Hopkins predicted ultimate land ruin if farmers listened to the teachings of the Middle West Soil Improvement Committee. According to Hopkins, the committee, financed by the National Fertilizer Association, engaged men from agricultural colleges to lend it prestige, and was getting columns of free advertising by use of "boiler plate" in country newspapers. He saw the committee as a giant plan of the fertilizer trusts to sell their products under the guise of instructing the farmer (17). Fertilizer interests retaliated with many equally caustic articles about Hopkins and his ideas in *American Fertilizer* and *Commercial Fertilizer* from 1912 through 1915. Hopkins, on a year's leave of absence from Illinois in 1914, served as director of agriculture of the Southern Settlement and Development Organization (20). This brought great blasts from the southern-based *Commercial Fertilizer*, one statement being "Dr. Hopkins is a leader of the blind, although not a blind leader, and, we repeat, it is a pity he so prostitutes his undoubted talents to lead farmers of his state and elsewhere so far afield on the great question of fertilizers by intensive methods so largely dependent on 'complete fertilizer'" (19).

Regardless of the problems in Illinois, the Middle West Soil Improvement Committee was deemed a huge success, and both the committee and the National Fertilizer Association became interested in broadening its scope. At a meeting in New York City in 1915 it was decided to add the states of West Virginia, New Jersey, Pennsylvania, Delaware, New York, Maine, Massachusetts, Vermont, New Hampshire, Rhode Island,

and Connecticut. The words "Middle West" were dropped from its title, but the headquarters remained in Chicago (22).

The Southern Fertilizer Association appointed a Southern Soil Improvement Committee about 1913 and patterned it more or less after the Middle West committee. Funding was apparently a problem and it got off to a slow start, not hiring a full staff until about 1917 (23).

Fertilizer Journals

The strong voices of the fertilizer industry and the fertilizer trade associations were the two independent fertilizer journals, *The American Fertilizer* and *Commercial Fertilizer*. *The American Fertilizer* was first published by the Ware Brothers Company of Philadelphia in 1894; it continued to appear monthly for nearly 60 years. *Commercial Fertilizer* was begun in 1910 by the Walter W. Brown Publishing Company at Atlanta. It, too, was published monthly and continued on a regular basis for 60 years, but placed greater emphasis upon the South. Both journals also published annual yearbooks.

The journals duly reported all matters of interest to the industry. These included such topics as the annual meetings of the trade associations, articles and editorials dealing with industry problems, advances made in public institutions relating to fertilizer research and use, and the major debates and squabbles at the time. Each journal contained large numbers of advertisements on manufacturing equipment and products and raw materials offered. Yearbooks concentrated mostly on production and consumption data and lists of manufacturers and where their plants were located. The *Commercial Fertilizer* yearbooks also contained authored summary-type articles dealing with various phases of fertilizer manufacture and use.

Summary

During the 1870-1920 period, use of fertilizer became common in the states east of the Mississippi River, which accounted for 94 percent of the U.S. fertilizer consumption.

All land with significant agricultural value, including the Great Plains and the Far West, was settled by the turn of the century. Total farm output of the Nation increased substantially until about 1910. By this time, few new lands were being brought into production, and farmers, with the help of machinery, were cultivating practically all the acreage on their farms. Farm output changed little from 1910 through 1920. The simple reason was that output could not expand further with no more cultivatable acreage available. During the 50-year period, technological advances in farm mechanization reduced farm labor and permitted farmers to cultivate larger acreages and support the growing U.S. population. These included the development of gang plows with as many as four bottoms, grain combines, the self-tying binder, and improvements in grain drills and planters. Steam engines came into use to power stationary threshers and farm tractors. The gasoline engine tractor appeared about 1890 and was mass produced by 1910. Motor trucks and self-propelled harvesting machines were in use by 1915 (36).

Average crop yields showed no increase from the 1870's, hovering around 13 bushels of wheat per acre, 24 bushels of corn, and 180 pounds of cotton (36). Genetic limitations of the crop varieties grown, the inability of farmers to cope adequately with plant diseases and insects, and the inadequate use of fertilizers and lime collectively placed a ceiling on yields even in areas of adequate moisture. Although fertilizer use increased from 1870 through 1920, average per acre use of plant nutrients was very low compared to today.

REFERENCES

1. Alvord, H. E., and C. E. and H. J. Patterson. 1890. Commercial fertilizers. *Expt. Sta. Rec.* 2(5): 228-231.
2. Anon. 1889. Office of Experiment Stations Circular No. 7. *Expt. Sta. Rec.* 1(1):50.
3. _____. 1894. Associated fertilizer manufacturers. *Am. Fert.* 1(4): 228-230.
4. _____. 1895. The requirements of the fertilizer industry in the United States. *Am. Fert.* 3(5):262-267.
5. _____. 1897. Agricultural facts of the year 1869. *Am. Fert.* 7(3): 113-115.
6. _____. 1898. Analysis of fertilizers and license of sales. *Am. Fert.* 8(6):249-254.
7. _____. 1902. Home-mixed fertilizers. *Am. Fert.* 16(3):7.
8. _____. 1902. Fertilizer laws. *Am. Fert.* 16(3):20-22.
9. _____. 1902. "Ammonia" to be abolished. *Am. Fert.* 17(6):32.
10. _____. 1903. Derivation of animal ammoniates. *Am. Fert.* 19(3):5-23.
11. _____. 1904. The manufacturers' protest. *Am. Fert.* 20(2):5-7.
12. _____. 1904. Fertilizer manufacturers association. *Am. Fert.* 21(4): 24-25.
13. _____. 1905. Sulphates of ammonia. *Am. Fert.* 22(2):5-9.
14. _____. 1911. Germany's potash treasure. *Comm. Fert.* 2(2):14.
15. _____. 1912. The German potash industry. *Am. Fert.* 37(1):36-37.
16. _____. 1912. Potash controversies close. *Comm. Fert.* 4(1):13.
17. _____. 1913. The cruel war in Illinois. *Comm Fert.* 6(2):14-15.
18. _____. 1913. The National Fertilizer Association. *Am. Fert.* 39(7):49-51.
19. _____. 1913. Science mixed with demagogy. *Comm. Fert.* 6(3):11-12.
20. _____. 1914. New southern mission of Dr. Hopkins of Illinois. *Comm. Fert.* (2):23-24.
21. _____. 1914. Cyanamid development in America. *Comm. Fert. Part II, 1914 Yearbook* 8(5):59-60.
22. _____. 1915. Soil improvement committee of the National Fertilizer Association. *Comm. Fert.* 11(4):27-29.
23. _____. 1916. Soil improvement of the Southern Fertilizer Association to be enlarged. *Comm. Fert.* 13(5):11-12.
24. _____. 1917. Alsatian potash. *Am. Fert.* 46(11):68-72.

25. ____. 1918. Largest air explosives plant in the world starts operation. *Comm. Fert.* 17(5):66.
26. ____. 1918. Potash production of the United States last year. *Comm. Fert.* 16(5):50.
27. ____. 1918. Some availability studies with ammonium phosphate and its chemical and biological effects on the soil. *Comm. Fert.* 16(4):40,44,46,50.
28. ____. 1923. Editor takes issue with home-mixing. *Comm. Fert.* 26(3):30-31.
29. ____. 1932. Nitrate deposits inadequate for commercial use. *Comm. Fert.* 45(2):20-21.
30. Bear, F. E. 1948. Historical introduction. In *Diagnostical techniques for soils and crops.* pp. ix-xxiii. American Potash Institute, Washington, D.C.
31. Bell, H. G. 1912. Middle West Soil Improvement Committee. *Comm. Fert.* 5(1):40-47.
32. Brand, C. J. 1940. A brief history of the National Fertilizer Association. *Comm. Fert.* 61(1):12-14,16.
33. ____. 1947. Some fertilizer history connected with World War I. *Agr. Hist.* 21:46-52.
34. Chazal, P. E. 1904. *The Century in Phosphate Fertilizers–A Sketch of the South Carolina Phosphate Industry.* Lucas-Richardson, Charleston, S.C.
35. Clark, K. G. and F. E. Bear. 1948. Use of natural organics in mixed fertilizers. *Am. Fert.* 108(3):7-10,24,26,28,30.
36. Cochrane, W. W. 1979. *The Development of American Agriculture.* Univ. of Minnesota Press, Minneapolis.
37. Collings, G. W. 1941. *Commerical Fertilizers.* The Blakiston Co., Philadelphia.
38. Cottrell, A. 1923. *The Manufacture of Nitric Acid and Nitrates.* Gurney and Jackson, London and Edinburgh.
39. Davis, R. O. E. 1949. Forty years of fertilizer research. *Chem. Eng. News* 27:410-412.
40. Duecker, W. W. and J. R. West. 1959. History of the manufacture of sulfuric acid. In *Manufacture of Sulfuric Acid.* Ed. by W. W. Duecker and J. R. West. pp. 9-12. Reinhold Publishing Corp., New York.
41. Eddy. E. D. 1956. *Colleges of Our Land and Time.* Harper & Brothers, New York.
42. ____, and R. Frank. 1959. Review of the sulfuric acid industry. In *Manufacture of Sulfuric Acid.* Ed. by W. W. Duecker and J. R. West. pp. 1-8. Reinhold Publishing Corp., New York.
43. Ernst, F. A. 1927. Atmospheric nitrogen fixation, 1902-1927. *Am. Fert.* 66(10):21-24.
44. Fisher, H. J. 1950. 75 years of real service to agriculture. *Comm. Fert.* 80(4):32-33, 35-36,38.
45. Fite, G. C. 1979. Southern agriculture since the Civil War: an overview. *Agr. Hist.* 53(1):3-21.
46. Hall, A. D. 1909. Theories of manure and fertilizer action. *Am. Fert.* 30(3):23-30.
47. ____. 1915. *Fertilizers and Manures.* E. P. Dutton & Company, New York.
48. Haynes, W. 1954. Manufacture of sulfuric acid. In *American Chemical Industry.* Vol. I. pp. 253-268. D. Van Nostrand Company, Inc., New York, Toronto, London.

49. _____. 1945. The World War I period: 1912-1922. In *American Chemical Industry*. Vol. II. pp. 164-181. D. Van Nostrand Company, Inc., New York, Toronto, London.
50. _____. 1945. The World War I period: 1912-1922. In *American Chemical Industry*. Vol. III. pp. 172-186. D. Van Nostrand Company, Inc., New York, Toronto, London.
51. _____. 1949. The chemical companies. In *American Chemical Industry*. Vol. VI. pp. 31-43, 391-394, 440-448. D. Van Nostrand Company, Inc., New York, Toronto, London.
52. Hilgard, E. W. 1906. *Soils*. The MacMillan Co., New York.
53. Hopkins, C. G. 1910. *Soil Fertility and Permanent Agriculture*. Ginn and Company, Boston, New York, Chicago, and London.
54. Horsfall, J. G. 1969. How Johnson related to science and society. In *How Crops Grow a Century Later*. Ed. by P. R. Day, Connecticut Agr. Expt. Sta. Bull. 708. pp. 1-6.
55. Jacob, K. D. 1940. New and old methods of processing phosphates. *Am. Fert.* 93(8):7-9.
56. _____. 1964. History and status of the superphosphate industry. In *Superphosphate: Its History, Chemistry, and Manufacture*. pp. 37-94. U.S. Dept. of Agr. and Tennessee Valley Authority, U.S. Gov't. Printing Office, Washington, D.C.
57. Jones, W. J., Jr. and H. A. Huston. 1914. *Composition of Maize at Various Stages of Growth*. Purdue Agr. Expt. Sta. Bull. 175.
58. Landis, W. H. 1927. Twenty-five years of progress in the cyanamid industry. *Am. Fert.* 66(12):58,60,62,64,66.
59. Lyon, T. L., E. O. Fippin, and H. 0. Buckman. 1915. *Soils, Their Properties and Management*. MacMillan Co., New York.
60. Mansfield, G. R. 1922. Nitrates. *Min. Res. of U.S. Part II, non-metals*. pp. 39-40.
61. _____. 1922. Potash. *Min. Res. of U.S. Part II, non-metals*. pp. 87-98.
62. Mappus, H. F. 1935. *The Phosphate Industry of South Carolina*. Master of Science thesis. Dept. of Chem. Univ. of South Carolina.
63. Mehring, A. L. 1934. *Changes in Composition of American Fertilizers, 1880-1932*. U.S. Dept. of Agr. Circ. 315.
64. _____. 1939. Magnesium content of fertilizers. *Comm. Fert. 1939 Yearbook*. pp. 32-41.
65. _____. 1944. *Double Superphosphate*. U.S. Dept. of Agr. Circ. 718.
66. _____. and A. J. Peterson. 1934. The development of mixed fertilizers in the United States. *Comm. Fert. 1934 yearbook*. pp. 33-44.
67. _____, J. R. Adams, and K. D. Jacob. 1957. *Statistics of Fertilizer and Liming Materials in the United States*. U.S. Dept. of Agr. Statistical Bull. 191.
68. Miller, M. F. 1929. Fertilizer use in the Corn Belt. *Am. Fert.* 71(7):48,51,52,54,56,58.
69. Noyes, R. 1966. *Potash and Potassium Fertilizers*. Chemical Process Monograph No. 15. Noyes Development Corp., Park Ridge, N. J.
70. Paget, E. M. 1904. The packing house industry. *Am. Fert.* 21(3):22-28.
71. Phalen, W. C. 1914. Certain fertilizer materials. *Comm. Fert. 1914 Yearbook. Part II* 8(5):32-36.
72. Phelps, C. S. :892. Results of experiments with fertilizers of different classes. *Expt. Sta. Rec.* 5(6):573-574.
73. Reed, H. S. 1942. *A Short History of Plant Sciences*. Chronica Botanicca Co., Waltham, Mass.

74. Ridler, E. S. 1959. Chamber process for the manufacture of sulfuric acid. In *Manufacture of Sulfuric Acid.* Ed. by W. W. Duecker and J. R. West. pp. 103-134. Reinhold Publishing Corp., New York.
75. Ross, B. R. 1926. The chemist as detective and policeman, or fertilizer, feed, and insecticide control. In *Chemistry of Agriculture.* pp. 358-374. The Chemical Foundation, Inc., New York.
76. Rossiter, M. W. 1975. *The Emergence of Agricultural Science: Justus Liebig and the Americans, 1840-1880.* Yale Univ. Press, New Haven, London.
77. Shannon, F. A. 1945. *The Farmer's Last Frontier: Agriculture, 1860-1897.* Harper Torchbooks, Harper and Row, New York, Evanston, London.
78. Sherman, M. S. 1960. USDA's 50 years of fertilizer technology research. *Comm. Fert.* 101(2):33-34.
79. Stocking, G. W. 1931. *The Potash Industry, a Study of State Control.* Richard R. Smith, Inc., New York.
80. Taylor, R. H. 1947. The sale and application of commercial fertilizers in the South Atlantic States to 1900. *Agr. Hist.* 21:46-52.
81. Terne, B. 1896. Home-made fertilizers vs. trade manufactured fertilizers. *Am. Fert.* 4(4):185-193.
82. Thorne, C. E. 1890. Commercial fertilizers. *Expt. Sta. Rec. Vol. III.* pp. 121-127.
83. ____. 1914. *Farm Manures.* Orange Judd Co., New York.
84. True, A. C. 1929. *A History of Agricultural Education in the United States, 1785-1925.* U.S. Dept. of Agr. Misc. Publ. 36.
85. ____. 1937. *A History of Agricultural Experimentation and Research in the United States, 1607-1925.* U.S. Dept. of Agr. Misc. Publ. 251.
86. Turrentine, J. W. 1913. *Nitrogenous Fertilizers Obtainable in the United States.* U.S. Dept. of Agr. Bull. 37.
87. ____. 1941. Liebig and the potash industry. *Am. Fert.* 94(6):6-8,24.
88. U.S. Dept. Agr. 1889. *Expt. Sta. Rec. Vol. I.* Louisiana, pp. 65-66; Virginia, 158-160; North Carolina, 284-285.
89. ____. 1890. *Expt. Sta. Rec. Vol. II.* Georgia, pp. 550-551; Indiana, 634- 637; Alabama, 710-711; Delaware, 716-718; Maryland, 726-728.
90. ____. 1891. *Expt. Sta. Rec. Vol. III.* Ohio, pp. 241-242; New Jersey, 292-295.
91. Vickery, H. B. 1969. Samuel W. Johnson and how crops grow. In *How Crops Grow a Century Later.* Ed. by P. R. Day. Conn. Agr. Expt. Sta. Bull. 708. pp. 7-24.
92. Waggaman, W. H. 1914. *The Manufacture of Acid Phosphate.* U.S. Dept. of Agr. Bull. 144.
93. ____. 1927. *Phosphoric Acid, Phosphates, and Phosphatic Fertilizers.* Chemical Catalog Co., Inc., New York.
94. Webster, W. H. H. 1910. Cyanamid industry in Canada. *Comm. Fert.* 1(1):27-28.
95. Wheeler, H. J. 1914. *Manures and Fertilizers.* The MacMillan Co., New York.
96. Whitney, M. 1906. *Soil Fertility.* U.S. Dept. of Agr. Farmers' Bull. 257.
97. ____, and F. K. Cameron. 1903. *The Chemistry of the Soil as Related to Crop Production.* U.S. Dept. of Agr. Bur. of Soils Bull. 22.
98. Wiley, H. W. 1899. *The Relation of Chemistry to the Progress of Agriculture.* Yearbook of the U.S. Dept. of Agr., 1899. pp. 201-258.
99. Wood, A. F. 1906. *The Present Status of the Nitrogen Problem.* Yearbook of the U.S. Dept. of Agr. 1906. pp. 125-136.

5

The Great Potash Search 1910-1935

One of the more interesting epics in U.S. fertilizer history was the great search for domestic sources of potash. It began in 1910 with the purpose of making this country independent of the German potash monopoly and culminated in the early 1930's in the discovery and initial development of the Carlsbad, New Mexico, potash beds. The great potash search was visualized as an orderly national investigation, spearheaded by the U.S. Geological Survey and the Bureau of Soils. Actually it took 20 years of hard work and never developed smoothly as expected. Finding a major deposit proved highly elusive.

The search had barely got underway when World War I prompted a German potash embargo that left the United States short of potash. As a result, prices skyrocketed and every possible source was exploited. The end of World War I brought the collapse of the hastily built domestic industry, except for Searles Lake. The wartime problems also brought a new determination to resume the search for a major potash deposit, particularly in the promising Permian salt basin in parts of Texas and New Mexico.

The German Potash Hassle

A bizarre series of circumstances prompted the search for domestic potash. Essentially the United States decision to search for potash was the outgrowth of a wrangle over prices of German potash shipped to the United States, first with the German potash syndicate and later with the Imperial German Government. On the one hand, the current syndicate had lost its control over production and pricing. On the other, an extremely aggressive U.S. fertilizer industry (the major export consumer of German potash) did everything it could to sidestep the syndicate and obtain potash on its own terms. The hassle that resulted finally involved the highest levels of both governments and created enough concern in the United States that a domestic search for potash was launched.

German potash syndicates had existed since 1879, although they were periodically re-formed to meet current situations. Their purpose was to control production and pricing, handle export sales, and serve as a worldwide informational medium to encourage consumption. The syndicates were made up of potash producers, with governmental participation to assure low prices to German consumers and the setting of export prices high enough to provide producer profits and pay for market development. The earlier syndicates generally had achieved their goals, although production control had always been a difficult problem and was never fully successful.

Early in the twentieth century syndicates increasingly lost control over production as new producers appeared faster than consumption increased. The number of mines increased to 28 in 1905, and four years later had reached 63. Some newcomers began sidestepping the syndicate, selling directly to foreign buyers at prices lower than set by the syndicate. Dissatisfaction grew among syndicate members over quota allotments. As capacity ran wild, even the syndicate began offering discounts on large volume purchases, and profits largely disappeared (49).

Dissension peaked as the time approached for renewal of the five-year syndicate contract. The rumor was out that reinstatement of the syndicate would fail at the final meeting on June 30. When this news reached U.S. fertilizer manufacturers, buying groups embarked en masse for Berlin, prepared to make on-the-spot bargain-counter deals. By the evening of June 30, the Hotel Adlon in Berlin, where the syndicate meeting was being held, was jammed with representatives of the United States and other countries anticipating collapse of the syndicate. As expected, the syndicate members failed to reach agreement.

The collapse of the syndicate and its disastrous effects brought immediate pressure by the German Government to try to correct the situation. In December 1909, the syndicate sent a commission to New York to negotiate with the U.S. contractors. Both sides were willing to give a bit, but an agreement could not be reached (49).

Negotiations eventually involved the foreign offices of both countries, but nothing was resolved. Germany finally developed what was to become known as the Potash Law of 1910 which placed the German potash industry under control of the Imperial Government. This law stipulated prices on future sales both for domestic consumption and export. A tax was levied on each ton of potash produced within the quota to offset the expenses of administering the law and marketing the products. However, if any producer exceeded his quota, an oppressive supertax was levied; in the case of muriate of potash this amounted to about $22 per ton in addition to the $15 per ton levied on product produced within the quota. This struck directly at U.S. firms which had made long-term contracts at very low potash prices since the German signers could not possibly supply the tonnages agreed upon and stay within the quotas allotted to them (29,49).

The industry convinced Department of State negotiators that the potash law would be discriminatory against U.S. interests and should be withdrawn. However, the German negotiators took the stand that the potash problem was a civil matter and not one for diplomatic procedure. Despite vigorous protestations by the State Department, the Germans did not budge. The minimum provisions of the Payne-Aldrich Act were extended to German, but by this time the potash controversy had received national attention, especially in the highly influential agricultural sector. The German Potash Law became effective May 25, 1910 (1,49).

The U.S. fertilizer industry was left with no alternative except to try to settle the potash dispute by civil procedures. A series of conferences with the syndicate in Hamburg led to an agreement in the fall of 1911. Under the terms of the settlement, all suits pending in U.S. courts involving liability for payment of the tax under the Potash Law of 1910 were withdrawn; U.S. contracts with the independent mines were to be assigned to the syndicate; new contracts with the syndicate covering full U.S. potash requirements for the 5-1/2 years were to be obtained at prices roughly the same as those prevailing before the execution of the 1909 contracts; independent mines not yet in the syndicate were to re-enter; and the German Government was to refund 60 percent of the supertax held in escrow in U.S. banks. All in all, the settlement was not too unfavorable to the U.S. companies. Contracts for muriate of potash were set at about $32.50 per ton. Although this was about $5 higher than had been offered by the syndicate in the New York negotiations, it amounted to a savings of about $5 per ton compared to the current syndicate prices (2,26,50).

Even though the fertilizer industry and farmers suffered some from the enactment of the Potash Law of 1910, in the long run they were to profit materially. This resulted from the awakening of the U.S. public and the nation's leaders to the possible perils of sole dependence upon a foreign monopoly as a supplier of potash.

The Potash Search, 1910-1914

The concerns built up during the uproar over the Potash Law of 1910 were translated into an immediate nationwide effort to find and develop our own domestic sources. It involved not only the Federal Government, but also the private sector and certain state institutions. The U.S. Congress passed legislation which became effective March 4, 1911, to undertake a survey to find domestic sources and to conduct work that would lead to their development. The legislation initially provided annual funding to the U.S. Geological Survey of $20,000, and the Bureau of Soils of $12,500, to carry out the investigations (20). Although not provided with Federal funding, commercial companies, private individuals, and some state institutions were interested and anxious to become involved on their own.

The idea of discovering domestic potash deposits in this country was not entirely new. In 1895 an article appeared in the *American Fertilizer* by Dr. Otto Meyer of Raleigh, North Carolina, entitled "Why not keep a lookout for potash deposits?" Meyer gave a good analysis of the German Strassfurt deposits, and suggested the first place to turn attention to in the United States would be the brine deposits in Ohio, West Virginia, Pennsylvania, and Michigan, and that boring for potash salts might be made in other areas. Whitman Symmes, a mining engineer for the California Borax Company, apparently first noted the presence of potash in Searles Lake, California, in 1898 but could not interest his company in following up the lead (23, 42).

Following is a list of potash minerals found in nature, several of which are used in fertilizer potash production:

Mineral	*Composition*	*% K_2O*
Chlorides		
Sylvite	KCl	63.1
Carnallite	$KCl \cdot MgCl_2 \cdot 6H_2O$	17.0
Kainite	$KCl \cdot MgSO_4 \cdot 3H_2O$	18.9
Hanksite	$KCl \cdot 9Na_2SO_4 \cdot 2Na_2CO_3$	3.0
Sulfates		
Polyhalite	$K_2SO_4 \cdot MgSO_4 \cdot 2CaSO_4 \cdot 2H_2O$	15.5
Langbeinite	$K_2SO_4 \cdot 2MgSO_4$	22.6
Leonite	$K_2SO_4 \cdot MgSO_4 \cdot 4H_2O$	25.5
Schoenite	$K_2SO_4 \cdot MgSO_4 \cdot 6H_2O$	23.3
Krugite	$K_2SO_4 \cdot MgSO_4 \cdot 4CaSO_4 \cdot 2H_2O$	10.7
Glaserite	$3K_2SO_4 \cdot Mg_2SO_4$	42.6
Syngenite	$K_2SO_4 \cdot CaSO_4 \cdot H_2O$	28.8
Aphthitalite	$(K, Na)_2SO_4$	29.8
Kalinite	$K_2SO_4 \cdot Al_2(SO_4)_3 \cdot 24H_2O$	9.9
Alunite	$K_2 \cdot Al_6(OH)_{12} \cdot (SO_4)_4$	11.4
Nitrates		
Niter	KNO_3	46.5

Activities of the U.S. Government Agencies

One of the first steps taken by the U.S. Geological Survey after funds were made available by Congress was to make a listing of the possible potash sources in the country. Mineral sources listed were igneous rocks (principally feldspar and leucite); the greensand marls of New Jersey and Delaware; alunite, which was known to occur at various places in this country; and salines in brines and salt beds. Organic sources listed were wood ashes; beet sugar refinery wastes; molasses residues from alcohol distillation; seaweeds, and wool scourings from woolen mills (19).

The Geological Survey and the Bureau of Soils agreed upon a cooperative approach to avoid unnecessary duplication of work. The Survey directed its attention to exploration for natural potash sources mostly in the arid western states, including drilling for buried potash salts. The Bureau of Soils concentrated much of its work on obtaining potash from the giant kelps (seaweed) off the Pacific Coast, and on developing possible processes for recovery of potash from various organic and mineral sources, including alunite, feldspar, and greensand. It also assisted the Geological Survey in its nationwide studies of brines as possible potash sources (19, 42, 43).

Both agencies made their analytical services available to private interests to encourage and assist them in their potash activities. The analytical load continued to grow and the agencies arranged the establishment of a cooperative laboratory at the Mackay School of Mines, University of Nevada, Reno, to examine and assay samples, and to handle inquiries. George J. Young of the School of Mines was in charge. He was assisted by A. R. Metz, a chemist from the Bureau of Soils. Samples from the public sector were analyzed free of charge and the results were kept confidential if requested. Appended to the replies reporting the results was a brief account of potash, its occurrence in nature, and its identification in the field (3, 19).

Work of the Geological Survey—The Geological Survey chose not to confine its work to any particular locality or type of potash deposit during this period, but attempted to uncover promising leads and weed out those that offered little hope for commercial development. Investigations accordingly included a study of the salt deposits, brines, and bitterns east of the Rocky Mountains; examination and hand drilling of various dry or partly dry lakes, playas, flats, and marshes in the arid Western States; deep drilling of possible underground potash deposits in Nevada and other likely locations within the Great Basin; and investigations of certain occurrences of alunite and leucite in the Western States. The Survey was assisted by the Bureau of Soils in the first two investigations (19).

Logically, since all of the German deposits were associated with beds of common salt, one of the first investigations involved examination of known deposits of salt and brines east of the Rocky Mountains to determine if any of these offered commercial possibilities as potash sources. The project, conducted by W. C. Phalen of the Survey and J. W. Turrentine of the Bureau of Soils, involved collection of brine samples from well drillers for oil or water, visits to all operating salt mines and brine wells, and obtaining samples of bitterns being discarded from salt or bromine operations. None of the many samples collected contained enough potash to suggest commercial consideration of potash recovery (41, 42).

Another investigation was undertaken by the Survey in 1911 to determine the potash possibilities in the "Red Beds" of the Laramie Basin in southern Wyoming. Gypsum deposits had long been known in the area, and some deep water wells and springs had been found by the University of Wyoming to contain large amounts of alkaline salts. Water samples collected and analyzed for potash by the Survey showed that the waters contained less potash than ordinary sea waters, indicating that potash deposits were highly unlikely (19).

The Geological Survey concentrated a great deal of its earlier studies on the Great Basin which occupies all of Nevada, the western third of Utah, parts of eastern California, and the southern portions of Idaho and Oregon. This huge area appeared ideal for accumulation of soluble potash salts since all drainage is internal (no water escaping to the ocean). Furthermore, the Great Basin is made up of smaller basins separated from each other by mountains. The sub-basins seemed particularly likely locations for potash deposits since the soluble potash salts resulting from weathering were confined entirely within the sub-basin area. The Survey was interested both in deep underground salt deposits and surface deposits such as brines and salts in the dry or desiccated lakes, alkaline flats, and marshes.

The Survey's first deep drilling attempt to find potash was in the old Lake Lahontan drainage basin (a sub-basin of the Great Basin occuping most of Nevada), primarily because earlier surveys had led geologists making the surveys to predict that immense amounts of saline materials must be present somewhere in the old lake basin. As a result, the Geological Survey selected a site for deep drilling at Carson Creek near Fallon, Nevada, where Lake Lahontan waters had been deepest. Drilling started in November 1911 and was stopped in October 1912 at a depth of 985 feet with no potash found in the sediments. Undaunted, the Survey subsequently made test drillings in Silver Peak Marsh, Columbus Marsh, and Smoke Creek Desert, all in Nevada, and at the south end of Death Valley, California. No concentration of potash was found in any of these (19, 42, 47).

Extensive reconnaissance studies, headed by G. S. Gale of the Geological Survey, were made of deposits of surface salts and brines throughout the Great Basin. Surveyors used hand operated drilling apparatus to obtain samples from dry lakes and marshes. In the selection of sampling sites, all available information was used to help guide the survey. These included past geological surveys, studies by state institutions, and analysis of samples sent in by the private sector. Although minor amounts of potash were found across the region, only two locations, Searles and Owens Lakes in California, were considered to contain enough potash to justify commercial development. Searles Lake had already been sampled for potash by private interests and the brines found to be unusually high in potash, but the discovery had not been publicly reported at the time the Survey collected its samples. The Survey also sampled Great Salt Lake and noted its potash content but apparently did not consider it to be sufficient for commercial recovery (20, 21, 42).

Two potash-bearing minerals also attracted the early attention of the Geological Survey. These were alunite, a potassium aluminum sulfate, and leucite, a potassium aluminum silicate. Both were considered to be of potential commercial importance, Alunite had been identified at several locations in Colorado; at Patagonia, Arizona; Bovard, Nevada; and Marysvale, Utah. The large Marysvale deposit of nearly pure alunite particularly attracted the attention of Survey geologists H. S. Gale and R. S. Butler in late 1910 and 1911. F. C. Shannon, another Survey geologist, explored the deposits in Arizona and Nevada at the same time (8, 42). Leucite had long been known in the Leucite Hills of Wyoming. Leucite-containing volcanic rocks in Sweetwater County, Wyoming, were found to contain considerable potash by A. R. Schultz and W. Cross of the Geological Survey in 1912 (46).

Numerous samplings were made of desiccated and dry lakes in the Permian salt basin of Texas and New Mexico, including one close to Carlsbad that was destined to become a waste dump for a potash mine. None contained enough potash to create excitement. Also, after private interests discovered potash in the alkaline lakes of western Nebraska, the Geological Survey sampled and studied a number of ponds and lakes in Cherry, Sheridan, Morrill, Garden, and Boxbutte Counties. Analysis of the samples confirmed high percentages of potash in some of the ponds and lakes (42).

Bureau of Soils Kelp Investigations—The Bureau of Soils concentrated a large portion of its field and laboratory work on developing the kelps off the Pacific Coast as a sound potash source. Starting in the spring of 1911, the Bureau surveyed kelp beds along the coast from southern California to the Alaskan Peninsula, determined the occurrence of different species, mapped and measured kelp groves, and estimated the quantity of potash contained in them. The wet kelps as cut were found to contain from 5 to 10 percent potassium chloride and, when thoroughly dried, 25 to 40 percent. Two species of giant kelps were identified, *Macrocystis pyrifera* in the southern waters and *Nereocystis lukteana* in the more northern waters.

The southern kelp, *Macrocystis*, was found to be a perennial which would permit several harvests per year. It grew in waters at depths of 35 to 50 feet and the stems ranged from 30 to 200 feet in length. The kelps were found to grow best along exposed coasts with rocky bottoms where there was a constant renewal of sea water. Some 230 square miles of *Macrocystis* groves were noted and these were estimated at being able to produce annually about 22 million tons of wet weed equivalent to a million tons of potassium chloride. Laboratory studies showed that kelp was capable of yielding in addition to potash a number of byproducts such as iodine and organic chemicals. The Bureau found that the kelp could be cut 4 to 8 feet under water with mechanical mowers from which it was lifted into barges. Methods for recovering potash from the kelp were studied, including leaching and charring (9, 43, 50).

Activities of the Private Sector

Private companies and individuals made a number of major contributions to the search for potash from 1910 into 1914. In fact, it was largely the private sector discoveries made during the period that were destined for commercial development during the World War I years. However, most of the private sector discoveries probably would not have been made without the interest generated by the Government agencies and the services rendered by them through analytical services, verification of the discoveries, and the provision of geological and other information. As evidenced by analyses of the great numbers of private prospecting samples sent to the Government laboratories, the private sector also experienced mostly failures in attempts to discover meaningful potash deposits.

The first major effort by a private company to discover underground potash deposits by deep drilling was made by the Railroad Valley Company of Tonapah, Nevada. The company began exploring the Railroad Valley in Nye County, Nevada, in 1911. The valley's surface was covered with salt crusts and brines containing 5 to 15 percent potash. Although not present in great quantities, the surface potash convinced the company that substantial potash deposits must exist at deeper levels. The company conducted extensive underground exploration operations over a period of about three years, drilling more than 10,000 feet in seven wells. So convinced was the company that valuable potash deposits existed that W. R. Free, formerly of the Bureau of Soils, was hired as consulting geologist. However, no segregated stratum rich in potash was found (42, 43, 44).

Searles Lake—The breakthrough was the discovery of potash in the brines of Searles Lake, California. Although presence of potash in the brines apparently had been first recognized by Whitman Symmes of the California Borax Company in 1898, it was left to C. E. Dolbear and others of the California Trona Company in 1911 to determine definitely the potential of Searles Lake as an important source of potash.

Searles Lake is in the extreme northwest corner of San Bernardino County in the Mojave Desert about 190 miles northeast of Los Angeles. It is not really a lake, but an old lake bed covered with water only a short time in the winter. It consists of a deposit of crystalline, porous salts impregnated with brine that make up about one half of the lake's volume.

Searles Lake covers roughly 12 square miles and its depth averages between 60 and 75 feet. The upper brine of the lake contains about 5 percent potassium chloride, 1.6 percent borax, 4.8 percent sodium carbonate, 6.4 percent sodium sulfate, and 16 percent sodium chloride (22).

The lake was named after John W. Searles, a gold and silver prospector, who passed through the region in 1863. Searles noted a similarity between the lake and one containing borax in Nevada and staked out claims. He returned in 1870 with partners and formed the San Bernardino Borax Mining Company. A considerable amount of semi-refined borax was reclaimed from the lake's crust and carted to Los Angeles in high-wheel wagons drawn by a string of mules. Searles could not compete with borax from the mineral colemanite, which was discovered in the hills around Death Valley, and operations were stopped in 1895 when the property was bought by the Pacific Coast Borax Company. Apparently the California Borax Company operated the deposit briefly around 1898 when Whitman Symmes noted the presence of potash in the brines (23, 42).

In 1908, the mining holdings passed into the hands of the California Trona Company, formed by C. E. Dolbear and seven others to produce soda ash and caustic soda. The original financing of the company was inadequate and a loan was arranged with the British-controlled Consolidated Gold Fields of South Africa, Ltd. California Trona ran into operation troubles and was unable to repay the loan. The operation failed in 1909. Guy Wilkerson, American manager of the Gold Fields' interests, bought up the stocks in order to keep the property intact. Although no soda shipments were made, the company staved off loss of its claims through a continuing prospecting program. It was in this program that Dolbear and others in the company established the high potash content of the brines and turned the company's interest to reclaiming potash. Analysis of the brines, indicating an average potassium chloride content of around 13.8 percent, was reported to the company in May 1911, but for company reasons was kept secret (18, 23).

H. S. Gale and E. E. Free of the Geological Survey, apparently unaware of California Trona's activities, also collected brine samples from several of Searle's old wells in the lake early in 1912, and in March announced publicly that the samples averaged 10.7 percent potassium chloride in the dissolved salts contained in the brine. Dolbear pointed out that the Government agencies were not the first discoverers and the record was set straight. The two sets of analyses left no question as to the value of the Searles Lake brines as a potential commercial source of potash (18, 43).

Two things happened following the confirmation of the Searles Lake potash deposit. First, the Federal Government in early 1913 withdrew some 133,000 acres of public domain in the desert basins showing presence of appreciable levels of potash salts, including the unclaimed

Pumping plant and pipelines used in recovery of potash from Searles Lake in California. *(G.R. Mansfield--USGS)*

areas of Searles Lake (42). Second, a new block of speculators flocked to Searles Lake to take claims on unclaimed portions of the lake; they apparently also intruded on previous claims. The speculators were accompanied by armed men with instructions to fight for the property. This was stopped when the U.S. Circuit Court ordered forced evacuation of the claim jumpers by Federal marshals. California Trona obtained a clear title to the northern part of the lake (4, 23).

In June 1913, the California Trona Company was taken over by the American Trona Corporation whose purpose was to produce potash, soda ash, borax, and sodium sulfate from Searles Lake. Most of the money came from the Gold Fields group, although American capitalists held minority interest. The new, well-financed company immediately began preparations for production. A 31-mile railroad spur was built to the site; a company town, Trona, was constructed to provide housing and facilities for employees; water was piped in, and a plant was constructed in 1914 for separation of the various salts from the brine. The process selected, however, failed to effect economical separation of the salts and the plant was shut down. Work on developing a better process began. The whole venture might have been abandoned except for the impact of the war and the rapid rise in potash prices (25, 39, 43).

Alkali Lakes of Western Nebraska—Two college students, Carl L. Modisett and John H. Show made a discovery in western Nebraska that was to provide the United States with its major source of potash during the war years. With hardly a dime between them, the young men had the perseverance and drive to conduct their own exploration, develop a recovery process, and build a company that would become an important potash producer.

The lakes in which Modisett and Show found potash were in the Sand Hills region of northwestern Nebraska in an area between the Niobara and North Platte Rivers. Scattered among the sand hills are depressions, apparently resulting from wind erosion, that contain numerous shallow lakes ranging up to 500 acres in size. Most have no surface outlets and are underlain by an impervious layer of hardpan or mud. The shallower lakes are strongly brackish due to salts leaching in from the surrounding areas. The dry salts obtained from the brines of the shallower lakes analyzed as high as 35 percent K_2O, largely in the form of potassium carbonate. The brackish lakes at the time were looked upon by the landowners as nuisances since they took up valuable grazing land and were unusable as water for the livestock (22, 44).

The discovery of potash in these lakes resulted from chemical analysis of alkali crust samples picked up by ranchers in the summer around the edges of the lakes and sent in to the University of Nebraska at Lincoln. In the fall of 1909, Modisett, a chemistry student charged with making the analysis, noted a high content of potash in some of the samples. After reading about the troubles the U.S. fertilizer industry was having over German potash, Modisett and Show, also a chemistry student, decided to analyze for potash all of the western salt and water samples they could find. The tests verified the earlier observations. Confident that they had solved the American potash problem, they determined to explore the lakes firsthand. After pooling their savings and enlisting the help of some former students, they set forth for the sand hills. Upon reaching Alliance, the party hired a wagon and team and traveled about 100 miles, collecting samples as they went, from crystal deposits, brines, and subsurface muds and sands of 14 lakes. They also measured the lake depths and surface areas. To cut costs they camped in abandoned sod houses (5, 23).

During the next few months, Show analyzed the samples, and Modisett calculated the amount of potash in each, using the area and depth measurements they had obtained on the trip. They selected Jesse Lake, 13 miles east of Alliance, as the best bet (it later proved to be the richest potash-bearing lake in the whole area), and filed claims on it in 1912. To double check their analyses, Modisett sent samples to the Geological Survey. It verified the results and sent R. B. Dole to look over the area and collect further samples (5, 23, 42).

Modisett and Show then worked out a recovery process involving evaporation of the water from the brine and recovering the crude salt. Using what funds they could borrow, they bought some old boilers and a pump for test use at Jesse Lake. In 1914, they incorporated as the Potash Products Company with a handful of backers willing to risk money on the scheme. Construction was started on a small reduction plant at nearby Hoffland, located on the railroad. Brine pumped from the lake was piped to the plant, which was completed in 1915.

Calcining cylinder of potash mill operated by Mineral Products Corporation at Marysvale, Utah, in 1916. *(V.C. Heikes--USGS)*

Surprisingly, no one besides Modisett and Show and their few backers caught the potash fever until later (5, 23).

Alunite at Marysvale, Utah--Europe had mined alunite, $K_2 \cdot Al_6(OH)_{12}(SO_4)_4$ [$K_2SO_4 \cdot Al_2(SO_4)_3 \cdot 4Al(OH)_3$], for centuries to produce potash-alum. In this country, alunite was known to occur in gold and silver mill tailings and in small deposits, but it was present either in too small amounts or was too contaminated with quartz and other gangue materials to make its recovery commercially appealing. The situation suddenly changed in the fall of 1910 when a large outcropping of "pink spar," long observed by prospectors in the mountains near Marysvale, Utah, was identified as almost pure alunite (32).

The main deposit is in the Tushar Mountains at the head of Little Cottonwood Canyon seven miles southwest of Marysvale at elevations of 9,000 to 11,000 feet. The main vein, containing 90 percent pure alunite, is 17 feet wide, at least 800 feet deep, and some 1,800 feet long. Other deposits, usually of lower quality, occur as lesser veins, lenses, and dikes. Pure alunite contains 11.4 percent potash (K_2O), 37 percent aluminum oxides, 38.6 percent sulfur trioxide, and 13 percent water (8, 32).

The pink spar outcropping was identified as alunite when Tom Gillan, an old-time prospector, sent a sample of the ore to the Assay Office at Salt Lake City for analysis. The sample contained about 10 percent K_2O. The results of the analysis came to the attention of a man named Custer, otherwise unidentified, of Salt Lake City, who immediately grubstaked Gillan to do further prospecting and stake out claims. Custer sent samples of the ore to people who he thought might be interested in the deposit, and to the Geological Survey. One came into the hands of C. H. MacDowell, president of the Armour Fertilizer Works. He and H. F. Chappell, vice president of the General Chemical Company and a descendent of the first families to manufacture superphosphate in Baltimore, had examined some European alunite samples and had jointly become interested in alunite as a possible source of potash for fertilizers. Chappell went to Salt Lake to see Custer, then visited the claims with Custer and Gillan, and took a year's option on them. Chappell and MacDowell decided to proceed with the development of the deposit, with Chappell assuming two-thirds of the costs and MacDowell the remainder. They sent a young engineer to make a thorough study of the area and supervise the development work. The Gillan-Custer claims on the main vein were bought up, and they formed the Minerals Product Company which began construction of a plant in 1914 (32).

Kelp Production—Largely as the result of interest stirred up by the Bureau of Soils, two companies began harvesting and processing West Coast kelp in 1911. The Pacific Kelp Mulch Company located an operation at East San Pedro, California. It developed a machine that harvested the kelp rapidly and in quantity. The kelp was taken by barge to the plant where it was unloaded onto a conveyor belt. After steaming to remove adhering sodium chloride, the kelp was chopped into pieces six to eight inches long and loaded in railcars. The product, of which more than 100 carloads was produced the first year, was marketed to farmers and fruit growers as a combined mulch and fertilizer. Coronada Chemical Company began a smaller operation at Cardiff, California, 25 miles north of San Diego. The kelp presumably was cut by hand from a boat, and unloaded from barges by the simple expedient of dumping the kelp close to the shore and letting the tides carry it to the beach. Here it was raked up and hauled farther up the beach and spread out for sun drying. Dried kelp was loaded on a hayrack and dumped into furnaces for ashing. The ash was sold in bulk form as a fertilizer. By the end of 1913, eleven companies had laid plans to engage in the kelp industry, although only a few of the plans materialized (42, 43).

Cement Plant Dusts—The first U.S. company to recover potash as a by-product from the dusts evolved during cement manufacture was the Riverside Portland Cement Company at Riverside, California, in 1913. At first, the company was concerned only with preventing the daily discharge of more than 100 tons of dust to surrounding orange groves. Indignant orange grove owners had sued the company on the basis that not only was the dust a nuisance, but it also damaged the trees and the crop. Rather than shut down, the company began looking for ways to relieve the problem (22).

Manufacture of Portland cement involves calcining a mixture of lime and clay in a rotary kiln to form a clinker that is ground to produce the final product. The clays used contain small amounts of potash, usually not over 1 percent, which during calcination react with the sulfur dioxide released by the fuels used to heat the kiln to form potassium sulfate. As the flue gases cool, the potassium sulfate condenses into fine, solid particles which are discharged along with other dusts into the atmosphere unless the dusts are removed (22, 50).

Although the percentage of potash in the clays is small, the large amount used generates considerable potash. This fact was noted in 1904 by W. F. Hillebrand of the Geological Survey, who pointed out that thousands of tons of potash from cement kilns was going to waste. Cement companies were interested, but there was no practical way to recover the dust. In 1912, Dr. F. G. Cottrell, then chief metallurgist of the Bureau of Mines, published a paper in which he described an electrostatic means for dust precipitation. Dr. Walter Schmidt of Western Precipitation Company, Los Angeles, applied the engineering knowledge that made the method practical (23).

The Riverside Cement Company had the Western Precipitation Company install a Cottrell precipitator at one of its kilns on an experimental basis in 1913. It worked so well that all 12 kilns were placed on the system the following year. About 90 percent of the potash in the dust was recovered, with the dust containing about 10 percent K_2O. The Riverside plant was the only cement plant recovering potash until after the war started. It probably was the first plant to use the Cottrell method (22, 23, 50).

Activities of the University of Texas

Discovery of potash in a deep water well at Spur, Texas, in 1912 by J. A. Udden of the Bureau of Economic Geology and Technology of the University of Texas was another important event in the history of U.S. potash production. The discovery, plus Udden's strong conviction that the potash came from an underground deposit similar to those in Germany, focused attention on the Permian salt beds as a possible major potash source.

The Permian salt basin, in which Udden's discovery was made, contains solid beds of salts ranging up to 3,500 feet thick. The beds extend from western Texas and southeast New Mexico through Oklahoma into Kansas. They were formed as shallow inland seas dried up. The most common salts in the basin are common salt and gypsum which attracted the attention of early explorers and geologists. Also, when interest in potash developed, numerous small alkali lakes and ponds scattered over the vast area were sampled for potash but with disappointing results (48).

The Spur well is east of Lubbock in Dickens County. It attracted Udden's attention because it was the deepest boring in the state. The well was being sunk to a depth of 4,500 feet by the S. M. Swenson Company, well drillers, to obtain a deep source of potable water. Udden visited the site to secure a log of the well and to arrange for samples of the strata penetrated. Some 330 bits of cuttings and pieces of well core were obtained, and with the assistance of the Geological Survey were analyzed. No potash was found, but the presence of much salt and anhydrite in the upper 1,200 feet led Udden to suggest that analysis be made of the well waters at various depths. Analysis of a sample of water taken at the 2,200-foot depth showed a definite concentration of potash indicating the presence of a potash-bearing layer (43, 48).

Udden was sufficiently encouraged to obtain drill logs and cuttings from 15 other wells in 11 Texas counties. No signs of potash accumulations were found in 12 of the wells, but one well each in Potter, Randall, and Oldham Counties, lying in a triangle west of Amarillo, showed promise. Cuttings from the wells in Potter and Randall Counties contained red salt crystals at depths ranging from 875 to 1,500 feet; analysis showed they contained 9 to 10 percent potash. The dump from the Oldham County well also yielded small bits of cuttings that were thought to contain potash. None of the red salts from the three wells was of sufficient quantity to permit identification of the potash minerals present (43, 48, 52).

Udden concluded from his investigations that the Texas Panhandle and adjacent eastern New Mexico likely had potash in commercial quantities at depths of 700 to 1,700 feet. His conclusions received considerable publicity and caused an intensification of the search for underground potash deposits in the Permian salt basin, mostly in western Texas and eastern New Mexico (52).

Potash Famine and Wartime Exploitation

The outbreak of World War I in the summer of 1914, followed by the British blockade and by the German embargo on all exports of potash salts in January 1915, rapidly changed the U.S. potash situation. Imports of German potash dried up quickly (Table 5.1) as potash in the transportation pipeline or stored in neutral countries was exhausted. The United States was ill-prepared to cope with the sudden shortage. Except for limited amounts obtained from kelp, cement dust and old-time organic sources such as tobacco stems, production of domestic potash was nonexistent. The domestic potash search, underway for only four years, had shown a great many places where potash did not exist in commercial quantities. The only promising sources uncovered by the prewar search were Searles Lake and Owens Lake in California, the alkali lakes of western Nebraska, alunite in Utah, kelp, and cement dust.

Table 5.1. U.S. Potash Imports and Prices (50,26).

Year	Potash imports	Wholesale price
	tons K_2O	$ /ton K_2O
1910	240,000	66
1913	255,101	70
1914	193,878	76
1915	42,519	314
1916	1,726	436
1917	504	429
1918	261	411
1919	28,484	246
1920	197,795	180

Skyrocketing potash prices (Table 5.1) sparked a frenzy of exploitation of all the known potash sources thought to have commercial possibilities as well as for any new sources that might offer even the remotest opportunity to yield a fast dollar. Few companies or individuals expected the high prices to continue after the war when imports returned, but many hoped to remain competitive after the bottom fell out. Practically everyone expected huge, rapid returns on investments. Others threw all caution to the winds and pursued will-of-the-wisps that probably could not have succeeded if high prices had prevailed indefinitely (50).

The search for potash continued throughout the wartime period in both the public and private sectors. Great efforts were directed to developing methods for reclaiming and refining potash salts from a wide range of natural and by-product sources. Much time was spent on sources that had little chance of success or, if successful, would have supplied very little potash. Nevertheless, considerable potash was produced from several sources. These are listed in Table 5.2, along with annual production data (40).

As shown in the table, the natural brines were the major potash source. Those contributing most of the potash were the Nebraska lakes; Searles Lake; Salduro Marsh, Utah; and Great Salt Lake. Other mineral sources of importance were alunite from Utah, cement plant dust, and blast furnace dust, although the latter contributed little. Of the organic sources, kelp, alcohol distillery wastes, and sugar beet refinery wastes were the main contributors. Wood ashes, a by-product of the hardwood lumber industry, was the only remaining source of note. Even though a great deal of effort and money went into research and attempts to produce potash from greensands, leucite, feldspars, sericite, and miscellaneous organic wastes, their combined production from 1915 through 1920 was less than 1,000 tons of K_2O.

Table 5.2. U.S. Potash Production by Sources (40).

Source	1915-16	1917	1918	1919	1920	Total
			Short tons of K_2O			
Mineral:						
Natural brines	4,858	20,652	39,716	21,590	37,515	124,331
Alunite	1,518	2,402	2,621	2,294	2,076	10,911
Cement mill dust	504	1,621	1,549	1,258	1,147	6,079
Blast furnace dust	11	185	205	94	173	668
Silicate rocks	25	—	105	127	51	308
Organic:						
Kelp	1,574	3,572	4,804	132	205	10,287
Distillery waste	1,799	2,846	3,467	2,892	3,253	14,257
Beet sugar waste	46	369	1,374	3,601	3,394	8,784
Wood ashes	412	621	673	484	263	2,453
Miscellaneous	63	305	289	2	—	659
Total	10,810	32,573	54,803	32,474	48,077	178,737

Producers from Natural Brines: 1915-1920

Searles Lake—The American Trona Company, which had built a plant at Searles Lake and had about given up the venture when the process selected had failed, found new life with the coming of the German potash embargo. The company established an experimental plant in New York City to develop a new process, using natural brine shipped from Searles Lake. The process involved evaporation of the natural brine to crystallize out the surplus sodium chloride and sodium sulfate to the point that the solution was practically saturated with potassium chloride and sodium borate. The two were separated by crystallization upon cooling (39, 44).

Success of the process led the company to hurriedly erect two plants, one at Searles Lake to produce the concentrated salts, and the second at San Pedro to refine the concentrated salts. About 1,000 tons of low-grade potash salt was produced in 1916. Production was rapidly increased to around 700 tons per month. In 1918 the plants were duplicated, and in 1919 a quick-cooling process was developed and put in operation. It gave cleaner separation of the potash and the borax, but the cost was high and several years of development were required before the potash and borax could be produced at reasonable cost (22, 39).

A new potash-borax venture was launched at Searles Lake in 1916 when the Pacific Coast Borax Company and the Solvay Process Company joined to form the Boro-Solvay Company. Pacific Coast Borax owned 2,240 acres on Searles Lake (compared to 14,000 possessed by the Trona Company) under patents issued 40 years previously to J. W. Searles. When potash prices skyrocketed, the Borax Company engaged in extensive drilling on its property and succeeded in tapping the main brine deposit of the lake. The company took up the matter with the Solvay Company of Syracuse, New York, which had worked out a process for recovery of potash from brines. In 1916, two tank cars of the brine were shipped to the Alameda works of the Borax Company to test out the process. The results were so encouraging that the company town of Borosolvay was built and construction of a plant started. The process, however, presented problems, and potash production in 1917 was not impressive. By 1918 the problems had been worked out and production of potash (K_2O) rose to around 200 tons per month (6, 22, 25, 27).

During 1918, combined production of the Trona and Boro-Solvay companies reached 10,000 tons of potash. Only the Nebraska lakes produced more potash from natural brines. Some of the potash was refined to produce high-grade potassium chloride, but most was marketed as a crude product containing some borax. Both firms also marketed borax. In 1920, when potash prices had declined, Boro-Solvay shut down and never reopened (27).

Nebraska Lakes—The Potash Production Company, incorporated in 1914 by Modisett and Show, the discoverers of potash in the western Nebraska lakes, finally got its plant into production in mid-1915. The operation consisted of sinking wells into the porous strata at the bottom of Jesse Lake, where the brine was richest, and pumping brine directly to the plant on the railroad at Hoffland three miles away. The brine was concentrated by vacuum evaporators, and the concentrated liquor then was allowed to stand in vats until the salts crystallized. These salt crystals were shoveled out and partially dried, and the leftover mother liquor returned to the system. Moist salts were shipped to industrial users where they were refined (22, 23).

The name of the company was changed in 1917 to the Potash Reduction Company, which improved and enlarged the plant. Annual production reached 10,000 to 12,000 tons of crude salts (analyzing about 28 percent K_2O) each year, thus making it the largest potash producer in the Nebraska lakes area. The two venturesome former chemistry students and their handful of investors received huge returns. Modisett and Show apparently became wealthy; other shareholders reportedly received monthly dividends equal to their original investment. The operation had started early and its production peaked well before prices declined (5, 23).

Two other Nebraska lake companies were producing potash in the fall of 1916. These were the Palmer Alkali Company, with a plant near Lakeside, and the American Potash Company of Omaha, which operated from a small lake near Antioch. Hord Alkali Products Company (later the Hord Company), which opened a plant in early 1917 near Lakeside, became the second largest producer in the Nebraska area. This company was unusual in that it was developed by local interests–Heber Hord and his sister who owned a large ranch that encompassed some of the lakes. Other companies of some importance were Nebraska Potash Company, Omaha Potash Refining Company, and Commonwealth Potash Company (5, 22, 23).

By 1918, nineteen companies reported production of potash from the Nebraska lakes, and four more were constructing plants. Production that year amounted to 116,600 tons of crude salts equivalent to 28,800 tons of K_2O. This represented 53 percent of the total potash output in the United States. Apparently none of the crude salts were refined by the producing companies. Also, most latecomers to the area were forced to evaporate brines from lakes containing low salt concentrations, which greatly increased costs (27, 40).

Great Salt Lake, Utah—The waters of Great Salt Lake, a surviving remnant of old Lake Bonneville, had long been known to be loaded with salts, especially sodium chloride which had been variously recovered. H. S. Gale of the Geological Survey was first to sample the lake as a possible potash source in 1913. Great Salt Lake has a solids content of 14 to 26 percent, depending on the lake level. Of this, 3.16 percent is KCl, 75.9 percent NaCl, 10.9 percent $MgCl_2$, and 9.5 percent Na_2SO_4.

Two companies were organized in 1915 and early 1916 to recover potash from the lake (22). The Utah Chemical Company was a subsidiary of the Cotton Oil Company which was allied with the Virginia-Carolina Chemical Company. It built a small plant to extract the potash from the mother liquor left over after removal of common salt by the Inland Salt Company at Saltair near Salt Lake City. The plant, located next to the saltworks, began production in February 1916. Liquor from the saltworks, containing about 3 percent K_2O, was first evaporated to remove the sodium sulfate and most of the remaining sodium chloride. The mother liquor left after this operation was evaporated to dryness and the salts contained 9 to 12 percent K_2O. Product was shipped without further refining (22, 23).

The Salt Lake Chemical Company, a subsidiary of the Diamond Match Company, started building a plant in early 1916 near Grantsville 30 miles west of Salt Lake City. The objective of the parent company was to obtain potash for making potassium chlorate for its match manufacture. Water from the Great Salt Lake was pumped to a series of natural, clay-bottomed sloughs which were divided into evaporation ponds. No further information seems available on subsequent processing. The first shipment from the plant was in late 1916 (22, 23).

Salduro Marsh, Utah—The Solvay Potash Company acquired property in the Salduro Marsh, Utah, in 1916 and began potash production in 1917. The company had been quietly prospecting many western salt deposits and selected Salduro Marsh as a likely place for commercial potash production (25, 27).

Salduro Marsh, another remnant of old Lake Bonneville, is an extensive salt field 110 miles west of Salt Lake City. It contains about 125 square miles that is covered to a depth of 3 to 5 feet with a deposit made up largely of sodium chloride. Beneath this deposit is a 6-foot-deep, soft clay substratum that also contains salts. A brine flows freely in the clay and in the lower part of the overlying salt deposit. The brine, although nearly saturated with sodium chloride, contains about 7 percent potassium chloride and 9 percent magnesium chloride, but very little sulfate of any kind. During the winter, the marsh surface is often covered with water, but in the summer the surface is always dry (22, 50).

The salt deposit first came to the attention of the engineers constructing the Western Pacific Railroad across the desert. The salt crusts were originally staked as salt claims by local people who organized the Montello Salt Company of Ogden, Utah. After several years of unsuccessful attempts to produce common salt, this company leased the property to the Capell Salt Company of Salt Lake City. A small saltworks was erected and salt was gathered for a year or two, after which Solvay took over the property (22).

Solvay's first attempts to separate and crystallize potassium chloride from the brine were not successful. The company finally hit upon a plan of letting nature do most of the work through solar evaporation. Concentric canals were dug in the marsh and the brine was moved toward the center by pumping over the dikes separating the canals. The brine became increasingly more concentrated until the potassium chloride finally would crystallize out. After drying, the potash was ready for marketing. Two grades were produced, a refined grade containing 85 percent KCl, and a crude grade, heavily laden with sodium chloride, containing 25 percent KCl (23, 50).

Other Operations

By-product Brine Projects—Small quantities of potash were produced at different times from other brine operations, mostly as a by-product. Inyo Development Company, backed by Stauffer interests, and Natural Soda Products Company, both at Owens Lake in Inyo County, California, marketed some potash as a by-product from mother liquors left over from their soda operations. Whitney Chemical Company at San Mateo, California, and Oliver Chemical Company at Mount Eden, California, produced some potash from the mother liquors of saltworks. United Mineral Products Company obtained a little potash from a brine taken from a dry lake near Hartsell, Colorado, and a small operation at Quitchipa Lake near Cedar City, Utah. Others probably existed (22, 23, 27).

Alunite, Marysvale, Utah—The high potash prices prompted C. H. MacDowell and H. E. Chappell to commercialize their alunite claims at Marysvale, Utah. Chappell reviewed the European literature on alunite refining, and developed a process for potash recovery. The Mineral Products Corporation, which they had formed earlier, was reorganized as an operating firm in 1915, with additional financial backing from U.S. Smelting and Mining Company, O. Armour, H. J. Baker and Brothers, and E. Klepstein. The company began producing potash from the main alunite vein in September 1915, with about 1,500 tons of K_2O being recovered that year (22, 32, 44).

The Minerals Product mine was at the head of Little Cottonwood Canyon where the ore was hauled by wagon from the vein to the edge of the canyon. Here it was dumped onto an aerial tramway over a mile long where it was dropped 1,900 feet to creek level. Using the process developed by Chappell, the ore was crushed, mixed with coal, and roasted in a rotary kiln. The calcined material was mixed with water in a digester and the leachate, containing potassium sulfate, was drawn off, filtered, and concentrated in a vacuum evaporator. After drying, the potash product contained about 95 percent pure potassium sulfate. The filtered cake left after the leaching was almost pure alumina (22, 32, 44).

The plant burned in 1916 but was immediately rebuilt and continued operation through 1920. Toward the end of its operation, the plant and mine were taken over and operated briefly by the Armour Company. Over the years the company gradually sold off the accumulated alumina tailings. All told, the overall operation was a profitable undertaking (23, 28).

Several other companies mined alunite in the Marysvale area. Nearly all of the material was calcined to produce a crude potash product containing about 16 percent K_2O for use in mixed fertilizers. Only the Florence Mining and Milling Company of Philadelphia actually built a calcining plant at Marysvale. The Company, whose product first appeared in 1917, also provided custom calcining for other companies. Other calcining was done in plants near fertilizer use areas. In 1917, Swift and Company built a calcining plant at Harvey, Louisiana, that used Marysvale alunite. American Smelting and Refining Company began producing potash-alum (potassium aluminum sulfate) from a plant at Murray, Utah. Caraleigh Phosphate and Fertilizer Works at Raleigh, North Carolina, used alunite as a source of potash, but contracted its calcination with the Florence Mining and Milling Company (22, 23, 27, 28).

Production of potash from alunite peaked in 1918, at 2,600 tons of K_2O, or 4.3 percent of the total domestic potash production that year. Total production of potash from alunite through 1920 was 11,000 tons of K_2O (40).

Cement Dust—Successful recovery of cement kiln dust as a source of potash by the Riverside Portland Cement Company in California using the Cottrell electrostatic precipitator encouraged other cement companies to follow in its steps. Meanwhile, the Riverside company had installed a hot water leaching system through which 80 percent of the potassium was recovered as high grade potassium sulfate by crystallization. Potash recovery became so profitable that in 1917 the company stored its cement clinker and concentrated entirely on potash production (22).

The second cement company to use the Cottrell method and market potash was the Security Cement and Lime Company near Hagerstown, Maryland. Company officials visited the Riverside plant and planned certain innovations in the dust recovery process. Tests were started in 1915 and the first unit came onstream in June 1915. Four others followed shortly thereafter. The venture was highly successful. The company was proud of its achievement and took the unusual step of publishing cost data and engineering details to encourage other cement companies to begin potash production (22).

In 1918, twelve of the country's 110 cement manufacturers reported recovery of potash-containing dusts. Two more installed facilities and began production in 1919. During 1918, the peak year, 1,549 tons of potash recovered in the dusts, accounted for 2.8 percent of the nation's K_2O production (27, 40).

Blast Furnace Dust—Some interest during the war period was focused on recovery and use of blast furnace dust as a source of potash. The iron ore, coke, and limestone charged into the furnaces contain a small amount of potash which is volatilized and passes out with the furnace gases. About 5 percent of the potash in the gases condenses and collects in dusts that settle out in the stoves and boiler flues where the blast furnace gas is consumed. (Although use of Cottrell precipitators was urged to increase the dust yield, none apparently was installed.) This dust, containing 6 to 9 percent water-soluble potash, mostly as potassium sulfate, was collected at some plants and marketed as a potash material. The sales were almost pure profit since the dust in any event had to be collected and removed periodically. Apparently some dust was refined to produce high quality potassium sulfate (22, 27).

The first company to market blast furnace dusts as a source of potash apparently was Bethlehem Steel Company at South Bethlehem, Pennsylvania, in 1915 or 1916. The Carnegie Steel Company, Pittsburgh; the Railroad Company, Birmingham, Alabama; and Thomas Iron Company, Hokendauqua, Pennsylvania also were marketing the dust by 1918. Several others began production in 1919 and 1920, but overall production was insignificant, only 668 tons of K_2O through 1920 (22, 27, 40).

Potash-Bearing Aluminum Silicates—Huge amounts of potassium occur in potash-bearing aluminum silicate rocks and sedimentary deposits. These materials had unusual appeal to Federal agencies and other wishful thinkers during the potash famine, due in part to their abundance throughout the eastern United States where most of the potash was being consumed. Unfortunately, there were many stumbling blocks. First, although the minerals in pure state contain appreciable amounts of potassium, such deposits seldom exist in nature; even the most promising deposits of any size contained only 7 to 10 percent K_2O. Second, complex and costly processing is required to obtain soluble potash from the aluminum silicates. The technology could be economical only if alumina also was recovered. Nonetheless, a great deal of time and money went into these efforts (22, 27, 28, 40).

Amazingly, the problems facing recovery of potash from the aluminum silicates greatly stimulated inventors to try their hand at developing recovery processes. No less than 150 U.S. patents were issued by 1920 on recovery processes or some phase of a recovery process. The recovery processes generally involved fusion, refining, concentrating, crystallizing, drying, grinding, sorting, and bagging. When it finally became apparent that potash extracted from the aluminum silicates as the sole product could not possibly compete with other sources, patent efforts shifted to include recovery of alumina or some other by-product (22, 27, 28, 40).

Deposits receiving the most attention were (1) the leucite rock deposits of the Leucite Hills, Sweetwater County, Wyoming, containing about 10 percent K_2O; (2) the greensands (containing glauconite, a potassium iron aluminum silicate) in New Jersey, Delaware, and Maryland, which contain about 7 percent K_2O; (3) the feldspar deposits from Maine to North Carolina, containing up to 10 percent K_2O; and (4) the sericite (a variety of muscovite) micas and shales of north Georgia, averaging about 9 percent K_2O (22, 44).

One of the largest money losers in the aluminum silicate endeavor was the Liberty Potash Company, which had focused on the leucite deposits in Wyoming. This company, along with a couple of others that never got beyond the organizational stage, was entranced by a 1912 Geological Survey study of the Leucite Hills that noted the occurrence of large amounts of leucite in the volcanic rocks of the area and speculated that the leucite might be a valuable source of potash (46). The Liberty Company, incorporated by western capitalists in 1917, built a million-dollar plant at Green River. It used a process in which the leucite ore was ground with salt, fused in rotary kilns, and the potash recovered from the fumes as dust in bag collectors. Problems developed in obtaining equipment and labor, and from a takeover of the company's power plant by the Government for war purposes. The plant finally got into operation after the Armistice, but only for a short time before technical difficulties forced it to close (23, 28).

With regard to greensands, deposits in New Jersey greensands received the most attention from possible commercial developers since they were somewhat higher in potash than those of Delaware and Maryland. Furthermore, the New Jersey deposits were 20 to 30 feet deep in places and could be mined easily by dredge or steam shovel. The first company to recover potash regularly from greensand was the Waverly Chemical Company at Camden, New Jersey, which produced small amounts of hydrated potassium carbonate for the cut-glass industry. The Atlantic Potash Company, formed in late 1916, bought a cement plant in Stockerton, Pennsylvania, in order to use four old kilns to process greensand mined at Marlton, New Jersey. The potash was volatilized in the kilns and condensed. Production was initiated in 1918, but lasted only a few months. Starting in 1916, the Kaolin Products Company produced some greensand potash at a pilot plant at Jones Point, New York, in anticipation of large scale production at New Brunswick. However, money problems forced the company to reorganize, first as the American Potash Corporation and later as the Eastern Potash Company. In addition, the war ended about the time the New Brunswick plant was completed. As a result, the only potash produced was from intermittent operation of the Jones Point pilot plant. Other companies developed plans for potash production from greensand, but R. S. Ryan and Company was the only one to build a plant. Its facility never went into production due to the ending of the war (22, 23, 27, 28).

In the case of feldspars, apparently no company seriously attempted to extract potash from them, except as a by-product from cement plants. Numerous processes were proposed and patented, and the Bureau of Soils built and operated an experimental plant to test processes. A major deterrent was that high quality feldspar did not occur in deposits large enough to justify commercial consideration.

Sericite had been found in abundance in practically pure form in beds and lenses in Pickens and Gilmer Counties in north central Georgia, along with potash-rich shales. These were investigated both by the Geological Survey and the Armour Company. The Pickens Mineral Company was incorporated in 1916 to obtain operating leases on the deposits of sericite in Pickens and Gilmer Counties. During the same year the American Potash Company of Atlanta had obtained options on large acreages of land containing Georgia shales from which it proposed to manufacture potash. The Georgia Potash and Chemical Company in 1918 also acquired large acreages of Georgia sericite and shale lands. None of the companies reached the production stage (23, 27, 44).

Only 308 tons of K_2O was produced from the aluminum silicates through 1920, making them the potash fiasco of the war years. Millions of dollars were spent and much effort was wasted (40).

Kelp—The high potash prices of 1915 brought a surge of activity in the kelp industry, with new companies springing up overnight. In 1916, at least 10 kelp plants were in operation off the coast of California, and several additional companies had indicated intentions of building plants. Four plants were operating off the coasts of Oregon and Washington, and three or four Canadian companies were either operating or in late stages of planning (22, 44).

Kelp operations were no longer limited to small companies. Several large national companies also moved into the industry including the Hercules Powder Company, Swift and Company, Lorned Manufacturing Company, and the Diamond Match Company. Hercules Powder was the largest of the kelp companies, producing both potash and acetone that was needed in its munitions activities. Swift produced both dried and ground kelp for its own mixed fertilizer plants, located mostly in the Eastern States. The Lorned Company, a subsidiary of Simmons Hardware Company of St. Louis, produced highly refined potassium chloride. Diamond Match produced potassium chlorate needed in match manufacture. In addition, the Bureau of Soils had obtained a $175,000 grant from Congress to built a small experimental plant to develop improved methods for obtaining potash, iodine and other byproducts from kelp. This plant, located at Summerland, California, began production in 1917 (22, 27, 50).

Practically all of the companies harvested their kelp using cutter boats equipped with below-surface mechanical mowers. The wet kelp was then transferred to barges by hoists and unloaded at the dock also using hoists. Here it was then chopped or macerated, conveyed to storage where it remained for a short time but not long enough to permit fermentation, and then processed (22).

Several processing methods were used. The simplest and most used was to dry the kelp with furnace heat and the grind it finely. The product, which was sold primarily for use in mixed fertilizers, contained about 1.2 percent nitrogen, 0.6 percent available P_2O_5, and 14.5 percent K_2O. The next most used procedures were either to ash or char the kelp. Ashing initially was done by burning the kelp in open air. However, because of the smoke and odors, this was replaced by charring the kelp in furnaces. The charred kelp contained 28 to 30 percent K_2O which was higher than the potash content of ashed kelp since the ashing volatilized part of the potash. The ashes and char were either sold directly as a fertilizer material, or refined to produce high grade potassium chloride which was sold primarily for nonfertilizer uses. To produce the refined potash, the ash or char was leached, concentrated by evaporation, and the potassium chloride recovered by fractional crystallization. Another method was to leach partially fermented kelp to remove the soluble materials including the potash, but at the same time save the organic fraction for other uses (22).

Production of potash from kelp increased rapidly, reaching around 3,600 tons of K_2O in 1917 and 4,800 tons in 1918. During both of these years, kelp was the second largest domestic potash source in the country, exceeded only by the natural brines. Kelp accounted for 11 percent of the Nation's potash and 9 percent in 1918. Total production through 1920 amounted to 10,000 tons of K_2O (40).

Molasses Distillery Waste—Some distillers use molasses left over from sugar manufacture to produce alcohol. After the alcohol is extracted, a very dilute waste or "slop" is left that contains the nonsugars and inorganic salts originally present. This waste had been used as a source of potash in Europe before the advent of German potash, but had not been used in the United States before the potash pinch. During the war years, some 25 molasses distilleries were operating in the country, mostly using molasses from cane sugar manufacture. About one-third of these recovered potash, making the alcohol industry the leading potash by-product producer during the war years (22).

The dilute waste solution contained about 1 percent K_2O as potassium carbonate, potassium sulfate, and potassium chloride. To obtain the potash salts, most of the water was removed by passing the solution through evaporators, after which the residue was carbonized in ovens or rotary kilns. The ash made up of the crude salts contained from 20 to 38 percent K_2O. This was marketed primarily for use in fertilizers, although some was refined (22, 27).

Probably the first distillers to produce potash were the United States Industrial Alcohol Company at New Orleans based on sugar cane molasses, and the Western Industries Company at Agnew, California, which used Hawaiian cane molasses and some local sugar beet molasses. Four distillers were producing potash in 1917, and eight in 1918. Potash from the wastes amounted to about 1,800 tons of K_2O in 1916, 2,800 in 1917, and 3,500 in 1918. In 1918, distillery waste accounted for 6.3 percent of total U.S. production. Through 1920, distillery waste accounted for 14,000 tons of K_2O (22, 23, 40).

Beet Sugar (Steffens) Waste—In beet sugar manufacture, the molasses left after the raw sugar is extracted usually is subjected to a second step to reclaim additional sugar This is the "Steffens process," in which sugar present in the molasses is precipitated by adding lime as calcium saccharate. The residual liquor, called Steffens waste, is about 97 percent water plus nonsugars and dissolved salts. To recover the potash, the Steffens waste was evaporated first in the plant's sugar evaporators to obtain a solution made up of about 55 percent solids. It was then further evaporated in drum dryers to produce a deliquescent solid containing 10 to 12 percent K_2O and about 5 percent nitrogen. This sometimes was marketed as a source of plant nutrients. More often, however, the material was charred or ashed to produce a product containing 30 to 35 percent K_2O but with no nitrogen, since the organic fractions containing the nitrogen were burned off. The waste usually is high in potassium carbonate, but also contains potassium chloride and potassium sulfate (22, 50).

U.S. production of potash from Steffens waste began in 1916. There seems to be no record of who first used it to produce potash. However, in 1918 the following eight companies were in production: the American Beet Sugar Company, Oxnard, California; Spreckels Sugar Company, San Francisco; Great Western Sugar Company, Denver; Columbia Sugar Company, Bay City, Michigan; Holland-St. Louis Sugar Company, Decatur, Indiana; Holly Sugar Company, Huntington Beach, California; Larrowe Construction Company, Mason City, Iowa; and the United Construction Company, Blissfield, Indiana. Only 369 tons of K_2O was recovered from Steffens waste during 1917 and 1,374 tons in 1918. However, more than 3,000 tons was produced in 1919 and in 1920 (27, 40).

Wood Ashes and Other Sources—The production of potash from wood ashes, which had flourished in this country prior to the introduction of German potash, was revived. Renewed production came primarily from sawmill wastes in the hardwood forests of Wisconsin and Michigan. The sawmills normally burned their wastes (butts, slabs, and sawdust) in large incinerators or used them as boiler fuel. With the advent of the war, a large number of small companies were formed to recover the potash from the ashes that otherwise would have been discarded. Recovery methods were those that had been developed in the earlier period when potash from ashes was in high demand domestically and internationally for nonfertilizer uses. Essentially, the recovery process involved leaching the ashes in tubs with hot water and evaporating the leachate. The leachate was sold as a fertilizer material or heated to burn off carbon and produce a higher grade product. Lime was sometimes added to the leachate to make caustic potash for use by soapmakers and laundries (22).

Some 70 small firms engaged in the potash wood ash business, with all except six being located in Michigan and Wisconsin. Yet, actual potash production was small. The peak year, 1918, saw only 673 tons of K_2O produced, 533 of which was crude potassium carbonate and the remainder caustic potash (22, 40).

Interest was by no means restricted to hardwood ashes. Ashes from a considerable number of woody plants, including banana stems, and organic wastes were analyzed for potash. Sagebrush, a woody shrub which grows abundantly in many parts of the West, aroused a furor of interest when it was found that the ashes sometimes contained as high as 20 to 30 percent K_2O. Many westerners visualized a potash bonanza from the lowly sagebrush. Unfortunately, reaping the bonanza was not as certain as it seemed. The sagebrush burned with such intense heat that large amounts of the potash were driven off unless great care was taken. Nevertheless, several projects were undertaken where large acreages of land were being cleared. Projects were launched near Pioche, Nevada; southern Idaho; central Utah; and at Needles, California (22,44). Apparently some potash was recovered, but the projects did not thrive.

Many other potash sources were tapped during the war period. Wool scouring waste from textile mills, after removal of oils, was used as a potash source by the Arlington Mills at Lawrence, Massachusetts, and by the Diamond Match Company, also at Lawrence. Ground tobacco stems continued to be used in mixed fertilizers both as a source of potash and a conditioner. Ashed cottonseed hulls were produced by the Phoenix Chemical Works, the Gulf Fertilizer Company, and the Armour Fertilizer Works at its East St. Louis plant (22,23).

The Potash Search, Related Activities: 1915-1920

The potash search continued during the 1915-1920 period, but with certain modifications brought on by the pressures of the war. The Geological Survey extended its exploration into new areas in both the Western and Eastern States. The Bureau of Soils concentrated its efforts on kelp and by-product potash sources. The private sector, for the most part, focused on the natural deposits and byproducts that seemed to offer the greatest opportunities for immediate returns.

Activities of the Geological Survey

The Geological Survey spread its potash activities over several fronts in the West. Included were investigations of the Alkali, Abert, and Sumner Lakes in southern Oregon; a soda lake in the San Luis Valley in Colorado; and the salt cliffs along the Virgin River near St. Thomas, Utah–all with negative results. The Salduro Marsh area was surveyed following the announcements of the Solvay Process Company that it intended to initiate potash production. Four deep drillings were made in the Smoke Creek Desert in Nevada, with no indications of a potash deposit. Various deposits of alunite were investigated, mostly in Nevada. A field geological survey was made of the Permian salt basin in Texas and New Mexico, and on the basis of J. A. Udden's studies a site was selected at Cliffside, Texas, eight miles northeast of Amarillo, for a deep drilling. A churn-drill hole was completed in 1917 to a depth of 1,700 feet with no indications of a potash stratum (22, 44, 47).

In the eastern United States the Survey collected samples of the greensand deposits in New Jersey, Delaware, and Maryland and, with the help of earlier geological surveys, was able to identify the richest deposits. Feldspar deposits from Maine through North Carolina were surveyed and sampled; the Survey noted the most promising areas and warned potential developers that no high grade deposits existed. The sericite deposits of north Georgia were pinpointed. Also, wood ash potash producers were surveyed to determine the number and location of companies in production and how much potash was being produced (22, 27, 44).

Activities of the Bureau of Soils

The Bureau of Soils concentrated a good part of its work during the 1915-1920 period on kelp, placing major emphasis on recovery of kelp products in addition to potash. It was becoming increasingly apparent that a long-time kelp industry could not survive based on potash alone; other products needed to be recovered to help defray costs. As a result, Congress granted the Bureau $175,000 in 1916 to construct and operate a small plant for experimentation. The plant located at Summerland, California, went into operation in February 1917 with the understanding that the products produced would pay for the operation of the plant. J. W. Turrentine was in charge of the operation, which continued into 1921 (22, 27, 51).

Several methods of processing were devised and tested. In general, after the kelp was harvested and dried, it was subjected to destructive distillation, leached to remove water-soluble constituents, and the water solution evaporated for crystallization of potash salts and recovery of iodine. The charred residue was treated to convert it into an active bleaching agent. These products were placed on a full manufacturing basis, utilizing about 100 tons of raw kelp per day. Cost data were obtained and various process improvements were made (51).

Paradoxically, the major achievement of the project came too late to help the ailing kelp industry. This was the invention of a vacuum-cooler crystallizer system. It was very rapid, utilized the heat of crystallization, increased evaporation, and yielded a free-flowing, easy-to-filter slurry of crystals in suspension. It reduced the period of cooling and crystallization from days to minutes, and yielded a final product containing 98 percent potassium chloride. The system soon was adopted in the United States and Europe and the almost pure potassium chloride became a standard product (51).

The Bureau also had several projects in addition to the kelp project. It continued its interest in feldspar as a source of potash, and built a small experimental plant at Arlington, Virginia, to test a number of recovery processes. It made a survey to determine the amount of potash emitted in cement plant dust, and gathered statistics, in cooperation with the Bureau of Mines, to determine the quantity of potash generated in blast furnace operations and the amount actually being recovered. Development of methods for recovering potash from wool scourings, greensand, and alunite also were undertaken (22, 44, 45).

Post-War Collapse of the Industry

The earlier-than-expected ending of the war in November 1918 had an immediate effect upon the rapidly growing domestic potash industry. Most producers and purchasers expected imports to resume quickly. Anticipating lower prices, consumers ceased buying and placing orders. As a result, producers ended the year with an inventory nearly equal to a third of a year's production. Prices dropped from an average of $411 per ton of K_2O f.o.b. plants to $246 in 1919, which in many cases was below the cost of production. During the peak production year of 1918, some 55,000 tons of K_2O had been produced by 128 companies; these numbers fell in 1919 to 32,000 tons produced by 102 companies, some of which produced for only part of the year.

High-cost producers were first to feel the blow. Those working the Nebraska lakes declined from 19 to 10, the kelp producers from 8 to 2, and the companies producing potash from wood ashes from 51 to 35. Attempts were made to have the Government level a protective tariff on potash imports, but the maneuver failed because the farmers and the fertilizer industry favored low cost potash regardless of source (26, 27, 28).

Imports from Europe Resumed

Cessation of hostilities ended the German potash monopoly with the return to France of the Alsace-Lorraine area (ceded to Germany in 1871) where the Alsace potash mines were located. American potash consumers, as a result, looked forward gleefully to keen competition between the two countries for the U.S. potash market. As expected, Germany immediately moved to prepare for renewal of export shipments. A Federal potash council was formed to limit production to the most efficient mines, and the potash syndicate was given sole responsibility for marketing potash at home and abroad. However, disorganized internal conditions delayed large export shipments until 1920. France, on the other hand, faced problems of organizing an industry; getting the Alsace mines, which had been flooded and were in dire need of repairs, back into production; and creating an export marketing organization (31, 49, 50).

European imports did not arrive in the amounts expected–only 8,000 tons of K_2O in 1918 and 40,000 tons in 1919. U.S. producers were able to market their accumulated stocks, and a few plants, mostly at the Nebraska lakes, were temporarily brought back into production. Domestic production rose to 48,000 tons of K_2O. By this time, however, Germany and France had gotten their houses in order and flooded the U.S. market with 225,000 tons. The price fell to $180 per ton, but much more potash was on hand than farmers, hit with a postwar depression, and industrial consumers were willing to buy. As a result, imports fell in 1921 to 79,000 tons, and domestic production decreased to 10,000 tons, with only 20 producing companies still remaining; the price declined to $102 per ton of K_2O. In 1922 imports again rose, reaching 201,000 tons, and the price fell to an unbelievable $41 per ton as both Germany and France competed fiercely for the U.S. market. Domestic production by 12 producers in 1922 was 12,000 tons. Most came from the American Trona Company's operation at Searles Lake and the remainder from producers of potash from distiller and sugar beet refinery wastes and as a by-product in manufacture of magnesium chloride; all other producers were out of business (26, 28, 34, 40).

The German potash policy in 1923 and 1924 was to increase the potash market both at home and abroad by lowering the price. This also was essential to meet French competition and discourage the search for and production of potash by other countries, including the United States. France, which had mounted an energetic and successful drive to gain world markets, also suffered from German competition. It soon became apparent to both countries that this kind of competition was mutually destructive. As a result, they agreed in August 1924 to divide the largest export market, the United States, with 67.5 percent being allotted to Germany and 32.5 to France. The agreement was extended the following year to include the world market, with 70 percent going to Germany and 30 percent to France. In addition, a joint German-French potash cartel was set up to handle and promote sales abroad. This was the N. V. Potash Export My. with headquarters in Amsterdam. A principal office was established in New York City for sales and market development in the continental United States, Puerto Rico, Hawaii, and Cuba. A wholly owned subsidiary, the Potash Company of Canada, Ltd., was established in Montreal to serve Canada. The agreements between Germany and France, which together produced 99 percent of the world's potash, dashed all hopes of the U.S. farmers and fertilizer industry that extreme competition between the two world producers would force potash prices to unrealistically low levels (49). It turned out, however, that the prices fixed by the cartel remained reasonable. The average U.S. wholesale price per ton of K_2O from 1924 to 1929 ranged between $39 and $52. Imports increased from around 200,000 tons of K_2O in 1924 to 330,000 tons in 1929 (14, 26, 50).

Decline of Domestic Potash

As a result of the prices established for German and French potash, the number of companies producing domestic potash continued to decline. Twelve were producing from 1922 through 1924, nine from 1925 through 1928, and only five in 1929. Only two companies operated continuously throughout the period. These were the American Trona Corporation at Searles Lake (reorganized in 1926 as the American Potash and Chemicals Corporation), and the U.S. Industrial Chemicals, Inc., which produced potash from distillers' waste in Baltimore. Up until

1927, when American Potash and Chemicals doubled its capacity, Searles Lake potash made up 85 percent of the total U.S. production and the Baltimore plant 10 percent. Two companies, the Carnegie Steel company and the Lavino Furnace Company, marketed potash from blast furnace dusts over much of the period, mostly from Pennsylvania operations. Potash from cement dusts and Steffens waste appeared intermittently and tiny amounts were produced from other sources including by-product potash from magnesium chloride operations and alunite and greensand processing (10, 11, 12, 14, 16, 35, 36).

The American Trona Corporation and its successor owed their unusual and long lasting success to good management, continual improvements in technology, and diversification into other chemicals obtainable out of the Searles Lake brines. Costs were reduced continually and output increased. Production of borax was begun commercially in 1919, and the following year the company produced 9,600 tons of potassium chloride and 4,600 tons of borax. In 1926, annual output had reached about 32,000 tons of potassium chloride, containing over 60 percent K_2O, and 15,500 tons of borax. Following the reorganization of American Trona into the American Potash and Chemical, the new management immediately rebuilt and doubled the size of the plant, and in 1929 the plant was again doubled (12, 13, 25, 35).

U.S. Industrial Chemicals produced potash as a by-product from its huge Baltimore industrial alcohol plant–then the second largest of its kind in the world. The company had an immense problem in disposing of its molasses stillage left over after alcohol removal and turned to recovering potash during the war years. The potash operation was closed down after the war but was renewed and continued into the 1930's (10, 15, 25).

The demise of most of the by-product potash producers must have been a severe blow to those who believed that a large domestic potash industry could be built around by-product potash. The Bureau of Soils held firmly to the by-product thesis as expressed in 1923 by J. W. Turrentine who was then in charge of the Bureau's potash activities:

We have in sight, we feel, the early and successful solution of the essential and most pressing phases of our potash problem. From industrial wastes, in industries already operating on a successful basis, wherein through the installation of more economical methods and machinery byproducts can be developed, we expect to recover a large portion of our present and future potash requirements. I refer particularly to the blast furnace, the cement, the distillery, and the borax industries . . . . The greensands of New Jersey, the potash shales of Georgia, the leucites of Wyoming, and the alunites of Utah contain in aggregate inexhaustible quantities of potash. . . . The problem is one of byproducts–other values to be recovered with the potash to cheapen its cost of manufacture . . . (35, p. 177).

Turrentine's personal views on the matter were even stronger as expressed in his book, *Potash, a Review, Estimate, and Forecast,* published in 1926 (50).

Renewal of the Potash Search

The search for natural potash deposits of the type and magnitude of those in Germany virtually came to a stop in 1917 when the Geological Survey's deep well at Cliffside, Texas, and one drilled by the E. J. Longyear Company near Carlsbad, New Mexico, showed negative results. The latter was within a few miles of where the United States Potash Company later opened its potash mine (47).

Although it stopped its deep drilling operations, the Geological Survey maintained a laboratory at Cliffside in cooperation with the University of Texas for the purpose of collecting and analyzing samples from privately drilled deep wells in the Permian salt basin. The analyses frequently showed presence of potash. The first identification of a potash-bearing mineral in the basin was in a sample taken in 1921 from a deep well in Midland County, Texas. The mineral was polyhalite, which contained about 15.6 percent K_2O when pure. In 1922 the University of Texas discontinued its active cooperation in the search from lack of legislative support. The Survey then moved its survey headquarters to Midland, Texas, wisely choosing to concentrate most of its efforts on the western Texas area and southeastern New Mexico (34, 35, 36).

The discovery of oil in 1923 in Reagan County, Texas, greatly encouraged the drilling of deep wells. By the end of 1924, records and samples of cuttings and brines had been obtained from 30 deep wells in 20 counties in southwestern Texas and adjoining New Mexico. They indicated widespread presence of polyhalite deposits. The Geological Survey concluded that the most promising area for deposits having commercial possibilities extended from Lea County, New Mexico (Lea County borders on the Texas-New Mexico state line and is the first county east of Eddy County in which Carlsbad is located) southwestward to Crockett County, Texas. Interest in this area was further heightened with the identification of the important potash mineral sylvite (when pure, sylvite contains 63.2 percent K_2O) in 1924 by D. C. Darton from a Texas well (34, 35, 36, 37).

In the meantime, it had become increasingly apparent that commercial oil and water drilling operations provided little or no information on the depth, thickness, and composition of potash-bearing strata. Churn drills, lubricated with water, were used in all of these earlier drillings. As a result, any potash strata that might be present were broken up, usually beyond recognition, and the soluble potash salts, except for polyhalite which was less soluble, were dissolved more or less completely in the water lubricant. To get around these problems the European potash producers had turned to core drilling, which not only extracted unbroken cores but used a lubricant made up of salt solutions which prevented dissolution of the potash salts. High costs involved in core drilling had prevented the Geological Survey and private interests from adopting the method in this country, but interest in core drills was revitalized as evidence mounted that a potash deposit might exist in the Permian salt basin (26).

The national interest caused the Federal Government to encourage core drilling. Senator Morris Sheppard of Texas began as early as 1923 to seek public funding from Congress. This was finally granted in 1926 after considerable foot-dragging by Congress who hoped that the private sector would purchase and use the equipment. The bill provided an appropriation of $100,000 annually for a five-year period to supply the Geological Survey and the Bureau of Mines with the funds needed to obtain the equipment and carry on the exploration. By agreement between the two agencies, the Geological Survey selected the drilling sites and examined the cores, and the Bureau of Mines negotiated all contracts and conducted the actual drilling operations. Government drilling began in early 1927 (26, 47).

Discovery of Carlsbad, N.M. Deposits

Meanwhile, a 1925 discovery in Eddy County, New Mexico, would soon change the Nation's potash outlook. V. H. McNutt, a consulting geologist for the Snowden and McSweeney Company, discovered on public domain land east of Carlsbad what appeared to be a rich potash deposit. McNutt had selected the site for a wildcat oil well and was supervisor of the project. The drill penetrated a thick layer of salts, cuttings of which were pink-colored with dark red streaks. Analysis of samples by a commercial company, confirmed by the Geological Survey, showed an abundance of polyhalite and the presence of sylvite–the first time either had been identified in New Mexico. McNutt was so convinced of the importance of his discovery that even before the analyses were completed, he acquired potash prospecting rights for 2,500 acres of land (25, 47).

Since the Snowden and McSweeney Company was primarily an oil company, Snowden, McSweeney, and some of their associates personally advanced funds to purchase and operate core drilling equipment. A core drilling was made in 1926 about 500 feet from the wildcat oil well and revealed a deposit of sylvinite (mixture of potassium chloride and sodium chloride) equal in purity to those being mined in Europe. Snowden and McSweeney immediately formed the American Potash Company. Further drillings in 1927 showed the sylvinite deposit to range from 6 to 12 feet in thickness, which encouraged the new company to seek additional funds. This was done by convincing the Snowden and McSweeney Company stockholders to advance funds to the potash company.

Drilling rig used in American Potash Company's second core test in Eddy County, New Mexico, 1927. (G.R. Mansfield--USGS; photo furnished by J.P. Shannon)

Standard percussion tool Texas oil rig of early 1920's used to generate subsurface data to correlate data on formations of West Texas and southeastern New Mexico. (W.B. Lang--USGS)

Also, McNutt was sent to Europe to inspect potash mines to help in evaluating the New Mexico discoveries, and to learn something about potash mining (25).

Core drillings in the Carlsbad area were not limited to the Snowden-McSweeney interests. The Geological Survey began to look for sites in the Carlsbad area, and in 1927 the Bureau of Mines started drilling at one of the three sites selected by the Survey. The first two drillings showed the presence of sylvite, carnallite, langbeinite, and kainite in beds that were relatively rich, but too thin to be of commercial value. The third revealed a bed of polyhalite 9 feet thick containing 11 percent K_2O. The Gypsy Oil Company, which had become interested in potash in the Carlsbad area, began core drilling on the first of four sites selected on state-owned land. Over in Texas, Max Agress of Dallas had organized a potash exploration company and obtained a 5-foot core of almost pure polyhalite at a depth of 2,100 feet in Midland County, Texas, The Standard Potash Company was organized to develop the deposit, but apparently did not carry through with its plans (24, 37, 47).

Thirty-one core drillings had been made in the Permian salt basin by the end of 1928: 20 in Eddy County, New Mexico; 10 in Texas, of which seven were made by the Government; and one in Kansas. In Eddy County, three of the drillings had been made by the Government, 14 by the Snowden-McSweeney interests, and three by the Gypsy Oil Company. These showed beds containing polyhalite and sylvite mostly ranging from 2 to 8 feet in thickness and carrying 10 to 20 percent K_2O. The drillings in Texas encountered only beds of polyhalite, a couple of which were thick enough to suggest commercial consideration if a cost-effective recovery method could be developed. The core drilling in Kansas was made by a private company, also called the American Potash Company (37).

In 1929, the name of the American Potash Company (New Mexico) was changed to the United States Potash Company to take over the development and operation of the promising ore rights. Snowden and McSweeney tried without success to raise additional funding for the new company, but again had to raise what money they could from their own pockets and those of their close associates. Drilling was begun in December 1929 about 20 miles east of Carlsbad where the core drilling had indicated greater promise. By the summer of 1930 the company was in dire financial straits. The sinking of the shaft had used up all financial reserves, and no one with capital had come forward to help keep the operation going. As the project was about to be abandoned, John Snowden was approached by representatives of the Pacific Coast Borax Company. In September 1930 the potash company sold half of its common stock to the borax company, a move that provided sufficient funds to continue the development (25).

The four-compartment shaft underway was completed in January 1931 to a depth of 1,062 feet (a second shaft was later added nearby to conform with state safety laws). Several major obstacles had to be overcome during the sinking of the shaft, including soft overburden, gas pockets, and an overabundance of water. However, a substantial body of sylvinite, 10 feet thick and containing 25 percent K_2O, was exposed at a depth of 986 feet. This was mined initially using methods common to the metal mining industry. The ore produced was ground, sized, and sent to market as manure salts. By the end of 1931, 11,000 tons of K_2O had been produced (17, 25).

Successful Mining and Production

By 1932, further exploration firmly established the exceptional grade and substantial tonnage of the deposit, and the company moved to establish a refinery. This was designed by Pacific Coast Borax personnel and built close to the Pecos River to gain an ample water supply. Pacific Coast Borax also provided a narrow-gauge railroad to connect the refinery with the mine some 17 miles distant. The refining process used selective leaching of the sylvinite to separate the potassium chloride from the sodium chloride. Potassium chloride was recrystallized from the enriched mother liquor to obtain pure potassium chloride crystals. The crystals were washed, dried, crushed and screened before shipment. Production in 1932 amounted to 97,000 tons of manure salts and 10,700 tons of high grade potassium chloride (17, 25, 47).

The second company to mine in the Carlsbad area was the Potash Company of America, formed in 1931 by a group of Denver financiers. The company secured prospecting permits on both U.S. Government and New Mexico public lands and sank some 15 core-drill wells and several churn-drill wells. A favorable mine site was located, and a three-compartment shaft started in February 1933. The sylvinite deposit was struck at a depth of 998 feet, averaging about 6-2/3 feet in thickness. A second shaft was sunk about 700 feet from the first to allow for ventilation and safety. Problems similar to those of the United States Potash Company were encountered during the sinking of the shafts, except that the water problem appeared worse. Initial shipments of manure salts began in 1934, and a refining unit was added in 1935 (7, 26, 33). No other companies produced potash from the field until the 1940's.

Ninety-seven core drillings had been made in the Permian salt basin by the mid-1930's, 74 by private interests and 23 by the U.S. Government. Of these, 74 were made in New Mexico of which 71 were by the private sector and three by the Government. Of the remaining 23 core drillings, 22 were drilled in Texas and one in Kansas. Polyhalite was the most common potash mineral. It was found over a 40,000-square-mile area. Substantial amounts of sylvite, carnallite, and langbeinite were found in addition to the polyhalite over an area of about 3,000 square miles, all in New Mexico. The area containing what was considered

United States Department of Agriculture,

OFFICE OF THE SECRETARY

Report No. 100.

[Contribution from the Bureau of Soils, Milton Whitney, Chief.]

POTASH FROM KELP.

BY

FRANK K. CAMERON,

In charge Chemical, Physical, and Fertilizer Investigations.

Part I.—Pacific Kelp Beds as a Source of Potassium Salts.—By Frank K. Cameron.

Part II.—The Kelp Beds from Lower California to Puget Sound.—By W. C. Crandall, Collaborator in Kelp Investigations.

Part III.—The Kelp Beds of Puget Sound.—By George B. Rigg.

Part IV.—The Kelp Beds of Southeast Alaska.—By T. C. Frye.

Part V.—The Kelp Beds of Western Alaska.—By George B. Rigg.

Maps under separate cover (portfolio).—Kelp Groves of the Pacific Coast and Islands of the United States and Lower California.

This 1915 publication of more than 100 pages and four accompanying volumes of engineering drawings of harvesting and processing equipment documented much of the kelp-for-potash work. *(Scripps Institute of Oceanography)*

mineable potash (as much as 14 percent K_2O in beds 4 feet or more in thickness) was limited to about 35 square miles extending 17 miles north and south in Eddy County, New Mexico, but not in a continuous band (48, 51).

Looking back, one can only consider that the discovery of a major world deposit of mineable potash in a tiny 35-square-mile pocket in a 40,000-square-mile basin was an amazing feat aided by incredible good luck. Not only was the deposit hidden hundreds of feet underground, but there were no surface features to aid in the search. J. A. Udden's conviction paid off, and the Nation's long cherished dream of finding a domestic Strassfurt appeared to have been realized.

REFERENCES

1. Anon. 1911. Cheap potash for Americans. *Comm. Fert.* (6):16.
2. _____. 1912. Potash controversies close. *Comm. Fert.* 4(1):13.
3. _____. 1912. The Nevada potash laboratory. *Am. Fert.* 36(6):35-36.
4. _____. 1913. Potash desperadoes. *Comm. Fert.* (1):20,22.
5. _____. 1918. Romance of the Nebraska potash lakes. *Comm. Fert.* 15(6):58,60,62.
6. _____. 1918. Enormous deposits of potash on which America may draw. *Comm. Fert.* 16(1):58-60.
7. _____. 1936. Potash Company of America introduces new red muriate. *Am. Fert.* 84(3):10.
8. Butler, B. S. and H. S. Gale. 1912. *Alunite, a newly discovered deposit near Marysvale, Utah.* U.S. Geol. Sur. Bull. No. 511.
9. Cammeron, F. K. 1912. Possibilities of potash in the United States. *Comm. Fert.* (4):26-29.
10. Coons, A. T. 1925. Potash. *Min. Res. of U.S. Part II.* pp. 213-221.
11. _____. 1926. Potash. *Min. Res. of U.S. Part II.* pp. 119-125.
12. _____. 1927. Potash. *Min. Res. of U.S. Part II.* pp. 43-50.
13. _____. 1928. Potash. *Min. Res. of U.S. Part II.* pp. 89-96.
14. _____. 1929. Potash. *Min. Res. of U.S. Part II.* pp. 139-145.
15. _____. 1930. Potash. *Min. Res. of U.S. Part II.* pp. 59-67.
16. _____. 1931. Potash. *Min. Res. of U.S. Part II.* pp. 23-32.
17. Cramer, T. M. 1938. Production of potassium chloride in New Mexico. *Ind. Eng. Chem.* 30(8):865-867.
18. Dolbear, C. E. 1913. The Searles Lake potash deposit. *Am. Fert.* 38(4):46-49.
19. Gale, H. S. 1911. Progress of search for potash in the United States. *Am. Fert.* 35(13):21-37.
20. _____. 1911. The search for potash in the Desert Basin region. In *Contributions to economic geology.* U.S. Geol. Sur. Bull. 530. pp. 295-305.
21. _____. 1913. *Salines in the Owens, Searles, and Panamint basins, southeastern California.* Geol. Sur. Bull. No. 580. pp. 251-323.
22. _____. 1916. Potash. *Min. Res. of U.S. Part II.* pp. 73-171.
23. Haynes, W. 1945. The World War I period: 1912-1922. *American Chemical Industry,* Vol II. pp. 141-168. D. Van Nostrand Company, Inc. New York.
24. _____. 1948. The merger era. *American Chemical Industry,* Vol. IV. pp. 85-95. D. Van Nostrand Company, Inc. New York.

25. _____. 1949. The chemical companies. *American Chemical Industry*, Vol. VI. pp. 31-43, 391-394, 440-448. D. Van Nostrand Company, Inc. New York.
26. Hedges, J. H. 1935. Potash. *Minerals Yrbk.* pp. 1137-1159.
27. Hicks, W. B. 1918. Potash. *Min. Res. of U.S. Part II.* pp. 385-445.
28. _____. and M. R. Nourse. 1919. Potash. *Min. Res. of U.S. Part II*, pp. 77-94.
29. Jenkins, W. C. 1911. Serious aspect of German potash contracts. *Am. Fert.* 34(7):34-38.
30. MacDowell, C. H. 1911. The potash controversy. *Am. Fert.* 34(4):31-36.
31. _____. 1920. What about potash? *Am. Fert.* 52(4):72-74.
32. _____. 1943. Potash from alunite. In *Haynes, Am. Chem. Ind., the World War I period.* Vol. II. Appendix 26. pp. 370-372.
33. Magraw, R. M. 1938. New Mexico sylvinite. *Ind. Eng. Chem.* 30(8): 861- 864.
34. Mansfield, G. R. 1922. Potash. *Min. Res. of U.S. Part II.* pp. 87- 98.
35. _____ and L. Boardman. 19Z3. Potash. *Min. Res. of U.S. Part II.* pp. 167-204.
36. _____. 1924. Potash. *Min. Res. of U.S. Part II.* pp. 27-61.
37. _____ and W. B. Lang. 1929. Government potash exploration in Texas and New Mexico. Trans. *Am. Inst. Mining & Met. Eng. 1929 Yrbk.* pp. 241-255.
38. Meyer, O. 1895. Why not keep a lookout for potash deposits? *Am. Fert.* 2(1):13-14.
39. Mumford, R. W. 1938. Potassium chloride from the brine of Searles Lake. *Ind. Eng. Chem.* 30(8):872-878.
40. Nourse, M. R. 1920. Potash. *Min. Res. of U.S. Part II.* pp. 97-121.
41. Phalen, W. C. 1911. *The occurrence of potash in the bitterns of the eastern United States.* U.S. Geol. Sur. Bull. No. 530. pp. 313-329.
42. _____. 1912. Potash salts: summary for 1912. *Min. Res. of U.S. Part II.* pp. 877-908.
43. _____. 1913. Potash salts: summary for 1913. *Min. Res. of U.S. Part II.* pp. 85-107.
44. _____. 1915. Potash salts. *Min. Res. of U.S. Part II.* pp. 95-133.
45. Ross, W. H. 1917. Fertilizers from industrial wastes. In *1917 Yrbk. of Agriculture*, USDA. pp. 253-263.
46. Schultz, A. R. and W. Cross. 1912. *Potash-bearing rocks of the Leucite Hills, Sweetwater County, Wyo.* U.S. Geol. Sur. Bull. No. 512.
47. Smith, H. I. 1933. Three and a quarter centuries of the potash industry in America. *Eng. & Min. Jour.* 134(12): 514-518.
48. _____. 1938. Potash in the Permian salt basin. *Ind. Eng. Chem.* 30(8):854-864.
49. Stocking, G. W. 1931. *The Potash industry, a Study of State Control.* Richard R. Smith, Inc., New York.
50. Turrentine, J. W. 1926. *Potash, a Review, Estimate, and Forecast.* John Wiley & Sons, Inc., New York.
51. _____. 1943. *Potash in North America.* Reinhold Publishing Company, New York.
52. Udden, J. A. 1915. *Potash in the Texas Permian.* Texas University Bull. 17.

6

Launching the Fixed-Nitrogen Industry 1890's-1930's

The period from about 1890 into the early 1930's saw the development of processes for fixing atmospheric nitrogen and the successful launching of a world fixed-nitrogen industry. For the first time, atmospheric nitrogen, constituting about 78 percent of the earth's atmosphere, could be rendered available for use in food production and needed industrial chemicals, and also for producing military explosives. In one great leap, man had provided a tool for vastly improving his own welfare but which, at the same time, could aid in his own destruction.

Toward the end of the 19th century, a few far-sighted people were becoming concerned that natural sources of fixed nitrogen would not meet the agricultural needs of an expanding population and the competing requirements of industry and defense. The two major commercial sources, Chilean nitrate and by-product ammonia from coke ovens, were inadequate. The only answer seemed to be in finding a practical way to convert molecular nitrogen (N_2) in the air into an active or available form—a feat that man had never been able to accomplish.

This chapter reviews events leading to the establishment of a fixed-nitrogen industry in this country. It starts with the early research, done mostly in Europe, that laid the groundwork for commercial nitrogen fixation, and then follows the early and often abortive steps taken to build an industry in this country. The rush to develop a wartime fixed-nitrogen capacity is discussed as are problems that arose when the government tried to get its hurriedly constructed wartime plants used for peacetime production of fertilizers. The chapter closes with the successful launching of a synthetic ammonia industry by U.S. companies.

Sir William Crookes' Plea to World Scientists

The need for a way to get atmospheric nitrogen into a form usable by plants as a fertilizer was forcibly brought to the attention of the western world's chemists and chemical engineers by Sir William Crookes in his much published presidential address before the 68th annual meeting of the British Association for the Advancement of Science in 1898. Crookes, a prestigious chemist who earlier had done some research on fixation of nitrogen by electric arcs, voiced his fears that world population growth would soon outrun food supplies. He saw that an increase in wheat production could be achieved only by increasing the available supplies of nitrogen fertilizers. He pointed out that the Chilean nitrate deposits were being depleted, and that the richer and more cheaply worked deposits would be exhausted in a few years. The answer to the dilemma was to tap the atmospheric inert nitrogen through development of a nitrogen-fixation process. He indicated that such an accomplishment would be one of the great discoveries of the world, and that the challenge would yield to the ingenuity of chemists.

Crookes' address found ready and sympathetic acceptance among most scientists and stimulated a number of the foremost chemists to attack the problem. His conclusions relative to the Chilean nitrate supply proved to be overly pessimistic as a result of the discovery of new deposits in Chile and development of the Guggenheim process which permitted use of lower grade ore. Nevertheless, Crookes' speech greatly encouraged research and development on nitrogen fixation processes (10, 20, 56).

Nitrogen-Fixation Processes

Four markedly different nitrogen-fixation processes emerged during the first 15 years of the new century. These were: (1) the electric arc process which combined nitrogen with oxygen in the air to form nitric oxide (NO); (2) the cyanamide process whereby calcium carbide (CaC_2) was reacted with nitrogen at a high temperature to form calcium cyanamide ($CaCN_2$); (3) the cyanide process where heated nitrogen gas was passed over sodium carbonate and a catalyst in a heated retort to form sodium cyanide (NaCN); and (4) the ammonia synthesis process in which nitrogen and hydrogen were combined under high temperatures and pressures in the presence of a catalyst to form ammonia (NH_3). Only the latter process has survived as a major means of fixing atmospheric nitrogen, although both the arc and cyanamide processes were important initially.

The Arc Process

Much of the groundwork for development of the arc process was laid soon after discovery of nitrogen as an element in the last half of the 18th century. Priestley, Cavendish, Lavoisier, and others had found that nitrogen could be made to combine with oxygen in trace amounts by sparking or passing an electric discharge through air. In 1800, Sir

Humphrey Davy produced a trace of nitric oxide by passing air over platinum wire heated by an electric current. In 1870, Berthelot showed that an electric arc could be used instead of a spark to produce nitrogen oxide. Others also demonstrated in the 1890's that nitrogen and oxygen could be combined using electric discharges (10, 13, 30).

Mechanical means had been developed by the end of the century for generating large amounts of electric energy. The use of low-cost hydropower to drive the generators helped bring the cost down. Along with the knowledge of the earlier work on formation of nitrogen oxides from air, this led C. S. Bradley and D. R. Lovejoy of the Ampere Electrochemical Company (a research and development organization of Ampere, New Jersey) in 1901 to develop the first arc process for nitrogen fixation. This consisted of arcing a direct current of 10,000 volts between poles to produce nitrogen oxides. In 1902, the Atmospheric Products Company was organized to take over the Bradley-Lovejoy patents and exploit the process, and a small plant was built at Niagara Falls, New York. The reaction took place in a furnace consisting of a fixed iron shell surrounded by a revolving concentric cylinder. The cylinder was driven at 500 revolutions per minute giving 414,000 brief arcs per minute. Air was passed through the space between the cylinder and the shell, and subjected to the arcs to produce the nitric oxide. The effluent air carrying the oxide was cooled, the nitric oxide converted into dilute nitric acid and eventually into calcium nitrate. The operation proved too costly, however, and was abandoned in 1904 (13, 30).

C. Birkeland of Norway in 1903 noted that a high tension alternating current arc passing through a magnetic field placed at right angles to the current was distorted to form a disk-like arc that was particularly effective in oxidizing nitrogen. He and S. Eyde, an engineer, designed a large furnace using the principle. An experimental unit was set up at Oslo in 1904, and the Norsk Hydro-Elektrish Kvaclstof, A.S. was formed to develop and operate the process. A larger installation was made near Vasmoen and, in 1905, the first full-scale plant was placed in operation at Notodden. It used electric power generated from a waterfall. The plant produced nitric acid, most of which was converted to calcium nitrate for the fertilizer market. Norsk Hydro then developed a plant at Rjukan, the most powerful waterfall in Norway (13, 30).

Several other successful arc processes were developed. The Badische Anilin und Soda Fabrik (BASF) of Germany developed the Schonherr process which was also installed at Rjukan, in a plant shared with Norsk Hydro. Two European-developed processes, the Pauling process and the Wiegolaski process, were placed in operation in the United States. Although a number of countries installed arc processes, the largest plants were located in Norway since only this country had the huge amounts of cheap hydropower required (67,000 kilowatt-hours to produce one metric ton of fixed nitrogen) (13, 15).

In the United States, a small arc plant using the Pauling process, but a different system of electrodes, was placed in operation in 1912 at Nitrolee, South Carolina, by the Southern Electrochemical Company, a subsidiary of the Southern Power Company backed by James B. Duke. The arc plant drew power from Southern Power's Great Forks and Rocky Creek hydroelectric plants. The plant attempted to manufacture calcium nitrate for fertilizer, but could not compete with textile mills for the needed power and was abandoned in 1916 (13, 22).

The second and last U.S. venture using the arc process was a small plant built near Seattle, Washington, in 1917 to produce sodium nitrite. The American Nitrogen Products Company was founded by a group of Norwegians working in Seattle for the Norway Pacific Construction and Drydock Company. They selected the process developed by F. H. A. Wielgolaski, and patented in Norway and Germany. Electric energy was obtained from a waterfall in Snohomish County, the rights to which had been secured by the company from the Federal Government. Annual nitrogen fixation was about 300 tons, with production continuing until 1927 (15, 22).

The Cyanamide Process

The cyanamide process for fixing atmospheric nitrogen was discovered in the late 1890's by two German chemists, Adolph Frank and Nikodem Caro, attempting to produce cyanides of alkaline earth metals to replace the more costly metal cyanides used in gold recovery. They found that calcium carbide reacted with nitrogen at around 1,000°C to form calcium cyanamide. Frank and Caro were not interested in the cyanamide until 1901 when Frank's son, Dr. Albert Frank, found that it might be useful as a fertilizer. Trials were conducted with satisfactory results. In order to secure advantages of cheap electric power, Frank and Caro's company, Cyanidgesellschaft GmbH *(Gesellschaft mit beschrankter Haftung)* of Berlin, joined with a large Italian company producing carbides to organize Societa Generale per la Cianamide. The new cyanamide company became the licensing company for all plants using the Frank-Caro process. A calcium cyanamide plant was built in 1907 at Piano d'Orta, Italy, using power generated from the Pescaro River (13, 37, 57).

Because of the vast power saving of the cyanamide process over the arc process (19,000 kilowatts per metric ton of fixed nitrogen versus 67,000 kilowatts for the arc process), the cyanamide process was rapidly adopted by several countries. Within a few years, plants were operating in Germany, Dalmatia, France, Switzerland, Norway, Japan, and at Niagara Falls, Canada (13, 38, 57).

The manufacture of calcium cyanamide proved relatively simple. Limestone was first burned to form calcium oxide and then fused with coke in an electric furnace at high temperature to form calcium carbide.

The carbide was drawn off in molten form, cooled, ground, and then heated to 1,000°C and treated with pure gaseous nitrogen (N_2). Pure nitrogen was obtained at first by passing air over heated copper, and later by liquefaction of air and consequent distillation. After the charge of carbide was heated with the nitrogen for several hours, the resulting calcium cyanamide was finely ground and sprayed with water to destroy any remaining carbide (15,32,38).

The American Cyanamid Company, a U.S.-based company, began production at Niagara Falls, Canada, in 1909 and sold its product as fertilizer in the United States (Chapter 4). The selection of the Canadian site was due to the company's inability to obtain enough hydropower in the United States to meet its needs. Starting in 1916, the company began converting part of its cyanamide production to ammonia at Warners, New Jersey, in order to produce ammonium phosphate fertilizer (Chapter 4) since the demand for cyanamide as a fertilizer was limited. During 1917 and 1918, most of the cyanamide was converted to ammonia for war uses. The U.S. Government began construction of a very large cyanamide plant in 1917 at Muscle Shoals, Alabama, and two others in Ohio in 1918, for production of nitric acid and ammonium nitrate for war uses. Only the Muscle Shoals plant was completed but it was never placed in production. Construction of the two Ohio plants was abandoned (30, 35).

In 1918, some 35 calcium cyanamide plants operating worldwide produced 325,000 metric tons of nitrogen (15).

The Cyanide Process

Various cyanide (CN) processes were developed in the 19th century to produce cyanides of sodium, potassium, calcium, and nonalkaline metals with the aim of producing the individual chemicals rather than as a means of fixing nitrogen from the atmosphere for multiple uses. About 1914, however, John E. Bucher of Brown University in Rhode Island began experimenting with a sodium cyanide process with the intention of autoclaving the cyanide in the presence of steam to form ammonia. As heated nitrogen gas was passed over briquettes of finely divided sodium carbonate and iron in an externally heated, the briquettes reacted with the nitrogen to form NaCN. This type of fixation theoretically required considerably less energy than the cyanamide process (13, 19).

The Nitrogen Products Company was formed to exploit the process and semi-commercial plants were set up at Greene, Rhode Island, and at the Mathieson Alkali Works at Saltville, Virginia. A wartime plant was built by the U.S. Government at Saltville. Unfortunately, it proved more costly to produce ammonia from cyanide than from cyanamide. An improved process eventually was developed using an inclined rotating cylinder as a reaction chamber. The company built a plant at Cudahy, California, which used this process for several years for production of sodium cyanide (19, 22).

Ammonia Synthesis

The synthesis of ammonia from nitrogen and hydrogen appears to be a relatively simple reaction, as follows:

$$N_2 + 3H_2 \leftrightarrow 2NH_3$$

The reaction is reversible, a fact that wasn't known for a long time, and the reaction is exothermic (produces heat) when the ammonia is formed. Synthesis conversion is greatest at high pressures and low temperatures in the presence of a catalyst. In practice, pressures of 100 atmospheres or more are used. Temperatures range from 350° to 550°C which represents a compromise to obtain an adequate reaction rate and at the same time retain the life and effectiveness of the catalyst. The reaction never goes to completion, requiring that ammonia be removed continuously from the system and that equivalent additions of nitrogen and hydrogen be made.

Early investigators were unable to combine nitrogen and hydrogen, even under pressure, and the general opinion developed that the two elements would not react except in nature. However, it was soon discovered than an electric spark or an electric discharge into a nitrogen-hydrogen mixture would produce a trace of ammonia. It also was found that ammonia could be decomposed slightly by heating and that an iron catalyst helped somewhat in the decomposition. The most extensive ammonia decomposition studies were made by Ramsey and Young in England in 1884. They showed that while ammonia would decompose, complete decomposition was impossible. Nevertheless, many chemists of the period persisted in the view that the reaction would proceed to completion. Le Chatelier, also in 1884, enunciated his principle "that if a system is in stable equilibrium, and one of its conditions is changed, then the equilibrium will shift in such a way as to restore the original condition." This thinking, along with knowledge of thermodynamics and kinetics, opened the door of chemical equilibrium to a whole new generation of chemists. Application of the principle to the ammonia reaction was inevitable (13, 20, 26).

The Haber-Bosch Process—In 1903, Fritz Haber, an assistant professor at the Karlsruhe Technical University in Germany, accepted a four-year grant from the Margulies brothers of Vienna, owners of a chemical plant, to undertake research on the formation of ammonia from its elements. Haber and a student, G. van Oordt, began investigations on ammonia synthesis and for the first time attained a real equilibrium on both sides of the equation (synthesis and decomposition) by passing the gases over heated porcelain with iron wire as a catalyst. At one atmosphere pressure and 1,020°C, the equilibrium concentration of the ammonia by volume was found to be 0.12 percent. They then calculated the ammonia equilibrium levels to be expected at other temperatures which showed a sharp increase of ammonia concentration as the temperature decreased (6, 20, 26, 49).

Walter Nernst, a chemical theorist at the University of Berlin, tested his new heat theory against Haber's experimental data. He disagreed with Haber's data, claiming that the ammonia equilibrium data were too high. Nernst called on Haber to recheck or retract; Haber opted to repeat his experiments, which confirmed his earlier results. Haber and R. Le Rossignol, his assistant, then extended the research to include the effect of pressures up to 200 atmospheres, the highest they could go with the equipment available. Remarkably high ammonia yields were obtained at 200 atmospheres and temperatures of 500° to 600°C in the presence of a catalyst. Nernst, still not satisfied with Haber's data, proceeded to collect experimental data of his own with the help of his associates Jost and Jellinek. They undertook experiments using pressures ranging from 40 to 75 atmospheres and temperatures from 685° to 1,040°C using a manganese catalyst (20, 26, 49).

Haber and Nernst never fully agreed with each other, but their rivalry resulted in an understanding of the ammonia synthesis reaction without which a practical process could not have been developed. Nernst, however, took the view that ammonia yields would be too low to justify further work while Haber took the opposite view, and moved on to discover a better catalyst. He came up with osmium as one possibility, and uranium as a second. In 1909, he was able to report that he had obtained 6 volume percent of ammonia using his osmium catalyst at 200 atmospheres pressure. Haber also had found that a synthesis catalyst functioned best at temperatures from 400° to 600°C, above which the catalyst life was short and below which the catalyst became relatively ineffective in promoting the reaction (6, 20, 49).

As a result of all of this work, Haber had most of the basic information needed to develop a commercially feasible process. Besides information on pressures, temperatures, and catalysts, he conceived the idea of recirculating the unconverted nitrogen and hydrogen in the reactor and catalyst chamber after removal of the ammonia, and adding make-up nitrogen and hydrogen without reducing the pressure on the system. Also, the heat released from the synthesis reaction when the gases passed over the catalyst was used to preheat the make-up gases before their introduction into the system. In 1908, Haber and Le Rossignol designed and tried out laboratory apparatus incorporating the above principles (20, 49).

Haber approached Badische Anilin-und Soda Fabrik (BASF) in 1908 for financial backing. BASF, a leading German producer of dyestuffs then investing a large sum in an arc plant built and operated jointly with Norsk Hydro in Norway, retained Haber as an advisor, apparently on the arc plant. The company would not, however, support his work on high pressure synthesis. Yet, when the high ammonia yield was obtained in 1909 using osmium as a catalyst, BASF sent Carl Bosch and A. M. Mittasch to Karlsruhe in July to observe a laboratory demonstration of the process. The company was convinced that the process was worth the risk of development and obtained rights to Haber's major patents on a royalty basis. BASF immediately sold its interest in the Norway arc plant and concentrated all effort on developing the Haber process for commercial production. Carl Bosch, 35, was made project leader (6).

Bosch was faced with three immediate problems. They were developing processes to produce cheap hydrogen and nitrogen of high purity; finding a cheap and rugged synthesis catalyst that would replace the costly and rare osmium or uranium; and developing suitable equipment for the ammonia synthesis chamber that could withstand a combination of high pressure and temperature never before encountered commercially. The first problem was solved by using water gas. (The water gas was made by blasting coke with air to raise it to a red heat. The air was then replaced with steam to gasify the coke to carbon monoxide and hydrogen. Blasting with steam continued until the coke was cooled and then the cycle was repeated. The gas collected from the steam blast was rich in hydrogen.) The basic water-gas reaction is:

$$C + H_2O \rightarrow H_2 + CO$$

Most of the nitrogen was provided by the combination of water gas and lean gas plus pure nitrogen, obtained by cryogenic air separation, the latter being required to adjust the composition of the hydrogen-nitrogen mixture needed for synthesis. The second problem, a suitable synthesis catalyst, required a tremendous experimental program. Under the supervision of A. Mittasch, 2,500 different formulas and materials were tested in more than 6,500 runs by 1911. Mittasch selected a mixture of magnetite and aluminum and calcium oxides. The equipment problem was extremely difficult. Bosch set up an entire workshop to test and manufacture high pressure equipment. Properties of steels and alloys were studied with mild steel being selected for the first pilot plant. This failed after a few days of operation because hot hydrogen decarbonized the steel. The problem was solved by using soft iron in the interior of the reactor and mild steel for the outer wall. Many other problems arose and were solved during design, construction, and operations (6, 49).

Construction of the first commercial plant at Oppau began in 1911, and production of 7,000 metric tons of fixed nitrogen per year was attained in 1913. The plant was enlarged during the war and produced 60,000 tons of fixed nitrogen in 1917. In 1916, when the battle of Verdun raised the demand for explosives to an unheard-of level, a second and very large ammonia synthesis plant was started at Leuna which, before the war ended, was producing about 200,000 metric tons of N annually (6, 20).

Although the Haber-Bosch process has been modified many times over the years, the original basic principles have never changed. The process replaced all other commercial nitrogen-fixation processes and the basic process is still used in all of the world's ammonia plants. Both Haber and Bosch were awarded Nobel Prizes for their great achievements.

Early U.S. Attempts to Master the Process—The first inkling most American and world chemists had that ammonia synthesis had reached the stage of commercial exploitation was at the 8th International Congress of Applied Chemistry in New York City in September 1912. Dr. H. A. Bernthsen, a BASF chemist who spoke perfect English, described the early work of Haber and Nernst, the research on development of synthesis catalysts, and the commercialization of the process by BASF. He announced publicly for the first time that the Oppau plant was under construction (4).

Bernthsen, during his trip, approached several U.S. producers of anhydrous ammonia to try to interest them in American rights to the synthesis process. The abnormally high pressures and temperatures and the huge capital outlay discouraged any interest. Furthermore, ammonia use in the United States at the time was primarily for refrigeration, and the by-product coke industry was supplying all that was needed (10, 22).

Apparently the only U.S. company that had any prior knowledge of the Haber-Bosch process, or any interest in it, was the General Chemical Company, which had close prewar ties with BASF. In 1913, the company began quietly working on an ammonia synthesis process of its own by making sufficient modifications of the Haber-Bosch process to circumvent BASF patents and thus avoid paying for their use. Developing a workable process outside of the patents was not easy since BASF had taken out strong, broad patents relating to the process, apparatus, temperatures, pressures, and the like. They had carefully avoided any reference to synthesis catalysts or their preparation, and omitted key details that were necessary for successful operation of a synthesis plant. General Chemical's research staff did enough work between 1913 and 1915 to justify building an ammonia synthesis pilot plant. The company also thought it had developed a workable synthesis catalyst (10, 22).

The General Chemical Company, with Dr. W. H. Nichols as board chairman, was an outgrowth of Nichols Chemical and Nichols Copper companies of which Nichols Chemical manufactured sulfuric acid. In 1899, Nichols made the first important chemical company merger in the United States by combining 12 companies to form the General Chemical Company. General Chemical first became involved with BASF about

1910, over a contact process to manufacture sulfuric acid. Nichols' research staff had been working on a contact process but he thought the BASF contact process was superior. He went to Germany to work out a deal, but BASF terms were so stiff that he decided to use the process developed by his own company. BASF brought an infringement suit which was settled out of court by an agreement that both parties would exchange patents, operating data, information on any improvements, and the privilege of mutual inspection of each others' plants. Interestingly, General Chemical's contact process actually proved superior. The period of prewar exchanges appears to have directly or indirectly given General Chemical access to a great deal of information on the Haber-Bosch process and on what BASF was doing in synthetic ammonia (21).

The importance of the Haber process was not lost on the Bureau of Soils which had established a small fixed-nitrogen laboratory at Arlington Farm research station in Virginia. (Arlington Farm occupied 300 acres near where the Pentagon now stands.) In 1914, the Bureau installed laboratory apparatus to study Haber's process and this eventually led to the building of a pilot plant. Research at the laboratory also proceeded on electrolytic oxidation of ammonia in an attempt to produce ammonium nitrate (10, 54).

Oxidation of Ammonia to Nitrogen Oxide

Oxidation of ammonia to produce nitric acid was another problem of real concern that arose after World War I began. The United States had little knowledge in this area, yet it needed to produce nitric acid and nitrates from ammonia obtained by autoclaving cyanamide or from by-product coke ovens. The possibility of an ammonia synthesis plant being constructed made the problem even more critical.

A number of catalysts had been discovered in Europe which were capable of promoting ammonia oxidation. Two of these, platinum and iron oxide, had been used commercially. Platinum was first found effective in ammonia oxidation by the French chemist, Kuhlmann, in 1839, but had been forgotten until 1900 when W. Ostwald of Germany independently rediscovered the process. Iron oxide had been shown capable of catalyzing ammonia oxidation by Schonbein and Liebig in the 1850's (55).

Ostwald took patents on his platinum process but did not attempt to adapt it to commercial use. In his process an ammonia-air mixture was passed over platinum wire, covered partially or entirely with platinum sponge or platinum black, which was wound around a carrier and preheated. The Ostwald process became the model upon which all other platinum-contact processes were based. The process was first installed in 1908 in a plant at Gerthe, Germany, to oxidize ammonia from by-product coke ovens. The second installation was in Belgium where ammonia from calcium cyanamide was oxidized for the first time.

Numerous modifications were made by others in the arrangement and fabrication of the platinum, number of meshes in the platinum gauze, the geometry of the catalyst bed, flow and velocity of the gas mixture, and the temperatures used. Also, many schemes and types of towers were devised to convert the nitric oxide to other nitrogen oxides and absorb them in water to form nitric acid. Platinum was used exclusively as the ammonia oxidation catalyst in all countries except Germany (55).

Many German companies, including BASF in its ammonia synthesis plants, mixed iron oxide with bismuth and granulated the mixture. The contact mass was then spread out in layers about 4 inches thick on perforated plates in reaction towers about 18 feet high. The ammonia-air mixture was preheated to 700° to 800°C and passed tangentially over the plates to produce nitric oxide (55).

In 1914, the United States did not have an ammonia oxidation unit in operation. However, by 1919, the United States was producing the equivalent to 225,000 tons of 100 percent nitric acid annually–all of it using a platinum catalyst. The first experimentation was begun by W. S. Landis of the American Cyanamid Company at its plant at Niagara Falls, Canada. The results were so successful that American Cyanamid constructed a plant to supply nitric acid for use in manufacturing sulfuric acid at its Ammo-Phos fertilizer plant at Warners, New Jersey, in 1916. The ammonia was supplied directly from the cyanamide decomposition autoclaves and was passed over electrically heated platinum gauze made up of about 80 meshes of wire per inch. The gauze was laid out flat in the bottom rectangular aluminum chambers and the gas mixture was passed downward through the chamber and out of the bottom. The Landis modification of the Ostwald process was installed in U.S. Nitrate Plant No. 2 at Muscle Shoals, Alabama (33, 37, 55).

The Bureau of Mines, in cooperation with the Semet-Solvay Company at its Syracuse, New York, by-product coke oven plant, set up a laboratory to investigate coke oven ammonia oxidation on a manufacturing scale. Various catalysts were studied, but platinum was finally selected. At first the laboratory heated platinum gauze electrically, but later found it could dispense with the heating by using three superimposed flat gauzes. However, the temperature varied greatly at times making for instability of operation. A much more satisfactory arrangement was devised by C. H. Jones and C. L. Parsons of the Bureau who arranged three or four layers of gauze in a cylinder within a circular chamber. The gases were forced downward on the inside of the gauze cylinder and moved outward through the gauze layers and impinged on the walls of the converter. Radiation maintained an even, red hot temperature without introducing electric heat (33, 55).

H. A. Curtis at the Ordnance Department laboratory at Sheffield, Alabama, also conducted research on ammonia oxidation and conversion to nitric acid. His work included testing the effect of wire gauze mesh size, working with an experimental tower system to speed

Frank Washburn of American Cyanamid was a key figure in American efforts to gain self-sufficiency in nitrogen production in the World War I era. *(American Cyanamid Company)*

conversion of NO to NO_2, and increasing the rate of adsorption of the oxides in water to form nitric acid (10). The Jones and Parson platinum catalyst system was installed in the nitric acid unit of the U.S. Nitrate Plant No. 1 at Sheffield (44).

Initiating a Wartime Fixed-Nitrogen Program

Except for nitrogen from natural organics, the outbreak of World War I in 1914 found the United States dependent largely upon Chilean nitrate to meet its major agricultural, industrial, and military needs. Production of by-product ammonia from coke ovens was modest; the cyanamide plant located at Niagara Falls, Canada, produced only a small amount of fixed nitrogen, and the arc plant at Nitrolee, South Carolina, produced nothing. Not counting the natural organics, the United States only produced about one-fourth of the nitrogen it used, and most of this was by-product ammonia. The gravity of the situation, especially if the United States should be drawn into the war, was not lost upon the War Department which began to consider involving the government in establishment of a fixed-nitrogen industry (10).

Three Years of Delay and Debate

General William Crozier, Chief of the Ordnance Department, sent a report to the Secretary of War in 1915, suggesting that an inquiry be made into establishing domestic sources of nitrates. The inquiry was to focus on possible hydropower sites and the building of nitrogen-fixation plants to supply nitrates for explosives in wartime and for agricultural and industrial uses in peacetime. Crozier also sought advice from Frank Washburn of the American Cyanamid Company on the possibilities for building cyanamide plants in the United States. Washburn indicated that such plants could be built. He even offered to supply the know-how and construct them if the government would relax restrictions on the use of rivers to produce hydropower. At about the same time, L. Baekeland, chairman of the Ordnance and Explosives Committee of the Naval Advisory Board, also recommended the government construct a nitrate plant, presumably using the arc process. Since no funds were available, nothing came of either proposal. The press, however, became interested and newspaper coverage aroused public support (10).

Various bills involving both nitrate production and waterpower were introduced and debated in Congress. Most died in committee, and none was enacted. However, a number of key points were discussed in the debates. These included government versus private ownership and operation, the use of the facilities to produce fertilizers during peacetime, and the kind of process to use and where to locate the facilities. Surprisingly, no one raised the possibility of ammonia synthesis during the discussions. Some bills favored specific certain companies (10, 22).

Senator E. D. Smith of South Carolina introduced a bill in March 1916, that provided for large scale production of synthetic nitrogen in the United States. It was incorporated into the National Defense Act of June 1916, as section 122. This authorized the President of the United States to conduct investigations to determine the best and most available means of producing nitrates and other products for munitions of war, and for the manufacture of fertilizers and other useful products from whatever power source was considered best. It included the right to select sites on navigable rivers or public lands for carrying out the purposes of the act. It also authorized the construction, maintenance, and operation of dams and locks, and improvements to navigation, powerhouses, and other plants and equipment. A sum of $20 million was appropriated to carry out the act. The plants were to be constructed and operated solely by the government (10, 28).

Even before the act reached its final form, a manufacturing process and location had to selected. The Secretary of War, in early 1916, requested the National Academy of Sciences with the help of the American Chemical Society to form a nitrate committee to examine and recommend nitrogen-fixation processes. In its preliminary report in June, 1916, the prestigious committee simply stated that there were numerous processes that needed to be investigated thoroughly, and recommended in the meantime that the Army should stockpile Chilean nitrate (10).

While the committee contemplated and Congress debated, the War Department struck out on its own. The Department borrowed Charles L. Parsons, chief chemist of the Bureau of Mines and an expert in nitrates (the same Parsons of the Jones-Parsons team that developed an ammonia oxidation process), to serve as its advisor. Parsons' first report to General Crozier placed the different nitrogen-fixation processes in perspective, and pointed out that the General Chemical Company was working on a process of its own and had knowledge of the BASF ammonia synthesis developments. Parsons recommended building hydropower, cyanamide, and ammonia synthesis plants at a site for exclusive use of the government. In October 1916, the War Department sent Parsons and Eyston Berg, an engineer of Norwegian birth who had long been familiar with European nitrogen fixation developments, to study fixation and nitric acid processes in the allied European countries. Parsons and Berg made their information available to the nitrate committee of the National Academy of Sciences. However, the committee wanted more time to continue its studies which meant it would be 5 or 6 years before the United States could begin building a fixation plant (10).

Even with no decision on the fixation process, it was apparent that a nitrate plant requiring a hydropower facility probably would be built. Accordingly, President Wilson on January 15, 1917, established an Interdepartmental Board made up of the Secretaries of War, Interior, and Agriculture to investigate and recommend sites. Members of the three departments toured the Southeast in the spring of 1917 looking for a site "that should be in the interior of the country, away from the possibility of coastal attack, preferably shielded by mountains. It should be near supplies of coke and limestone, provided with potential water-power, and near an existing railway line." Thirty locations were listed by the committee as possible choices. The top four, in decreasing order of merit, were Chattanooga, Tennessee; Knoxville, Tennessee; Sheffield, Alabama; and North Birmingham, Alabama (10). (Parsons in his final report to the Nitrate Committee recommended southwest Virginia or adjoining territory in West Virginia) (10).

With time running out, the War Department discontinued the slow-moving National Academy Nitrate Committee and on March 7 appointed a committee of its own. The more effective nonacademic members of the old committee were retained, and three new civilian members were added, including Parsons. To make sure that the committee would move along, it was headed by General Crozier and other top military people. Their first job was to review all of the various reports, investigations, and recommendations that had been made and to arrive at a course of action (10).

Parsons had been in contact with W. H. Nichols, Chairman of General Chemicals, who, by this time, was planning to build a small 7-1/2 ton-per-day ammonia synthesis plant based on the Haber process, and was having difficulty in obtaining the necessary materials for construction. Nichols offered to place the results of all of General Chemical's research investigations in the hands of the government, allow the government to use their process, and provide full assistance in designing, building, and operating a plant. Nichols also wanted a royalty paid on each ton of nitrogen produced (10).

Parsons also visited the Nitrogen Products Company Bucher (cyanide) process plant at Saltville, Virginia. The company also offered its process to the government, but Parsons, although impressed, thought more experimentation was needed (10).

The United States entered the war on April 7, 1917, with no decisions on the nitrate supply problem. However, Parsons submitted his final recommendations to the now-desperate nitrate committee on April 30. After reviewing the various reports and recommendations, including Parsons' final report, the committee released its own recommendations on May 11, the first five of which were based on those made by Parsons in his report. In brief, the recommendations were:

1. That the government negotiate with the General Chemical Company for the right to use its synthetic ammonia processes.

2. That, contingent upon the negotiations, funds be set aside to build a synthetic ammonia plant, preferably in southwest Virginia, to produce about 60,000 pounds of ammonia per day.

3. That funds be set aside to build a plant to produce about 24,000 pounds of 100 percent nitric acid per day by oxidation of ammonia.

4. That the War Department proceed at the earliest practical date with the construction of the oxidation plant, and with the conclusion of the synthetic ammonia plant.

5. That the government negotiate with the Nitrogen Products Company for the right to use that company's patent and proceed with experimentation toward the industrial development of the Bucher process for production of ammonia through cyanide.

6. That funds be allotted for active investigation of processes for industrial production of nitrogen compounds useful in the manufacture of explosives or fertilizers–this under the supervision of the War Department.

7. That the government promote installation of by-product coke ovens by directing priority for materials or parts.

8. That more extensive installation of nitrogen fixation processes and waterpower development be postponed until plants recommended above are in operation.

9. That building an ample reserve of not less than 500,000 tons of Chilean nitrate was urgently necessary (10, 22).

General Chemical submitted its second offer on June 5, which was accepted immediately. This offer required no royalties as long as the products were used for war materials; however when the product was used for fertilizers the government would pay a royalty of $5 per ton of ammonia. All the General Chemical project staff would be placed at the disposal of the government as would all information pertaining to the process. The proposal allowed free use of patents and apparatus developed by the company. In return, the government was to turn over to General Chemical any modifications or improvements in the process or apparatus which it might make in using the process (10, 22).

The Final Decision

On July 6, 1917, the Interdepartmental Board recommended to the President that he accept the first six recommendations of the Nitrate Supply Committee's report for implementation. On July 21, a separate branch of the Ordnance Department was created to handle the program; this was Division T (later changed to the "Nitrate Division") headed by Colonel J. W. Joyes. Joyes moved rapidly to recruit a staff and get the wartime nitrate program underway. Outstanding chemists and engineers with advanced degrees were recruited and commissioned as Army officers, and a nontechnical support staff was recruited from the enlisted ranks. Harry A. Curtis, who was to play an important role in future years, held the rank of major (10, 22 pp. 89-100).

The Government Nitrate Plants

One of the first requirements in the government nitrogen program was for the President to exercise the authority granted to him under the National Defense Act and select a site for the ammonia synthesis plant. After considering the list of possible sites developed by the Interdepartmental Committee, President Wilson announced on September 28, 1917, the selection of Sheffield, Alabama, as the location for the modified Haber plant. This was to be the first ammonia synthesis plant outside of Germany (10, 22).

U.S. Nitrate Plant No. 1

Construction of the plant, designated as U.S. Nitrate Plant No. 1, began in October 1917 under the supervision of General Chemical Company personnel and with J. G. White Engineering Company as contractor. Support facilities were built for the 1,100 construction workers and a village was built for permanent operating and supervisory employees and their families. Some 1,900 acres of land were acquired at the site, including some old foundry buildings already on the land. This large acreage was deemed essential since the original plans also called for construction of production facilities for smokeless powder, picric acid, and TNT. The ammonia synthesis plant consisted of two 7-1/2 tons of ammonia per day units and one 15-ton unit. In addition, a 2-1/2 ton-per-day nitric acid plant was built along with a small ammonium nitrate plant. A coal-fired steam plant was built to provide electricity (10, 22).

By the time construction began on the ammonia synthesis plant in October, it was already apparent that difficulties lay ahead. Colonel Joyes and some of his staff had visited General Chemical's Laurel Hill pilot plant in August. They found that the synthesis process was not as well developed as the company had indicated, and considerable research and testing were still needed. As a result the Nitrate Division established a research facility at Sheffield in October; it was headed by Major Curtis and staffed with 23 military personnel who were trained chemists. The laboratory was located in a vacant foundry building on the reservation. The Nitrate Division also sent a number of people to the Laurel Hill laboratory to train under and work with the General Chemical chemists on improving of the process. However, as construction work proceeded at Sheffield, problems requiring professional knowledge emerged so rapidly that in the spring of 1918 the entire Laurel Hill group was transferred to the Sheffield laboratory. Problems occurred in practically every phase of the operation, often requiring radical design changes or modifications (10,22).

Regardless of the problems work proceeded rapidly on the plant. On June 4, 1918, the powerhouse boilers were fired and the oxidation unit produced its first nitric oxide on July 1, using shipped-in ammonia. On July 15, the first nitric acid was produced. The first synthetic ammonia was produced during a short run on September 16. The first ammonium nitrate liquor was made on October 28 and this was converted to solid ammonium nitrate on November 12. Due to the many problems, only one 7-1/2 ton unit was completed when the Armistice was signed on November 11, and even this unit could not sustain operation for any period of time. The biggest problem was that the synthesis catalyst was quickly and permanently destroyed by impurities in the synthesis gas. Furthermore, the catalyst was very difficult to prepare (10, 22, 29).

It was apparent by mid-1918 that the synthesis catalyst would never work satisfactorily. The Nitrate Division hurriedly took over the Bureau of Soils' personnel and fixed-nitrogen laboratory at Arlington Farm, Virginia, to find and prepare a better catalyst for the Sheffield plant. Dr. R. O. E. Davis of the Bureau of Soils was initially in charge of the investigations (10).

Immediately following the Armistice, construction of the Sheffield plant was cut to one shift of 200 men per day. Both the plant and laboratory were closed permanently in January 1919. The plant was kept in standby condition because the War Department still had every intention of bringing it into full operation. However, only one 7-1/2 ton unit was "completed". Total cost to the government was about $19 million (10, 22).

Differences: Sheffield and Oppau Plants

Although it was known that General Chemical's modified Haber plant differed considerably from the German plants, no comparisons were possible until members of the United States Fixed Nitrogen Commission visited the German Oppau plant in 1919. The differences and similarities were published in a series of papers by R. S. Tour, a Commission member working on plans to make the Sheffield plant effective at the time of the visit, in *Chemical and Metallurgical Engineering* in 1922 (50).

Tour's comparisons between the German Oppau plant and the Sheffield plant showed that both plants used water gas as a source of hydrogen. The Oppau plant used nitrogen drawn from the air during the water gas preparation of the mixture of hydrogen, carbon monoxide, and carbon dioxide. In addition the Oppau plant also produced pure nitrogen by distillation of liquid air that was used to adjust the volumes of hydrogen and nitrogen in the synthesis gas to the desired 3:1 ratio. At Sheffield only the nitrogen from the water gas preparation was used. Both plants converted the carbon monoxide in the gas mixture to hydrogen and carbon dioxide by using steam in the presence of an iron-containing catalyst. Removal of carbon dioxide in both plants was by water scrubbing with a cuprous solution. Sheffield, however, removed most of the carbon monoxide by scrubbing with a hot, concentrated caustic solution followed by scrubbing with a cuprous solution. So many difficulties arose that the hot, caustic scrubbing was abandoned for a cold, caustic scrubbing similar to that at the Oppau plant.

Ammonia synthesis at Oppau was carried out under a pressure of 200 atmospheres and a temperature of 500° to 600°C using a rugged metal catalyst made up mostly of pure iron. At Sheffield, the pressure was 100 atmospheres, the temperature 400° to 450°C, and the catalyst was made up of spongy iron with some metallic sodium and sodamide incorporated. This catalyst was the greatest weakness of the Sheffield plant. At Oppau, the ammonia synthesis chamber was constructed of materials that would withstand the high temperature and pressure used and at the same time retain heat. At Sheffield, even though the pressure and the temperatures were lower, heat retention of the chamber was very low, and the chamber was not protected from attack by the hot gases.

Ammonia removal at Oppau was achieved by water scrubbing of the synthesis chamber gases to form aqua ammonia. The scrubbing, however, left a water vapor in the chamber gases which reduced the efficiency, but apparently not the life of the catalyst. At the Sheffield plant, where the catalyst was extremely sensitive to water vapor, the ammonia was removed by refrigeration to form anhydrous ammonia.

Although the Oppau and the Sheffield plants had many similarities, there were also some marked differences. This was to be expected since information in the German patents had to be modified to evade patent infringements if General Chemical was to be successful in developing its own process. Also, the company was limited to operating information obtained by BASF before 1914. Further, General Chemical was entirely on its own when trying to fill some of the key gaps purposely concealed by BASF. Although the incomplete Sheffield plant was mothballed, many of the problems inherent in the plant were overcome during construction and initial testing of equipment. In addition, the Nitrate Division had worked hard to find and prepare a workable ammonia synthesis

The U.S. Government built a nitrate plant based on the cyanamide process at Muscle Shoals during World War I. This shows the ammonia columns in the liquid air building. *(TVA)*

catalyst, even with the information R. S. Tour had gotten firsthand on the German Oppau plant. In any event, the accumulated information and experience was sufficient to enable General Chemical through its subsidiary, Atmospheric Nitrogen, to build and operate an ammonia synthesis plant at Syracuse, New York, within about three years after work ceased at Sheffield.

U.S. Nitrate Plant No. 2

By October 1917, barely a month after the President announced his selection of Sheffield as the site for Nitrate Plant No. 1, the War Department was urgently proceeding to establish a second nitrate plant. Concern had grown that Chilean nitrate imports might be cut off, and it was apparent to the War Department that the need for explosives had been badly underestimated. Second thoughts were also rising as to whether Nitrate Plant No. 1 would be operable as soon as originally thought. The decision was made to use the tried and proven calcium cyanamide process in U.S. Nitrate Plant No. 2. The plant was constructed at Muscle Shoals, Alabama, bordering the Tennessee River about 3 miles from Nitrate Plant No. 1. The plant was to be designed to produce an unheard of 600 tons of crude calcium cyanamide per day. It would be converted on-site into 150 tons of ammonia, and this, in turn, to 260 tons of nitric acid and 300 tons of ammonium nitrate (10, 22).

The high electric power needs of the plant were to be met initially by constructing a coal-fired steam plant and then by a hydropower plant as soon as a dam could be constructed across the Tennessee River. American Cyanamid Company was approached with a proposition to design, build, and operate the plant because the company held the American patent rights to the Frank-Caro process, it was U.S. based, and it owned a plant in Canada. The company had firsthand knowledge not only of cyanamide production but also of converting cyanamide to ammonia and ammonia to nitric acid. Furthermore, General Crozier had been in frequent contact with Frank Washburn of American Cyanamid in the past, and Washburn already had submitted proposals for construction of a cyanamide plant. However, when approached with the U.S. Nitrate Plant No. 2 proposal, which called for government ownership of the plant, Washburn was hesitant inasmuch as his earlier proposals had been developed with the idea that the plant would eventually become property of the company. Washburn finally agreed reluctantly, but on the basis that his company form the Air Nitrates Corporation, a subsidiary, to take on the project (10).

Muscle Shoals was selected as the site for Nitrate Plant No. 2 to capitalize on the hydropower potential of the Tennessee River at this point. The river fell more than 100 feet over a series of rapids covering a distance of about 20 miles. Not only would the dam provide the needed hydropower for the cyanamide plant, but it also would make the river navigable for its entire length–a problem which had held back development of parts of the Tennessee Valley for over a century. In fact, Washburn tried to obtain the site before he built his plant at Niagara Falls, Canada, but was stymied because the government insisted that he also build costly navigation locks. The dam, named after President Wilson, was to be constructed by the Corps of Engineers and have a minimum hydropower generating capacity of 90,000 kilowatts. Until the dam and power-generating facilities could be completed, power was to be supplied by a 60,000-kilowatt coal-fired steam plant to be constructed at Muscle Shoals. Any deficiency was to be made up by the Alabama Power Company from a hydroplant on the Coosa River and a steam-generating plant known as Warrior Station on the Black Warrior River. Alabama Power agreed to build a transmission line to and a substation in Muscle Shoals, in return for the government building an additional steam plant at the Warrior Station. Also, the government would pay for the power it received at the Muscle Shoals substation (10, 22).

The Air Nitrates Corporation contracted the building of the Muscle Shoals steam plant to J. G. White Engineering Corporation; the erection of the plant buildings to Westinghouse, Church, Kerr, and Company of New York; and the construction and installation of equipment to the Chemical Construction Company. The first material was delivered in December 1917, but actual construction of the plant was slowed due to an exceptionally cold winter (8°F and below) and an outbreak of influenza. Some 19,000 workers were employed during the peak construction period. The plant was sufficiently complete to permit operation at one-fifth capacity in November 1918, which was a remarkable feat considering the handicaps and the huge size of the plant and support facilities. The plant had a cyanamide capacity seven times larger than Cyanamid's already enlarged Niagara Falls plant. Temporary facilities were built to accommodate 20,000 people with lodgings, restaurants, offices, police headquarters, hospitals, theaters, fire departments, and so forth. Also a permanent village was built to accommodate the expected 12,000 permanent employees and family members. The plant and support facilities occupied a 2,200-acre site that was formerly corn and cotton fields (17).

The plant was completed after the Armistice using only one 8-hour shift of workers, and after completion each section was given a test run and placed in standby. The Muscle Shoals steam plant was completed in August 1919, and its power was sold thereafter to the Alabama Power Company. Work on Wilson Dam, under the direction of the Corps of Engineers, started early in 1918 and continued into 1921 when funds ran out. Additional funds were obtained in 1922 and the dam was completed in 1924. Total cost of Nitrate Plant No. 2 was $75 million, not including Wilson Dam (10, 22).

The cyanamide plant was laid out by W. S. Landis of American Cyanamid, following closely the pattern of the Niagara Falls plant. The conversion of cyanamide to ammonia, the oxidation of ammonia, and the manufacture of nitric acid followed the pattern and processes perfected by Landis and used at the company's Ammo-Phos plant at Warners, New Jersey (22).

The manufacturing steps followed at Muscle Shoals (17) were essentially as follows:

1. Limestone from a local quarry was crushed and heated to 1,100°C in a rotary kiln.

2. The CaO was fused with coke in an electric furnace to form calcium carbide (CaC_2). The molten carbide was removed through the bottom of the furnace, pulverized, and a calcium fluoride catalyst added.

3. Pure nitrogen gas obtained by distillation of liquid air was brought into contact with the calcium carbide, which had been heated to 1,000°C, to form calcium cyanamide ($CaCN_2$) using ovens in which the charge remained for 24 hours.

4. The resulting cyanamide contained unreacted calcium carbide which was destroyed by grinding and spraying with water.

5. The calcium cyanamide was then converted to ammonia by treating it with superheated steam in an autoclave under pressure. The ammonia was recovered from the steam-ammonia mixture by fractional distillation.

6. Part of the ammonia was converted to nitric acid, using the Landis modification of the Ostwald process in which the ammonia gas mixed with air (1:9 ratio) was introduced into tops of aluminum catalyzer boxes containing a sheet of electrically heated platinum gauze suspended near the bottom outlet. In the process the ammonia was converted to nitric

oxide (NO) and passed through cooling towers containing tubes through which cold water circulated. The gas, cooled to 30°C, contained a mixture of NO and NO_2 which, when passed to oxidation towers, was converted to N_2O_4. This gas was passed through absorption towers, made of acidproof brick and filled with spiral rings, where water sprayed in at the top trickled downward, absorbing the N_2O_4 to form nitric acid. The acid solution was progressively recirculated through additional towers until a strength of 50 percent acid was reached.

7. Ammonium nitrate was produced by neutralizing the nitric acid with ammonia gas. The neutralized solution was then discharged into pans equipped with steam pipes and evaporated until the crystallizing point was reached. It was then discharged into crystallization kettles equipped with an agitator and jacketed so that the solution could be heated or cooled. Upon crystallization, a gate at the side of the kettle was opened and the crystals were swept out onto a clean floor.

The overall production capacity of Plant No. 2 was achieved by replicating a number of small units. As an extreme example, 696 individual catalyst boxes arranged in 24 units of 29 boxes each were required to oxidize the ammonia to nitric oxide.

U.S. Nitrate Plants 3 and 4

Even with the country's planned fixed-nitrogen capacity greatly expanded with the decision to build U.S. Nitrate Plant No. 2, reverses on the battlefields of France brought a decision in February 1918 to construct an additional cyanamide plant. A month later, still another cyanamide plant was added to the list. These were to be half the size of the Muscle Shoals plant, one to be constructed at Toledo, Ohio, and the other at Cincinnati. Air Nitrates was to assume major responsibility for the two plants, with the Army being responsible for expediting materials, labor, and transportation. Signing of the Armistice brought immediate cancellation of construction of both plants with no intention of renewal (10, 22).

The Bucher-Cyanide Plant

The Bucher cyanide process for nitrogen fixation, which had so appealed to Parsons that he obtained funds for further research, was placed in operation in a small government-built plant at Saltville, Virginia. However, the purpose of the plant was changed from production of fixed nitrogen for explosives to providing sodium cyanide for use in manufacture of poison gases. The plant was in actual operation for only about a month before it was abandoned and sold for salvage. Numerous problems had developed and cost of production in terms of ammonia turned out to be higher than that from calcium cyanamide (10, 13).

The Fixed-Nitrogen Research Laboratory

The Fixed-Nitrogen Research Laboratory (FNRL) was established in March 1919 by the Secretary of War. It led the dual purpose of continuing government research on nitrogen fixation and perfecting ways to get maximum peacetime and national defense returns from Nitrate Plants 1 and 2. In December 1918, the Secretary of War appointed Arthur G. Glasgow, a civilian consultant, to survey the nitrogen situation in the United States and Europe. He made his report in January 1919, and was made Fixed-Nitrogen Administrator, reporting directly to the Secretary, and responsible for all U.S. Government fixed nitrate activities including those of the Nitrate Division. His first act was to establish the FNRL as the center of all government research on fixed nitrogen (10).

The FNRL had its roots in the earlier Nitrate Division laboratories at Laurel Hill and Sheffield, the Bureau of Mines laboratory at Syracuse, and the Bureau of Soils fixed-nitrogen laboratory at Arlington Farm. Dr. A. B. Lamb, a Harvard chemistry professor who had studied before the war under both Haber and Ostwald, was appointed the FNRL director with R. C. Tolman and W. C. Bray as associate directors. (In 1920, Lamb returned to Harvard and Tolman became director.) The Arlington Farm laboratory space was returned to the Bureau of Soils. FNRL used laboratory space vacated by the Chemical Warfare Service at American University in Washington, D.C. The Haber process pilot plant and other equipment were moved from Arlington Farm to American University along with Bureau of Soils personnel who wanted to join the new organization. The FNRL had a staff of 108. Of these 77 were technically trained, and some were among the Nation's top chemists. In early 1921, the Nitrate Division of the Army Ordnance Department was dissolved. In July, FNRL was turned over to the Bureau of Soils but remained on the American University campus. F. G. Cottrell was appointed director, a position he held until FNRL was terminated as a separate entity in 1926 and blended into the Bureau's overall fertilizer program (10).

The research of the FNRL was confined essentially to three areas: (1) synthetic ammonia, involving practically all aspects of the Haber process and its use; (2) the cyanamide process, particularly the manufacture and testing of nitrogen fertilizers in addition to calcium cyanamide that could be made following the conversion of cyanamide to ammonia; and (3) the arc process, primarily basic research. Most of the research was directed at ammonia synthesis since it was obvious from the outset that this process would dominate all others in the future. Work on cyanamide was aimed primarily at improving the position of the Muscle Shoals plant for peacetime operation. Research on the arc process, which was very limited, was in deference to the National Defense Act which specified that research should be done on all nitrogen-fixation methods (34, 52).

Ammonia Synthesis Research

Undoubtedly FNRL's greatest contribution was in the field of ammonia synthesis catalysts, both in the understanding of the mechanisms and behavior of the catalysts under different conditions, and in the development of a superior catalyst. Starting at Arlington Farm, all likely catalysts referred to in the literature were investigated by A. T. Larson and others. Special apparatus had to be developed for catalyst preparation and testing. Pure metal catalysts–iron, cobalt, nickel, tungsten, and molybdenum–proved unsatisfactory as did mixed metal catalysts. Most of these had specific temperature ranges where they behaved best, and some behaved differently at the very high pressures necessary for the ammonia synthesis reaction. Iron alone, for example, decreased sharply in effectiveness as pressure increased (39, 40).

It was known from the early work in Germany that small amounts of metal oxides mixed with pure iron enhanced its efficiency under increased pressures. As a result, the FNRL investigations with iron were expanded to include the effect of promoters on increasing its catalytic activity. Action of 16 reducible oxides was studied, of which only five–aluminum, silicon, zirconium, thallium, and cerium–showed highly beneficial effects. Oxides of sodium, potassium, and magnesium showed intermediate advantages when mixed with the iron. Iron in a mixture with two promoters–potash-alumina, potash-zirconium, or potash-silica–made a very reactive synthesis catalyst. The catalyst iron-alumina-potassium oxide was most satisfactory and was subjected to further studies to determine the conditions of temperature, pressure, gas flow velocity, and water vapor content which would maximize its yield. The most effective catalyst mixture as finally developed was an iron oxide matrix containing 3 percent alumina and 1 percent potassium oxide. This catalyst mixture was to see broad commercial use (39, 40).

The FNRL modifications of the Haber process involved a number of novel features. Unfortunately, the process (known as the "American process") was based on electrolytic hydrogen, an expensive feedstock. Its most novel approach was in removing impurities from the synthesis gases by first passing the gases over a rugged but relatively inefficient catalyst which removed the small amount of ammonia formed in the system. The catalyst and the ammonia retained the impurities that normally would poison the more sensitive, regular synthesis catalyst used in most ammonia production. Oil as a contaminant was kept out of the regular synthesis loop by using a compressor whose sole lubricant was ammonia; thus, all gases on the regular synthesis loop were essentially free from impurities (5, 16).

Research on Cyanamide and New Fertilizers

The focus of the FNRL program relating to Nitrate Plant No. 2 was on peacetime production of fertilizers. One of the first steps taken by A. B.

Lamb, director of FNRL, was to arrange a conference between the laboratory leaders and Washburn and Landis of American Cyanamid to discuss fertilizer production at the Muscle Shoals plant. It soon became apparent that calcium cyanamide was far from a perfect fertilizer material. As evidence of this Cyanamid even built a plant at Warners, New Jersey, to convert part of its cyanamide to ammonia in order to produce ammonium phosphate fertilizers. Cyanamide was disagreeable to handle, reduced germination if seeding occurred soon after application, was toxic upon contact with leaves, and only slowly became available for plant uptake following application. Washburn and Landis pointed out that marketing a large amount of cyanamide for direct application to the soil was unlikely, due to the resistance of farmers to the product and also to their preference for mixed fertilizers over single-nutrient materials. Marketing cyanamide to fertilizer mixers also did not offer a very large market because additions of cyanamide in excess of about 60 pounds per ton of mixed product resulted in reversion of the soluble phosphate into insoluble forms, thus lowering the grade and reducing the market value of the product. According to Washburn and Landis, the best bet for marketing the output of Plant No. 2 was to go ahead and produce ammonium nitrate even though the hygroscopicity problem would have to be overcome and farmers would have to be educated in its use (35, 36).

The FNRL decided to place priority upon finding economically feasible ways to convert calcium cyanamide to other, more desirable nitrogen materials. The program that unfolded was to look into all feasible nitrogen fertilizer materials, if necessary, to develop methods for their manufacture, and to evaluate their comparative effectiveness as fertilizers (36). Ammonium sulfate was considered one possible material since ammonia from the Muscle Shoals plant could be combined with sulfuric acid shipped from the large acid plants of the smelting industry located near Ducktown, Tennessee. Products subjected to process investigations were urea (53), ammoniated superphosphate (31), ammonium phosphates (25), a nonhygroscopic ammonium nitrate fertilizer (47), calcium nitrate, and the double salt ammonium nitrate-ammonium phosphate (11). Another product "Urephos" received a great deal of attention (8). Supposedly, this was a urea phosphate formed by reacting an excess of sulfuric acid with calcium cyanamide and neutralizing the unreacted acid with phosphate rock. Unfortunately, insoluble guanylurea was formed instead of urea.

The various fixed-nitrogen fertilizer materials were evaluated first in greenhouse pot experiments by the Bureau of Plant Industry (9). These showed that the cyanamide derivatives, guanylurea sulfate and dicyandiamide, were toxic to beans and wheat, and that urephos was of little value. Excellent results were obtained with calcium cyanamide, urea, ammonium nitrate, and ammoniated superphosphate. Products that were known or found to be nontoxic were evaluated in conventional small plot field experiments on farmlands available on the government reservations at Muscle Shoals and Sheffield. Dr. Frank Allison, later one of the Nation's experts on changes that nitrogen undergoes in soils, supervised the field research. The two government reservations were selected for the experiments because it was expected that the nitrogen fertilizers produced at Plants 1 and 2 would be used in the South, where the bulk of the nitrogen-containing fertilizers were then consumed. Furthermore, land, labor, and equipment for conducting the experiments were available at the sites. Three different sets of field experiments were conducted, starting in the spring of 1919. They involved two seasons of testing with corn and cotton, and one with mainly wheat and rye as overwinter crops. Tests with summer crops involved about 20 acres of land divided into several hundred 1/40- and 1/20-acre plots (1, 3).

This was probably the first extensive testing in the United States of the new concentrated nitrogen fertilizers produced by commercial nitrogen fixation. Products tested were cyanamide, calcium nitrate, ammonium nitrate, urea, urephos, ammoniated superphosphate, and ammonium phosphates. Ammonium sulfate and sodium nitrate were used as standards for comparison. Rates per acre ranged from 10 to 80 pounds of N, and all straight nitrogen plots received basic applications of superphosphate and potash. Nitrogen and phosphorus carriers were compared with equal amounts of N and P from ammonium sulfate and superphosphate. In general, the data indicated that the nitrogen sources were equally effective except calcium cyanamide which reduced germination and especially cotton yields. Urephos was soon ruled out as being ineffective. Individual studies confirmed that cyanamide converted very slowly to nitrates in the soil, damaged seedlings due to the presence of dicyandiamide, and reduced the availability of phosphorus when mixed with superphosphate (2, 3, 43).

Arc Process

Basic research on the arc process focused on the nature of corona discharge in arc plants, and the products resulting from the arc discharge. The latter included nitrogen oxides and ozone, as well as the reaction between ozone and nitrogen tetraoxide. The research yielded nothing of practical significance (10).

The Muscle Shoals Controversy

It took the United States nearly three years to reach a decision on building U.S. Nitrate Plants 1 and 2, less than a year to construct them, and about 14 years of intense wrangling to decide what to do with them. The core of the controversy initially hinged around the intention of the National Defense Act of June 1916 that the plants would be used during peacetime to produce fertilizers for American agriculture, and that they would be owned and operated by the Federal Government. Later, the concern shifted to Wilson Dam and the control of its hydropower. The real plum, at least behind the scenes, was not the nitrate plants but the hydropower. The huge Nitrate Plant No. 2 was already obsolete by the end of World War I due to the highly successful operation of the low-power-requiring Haber Bosch plants in Germany.

The Problem of Nitrate Plants 1 and 2

Arthur G. Glasgow, Fixed Nitrogen Administrator, was charged by the War Department with formulating a plan for the postwar use of the Muscle Shoals and Sheffield plants. Action on Plant No. 1 at Sheffield was not long in coming. Shortly after the Armistice, General Chemical proposed to the War Department to operate the plant for one year, provided that if the plant lost money the company would have the opportunity to recoup its losses in a second year. The company also offered to turn all profits over to the government after deducting costs of experiments, fixed charges, and operation. The intention of the company, of course, was to finish perfecting the process and to gain enough knowledge to build a Haber-type plant of its own. However, the government wanted the company to spend at least $500,000 on the plant and guarantee its success, in return for which General Chemical would get free use of the plant for three years. The company and the War Department were unable to reach an agreement (22).

While negotiations were underway on the Sheffield plant, Glasgow tried to work out an agreement with Washburn of American Cyanamid to operate the Muscle Shoals cyanamide plant in early 1919. Washburn pointed out that the Niagara Falls plant was quite capable of meeting the limited demand for cyanamide as a fertilizer. Glasgow then proposed to salvage two sulfuric acid manufacturing units from another ordnance plant so that American Cyanamid might be able to convert cyanamide-derived ammonia into ammonium sulfate. However, Washburn believed that ammonium sulfate produced in this way would not be able to compete with that produced at by-product coke oven plants. In short, Washburn would not lease the plant for peacetime production of nitrogen fertilizers unless the government subsidized the operation. Glasgow then approached leading fertilizer companies with leasing proposals, but not a single offer materialized. The same results followed efforts to attract New York financiers and coke oven interests. How Glasgow planned to get around the requirement of the National Defense Act that government built nitrogen-fixation plants be operated solely by the government is not known (22).

The Secretary of War in the meantime had appointed a U.S. Fixed Nitrogen Commission to inspect European plants and, in this country, to study the supply, demand, and use of nitrogen fertilizers that might be produced from the government nitrate plants. The Commission's recommendations were that Plant No. 1 be made effective, Plant No. 2 be converted to a fertilizer operation, and that Wilson Dam be completed and the power made available to Plant No. 2. All government nitrogen-fixing activities were to be placed in the hands of a government-owned industrial corporation to carry out the operations effectively (22).

The Secretary of War, Newton D. Baker, drafted a bill encompassing the Commission's recommendations and obtained the backing of Senator J. W. Wadsworth of New York, chairman of the Senate Committee of Military Affairs, and Congressman J. H. Kahn of California, chairman of a similar committee in the House (22, 28). This activity caused members of the U.S. Congress representing agricultural states to realize that the government-operated plants could produce cheap nitrogen fertilizers, and that such fertilizer produced and distributed by the government was powerful political ammunition that would have the full support of the farm bloc. This realization, bolstered later by the electric power issue, was responsible for launching the Muscle Shoals controversy that was to rage for years. (That controversy has been thoroughly documented in P. J. Hubbard's 1961 book, *Origins of the TVA: The Muscle Shoals Controversy, 1920-1932*.)

The Wadsworth-Kahn bill was introduced in Congress in November 1919. The bill was strongly supported by the major farm organizations and the U.S. Government agencies. Its opponents initially included Washburn of American Cyanamid and the U.S. fertilizer industry. No formal action was taken on the bill during the 1920 sessions, although it was brought up in various committees and prompted numerous congressional debates. At the same time, the Republicans launched a major diversionary tactic aimed at embarrassing the Democrats in the upcoming election by charging fraud during construction of Nitrate Plant No. 2–a charge they could not prove. Numerous amendments were offered to the Wadsworth-Kahn bill and it finally passed the Senate in January 1921, primarily due to strong southern support. However, the bill never got out of committee in the House. The incoming Republican administration was so strongly opposed to the idea of government operation through a public corporation that the bill was promptly killed in the new Congress.

Henry Ford Becomes a Bidder

The War Department negotiations with U.S. companies and the debates over the Wadsworth-Kahn bill excited only minimal public interest in the Muscle Shoals issue. This suddenly changed in July 1921, when Henry Ford, the father of the Model T automobile, submitted a bid to the Ordnance Department for the Muscle Shoals and Sheffield properties. Ford offered to purchase Nitrate Plants 1 and 2 along with all lands, the steam plants, and other properties for $5 million. Also, if the government would complete construction of Wilson

Dam and later constructed dam No. 3 about 15 miles upriver, he would lease them and their hydropower facilities for 100 years. Ford indicated he would pay 6 percent interest annually on additional funds needed to complete the facilities, provided the additional funds did not exceed $20 million for Wilson Dam and $8 million for dam No. 3. In addition, Ford would establish a fund that would amortize the entire cost of the power facilities. He claimed that the annual contribution to such a fund would be about $46,000 (28).

In return for acceptance of his terms, Ford would operate the Muscle Shoals Nitrate Plant No. 2 at its approximate maximum capacity in the production of "nitrogen and other fertilizer compounds," and maintain the plant in readiness for national defense. Ford would limit his profits on fertilizers to 8 percent. A Ford-owned company would be formed specially for the new operation with a board made up of representatives of farm organizations, the Department of Agriculture, and Ford's Muscle Shoals company. Disputes would be referred to arbitration by the Federal Trade Commission. The War Department turned down the offer mainly because Ford's estimate of the amount of money it would take to complete the dams was entirely too low (28).

Meetings involving the Corps of Engineers were conducted in Washington to try to resolve the differences relating to the cost to complete construction of Wilson dam and the power facilities. The meetings were started in mid-September and by mid-November had gotten nowhere. Ford suspended negotiations and announced that he and Thomas Edison, the inventor, would make an inspection tour of Muscle Shoals to gain "firsthand" information. Ford and Edison traveled to Muscle Shoals on December 2 in a dramatic move to gain public support for Ford's offer and to get things moving in Congress. Ford scheduled a special train nonstop from Dearborn to Muscle Shoals. It was loaded with reporters, whom he told enroute that his attempt to acquire the Shoals was based primarily on his desire to provide cheap fertilizers for the American farmer, and that he was considering using the excess power for the manufacture of one or more products, including aluminum, steel, and automobile parts.

Ford made his appeal for major national support of his project at Florence, Alabama, across the river from Muscle Shoals, by injecting anti-Wall Street themes such as eliminating the gold standard and substituting in its place national wealth (which his scheme for Muscle Shoals would help build). In another major speech before leaving the Muscle Shoals area, he stated that congressional acceptance of his offer would mean the creation of the greatest prosperity that the economically blighted region had ever known. Then he tossed the responsibility for the success of the project into the lap of Congress, saying that he had made the offer and it was up to Congress to give him the opportunity to carry it out (28).

Ford's visit created tremendous support in the South. In January, he greatly added to the excitement by a news release stating that if his offer were accepted he would build a great industrial center at Muscle Shoals. This would stretch out over 75 miles, and be so planned as to protect the health and welfare of the workers and their families. Ford's reference to a "Detroit of the South" projected him in the eyes of many as the economic savior of the region. By February 1922 the area was overrun with speculators and adventurers. Land values skyrocketed and real estate changed hands many times. Evidence of the boom still exists in the area in names like Ford City, Nitrate City, and the Dearborn Building. City blocks were laid out with streets and sidewalks, many resting in cottonfields until about 1980.

Ford modified his offer in January 1922 as it related to the cost of the completion of the dams and hydropower facilities by agreeing to pay the remaining costs of construction without limitations, for an annual rental of 4 percent of cost with an option to purchase at the expiration of the 100-year lease. Secretary Weeks, after objecting, submitted the offer to Congress where it created strong reactions both for and against. It was strongly backed by the farm bloc, the Southern States, and labor organizations, and opposed by the War Department, the National Fertilizer Association, and the private power bloc (28).

Ford did not remain the sole bidder for long. In the midst of the House hearings on the Ford offer in February 1922, the Alabama Power Company submitted a proposal to lease the power site at Wilson Dam for 50 years and complete the construction of the project at its own expense. The company agreed to purchase all other generating and transmission equipment for $5 million, to be paid in annual installments. The offer contained no provision for the nitrate plants other than the company was to furnish the government free of charge a limited amount of power. Although strongly supported by Secretary Weeks, the offer did not receive much attention (28).

As time passed, enthusiasm on the Ford offer cooled. Not only was the opposition in Congress more organized, but it was becoming increasingly apparent that Ford's primary interest was to obtain the hydropower that would be generated at Wilson and possibly other dams on the Tennessee River. Furthermore, as shown by his much publicized plans for the Muscle Shoals area, Ford planned to use a good part of this power to operate his own industries to be developed in the immediate area. Nonetheless, the bill passed the House in March 1924. Senator George Norris, however, used his powers as chairman of the Senate Agricultural Committee and kept it from reaching the Senate floor before Congress recessed in June. Ford gave up in disgust and notified the President in October that he was withdrawing his offer, stating that "a single affair of business which should have been decided by anyone within a week has become a complicated political affair" (7, 28).

Enter the Power Companies and George Norris

Meanwhile, in January 1924, nine southern power companies headed by Alabama Power Company submitted a proposal to lease Wilson Dam and the proposed No. 3 dam, if and when constructed, for $3.2 million annually. Also, the companies would pay $4.5 million outright for the Muscle Shoals steam plant, but no mention was made of Nitrate Plants 1 and 2. Southern Democrats were quick to attack the proposal for not including fertilizer production, and the power companies hurriedly tossed in a proposal to build a Haber-type ammonia plant that wouldn't use much power. However, maneuvering in Congress over the Ford offer precluded any action on the power companies' proposal (7, 28).

In April, Senator George Norris of Nebraska, chairman of the Senate Committee on Agriculture through which all of the Muscle Shoals bills had to pass in order to reach the Senate floor, introduced his first Muscle Shoals bill which provided for a government corporation to control and operate the Muscle Shoals projects. Also, it authorized completion of Wilson Dam and construction of dam No. 3. The corporation was to manufacture fertilizers for farmers at cost and would be free to sell any power in surplus of the needs of Nitrate Plant No. 2 to states, counties, and municipalities. The Norris bill also provided for research and experimentation to cheapen the cost of producing fertilizers. Although this Norris bill was strikingly similar to the plan that was finally adopted in 1933, it, like the Alabama Power offer, got nowhere. However, in June 1922, Norris introduced an amendment to the Army Appropriation bill which did succeed in providing funds for completion of Wilson Dam (7, 28).

The fertilizer issue would not stay dead, although the real issue on the Muscle Shoals properties was the hydropower from the Tennessee River. The farm bloc, especially the Farm Bureau through its Washington representative C. H. Gray, and the southern interests were just too powerful. As a result, practically all future bills included fertilizers in one way or another. President Coolidge in his message to Congress in December 1924, even declared that support of agriculture was the chief problem to consider in connection with the Muscle Shoals property (7, 28).

A Muscle Shoals bill containing the Coolidge ideas was submitted to Congress by Senator Underwood of Alabama in December 1924. This bill placed practically all of the emphasis on production of fertilizers and munitions with a private industry lessee paying an annual fee of four percent of the total cost of Wilson Dam and, in return, being free to sell any excess power left over from that used in the nitrate plants. Also, the bill stated that if private industry failed to respond, the project would be operated by a government corporation. After rough handling by both the Senate and the House, the bill was passed by both and sent to a joint conference committee in March 1925 to iron out a few differences.

Senator Norris was able to tie up the bill by charging that the conferees in attempting to compromise the differences had introduced new matter. The bill was allowed to die in conference (7, 28).

The long and fruitless debates over Muscle Shoals led many to believe that Congress should not attempt to deal with the matters relating to technical issues, but should only consider the big issue of public versus private operation. Coolidge therefore appointed a five-man Muscle Shoals Commission to ascertain the most favorable conditions under which the project should be leased. The commission was bombarded by pressure groups and ended up in a split with three members favoring the fertilizer aspects about as laid out in the Underwood bill. The other members, both technical people, advised that Muscle Shoals be used primarily for the power which was to be produced and distributed by a private company, and that fertilizer should be produced by a private company using a Haber-type process to fix nitrogen. Coolidge, although he bought the minority idea because it offered no alternative for private operation, was thoroughly disgusted with the Muscle Shoals issue generally, saying, "The problem of Muscle Shoals seems to me to have assumed a place all out of proportion with its real importance. It probably does not represent in market value much more than a first-class battleship, yet it has been discussed in the Congress over a period of years and for months at a time" (28).

The President's acceptance of the minority report resulted in adoption in January 1926 of what was known as the Snell resolution which set up a joint congressional committee to seek bids from private firms for Muscle Shoals facilities. Only two bids were finally considered as responsible: one by the power company combine and the other by American Cyanamid Company (now a huge company with multiple interests, and a new chairman). The power combine proposed to form separate corporations to handle power and fertilizers and offered $200 million for a 50-year lease. Cyanamid's offer involved giving the company practically complete control of the entire Tennessee River with Cyanamid building a Haber-type plant as a base for nitrogen fertilizers. Total payment to the government would be $86 million over 50 years. The joint committee recommended acceptance of the power companies' proposal and it was introduced into Congress as the Deneen-Morin bill. The bill got nowhere in either the Senate or the House, being delayed in committee in both. The Cyanamid offer gained support and was introduced into Congress in January 1928 as the Madden-Willis bill. It fared badly in the Senate and House committees when it became apparent that Cyanamid was really only interested in the electric power aspect. This was the last private sector bid to be made for Muscle Shoals (7, 28).

By the late 1920's it was clear to almost everyone except a few farm bloc diehards that the nitrate plants at Muscle Shoals and Sheffield were of no value either for nitrogen fertilizer production or for munitions. The country had a number of successful private sector Haber-type plants, making the cyanamide plant useless for its intended purposes. The only real value of the Muscle Shoals project was in its steam plants and the hydropower facilities (7, 28).

A modified Norris bill passed Congress in March 1928. Deleted were provisions relating to unified development of the Tennessee River, and fertilizers were relegated to research only. Passage of the bill in Congress had been greatly aided by the Federal Trade Commission's exposure of questionable activities of the private power industry. President Coolidge pocket vetoed the Norris bill, apparently because it placed the government in the public power business (7, 28).

The Norris bill was practically assured of passage by Congress again in 1930. Support of the Cyanamid proposal had been largely eliminated as a result of an unfair lobbying charge based on collusion between Cyanamid, the Farm Bureau, and possibly the power companies. In his 1930 bill, Norris gave up his idea of fertilizer research and agreed to private leasing of the nitrate plants plus granting the lessee purchase rights on power to operate the Muscle Shoals plant. Norris was able to retain public-owned operation of the power facilities and transmission lines. Passage of the bill came in February 1931, but President Hoover vetoed it in March.

Unlike Coolidge, Hoover went to considerable effort to justify his veto–the main reason being his opposition to government operation. Hoover, however, could not resist setting up another commission somewhat as Coolidge had done back in 1924 to formulate a plan for the disposal of the Muscle Shoals facility in conformity with his ideas. This time the commission consisted of nine members, three appointed by the President and three each by the Governors of Alabama and Tennessee. Some 130 large companies were contacted to submit offers on the power and fertilizer facilities; only seven even bothered to submit a bid, and none of the bids was considered as satisfactory.

The Tennessee Valley Authority Act

The Muscle Shoals controversy for all practical purposes came to an end in November 1932 when Franklin Roosevelt, a public power advocate, was elected President. Norris didn't even bother to introduce his bill during the lame duck session of Congress. Norris and Roosevelt visited Muscle Shoals in January 1933, and in February Roosevelt announced his plan for unified development of the entire Tennessee River watershed making up parts of seven states. Most of the earlier concepts of Norris were included. In May 1933, the Congress enacted Roosevelt's recommendations which were incorporated in the Tennessee Valley Authority (TVA) Act (7, 28).

The act created a U.S. Government corporation having extremely broad powers for the unified development of the Tennessee watershed including the Muscle Shoals facilities; construction of dams and hydropower facilities, power plants, and transmission lines; and power sales. It also covered navigation, flood control, agriculture, forestry, and use of facilities for national defense. Very broad powers were granted relative to fertilizers and Nitrate Plants 1 and 2. TVA could lease Nitrate Plant No. 2 to any responsible farm organization for manufacture of fertilizer or fertilizer ingredients, or the plant could be used by the corporation to fix nitrogen, produce fertilizers (including phosphate or potash), or be maintained in standby condition. Plant No. 1 could be used for whatever the corporation wanted. The corporation was authorized to cooperate with experiment stations, demonstration farms, farmers, and others on the use of new fertilizers, and the fertilizers could be distributed to assist in erosion control. Alterations could be made to the existing plants, or new plants could be constructed. Laboratories or experimental plants could be established, and experiments on fertilizers undertaken (7, 28).

Although the controversy over what to do with the Muscle Shoals and Sheffield facilities ended with the passage of the TVA Act, a new controversy was eventually to arise and persist for years between the fertilizer industry and TVA over the agency's fertilizer programs.

During the controversy of the 1920's the National Fertilizer Association, representing the U.S. fertilizer industry, consistently opposed all bills or schemes, public or private, to produce nitrogen fertilizers at Muscle Shoals. The association, which exerted only minimal political influence compared with the farm bloc organizations, kept close to the facts which were usually favorable to its side of the issue. For example, the association was quick to point out that Nitrate Plant No. 2 was an obsolete and costly way to fix nitrogen, that a subsidized fertilizer production at Muscle Shoals would injure the already established private industry, and that the government eventually through pressures for unrealistically low priced fertilizers would in effect be fixing fertilizer prices. Diversion of cheap power from Wilson Dam to produce cyanamide-based fertilizers was considered unrealistic and as an attempt to justify the $75 million "white elephant" cyanamide plant (7, 28, 42).

Domestic Synthetic Ammonia Production: 1921-1932

The first commercial synthetic ammonia plant in this country was that of the Atmospheric Nitrogen Corporation at Syracuse, New York, in 1921. Formed in 1919 by W. H. Nichols of the General Chemical Company, the Atmospheric Nitrogen Corporation built and operated the plant using General Chemical's modified Haber-Bosch process and the experiences gained by the company in designing, building, and attempting to operate U.S. Nitrate Plant No. 1 at Sheffield (23). In 1921, General Chemical and its Atmospheric Nitrogen subsidiary became part of Allied Chemical and Dye Corporation, then a holding company, which took over five large, well established domestic chemical manufacturers (24).

The Syracuse plant's initial production capacity of 15 tons of ammonia per day later was increased to about 40 tons. The plant first used a de Jahn (General Chemical) ammonia synthesis catalyst that was a marked improvement over that used at Sheffield. This catalyst was later replaced by catalyst of iron oxide, alumina, and potassium oxide developed in A. T. Larson's Fixed Nitrogen Research Laboratory and referred to as the Larson catalyst. In other respects the Syracuse plant followed essentially the final process at Sheffield, but with some additional improvements. Water gas was the source of hydrogen, synthesis was accomplished under 100 atmospheres pressure and 500°C, and the ammonia was removed through refrigeration. The operation was successful, and the ammonia produced was sold primarily for refrigeration purposes (23, 51).

The second commercial plant was built by the Mathieson Alkali Works at Niagara Falls, New York, in 1922. The plant, based on the FNRL "American" process, obtained by-product hydrogen from electrolytic cells used to produce chlorine. The nitrogen was obtained by burning the hydrogen in air. The Larson catalyst was used initially; the synthesis pressure was 300 atmospheres and the temperature was 500°C. The production capacity was 10 tons of ammonia per day (23, 51).

In 1924, the Niagara Ammonia Company began production at Niagara Falls using the Casale (Italian) modification of the Haber-Bosch process. By-product hydrogen was obtained from an adjacent electrochemical plant, and nitrogen was obtained by burning hydrogen in air. Synthesis took place at 600 atmospheres pressure and 500°C, and the ammonia was removed by condensation through water cooling. Capacity was 12 tons of ammonia per day (23, 51).

In the mid-1920's, the Pacific Nitrogen Corporation, with the help of FNRL personnel, built a plant based on the American process in Seattle, Washington. A similar plant was built by Midland Ammonia Company in Michigan. A couple of smaller plants based on electrolytic or waste hydrogen using the Mount Cenis and Nitrogen Engineering Corporation processes were also built in the mid-1920's. These plants obtained their nitrogen directly from the air. All capacities were less than 10 tons of ammonia per day (10, 48).

In 1924, E. I. Du Pont de Nemours Company secured rights to use the Claude (French) modification of the Haber-Bosch process. A subsidiary, Lazote, Inc., was formed and a site was selected at Belle, West Virginia. The plant began production in 1926, initially producing 25 tons of ammonia per day. Water gas from bituminous coal was the source of hydrogen. Nitrogen came from producer gas obtained while manufacturing water gas. The synthesis step involved a very high pressure of 1,000 atmospheres and a temperature around 600°C. In 1929 the Lazote name was dropped in favor of the Du Pont title, and the plant capacity was increased to 120 tons of ammonia per day. Du Pont was the first U.S. company to produce urea as a fertilizer (23, 51).

Construction in late 1920's of Allied Chemical's Hopewell, Virginia, ammonia plant. (*Allied Fibers*)

Allied Chemical and Dye, encouraged by the successful operation and market position of the Syracuse plant and of its subsidiary, Atmospheric Nitrogen, decided in 1927 to build the Nation's largest synthetic ammonia plant at Hopewell, Virginia. The plant basically used the old General Chemical process which obtained hydrogen from water gas and nitrogen from the producer gas. The plant was producing 270 tons of ammonia per day by 1930 and Allied decided to move much of the nitrogen into the fertilizer trade (previous to this, most of the ammonia produced by the small plants went into industrial uses). Considerable ammonia was also used to manufacture synthetic sodium nitrate, marketed under the trade name "Arcadian sodium nitrate" by the Barrett Company (23). The first sodium nitrate produced by Allied was made by oxidizing ammonia with air in a sodium carbonate solution circulating through towers. This was soon replaced with a process involving the reaction of sodium chloride with nitric acid (12).

In 1929, Shell Chemical Company, a subsidiary of Shell Union Oil Corporation and Royal Dutch Petroleum Company, built at Pottsburg, California, the first U.S. ammonia plant to use methane as a source of hydrogen, it may also have been the first such plant in the world. The company used the Mount Cenis modification of the Haber process which had recently been developed in Germany (18). This modification was a low pressure process using 100 atmospheres at 400°C and an iron cyanide catalyst. Its capacity, using two units, was 60 tons of ammonia per day. The end products were ammonium sulfate, anhydrous ammonia, and aqua ammonia. The company was the first to apply anhydrous and aqua ammonia in irrigation water as a fertilizer. It was also the first to inject anhydrous ammonia directly into the soil (23, 45).

American chemical engineers rapidly gained knowledge and made improvements in the operation of synthetic ammonia plants, both through the Fixed Nitrogen Research Laboratory and the design and operation of private plants. Most improvements were made in the purification of gases, in catalysts, and in handling and coping with high pressures and temperatures. L. C. Jones and C. C. Brown formed the Nitrogen Engineering Corporation, an engineering firm, which was later owned by American Cyanamid under the name Chemical Construction Company. Nitrogen Engineering Corporation built the early Mathieson electrolytic hydrogen ammonia synthesis plant at Niagara Falls. By 1928, the company was building a large synthetic ammonia plant in Norway, and had been awarded a contract in France by the Etablissements Kuhlmann. By 1930, it had constructed 14 plants using the "NEC" process and was the third largest ammonia synthesis plant contractor in the world, exceeded only by the Casale and the BASF (Haber-Bosch) interests (23, 27, 48).

Summary

The advent of a relatively low cost method for fixing atmospheric nitrogen–ammonia synthesis–provided the last major building block needed for production of modern fertilizers. Nitrogen, which had been sparingly used in fertilizers, now became plentiful and at prices low enough to justify widespread use on grain crops whose yields, as Crookes had indicated, had improved but slightly over the centuries primarily due to an insufficiency of nitrogen. Ammonia synthesis offered mankind the first real hope that the world's bread crops could meet food needs. Once it had firmly established an ammonia synthesis industry, the United States found itself in an envied position in the world of fertilizers. Along with adequate domestic supplies of P and K, the United States could now meet within a short time frame all of its domestic requirements without imports–a fact that was soon to be appreciated in World War II. Furthermore, the future would see the United States become the world's largest producer and consumer of fixed nitrogen.

REFERENCES

1. Allison, F. E. 1920. *Field experiments with nitrogenous fertilizers on winter crops.* Fixed Nitrogen Research Lab. Tech. Rpt. No. 49.
2. ____, and J. M. Braham. 1922. *Field experiments with nitrogenous fertilizers conducted during the season 1921 at Muscle Shoals and Sheffield, Alabama.* FNRL Tech. Rpt. No. 86.
3. ____, and J. E. McMurtney. 1924. *Field experiments with atmospheric nitrogen fertilizers.* U.S. Dept. Agr. Bull. 1180.
4. Anon. 1912. General lecture by H. A. Bernthsen on synthetic ammonia. *Met. and Chem. Eng.* 10(9A):637-642.
5. ____. 1924. The American process for nitrogen fixation. *Chem. and Met. Eng.* 30(24):948.
6. Appl, M. 1976. A brief history of ammonia production from early days to present. *Nitrogen* (100):47-58. Mar.-Apr. 1976.
7. Bowker, H. 1928. Past and pending legislative proposals regarding Muscle Shoals. *Comm. Fert.* 37(6):30-33,58.
8. Braham, J. M. and E. B. Vliet. 1919. *The manufacture of urephos: chemical changes produced by treating lime-nitrogen with excess sulfuric acid.* FNRL Tech. Rpt. No. 17.
9. ____. 1920. *Pot tests on various nitrogenous fertilizers.* FNRL Tech. Rpt. No. 33.
10. Clarke, M. 1977. *The Federal Government and the fixed nitrogen industry, 1915-1926.* Oregon State Univ. PhD thesis. Copies available through University Microfilms International, Ann Arbor, Michigan.
11. Clarkson, A. L. and J. M. Braham. 1920. *Double salt studies in the system ammonium nitrate/ammonium phosphate/water.* FNRL Tech. Rpt. No. 47.
12. Crittenden, E. D. 1964. Synthetic sodium nitrate–production and use. In *Fertilizer Nitrogen,* ed. by V. Sauchelli. pp. 331-343. Reinhold Publishing Corp., New York.
13. Curtis, H. A. 1932. A history of nitrogen fertilizer processes. In *Fixed Nitrogen,* ed. by H. A. Curtis. pp. 77-89. Chemical Catalog Co., Inc., New York.

14. Emmett, P. H. 1932. Synthetic ammonia. In *Fixed Nitrogen*, ed. by H. A. Curtis. pp. 150-239. Chemical Catalog Co., New York.
15. Ernst, F. A. 1927. Atmospheric nitrogen fixation, 1902-1927. *Am. Fert.* 66(10);21-24.
16. ____, F. C. Reed, and W. L. Edwards. 1925. A direct synthetic ammonia plant. *Ind. Eng. Chem.* 17(8):775-778.
17. Fairlea, A. M. 1919. Muscle Shoals nitrate plant. *Chem. and Met. Eng.* 20(1):8-17.
18. Frear, G. L. and R. L. Baber. 1963. Ammonia. In *Kirk-Othmer Encyclopedia of Chemical Technology*. 2nd ed. Vol. 2, pp. 258-298.
19. Guernsey, E. W. 1932. The alkali cyanide method of nitrogen fixation. In *Fixed Nitrogen*, ed. by H. A. Curtis. pp. 311-336. Chemical Catalog Co., Inc., New York.
20. Haber, L. F. 1968. Fritz Haber and the nitrogen problem. *Endeavour* 37(102):150-153.
21. Haynes, W. 1954. Early industries mature. In *American Chemical Industry*. Vol. I. pp. 160-164. D. Van Nostrand Co., Inc., New York, Toronto, London.
22. ____. 1945. The World War I period: 1912-1922. In *American Chemical Industry*. Vol. II. pp. 141-168. D. Van Nostrand Co., Inc., New York, Toronto, London.
23. ____. 1948. The merger era. In *American Chemical Industry*. Vol. IV. pp. 85-95. D. Van Nostrand Co., Inc., New York, Toronto, London.
24. ____ 1949. The chemical companies. In *American Chemical Industry*. Vol. VI. pp. 31-43, 391-394. D. Van Nostrand Co., Inc., New York, Toronto, London.
25. Heatherington, H. C. and J. M. Braham. 1920. *The manufacture of ammonium phosphate*. FNRL Tech. Rpt. No. 30.
26. Honti, G. D, editor. 1976. *The nitrogen industry*. Akademiai Kiado, Budapest.
27. Howard, P. E. 1932. Nitrogen statistics. In *Fixed Nitrogen*. ed. by H. A. Curtis. pp. 467-489.
28. Hubbard, P. J. 1961. *Origins of TVA, the Muscle Shoals Controversy, 1920-1932*. Vanderbilt Univ. Press, Nashville, Tennessee.
29. Jones, C. H. 1920. Nitrogen fixation by the Haber method. *Am. Fert.* 52(13):120-144.
30. Krase, N. W. 1932. The arc method of nitrogen fixation. In *Fixed Nitrogen*, ed. by H. A. Curtis. pp. 132-149.
31. ____, G. C. Backus, and J. M. Braham. 1919. *The manufacture of ammoniated superphosphate*. FNRL Tech. Rpt. No. 28.
32. Krase, H. J. 1932. The cyanamide method of nitrogen fixation. In *Fixed Nitrogen*, ed. by H. A. Curtis. pp. 296-310.
33. ____, 1932. Oxidation of ammonia. In *Fixed Nitrogen*. ed. by H. A. Curtis. pp. 366-408.
34. Lamb, A. B. 1920. The Fixed Nitrogen Research Laboratory. *Chem. and Met. Eng.* 22(21):977-979.
35. ____ and R. C. Tolman. 1919. *Preliminary report on utilization of U.S. Nitrate Plant No. 2*, FNRL Tech. Rpt. No. 1.
36. ____. 1919. *Suggestions for chemical research on cyanamid*. FNRL Tech. Rpt. No. 2.
37. Landis, W. S. 1916. The production of ammonia from cyanamid. *Met. and Chem. Eng.* 15(2);87-90.
38. ____. 1927. Twenty-five years of progress in the cyanamid industry. *Am. Fert.* 66(12):58,60,62,64,66.

39. Larson, A. T. and A. P. Brooks. 1926. Ammonia catalysts. *Ind. Eng. Chem.* 18(12):1305-1307.
40. _____, R. S. Tour, A. P. Brooks, W. L. Newton, and W. Hawkins. 1922. Contributions to the study of ammonia catalysts. Parts I-IV. *Chem. and Met. Eng.* 26(11):493-497; 26(12): 555-560; 26(13):588-593; 26(14):647-654.
41. Mehring, A. L., J. R. Adams, and K. D. Jacob. 1957. *Statistics of fertilizers and liming materials in the United States.* U.S. Dept. of Agr, Statistical Bull. 191.
42. MacDowell, C. H. 1925. The problems of Muscle Shoals. *Am. Fert.* 63(6):21-24; 63(7):21-30.
43. McMurtney, J. E. and F. E. Allison. 1921. *Field experiments with nitrogenous fertilizers conducted during the season of 1920 at Muscle Shoals and Sheffield, Alabama.* FNRL Tech. Rpt. No. 63.
44. Parsons, C. L. 1919. Commercial oxidation of ammonia to nitric acid. *Ind. and Eng. Chem.* 11(6):541-552.
45. Rosenstein, L. 1931. Why Shell built its ammonia plant in California. *Chem. and Met. Eng.* 38(11):636-637.
46. Ross, W. H. and A. R. Merz. 1932. Synthetic nitrogen fertilizers. In *Fixed Nitrogen*, ed. by H. A. Curtis. pp. 409-466.
47. Scalione, C. C. and H. R, Beard. 1919. *Method of reducing the hygroscopicity of ammonia.* FNRL Tech. Rpt. No. 18.
48. Slack, A. V. 1973. History and status of ammonia production and use. In *Ammonia*, ed. by A. V. Slack and G. R. James. pp. 5-142. Marcel Dekker, Inc., New York.
49. Timm, B, and W. Danz. 1964. History of nitrogen fixing processes. In *Fertilizer Nitrogen*, ed. by V. Sauchelli. pp. 40-57. Publ. by Reinhold Publishing Corp., New York.
50. Tour, R. S. 1922. The German and American synthetic ammonia plants. Parts I-V. *Chem. and Met. Eng.* 26(6): 245-248; 26(7):307-311; 26(8):359-362; 26(9):411-415; 26(10):463-466.
51. _____. 1927. Synthetic ammonia costs in America. *Trans. Am. Inst. Chem. Eng.* 20:213-249.
52. Tolman, R. C. 1921. Government fixed nitrogen research. *Chem. and Met. Eng.* 24(14):595-599.
53. _____ and N. W. Krase. 1919. *Preliminary experiments in the formation of urea from ammonia and carbon dioxide.* FNRL Tech. Rpt. No. 21.
54. True, A. C. 1937. *A history of agricultural experimentation and research in the United States.* U.S. Dept. Agr. Misc. Publ. 251.
55. Waeser, B. 1926. *The Atmospheric Nitrogen Industry.* Vol. II. pp. 609-648, 649-684, Transl. by E. Fyleman. P. Blakiston's Son and Company, Philadelphia.
56. Washburn, F. S. 1913. Agricultural Fertilizers from the air in relation to water power development. *Am. Fert.* 39(12):39-46.
57. Wheeler, A. J. 1927. Air-nitrogen fertilizers. *Am. Fert.* 67(5):19-26.

7

Production of Phosphate Rock, Sulfur, and Sulfuric Acid 1920-1980

The period prior to 1920 saw the discovery and mining of the South Carolina phosphate rock deposits, the largest known in the world up to that time. This was followed by discovery of the greater deposits in Florida (including the fabulous central Florida field), Tennessee, and the western states. This earlier period also saw major changes in sources of sulfur resulting in reduced dependence on imports of elemental sulfur and sulfur-bearing pyrites, and recovery of sulfur from smelter gases and from domestic pyrites. The discovery of elemental sulfur along the U.S. and Mexican Gulf Coast was made possible with the development of the Frasch hot-water process.

U.S. phosphate rock production from 1920 through 1980 increased nearly 14-fold, reaching an annual output of nearly 60 million short tons; this was 39 percent of the world's production, making the United States the world's leading producer. Production climbed steadily over the 60-year period except for sharp declines during certain years in the 1920's and in the early 1930's due to the Great Depression and a smaller decline in 1970 as production was realigned with demand. The United States continued to be a major rock exporter throughout the period. It also became a major exporter of phosphate rock in the form of concentrated superphosphate, ammonium phosphates, and of phosphoric acid in the 1960's.

Frasch sulfur throughout the 1920-1980 period was the mainstay of the U.S. sulfur industry, although recovered sulfur mostly from sour natural gas and refinery gases became increasingly important beginning in the 1960's. Imports of Frasch sulfur from Mexico and recovered sulfur from Canada also increased sharply in the 1960's and in the 1970's, just about offsetting exports. Sulfuric acid production kept abreast of needs, increasing nearly 10-fold in six decades.

This chapter deals with nearly all aspects of production of phosphate rock, sulfur, and sulfuric acid as related to fertilizers, including sources,

Table 7.1. Production of Phosphate Rock (30, 101, 40, 42, 8, 72).

Year	Florida 1000 tons	Florida %U.S. total	Tennessee 1000 tons	Tennessee %U.S. total	Western States 1000 tons	Western States %U.S. total	U.S. exports 1000 tons	Total U.S. production 1000 tons	World production 1000 tons[1]
1920	3,705	82	683	15	62	1	1,198	4,513	–
1930	3,574	82	672	16	74	2	1,373	4,320	12,870
1940	3,130	71	1,093	25	179	4	842	4,402	10,780
1950	9,629	77	1,649	13	1,170	10	1,971	12,448	25,760
1960	13,800	70	2,172	11	3,647	19	4,473	19,618	46,110
1970	31,278[1]	81[1]	3,163	8	4,297	11	11,738	38,739	94,083
1980	52,076[1]	87[1]	1,900 est.	3	6,000 est.	10	15,736	59,982	152,614

[1]Includes North Carolina (during these years North Carolina produced about 7% of U.S. total production); short tons.

locations, companies involved, methods of mining, processing, transportation and main uses.

Phosphate Rock Production by States

Table 7.1 shows marketable phosphate rock production at 10-year intervals for each of the principal producing regions: Florida (includes North Carolina), Tennessee, and the Western States. Included also is each region's share of the national production. Not included are data for South Carolina which still produced a small amount of rock in 1920 and token amounts in 1922 and 1925.

During the 1920-1980 period Florida consistently produced 70 to 82 percent of the marketable phosphate rock mined annually in the United States with most of the production coming from the central land-pebble district. Production of hard rock declined from 12 percent of the marketable Florida phosphate produced in 1920 to less than 1 percent in 1940; mining of hard rock ceased in 1966. Several companies began reclaiming soft rock that had been dumped as a waste during the boom days, selling it for livestock and poultry feed and for direct application to the soil. Soft rock was produced continuously from 1931 through the 1970's but seldom exceeded 60,000 tons annually. Mining of the north Florida deposit in Hamilton County in the late 1960's was a major addition to Florida's production capacity. An even more important development, also occurring in the late 1960's, was the opening of a mine in a recently discovered field having appreciable mineable deposits in Beaufort County, North Carolina.

Tennessee's share of the Nation's total phosphate rock production increased from 15 percent in 1920 to 25 percent in 1940, then declined steadily to about 3 percent in 1980. Marketable tonnage increased from 683,000 short tons in 1920 to 3.3 million in 1969, then dropped to around 2 million in 1980. Blue rock production from underground mines in the Highland Rim amounted to 88,000 tons in 1920 and then declined until 1937 when mining ceased. Brown rock, by far the dominant source in the 1920-1937 period, was the only phosphate rock source mined in Tennessee after 1937. The grade of the brown rock decreased until 1960, after which it was used only in electric furnaces to produce mostly nonagricultural products.

The Western States remained relatively minor phosphate rock producers even though production increased 100-fold from 1920 to 1980. The West's annual share of the U.S. marketable production remained in the single-digit range until the late 1940's. The share peaked at 19 percent in 1960, and then declined to about 10 percent by 1980. Tonnages of rock mined, however, increased steadily through 1980. The remoteness of deposits from major farming areas held back use of western phosphate for fertilizers. Since 1950, western rock has been used increasingly to produce electric furnace phosphoric acid from which high-value, nonagricultural products are manufactured. Slightly more than half of the phosphate rock produced in 1979 went this route.

Phosphate Rock Reserves

Various estimates have been made of the U.S. and world phosphate rock reserves. The most recent estimate of measured reserves and identified subeconomic resources for the United States in million short tons are in Table 7.2. Improvements in processing technology, some of which are underway, could make some of the subeconomic resources commercially economic in the future (98).

Exports

The United States had a virtual monopoly on world exports of phosphate rock prior to 1923 at which time phosphate rock from French Africa–Tunisia, Algeria, and Morocco–became a serious competitor. However, the United States remained the world's leading exporter throughout the 1920-1980 period, even though additional competition on the world market also developed from the USSR, the Pacific islands, South Africa, and Israel. Major competition in the 1970's was from the USSR, Morocco, and Tunisia (37, 69).

Exports by the United States during the 1920-1980 period usually ranged between 20 and 30 percent of the marketable production, being lower during the World War II years and higher when demand temporarily exceeded the world supply. Most of the rock exported was

Table 7.2. U.S. Phosphate Rock Reserves (98).

	Measured reserves	Identified subeconomic resources	Total identified resources
Central Florida	1,000	700	1,700
North Florida	200	60	260
North Carolina	1,000	200	1,200
Tennessee	20	-	20
Idaho	800	500	1,300
Utah	100	100	200
Wyoming	50	50	100
Montana	50	50	100
Total	3,200	1,660	4,880

Phosphate rock being loaded on ship at Tampa. A significant portion of the ore mined in Florida is exported. *(F.J. Myers--TVA)*

from Florida, although considerable western phosphate moved to Canada, starting in the 1930's. In 1955, Florida supplied 84 percent of the total exports, and Montana 15 percent. In 1975, Florida (including North Carolina) supplied 91 percent of the exports and the western states 9 percent. In addition to direct exports of phosphate rock, considerable phosphate in the form of finished fertilizers and intermediates also was exported. Export of concentrated superphosphate in 1970 amounted to 325,000 tons of P_2O_5 equivalent, or 22 percent of its total production; the corresponding 1979 figure was 732,000 tons or 40 percent. Ammonium phosphate exports, principally diammonium phosphate, amounted to 470,000 tons of P_2O_5 in 1970, or 22 percent of the total production: this increased to 2.8 million tons, or 53 percent, in 1979. Phosphoric acid exports also had become important by 1979 when 804,000 tons of P_2O_5 equivalent, or 8 percent of the total produced, was exported (8, 41, 72, 84, 96, 105).

Uses

In the United States, agriculture used far more than 90 percent of mined phosphate rock prior to 1930 and 70 to 82 percent thereafter. Of the rock going into agriculture, 80 to 95 percent is used in production of fertilizers. In 1930, 87 percent of all of the rock consumed in the United States for all uses went into normal superphosphate; this share dropped to 80 percent in 1940 and 60 percent in 1950. A Bureau of Mines breakdown of the total phosphate rock consumption in 1955 shows normal superphosphate using 49 percent, concentrated superphosphate 18 percent, direct application 7 percent, stock and poultry feeds 2 percent, and fertilizer fillers 1 percent. Agriculture used 77 percent and industrial uses accounted for the remaining 23 percent (55, 57, 72, 84).

Still more changes in agricultural uses took place after 1960. Use of phosphate rock for direct application declined to less than 1 percent of the total consumption by the 1970's, use as a fertilizer filler vanished by the early 1960's, and consumption as livestock feeds remained minimal. Use in normal superphosphate decreased as concentrated superphosphate and ammonium phosphates came to the forefront. For example, in 1965, of the total P_2O_5 in phosphate rock consumed in fertilizers (including exports of finished materials), 29 percent went into normal superphosphate, 38 percent into concentrated superphosphate, and 28 percent into ammonium phosphates; in 1979, 5 percent was consumed in normal superphosphate, 24 percent in concentrated superphosphate, and 69 percent in ammonium phosphates, principally diammonium phosphate (7, 33, 95, 96).

Advances in Mining and Beneficiation

Major technological advances in phosphate rock mining and beneficiation prior to 1950 helped revolutionize phosphate rock production, particularly in the Florida and North Carolina deposits. These were the development of flotation and related beneficiation procedures to separate and reclaim small size phosphate particles remaining after removal of the larger phosphate-bearing fraction by wet screening, and the introduction and use of draglines to remove both overburden and the phosphate-containing matrix. Both advances reduced the cost of producing marketable phosphate rock. Use of flotation technology greatly prolonged the life of the deposits.

Phosphate Mining with Draglines

The major technological advance was the introduction of dragline excavators, which were used widely in the open-pit mining of other minerals. Basically a dragline consists of a long boom that supports a bucket suspended by cables. Draglines are semi-mobile; when set in a fixed position, they work over a large area and mine to a considerable depth. A small dragline was first used in phosphate mining in 1914 to remove overburden in the brown rock field in Tennessee. The first use of a dragline in Florida was in 1920. Under a contract with the Southern Phosphate Company, the W. F. Carey Company used a dragline to remove overburden in the pebble field (5, 65).

Early Florida draglines were powered by steam or internal combustion engines and were moved on wheels, rollers, or rails. However, the draglines were soon powered with electricity. Booms ranged from 50 to 100 feet in length and buckets had a capacity of about 4 cubic yards. (In Tennessee, draglines were much smaller, using buckets of 2-3 cubic yard capacity.) By 1928, tracked treads like those used on bulldozers today began appearing on the draglines; the size of buckets had reached

8 cubic yards, and booms were extending to 125 feet. Draglines were used in the 1940's to remove both the overburden and the matrix. Size continued to increase. In 1946, a dragline with a 24-cubic-yard capacity and a 215-foot boom made its appearance. By 1965, draglines were operating with 30 to 55 cubic yard buckets. The Florida draglines were topped, however, by Texas Gulf Sulphur's mammoth equipment in North Carolina; its bucket capacity was 72 cubic yards.

Today's larger draglines are repositioned by use of unique walking shoes. The walking draglines have large, circular tubs beneath the superstructure and rest upon the ground during actual operation. Mobility is provided by fitting walking shoes on either side of the central housing. When the machine is not being propelled, the shoes are raised with the weight being borne entirely by the tub. To move the dragline, the tub and superstructure are raised, leaving the weight on the shoes. The dragline moves horizontally along the line of travel, driven by a system of shafts and rotating cranks attached to the shoe links, and the tub is set down behind its original position (21, 65, 98).

Maximum economies from large draglines are achieved where there is a sizable overburden and a deep deposit of phosphate ore. The pebble deposits of Florida and North Carolina are particularly suited to the large draglines because of the flat terrain. Western producers found no use for draglines due to the sloping and faulted nature of the phosphate beds (21, 98).

Beneficiation by Flotation

In early mining, the pebble fraction was beneficiated by washing and screening operations. Slimes and low-grade fines containing considerable phosphate were discarded. About 1920, investigators conceived the idea of separating unwanted silica particles from phosphate particles of the same specific gravity by means of flotation. The process involved mixing surfactants with water containing finely-divided phosphate and silica particles and blowing air through the resulting mixture. The surfactant selectively coated the surface of the fine phosphate particles and floated them to the top in a froth where they were removed by skimming (39, 64).

Shortly before 1920 Broadbridge and Edser in England became the first to successfully float phosphate. They obtained a U.S. patent on the process in 1925. (Prior to Broadbridge and Edser's work it had always been considered that a polar, nonmetallic mineral such as phosphate would not float.) The process was developed on a commercial scale by the Phosphate Recovery Corporation, a company set up and jointly owned by the International Agricultural Corporation (now IMC) and the Minerals Separation North American Corporation. A laboratory flotation operation using oleic acid was set up at Mt. Pleasant, Tennessee, and encouraging results were obtained with the first test. In 1926, the work was transferred to Mulberry, Florida, and further experiments conducted through 1928 by a team of researchers resulted in a workable process. The flotation cells developed in this research were patented in 1930 by Trotter and Wilkinson. These worked well with a fine −28 +200 mesh fraction but not with a coarser −1 mm +28 mesh material. (The expression −28 +200 mesh is the conventional notation for sizing materials that will pass through a screen having 28 openings per inch but not through a screen having 200 openings per inch. Similarly −1 mm +28 mesh refers to objects passing through screens having one millimeter square openings but not passing one having 28 openings per inch.) The process was first commercially used in Phosphate Recovery Corporation Plant No. 2 near Mulberry where approximately 90 percent of the phosphate in the fine fraction was recovered (4, 48, 64). John T. Burrows, Vice President of the International Agricultural Corporation, announced the breakthrough in the perfection of flotation at the 5th annual convention of the National Fertilizer Association at New London, Connecticut, in June 1929 (9).

By this time it was apparent that the coarser −1 mm +28 mesh fraction could not be beneficiated using the developed flotation procedure. In 1929, Chapman and Littleford applied for a patent covering agglomerate tabling of this fraction and the patent was granted in 1934. In this process the feed containing the coarser phosphate was dewatered to 60 to 75 percent solids and mixed with the surfactant reagents. The feed was then diluted to 35 percent solids and passed over a standard shaking, riffled table. The vibrating table caused the sand particles to travel between longitudinal ribs along the bottom of the table to one end while phosphate floated in a thin layer of water over the sides of the table. This process was used by the Phosphate Recovery Corporation (5, 65).

Several methods other than agglomerate tabling were developed to separate the phosphate from the coarse fraction following treatment with surfactants–underwater screening, spray belts, and Humphrey spirals. International Minerals and Chemical Corporation replaced agglomerate tabling with Humphrey spirals to lower costs and save space. The phosphate was separated from the silica in a water suspension which traveled down a nest of spirals in such a way that the lightest solids concentrated on the inner rim, while the heavier moved toward the outer rim. Because of its higher specific gravity, phosphate concentrated on the outer rim (64, 65).

A double flotation process was developed by Arthur Crago in 1942 in which the fatty acid concentrate left after the regular flotation treatment was removed with sulfuric acid. The phosphate concentrate was then washed and subjected to a second flotation using amine as a reagent. This floated silica away from the phosphate leaving a high-grade concentrate (65).

Use of flotation and other improved beneficiation methods was adopted by all phosphate producers in the central pebble district in

Florida. Flotation was used on newly mined matrix and to reclaim waste phosphate from abandoned tailing ponds (38).

Florida Phosphate Rock

Florida phosphate rock has dominated U.S. and world markets since around 1895 when it first exceeded South Carolina production. By 1910, as hard rock mining leveled off, the central field dominated Florida production. The central field continued in this position through 1980, although its monopoly was broken in the late 1960's with the opening of the north Florida deposit. During the 1920-1979 period Florida production increased nearly 15-fold, from 3.3 million to around 48 million tons.

Hard Rock

The Florida hard rock field, on the west side of the Florida peninsula and north of the central pebble field, was a major source of phosphate rock exports prior to World War I (Chapter 3). However, during the war exports practically ceased; production dropped sharply, rebounded briefly after the war, and then declined from around 200,000 tons annually in the early 1920's and to less than 100,000 tons in 1950. Production ceased in 1965. Hard rock mining costs were high, and stiff competition was encountered in the export market from the land-pebble field and from North Africa. An attempt was made to increase exports through the formation of Hardphos, a hard rock trade association, through which the member companies sought to negotiate an agreement with the North African producers aimed at price stabilization. This failed but Hardphos joined with the Phosphate Export Association, the trade association representing the Florida pebble trade group, and the North African group to form the International Phosphate Cartel. This was only partially successful; it ran into difficulties with the Federal Trade Commission, and was eventually disbanded (69, 70, 72).

Hard rock mining in the late 1920's consisted of stripping the overburden by hydraulic methods and recovering the matrix from underwater in artificial ponds by dipper dredges. The deepest mining possible with the dredges was 35 feet below water level. The matrix was hauled by one-bucket cable cars to washers at the edge of the pits. The introduction of small draglines in 1932 permitted mining up to 50 feet below water level. Hydraulic removal of overburden continued since the overburden was often 70 feet thick (104).

The number of companies mining hard rock, which had been as high as 30 in its boom days, declined to 3 in 1928. These were the J. Buttgenbach Company with mines at Dunnellon and Hernando; C. and J. Camp, mining at Dunnellon; and the Dunnellon Phosphate Company with mines at Inverness and Dunnellon. In 1950, only one company was mining–the Kibler-Camp Phosphate Enterprise, Ocala. The Kibler-Camp mine had been jointly worked since 1935 by the Belgian-owned J. Buttgenbach and Company with K. B. Kibler as manager in later years. Kibler in 1949 acquired the interest in the company held by the Belgian partner and later merged with C. and J. Camp to form the Kibler-Camp Phosphate Enterprise. Kibler-Camp in 1950 landed a contract with the Virginia-Carolina Chemical Corporation to furnish hard rock for an electric furnace which the latter company had just erected at Charleston, South Carolina. This proved to be the principal hard rock outlet that kept Kibler-Camp in operation. However, hard rock production ceased in 1965 and the carryover inventory was sold in 1966 (5, 51, 53, 56).

Hope for continued hard rock mining persisted briefly, but this too was soon to vanish. The Tennessee Valley Authority in 1955 began purchasing hard rock reserves to assure a long-term supply of high-grade phosphate rock for blending with unbeneficiated Tennessee brown rock for use in its electric furnaces at Muscle Shoals, Alabama. By 1961, 4800 acres of prospected hard rock land had been selected and purchased. The agency, however, found it advantageous to continue to purchase high-grade land pebble rather than to immediately mine its own hard rock. By 1970, TVA had determined that furnace-based fertilizers were too costly to produce, and the hard rock holdings were eventually sold at public auction. No interest was shown in the phosphate and the entire 4,800 acres were bought by real estate speculators. So ended the Florida hard phosphate rock field.

Soft Rock

Florida soft rock, which occurs in combination with Florida hard rock and as separate deposits, was mined and marketed briefly in the 1890's and again for a brief period starting in 1918. Most soft rock, however, was discarded in waste ponds during the mining of hard rock. In 1931, a continuing market was found for direct application to the soil, use as a filler in fertilizer, and as a livestock and poultry feed supplement. The material was low in phosphate content, high in iron and aluminum, and of no value in manufacture of phosphatic fertilizers. Small companies began recovering the soft rock from the old waste ponds in 1931. The surface portions of the old ponds were cut up mechanically and exposed in place to the sun for drying. The dry material was hauled to storage sheds where it was ground and screened before shipping. Tonnages marketed never exceeded 100,000 tons a year and from 1960 on, production declined to around 30,000 tons annually (5, 55, 57, 72).

Some of the small companies operated for years in the field. Companies operating in 1950 were Colloidal Phosphate Company, Ocala; Sea Board Phosphate Company, Dunnellon; Soil Builders, Inc., Hernando; and Superior Phosphate Company, Dunnellon (56).

International Minerals' mining operation in Florida. *(F.J. Myers--TVA)*

Florida Pebble

More than 70 percent of the phosphate rock produced in the United States during the 1920-1950 period came from the central Florida mines. Production costs were lower than anywhere else in the country in the 1920's and became even more competitive with the advent of flotation and use of large draglines.

Companies mining pebble phosphate from 1920 through 1950 were predominately old-line fertilizer or mining companies with very few changes in ownership occurring. Eight companies were active in the field in 1927: Amalgamated Phosphate Company with mines at Brewster and Green Bay; American Agricultural Chemical Company mining at Pierce; Coronet Phosphate Company mining at Pembroke and Plant City; Florida Phosphate Mining Company with mines at Bartow and Nichols; Southern Phosphate Corporation mining at Eston Park; and Swift and Company mining near Bartow (51). Seven companies were operating in 1938. Phosphate Mining Company had dropped out, and Amalgamated Phosphate Company reverted to American Cyanamid Company, its former owner (5).

Seven companies were operating in the pebble field in 1950: American Agricultural Chemical Company at Pierce; American Cyanamid at Brewster; Coronet Phosphate at Plant City; Davison Chemical Company at Bartow (Davison in 1947 became owner of the Southern Phosphate Company); International Minerals and Chemical Corporation (name changed from International Agricultural Corp. in 1942); Swift and Company at Bartow and Fort Meade; and the Virginia-Carolina Chemical Corporation at Nichols (the company began on holdings mined prior to 1920 by subsidiaries) (5, 56).

The large amounts of high-grade phosphate rock available in the central Florida field led the mining companies and a few large fertilizer producers to locate concentrated superphosphate plants in or near the area along with supporting sulfuric and phosphoric acid plants. The first to install such facilities in the area were Swift and Company and Armour Agricultural Chemical Company, both of which began operations in 1949. The International Minerals and Chemical Corporation followed in 1952, Virginia-Carolina in 1953, Davison Chemical and F. S. Royster Guano Company in 1954, and American Cyanamid in 1957 (50).

The following were mining in the central pebble field in 1962: American Agricultural Chemical Company; American Cyanamid Company; Armour Agricultural Chemical Company; Davison Chemical Company (now a division of W. R. Grace and Company); F. S. Royster Guano Company; International Minerals and Chemical Corporation; Smith-Douglas, Inc.; U.S. Phosphoric Products (Tennessee Corporation); and Virginia-Carolina Chemical Corporation (10, 101).

A number of new companies appeared by the mid-1960's. The major oil companies, some of which already were producing ammonia, began moving into the rapidly expanding phosphate business. Frasch sulfur producers and others likewise became interested in phosphate rock mining and phosphate fertilizer production. The larger, old-line fertilizer companies operating in the pebble field also caught the fever and began expanding (77). Production of marketable Florida pebble jumped from 13.8 million tons of material in 1960 to 33 million in 1968 (7). Overproduction resulted, prices fell, and many of the newcomers sold out, resulting in further changes in ownership.

Major ownership changes had occurred in the Florida pebble district by 1970. American Agricultural Chemical, which had been in the pebble field since the turn of the century, was taken over by the Continental Oil Company as its Agrico Division in 1963. The operation in turn was taken over in 1971 by the Williams Companies, but the Agrico name was retained. Mobil Oil acquired Virginia-Carolina Chemical Corporation in 1963, and the Borden Company took over Smith-Douglas in 1964. The Tennessee Corporation, parent company of the United States Phosphoric Corporation, was acquired by Cities Service Oil Company in 1962. Cities Service also mined pebble under its own name in the early 1970's. Davison Chemical, one of the first companies to manufacture superphosphate in the United States and also an early miner in the pebble field, sold out to W. R. Grace and Company. Armour and Company sold its Armour Agricultural Chemical Company to U.S. Steel which in turn reorganized its fertilizer activities into USS Agrichemicals. Kerr-McGee and American Cyanamid joined to form Brewster

Phosphates to mine phosphate. CF Industries in 1971 absorbed Central Phosphates, Inc., of Plant City and later took over the Bonnie complex from International Minerals to produce phosphoric acid, concentrated superphosphate, and ammonium phosphates. Farmland, another large cooperative, also bought a fertilizer production center at Pierce but did not mine phosphate (11, 16, 17, 19, 22, 24, 25, 77).

The rapid changes among Florida pebble producers appeared to have subsided by 1979. The following 13 companies were mining phosphate rock; of these, eight (asterisks) also produced phosphatic fertilizer materials in conjunction with their mining operations. *Agrico Chemical (Williams Bros.), *Borden Chemical Company, Brewster Phosphates, *C. F. Industries, Florida Phosphate Corporation, *Gardinier, *W. R. Grace and Company, *International Minerals and Chemical Corporation, Mobil Chemical Company, *Occidental Agricultural Chemical, Swift Chemical Company (Esmark), T-A Minerals Corporation, and *USS Agrichemicals (7).

The Phosphate Rock Export Associations

The Florida pebble producers were represented by an aggressive phosphate rock export association until the early 1940's when it ran afoul of the Federal Trade Commission. The Webb-Pomerene Act of 1919 permitted American companies to form export associations in order to compete better with foreign firms on the world market. As a result, the Phosphate Export Association (PEA), representing the pebble producers, and the Hardrock Export Association (Hardphos) were formed. To protect members, the two associations fixed minimum export prices and, among other things, negotiated export sales. Production quotas for members were determined by mutual agreement. The associations also could fine members for breaking rules and regulations. One effort was directed toward negotiating an agreement on price stabilization with the North Africa phosphate producers. It failed to materialize until 1933 when PEA and the North Africa group formed the International Phosphate Cartel which Hardphos later joined. The cartel's operation, which was unofficially terminated in 1939 by World War II, apparently was moderately successful but was hampered by competition from nonmembers–in Curacao, Egypt, the Pacific, and Russia (70).

In 1944 hearings, the Federal Trade Commission questioned the two associations' participation in an international cartel that sold rock on international markets at fixed prices and fined members for exceeding quotas. In addition, it appeared to the Commission that the associations were stabilizing domestic prices and entering into agreements to share the domestic market. Further, the Commission was concerned that the associations were preventing new companies from moving into the pebble and hard rock fields. Allegedly, the flotation process was licensed exclusively to PEA members, which prevented outsiders from mining in the pebble field. Hardphos was charged with restricting use of the Fernandina terminal to Hardphos members only (70).

The outcome was that the Federal Trade Commission concluded that the activities of the two associations violated either the antitrust laws or the Webb-Pomerene Act, or both. It ordered the two associations to rescind all agreements with the international cartel; desist from restricting production, potential production, or marketing of rock; and to give up the practice of using domestic sales contracts also used by other members. PEA complied with the Commission's recommendations by voluntarily dissolving itself in October 1945, and Hardphos submitted a required letter of compliance (70).

The North Florida Field

Occidental Petroleum Corporation through its Occidental Agricultural Chemical subsidiary in 1965 opened its Suwanee River mine in Hamilton County, north Florida. Occidental got into the fertilizer business in 1963 when it acquired the Best Fertilizer Company and International Ore and Fertilizer Corporation (Interore), the world's largest international marketer of fertilizer. Occidental's opening of the north Florida mine and the building of an accompanying phosphate fertilizer complex was of signal importance in that the north Florida reserve had previously gone undeveloped (16, 22).

The presence of phosphate in north Florida had been known since 1885 when the area was explored for phosphate by Dr. Lawrence C. Johnson of the U.S. Geological Survey (Chapter 3). Apparently no commercial mining was done in the area until Occidental's Suwanee River mine was commissioned. The north Florida deposit, although less extensive, is similar to the deposits in Polk and Hillsborough Counties in central Florida (30); however, there are key differences, such as greater reactivity and the sand-size particles.

Occidental secured phosphate mining rights on 30,000 acres in Hamilton County, 4,000 of which were developed for the Corporation's Suwanee River mine. The first ore was shipped in March 1966 from the Corporation's newly built shipping terminal at Jacksonville to which the ore is transported by rail. The Suwanee River mine initially had a rated capacity of 1.5 million tons of phosphate rock but this was doubled in 1968. The accompanying fertilizer complex produced wet-process phosphoric acid, concentrated superphosphate, and superphosphoric acid. In expectation of a deal with the USSR whereby Occidental would barter superphosphoric acid for ammonia and potash, the Corporation developed a second mine at Swift Creek, also in Hamilton County, in 1975. The mine was designed to produce 2.5 million tons of rock annually with the rock being converted to superphosphoric acid and other products in a new chemical complex. A U.S. embargo on shipment of superacid to Russia delayed opening of the new mine and complex (16, 19, 97). (The embargo was lifted in 1981.)

Overcoming Environmental Problems

Tremendous effort was required to overcome environmental problems in the central Florida pebble district arising from the mining and beneficiation of phosphate rock and its processing into fertilizer materials. Awareness of the problem and possible solutions were first expressed in 1929 when the Coronet Mining Company leveled a mined-over area and built a golf course on it as a demonstration. This was followed in 1937 by the International Agricultural Corporation building an "oasis" of palms, a swimming pool, and a golf course on abandoned spoil lands. The first serious expression of concern outside the industry was by the Lakeland Chamber of Commerce which sent a proposed reclamation bill to the state legislature in 1947. Although nothing was done toward passing the bill, the industry agreed to undertake some reclamation projects. Most notable perhaps was a 1949 project by American Cyanamid to reclaim a 220-acre spoil area for agricultural uses (5).

A new surge of public concern developed in the 1950's in Polk and Hillsborough Counties where mining had centered on about 130,000 acres over the years and also where concentrated superphosphate production was getting underway. The other major industries in the area–tourists and citrus–just didn't mix with phosphate mining and processing. The chief concern at this time was fluoride gas emissions from phosphoric acid plants and of SO_2 emissions and sulfuric acid mists from associated sulfuric acid plants. As a result, the Florida State Board of Health established an air pollution control district in the area to investigate the problems. To protect its own interests, the phosphate industry formed the Florida Phosphate Council and after some delay decided to begin reducing the emissions. Good progress was made and by the end of the 1960's the emissions were reduced by 90 percent (5).

The environmental problems, however, were much broader than air pollution. Overburden and silica tailings from the flotation and other beneficiation processes dumped into mined-out areas made the land useless for other purposes. Slimes from the washing operation were collected and held in settling ponds. The settling ponds particularly were a problem since they required years to dry out. In the meantime, the slimes had to be contained in the ponds by earthen walls and dams, which were subject to breaking and pouring slimes over the adjacent lands, injuring citrus groves or escaping into and polluting streams (98).

Although slime pond breakages were fairly common, none created more attention than a break in December 1971 at Cities Service's Fort Meade operation. Some 2 million gallons of the milky slime suspension poured into Peace River, contaminating it and killing fish all the way to

Gypsum stacks (above) in Florida mining area
and reclamation of clay settling area in progress (below). *(Florida Phosphate Council)*

Charlotte Bay 75 miles distant. As a result, the State of Florida forced a shutdown of Cities Service's operations and filed a suit for $20 million. The Bureau of Mines stepped up research to find an economic way to dewater the slimes, but found none; the Florida Pollution Board tightened requirements for construction, operation, and maintenance of settling ponds; and the industry devoted considerable effort to preventing wall breakages (95). Progress continued in the 1980's.

Reclamation of spoil banks, although dealt with in a demonstration manner earlier, became a public issue as urban encroachment highlighted the problem. A Land Use and Reclamation Committee was formed, but this time the industry, through the Florida Phosphate Council, adopted a reclamation policy and instituted a system of simultaneous mining and reclamation. The system involved removing the overburden and matrix from an area that would become a lake and then pivoting short mine cuts around the area and distributing the overburden in the previously mined cuts to about ground level and grading with a bulldozer. This system greatly reduced reclamation costs and the leveled land had value for citrus and other crops and for recreation. About 70 percent of the mined-over land can be restored in this manner (5).

In 1971, Florida initiated a severance tax on mined phosphate. In 1975, the severance tax was 5 percent of the established value of the mineral at the point of severance with a credit for ongoing reclamation efforts. This was to encourage reclamation not only on lands being currently mined but also on those mined in the past (96).

A Pandora's Box opened as mining companies sought permits to open new mines in 1973 and 1974 as demand for phosphate increased sharply and exceeded existing capacities. Counties, the State, and the Federal Government all got into the permit-granting act. Counties required zoning permits, approval of master plans, and the granting of operating and building permits. The State assessed the regional impact and required and issued permits for air quality, industrial waste waters, dredge and fill, drainage wells, dam construction, potable water supply, and sanitary wastes. The Water Management District required permits on consumptive water use, water well construction, and management of storage and surface waters. The State Department of Natural Resources was involved in reclamation standards. At the Federal level, EPA was involved in water quality permits and air quality standards while the Army Corps of Engineers issued dredge and fill permits and dam construction permits on waters of the United States. Environmental impact statements were required to meet the National Environmental Policy Act. With all of the various permits that had to be obtained and the often overlapping requirements that had to be met, the phosphate companies found that several years and considerable expenditures were required to get a new mine in operation. Mine openings as a result were delayed or suspended (36, 96, 98).

Other phosphate mining states, with the possible exception of North Carolina, had fewer environmental problems to cope with partly because they had fewer mines and they generally were not in heavily populated areas.

North Carolina Phosphate

One of the most potentially important phosphate deposits in the United States was opened in 1966 when production began at Texas Gulf Sulphur's Lee Creek mine in Beaufort County, North Carolina. As in north Florida, presence of phosphate deposits in North Carolina had been known since before 1890. These occurred in a belt containing scattered, uneconomic deposits extending inland about 25 miles from the coast all the way from the South Carolina border northeastward to the Neuse River. About 25,000 tons had been mined in the 1890's, but the rock could not compete with either the South Carolina or the Florida rock. The northern edge of these deposits on the Neuse River was only about 30 miles southwest of the Pamlico River where the major new deposit was located (Chapter 3).

Studies by the U.S. Geological Survey in Beaufort and Hyde Counties in 1957 disclosed extensive phosphate rock deposits. Phosphate-bearing sands containing 8 to 31 percent P_2O_5 ranging from a few feet to 90 feet in thickness were found under an overburden ranging from 45 to 250 feet in depth. The deposits extended over an area of about 450 square miles from the south shore of the Pamlico River into Hyde County, apparently an old basin. Several companies immediately became interested in the area, but only Texas Gulf Sulphur Company proceeded with the development of a mine and phosphate complex (85).

The Texas Gulf Sulphur mine lies under water at Lee Creek. It has a 100-foot-thick overburden. The mining procedure is similar to that used in the Florida pebble fields except that a 30-inch hydraulic dredge removes the upper 40 feet of overburden. A 72-cubic-yard dragline and a 45-cubic-yard dragline are used to strip the remaining overburden and to mine the 40-foot-thick pebble matrix. A small dragline is used to move the matrix to the sluice pit (98).

Capacity of the mine in the mid-1970's was 3.5 million tons of material; annual increases took capacity to 5 million tons by 1980. Shipments of phosphate rock began in the spring of 1966. The phosphate complex produces 54 percent wet-process phosphoric acid, superphosphoric acid, diammonium phosphate, concentrated superphosphate, feed-grade phosphate, and sulfuric acid. Although Texas Gulf Sulphur (later Texasgulf, Inc.) uses most of its rock and phosphate products internally, the Lee Creek location near the coast is favorable for exports to western Europe (18, 97, 98).

More than 90 percent of the total phosphate rock exported from the United States in recent years has been Florida and North Carolina pebble. To expedite marketing of the huge tonnages of rock involved in the export market, the Phosphate Rock Export Association (Phosrock) was formed in 1971 with headquarters at Tampa. Original members were Agrico, American Cyanamid, W. R. Grace, International Minerals and Chemical, and Occidental Chemical (95).

Beneficiated rock not used in fertilizer manufacture within or near the central pebble district was shipped by rail to terminals at Tampa and Boca Grande for both overseas export and for transport to fertilizer plants on the inland waterways. Rock also was shipped directly by rail from the beneficiation plants to fertilizer plants elsewhere in Florida and the eastern United States. Practically all of the domestic use of Florida phosphate in the 1970's was for fertilizer manufacture; only 1 or 2 percent went to industrial uses and 0.6 percent into defluorinated animal feeds (96, 97, 98, 99).

Tennessee Phosphate Rock

The Tennessee phosphate rock industry during the 1920-1980 period was characterized by uncertainty. During the 1920's about 90 percent

Equipment used by Texas Gulf to mine phosphate in North Carolina. *(Texas Gulf Chemicals)*

of the phosphate mined was brown rock coming mostly from Williamson and Maury Counties. The remainder was blue rock coming largely from an underground mine in Lewis County operated by the Charleston (South Carolina) Mining and Manufacturing Company (later renamed Charleston Mining Company). Blue rock mining ceased in 1937. A small amount of white rock was mined in Perry County by a power shovel for the Tennessee Valley Authority in 1934; it was barged on the Tennessee River to Muscle Shoals. After 1937 all mining was confined to brown rock, but by 1940 the good quality rock was exhausted (31).

Tennessee phosphate rock production from 1921 through 1936 vacillated from 300,000 to 700,000 tons of material annually except for the worst depression year of 1932 when it fell to 216,000 tons (72). Thereafter, production climbed slowly but steadily, reaching around 3 million tons in 1970 and then declining rapidly during the remainder of the 1970's (7, 32, 40, 42, 43).

Mining Brown Rock

The spotty occurrence of the brown rock deposits along with variations in thickness of the matrix and the frequent presence of limestone outcrops made mining much more costly and difficult than in the Florida pebble field. Mining of brown rock during the 1920-1980 period centered largely around use of small draglines having bucket capacities of 2 or 3 cubic yards and booms 50 to 75 feet long. The overburden averaged about 8 feet in thickness and the ore about 6 feet, although variations of both occurred, ranging up to about 20 feet maximum. During the earlier part of the period, where the matrix was thin or limestone outcropped, ore was removed by pick and shovel. (Also in the early 1930's TVA paid farmers to dig or pick up phosphate lumps and boulders from their farms and deliver them to collection points. This failed since farming and mining didn't mix.) The mined matrix usually was transported to washers by truck or rail, although in some cases it was pumped to the washer as a slurry (31, 64, 98).

Waning Brown Rock and Attempts at Beneficiation

When it became apparent that high-grade brown phosphate rock was rapidly approaching exhaustion and that flotation of the brown rock was not working out as hoped, it appeared that mining of brown rock was doomed to an early end. The grade of the ore was too low; the amounts of impurities, especially iron and aluminum, too high; and beneficiation too costly to compete with Florida pebble for use in superphosphate manufacture.

Considerable effort and research were devoted to increasing the grade of the mined brown rock to meet market demands as the high-grade ore became depleted. A good part of this was directed to the use of flotation which was not highly successful since the degree that brown rock could be upgraded did not justify the extra expense. The Phosphate Recovery Corporation that had built two flotation plants in Florida installed its third plant at Wales, Tennessee, in 1931; another was built at Mt. Pleasant, but both plants were abandoned. The double-flotation process also proved uneconomical on the lower grade brown rock ores. Consequently, brown rock producers relied upon washing, screening, and hydro-separation to upgrade the ore, Although this was inadequate for producing phosphatic fertilizer materials by acidulation, such ores were satisfactory for use in electric furnaces.

The coming of the electric furnaces greatly extended the life of Tennessee phosphate rock production. TVA constructed an improved beneficiation plant (but did not include flotation) in 1942 to upgrade some medium-grade ores in the Bear Creek area in Maury County for use in its electric furnaces at Muscle Shoals, Alabama. However, when the ore in the Bear Creek area was exhausted nine years later, the agency sold the lower grade ores of its remaining reserves. Instead, it turned to upgrading the unbeneficiated brown rock with high-grade phosphate rock shipped from Florida to Muscle Shoals. This practice was continued by TVA until its last furnace was closed in 1976 (2, 31, 49, 64). (TVA eventually sold its reserves remaining in Maury and Williamson Counties at public auction to furnace producers still active in the area.)

Electric Phosphorus Furnaces Become Important

The first electric phosphorus furnaces in the United States were built at Niagara Falls in 1896. However, they were not commercially important until the 1920's when the Federal Phosphorus Company (Swann Corporation from 1932-1935) at Anniston, Alabama, developed a number of useful and profitable compounds from furnace-grade phosphoric acid. T. Swann, owner of Federal Phosphorus, planned as early as 1931 to build furnaces in the brown rock field in Tennessee, but the depression and a developing merger with the Monsanto Chemical Company delayed the move. The Monsanto Company, which took over the Swann Corporation, built a sinter plant near Columbia in 1935 to serve the Anniston furnaces and then in 1937 installed three 8,000-kilowatt furnaces also at Columbia.

Meanwhile the newly-formed TVA decided to use furnaces to produce high-analysis phosphate fertilizers and also serve national defense needs for elemental phosphorus. The agency began buying brown rock in 1934 and shipping it to Muscle Shoals 60 miles away. By 1941 TVA was operating four furnaces at Muscle Shoals; Monsanto, four at Columbia; and Victor Chemical Works, four at Mt. Pleasant. In 1945, 51 percent of the marketable production of Tennessee rock was used in electric furnaces. Over 24 electric furnaces were being operated in the United States by seven producers in 1951 with the greater share of their phosphate coming from the brown rock field (1, 2, 47).

Major factors responsible for the rapid increase in electric furnace use had been first the presence of low-cost electricity in the brown rock area furnished by TVA, and in the West by electricity generated entirely from hydropower; and second, the ability of the furnaces to economically use low-grade, less-costly phosphate rock high in silica and other impurities. Low-grade rock was processed close to the mine to avoid high shipping costs. The presence of silica was a definite advantage since it along with coke was essential for a reaction of the following type to take place in the furnace:

$$Ca_3(PO_4)_2 + SiO_2 + C \rightarrow CaSiO_2 + P_2 + CO$$

The industrial products of high purity that could be produced from phosphoric acid derived from elemental phosphorus brought much higher prices and yielded greater profits than when used in fertilizers.

Companies Operating in the Brown Rock Field

In 1928, 14 companies were operating in Tennessee, employing about 1,000 people. These were American Agricultural Chemicals mining at Spring Hill; Armour Fertilizer Works mining near Columbia; Charleston (S.C.) Mining and Manufacturing Company with mines at Gordonsburg and Mt. Pleasant; J. K. Davis mine near Mt. Pleasant; Federal Chemical Company with mines at Southport, Century, and Ridley; Harsh Phosphate Company mine near Nashville; Hoover and Mason Phosphate

Company mine at Mt. Pleasant; International Agricultural Corporation mines at Mt. Pleasant and Wales; J. J. Jones mine at Mt. Pleasant; S. T. Jones mine at Mt. Pleasant; W. A. Kittrell Company mine at Mt. Pleasant; Ligon and Huff mine at Mt. Pleasant; and New England Phosphate Corporation mine at Twomey. Most of the phosphate rock went into the manufacture of normal superphosphate at plants near points of use in the Tennessee, the adjoining states, the Midwest, and inland states to the east. Tennessee in 1928 also provided over 40,000 tons for direct application to the soil. About 21,000 tons was sold to increase the phosphorus content of pig iron produced in blast furnaces, and some went into poultry and livestock feeds and into fillers for fertilizers (52).

Eight companies and TVA were mining in Tennessee in 1950, all in the brown rock field. These were the Armour Fertilizer Works mining at Columbia; Federal Chemical Company at Mt. Pleasant; Harsh Phosphate Company at Nashville; Hoover and Mason Phosphate Company at Mt. Pleasant; International Minerals and Chemical Corporation at Columbia; Monsanto Chemical Company at Columbia; Owens Agricultural Phosphate Corporation at Centerville; TVA, near Columbia; and Virginia-Carolina Chemical Corporation (formerly Charleston Mining Company which merged in 1942 with Virginia-Carolina Chemical Corporation) at Mt. Pleasant (56).

Direct application of phosphate peaked in the early 1950's at more than 1 million tons per year, mostly from Tennessee. Illinois used about half the total, followed by Missouri.

Of those mining in 1950, only Armour, Monsanto, and TVA were still mining in 1967. New mining companies were Hooker Chemical Company, Mobil Chemical Company which had acquired Virginia-Carolina Chemical, Stauffer Chemical which had taken over Victor Chemical Works, and the Presnell Phosphate Company. The continuing shift to nonagricultural uses based on electric furnace phosphorus was increasingly apparent. In 1960, 90 percent of the rock was going into nonagricultural uses. Of the remainder going into agriculture, 6 percent went into superphosphates and 3 percent was used for direct application. In 1971, all of the brown rock produced went into the electric furnaces of which only the 5 percent consumed by TVA furnaces went into fertilizer production (33, 40, 41, 95).

Brown rock production, which had peaked at around 3.2 million tons in 1970, declined to 2.3 million tons in 1975, and to 1.9 million in 1980. The sharp fall in the 1970's was due largely to the decline in use of sodium tripolyphosphate in detergents brought about by tightening water quality controls. Only four companies were mining in Tennessee in 1980: Hooker Chemical Company, owned by Occidental Chemical Corporation; Monsanto Chemical Company; Stauffer Chemical; and Presnell Phosphate Company (8, 95, 96).

Western Phosphate Rock

Status of Mining Prior to 1920

Western phosphate rock, mined sparingly since 1906 in southeastern Idaho and adjoining areas in Utah and Wyoming (Chapter 3), never exceeded 20,000 long tons of material in any one year prior to 1920. At the start of 1920 only two companies were operating; the San Francisco Chemical Company was working the Waterloo mine at Montpelier, Idaho, and P. B. and R. S. Bradley of Boston was mining in Rich County, Utah (94). However, 1920 saw a spurt in demand for western rock; prices soared one-third in a year's time and sales increased 230 percent. This was due in part to a high water freight rate on Florida rock shipped to the west coast that had been placed in effect to discourage ocean shipment during World War I but had not been repealed. Western rock as a result became competitive on the Hawaiian and Japanese markets and moved into these markets.

Mining Activities:1920-1950

The Anaconda Copper Mining Company in Anaconda, Montana, began buying Idaho phosphate rock for conversion to concentrated superphosphate as a way to utilize sulfuric acid derived from its smelter fumes. To meet the sudden increase in rock demand, two additional companies began mining in 1920. Others entered the field in 1921, bringing the total to eight in Idaho and one in Montana. However, the high water rates from Florida to the west coast were repealed, and western production fell from 62,000 tons in 1920 to 7,000 in 1921 and to 5,000 in 1922. Most of the companies dropped out of the entire western field by 1922 (68). Those remaining were the San Francisco Chemical Company at Montpelier, the Anaconda Copper Mining Company at Conda, Idaho (near Soda Springs), and the small Lakesville Phosphate Company near Cokesville, Wyoming (89).

A decision of Anaconda to mine its own phosphate was a major event affecting the development of the western deposits. The original intention was to establish a mine in Montana but no suitable deposits were found. As a result, the company in 1919 and 1920 purchased claims held by the Southern California Orange Grove Fertilizer Company in Caribou County, Idaho, just east of Soda Springs. Underground development began in 1921, a railroad spur was constructed, a townsite laid out, and a crushing plant was built. Rock was shipped by rail to Anaconda, Montana, where the superphosphate plant was constructed. Anaconda for years was the largest phosphate miner in Idaho, greatly increasing its production in 1931. Besides wet-process phosphoric acid, the company produced concentrated superphosphate and some ammonium phosphates. The concentrated products were necessary to hold down freight costs to the distant using areas. Anaconda's Idaho mine was operated until 1959 when it was sold to the J. R. Simplot Company (89).

Although a small amount of phosphate had been mined in Montana in the early 1920's, sustained production was not achieved until 1930 when the Dissett Brothers started mining near Phillipsburg, and the Montana Phosphate Products of Trail, British Columbia, near Garrison. The total output of these two mines was shipped to the Consolidated Mining and Smelting Company (Cominco) at Trail. Like the Anaconda Company, Cominco had a large supply of sulfuric acid from its smelting operations and, in order to dispose of it, went into production of concentrated superphosphate. The Trail, British Columbia, outlet was consuming a large part of the western rock production by 1931. Cominco obtained some of its rock from Idaho through a subsidiary, Solar Development Company, near Paris for 4 years starting in 1930. Most of its rock came from Montana, either purchased from independent miners or mined by Cominco subsidiaries. Its largest producing subsidiary was the Montana Products Company, which for several years in the early 1940's was the largest phosphate rock miner in the West (54, 55, 56, 90).

The San Francisco Chemical Company, which had operated its Waterloo mine at Montpelier steadily from 1907, closed the mine in 1929. From 1930 through 1944 the company mined no phosphate but in 1945 started development on an open pit mine at the same location. The mine was operated until the rock supply was exhausted in 1958. The company then took over a number of old patent claims under private ownership on phosphate lands astride the Wyoming-Utah line in Lincoln County, Wyoming, and Rich County, Utah. These properties were near the Union Pacific Railroad junction of Sage, Wyoming. The company began development of an open pit mine on the Leefe group of claims in the Beckworth Hills on the Wyoming side of the line and transferred its main operations from the Waterloo mine to this site. Production began in 1947. The San Francisco Company also mined and processed rock from a number of other locations in north-central Utah and adjacent Wyoming. In addition to the Leefe mine, two others were of significant importance: the Cherokee mine in Rich County, Utah, which opened in 1957, and the Vernal mine in Uintah County, Utah, which opened in 1961 (60, 90).

The J. R. Simplot Fertilizer Company operated a government-financed concentrated superphosphate plant at Pocatello, Idaho, during World War II and purchased the plant in 1946. The wartime plant used phosphate rock produced by the San Francisco Chemical Company at its Waterloo mine. Simplot also opened the Gay mine on the Fort Hall Indian Reservation 16 miles from the Pocatello plant in 1946. The existence of the Fort Hall deposits apparently was discovered by G. R. Mansfield of the U.S. Geological Survey in 1920. Most of the deposits were leased to the Simplot company and the FMC Corporation which through its Westvaco subsidiary operated an electric furnace at Pocatello; Simplot did the mining for both companies. The Gay mine was to become the highest producing mine in Idaho. Simplot used the high-grade rock from the mine to manufacture fertilizers and the low-grade shales by Westvaco to feed its furnaces (56, 67, 88).

Seven companies were mining phosphate in the Western States in 1950. They were J. R. Simplot at Fort Hall, Idaho; Anaconda Copper Mining Company at Conda, Idaho; the Montana Phosphate Products Company operating several mines in the Garrison district, Montana; George Relyea, Garrison district; Anderson Bros. Mining Company, Garrison district; Pearl and Toland Phosphate Company, Rich County, Utah; and the San Francisco Chemical Company, Sage, Wyoming (56). Marketable production in 1950 from the Idaho mines was 642,000 tons and from mines in Montana was 235,000 tons. Together these amounted to about 10 percent of the U.S. total (72).

The Gay mine, opened on the Fort Hall Indian Reservation in 1946, was to become the largest producing mine in Idaho. This photograph is from the early 1950's.
(J.R. Simplot Company)

Mining Activities: 1950-1980

In the 1960's, Stauffer Chemical Company, which had earlier taken over the Victor Chemical Works furnace at Silver Bow, Montana, acquired the properties of San Francisco Chemical Company mines in Wyoming and Utah as well as Victor's mines in Montana. Stauffer also had taken over the Garfield, Utah, phosphate complex from Western Phosphates, Inc., and mines in Utah and Wyoming that supplied the complex with phosphate rock (90).

Central Farmers Fertilizer Company (later CF Industries), a midwestern cooperative, through TVA's activities became sold on calcium metaphosphate fertilizer produced using electric furnaces. The cooperative in the 1950's built a furnace in Georgetown Canyon, Idaho, and engaged in developing a mine. Plans were changed to produce concentrated superphosphate instead of calcium metaphosphate from the furnace phosphorus. Production got underway in 1959 but the plant was shut down in 1963. The El Paso Products Company bought up the co-op's Georgetown Canyon facilities and equipment and moved most of the plant facilities to Conda, except for the furnace and related buildings which were abandoned. El Paso developed a mine in Maybie Canyon, the leases of which had been acquired from Central Farmers, to supply the Conda complex (based on wet-process phosphoric acid) with phosphate, and in 1965 an open-pit mine was placed in operation. El Paso Products dropped its Idaho activities in 1967 when fertilizer production became unprofitable due to overcapacity. Beker Industries acquired the Conda complex from El Paso Products and also the assets of the Mountain Fuel Supply Company which included a mine in Dry Valley. The Beker subsidiary, Agricultural Products Corporation, began production in 1972 (32, 66, 90, 101).

The Monsanto Company, another major phosphate miner in the West, processed all of its rock for use in electric furnaces and opened its first western furnace at Soda Springs, Idaho, in 1952. The company's Ballard mine, an open-pit mine located near Soda Springs, was developed solely to meet the needs of the company's furnaces which had increased in number and size over the years. To meet the growing needs, a second mine was located in the Wooley Range north of the Ballard mine near Henry, Idaho. The ore was trucked to Soda Springs for processing (90).

Mining Methods—In recent years, except for a couple of small underground mines in Montana, only open pits have been used in mining western rock. The western open-pit mining differs considerably from that practiced in Florida, North Carolina, and Tennessee. The sedimentary deposits in the West are variously faulted and folded, and are usually inclined. As a result, most of the mines in Idaho use scrapers and bulldozers to remove overburden and to mine the ore-except for one where power shovels are used. Also in Idaho, phosphate ore suitable for the manufacture of wet-process phosphoric acid (31-32 percent P_2O_5) is separated from the lower grade shales (24-26 percent P_2O_5) suitable for use in electric furnaces. In Utah, the rock is surface mined after the overlying limestone cap is blasted and removed. In the underground mines in Montana the ore is broken up within the mine and then removed by chutes which slope downhill and serve as outlet tunnels to the surface. All western rocks are moved by truck or rail to the processing plants. Rock going into wet-process acid plants is calcined to reduce the hydrocarbon content; shales going into electric furnaces are nodulized (76, 88, 98).

Phosphate Fertilizer Complexes—Phosphate fertilizer complexes based on western rock were mostly located at ore smelting sites, some at a considerable distance from the phosphate mines, where SO_2 was being recovered and converted to sulfuric acid primarily to abate a severe air pollution problem. The production of the phosphate fertilizers thus became a way to dispose of the sulfuric acid and hopefully to realize some profits as a result. Besides the Anaconda complex near Butte, Montana, and the Cominco complex at Trail, British Columbia, the Bunker Hill Company developed a phosphate complex in 1964 near Kellogg, Idaho, in the northern part of the state to use sulfuric acid produced as a by-product of its zinc smelter operation. A complex built at Garfield, Utah, used sulfuric acid produced at Garfield from copper smelting. The fertilizer complex was initially operated by Western Phosphates, Inc., but was later acquired by Stauffer which used rock from its mines in Utah and Wyoming. Two complexes apparently not tied to by-product sulfuric acid were the J. R. Simplot Company operation at Pocatello, Idaho, using rock from its nearby mine at Fort Hall, and the El Paso Products complex built in 1964 at Conda, Idaho, also using rock from its nearby mine. The latter complex was taken over by Beker Industries in 1972 (32, 33, 41, 44, 90, 95).

Western rock increasingly was consumed in electric phosphorus furnaces following the first furnace operation by Westvaco Chemical Division of the Food Machinery & Chemical Corporation at Pocatello in 1949 until 1970 when the market for furnace phosphate in detergents decreased. Low-cost hydropower, a plentiful supply of inexpensive high silica phosphate shales, and the low cost (per unit of P_2O_5 equivalent) of shipping elemental phosphorus long distances by rail to industrial customers encouraged furnace use. In 1956, eight furnaces were in operation and by 1969 well over one-third of the Nation's total elemental phosphorus capacity was based on western rock. Companies operating furnaces in the western rock mining areas in 1969 were the FMC Corporation (Westvaco) at Pocatello; Monsanto at Soda Springs; and Stauffer at Silver Bow, Montana (33, 41, 90, 95).

End Uses of Western Rock—End uses of western rock changed considerably over the years. Prior to 1945, 95 percent of the mined rock was used to make fertilizers, primarily superphosphates. With the coming of the electric furnaces in response to the increasing demand of the highly profitable nonagricultural products, tonnages of phosphate rock going into industrial uses increased materially. By 1955, only 38 percent of the total marketable western rock consumed domestically went into agricultural uses (practically all into fertilizers) as compared with 62 percent going into industrial uses. However, in 1971, industrial uses peaked at 65 percent of the total phosphate rock marketed, and by 1975 they had fallen to 58 percent (8, 99).

Companies mining phosphate rock in Idaho during 1980 were the Beker Industries at Dry Valley, Monsanto Industrial Chemicals Company at Henry, J. R. Simplot Company at Fort Hall, and Stauffer Chemical Company at Wooley Valley. In Montana, the only company mining was Cominco-American, Inc., at Garrison. Stauffer Chemical was operating only at Vernal, Utah, having discontinued its operation at Leefe, Wyoming, in 1978 (8, 99).

Sulfur and Sulfuric Acid Production

Although sulfur is a plant nutrient and is used in one form or another to overcome sulfur deficiencies, its main use in the fertilizer field is as a raw material to manufacture sulfuric acid for use in making phosphatic fertilizers. The fertilizer industry thus has been the Nation's major consumer of sulfuric acid throughout the 1920-1980 period. Sulfuric acid accounted for about 75 percent of the domestic sulfur consumption from all sources during the 1920 to 1955 period, 80 percent in 1960, and 85 percent in the 1970's. Consumption of all forms of sulfuric acid was about 4 million short tons in the 1920's, 14 million in 1950, 30 million in 1970, and 43 million in the late 1970's (8, 35, 43).

Fertilizers have used proportionately more of the Nation's sulfuric acid production as time advanced, growing from 25 to 35 percent in the 1920's and 1930's to 38 percent in 1950, 43 percent in 1960, and around 60 percent in the 1970's. Prior to the 1950's practically all sulfuric acid going into fertilizers was used to produce normal superphosphate and ammonium sulfate. The establishment of wet-process phosphoric acid as an important intermediate in the manufacture of phosphatic fertilizers by 1960 soon eliminated normal superphosphate as an important user of sulfuric acid. Concentrated superphosphate by 1965 had replaced normal superphosphate as the major source of P_2O_5. Although concentrated superphosphate remained an important phosphatic fertilizer it did not increase greatly in tonnage. The leading materials by far were the ammonium phosphates, including diammonium phosphate, which increased strongly in the mid-1960's. Phosphoric acid as the intermediate grew from 1.3 million tons of P_2O_5 equivalent in 1960 to 10 million in 1980. By the late 1970's, phosphatic fertilizers were using 61 percent of the total domestic production of sulfuric acid and ammonium sulfate 1 percent (7, 8, 43, 62, 63).

Advances in Sulfuric Acid Manufacture

The old lead chamber process that dominated sulfuric acid manufacture in this country prior to 1920 (Chapter 4) gradually gave way to the simpler, less costly contact process. In 1921, chamber-produced acid amounted to 2 million short tons of 100 percent H_2SO_4 equivalent while contact plants produced only 686,000 tons. Chamber acid peaked in 1929 at 3.3 million tons and by the early 1930's contact production exceeded that from the chamber process (7, 8, 43, 46).

The slow demise of the chamber process was due to the fact that existing chamber plants were well suited for producing acid from SO_2 obtained by roasting pyrites or the smelting of nonferrous ores. Most superphosphate manufacturers making their own acid stayed with the process longer than producers for nonfertilizer uses since the more concentrated, pure contact acid was of little or no advantage in normal superphosphate manufacture. Besides, the old chamber plants were fully depreciated. In 1938, 60 plants were producing acid solely by the contact process, 91 solely by the chamber, and 10 plants using both processes. About 70 of the 91 plants devoted solely to the chamber process were operated by fertilizer companies–only 3 or 4 of which had contact plants. After World War II, contact plants increased both in size and numbers. Few chamber plants were in operation after 1960 and chamber acid disappeared entirely in 1977 (46, 71, 83, 102).

The introduction and use of vanadium catalysts in contact plants in the mid-1920's for promoting the reaction of SO_2 with oxygen to form SO_3 was a major technological advance in sulfuric acid manufacture. The vanadium catalysts were rugged and less subject to poisoning, which greatly simplified gas purification. As a result, they reduced both capital and operating costs.

The use of vanadium as a catalyst was first proposed by R. Meyers in Germany in 1899, and the basic patents were issued to de Haen in 1901 and 1902. Badische Analin und Soda Fabrik in Germany in 1915 apparently produced the first effective vanadium catalyst for the contact process. The Monsanto Company produced, used, and marketed the first catalyst in this country. A year or so later the Selden Company produced a commercial vanadium catalyst, followed by the Chemical Construction Company. After 1925, vanadium catalysts gradually replaced platinum catalysts in contact plants (34).

Sources of Sulfur

The relative importance of various sources of sulfur used in the manufacture of sulfuric acid shifted greatly during the 1920-1980 period as indicated in Table 7.3. Pyrites, which had been a major source up until about 1915, decreased steadily in importance. Frasch-process elemental sulfur provided 85 percent or more of the total sulfur produced from all sources through 1950, but declined to 74 percent in 1970, and then fell sharply. By 1979, recovered elemental sulfur and sulfur from by-product sulfuric acid were gaining in importance. Imports of Frasch sulfur from Mexico became substantial after 1970, as did recovered elemental sulfur from Canada in the mid-1960's. By 1979, Frasch sulfur consumption in the United States was 49 percent of the total from all sources, recovered elemental sulfur 39 percent, pyrites 3 percent, by-product sulfuric acid 8 percent, and other forms 1 percent (92).

Frasch Sulfur—Sulfur mined in the United States by the Frasch method was limited to sulfur-bearing salt domes in the Gulf Coast areas of Louisiana and Texas until mining began on the west Texas evaporite basin deposits in the late 1960's. U.S. imports from Frasch-mined Mexican salt dome deposits on the Isthmus of Tehuantepec began in the 1950's.

Three mines were operating in the Gulf Coast area at the beginning of the 1920's (Chapter 3). These were Frasch's original Sulphur Mine in Louisiana which came into preliminary production in 1895, Freeport Sulphur Company's Bryanmound mine in Texas opened in 1912, and Texas Gulf Sulphur Company's Big Hill mine that opened in 1919. Sulphur Mine, still operated by Frasch's original Union Sulphur Company, was rapidly approaching exhaustion. The vision of tight sulfur supplies and higher prices, along with the fact that the Frasch patents had expired, resulted in a rush by companies, including Union Sulphur, to find new domes containing sulfur. It soon became apparent that not many salt domes had sulfur deposits and of these only a few were commercially desirable. Once steaming began, it became apparent that the Frasch process did not work equally well on all domes. Between 1924 and 1928, 64 previously unknown salt domes were discovered but only four had deposits worthy of commercial development (45, 78).

Although at least a dozen companies at one time or another mined Frasch sulfur in Texas and Louisiana, only four were active over most of the 1920-1980 period–Texas Gulf Sulphur Company, Freeport Sulphur Company, Duval Texas Sulphur Company, and the Jefferson Lake Sulphur Company. Each underwent modifications of the corporate name as well as changes in ownership. Texas Gulf Sulphur, however, got through without change until the 1970's when it became Texasgulf, Inc. Texas Gulf operated almost entirely in Texas while Freeport concentrated mostly in Louisiana. The Duval Texas Sulphur Company,

Table 7.3. U.S. Sulfur Production, Exports, Imports, and Consumption (72, 75, 54, 56, 63, 73, 92).

	1920	1930	1940	1950	1960	1970	1979
Frasch Sulfur			*1,000 long tons of S*				
Production	1,278	2,605	2,774	5,193	5,037	7,082	6,257
Exports	486	620	780	1,505	1,819	1,459	1,963
Imports	-	-	-	-	590	539	1,129
Recovered							
Production	-	-	-	142	767	1,457	4,006
Imports	-	-	-	-	138	1,016	1,267
Pyrites							
Production	126	126	266	393	416	339	400
Imports	156	178	195	92	149	133	-
By-product sulfuric acid							
Production	286	275	194	216	345	537	1,167
Total U.S. production	1,691	3,006	3,235	5,986	6,661	9,557	11,910

organized in the 1920's, became Duval Corporation in 1963 and became a subsidiary of Pennzoil in 1966. Duval operated entirely in the Gulf Coast area of Texas until 1968 when the company also began mining sulfur in west Texas. Duval abandoned the Gulf Coast in the early 1970's and concentrated in west Texas where it operated the huge Culbertson (Rustler Hills) mine. The Jefferson Lake Sulphur Company (originally Jefferson Lake Oil Company) was formed in 1932. It was taken over by the Occidental Petroleum Corporation in 1964 but retained the Jefferson Lake name. Jefferson Lake operated in both Texas and Louisiana. Frasch's Union Sulphur Company, failing to find another productive sulfur deposit, dropped out of the sulfur business and became Union Texas Oil Company (3, 16, 62, 63, 73).

Severe upturns and downturns struck the Frasch sulfur industry in the mid-1960's as they did most other fertilizer and related industries. From 1959 through 1964 prices remained low, around $20 per ton, and production bottomed out at around 5 million tons annually. As demand improved and prices rose rapidly to $40 per ton by 1968, production increased to 7.4 million tons. At first production was increased through minimum plant investments; however, as prices continued to rise, more was produced from the less efficient domes by increasing the amount of hot water per ton of sulfur removed. New domes that were considered marginal were opened and old domes that had been abandoned due to increasing operating costs were reopened. With optimism high as to the future of fertilizers as a result of the Green Revolution, it appeared that high prices and profits from Frasch sulfur would go on forever and oil companies entered the field as they did in other fertilizer-related activities generally. In addition to Pennzoil's and Occidental Petroleum's taking over two of the long-time producers, Union Texas Petroleum, Atlantic Richfield Company, Pan American Petroleum, and John H. Phelan Oil Company all became involved in Frasch mining. Frasch production rose from 4.9 million long tons in 1963 to 7.5 million tons in 1968 (7, 20, 73, 91).

Sulfur prices declined from the 1968 peak of $40 to $24 per ton in 1970 and to $17.50 in 1972 (92). Producers had no choice but to try to overcome the oversupply situation. The strategy was to concentrate on the larger, more efficient mines and close the others. Many companies dropped out during the adjustment period. At the beginning of 1970, eight companies were operating 19 mines as follows: Texas Gulf Sulphur, eight mines in the Texas Gulf Coast area; Freeport Sulphur, four mines in Louisiana; Jefferson Lake, one in Louisiana; Duval, three in Texas, two of which were in west Texas; Union Texas Petroleum, one in Louisiana; U.S. Oil of Louisiana, one in Louisiana; Atlantic Richfield, one in west Texas; and Pan American Petroleum, one in west Texas. By the end of 1970, five mines had gone out of production and one company had left the field. Total production during the year was 7.1 million tons (73). By 1975, only five companies were active although 13 mines remained in production. These were Texasgulf Inc., with one mine in Louisiana and five in the Gulf Coast area of Texas; Freeport Minerals with four in Louisiana; Jefferson Lake, with one in Louisiana; Duval, with one in west Texas; and Atlantic Richfield with one in the new west Texas field. Total production was 7.2 million tons, mostly from the 11 mines operated by Duval, Freeport, and Texasgulf (7, 20, 91).

Natural gas, used in the Frasch process to heat water for extraction of the sulfur from underground deposits, came into short supply in the early 1970's, and prices escalated from around 30 cents per thousand cubic feet to 60 cents in 1975 and to around $2.00 in 1980. This adversely affected the Frasch industry and its customers, since about 1,000 gallons of heated water is required to extract a ton of sulfur even under favorable mining conditions and considerably more under less favorable conditions. Sulfur prices increased from $17.50 per ton in 1972 to $42 in 1975 and to $54 in 1979, due largely, at least in the later years, to the increase in natural gas prices. Frasch production fell from a peak of 7.9 million tons in 1974 to 5.6 million in 1978 as producers closed inefficient mines. From 1976 to 1978 four mines were closed. The tonnage climbed to 6.3 million in 1979 and 1980 (8, 28, 92).

In 1979, five companies were operating eight mines: Texasgulf with three mines in the Gulf Coast area of Texas; Freeport with two in Louisiana; Jefferson Lake with one in the Texas Gulf Coast; Duval in west Texas with the largest sulfur mine in the world; and Farmland, operating the former Atlantic Richfield mine in west Texas. Production in 1979 was 3.9 million tons from Texas and 2.5 million from Louisiana (92).

Major Gulf Coast Mines—Some 330 salt domes have been identified on the Gulf Coast of Texas and Louisiana, but only about 30 have produced sulfur commercially. Only 18 have yielded more than 1 million long tons of sulfur (6). Producing capability, costs of production per ton of sulfur, and length of effective life vary greatly among the producing domes, some of which are described below.

Sulphur Mine dome, the original Frasch mine in Calcasieu Parish, Louisiana (Chapter 3), was operated by the Union Sulphur Company from 1895 until 1924, producing more than 9.4 million long tons of sulfur. The dome in its last few years as it approached exhaustion had become less profitable to operate. However, in 1966, Union Texas Oil Company, the successor of Union Sulphur after it ceased mining sulfur, resteamed the dome and resumed production. The output was erratic and costly and operation ceased in February 1970 (20, 45, 73).

Bryanmound near Freeport, Texas, was found to contain sulfur during exploration for oil in 1905. Freeport Sulphur Company was formed in 1912 to exploit the dome. It remained in production from 1912 through 1935, producing 5 million tons of sulfur (45).

Big Hill (later renamed Gulf Dome) in Matagordo County, Texas, was the third Frasch mine to come into operation. Sulfur was noted during exploration for oil in the early 1900's. The Gulf Sulphur Company eventually was formed to develop the discovery, but progress was slow until World War I when the U.S. Government urged completion of the project. In 1918, the company name was changed to Texas Gulf Sulphur Company. Production began in 1919 and continued without interruption until 1932 with a total production of 12 million tons. The mine was operated briefly in 1936 by Texas Gulf Sulphur and again from 1965 to 1970 with limited production (45, 73).

Hoskins Mound in Brazoria County, Texas, had been variously drilled for oil before the Texas Coast Development Company located an extensive deposit of sulfur. Not interested in mining the sulfur, the Texas Coast company negotiated its sulfur rights to Freeport Sulphur. Mining began in 1923, but difficulties encountered in removal of the sulfur were not solved until 1927. Mining at Hoskins Mound ceased in 1955 with a total production of 10.8 million tons (46, 74).

Boling Dome, 60 miles southwest of Houston, was destined to become one of the most productive sulfur mines in the world. It was discovered in 1922 by a small oil driller, the Gulf Production Company. It was first

Aerial view of the Caminada sulfur mine of Freeport Sulphur. It is about eight miles off the Louisiana coast in 50 feet of water. *(Freeport Sulphur Company)*

steamed for sulfur by the Union Sulphur Company in 1928 in its search for a new mine to replace Sulphur Mine, but such small tonnages were produced that the company dropped the project. Texas Gulf Sulphur took over the deposit in 1929, and it was still being mined by the company (now Texasgulf, Inc.) in 1980, by which time it had produced 77.8 million tons of sulfur (28, 45, 74, 79).

Grande Ecaille dome was buried under the tidal marshes of the Mississippi River Delta about 40 miles south of New Orleans in an area frequented mostly by mosquitoes and snakes. It was explored by a consortium of oil companies with the Humble Oil Company doing the drilling. A considerable deposit of sulfur was found and the sulfur rights were sold to Freeport Sulphur. Freeport began mining in 1933 after solving unusual problems not previously encountered in Frasch mining. A canal was constructed from the Mississippi River to the dome. Mud from the excavation was used as fill at the mouth of the canal upon which Port Sulphur, a town and shipping terminal, was built. Buildings at the dome were constructed on piling and low-salt water was pumped from the Mississippi to support the mining operation. Faults in the dome held down production for many years, but these were cured by mudding in the late 1940's. From 1933 to 1966, 31.4 million tons of sulfur had been produced. Production stopped in December 1978 (20, 45, 82, 92).

Long Point, 34 miles southwest of Houston, was first brought into production in 1930 by Texas Gulf Sulphur and was operated by the company until 1938, producing only 400,000 tons of sulfur. In 1940, Jefferson Lake leased the sulfur rights on a share basis and began mining in 1946. The mine was still operating in 1980, by which time it had produced 9.5 million tons. Jefferson Lake was acquired by Occidental in 1965, and thereafter the sulfur was shipped by rail to Occidental's phosphate complex in north Florida (28, 46).

Orchard Dome, also southwest of Houston, was explored for oil by Gulf Oil Company, with Texas Gulf Sulphur holding sulfur exploration rights. Texas Gulf further explored the dome without finding a substantial showing of sulfur. Duval Corporation then procured the sulfur rights on a royalty basis, found a good deposit, and began production in 1938. By the end of 1966 some 5.2 million tons had been produced. The dome was then largely exhausted; due to high sulfur prices, however, mining continued until 1970, adding another 0.3 million tons (20, 46, 73).

Moss Bluff Dome in Liberty County east of Houston was acquired from Gulf Oil Company in 1927 by Texas Gulf Sulphur. Due to various delays, including World War II, it wasn't until 1948 that production began. By December 1980, the mine, still in production, had produced 9.6 million tons (28).

Garden Island Bay, located at the tip of the Mississippi Delta in Louisiana, had been explored by the Texas Company (now Texaco) which noted a large sulfur deposit. Freeport Sulphur, having experience at Grande Ecaille in developing a mine on marshland, obtained the sulfur rights in 1951. The mining operations and support activities were located on a concrete mat built on pilings 16 feet above the surrounding marshes. Mining began in 1953 with the molten sulfur being poured directly into special insulated barges and transported on the Mississippi River to Port Sulphur, which also served the Grande Ecaille mine. Garden Island was still operating in 1980 after 20 million tons of sulfur had been removed (28, 46).

Grand Isle, the Nation's first offshore sulfur mine, is under 50 feet of water in the Gulf of Mexico 7 miles off the Louisiana coast from Grand Isle and 22 miles from Port Sulphur. The deposit was discovered by Humble Oil while prospecting for oil in 1949 and was confirmed as a major deposit by Humble in 1954 when it drilled 10 sulfur prospect holes. Freeport Sulphur acquired the sulfur rights in 1956 and began production in 1960. Molten sulfur from mobile production platforms was transported directly by pipeline to the Grand Isle base and transferred to insulated barges for shipment to Port Sulphur. By 1980, 21 million tons had been produced and reserves remaining were estimated at 30 million tons (20, 28, 63).

West Texas Evaporite Basin Deposits—The west Texas sulfur deposits occur at various locations in the Delaware Basin and adjacent platforms. The basin is underlain by thick beds of anhydrite ($CaSO_4$) laid down by evaporation of inland sea water. Sulfur accumulated in deposits as a result of a series of much different geological events from those which occurred under the caprocks of the salt domes of the Gulf Coast. Evidently all of the west Texas sulfur deposits were formed in lenses and fissures resulting from the collapse of the anhydrite from the underside of the anhydrite beds. Ground water moved upward from underlying aquifers and dissolved more anhydrite to form caverns. Oil from underlying oil sands penetrated the area containing the rock fragments from the collapsed anhydrite. The oil, as was the case in the salt domes, provided the hydrogen that permitted anaerobic bacteria to convert the sulfur in the anhydrite to hydrogen sulfide gas, leaving behind gray limestone. The hydrogen sulfide, trapped under the overlying anhydrite bed, was later oxidized to elemental sulfur that was deposited in the pores of the gray limestone. Although several of the west Texas deposits were found mineable by the Frasch method, only one, that in Culbertson County, turned out to contain a very large amount of sulfur (6).

The sulfur deposits in Culbertson and Reeve Counties in west Texas had been known for a long time. In 1904, G. B. Richardson of the U.S. Geological Survey reported sulfur deposits at several locations including Rustler Springs. He noted at or near the surface sulfur which was associated with beds of gypsum and limestone. Richardson suggested that mining on a small scale probably would be profitable. In 1916, due to high sulfur prices, renewed interest developed and W. B. Phillips, a Geological Survey engineer, visited a number of locations and claims. His conclusion was: "There is a good deal of sulphur in Culbertson County and some of it can be cheaply mined .... The prospecting and opening of these sulphur deposits requires considerable capital. This country is no place for a man without means" (93, p. 415). One mine in Culbertson County, owned by Michigan Sulphur and Oil Company, reported production of a small amount of sulfur in 1916. The next activity in west Texas apparently was in 1944 when the Pecos Orla Sulphur Company mined sulfur at the Michigan Claims in Culbertson County (58, 93).

In 1967, Duval Corporation, Standard Oil and Gas Company, Humble Oil and Refining Company, Sinclair Oil and Gas Company, and Texas American Oil Company all were reported drilling for sulfur in Pecos County. Several mines soon came into production using the Frasch process. Production began in 1969 by the Duval Corporation at Culbertson (Rustler Hills) mine in Culbertson County. Also by 1970, Atlantic Richfield was operating a mine 20 miles northeast of Fort Stockton in Pecos County, and Duval opened a small mine also near Fort Stockton which was soon closed. Texasgulf, Inc., opened its Comanche mine near the Atlantic Richfield mine in 1975. Farmland Industries, took over the Atlantic Richfield mine in 1976. In 1980, Duval also started a small mine at Phillips Ranch, 6 miles west of its Rustler Hills mine (28, 73, 91, 92).

Duval Corporation's Culbertson (Rustler Hills) operation, one of the world's largest, is 43 miles northwest of the town of Pecos (55 miles south of Carlsbad, New Mexico). The mine began producing in September 1969 on a carefully selected 600-acre tract where the majority of the sulfur reserves were located. The thickness of the deposits ranged from the equivalent of 2 feet to 80 feet of solid sulfur. The sulfur was encountered at depths ranging from 240 feet to 1,237 feet. The capacity of the plant permitted a production of 5,500 long tons per day. From 1969 through 1980, the mine had produced 19.6 million tons of sulfur (28). This amounted to 50 percent of all the sulfur produced in Texas during the same period, and roughly about 30 percent of all Frasch sulfur produced in the United States.

Mexican Frasch Sulfur—The existence of sulfur associated with salt domes on the Isthmus of Tehuantepec in Mexico was noted during oil drilling in 1902. It wasn't until 1954, however, that the first Frasch sulfur was produced by the Mexican Gulf Sulphur Company at the San Cristóbal dome. Yields were disappointing and the mine was abandoned in 1957. The first major producing mine owned by the Pan American Sulphur Company opened at Jaltipan dome in 1957. Another important mine at Nopalapa dome, operated by Cia Exploradora del Istmo, a Texas Gulf Sulphur Company subsidiary, also began production in 1957. Two other mines were operating by 1960, but the Pan American and Cia Exploradora operations were dominant. Pan American and Cia Exploradora del Istmo have produced about 2 million metric tons annually since the early 1960's. Much of the sulfur was exported, with over half going to the United States in recent years. The nearby port of Coatzacoalcos on the Gulf of Mexico was used for export shipments; most of that going to the United States was received at Tampa (3, 46, 62, 73, 92).

Recovered Elemental Sulfur—Elemental sulfur recovered primarily from purification of sour natural gas and from petroleum refineries became an increasingly important sulfur source in the United States in the 1960's. Small amounts also were recovered from coke oven and other gases. Recovery of sulfur from sour gas and petroleum is nondiscretionary in that the hydrogen sulfide must be removed before the products can be used.

The first recovered elemental sulfur in this country appeared in the 1920's and 1930's when it was removed from a slurry resulting from purification of manufactured fuel gases. The slurry contained very finely divided sulfur which was recovered through steam distillation. About 1,500 long tons of sulfur was recovered in this manner in 1934. By the

1940's, elemental sulfur was being recovered from coke oven gases, petroleum refinery gases, and natural and other gases containing objectionable amounts of hydrogen sulfide. In 1944, this amounted to some 20,000 tons of sulfur. About 60 percent of this was marketed as a partially dehydrated paste containing 35 to 52 percent S and the remainder as dry material (58, 80, 83).

By 1950, a strong industry was developing around reclaiming sulfur as a by-product from petroleum refinery gases and sour natural gas. This was stimulated by a shortage of Frasch sulfur-the first the Nation had encountered since Frasch's Sulphur Mine came into full production. During 1950, two new refinery gas plants were located in California and New Jersey, and four were built to scrub sulfur from natural gas in Arkansas and Wyoming. In 1949, 60,000 tons of recovered sulfur was produced; in 1950, 140,000 tons; and in 1955, 400,000 (62, 86, 87).

Recovery of sulfur from refineries and natural gas from 1950 onward was accomplished using the Claus process. In this process, the hydrogen sulfide in the gases is extracted using an amine reagent in aqueous solution. On heating the solution, the H_2S can be separated as a fairly pure gas. Recovering the sulfur involves converting roughly one-third of the H_2S to SO_2 by oxidation as follows: $2H_2S + 3O_2 \rightarrow 2SO_2 + 2H_2O$ and then reacting the remaining H_2S with the SO_2 to form sulfur as follows: $2H_2S + SO_2 \rightarrow 3S + 2H_2O$. The latter reaction occurs in the presence of a catalyst such as bauxite or alumina. The basic Claus process was discovered in 1883 (13).

Most recovery plants were operated by oil companies and initially they were quite small. By 1954, 33 plants in 33 states produced 360,000 tons of sulfur. The first large plant had a capacity of 102,000 tons per year. It was built by Ralph M. Parsons Company for Getty Oil Company at Delaware City, Delaware, in 1956. Other large plants followed in 1960-61, including a 133,000-ton-per year Texaco plant at Long Beach, California; a Shell Oil Company 50,000-ton plant at Wood River, Illinois; and an Allied Chemical 66,000-ton plant at Richmond, California (29, 61, 63).

Production of recovered sulfur in 1960 reached 767,000 tons from 60 plants in 19 states, with 60 percent coming from oil refineries and the remainder from sour gas purification. Production doubled by 1970 to 1.5 million tons produced by 99 plants in 21 states. The five largest producers were Cities Service Oil Company, Getty Oil Company, Pan American Petroleum Corporation, Shell Oil Company, and Stauffer Chemical Company. Their 23 plants accounted for 43 percent of all recovered sulfur production (63, 73).

The almost constant yearly increases in tonnages of recovered sulfur peaked in 1978 at around 4 million tons. In 1979, this tonnage was produced by 56 companies at 152 plants in 28 states, Puerto Rico, and the Virgin Islands. By source, 57 percent came from 82 refineries or satellite plants owned by 56 companies treating refinery gases, one coking operation, and two utility plants. The remaining 43 percent was produced at 67 natural gas treatment plants operated by 27 companies. The five largest recovered sulfur producers in 1979 were the Atlantic Richfield Company, Chevron U.S.A., Exxon Company U.S.A., Shell Oil Company, and Standard Oil of Indiana; together, their 44 plants produced 61 percent of the total (92).

The crude oils refined originally in the United States were sweet, light crudes of the Gulf Coast and Texas containing about 0.3 percent sulfur by weight. With U.S. domestic oil peaking in 1970, U.S. companies looked for and purchased similar crudes from abroad. Since these crudes also were in high demand in other countries, the reserves were diminished and the light crudes came into short supply and were more costly. As a result, United States companies stepped up purchase of heavy crude from Saudi Arabia and elsewhere which contained more sulfur (however, in 1980, 50 percent of U.S. oil imports were still low in sulfur). Oil from Alaska that partly replaced the Texas light crudes also contains considerable sulfur. Along with tighter SO_2 emission standards, this resulted in the refineries greatly increasing the tonnage of sulfur recovered until high oil prices triggered a decline in petroleum use (29).

Recovered Sulfur from Canada—The United States imports a considerable amount of recovered elemental sulfur from Canada. Imports began around 1960 and exceeded 1 million long tons annually in the 1970's. The Canadian producers derived almost all of this tonnage from sulfur recovery units associated with natural gas processing plants, mostly in Alberta, Canada, which recovered only 245,000 tons of sulfur in 1960, but increased production rapidly as demand for natural gas increased, peaking at 7 million tons in 1973. Production, however, declined to 6 million tons of sulfur by 1979. The sulfur content of the Canadian sour gas averages about 15 percent, but from some locations it is about 30 percent (7, 63).

Continuing high demand for Canadian natural gas, which was distributed by pipelines into the Western States and Midwest and as far east in Canada as Ontario, resulted in accumulation of huge inventories of sulfur at times. Canada in 1967 replaced the United States as the world's largest exporter of elemental sulfur. All sulfur shipped overseas is in solid form, going by rail to Vancouver where it is loaded in ocean-going vessels. Molten sulfur is moved by rail from central liquid shipping points in Alberta to the United States and parts of Canada. In 1975, there were 45 natural gas processing complexes–42 in Alberta–which accounted for 86 percent of the Canadian output, 2 in British Columbia, and 1 in Saskatchewan. Most producers were subsidiaries of major oil companies (23, 26, 63, 91).

Transportation and Distribution of Elemental Sulfur—The traditional method of handling elemental sulfur involves filtering the molten sulfur to remove impurities followed by cooling and solidification in vats. Solidified material was broken up and shipped to the point of use. A major innovation was made with the introduction of handling and shipping in molten form. The idea for and early experimentation in handling and transport of molten sulfur was developed by Freeport Sulphur in the late 1940's and early 1950's in its efforts to transport sulfur from its Frasch mines in the swamps of the lower Mississippi Delta to the company terminal at Port Sulphur (23).

The development of molten sulfur handling and transportation gave both sulfur producers and sulfuric acid manufacturers the opportunity to streamline operations. Most elemental sulfur, including recovered sulfur, is initially in liquid state and ultimately must be in liquid state for manufacture of sulfuric acid. Savings in labor and other advantages resulted in its rapid adoption of the system, even though it required specialized shipping, handling, and storage facilities, usually insulated and equipped for heating (23, 62).

The first long barge shipment of molten sulfur was made from Point Sulphur on the lower Mississippi River in May 1955. It arrived at St. Louis, 1,100 miles upstream, 8 days later. The hold of the barge consisted of a large tank within the barge hull surrounded by air space and lined with 4-inch foam glass insulation and covered with a layer of asbestos board. Some later barges were equipped with steam coils to maintain the desired temperature (240°-320°F). Suitable handling and storage facilities along with specially equipped vessels, barges, road and rail tankers were developed rapidly to meet the domestic needs of the new system. By 1963, 85 percent of the elemental sulfur used in this country was transported in molten form (3, 23, 62).

The first ocean-going vessel equipped for molten sulfur transport was the *SS Marine Sulphur Queen* built for Texas Gulf Sulphur. It hauled molten sulfur from the company's main terminal at Beaumont, Texas, to regional terminals at U.S. Gulf and East Coast ports. This ship was lost off the Florida coast in February 1963 while carrying a cargo of molten sulfur. Texas Gulf Sulphur in 1964 launched a replacement carrier, the *Marine Texas*. Freeport Sulphur also launched new ocean-going carriers, including one of 20,000-ton capacity (3, 14, 23).

Exports of molten sulfur, although receiving approval of western European countries, were delayed until 1964 when large, long-distance ocean-going vessels could be specially built to meet U.S. and Mexican Frasch producers' needs. In the United States, Sulexco, a jointly-owned sulfur export sales organization formed in 1958 by the four major U.S. Frasch producers, chartered two British-built and -operated vessels, the *SS Naess Texas* and the *SS Naess Louisiana* to transport liquid sulfur from the U.S. Gulf Coast ports to terminals in Rotterdam and Dublin. The *SS Naess*, the first liquid sulfur tanker built for transatlantic service, was 620 feet long, 85 feet wide, and carried 25,000 tons of sulfur at a draft of 32.5 feet. Waste heat from the engines was used to produce steam for coils in four sulfur tanks, each 92 feet long, 43 feet wide, and 34 feet high (12, 14, 23). (Sulexco did not limit its exports to Rotterdam and Dublin or to transport by the two large vessels. It shipped to 60 countries, with the major customers being the United Kingdom, Australia, Brazil, New Zealand, and West Germany.)

Three main terminals were responsible for the molten shipments of Frasch sulfur. These were Port Sulphur, Louisiana, built and used by Freeport Sulphur; Beaumont, Texas, built and used by Texas Gulf Sulphur; and Galveston, Texas, built and used by the Duval Corporation to handle deliveries from the Culbertson County mine in west Texas. Each terminal had storage installations for both solid and liquid sulfur, including handling systems and loading points for ocean-going tankers and dry cargo ships, barges, and truck and rail tankers (15, 23).

Florida became the world's largest elemental sulfur market by the 1970's as a result of the concentration of sulfuric acid plants in and around the mining districts. Most of the sulfur going into central Florida is shipped in molten form from terminals in Texas and Louisiana and from the terminal in Mexico. (Only small amounts of recovered sulfur are used in Florida.) Five sulfuric acid plants were operating in or near the central Florida pebble district in 1964. By 1980, some 30 sulfuric acid plants were operating in the central and north Florida pebble districts.

Molten sulfur is transported routinely in barges and ocean-going vessels.
(Texasgulf Chemicals Company)

They consumed some 5 million tons of sulfur or 37 percent of all of the sulfur consumed in the United States. Tampa was the main port servicing the sulfur needs of the central district. Occidental shipped molten sulfur produced by its Jefferson Lake subsidiary by rail to its north Florida operation (8, 27, 33).

Pyrites—Domestically mined and imported iron pyrites accounted for 80 percent or more of the sulfuric acid produced in the United States from 1900 to 1917 (Chapters 3, 4), but steadily declined in importance thereafter. In the period 1920-1980, pyrites ceased to be a sulfur source of any significance, being replaced by Frasch and recovered elemental sulfur and by-product sulfuric acid, as shown in Table 7.3.

Domestic production in the first half of the 1920's centered largely on pyrite ores from California and Virginia mined primarily for their sulfur content. These two states produced 95 percent of the pyrites mined in the country, the remainder coming from New York and Ohio. Imports during the 1920's, mainly from Spain, were used largely by sulfuric acid plants along the eastern seaboard. Smaller amounts were imported from British Columbia, feeding sulfuric acid plants in Washington and the San Francisco Bay area (59, 79, 80).

Traditionally, pyrites had been mined separately from other minerals, but from the mid-1920's on, pyrite production increasingly became a by-product of copper, zinc, and lead smelting. Beneficiation of some of the nonferrous ores yielded a concentrate of pyrites fines. The pyrite (FeS_2) and pyrrhotite (FeS) concentrates were recovered by selective flotation in a mill which also yielded the zinc, copper, or lead concentrates. The pyrite concentrates were roasted at the location of the smelter and the SO_2 gas generated was mixed with the smelter gases and converted to sulfuric acid. Also, iron concentrates of a third type were separated magnetically and added to the others for roasting. By-product pyrites were much cheaper to produce than pyrites mined solely for their sulfur content (81).

The shift to flotation pyrite fines was made possible through improvements in pyrite burners and roasters where the ore was burned to release SO_2. Originally, lumps of pyrite were burned on a batch basis in individual ovens that could not utilize finely divided ore. The first type that could better utilize fines involved a vertical cylinder containing a series of hearths, one above another. The ore was fed in at the top and was moved from one hearth to the next below by revolving arms as it burned. The gases moved upward and the spent cinders accumulated in the bottom and were discharged.

Flash roasting apparently was a major advance. This process was designed specifically to handle flotation fines. The fines, suspended in a stream of air, were introduced into a cylindrical roaster along with a small secondary stream of air that kept the solids in suspension long enough for them to burn completely. The exhaust gases and some entrained fines left through a top duct and were scrubbed to remove the fines. The spent coarser solids fell to the bottom of the roaster. Another type coming after World War II was the fluidized bed roaster which involved the suspension of the solid particles, usually as a slurry, in an upward-rising stream of gas. The result is a violently agitated or fluidized mass which behaves as a stream of water in that it exerts a hydrostatic head. The chemical reaction is almost instantaneous. Exhaust gases pass through a waste heat boiler and entrained solids are extracted by cyclones. Coarser particles discharge through an overflow port (103).

By 1937, about four-fifths of the pyrites produced in the United States came from flotation fines, and in 1954 virtually all of the pyrites produced were from this source. The principal producing states were Tennessee, California, Virginia, Vermont, Pennsylvania, and Colorado. Practically all of the SO_2 derived from pyrite roasting was used ito make of sulfuric acid (62, 83).

Although the numbers of companies and locations producing pyrites began declining around 1960, the tonnages of sulfur produced from pyrites remained about the same. In 1960, 9 companies were producing pyrites at 10 locations in 8 states, producing the equivalent of 416,000 long tons of sulfur. By 1970, 6 locations in 5 states produced 339,000 tons of sulfur equivalent, and in 1978-79 only 3 companies operated at 3 locations in 3 states, producing 400,000 tons. Imports of pyrites continued throughout practically all of the 1920-1980 period, the last recorded being in 1972. Imports never exceeded 200,000 tons sulfur equivalent in any year (63, 91, 92).

By-product Sulfuric Acid—Recovery of sulfuric acid as a by-product from smelting of nonferrous sulfide ores (copper, zinc, and lead) began in this country in 1908 at Ducktown, Tennessee, (Chapter 3) and continued throughout the 1920-1980 period. However, except for the beginning and ending of the 60-year period, the by-product acid was of relatively minor importance in comparison to the U.S. total sulfur production (Table 7.3). In 1920, the by-product acid accounted for 17 percent of the total sulfur produced in the United States but by 1940 it had declined to 6 percent and remained in the 4 to 6 percent range through 1974. Production increased after 1974, reaching 10 percent of the total U.S. sulfur production in 1979 as companies with smelters responded to the Clean Air Act (7, 8, 42, 92).

Prior to the early 1960's, zinc smelter plants produced up to about 70 percent of the by-product sulfuric acid in the United States, with most of the remainder coming from copper smelters (only one lead smelter recovered by-product acid). Copper smelters gradually produced more by-product acid until they exceeded that from zinc plants in 1972. By 1979, copper produced 70 percent of the by-product sulfuric acid (58, 62, 79, 92).

Largely because of the severe damage to vegetation and crops from SO_2 gas released during smelter operations and resulting lawsuits, there was considerable participation of smelting companies in by-product sulfuric acid production. In 1960, 16 plants in 13 states were producing by-product acid. In 1970, 18 plants were operating in 14 states with 5 copper smelters accounting for 41 percent of the acid production. The five largest by-product acid producers, accounting for 72 percent of production, were American Zinc Company, Kennecott Copper Corporation, New Jersey Zinc Company, Phelps Dodge Corporation, and St. Joseph Lead Company. In 1974, 12 companies produced acid at 22 plants in 13 states; 12 of the plants were smelting copper, the others, either zinc or lead. In the record production year of 1979, by-product acid was produced by 13 companies at 26 plants in 13 states. Thirteen acid plants were tied to copper smelters, and 13 to zinc and lead smelters and roasters. The five largest acid producers were American Smelting and Refining Company, Magma Copper Company, Kennecott Copper Corporation, Phelps Dodge Company, and St. Joseph's Minerals Corporation; their 13 plants produced 68 percent of the U.S. by-product acid (63, 73, 91, 92).

REFERENCES

1. Aall, C. H. 1952. The American phosphorus industry. *Ind. Eng. Chem.* 44(7):1520-1525.
2. Aldred, J. W. H. 1960. *Phosphatic raw materials for TVA's fertilizer and munitions program.* Unpublished report. Tennessee Valley Authority. March 30, 1960.
3. Babcock, C. O. 1963. Sulfur and pyrites. Bur. Mines *Min. Yearbook,* Vol. I. pp. 1075-1096.
4. Barr, J. A. 1934. Development and application of phosphate flotation. *Ind. Eng. Chem.* 26:811-815.
5. Blakey, A. F. 1973. *The Florida Phosphate Industry: A History of the Development and Use of a Vital Mineral.* Wertheim Comm., Harvard Univ. Press, Cambridge, Massachusetts.
6. Bodenlos, A. J. 1973. Sulfur. In *United States Mineral Resources.* U.S. Geol. Survey Paper 820, pp. 605-618.
7. Bridges, J. D. 1979. *Fertilizer Trends.* Tenn. Valley Auth., Muscle Shoals, Alabama.
8. ____. 1982. *Fertilizer Trends.* TVA, Muscle Shoals, Alabama.
9. Burrows, J. T. 1929, Phosphate progress. *Comm. Fert.* 39(1):50, 52-54.
10. British Sulphur Corporation. 1962. World phosphate rock production. *Phosphorus and Potassium,* Apr.-Dec. issue, 1962, pp. 1-2.
11. ____ 1964. Structure of the U.S. fertilizer industry. *Phosphorus and Potassium* 9:15-16.
12. ____. 1964. Sulexco - Sulphur Export Corporation. *Sulphur* 50:85.
13. ____. 1964. Sulphur recovery by the modern Parson's plant. *Sulphur* 50:89-90.
14. ____. 1964. Texas Gulf's 24,300 ton molten sulphur tanker. *Sulphur* 50:99.

15. ____. 1964. Boom in United States sulphur demand. *Sulphur* 52:20-23.
16. ____. 1964. Occidental Petroleum Corporation–rapid expansion and growth in 1963. *Sulphur* 53:42-43.
17. ____. 1966. Fertilizer marketing and major distributors. *Phosphorus and Potassium* 22:12-19.
18. ____. 1966. Texas Gulf Sulphur Company. *Phosphorus and Potassium* 22:53.
19. ____. 1966. Developments in Florida phosphate rock exploitation. *Phosphorus and Potassium* 25:19-22.
20. ____. 1967. Expanding production of Frasch sulphur in the U.S.A. *Sulphur* 70:17-22.
21. ____. 1968. Mining phosphate rock with dragline excavators. *Phosphorus and Potassium* 87:41-42,
22. ____. 1970. A phosphorus and potassium diary: 1962-1970. *Phosphorus and Potassium* 50:9-12.
23. ____. 1970. Liquid sulfur transportation. *Sulphur* 88:40-46.
24. ____. 1971. C F Industries absorbs Central Phosphates, Inc. *Phosphorus and Potassium* 53:7.
25. ____. 1971. The phosphate fertilizer industry in the United States, *Phosphorus and Potassium* 55:21-28.
26. ____. 1972. Sulphur from natural gas in Canada. *Sulphur* 98:26-35.
27. ____. 1980. Florida: The world's largest sulphur market. *Sulphur* 146:18- 21.
28. ____. 1981. The U.S. Frasch industry. *Sulphur* 153:22-27.
29. ____. 1982. Recovered sulphur production in the United States - the role of refineries. *Sulphur* 155:24-27.
30. Cathcart, J. B. 1980. The phosphate industry of the United States. In *The Role of Phosphorus in Agriculture*, ed. by F. E. Khasawneh, E. C. Sample, and E. J. Kampreth, pp. 19-42. Publ. by American Society of Agronomy, Crop Science Society of America, and Soil Science Soc. America, Madison, Wisconsin.
31. Chapman, O. C. 1969. The phosphates of Tennessee. In *Phosphoric Acid, Phosphates, and Phosphoric Fertilizers*, ed. by W. H. Waggaman. pp. 72-82. Hafner Publishing Co., New York and London.
32. Douglas, J. R. 1960. *Fertilizer Trends*. Tenn. Valley Auth., Muscle Shoals, Alabama.
33. ____, E. H. Harre, and E, L. Johnston. 1964. Fertilizer Trends. Tenn. Valley Auth., Muscle Shoals, Alabama.
34. Duecker, W. W. and J. R. West. 1959. *History of the Manufacture of Sulfuric Acid*, ed. by W. W. Duecker and J. R. West. pp. 9-12. Reinhold Publishing Co., New York.
35. Eddy, E. W. and R. Frank. 1959. Review of the sulfuric acid industry. In *Manufacture of Sulfuric Acid*, ed. by W. W. Duecker and J. R. West, pp. 1-8. Reinhold Publ. Co., New York.
36. Farm Chemicals. 1980. Phosphate report from Bone Valley. *Farm Chem.* 143(2):13-26, 31.
37. Food and Agriculture Organization of the United Nations. 1980. *FAO Fertilizer Yearbook* 1980.
38. Fuller, R. B. 1951. The history of development of phosphate rock mining. *Min. Eng.* 3(8):708-712.
39. Gray, A. N. 1944. *Phosphates and superphosphate*. Publ. under auspices of the International Superphosphate Manufacturers Asso. E. T. Heron and Co., London.

40. Harre, E. A. 1967. *Fertilizer Trends.* Tenn. Valley Auth., Muscle Shoals, Alabama.
41. ____. 1969. *Fertilizer Trends.* Tenn. Valley Auth., Muscle Shoals, Alabama.
42. ____. 1971. *Fertilizer Trends.* Tenn. Valley Auth., Muscle Shoals, Alabama.
43. ____. 1973. *Fertilizer Trends.* Tenn. Valley Auth., Muscle Shoals, Alabama.
44. ____, M. N. Goodson, and J. D. Bridges. 1976. *Fertilizer Trends.* Tenn. Valley Auth., Muscle Shoals, Alabama.
45. Haynes, W. 1942. *The Stone that Burns.* D. Van Nostrand Co., Inc., New York.
46. ____. 1959. *Brimstone, the Stone that Burns.* D. Van Nostrand Co., Inc., Princeton, N. J. and New York.
47. Hill, W. L. 1952. Elemental phosphorus and phosphoric acid in the fertilizer industry. *Ind. Eng. Chem.* 44(7):1526-1532.
48. Jacob, K. D. 1931. Recent developments in the phosphate industry. *Ind. Eng. Chem.* 23(1):14-18.
49. ____. 1953. Phosphate resources and processing facilities. In *Fertilizer Technology and Resources,* ed. by K. D. Jacob. pp. 117-165. Academic Press, Inc., New York.
50. ____. 1964. History and status of the superphosphate industry. In *Superphosphate: Its History, Chemistry, and Manufacture.* pp. 19-94. U.S. Dept. of Agr. and Tenn. Valley Auth.
51. Johnson, B. L. 1927. Phosphate rock. Bur. Mines *Mineral Resources of the U.S. Part II.* pp. 313-326.
52. ____. 1928. Phosphate rock. *Min. Res. of the U.S. Part II.* pp. 253-275.
53. ____. 1929. Phosphate rock. *Min. Res. of the U.S. Part II.* pp. 341-357.
54. ____. 1930. Phosphate rock. *Min. Res. of the U.S. Part II.* pp. 315-332.
55. ____. 1931. Phosphate rock. *Min. Res. of the U.S. Part II.* pp. 511-522.
56. Josephson, G. W. and N. G. Jensen. 1950. Phosphate rock. *Min. Yearbook.* pp. 1003-1020.
57. ____ and B. H. Stoddard. 1934. Phosphate rock. *Min. Yearbook.* pp. 947-967.
58. ____ and N. G. Jensen. 1944. Sulfur and pyrites. *Min. Yearbook.* pp. 1359-1372.
59. Julihn, C. E. and H. M. Meyer. 1926. Sulphur and pyrites. *Min. Res. of U.S. Part II.* pp. 295-301.
60. King, D. L. 1967. San Francisco Chemical Company, Crawford Mountains - Leefe Area, Utah and Wyoming. In *Anatomy of the Western Phosphate Field,* ed. by L. A. Hale. pp. 203-209. 15th Annual Field Conference of Intermountain Assoc. of Geologists, Salt Lake City.
61. Larson, L. P. and A. L. Marks. 1954. Sulfur and pyrites. *Min. Yearbook. Vol. I.* pp. 1118-1143.
62. ____ and A. L. Marks. 1955. Sulfur and pyrites. *Min. Yearbook. Vol. I.* pp. 1089-1109.
63. ____ and V. R. Roman. 1960. Sulfur and pyrites. *Min. Yearbook. Vol. I.* pp. 1059-1082.

64. Lebaron, I. M. 1965. Phosphate rock. In *Chemistry and Technology of Fertilizers*, ed. by V. Sauchelli. pp. 68-92. Reinhold Publishing Corp., New York.
65. _____. 1969. Florida pebble phosphate. In *Phosphoric Acid, Phosphates, and Phosphatic Fertilizers*, 2nd edition, ed. by W. H. Waggaman. pp. 50-71. Hafner Publishing Co., Inc., New York.
66. Lewis, R. W. and G. E. Tucker. 1960. Phosphate rock. *Min. Yearbook. Vol. I.* pp. 867-886.
67. Mansfield, G. R. 1920. *Geography, geology, and mineral resources of the Fort Hall Indian Reservation*, Idaho. U.S. Geol. Survey Bull. 713.
68. _____. 1922. Phosphate rock. *Min. Res. of U.S. Part II.* pp. 109-121.
69. _____. 1923. Phosphate rock. *Min. Res. of U.S. Part II.* pp. 239-273.
70. Markham, J. W. 1958. *The Fertilizer Industry; A Study of an Imperfect Market*. Vanderbilt University Press, Nashville, Tennessee.
71. Marshall, V. C. 1961. The sulphuric acid industry and its economic aspects. *British Chem. Eng.* 6(12):841-850.
72. Mehring, A. L., J. R. Adams, and K. D. Jacob. 1957. *Statistics on fertilizers and liming materials in the United States*. U.S. Dept. of Agriculture Statistical Bull. 191.
73. Merwin, R. W. 1970. Sulfur and pyrites. *Min. Yearbook. Vol. I.* pp. 1059-1071.
74. Meyer, H. M. 1923. Sulphur and pyrites. *Min. Res. of U.S. Part II.* pp. 1-6.
75. _____. 1924. Sulphur and pyrites. *Min. Res. of U.S. Part II.* pp. 1-5.
76. Norris, E. M. 1969. Western phosphates. In *Phosphoric Acid, Phosphates, and Phosphatic Fertilizers*. 2nd edition, ed. by W. H. Waggaman. pp. 84-99. Hafner Publishing Co., New York and London.
77. O'Hanlon, T. 1968. All that fertilizer and no place to grow. *Fortune*, June 1, 1968. pp. 91-95, 129.
78. Ridgeway, R. H. 1928. Sulphur and pyrites. *Min. Res. of U.S. Part II.* pp. 55-65.
79. _____. 1929. Sulphur and pyrites. *Min. Res. of U.S. Part II.* pp. 175-194.
80. _____. 1930. Sulphur and pyrites. *Min. Res. of U.S. Part II.* pp. 117-135.
81. _____. 1931. Sulphur and pyrites. *Min. Res. of U.S. Part II.* pp. 1075-1096.
82. _____ and A. W. Mitchell. 1933. Sulphur and pyrites. *Min. Yearbook*, 1932-33. pp. 699-675.
83. _____ and A. W. Mitchell. 1938. Sulphur and pyrites. *Min. Yearbook*. pp. 1151-1166.
84. Ruhlman, E. R. and G. E. Tucker. 1955. Phosphate rock. *Min. Yearbook. Vol. I.* pp. 875-893.
85. _____ and G. E. Tucker. 1957. Phosphate rock. *Min. Yearbook. Vol. I.* pp. 929-945.
86. Sands, A. E. and L. D. Schmidt. 1950. Recovery of sulfur from synthesis gas. *Ind. Eng. Chem.* 42:2277-2287.
87. Sawyer, F. G., et al. 1950. Sulfur from sour gas. *Ind. Eng. Chem.* 42:1938-1950.
88. Schmitt, W. O. 1967. The Gay mine, Fort Hall, Idaho. In *Anatomy of the Western Phosphate Field*, ed. by L. A. Hale. pp. 195-202. 15th Annual Field Conference of Intermountain Assoc. of Geologists, Salt Lake City.

89. Schwarze, D. M. 1967. History of the Conda operation–underground and strip mining. In *Anatomy of the Western Phosphate Field*, ed. by L. A. Hale. pp. 187-194.
90. Service, A. L. 1967. History and development of the phosphate industry in southeastern Idaho. In *Anatomy of the Western Phosphate Field*, ed. by L. A. Hale. pp. 175-185.
91. Shelton, J. E. 1975. Sulfur and pyrites. *Min. Yearbook. Vol. I.* pp. 1339-1357.
92. ____. 1979. Sulfur and pyrites. *Min. Yearbook 1978-79. Vol. I.* pp. 877- 897.
93. Smith, P. S. 1916. Sulphur, pyrite, and sulphuric acid. *Min. Res. of the U.S. Part II.* pp. 403-431.
94. Stone, R. W. 1920. Phosphate rock. *Min. Res. of U.S. Part II.* pp. 27-35.
95. Stowasser, W. F. 1972. Phosphate rock. *Min. Yearbook. Vol. I.* pp. 1027- 1041.
96. ____. 1975. Phosphate rock. *Min. Yearbook. Vol. I.* pp. 1163-1182.
97. ____. 1977. Phosphate rock. *Min. Yearbook. Vol. I.* pp. 699-722.
98. ____. 1977. *Phosphate rock.* Mineral Commodity Profiles. MCP-2. May, 1977. U.S. Dept. of Interior Bureau of Mines.
99. ____. 1979. Phosphate rock. *Min. Yearbook 1978-79. Vol. I.* pp. 677-697.
100. Tennessee Valley Authority. 1962. *Annual report of the Tennessee Valley Authority for the fiscal year ended June 30, 1962.* TVA, Knoxville, Tennessee.
101. ____. 1962. *Fertilizer Trends.* Tenn. Valley Authority, Muscle Shoals, Alabama.
102. Titlestad, N. 1945. Contact acid in the fertilizer industry. *Amer. Fert.* 103(6):15.
103. Thompson, R. B. and W. W. Jukkola. 1959. Pyrites and sulfide ore burners or roasters. In *Manufacture of sulfuric acid*, ed. by W. W. Duecker and J. R. West. pp. 61-84. Reinhold Publishing Corp., New York.
104. Waggaman, W. H. 1969. Florida hard rock phosphate. In *Phosphoric acid, phosphates and phosphatic fertilizers*, ed. by W. H. Waggaman. pp. 44-49. Hafner Publishing Co., New York and London.
105. Weigel, W. M. and B. H. Stoddard. 1925. Phosphate rock. *Min. Res. of U.S. Part II.* pp. 147-158.

8

Potash Production and Sources 1935-1980

The great search for domestic sources of potash that hopefully would make the United States independent of foreign imports, the subject of Chapter 5, appeared to have ended successfully in the 1920's with the discovery of substantial underground deposits near Carlsbad, New Mexico, and the start of mining there in 1931. This chapter relates the development of the underground potash deposits at Carlsbad and at Moab, Utah, and of the brine deposits at Searles Lake, California, and Salduro Marsh, Utah. Together, these made this country self-sufficient in potash for the first time. This chapter also recounts the discovery and development of the vast Canadian deposits, the depletion of the high-grade Carlsbad ore, and the decline of U.S. potash production. The skyrocketing demand for potash fertilizers resulted in the United States again becoming the world's largest importer of potash.

The Ever Changing U. S. Potash Situation

Prior to the opening of the first Carlsbad mine in 1931, domestic production was limited to the brines of Searles Lake, California, and to small amounts of by-product potash coming mostly from one producer in the cement industry and one in the distillery industry. Most potash needs were met by imports from Europe. With the opening of additional mines and expansion of capacities at existing mines and refineries, the country began an extended period of potash independence from 1935 to 1963. Consumption increased rapidly and steadily, and producers were assured of good returns on their investments.

The successful operation of International Minerals and Chemical Corporation's K1 mine in Saskatchewan in 1962 signaled a new era in the U.S. potash situation. The high-grade Canadian potassium chloride could be mined and refined at lower cost than the U.S. product and its favorable location with respect to the high-potash-using Midwest

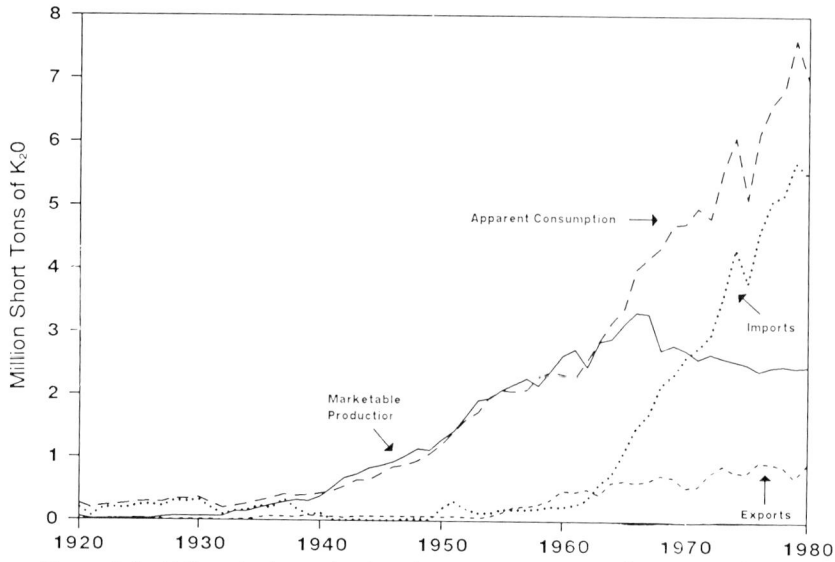

Figure 8.1. U.S. potash production, imports, exports, and consumption.

assured a ready market. Furthermore, the Carlsbad district, which accounted for 80 percent or more of the total U.S. potash production, was becoming depleted in high-grade ore, and mining and refining costs per ton of product were rising. Demand at the same time continued to increase rapidly. As a result, from 1966 on Carlsbad production began decreasing and imports from Canada shot up, paralleling the rapid gains in U.S. consumption. Potash production from Carlsbad became limited largely to the high-potash-using Southern States where it enjoyed a freight advantage over the Canadian product. At the same time, the Carlsbad potash found a sizable export market, primarily Latin America, Japan, New Zealand, and Australia.

Consumption of potash in the United States increased from around 3 million tons of K_2O in 1965 to over 7 million in 1979, 95 percent of which was consumed as fertilizer. As shown in Figure 8.1, imports provided an increasingly larger share of the potash consumed, rising from 32 percent in 1965 to 78 percent in 1980. This brought the domestic potash situation full circle in 60 years, from 1920 to 1980, starting and ending with heavy dependence upon imports.

Most potash produced in the United States and all of that in Canada is potassium chloride (sylvite). The potassium chloride in underground deposits occurs in the mineral sylvinite, a mixture of potassium chloride and sodium chloride, in strata usually underlain and overlain with sodium chloride. The sylvinite is mixed with small amounts of clays and other insoluble materials. Potassium chloride also occurs in natural surface and subsurface brines along with other salts. The mineral langbeinite, a double salt of potassium sulfate and magnesium sulfate, is found in beds mixed with sodium chloride and with sodium and potassium chlorides at Carlsbad, New Mexico. Part of the langbeinite is converted to potassium sulfate and the remainder is marketed as potassium magnesium sulfate; both are used as fertilizers.

Potassium chloride also is recovered from natural brines in Utah and Searles Lake, California, although a part is converted to potassium sulfate. Potassium chloride is refined at or near the mine site. The primary task is to separate the potassium chloride from the sodium chloride and other unwanted impurities or from other marketable salts. The refined potash is divided according to particle size or granulated by the potash producer. The product may be marketed by the producer by his own company or through a subsidiary, or it is wholesaled on the open market for domestic consumption or export.

The Expanding Domestic Industry: 1935-1966

Most building blocks for developing a strong U.S. potash industry were in place by 1935. The major underground potash deposit near Carlsbad had been verified, and both the United States Potash Company and the Potash Company of America were mining and refining high-grade sylvinite ore. The American Potash and Chemical Company was producing potash from brine pumped from Searles Lake. Also, domestic potash consumption, which had bottomed out in 1932 at 152,000 tons of K_2O as a result of the Great Depression, was showing definite signs of recovery (64).

From 193,000 tons of K_2O in 1935, production increased steadily to 1.3 million tons in 1950–a 7-fold increase in 15 years (see Figure 8.1). The next 15 years, 1951-1966, saw production reach 3.3 million tons– 2-1/2 times that of 1950 and 17 times the 1935 level. Imports of European potash, which had earlier greatly exceeded domestic production, fell behind U.S. production by 1938 and practically ceased with the coming of World War II. Although imports reappeared in 1950, tonnages remained modest–about 200,000 tons annually–until sizable imports began arriving from Canada in the early 1960's. Imports reached nearly 600,000 tons in 1963 and 1.5 million tons in 1966. At the same time, U.S. exports were increasing–from 65,000 tons in 1950 (5 percent of the U.S. production) to around 650,000 tons in 1965 (21 percent of U.S. production) (5,40,64).

The domestic demand increased rapidly and potash prices remained strong during much of the 1960's. U.S. production continued upward through 1966, when it set an all-time high of 3.3 million tons of K_2O. As a result, three mines operating in the Canadian field by 1966 were a factor in the market, but they were not overly burdensome.

The Producing U. S. Companies

By-product Potash Producers—Two by-product potash producers from World War I years continued to operate well into the 1940's. They were the U.S. Industrial Chemicals, Inc., which recovered potash from industrial distillery wastes at Baltimore, and the North American Cement Company which produced potash from cement dust near Hagerstown, Maryland. Production of these two companies were insignificant compared with the U.S. total production (37).

American Potash and Chemical Corporation—This company began operation at Searles Lake during World War I (Chapter 5). The successful Searles Lake operation was the result of a persistent effort to develop processes to recover potash and various other salts from the complex brines of the old lake. The Searles Lake brines occur in two definite layers. The upper layer was 70 feet thick and contained about 5 percent potassium chloride (KCl) along with other minerals. The lower layer was about 35 feet thick and contained about 3 percent KCl and other salts. The layers are separated by 10 to 15 feet of impervious mud. Wells were driven into the brine layers and the brine was pumped several miles to the processing plants. In the upper layer the wells were positioned near the bottom since the higher potash-bearing brines concentrate at the lower depth (37).

The upper layer provides brine for the main process at the plant which produces most of the potash. The raw brine is heated and then circulates through coolers which absorb heat and provide part of the energy for the evaporation of the brines (fuel for heat is a major processing cost). The brine is concentrated in large, triple-effect vacuum evaporators. As evaporation proceeds, burkeite ($Na_2CO_3 \cdot 2Na_2SO_4$) and sodium chloride are removed from the evaporators. After separation of the sodium salts the hot, concentrated liquor is rich in potash and borax. Following clarification it is sent to the potash plant where the KCl is separated from the borax using vacuum coolers. (A later process was added which permitted crystallization of the potash with the borax, and the slurry of the two treated with flotation reagent, the borax being floated from the potassium chloride.) A separate carbonation plant processed the brine from the lower strata to produce sodium carbonate and borax (37,46,63).

World War II brought about a major ownership change. The Alien Property Custodian disclosed in 1942 that 90 percent of the capital stock of the American Potash and Chemical Corporation was owned by German nationals–one of the owners being Wintershall, A.G., an important German potash producer (49). In 1946, the Custodian sold the German-owned shares to a group of investors of which Heyden Chemical Company became the principal stockholder. The new owners continued to operate under the American Potash and Chemical name (51).

United States Potash Company—When mining was initiated at Carlsbad by U.S. Potash in 1931 (Chapter 5), only run-of-mine manure salts was produced until a refinery could be placed in operation. Little was known in this country about underground mining of potash and the company turned to methods common in the metals mining industry. A four-compartment timbered shaft was finally sunk to a depth of 1,060 feet after overcoming a number of obstacles, including an overabundance of water, gas pockets, and unstable ground. A year later a second shaft was sunk to improve ventilation. The mining was done by driving drifts 8 feet wide into the ore body using air-driven rock drills. In a short time the drifts were widened to 20 feet and locomotive haulage was installed (26).

Within a year and a half, coal undercutters and electrically-driven auger drills were installed. The company, however, developed its own drills that had been adapted for use on potash ore. A room-and-pillar mining method replaced the earlier method with the rooms and breakthroughs 36 feet wide. After blasting, the ore was loaded mechanically onto shuttle cars, and then transferred to ore cars and transported to the shaft where it was loaded onto the skips and hoisted to the surface (26,82).

Construction of a refinery was completed in 1932 on the Pecos River. The refining process was patterned after the European method of solution and recrystallization of the potassium chloride to free it of sodium chloride and impurities. It was based on the principle that the solubility of potassium chloride in a solution of water or a sodium chloride-potassium chloride brine increases rapidly as the temperature increases while that of the sodium chloride remains practically unchanged (28,37). As first practiced at Carlsbad, a cool brine saturated with both sodium chloride and potassium chloride was heated to 110°C by circulating through condenser coolers and through heat exchangers heated with steam. The resulting hot brine was passed through a stationary bed of crushed crude salts from the mine, and the now potash-enriched brine was cooled by vacuum evaporators. The cooled brine, containing potassium chloride crystals, was pumped to settling tanks and the potash-free liquor decanted. The thickened crystalline slurry containing the potassium chloride crystals was filtered and the crystals were dried (28).

U.S. Potash merged with U.S. Borax Company to form the U.S. Borax and Chemical Corporation in 1956. The potash activities retained the U.S. Potash Company name (3).

Potash Company of America—The Potash Company of America (PCA), the second company to produce potash in the Carlsbad area (Chapter 5), began production in 1934. The company, managed by men with coal mining experience, adopted immediately the room-and-pillar mining method used in the coal industry. The company was destined to become the largest potash producer in the United States. It introduced and improved upon a number of the practices followed in potash mining, and was the first company in the world to use a flotation process to beneficiate soluble potash salts on a commercial scale (35,82).

A patent filed in France in 1928 noted that the flotation method could be carried out in a brine saturated with ore constituents (22). Up until this time it was thought that a highly ionized solution such as brine interfered with action of flotation agents and made it impossible to float saline materials without dissolving them too much. The flotation process used by the Potash Company of America and developed cooperatively with the Bureau of Mines involved floating the sodium chloride away from the potassium chloride (just the reverse of the process that was to become standard) using as reagents carboxylic acids in a circuit modified by lead or bismuth salts. The method was developed and patented in the United States by Arthur J. Weinig. The process floated not only the sodium chloride, which was present in the brine in greater quantities than the potassium chloride, but also clays and other impurities to produce a white, relatively pure potassium chloride (22,35,44).

PCA's refining plant began operating at the mine site in 1936. Essentially the steps were as follows. The ore was crushed to size and screened; part was shipped directly to market without processing, and the remainder was ground further in a hammer mill, pulped with brine, and milled by a ball mill. Flotation agents were added and the pulp went through a series of flotation cells into which air was introduced at the bottom to form a small bubble froth. Filmed sodium chloride particles were picked up and carried to the surface in the froth and scraped off automatically. Underflow containing the particles of potassium chloride was dewatered on vacuum filters and dried to produce a 60 percent standard potassium chloride product (43,44). In 1962, the original flotation plant was converted to the less costly amine flotation of potassium chloride (25).

By 1950, the potash not recovered during flotation was separated and the filter cake containing the potash was used in two processes. In one, the cake was melted in a furnace and solidified as a thin layer on a disc-type cooler from which it was scraped continuously to form granular particles. The granular product containing about 60 percent K_2O was sold on the infant granular fertilizer market. In the second process, the cake was redissolved and recrystallized to produce a 99.9 percent pure chemical grade of potassium chloride sold on the industrial market (82).

International Minerals and Chemical Corporation—As a result of the successes of the United States Potash Company and the Potash Company of America, several new companies were launched to exploit the Carlsbad deposits and to conduct additional exploration. Union Potash and Chemical Company was formed in 1936 to consolidate the interests of four of these companies: the Texas Potash Company, the General Potash Company, the New Mexico Potash Company, and the Carlsbad Potash Company. Union Potash began sinking a shaft in 1936 but lack of funds prevented its continuance. The company applied for three leases of 2,560 acres each on public areas explored by the merged companies and known to contain commercial deposits of sylvinite and langbeinite (36,37).

International Agricultural Corporation, which became the International Minerals and Chemical Corporation (IMC) in 1942, acquired an interest in Union Potash in return for financing development of the mine. As a result, the shaft was completed to a depth of 925 feet in 1938. The mine began operating in 1940, producing potassium chloride and potassium magnesium sulfate (langbeinite); the latter was marketed under the trade name "Sul-Po-Mag." Unlike the other two companies operating in the area, IMC marketed no crushed ore as manure salts (37,45,82).

Mining was done by the room-and-pillar method using the most advanced techniques. All operations were fully mechanized and all underground equipment was electrically driven. The company operated at two levels, mining langbeinite on the 850-foot level and sylvinite on the 900-foot level. The mining shafts serviced the 850-foot level which was connected with the 900-foot level by a slope equipped with a belt conveyor. Beginning in 1948, the pillars on the 900-foot level were mined and the degree of convergence was carefully followed (26).

IMC in 1942 became the first company anywhere to use amine reagents to float potassium chloride from sodium chloride commercially. The idea for floating the potassium chloride rather than the sodium chloride apparently was first suggested in this country in 1937. The process as developed by IMC and variously improved and modified became the most widely practiced method worldwide for removing potassium chloride from sylvinite (36,82). The company previously had considerable experience in developing and using flotation in beneficiation of phosphate rock in the late 1920's and the 1930's (Chapter 7).

IMC was active also in other lines of potash beneficiation. In the early 1950's, IMC and the U.S. Potash Company were both separating potassium chloride from sodium chloride by gravity to produce a granular product containing 50 percent K_2O (82). In 1963, IMC developed and placed in operation at its Canadian mine a heavy media process to separate potassium and sodium chlorides. The method involved introducing finely ground magnetite, which was recoverable, into the brine to aid in the gravity separation of the potassium chloride. The company also applied the method at its Carlsbad operation to recover langbeinite from mixed langbeinite-sylvinite ores (3,22).

The beneficiation of langbeinite ore did not present any serious difficulties. IMC, the first company to mine langbeinite, developed a successful fresh-water washing process in which the sodium chloride is washed away from langbeinite. Although langbeinite is water soluble, the rate at which it dissolves is slow. IMC also developed a continuous, countercurrent washing process which gave maximum solution of the unwanted salts in a minimum contact time. The solid langbeinite, 96 to

98 percent pure, was dried and marketed (38,82). The company also reacted the langbeinite with potassium chloride to form potassium sulfate (38,82).

Bonneville, Ltd.—Located on the Bonneville Flats near Wendover, Utah, Salduro Marsh had provided brines from which potash had been recovered during World War I (Chapter 5). Production ceased after World War I and the property was taken over by local speculators. In 1937, Bonneville, Ltd., formed by a group of New York investors, including Bradley and Baker Company, a long-time dealer in fertilizers in the East, renewed potash production. As before, the salts in the brine were crystallized by solar evaporation (46).

The brine was collected in a system of canals extending more or less radially from central points where pumping stations were located. The canals, totaling 50 miles in length, became filled by seepage with brine containing chlorides of sodium, potassium, and magnesium. The brine was pumped from the canals into primary evaporation ponds where deposition of sodium chloride was allowed to proceed until saturation of the brine with potassium chloride was reached. The KCl-saturated brine was then transferred to secondary ponds and evaporation continued until the point was reached where carnallite (KCl • $MgCl_2$ • $6H_2O$), an undesired potassium mineral, began to precipitate out. The remaining brine was then removed to waste ponds. Crude salts in the secondary ponds were harvested with bulldozers and trucks and transported to the processing plant where the potassium chloride initially was separated by crystallization. By 1950, however, the potassium chloride was being separated by flotation (37). Production from Salduro Marsh has remained modest, averaging around 55,000 to 60,000 short tons of K_2O annually. Bonneville, Ltd. was taken over by the Kaiser Chemical Corporation in the early 1960's (3).

World War II Potash Situation

World War II found the United States in a markedly different potash situation than existed at the start of World War I. At that time, the Nation depended entirely on imports from Germany. By 1939, the United States had an established industry; two plants were operating and another was nearing completion in the Carlsbad district, and two companies were recovering potash from brines. The 1939 production of 312,000 tons of K_2O increased to 525,000 tons in 1941, of which 82 percent came from Carlsbad, 17 percent from brines, and 1 percent from the two by-product sources. Steady increases in production, mostly from Carlsbad operations, brought production to 874,000 tons in 1945 (64). This remarkable increase in production, all privately financed, offset prewar imports and was sufficient to meet most of the considerably expanded wartime needs.

The War Production Board early in 1943 began to allocate potash to various users including domestic agriculture; the chemical industry; munitions production; and exports to Canada, Cuba, and certain lend-lease countries. Although small shortages developed, reaching about 10 percent in 1943-44, no serious damage resulted–a sharp contrast to the potash famine of World War I. Wartime price controls on potash were set by the Office of Price Administration. Even before these went into effect there had been no increase in wholesale prices (1,80).

One major impact of price controls was to preclude a rush to produce potash from a wide range of by-products, as had been the case in World War I. The Utah alunite deposits, however, received a lot of attention; this time the primary interest was aluminum rather than potash, and a plant was constructed with Federal Government funds (51). The venture was not economically successful and the plant was closed in 1946.

The postwar period saw no immediate need to add major new mines and none was opened until 1952. In Michigan, however, the Dow Chemical Company in 1946 began recovering a small amount of fertilizer-grade potassium chloride from its brine wells near Midland as a by-product of production of magnesium bromide and other salts (37). Potash recovery from the brine continued until 1970.

Although consumption in the late 1940's continued to increase modestly, exports about balanced imports with the increase being met by a series of expansions at the three Carlsbad mines. IMC built a new refinery, sank more shafts, and increased the size and effectiveness of its mining and plant operations. PCA also completed an expansion and improvement program; this included adding a new shaft, completing a new 24-cell flotation section, and providing a 26-mile water pipeline. U.S. Potash added a flotation unit in addition to its crystallization unit, and expanded the overall operation (52,53).

A considerable amount of prospecting got underway in the Carlsbad district and in an area in Grand County, Utah, where potash deposits had been identified earlier. Although little noted at the time, a tremendously important discovery of underground deposits of potash had been made in the Province of Saskatchewan in Canada. Plans well underway by the end of the 1940's to open new mines in the Carlsbad district would launch a period of rapid expansion of domestic potash production.

New Companies: 1950-1966

Duval Company—The Duval Sulphur and Potash Company began exploring in 1947 for a likely location for a potash mine in the Carlsbad area. By 1949, a site had been selected for what was to become the Saunders mine. Construction began on two shafts and the sylvinite deposit was tapped at 1,424 feet. A refinery was located adjacent to the mine with shipment of the refined product beginning in 1952. In 1961,

Duval began mining sylvinite at a second mine, the Wills-Weaver mine, 13 miles north of the Saunders mine where the new mine's ore also was processed. The Duval Sulphur and Potash Company in 1964 became the Duval Corporation, a subsidiary of the Pennzoil Company. In December 1964, the company started production of langbeinite at its recently completed Nash Draw mine near Carlsbad. Two 900-foot shafts were sunk to the sylvinite level which was mined later. The langbeinite bed, encountered at the 1,025-foot level, was reached by an inclined-slope tunnel from the 900-foot sylvinite level. A new plant was built next to the original refinery at the Saunders mine to process the langbeinite (26, 53, 57, 59, 60).

Southwest Potash Corporation—This company, a wholly-owned subsidiary of American Metal Company, Ltd., was formed in 1948 to hold Federal and state prospecting permits on lands in the Carlsbad district. An intensive core drilling program was launched, and some 60 test holes were sunk. Sinking of shafts began in 1950 to tap a sylvinite layer at the 1016-foot depth. The mine came on stream in 1952, producing at first only standard-grade potash (52,53,69). In 1957, the company became the first to produce granular potassium chloride using a compaction method. The granular product was introduced as K-Gran and promoted for use in bulk blends (19). In 1963, the company began production of potassium nitrate at Vicksburg, Mississippi, for both fertilizer and non-agricultural uses (2).

The company's name was changed in 1967 to that of the parent company, American Metal and Climax, Inc., and again in the early 1970's to Amax Chemical Corporation (19).

National Potash Company—Freeport Sulphur Company, a parent company of the National Potash Company, began drilling and investigating the Carlsbad area in 1948 and acquired potash leases and mining permits. National Potash was formed in 1955 by Freeport Sulphur and the Pittsburgh Consolidation Coal Company on an equal share basis to develop potash deposits in Lea County, New Mexico, a part of the Carlsbad district. Two 15-foot-diameter shafts were sunk to a depth of 1,800 feet and operations began in 1957. During the same year the company acquired another deposit 17 miles from the original mine to obtain a higher grade ore for upgrading that of the first mine. Production of the second mine, known as the Government Reserve Mine and located in Eddy County, began in 1964. Both mines produce sylvinite. In 1965, Freeport took over Consolidated Coal's interest in the potash company. Most of National Potash's output was sold to Central Farmers Fertilizer Company (CF Industries), a farm cooperative (3,52,72).

Texas Gulf Sulphur Company—Texas Gulf Sulphur Company began production from its Cane Creek mine near Moab, Utah, in 1964. This was the first major domestic underground deposit containing solid potash salts to be mined outside of the Carlsbad district, and was the result of years of exploration in the general area. Potash was first indicated the area in 1924 when a sample of well drillings from the Crescent Eagle well east of Green River, Utah, was turned over to the Geological Survey and was found to contain the potassium mineral carnallite. In 1925, a sample taken from a greater depth in the Crescent Eagle well was examined and the presence of sylvinite was noted (78). Prospecting for potash was conducted in 1942 when Potash Company of America entered into an agreement with the Utah Magnesium Corporation to drill a number of deep wells and prospect the holdings of the Magnesium Corporation near Crescent Junction in Grand County. Four wells were put down to a depth of 5,000 feet in 1943. These showed that, although carnallite was the most abundant potash mineral, sylvinite and polyhalite also were present (50,51). The Delhi Oil Company began exploration for potash near Moab in 1953, and upon completion of its investigations in 1956 reported substantial potash deposits (70,73).

Texas Gulf Sulphur in 1960 acquired a large, high-grade sylvinite deposit in the Cane Creek Anticline area near Moab from the Delhi-Taylor Oil Corporation. Construction was started in 1962 on a refinery based on flotation and having a capacity of 600,000 tons per year of KCl; also one mine shaft was put down to a depth of 2,789 feet. These were completed in 1964 and operations began in 1965. Difficulties were encountered in using conventional mining equipment in the heavily faulted deposits. Output was low, costs were high, and the mine operated at a loss. Output of the refinery was boosted in 1967 with the addition of a crystallizer unit to treat the low-grade sylvite fines, and a second mine shaft was completed in 1968. Production rose from 300,000 tons to 410,000 in 1968. Even with the increase in production, it became apparent to the company that the form of mining practiced at Cane Creek could never produce potash competitive with that produced in Canada (9,13,17).

Kermac Potash Company—In 1955, the Farm Chemicals Resources Development Corporation was incorporated with the National Farmers Union holding 50 percent of the shares; Kerr-McGee Oil Industries, Inc., 25 percent; and Phillips Chemical Company, 25 percent. Kermac Potash Corporation was formed in 1961 after Kerr-McGee had purchased Phillips Chemical's holdings, making Kerr-McGee and National Farmers Union equal partners (8). In 1965, Kerr-McGee Oil Industries changed its name to Kerr-McGee Corporation (58).

Kermac mines a zone of high-slime, low-grade sylvinite ore on the border of Eddy and Lea Counties near the eastern boundary of the Carlsbad district. The initial organization, Farm Chemicals Resources Development, selected the Eddy-Lea County border area for its operations apparently because of the large potash reserves remaining in this portion of the Carlsbad area. Before starting construction the company established reserves of some 80 million tons of ore averaging 17 percent K_2O, sufficient to assure the company of the longest life expectancy of any potash producer then mining at Carlsbad. The project was completed after 10 years of preliminary exploration and research, shaft sinking, and refinery construction. The first shaft was completed in 1957, and a second shaft, rotary drilled, was completed five years later. Plant facilities were delayed until 1965 due to potash recovery problems resulting from the high content (5 to 7 percent) of clay and insoluble matter in the ore (12).

Mining was done by the longwall system since the ore bed was only 4.5 feet thick. Three entries led into panels some 800 to 1,000 feet wide and 2,500 feet long. A coal-boring machine capable of working relatively thin deposits removed the ore over the 2,500-foot length. The broken ore was picked up by a loading machine and transported in shuttle cars to a conveyor belt for transport to a crushing center and storage prior to hoisting to the surface. The mining removed about 80 percent of the ore from each of the panels. Subsidence was gradual and no major roof problems were encountered (12).

The solution-crystallization procedure was used to separate the KCl from the NaCl. A special slime removal system was developed and tested at the Kerr-McGee research center at Oklahoma City. This consisted of a sequence of slime separation steps involving use of cyclones and spiral classifiers. Crystallization of the potassium chloride took place in a series of vacuum crystallizers. The potash crystals were withdrawn, slurried with a brine, and dewatered by centrifuging. The final product was distinguished by its high K_2O content (62.5 percent) (12). Annual capacity was around 300,000 tons of K_2O, although early estimates were higher (18).

Status of Mining and Beneficiation by Mid-1960's

The period from about 1930 through the mid-1960's was one of considerable challenge to U.S. potash producers, particularly those mining underground deposits. With so little known in this country about mining and refining underground potash deposits, the Carlsbad producers, especially the earlier ones, had to become innovators of the first order. Some of their developments, such as the separation of potassium chloride from sodium chloride by froth flotation, were used worldwide. Practices developed and improved upon at Carlsbad were used widely in the Saskatchewan field, an easy transfer since the companies that developed them also were among the developers and operators of the Canadian mines. By the mid-1960's, mining and refining methods and practices had become fairly well standardized although modifications often were required to adapt them to specific conditions.

Design of mine shafts remained highly flexible to meet the different capacities of mines and depths of ore zones. For example, in the Carlsbad area shaft diameters ranged from 8 to 18 feet and depths ranged from 800 to 1,800 feet. The first shaft of Texas Gulf Sulphur's mine in Utah, however, had a diameter of 22 feet and a depth of 2,789 feet. The potash mines were served with either one multiple purpose shaft, or with two shafts. With two shafts, one shaft served primarily for ventilation or included ventilation along with conveyance of men and materials; the second shaft was used primarily for hoisting ore to the surface. The methods for sinking and lining the shafts varied greatly according to geological conditions. Where water was encountered it was sealed off by grouting with concrete, or later by freezing the ground around the water-bearing strata. Linings in New Mexico under difficult conditions were reinforced concrete or thick concrete walls (28). (In Europe where geological conditions were less favorable than in New Mexico, freezing was common and the shafts were lined with reinforced concrete walls, single or double sheet steel cylinders or steel plates with or without use of sealants or inner linings of concrete or bitumen, or cast iron tubbing (81). Material removal during shaft sinking usually involved hand excavation, use of percussion drills, blasting, mechanical mucking, and even rotary shaft drilling (13).

The Potash Company of America in 1951 used a freezing method to sink a shaft at Carlsbad when grouting failed. A series of 28 holes was bored in the ground surrounding the 15-foot-diameter shaft. Each hole was cased with 6-inch tubing down which a 2-inch tube was inserted to within 18 inches of the bottom of the hole to permit free circulation of a refrigerated brine. Nevertheless, problems resulted when tubes ruptured, filling the area being frozen with brine. A new, more costly refrigerant had to be substituted and, due to the presence of the spilled brine, 2-1/2 months was required to freeze the shell of earth around the shaft to a depth of 250 feet. The shaft was sunk and lined without mishap after the freezing (62).

The room-and-pillar method of mining underground potash deposits was the standard method except under unusual situations. In this method, pillars are left to support the overburden as rectangular rooms are mined out. Dimensions of entry ways, rooms, and pillars differ among mines. (In one example cited, both rooms and breakthroughs were 36 feet wide, with pillars in the panel areas 36 by 82 feet.) Initial mining recovered around 60 percent of the ore. Pillar removal after the rooms are exhausted (first practiced by IMC in 1948) resulted in a total recovery of about 90 percent of the ore. Most producers by the mid-1960's removed the pillars (55).

The introduction and use of continuous mining machines was a major advance in potash mining. PCA appears to have been the first to install continuous miners. It placed two in operation at Carlsbad in 1951. In 1954, four Carlsbad mines reported using the miners. The continuous miners, of which there were several types, rapidly replaced the conventional mining operation which involved undercutting, drilling, and blasting to break up the ore. The new machines initially could mine 40 to 60 tons per hour, but by 1966 IMC had installed one miner, a borer type, in its Canadian plant that could mine 5 tons per minute (54,68,71).

Broken-up ore from the mining machines is gathered by mechanical loaders and loaded onto shuttle cars or conveyor belts for transport to a main conveyor belt which delivers the ore to the shaft. Here the ore is crushed by rollers into 3- to 6-inch chunks and placed in underground storage bins. From the bins it is automatically loaded onto skips, holding up to 24 tons each, and hoisted to the surface. Mining maintenance and other services needed in the overall mining operation are provided by facilities underground. Working conditions in most potash mines are nearly ideal, including freedom from gases and dusts (54).

Solution mining, which does away with shafts and the need for placing men and equipment underground, first became a commercial reality at Kalium Chemicals mine in Saskatchewan in 1964. Texas Gulf Sulphur converted its uneconomical underground Cane Creek, Utah, mine to a solution mine in 1972.

Development of a flotation process to separate the mineral sylvite (KCl) from halite (NaCl) was a major breakthrough in potash refining. As pointed out earlier, flotation, first applied commercially in the world's potash industry by the Potash Company of America, was a method whereby the sodium chloride in sylvinite was floated from the sylvite (KCl). This procedure was displaced by a flotation procedure developed by IMC for floating the KCl away from the NaCl. Since the IMC process required less of the costly flotation reagents, it was adopted rapidly in the United States and Canada as the new potash mines came on stream. Adoption was slower in other countries.

The basic steps of the sylvite flotation process had become fairly well standardized by the mid-1960's and included the following: (a) crushing ore and classifying it into coarse and fine particle fractions; (b) adding a saturated brine of potassium chloride and sodium chloride to produce a slurry containing 50 to 75 percent solids; (c) wet-grinding the ore to a size that liberated the sylvite from the sodium chloride crystals; (d) scrubbing the ground material and mechanically removing slimes consisting of clay and other insoluble materials adhering to the surfaces of the particles; (e) introducing the chosen sylvite conditioning agents including an aliphatic amine to selectively film the sylvite particles to make them hydrophobic so that they will float; (f) diluting the slurry to 20 to 25 percent solids; (g) introducing the slurry into a series of rough flotation cells where the slurry is circulated and contacted with air to form air bubbles which adhere to the sylvite particles and cause them to float. The sylvite float is raked mechanically from the top of the flotation cells; (h) the harvested sylvite (still containing some halite) is introduced to a "cleaner" circuit of flotation cells to further refine the

Continuous mining machines were introduced at Carlsbad, New Mexico, in 1951. *(Potash Company of America)*

sylvite; (i) drying the sylvite; and (j) screening the potassium chloride crystals according to size ranges to be marketed and granulating the fines into a desired size range (27,66).

The flotation process became considerably more important in refining potash salts than the formerly dominant crystallization process. Crystallization holds a definite advantage over flotation when used on high-slime ores, and is essential in recovering potash from natural brines. Crystallization also found use in recovering potassium chloride from tailings and brines left over from flotation (27).

Emergence of the Canadian Potash Industry

The discovery of the world's largest known deposit of high-grade potash ore in Canada and its consequent development greatly affected the U.S. potash situation. The appearance of Canadian potash on the U.S. market in the 1960's assured this country of a virtually unlimited supply at a critical time when demand for potash fertilizer was increasing rapidly and the supply of high-grade sylvinite ore in the Carlsbad deposits was running out. On the other hand, imports of the low-cost Canadian potash hastened the eclipse of the Carlsbad district by making reserves of the lower grade ores noncompetitive. Further, the United States had no other proven reserves likely to compete in most years with the Canadian imports.

Discovery and Exploration

Potash was first noted in southeastern Saskatchewan during oil drilling operations of the Imperial Oil, Ltd., in 1943 and 1944 near

Radville at depths of around 7,200 feet. Because of the great depth, no commercial interest was aroused. In 1946, however, a potash-bearing bed 11 feet thick containing sylvinite analyzing 21.6 percent K_2O was found at a depth of 3,500 feet at the Verbata Well No. 2 located near Unity in west-central Saskatchewan. This discovery immediately excited speculation on the possibility of commercial production (67).

In 1950, oil companies engaged in drilling began running logs of measurements of natural radioactivity of the formations penetrated. (All naturally-occurring potash deposits contain a small amount of the potassium-40, a radioactive isotope that emits gamma rays which can be detected and measured.) Neutron logs kept of the drill holes not only showed the presence of potassium but also gave some indication of the potassium content. The measurements greatly speeded prospecting and confirmed the existence of high-grade potash deposits over a large area of Saskatchewan (67,76).

The sylvinite beds in Saskatchewan and adjacent Alberta and Manitoba occur in the Devonian Prairie Evaporite formation which is about 200 miles wide and extends about 800 miles in a northwesterly direction with small extensions into North Dakota and Montana. The top of the formation ranges in depth from 2,000 to 3,000 feet along the northern edge to 9,000 feet at the North Dakota border. The sylvinite beds are very high grade, ranging from 25 to 35 percent K_2O, and their thickness averages 7 to 10 feet. The beds are uniform and free from structural deformities. Three major potash zones have been identified in the upper 200 feet of the Evaporite formation; they are separated by halite beds. The zones, in ascending order, are the Esterhazy, Belle Plaine, and Patience Lake. Sylvinite is the major mineral in all three zones; the latter two also contain carnallite in small quantities. Potash mining is restricted to the Province of Saskatchewan where the most significant deposits are found (67,76).

Commercial Development

Commercial production of potash in Saskatchewan was first attempted by the Western Potash Corporation, Ltd. (changed to Continental Potash Corporation in 1955), which began sinking a shaft near Unity in 1952. The plan was to bore a single shaft and extract the potassium chloride in solution by treating the sylvinite underground with unsaturated brine. Shaft construction was abandoned after reaching a depth of over 1,000 feet. Continental Potash revived the effort in 1955, but this time the shaft flooded at 1,675 feet. Operations, renewed once more in 1959, failed when the shaft ruptured. The project was abandoned in 1964 (10,67). This was the first encounter with the troublesome Blairmore Formation. The formation, 100 to 300 feet thick, is found at depths of 1,200 to 1,700 feet and contains strata of water-bearing, unconsolidated sands and clays where water pressures reach 500 to 600 pounds per square inch (81).

The Potash Company of America, the first of the Carlsbad producers to begin exploration in Saskatchewan, in 1953 selected a mining site 16 miles southwest of Saskatoon at Patience Lake. The shaft, begun in 1954, was sunk through ground that had been frozen by circulating refrigerant through 27 vertical holes surrounding the shaft (the same general plan the company had used successfully at Carlsbad in 1951). The company was able to pass its shaft through the Blairmore Formation by drilling and then lining the walls with a thick layer of concrete. Although the shaft was completed and production began in 1958. a thawing of the surrounding area caused severe leakage and led to closing of the mine. Two and a half years was required to repair the shaft by grouting. Continuing operations began in 1965 employing conventional mining methods and refining by flotation. Production capacity of the operation was 360,000 tons of potassium chloride annually. By this time, however, both IMC and Kalium Chemicals had mines on stream (10,67). In 1967, PCA merged with Ideal Cement Company of Denver to form Ideal Basic Industries, Inc., of which the Canadian subsidiary of the Potash Company became a division (61). Annual capacity of the plant was increased to around 750,000 short tons of KCl with the sinking of a second shaft in 1968.

International Minerals and Chemical Corporation became interested in the Saskatchewan deposits in 1955 and selected a mine site on the eastern side of the province 12 miles northeast of Esterhazy. Shaft sinking was started in 1957 with an effort made to control the water and quicksand of the Blairmore Formation by grouting. After two failures the decision was made to employ a practice commonly used in Europe; it involved freezing the troublesome strata, digging through it, and installing cast iron tubbing rings which are prefabricated but assembled in the shaft. IMC employed a German-Canadian group, AMC-Harrison Ltd., formed by using engineers from leading German shaft sinking firms. Shaft sinking is a highly specialized field and usually is done by companies having research, and engineering and design departments (81). Even so, a number of unexpected problems developed during sinking. The IMC shaft finally reached the deposit at 3,100 feet depth in June 1962. The mine began producing a month later, making it the first mine in the Canadian field to achieve continuous operation. Production initially was 1 million tons of product annually. Mining was done by a modified room-and-pillar method, the operation was trackless using only shuttle cars and belt conveyors, and all ore was excavated by continuous boring machines of the type tested initially at IMC's Carlsbad mine. The one shaft served the entire mine (10,56).

IMC in 1963 began sinking a shaft for its second or K2 mine, about 6 miles from the K1 mine. As a result of the experience gained in sinking the first shaft, the K2 mine, designed to produce 1.5 million tons of product annually, was brought into production in January 1967. Production capacities of both mines, however, were subsequently increased through modifications and improvements. The two shafts, K1 and K2, were connected underground at the level of the potash horizon mainly for ventilation reasons. Each mine has its own refinery based on flotation. In 1963, IMC also built a heavy media crystallization plant to produce white potash for the Japanese markets (3).

The heavy media process developed by IMC employed finely ground magnetite to aid in the gravity separation of halite (NaCl) crystals from sylvite (KCl). The halite is denser than sylvite (sp. gr. 2.13 versus 1.98) and in a liquid of intermediate specific gravity the halite will sink and the sylvite will float. IMC uses a suspension of finely ground magnetite as the intermediate fluid and introduces it into the brine of potassium and sodium chlorides. The process is continuous with separation of the two chlorides taking place in a hydrocyclone. The magnetite is recovered by washing it from the potash concentrate and salt tailing, and recycled. IMC uses the coarser fraction of the ground ore for the heavy media separation while the finer fraction is subjected to crystallization. A combination of heavy media treatment of the coarse fraction plus crystallization of fine particles can produce coarse and granular grades from the former and "white" potash from the latter; white potash has been in good demand for Japanese markets (3,22,65).

Experience gained by the early potash companies as they attempted to open mines in Saskatchewan and the successful operation of IMC's K1 mine encouraged other companies to continue or enter the development of the field. Furthermore, export demand was good, prices were stable, and the political climate of the Province of Saskatchewan was highly favorable at the time to private exploitation of the reserves. The Provincial Government in the early and mid-1960's encouraged foreign investment including ownership of the mines. In addition, the Provincial Government guaranteed low fixed royalties, 2-1/2 percent of the value of the potash, until 1981. All of this touched off a surge of development in the 1960's resulting in nine mines being operated by the end of 1969 with the tenth coming on stream in September 1970.

In October 1964, Kalium Chemicals Ltd., then a joint subsidiary of Pittsburgh Plate Glass Industries and Armour and Company (Armour dropped out later), brought a solutions mine into continuous production at Belle Plaine between Moose Jaw and Regina in the south central part of Saskatchewan. Although a number of attempts had been made at solution mining of potash, this was the first underground potash to be mined successfully by this method. The decision of Kalium Chemicals to investigate solution mining in the Saskatchewan field was brought about by the desire to avoid the troublesome Blairmore Formation and deep shafts which increased the cost of mining. Further, the rich potash deposits occurring at 5,000 feet or more in depth could not be mined using the shaft and conventional underground method. As a result,

In solution mining, crystallizers are used to extract the sylvite-halite mixture that was dissolved underground. *(Kalium Chemicals)*

Pittsburgh Plate Glass engineers were assigned the job of perfecting a solution mining process. After several years of research and testing, exploratory drilling began in 1960; a pilot plant was placed in operation in 1961, and construction of a commercial production facility was started in 1963. The various investigations resulted in several patents issued to J. B. Dahms, B. P. Edmonds, and E. P. Helvenston and assigned to Pittsburgh Plate Glass. The mine began preliminary operation in August 1964 from a bed 5,300 feet below the surface (7,10,66).

Solution mining as used by Kalium Chemicals involves, as a first step, pumping hot water or a dilute salt solution through a pipe placed in cased bore holes drilled from the surface to a point in the potash-lean halite bed just below the potash-rich sylvinite bed. The solution extracts the potassium chloride and sodium chloride, forming a cavity. The concentrated solution is removed through the pipe to the surface at first through the single cased hole. However, as the cavity enlarges, circulation of the dissolving solution into and out of the cavity is accomplished by providing two or more cased holes into each cavity, the dilute solution being injected through one and the concentrated solution removed from another. Usually, the dissolving solution remains in the cavity for several months until it becomes nearly saturated with KCl and NaCl. Composition of the extracting solution is controlled to extract KCl selectively from the ore to the maximum extent desirable (54).

Upon reaching the surface, the saturation solution is run to an evaporation-crystallization plant to refine the sylvite-halite mixture. The solution passes to evaporators where large quantities of water are

Table 8.1. Potash Developments in Saskatchewan, Canada (10, 3, 61, 42).

Location	Operating Company	Parent Companies	Construction Started	First Operation	Annual Capacity 1000 s. tons K_2O
Patience Lake	Potash Co. of America, Ltd.	Ideal Basic Industries, Inc., Denver	April 1954	May 1965	460
Esterhazy K1 mine	Int. Min. & Chem. Corp (Canada) Ltd.	Int. Min. & Chem. Corp.	June 1957	June 1962	
K2 mine	"	"	May 1963	April 1967	2,330
Belle Plaine	Kalium Chemicals, Ltd.	Pittsburgh Plate Glass Co.	May 1963	Oct. 1964	937
Allan	Allan Potash Mines	U.S. Borax, Swift, and Texas Gulf Sulphur	Aug. 1964	May 1968	900
Saskatoon	Duval Corp.	Pennzoil	Dec. 1965	May 1968	730
Lanigan	Alswinsal Potash of Canada, Ltd.	French & West German interests	Oct. 1964	Oct. 1968	600
Vade (near Saskatoon)	Cominco Ltd.	Canadian-owned, majority held by Canadian Pacific	Sept. 1965	March 1969	720
Viscount	Central Canada Potash Co., Ltd.	Noranda Mines Ltd., 51% CF Industries 49%	Jan. 1966	Sept. 1969	900
Rocanville	Sylvite of Canada	Hudson Bay Mining & Smelting Co., Ltd.	Jan. 1968	Sept. 1970	732

removed. Settling is accomplished in a thickener and crystallization is conducted in four baffle crystallizers, each one producing a specific particle size range. Fines are granulated. The product is white due to the absence of iron (3,29,54,66).

The massive expansion program of the Saskatchewan potash industry was over by 1971 with 9 companies operating 10 mines (Table 8.1). Annual production capacity of the 10 mines was around 7.6 million short tons of K_2O, exceeding that of any other country. About 30 percent of the capacity was in IMC's two mines at Esterhazy. Six of the companies had U.S. roots; in addition, Sylvite of Canada was marketing its product through Terra Chemicals of Sioux City, Iowa.

Of the 10 mines in operation, all except the Kalium Chemicals used conventional underground mining practices. Freezing and tubbing of shafts through the Blairmore Formation was used on the nine non-solution mines, with the entire shaft-sinking operation being contracted out to professional shaft-sinking companies under the direction of European engineers. All of the mines are equipped with the most modern mining machinery including continuous miners. Most of the refineries employ both flotation and crystallization processes to separate the KCl from the NaCl, especially as the demand for high-grade potash in clear liquid fertilizers increased. Nearly all of Canada's overseas shipments are handled in bulk loading terminals at Vancouver using Canadian Pacific and Canadian National railways for overland transport in Canada. Shipments to the United States are primarily by rail (3,11).

As the end of the 1960's approached it became increasingly apparent that the world's fertilizer industry had badly overestimated the demand for fertilizers and fertilizer materials. The Canadian potash industry, like those in most other countries, had expanded too fast and production capacity far exceeded demand. Potash prices declined sharply–from a Saskatchewan average of Can. $37.53 Canadian per short ton of K_2O to $19.87 in 1969. As 1969 progressed, the producers abandoned the customary seasonal pricing policy and sold potash for whatever it would bring (4).

The low prices for Canadian potash caused a bitter reaction in the United States, primarily because of the inability of Carlsbad potash to compete, resulting in a major layoff of potash workers in New Mexico. The U.S. Tariff Commission found that, under the Anti-dumping Act of 1921, the U.S. potash industry was being, or was likely to be, injured by unfair imports of potassium chloride from Canada, thus making potash subject to an anti-dumping duty. Several bills where introduced in Congress to impose quotas and tariffs on potash imports. The U.S. Justice Department, however, argued in March 1970 against imposition of anti-dumping penalties on the basis that the alleged dumping was primarily by U.S. owned companies operating in Canada. As a result, no penalty was enforced and none of the bills became law (4,14,61).

Saskatchewan Government Involvement

Although the Saskatchewan Government was able to stimulate development of the potash deposits by tax concessions and nongovernmental interference, it was not able to forestall or improve the bad market situation. With prices at an all-time low and production exceeding demand, the Saskatchewan economy began to suffer from tax and direct revenue losses and unemployment in the potash industry was increasing. To improve the situation, the Thatcher administration in Saskatchewan in April 1970 implemented a prorationing program that limited production to about 40 percent of capacity, and established a floor price of Can. $33.75 per ton of K_2O. However, companies were allowed to develop additional markets after all producers in the province had reached their 40 percent capacity figure. Prorationing was retained when the New Democratic Party under Allan Blakeney came into power in 1971, but at a uniform percentage of capacity and without the additional market option. Prorationing failed to firm prices on a short-term basis. It also stifled market growth during a time when world demand for potash was increasing. Buyers seeking additional potash, as a result, had to look somewhere other than Saskatchewan. For example, in 1971-72 Saskatchewan was operating at 48 percent of capacity while the United States operated at 89 percent and Western Europe at 82 percent (4,21,61).

The Blakeney administration added a "prorationing" fee of 60 cents per ton of product in 1972 and doubled it to $1.20 per ton in 1973. In 1974, the Provincial Government announced a new potash policy aimed at ensuring the people of Saskatchewan a fair share of benefits, encouraging expansions, and ensuring a degree of government ownership–all of which further worsened relationships between the potash producers and the Provincial Government. What followed was a potash "reserve tax" designed to absorb windfall profits on potash for the benefit of the province. The tax was determined by a complex formula involving the value of the potash property, size of the mine, capital improvement, grade of ore, and market price of potash. The Canadian Federal Government also in 1974 declared that the provincial taxes and royalties were nondeductible for Federal income tax purposes (4).

The Central Canada Potash (49 percent owned by CF Industries) in 1972 had challenged the province's prorationing regulations in the courts on the basis that the regulations denied sales to the company's captive outlet in the United States. Although the province lifted prorationing in 1974 due to increased potash demand, the government emphasized it had not abandoned the principle of prorationing or floor prices. In 1975, the Saskatchewan Court of Queen's Bench ruled that prorationing was unconstitutional and awarded Central Canada Can. $1.5 million. The Court of Appeals overturned the lower court's ruling. Central Canada in turn appealed to the Supreme Court of Canada which confirmed in 1978 that prorationing was unconstitutional; it did not, however, allow the claim for lost sales (21,24).

The reserve tax also was challenged by the potash producers in 1975 when a suit was launched against the Provincial Government alleging the reserve tax was primarily a production tax and as such could only be collected by the Federal Government. After intense negotiations, a compromise resulted in 1979 in the form of "potash resource payment agreements," thus ending several years of disputes. The agreements involved a base payment of Can. $6.00 per ton of K_2O on the first 300,000 tons, and $7.50 for each ton over this. Certain deductions were allowed the industry if the gross mine revenue the previous year was low and for additional capital investments. The new tax replaced all previous taxes (24).

In line with its new policy of 1974, the Saskatchewan government, following re-election of the New Democratic Party in 1975, prepared legislation to acquire assets of some or all of the province's producing potash mines. To implement this, the Provincial Government established a government corporation–the Potash Corporation of Saskatchewan (PCS)–with the intention of eventually owning 50 percent or more of the potash capacity. Also in 1975, the decision was made to acquire the assets of existing mines rather than to build new mines. In 1976, the Potash Development Act and the Potash Corporation of Saskatchewan Act were passed to give PCS authority to purchase or expropriate any kind of potash property on behalf of the government (4,21).

Several companies, apparently discouraged with their Canadian ventures, showed interest in selling their properties to the Provincial Government. In August 1976, PCS announced the purchase of the Duval mine from Pennzoil, Inc., for Can. $128.5 million and renamed it PCS Cory Ltd., a wholly-owned subsidiary of PCS. In March 1977, PCS obtained Sylvite of Canada's Rocanville mine for Can. $144 million, which included Sylvite's storage at Vancouver and at various locations in the United States; however, PCS was to continue supplying potash to Terra Chemicals at Sioux City. In June 1977, PCS reached an agreement with the French and West German owners of Alwinsal Potash of Canada, Ltd., to purchase the Lanigan mine for Can. $76 million. The agreement did not include the Potash Company of Canada, Alwinsal's marketing subsidiary. The final mine to be taken over was the Allan Potash Mines' Allan mine in January 1978, in which PCS obtained the 40 percent owned by U.S. Borax and the 20 percent owned by Swift; Texasgulf, Inc., retained its 40 percent share. The U.S. Borax and Swift shares were obtained for Can. $86 million, and in a separate agreement PCS agreed to provide Swift with potash for its U.S. market. Thus by 1979 only five potash operations (6 mines) were left in the hands of private industry. They were: Potash Company of America, Inc.; IMC (Canada) Ltd (2 mines); Kalium Chemicals, Ltd.; Cominco, Ltd.; and Central Canada

Potash. Based upon 1980 production capacity data, 36 percent of the total Saskatchewan production capacity was controlled by PCS. After the takeover, PCS increased the production capacity of the Cory and Rocanville mines together by 304,000 tons of K_2O (21,24).

Canadian Potash in Perspective

Canada's annual production capacity for potash reached 7.7 million tons of K_2O in 1971 after Sylvite of Canada's Rocanville mine came into production; capacity climbed 11 percent by 1980 to 8.7 million tons in 1980. However, during the same period actual production increased from 3.5 million tons of K_2O to 7.8 million, a gain of 54 percent. (In contrast, the domestic U.S. production changed very little during the same period.) In 1971, the Saskatchewan mines were operated at only 45 percent of capacity, and in 1980 at 90 percent capacity. In 1971, Saskatchewan accounted for 64 percent of North America's (United States and Canada) production capacity, and in 1980, 74 percent; actual production was 58 percent of the continent's total in 1971 and 76 percent in 1980 (5,6,39,42).

On the world scene, Canada in the 1965-66 fertilizer year became the world's major producer of potash. It then declined to sixth place during the early days of prorationing and remained in about the same position through 1972-73. In 1973-74, Canada moved to second place (USSR held first place), and in 1979-80 again became the world's largest producer. Canada was the world's largest exporter of potash from 1965-66 through 1979-80 fertilizer years. During the same period the United States became the world's leading importer of potash, with Canada eventually supplying around 95 percent (31,32,33,34).

Canada's position as a world potash producer appears to have been strengthened by the discovery of a high-grade sylvinite deposit northeast of St. John in New Brunswick in 1971. The sylvinite, occurring at depths of 2,000 to 3,400 feet, contains around 32 percent K_2O. In one deposit, the potash layer was 50 feet thick, but faulted and irregular. PCA indicated its intention to develop and mine the deposit and completed a 2,400-foot shaft by the fall of 1978. Others, including IMC (Canada) also have shown interest and obtained leases. The deposit is strategically located to serve the eastern United States and Canada, and for shipment to Europe (4,76,77).

Decline of U.S. Potash Production: 1966-1980

Seven companies were producing potash in 1966 from the underground deposits in the Carlsbad area, and one from an underground deposit at Cane Creek near Moab, Utah. Two companies were producing from brines-one at Searles Lake, California, and the other at Salduro Marsh near Wendover, Utah. Domestic potash production reached an all-time peak in 1966 of 3.3 million tons of K_2O (Figure 8.1). After 1966, domestic production was reduced nearly every year until 1975 when it leveled out at around 2.5 million tons of K_2O annually.

U.S. Becomes Leading Potash Importer

Three potash events happened more or less simultaneously: quality (potash content) of the Carlsbad ore declined as the higher quality ores were mined out, the newly launched Canadian potash industry expanded production rapidly, and domestic demand for potash in fertilizers increased by leaps and bounds. Low-cost Canadian potash flowed into the country in ever-increasing amounts, not only making up for the decrease in domestic production but keeping abreast of the burgeoning demand. Consumption from 1966 through 1980 increased from 4 to 7 million tons of K_2O, or 75 percent. At the same time, potash imports almost quadrupled, going from 1.5 million tons to 5.5 million tons of K_2O, with 95 percent coming from Canada (6).

Although the United States was the number one potash importer, it continued to export domestically-produced potash. In 1966, it exported 621,000 short tons of K_2O, or 19 percent of the total domestic production; by 1980, it was exporting 926,000 tons or 38 percent, making the United States fifth in rank among potash exporting countries (34). Principal purchasers were Latin America (primarily Brazil), Japan, New Zealand, and Australia. Most of the potash for export was shipped from the ports at Houston and Galveston, Texas, and Long Beach and San Diego, California. Ground transportation costs to these ports from the Carlsbad district apparently were about the same as from Saskatchewan to Vancouver, British Columbia (23,76).

The lower cost Canadian potash retained its advantage over Carlsbad potash in the Midwest, the largest and fastest growing market in the United States. In 1965, the nine states normally considered as making up the Midwest consumed 2.8 million tons of K_2O as fertilizer, or 48 percent of the total U.S. consumption. However, in 1980 these same states consumed 3.6 million tons, or 58 percent of the U.S. total (36). Canadian potash also had a competitive advantage over Carlsbad potash elsewhere in the northern half of the United States, although the northern Great Plains and the Western States use very little potash in fertilizers. The major domestic market for Carlsbad potash was the traditionally high potash using Southern States which accounted for over a million tons of K_2O annually. New Mexico and states closer to the Carlsbad mines where the freight advantage was greatest use very little potash fertilizer. Potassium sulfate and potassium magnesium sulfate demanded premium prices and had no competition from outside of the country.

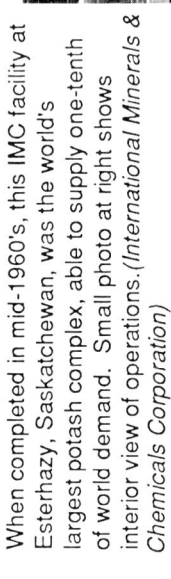

When completed in mid-1960's, this IMC facility at Esterhazy, Saskatchewan, was the world's largest potash complex, able to supply one-tenth of world demand. Small photo at right shows interior view of operations. *(International Minerals & Chemicals Corporation)*

Declining Quality of Carlsbad Ores

The potash (K_2O) content of the ore mined at Carlsbad gradually declined as the better quality ore was depleted. In 1939, the mined ore averaged 25.2 percent K_2O; in 1954, 21.0 percent; in 1959, 18.6 percent; in 1972, 16.3; and in 1977, 14.2 percent. In contrast, Saskatchewan ores were running 25 to 30 percent K_2O. The decrease in potash content of the Carlsbad ore resulted from depletion of what had become known as zone 1 or "first zone," the first sylvinite ore zone to be mined at Carlsbad and the highest in grade. At least 60 potash layers had been noted in the Carlsbad area but only 11 are considered significant. Practically all of the mining has been concentrated on six zones. Numbered in ascending order, zone 1, originally the richest zone, lies 800 to 1,800 feet in depth depending on location, with beds 4 to 10 feet in thickness. It was practically exhausted by 1970. Sylvinite of lesser quality is mined from zones 3, 7, and 10. Zone 4 contains langbeinite ore, and zone 5 mixed sylvinite and langbeinite ore. Not all of the ore zones are continuous over the entire 33-square-mile Carlsbad district. For example, zone 1 does not occur on the eastern fringe of the deposit (8,23,76).

As zone 1 became exhausted, the producers turned to less desirable zones. The potash content of the sylvinite zones 3, 7, and 10 was lower because the mineral sylvinite made up a smaller proportion of the ore. Also these zones, particularly 10, contain more insoluble clays and slimes which, along with the lower potash content, increase the cost of refining. Zone 4 ore was rich in the mineral langbeinite which was mined by two companies. One company mined the mixed langbeinite-sylvinite ore from zone 5. A good demand existed for the langbeinite, which is free of chlorides and contains three nutrients–K, Mg, and S. It was sold either as potassium magnesium sulfate or converted to potassium sulfate for use primarily on chloride-sensitive crops. It also was advantageous for irrigated soils where chloride accumulation is a problem and where magnesium is needed. Although advances and improvements in mining and refining made it possible to tap the less desirable zones, the general effect was to make Carlsbad potash less competitive with Canadian potash (18,23,76).

Changing U.S. Potash Producers: 1966-1980

Several changes occurred in operating companies and ownership between 1966 and 1980. Also, production capacities were reduced (Table 8.2). Only one new operation came on the scene, that of the Great Salt Lakes Minerals and Chemicals Corporation which processes brine from the northern arm of Great Salt Lake. Five of the 10 companies operating in 1966 were still operating under the same name and ownership in 1980. These were IMC, Duval Corporation, National

Table 8.2. U.S. Potash Producers and Annual Production Capacities (39, 6).

Location	1966 Producing Company	Annual capacity 1000 s. tons K$_2$O	1980 Producing Company	Annual capacity 1000 s. tons K$_2$O
Searles Lake, CA	American Potash & Chemical Corporation	220	Kerr-McGee, Inc.	235
Carlsbad area, N.M.	U.S. Potash Company	520	Mississippi Chemical Corp.	240
Carlsbad area, N.M.	Potash Company of America	620	Potash Company of America	620
Carlsbad area, N.M.	Int. Minerals & Chem. Corp.	450	Int. Minerals & Chem. Corp.	380
Carlsbad area, N.M.	Duval Corp.	450	Duval Corp.	130
Carlsbad area, N.M.	National Potash Company	350	National Potash Company	250
Carlsbad area, N.M.	Southwest Potash Corp.	450	Amax Corp.	450
Carlsbad area, N.M.	Kermac Potash Company	300	Kermac Potash Company	340
Moab, Utah	Texas Gulf Sulphur Company	350	Texasgulf Inc.	186
Wendover, Utah	Kaiser Aluminum & Chemical Corporation	66	Kaiser Aluminum & Chemical Corporation	60
Ogden, Utah			Great Salt Lake Minerals & Chemical Corporation	110
Annual capacity		3,776		3,001

Potash Company, Kermac Potash Company, and Kaiser Aluminum and Chemical Corporation.

Kerr-McGee Corporation—The American Potash & Chemical Corporation operation at Searles Lake was taken over by the Kerr-McGee Corporation in 1969. The company at the time of the Kerr-McGee takeover was held by U.S. investors of which Heyden Chemical Company was the major shareholder. Although Kerr-McGee doubled production capacity of soda ash in the early 1970's, no increase was made in potash capacity. The potash production capacity from the early 1960's through 1978 was held at around 235,000 tons of K_2O annually, but in 1979 and 1980 it was cut back to 72,000 tons (6,15,40,41).

U.S. Potash and Succeeding Companies—The Carlsbad property originally owned by the United States Potash Company, the first producer in the area, underwent numerous ownership changes. U.S. Borax and Chemical Corporation, owners since 1956, closed the mine in 1967 since it could not compete effectively with potash from a Canadian company, Allan Potash Mines, which was partly owned by U.S. Borax. A year later Continental Royalty Company bought the Carlsbad mine and refinery, which became its U.S. Potash and Chemical Company subsidiary. Production capacity, which had run as high as 540,000 tons of K_2O a year under U.S. Borax, was cut back to around 200,000 tons as zone 1 approached exhaustion. In 1973, the mine again changed hands, being taken over by Teledyne, Inc. Following a six-month scavenger operation, the mine was closed and sold to Mississippi Chemical Corporation in 1974. Mississippi Chemical began mining zone 7 and in 1977 doubled the mine and refinery capacities to 180,000 tons of K_2O annually as a result of modernization and expansion of the flotation circuit. Capacity was further increased in 1980 to 240,000 tons. (The mine closed in 1983. No one was able to make the operation profitable on a continuing basis once the high-grade ore was exhausted) (3,18,25).

Potash Company of America—The Potash Company of America (PCA), the second to produce potash in the Carlsbad area, was the major U.S. potash producer between 1966 and 1980. The company owned the largest reserve of high-grade zone 1 potash in the area. Although the ore grade had declined some by 1973, it still averaged 21-22 percent K_2O. PCA's production capacity throughout the period was around 620,000 tons of K_2O annually, which amounted to 14 percent of the total U.S. capacity in 1966 and 21 percent in 1980. Annual production varied, depending on the Saskatchewan potash situation as it affected PCA's Canadian mine. The ore was beneficiated using the potash flotation process along with a crystallization circuit to recover fines. PCA merged with Ideal Cement Company to form Ideal Basic Industries in 1968, the

Some of the Carlsbad facilities of Potash Company of America. *(F. J. Myers--TVA)*

merger including both the Carlsbad and Saskatchewan holdings. However, the PCA name was retained for the operating subsidiaries. In 1978, PCA acquired the adjoining closed Eddy County mines of Duval Corporation and National Potash Company. Both mines were based on mining depleted zone 1 ore which had been uneconomical for previous owners. The company continued to operate its Dumas, Texas, potassium sulfate plant based on treatment of potassium chloride with sulfuric acid (18,23,25).

International Minerals and Chemical Corporation—As early as the 1950's, IMC began running into problems of zone 1 ore depletion. IMC's mining was centered in the northern part of zone 1 for the first 10 years of its Carlsbad operation. The company then shifted operations to the southern part of the zone where the sylvinite was contaminated to varying extents by langbeinite. At first the sylvinite was mined selectively, avoiding pockets where the langbeinite concentrations were highest. By the 1960's, the langbeinite content of the ore from the zone had risen to 10 percent and provisions were made to recover it from salt tailings in the refinery. (Langbeinite had been mined and marketed by IMC since the 1940's.) (18).

IMC in 1967, when all doubt had vanished as to the success of its Canadian operation, halved its Carlsbad production leaving a capacity of about 450,000 tons of K_2O annually. Later in the same year the company began a new process (heavy media separation) to separate sylvinite from langbeinite in a mixed ore. Once separated, the sylvinite was concentrated by flotation and the langbeinite was washed to produce saleable "Sul-Po-Mag." Langbeinite from zone 4 was simply washed. In 1969, production of langbeinite exceeded that of potassium chloride. In 1980, langbeinite from zone 4 and the mixed zone 5 still accounted for the greater proportion of IMC's output. IMC's Carlsbad annual production capacity was further cut to 380,000 tons of K_2O annually in the 1970's. (IMC's Canadian production capacity during the same period was 2.5 million tons annually.) (5,18,23).

Duval Corporation—The Duval Corporation, which had been mining high-grade (22 to 25 percent K_2O) zone 1 ore at its Saunders mine since 1952, was forced to close the mine in 1969 due to exhaustion of its reserves (Duval had opened a mine in Canada in 1968.) The Wills-Weaver mine which provided a lower grade zone 1 sylvinite (18 to 20 percent K_2O) ran out in 1971. This left the company with one mine, the Nash Draw, that was opened in 1964 to mine langbeinite from zone 4. However, the langbeinite operation was soon switched over to include sylvinite from zone 7 as had been originally planned. The grade of sylvinite not only decreased rapidly but the slimes content also increased, making addition of more desliming steps necessary. Even then, recovery at the refinery was only 75 percent as compared with 93 percent earlier. In 1976, Duval opened its North Mine, which was closed two years later after mining of its remaining zone 1 sylvinite proved uneconomical. Thus, all of the company's production of potassium chloride at Carlsbad ceased. In late 1977, Duval also terminated production of potassium sulfate, continuing to market only langbeinite under the trade name of "K-Mag." The annual production of the langbeinite was expanded from 91,000 tons of K_2O to 130,000 tons. The company's total annual production capacity back in 1966 had been 450,000 tons of K_2O (18,23,25,74,75).

Amax Corporation—Southwest Potash Company underwent changes in name ending up in the early 1970's as the Amax Chemical Corporation. Amax faced the prospect of running out of high-grade zone 1 ore and began to also mine zone 3, a lower grade sylvinite ore. Ore from the two zones was blended for processing. Amax increased its ore reserves by about 15 percent in 1978 by leasing Federal land adjoining its mine. Only potassium chloride was produced, with granular products accounting for most of the output. Amax also started building solar ponds to recover potash from mine and recovery wastes. The company became a major exporter, shipping from a port at San Diego, California, primarily to Brazil, Mexico, and Japan. Amax, the second largest producer at Carlsbad, held its annual production capacity from 1966 through 1980 at 450,000 tons of K_2O (18,19,25).

National Potash Company—A wholly-owned subsidiary of Freeport Sulphur Company, National Potash in 1966 had two mines in operation, one in Lea County, opened in 1957, and the other in Eddy County which opened in 1964. However, when potash prices deteriorated in the late 1960's, the company mined only the higher grade, zone 1 ore of the Eddy County (Government Reserve) mine. This mine was shut down in 1976 when all recoverable ore had been mined, and the Lea County mine was reopened. The company ceased operations in 1982 (18,25).

Kermac Potash Company—The Kermac Potash Company, mining on the border of Eddy and Lea Counties in an area where zone 1 ore did not occur, mined only the high clay content zone 10 sylvinite ore. Because of the high slime content, the flotation process could not be used economically and a special crystallization process was developed by Kerr-McGee engineers to treat the ore. The process was inaugurated in 1965, but numerous problems held back production until further improvements were made and installed in 1968. In 1970, a compaction unit was added. The Kerr-McGee Corporation in 1968 became the sole owner of the Kermac Potash Company after purchasing National Farmers Union's interest. The annual capacity of the plant after the improvements was about 250,000 tons of K_2O (15,23,25).

Kaiser Aluminum and Chemical Corporation—The Kaiser Aluminum and Chemical Corporation's brine operation at Salduro Marsh (Bonneville Flats) in Utah, producing potassium chloride, remained a small operation throughout the 1966-1980 period. However, in 1979 a new pond system including 40 miles of canals, dikes, and baffles was being built to replace the smaller, old system. This boosted capacity somewhat from its former level 60,000 tons of K_2O annually (18,76,77).

Texas Gulf Sulphur Company—Texas Gulf Sulphur converted its mine at Cane Creek near Moab, Utah, from conventional underground mining to solution mining in 1970-71. Production began in March 1972. Although the mine had been put into production in 1964, the heavily faulted and undulating nature of the deposit made it difficult to use mechanized equipment. Low production and high costs resulted in operating losses. Further, it was evident that the mine could not compete with Canadian potash. As a result Texas Gulf became a shareholder of Allan Potash Mines in 1969 (17). To convert to solution mining, all underground equipment was removed, entrances were sealed, and wells were sunk to a depth of 2,800 feet. The mined-out area was flooded by pumping water down the wells. Brines normally pumped from the mine after 300 to 350 days contain about 40 percent potassium chloride and 60 percent sodium chloride. The brine is pumped through a pipeline to a series of 23 solar surface ponds built 3-1/2 miles from the mine at a site near the Colorado River. These are lined with polyvinyl chloride and covered with a 6-inch layer of salt from the old tailings to protect the plastic and support the heavy machinery used in the harvesting operation. After evaporation and harvesting, the salt mixture is transferred back to the original refinery at the mine site by slurrying and pumping it through the 3-1/2 mile pipeline. Flotation is used to separate the salts. As expected, solution mining resulted in a lower cost per ton of product. On the labor side, the solution mine employed 100 people versus 429 during conventional mining. Texas Gulf Sulphur became Texasgulf, Inc., in the late 1970's when one-third interest was acquired by the Canada Development Corporation which is owned by the Canadian Federal Government (17,76).

Great Salt Lake Minerals and Chemical Corporation—With the opening of its recovery facilities near Ogden, Utah, in 1970, Great Salt Lake Minerals became the latest company to recover potash from natural brines in the United States. The company tapped the brine supply from the northern arm of Great Salt Lake where the potassium content is about 50 percent higher than the southern part of the lake. (Great Salt Lake was divided into two sections when the causeway for the Southern Pacific Railroad was completed. The northern section has only restricted inflow of fresh water, hence it is richer in minerals.) The brine from the northern arm is conducted by a canal to a succession of flumes and pumps to 17,000 acres of solar evaporation ponds on the eastern shore. The first section of the salt ponds yields sodium chloride by precipitation. The remaining liquor flows to a second section, known as harvest ponds, where crude salts of potassium, sodium, and magnesium are removed. The remaining liquor is rich in lithium, magnesium, and bromine compounds (3,76).

Harvested salts include kainite and schoenite (mixtures of potassium chloride and magnesium sulfate), magnesium sulfate, and sodium chloride. Recovery of potassium sulfate involves conversion of the kainite to schoenite which is subsequently decomposed with water to yield potassium sulfate. The annual capacity is 110,000 tons of K_2O but production depends upon the water level of Great Salt Lake which has been rising (3,76).

The first investigation leading to the Great Salt Lake installation was undertaken in 1963 by the Lithium Corporation of America, a subsidiary of Gulf Resources and Chemical Corporation, whose main interest was to establish a new source of lithium. Upon noting the potassium and magnesium contents of the lake, the Lithium Company invited Salzetfurth A.G., the West German potash mining company, to join in exploiting the potassium and magnesium. In 1967, the Great Salt Lake Minerals and Chemical Corporation was formed as a joint venture by the Gulf Resources and Chemical Corporation and by Salzetfurth A.G. and its American subsidiary, Chemsalt, so that the ownership by Gulf Resources was 51 percent and Salzetfurth 49 percent (3,16).

Of the 11 companies producing potash in the United States in 1980, all but Great Salt Lake and Chemicals and the Duval Corporation were producing potassium chloride containing about 61 percent K_2O. Two companies, IMC and Duval, produced and sold langbeinite. Potassium sulfate was produced by five of the companies. In the late 1970's, 84 percent of U.S. potash production was as potassium chloride, the remainder being potassium sulfate and potassium magnesium sulfate (washed langbeinite). About 83 percent of the U.S. total potash production was coming from the Carlsbad district (Eddy and Lea Counties).

Court Suits

Prorationing, which caused so much trouble for potash producers in Canada, also moved into U.S. courts and affected U.S. producers. In 1976, the Antitrust Division of the U.S. Department of Justice in the northern Illinois U.S. District Court filed a criminal indictment charging five U.S. producers with restricting trade by curbing U.S. potash production and stabilizing U.S. prices at noncompetitive levels, and conspiring to coordinate United States and Canadian production and prices for potash. Also, the five were indicted on coordinating exports from the United States. The case related to the prorationing imposed by the Provincial Government of Saskatchewan during 1970-1974 and was limited only to that period. The criminal trial began in January 1977. The Potash Company of America and the National Potash Company were acquitted in February. In March, a mistrial was declared because of a hung jury. In May 1977, the three remaining companies, IMC, Amax, and Duval, also were acquitted by the Federal judge. A companion civil suit that also had been filed by the Federal Government against the same five companies was dismissed in June (76).

In the meantime the states of Illinois, Connecticut, and Minnesota and 30 other potash users had filed class-action civil suits, mostly in the same Illinois court, seeking damages for the high prices paid for potash during the Canadian prorationing period. The five producers acquitted in the Federal suits along with Kerr-McGee and Texasgulf were sued. A settlement agreement was reached in August 1977 between the potash producers and five of the plaintiffs, including the States of Illinois and Minnesota, which had purchased potash directly from the producers. Final settlement was scheduled for June 1978 for payment of about $3 million to the plaintiffs (76).

Potash Particle Size Grades

The term "potash grade" as used in this country and Canada refers to the particle size range of potassium chloride as it is marketed. In the United States, particle sizes are expressed as Tyler mesh numbers which indicate the number of sieve openings per linear inch. The three principal grades are standard, coarse, and granular, each of which contains 60 percent or more of K_2O, and a soluble grade containing 62-63 percent K_2O produced from crystallized potassium chloride resulting in a low content of insoluble impurities. Actual size ranges of the different grades vary somewhat among producers. Grades and their typical size specifications in terms both of Tyler mesh and millimeters are as follows:

| | Typical size range | |
Grade	Tyler mesh	mm
Standard	10-65	1.7-0.2
Coarse	8-28	2.4-0.6
Granular	6-20	3.4-0.8
Soluble	35-100	0.4-0.15

Source: Ruhlman, 1978 Bur. of Mines MCP:1(76).

Potassium sulfates also are produced in standard and granular grades. Size specifications of grades produced in the United States and Canada are tighter than in other countries (20).

Particle size was of little concern prior to the 1950's and the products typically were heavily laden with fine particles, roughly corresponding to the present standard grade. With the advent of ammoniation-granulation of mixed fertilizers in the early 1950's, it was found that coarse potash particles aided in the granulation of mixtures low in nitrogen and high in potash. The coarse potash particles served as nuclei for formation of granules which greatly increased the production rates from small-size plants converted from earlier ammoniation plants (19,47).

Growth of the infant bulk blending industry in the 1950's motivated production of a compacted, granular product made from fine particles of potassium chloride obtained from the flotation process. The first producer of a granular grade was the Southwest Potash Corporation in 1957. The company marketed the product as K-Gran and promoted its use in the rapidly growing bulk blend industry in the Midwest. Granular forms of materials were preferred because they had less tendency to segregate (tended to stay evenly mixed with other ingredients), and could be spread more uniformly. Also, granular diammonium phosphate, produced largely in –6 to +14-mesh (Tyler) size range, came into commercial production in 1959 and became a favorite material in the rapidly expanding bulk blend industry. As a result, granular potassium chloride had an excellent size match with granular diammonium phosphate and other granular nitrogen and phosphate materials used in the blends. (Hoffmeister of TVA in 1962 was the first to determine that particle size was by far the most important property that had to be matched to prevent unwanted segregation.) (19,48).

In 1961, deliveries of standard potassium chloride amounted to the equivalent of 1.1 million tons of K_2O while coarse and granular together amounted to 1.0 million (although separate data were not reported, delivery of coarse grade far exceeded granular). The standard grade continued to exceed the combined tonnages of coarse and granular grades until the mid-1960's while the coarse grade exceeded the granular in all years since 1961. In 1970, the standard grade accounted for 41 percent of the tonnage; the coarse grade, 24 percent; and the granular, 17 percent (remainder included refined and non-KCl products). Since 1970, coarse, granular, and soluble have increased markedly. By 1979, sales of potassium chloride for agricultural purposes showed that standard provided 18 percent; coarse, 41 percent; granular, 33 percent; and soluble, 9 percent, due to the increased use of fluid mixtures (30,55,77).

Much of the growth in use of the coarse and granular grades which has occurred in the United States especially since 1975, is attributed to the rapid increase in direct application of potash. The addition of compaction lines based on use of the standard grade or recycled fines has steadily increased granular potash capacity in the United States and Canada. Both coarse and granular grades are used in bulk blending; in recent years most of the potash used is in the granular grade even though it is more costly than the coarse grade. Fluid mixtures, both solution and suspension, obtain most of their potash from the soluble grade. Most granular potash going into bulk blends is potassium chloride, although smaller amounts of granular potassium magnesium sulfate and potassium sulfate are also used primarily in situations where chlorides cannot be tolerated (6,20).

Processes for Granulating Potash

A process to produce a granular 50 percent K_2O (80 percent KCl) product was in use around 1950 by the United States Potash Company and IMC at Carlsbad. This was an adaptation of the agglomerate tabling process used in the early 1930's for beneficiation of a coarser fraction of phosphate rock in Florida (Chapter 7). After removing the slimes, the brine containing an −8 +16 mesh (2.4 to 1 mm) ore fraction was conditioned with special reagents that floated the larger particles. It was then passed over agglomeration (concentration) tables where the difference in gravity between the potassium and sodium chlorides resulted in their separation. As the brine moved over shaking, riffled tables, the potassium chloride particles formed agglomerated flocs and moved across the tables' riffles while the heavier sodium chloride dropped to the face of the table and was removed at the end of the table (37,82).

As demand grew for larger particle sizes, various techniques and modifications were made to the flotation and crystallization process to increase particle size and process efficiency. However, costs increases and product size limitations made it desirable to investigate other methods. As a result, methods involving fusion and compaction were developed for transforming finely divided particles recovered in the flotation and crystallization procedures into larger particle sizes (54).

Patents were issued in 1953 and 1956 to E. W. Douglas and P. S. Dunn on the fusion method. The Potash Company of America apparently was the first to use the process commercially. Finely divided potassium chloride from both flotation and crystallization beneficiation was charged into a gas-fired furnace and melted at approximately 750°C. The molten material was drawn off continuously and directed to the surface of an internally water-cooled rotating disc upon which it formed a layer of potassium chloride 1/16 to 1/8 inch in thickness. Upon cooling, the layer of potassium chloride was shattered into large thin flakes by a scraper. The product was cooled, ground, and screened to the desired particle size range (55).

The compaction process, introduced around 1960, became the most used method for increasing the particle size of fine potassium chloride particles to granules of desired size range. Although different techniques were used, the most common process has been to feed preheated (49°-65°C) fine particles plus recycled fines into a pair of smooth-faced rolls which can exert pressures of 20,000 to 30,000 pounds per linear inch. Pressure is applied hydraulically to one of the rolls which compacts the potash against the second roll and fuses the particles into a sheet. The sheet is broken into flakes, screened to remove fines and oversize particles, and introduced into two granulating mills operating in parallel. These have rolls with sharp-edge corrugations to produce a granular, somewhat cubical product (54,55,79).

Domestic Potash Outlook: 1980

The future of potash production in the Carlsbad area appeared rather bleak by 1980. Continued reduction in potash contents of the ores resulted in steadily increasing costs per ton of product. Also, operating costs increased at some Carlsbad mines as a result of roof falls and gas problems not encountered earlier when mostly zone 1 ore was mined. In addition, taxes and tariffs associated with mining ores on the Federal and State lands in New Mexico became more burdensome as profits declined. (Federal royalties on public lands owned by the Government ran between 2.0 and 7.5 percent of the gross value of production. That mined on State lands was subject to a lease royalty of 5 percent of the value of the crude ore. Also, New Mexico severance and resource taxes were equal to almost 1 percent of the gross value of the beneficiated potash.) (25).

Competition of the Saskatchewan potash had dealt a severe blow to domestic potash except in market areas more distant from the Saskatchewan mines. However, the discovery of mineable sylvinite in the Province of New Brunswick and the decision of the Potash Company of America to mine the ore, added a new challenge to domestic production. The new deposits, located in southern New Brunswick, are in a strong position location-wise to provide potash to the eastern United States, both from the seaport at St. John and by land. There are few possibilities for any company mining in the Carlsbad area to extend mining operations through acquisition or leasing new land near its present operation, and practically no chance that a high-grade sylvinite deposit of any size exists anywhere in the district. Two companies still control large reserves, IMC with sylvinite/langbeinite averaging 5 to 6 percent K_2O, and Mississippi Chemical with a very large reserve of low-grade sylvinite averaging 15 percent K_2O. (Mississippi Chemical closed its operation in 1983 when potash prices were low.) (25).

The U.S. Bureau of Mines in 1978 published its estimates of tonnages of K_2O in identified world potash reserves based on average 1976 domestic mine prices. (Reserve is defined by the Bureau of Mines as that part of a resource for which rank, quality, and quantity have been reasonably determined and which is deemed mineable at a profit under existing market conditions.) The estimate showed that the United States mineable reserves based on 1976 prices amounted to 200 million short tons of K_2O; Canada with 10 billion (10,000,000,000) tons; the U.S.S.R. with 2 billion; East Germany, 300 million; West Germany, 200 million; Israel and Jordan (the Dead Sea), 240 million; and all other potash-producing countries combined, 300 million tons. The U.S. reserves were made up roughly of about 100 million tons of bedded deposits in New Mexico and 100 million in brines, primarily in California and Utah (76).

The Bureau of Mines study also included potash resources (potentially mineable deposits which could not be recovered profitably at current prices). Canada had an estimated resource of 64 billion short tons of K_2O; the U.S.S.R., 48 billion; Thailand, 9.9 billion; United States, 5.8 billion; East Germany, 4.7 billion; West Germany, 3.4 billion; Israel and Jordan, 1 billion; and all other, 1 billion (76).

Most potash resources in the United States occur as beds of sylvinite at depths of 5,000 to 10,000 feet in the North Dakota and adjacent Montana area, and in Michigan and Utah. These could be extracted only by solution mining. Two companies, Kalium Chemicals, a division of Pittsburgh Plate Glass, and Farmers Potash Company, a combine of Burlington Northern, Inc. and CF Industries, began exploratory drilling in North Dakota in 1976. IMC also leased acreage in the area. The potash is present in the Prairie Evaporite Formation that is the source of potash in Saskatchewan and underlies about 12,000 square miles in the two states. Beds vary in thickness from a few feet to 20 feet. Also, in 1978 new permits were issued for potash exploration of some 51,000 acres near Moab, Utah, which has been demonstrated by Texas Gulf Sulphur Company to be mineable by the solution method. The overall bed is estimated to contain some 500 million tons of K_2O, mainly as good-grade sylvinite. The estimated total resource of bedded potash in Utah is 2 billion tons of K_2O. In Michigan, Dow Chemical Company core-sampled bedded sylvinite near Midland, finding a salt layer containing potash deposits 400 feet thick at a depth of about 8,000 feet which may underlie about 13,000 square miles (76).

In general, unless solution mining can economically tap the deep or faulted deposits indicated above, it appears that the United States will need to depend increasingly upon imports, primarily Canadian, to meet its potash needs.

REFERENCES

1. Albright, H. M. 1941. American potash independence achieved. *Am. Fert.* 95(3):5-7, 24.
2. Anon. 1967. Southwest Potash: new route to KNO_3. *Chem. Eng.* Nov. 20, 1967, 118-119.
3. _____. 1971. World potash producers. *Ind. Minerals* 41:15-27.
4. _____. 1977. Potash industry reshaped in government hands. *Ind. Minerals* 113:15-23.
5. Bridges, J. D. 1979. *Fertilizer Trends*. Tenn. Valley Auth., Muscle Shoals, Alabama.
6. _____. 1982. *Fertilizer Trends*. TVA, Muscle Shoals, Alabama.
7. British Sulphur Corporation. 1964. Kalium Chemical Co. to start mining potash shortly. *Phosphorus and Potassium* 10:35-37.
8. _____. 1964. U.S. potash industry 1962/63. *Phosphorus and Potassium* 11:27- 29.
9. _____. 1965. The new Texas Gulf potash mine and refinery at Cane Creek. *Phosphorus and Potassium* 15:37-40.
10. _____. 1965. Canadian potash industry: History, recent developments, and outlook. *Phosphorus and Potassium* 18:30-33.
11. _____. 1967. Vancouver potash terminals expanding to handle greater throughput in 1967-68. *Phosphorus and Potassium* 29:39-40.
12. _____. 1967. Kermac Potash Co.'s Carlsbad operation. *Phosphorus and Potassium* 31:39-40.
13. _____. 1968. Second shaft for Texas Gulf Sulphur's Cane Creek mine. *Phosphorus and Potassium* 34:43-44.
14. _____. 1969. Potash dumping injury may be self inflicted. *Phosphorus and Potassium* 44:37-38.
15. _____. 1971. The United States potash industry at 90% of capacity. *Phosphorus and Potassium* 51:42-45.
16. _____. 1971. Significance of the Great Salt Lake project. *Phosphorus and Potassium* 52:45-49.
17. _____. 1972. Texas Gulf brings Cane Creek back on-stream. *Phosphorus and Potassium* 61:46-47.
18. _____. 1973. Potash in the United States. *Phosphorus and Potassium* 68:39- 42.
19. _____. 1977. Amax Chemical Corp. *Phosphorus and Potassium* 89:48-50.
20. _____. 1977. Sized potash. *Phosphorus and Potassium* 91:38-43.
21. _____. 1978. Saskatchewan potash-1. *Phosphorus and Potassium* 94:40-45.
22. _____. 1978. The beneficiation of potash ores. *Phosphorus and Potassium* 98:38-40.
23. _____. 1980. Potash production at Carlsbad. *Phosphorus and Potassium* 108:26-30.
24. _____. 1981. A review of recent developments and prospects for the 1980's. Phosphorus and Potassium 113:18-21.
25. _____. 1984. Carlsbad–what future potash? *Phosphorus and Potassium* 129:17-20.

26. Bruhn, H. H. and E. H. Miller. 1954. Potash mining methods. *Min. Eng.* 6(6):608-612.
27. Buehler, J. D. and N. G. Watson. 1966. Trends in potash technology. *Phosphorus and Potassium* 23:36-44.
28. Cramer, T. M. 1938. Production of potassium chloride in New Mexico. *Ind. Eng. Chem.* 30:865-867.
29. Dahms, J. D. and B. P. Edmonds. 1964. *Solution mining of potassium chloride.* U.S. Patent 3,148,000.
30. Eilertsen, D. E. 1970. Potash. Bur. Mines *Minerals Yearbook*, Vol. I, pp. 951-964.
31. Food and Agriculture Organization of the United Nations. 1970. *FAO Annual Fertilizer Review.*
32. _____. 1976. *FAO Annual Fertilizer Review.*
33. _____. 1978. *FAO Fertilizer Yearbook.*
34. _____. 1980. *FAO Fertilizer Yearbook.*
35. Gaudin, A. M. 1957. *Flotation.* 2nd edition, pp. 514-520. McGraw-Hill and Co., New York, Toronto, London.
36. Hargett, N. L. and J. T. Berry. 1980. *Fertilizer Summary Data.* Tenn. Valley Auth., Muscle Shoals, Alabama.
37. Harley, G. T. 1953. Production and processing of potassium materials. In *Fertilizer Technology and Resources*, ed. by K. D. Jacob, pp. 287-322. Academic Press, Inc., New York
38. _____ and G. E. Atwood. 1947. Langbeinite: mining and processing. *Ind. Eng. Chem.* 39:43-47.
39. Harre, E. A. 1967. *Fertilizer Trends.* Tenn. Valley Auth., Muscle Shoals, Alabama.
40. _____. 1969. *Fertilizer Trends.* Tenn. Valley Auth., Muscle Shoals, Alabama.
41. _____. 1971. *Fertilizer Trends.* Tenn. Valley Auth., Muscle Shoals, Alabama.
42. _____. 1973. *Fertilizer Trends.* Tenn. Valley Auth., Muscle Shoals, Alabama.
43. Hedges, J. H. 1936. Potash. Bur. Mines *Minerals Yearbook*, pp. 1007-1021.
44. _____. 1937. Potash. Bur. Mines *Minerals Yearbook*, pp. 1381-1398.
45. _____. 1938. Potash. Bur. Mines *Minerals Yearbook*, pp. 1239-1253.
46. _____. 1939. Potash. Bur. Mines *Minerals Yearbook*, pp. 1387-1402.
47. Hignett, T. P. 1960. General considerations on operating techniques, equipment, and practices in manufacture of granular mixed fertilizers. In *Chemistry and Technology of Fertilizers*, ed. by V. Sauchelli, pp. 269-298. Reinhold Publishing Corp., New York.
48. Hoffmeister, G. 1962. Compatibility of raw materials in blended fertilizers: segregation of raw materials. *Proc. 12th Annual Meeting, Fertilizer Industry Round Table*, Washington, D. C.
49. Johnson, B. L. and K. G. Warner. 1942. Potash. Bur. Mines *Minerals Yearbook*, pp. 1447-1460.
50. _____ and K. G. Warner. 1943. Potash. Bur. Mines *Minerals Yearbook*, pp. 1496-1511.
51. _____ and D. I. Marsh. 1946. Potash. Bur. Mines *Minerals Yearbook*, pp. 1017-1030.
52. _____ and E. M. Tucker. 1949. Potash. Bur. Mines *Minerals Yearbook*, Vol. I. pp. 1025-1041.
53. _____ and N. C. Jensen. 1950. Potash. Bur. Mines *Minerals Yearbook*, Vol. I, pp. 1034-1052.

54. Kapusta, E. C. 1968. Potassium fertilizer technology. In *The Role of Potassium in Agriculture*, ed. by V. J. Kilmer, S. E. Younts, and N. C. Brady, pp. 23-52, publ. by Am. Soc. Agronomy, Madison, Wisc.
55. ____ and N. E. Wendt. 1963. Advances in fertilizer potash production. In *Fertilizer Technology and Usage*, ed. by M. H. McVickar, G. L. Bridger, and L. B. Nelson, pp. 189-230, publ. by Soil Science Soc. Am., Madison, Wisc.
56. Kyle, A. J. 1964. Mining methods and equipment used in IMC's Esterhazy operations. *Canadian Min. & Met. Bull.* Trans. Vol. 67, 1964, pp 83-91.
57. Lewis, R. W. 1963. Potash. Bur. Mines *Minerals Yearbook*, Vol. I, pp. 913-927
58. Lewis, R. W. 1965. Potash. Bur. Mines *Minerals Yearbook*, Vol. I, pp. 763-771.
59. ____ and G. E. Tucker. 1961. Potash. Bur. Mines *Minerals Yearbook*, Vol. I, pp. 1011-1031.
60. ____ and G. E. Tucker. 1962. Potash. Bur. Mines *Minerals Yearbook*, Vol. I, pp. 999-1012.
61. Litvack, B. M. 1973. *The Canadian potash industry*. Report 62, Canadian Transport Commission, Systems Analysis Branch, Ottawa.
62. Lutz, J. E. 1952. Freezing method solves problem in Carlsbad, N.M. *Min. Eng.* 4(10):942-947.
63. MacDonald, R. A. 1980. Potash: occurrences, processes, production. In *Chemistry and Technology of Fertilizers*, ed. by V. Sauchelli, pp. 367 402, Reinhold Publishing Corp., New York.
64. Mehring, A. L., J. R. Adams, and K. D. Jacob. 1957. *Statistics on fertilizers and liming materials*. U.S. Dept. Agriculture Statistical Bull. 191.
65. Mitchell, J. B. 1970. Three ways to process potash. *Min. Eng.* 22(3): 60- 62.
66. Noyes, R. 1966. *Potash and potassium fertilizers*. Chemical Process Monograph No. 15, Noyes Development Corp., Park Ridge, N. J.
67. Pearson, W. J. 1960. Developments in potash in Saskatchewan. *Canadian Mining and Metallurgical Bull.* 582, pp. 759-764.
68. Ruhlman, E. R. and G. E. Tucker. 1951. Potash. Bur. Mines *Minerals Yearbook*, Vol. I, pp. 1078-1094.
69. ____ and G. E. Tucker. 1952. Potash. Bur. Mines *Minerals Yearbook*, Vol. I, pp. 825-844.
70. ____ and G. E. Tucker. 1953. Potash. Bur. Mines *Minerals Yearbook*, Vol. I, pp. 911-930.
71. ____ and G. E. Tucker. 1954. Potash. Bur. Mines *Minerals Yearbook*, Vol. I, pp. 933-949.
72. ____ and G. E. Tucker. 1955. Potash. Bur. Mines *Minerals Yearbook*, Vol. I, pp. 911-928.
73. ____ and G. E. Tucker. 1956. Potash. Bur. Mines *Minerals Yearbook*, Vol. I, pp. 939-955.
74. Singleton, R. H. 1975. Potash. Bur. Mines *Minerals Yearbook*, Vol. I, pp. 1195-1207.
75. ____. 1977. Potash. Bur. Mines *Minerals Yearbook*, Vol. I, pp. 739-761.
76. ____. 1978. Potash. Bur. Mines *Mineral Commodity Profiles*, MCP-ll.
77. ____. and J. P. Searls. 1978-79. Potash. Bur. Mines *Minerals*
78. Smith, H. I. 1933. Three and a quarter centuries of the potash industry in America. *Eng. Min. Jour.* 134:514-518.

79. Smith, R. 1979. Potash production. *Proc. of the 29th Annual mtg. of the Fertilizer Industry Round Table.*
80. Turrentine, J. W. 1945. Potash in war and peace. *Comm. Fert.* 1945 Yearbook, pp. 63-71.
81. Walli, J. R. O. 1964. *The application of European shaft-sinking techniques to the Blairmore formation.* Canadian Min. & Met. Bull., Febr. 1964.
82. White, N. C. and C. A. Arend, Jr. 1950. Potash production at Carlsbad. *Chem. Eng. Progress* 46(10):523-530.

9

Ammonia Synthesis 1932-1980

Production of ammonia in the United States on a commercial basis began in 1921. The industry was well on its way by 1932 with nine companies operating 10 plants (Chapter 6). Most plants were small, 25 short tons per day (tpd) or less. However, one plant operated by the E. I. du Pont de Nemours and Company at Belle, West Virginia, had a capacity of 120 tpd. Another by Allied Chemical and Dye Corporation at Hopewell, Virginia, had a capacity of 270 tpd. These two facilities were among the largest ammonia synthesis plants in the world. In California, the Shell Chemical Company had found methane to be a satisfactory source of hydrogen for use in ammonia synthesis, pointing to natural gas as a possible hydrogen-carbon source. Thus, the foundation was laid for an expanded domestic ammonia industry. This potential was soon tapped when the U.S. Government constructed 10 additional plants, some based on natural gas, to meet the projected munitions needs of World War II. Not only was capacity tripled but also a sizable ammonium nitrate production capacity was added. After the war, most of the plants were sold or leased to private industry.

By the early 1950's, synthetic ammonia largely replaced the previously important nitrogen sources: natural organics, sodium nitrate from Chile, and calcium cyanamide from Canada (the latter two had been declining in tonnage before 1950). Byproduct ammonium sulfate, which had been an important source since the mid-1920's, continued at the earlier levels but provided an ever shrinking share of the total nitrogen. After about 1960, synthetic ammonia accounted for 95 percent or more of the nitrogen in U.S. fertilizers.

Farmers in the late 1940's and the 1950's were rapidly learning the economic value of applying large amounts of chemical nitrogen on nonleguminous crops, especially corn and cotton. Also, they were increasing plant populations, obtaining improved crop varieties, and doing a better job of controlling plant pests–all of which assured higher returns from increased fertilizer use.

With the rapid increase in demand, production of ammonia rocketed from 3.2 million tons in 1955 to 19.7 million in 1980 (Table 9.1). Nitrogen (N) consumption as a plant nutrient in 1958 exceeded that of either

Table 9.1. Growth of U.S. synthetic ammonia industry, 1932-1980 (16, 26, 28, 12, 13, 33, 48, 55, 43).

Year	Plants	Companies	Production	Capacity
	No.	No.	1000 tons NH_3	
1932	11	9	-	380
1940	9	8	360	460
1946	18	10	730	1,600
1950	19	14	1,600	2,700
1958	57	42	4,000	4,260
1960	56	41	4,820	5,200
1964	74	62	7,600	8,000
1967	100	75	12,190	12,000
1969	109	73	12,770	18,400
1971	87	61	14,540	17,000
1975	93	59	16,420	18,500
1980	89	54	19,650	20,800

phosphate (P_2O_5) or potash (K_2O). (In the late 1970's, when the consumption of phosphate actually declined, nitrogen consumption nearly equalled that of phosphate and potash together.)

Fertilizer since World War II has been consistently the major user of ammonia. Major materials based on ammonia included anhydrous ammonia both for direct application and in the manufacture of NP and NPK fertilizers, ammonium nitrate, urea, nitrogen solutions, and fluid fertilizers. A multitude of nonfertilizer uses also developed, including industrial chemicals, explosives, animal feed supplements, plastics, and synthetic fibers (10).

During the years of fastest gains in fertilizer nitrogen consumption the percentage going into fertilizers increased and during slack periods the proportion going into nonfertilizer uses increased. Over the entire period, fertilizer was the dominant user of ammonia. The share of ammonia going into fertilizers for selected years was: 1949, 61 percent; 1958, 76; 1965, 81; 1968, 85; 1971, 72; and 1976, 75 (10,55).

This chapter reviews the development of the ammonia industry, including its remarkable growth, major technological advances, companies, plants and their locations, production capacities, ammonia storage and transport, and major industry problems.

The Formative Years: 1932-1950

The initial surge of ammonia plant construction was completed by 1932 at the very depths of the Great Depression. Consumption of nitrogen in fertilizers had fallen to half the 1930 level. Consumption improved slowly but it wasn't until 1939 that nitrogen use equalled the 1930 level. Only one new plant came into operation and this in 1939. The entrance of the United States into the World War II, however, brought a rush of new ammonia plant construction to meet expected munitions needs. Ammonium nitrate in excess of munitions needs became available as early as 1943 for use as a nitrogen fertilizer; this was the first time that sizable quantities of this material had become available to American farmers. Use of nitrogen fertilizer based on ammonia greatly increased after the war as the government began leasing and selling the plants to the private sector. Production of ammonia reached a level of 1.6 million tons in 1950.

Status of the Industry in 1932

The nine companies operating ammonia plants in 1932 and the locations of their 11 plants were as follows: Atmospheric Nitrogen Corporation (an affiliate of the Allied Chemical and Dye Co.) operating plants at Syracuse, New York and Hopewell, Virginia; the E. I. du Pont de Nemours and Company at Belle, West Virginia, and Niagara Falls, New York; Shell Chemical Corp. at Pittsburg, California; Pennsylvania Salt Manufacturing Co. at Wyandotte, Michigan; Mathieson Alkali Co. at Niagara Falls, New York; Raessler-Hasslecher Chemical Co., Niagara Falls, New York; Midland Ammonia Co., Midland, Michigan; Great Western Electro-Chemical, Pittsburg, California; and the Pacific Nitrogen Co. at Seattle, Washington. Most of these were among the original companies producing ammonia in the 1920's (Chapter 6). The two largest plants-at Hopewell, Virginia, and Belle, West Virginia–accounted for 87 percent of the nation's production capacity of 380,000 tons. Most of the plants ran considerably below their capacities throughout the depression years. Production of farm products exceeded demand, and government crop controls restricted acreages. Industrial demand for synthetic ammonia remained fairly modest. No new plants were built until 1939 when the Hercules Powder Company opened a 90 tpd plant at Pinole, California (51).

Wartime Expansion

The coming of World War II with its projected needs for large amounts of nitrates for munitions brought about the construction of 10 new ammonia synthesis plants in four years, the first coming on stream in 1941. Annual ammonia production capacity was increased by 970,000 tons, making the U.S. Government the owner of about 70 percent of the total annual U.S. capacity.

Table 9.2 lists the government-owned wartime plants. Four of the nine companies operating the plants were among the early ammonia plant pioneers: the E. I. du Pont de Nemours Co., Atmospheric Nitrogen

Table 9.2. Government-owned synthetic ammonia plants constructed during World War II (33-37,42,19,55).

Plant	Location	NH$_3$ capacity short tons/year	Sponsoring govt. agency	Wartime operator	Postwar operator
Morgantown	Morgantown, WV	260,000	Ordnance[1]	Du Pont	Olin-Mathieson
Ohio River	Henderson, KY	54,000	Ordnance	Atmos. N. Corp.	Spencer Chemical
Missouri[2]	Louisiana, MO	54,000	Ordnance	Hercules Powder	Hercules Powder
Dixie	Sterlington, LA	54,000	Ordnance	Comm. Solvents	Comm. Solvents
Buckeye	South Point, OH	160,000	Ordnance	Atmos. N. Corp.	Allied Chemical
Jayhawk	Pittsburg, KS	110,000	Ordnance	Military Chem. Works	Spencer Chemical
Ozark	El Dorado, AR	110,000	Ordnance	Lion Chemical Co.	Lion Oil
Cactus	Etter, TX	54,000	Ordnance	Shell Chemical	Phillips Chemical
Lake Charles	Lake Charles, LA	54,000	DPC[3]	Mathieson Alkali Works	Mathieson Chemical
Muscle Shoals	Muscle Shoals, AL	60,000	TVA	TVA	TVA

[1]U.S. Army Ordnance Department.
[2]Part of the ammonia equipment transferred in 1949 to the San Jacinto Ordnance Depot near Houston, TX and the plant operated by the San Jacinto Chemical Co.
[3]Defense Plant Corporation.

Corporation (Allied Chemical and Dye), Mathieson Chemical Corporation, and Shell Chemical Company. The remaining five had no previous experience in ammonia plant operation. The Dixie and Lake Charles plants in Louisiana, the Cactus plant in Texas, and the Jayhawk plant in Kansas were sited on pipelines or near gas wells so they could use natural gas as a feedstock. All others used water gas.

Several plants, including the Dixie plant, the Cactus, Jayhawk, and the Ozark, were equipped to produce ammonium nitrate. So was the TVA plant at Muscle Shoals, Alabama, using the World War I nitric acid and ammonium nitrate facilities. The Hercules Powder Company plant in California also was equipped to produce ammonium nitrate (33,37,42,55).

With the development and production of more powerful explosives based on organic compounds, the need of ammonium nitrate for munitions declined. Starting in 1943, much of TVA's and Hercules Powder Company's production was released for use as fertilizer. This presented a problem in that, after bagging, ordnance quality ammonium nitrate solidified into "tombstones," creating major problems in application. TVA, the U.S. Department of Agriculture, and Canadian interests (Canada also had leftover ammonium nitrate, much of which was exported to the United States) joined in a crash program to solve the problem and were able to come up with workable solutions. The government in 1944 and 1945 released more ammonium nitrate for fertilizer use, a good portion coming from TVA. Some of the ordnance plants produced ammonium nitrate only in solution form; this material had to be shipped to graining plants for conversion to solid form (21,32,42).

Following cessation of hostilities in 1945, several ordnance plants were declared surplus and advertised for sale or lease. These were the Ohio River, Dixie, Buckeye, Jayhawk, Ozark, Cactus, and Morgantown plants, along with the Defense Plant Corporation operation at Lake Charles, Louisiana. Four of the plants were disposed of quickly. But, development of a postwar world food shortage caused the Ordnance Department to operate the remaining plants along with 11 granulation facilities needed to produce solid ammonium nitrate. By 1950, all but two of the surplus ammonia plants had been sold or leased, leaving only the Morgantown and Missouri plants which were placed in private hands by 1954 (34,35,36,37).

By the end of 1950, 14 companies including TVA were operating 19 ammonia plants having an annual production capacity of 2.7 million tons of ammonia. During that year about 70 percent of the Nation's domestic nitrogen consumption was derived from ammonia synthesis, with practically all of the remainder coming from inorganic sources. Of the plants operating in 1950, eight had been operating in 1932, one was built by private industry in 1939, and the remainder were wartime plants. Of the 14 companies operating in 1950, seven had produced

Some of the equipment in small ammonia plant built at Muscle Shoals in early 1940's. Worthington circulators are in foreground and Cooper-Bessemer compressors in right background. (*G.L. Bracey--TVA*)

Grainer kettles from World War I nitrate plant at Muscle Shoals loaded for shipment in 1942 to ordnance plant in Ohio. *(G.L. Bracey--TVA)*

ammonia prior to 1932. Leading companies in ammonia production capacity in 1950 were, in declining order, Allied Chemical, Spencer Chemical, Du Pont, Lion Oil, and Phillips Chemical. They accounted for 53 percent of the total capacity (37,50,55).

Major Technological Advances Prior to 1950

The major technological advances made in ammonia production in this country during the 1930-1950 period were related to the development of the capability to use natural gas as a feedstock. Hydrogen for the plants of the 1920's was obtained by electrolysis of water, as electrolytic byproduct, and from water gas. These sources were characterized by high cost and limited availability, or both, and could not have supported an ammonia manufacturing industry of the magnitude that developed in the United States.

Shell Chemical Company, a subsidiary of the parent Holland company, first used methane (CH_4) as a feedstock in 1931 at its Pittsburg, California, plant (Chapter 6). However, Shell used the hydrogen contained in the methane and removed the carbon as a byproduct and did not use it in the water gas process, as will be explained later. Since California had no coal, companies generated gas for domestic consumption by cracking oil-gas, an intermediate distillate fraction obtained during petroleum refining, to produce methane. The Southern California Gas Company, which had generated gas for years, offered its services to Shell engineers and placed a full-scale gas-cracking unit at Shell's disposal. Shell used this plant for making refinements for removal of unwanted impurities and in thermal cracking of methane to form hydrogen and solid carbon which was removed by scrubbing with water and briquetted. The Pittsburg ammonia plant was equipped with the newly-designed purification and cracking units (38,55).

Steam reforming, rather than methane cracking, became the route for releasing hydrogen from natural gas, the chief ingredient of which is methane, for use in ammonia synthesis. The basic reaction is:

$$CH_4 + H_2O \rightarrow CO + 3H_2$$

Steam reforming involves a series of steps. Initially, sulfur-free natural gas that has been preheated is reacted with steam over a nickel catalyst at 800 to 900° C and 35 pounds per square inch (psi) pressure in the primary reformer. (After 1950, the pressure was raised to about 500 psi.) This produces a mixture of hydrogen, carbon monoxide and carbon dioxide. This mixture goes to the secondary reformer, a vessel filled with bulk nickel catalyst. Air is added to complete the steam-methane reaction (by combustion with hydrogen), and to supply nitrogen needed later for synthesis of ammonia. After being cooled to about 400° C, the gas goes to the shift converter where the carbon monoxide reacts with steam over an iron-chromium-based catalyst to form hydrogen and carbon dioxide. Later, a more efficient copper-based catalyst which is active at lower temperatures was used. This gas mixture is cooled and routed to an absorber where a solvent removes the carbon dioxide.

At this point, the hydrogen-nitrogen gas is passed over a nickel catalyst in the methanator to remove traces of carbon monoxide and carbon dioxide that could poison the ammonia synthesis catalyst. Finally, the mixture of hydrogen and nitrogen gases is subjected to a temperature of 400 to 450° C and a pressure of 3,000 to 5,000 psi in the converter to form ammonia ($N + 3H \rightarrow NH_3$). Plants using centrifugal compressors usually are limited to 1,500 to 3,000 psi, whereas plants using reciprocating compressors can operate at pressures as high as 10,000 psi. The gas mixture is fed continuously to the converter, and product ammonia is removed continuously by cooling and condensation. Usually, 10 to 20 percent of the mixture reacts in each pass through the converter. The conversion per pass increases as the pressure is increased. At the maximum pressure used commercially, more than 90 percent conversion can be obtained (51,55).

Catalytic reforming of methane to form hydrogen was not new. A U.S. patent was issued to A. Mittasch and C. Schneider of Badische Analin und Soda Fabrik in 1915 for production of hydrogen by steam-methane reaction. It was further developed in the 1920's by others and apparently was introduced in this country by the Standard Oil Company of New Jersey in 1930. A steam reforming plant using the German I. G. Farbenindustrie process was opened in 1931 at Baton Rouge, Louisiana, to produce hydrogen for use in petroleum refineries. Hercules Powder Company at its California ammonia synthesis plant in 1939 was first to apply steam reforming to natural gas. By 1952, 80 percent of U.S. synthetic ammonia was based on steam reforming (8,9,55).

The carbon monoxide left in the synthesis gas is reacted with steam in the presence of an iron and chromium oxide catalyst at 500 or more pounds per square inch and elevated temperatures to form hydrogen in the reaction as follows: $CO + H_2O \leftrightarrow H_2 + CO_2$ (53,55).

Natural gas has significant advantages over other feedstocks in ammonia production. First, in raw state it is relatively pure, containing very small amounts of carbon dioxide and hydrogen sulfide which are removed easily by scrubbing. Second, the hydrocarbon itself is mostly in the form of methane (CH_4), thus supplying a large amount of hydrogen. And third, in addition to the hydrogen it still carries on the main function of a carbonaceous feedstock, the reaction of the carbon with steam to form hydrogen. (With the advent of natural gas as an ammonia feedstock, countries short of natural gas turned to naphtha, a less desirable feedstock in that it contains more carbon in relation to hydrogen and also contains complex sulfur impurities which are difficult to remove due to the high carbon to hydrogen ratio. Naphtha also presents a problem of carbon formation in the catalyst.) (51).

The 1950's, Beginning of a New Era

From 19 plants with an annual capacity of 2.7 million tons of ammonia in 1950, a new surge of construction brought the number of plants to 56 and capacity to 5.2 million tons by 1960. This happened largely in response to rapidly increasing demand for nitrogen fertilizer for corn in the Midwest and cotton in the South and West. Row crop farming intensified as chemical nitrogen fertilizer replaced alfalfa and clovers grown in the crop rotations as a source of nitrogen. Also, prices received by farmers for their products remained high due largely to government price supports and other controls (15). In addition, the government allowed a rapid tax writeoff of new ammonia plant construction costs. Seventeen plants utilized the rapid writeoffs (49).

No difficult problems faced companies in constructing ammonia synthesis plants or gaining entrance into the industry. Needed technology was available through engineering firms that held patents or licenses on various individual "processes" (based on the original Haber-Bosch process but differing enough in pressure, temperature, catalyst, mechanical equipment, or gas purification methods to justify patents and separate identification). U.S. and foreign engineering firms actively competed for the market. The firms, besides providing the design, usually oversaw construction, trained operators, and aided in startup (45,51).

Use of natural gas as an ammonia feedstock became dominant in the 1950's. Of the 53 ammonia plants operating in 1957, 72 percent were using natural gas, 11 percent refinery gas, 9 percent water gas, and 2 percent coke oven gas. Natural gas pipelines were established or under construction over broad sections of the country (eventually 224,000 miles of natural gas main lines were in operation with the bulk of the construction undertaken in the 1940's and 1950's). Synthetic ammonia plants using natural gas no longer were confined to areas near gas fields but could also be located at or close to market areas. Further, unwanted sulfur-bearing impurities were being removed from gas at the source to avoid corrosion of pipes (25,51).

During the 1950's, 34 new ammonia plants came into production, of which 8 were operated by companies that were in the field prior to 1950. A wide range of primary interests was represented by the new companies, including oil, gas, chemical, explosives, and farmer cooperative organizations. Armour was the only old-line fertilizer company to start ammonia production during the period (16). Ammonia capacities of individual, single-train plants ranged from about 25 to 300 tpd with a number in the 60- to 120-ton range.

Most of the added ammonia capacity was in the Texas-Louisiana Gulf Coast area near gas wells and water transportation, or along natural gas pipelines, particularly in the Midwest. The New England and the Mountain States had the fewest plants and the least capacity (16,51). The five leading states in annual ammonia production capacities during 1960 were Louisiana, 586,000 tons; Texas, 557,000; California, 551,000; Ohio, 428,000; and Virginia, 400,000. Together they accounted for about half of the total U.S. ammonia capacity. Leading companies, in declining order, were Allied Chemical, Phillips Chemical, Lion Oil (a division of Monsanto), Spencer Chemical, and E. I. du Pont de Nemours; together, they represented 44 percent of U.S. capacity (16).

In 1960, roughly half of the ammonia synthesis plants also produced nitrogen fertilizer materials, either at the ammonia plant site or nearby. Essentially, the associated plants became a nitrogen fertilizer complex. Many were equipped with nitric acid plants and even a few had wet-process phosphoric acid facilities so that they could produce ammonium phosphates. The building of nitrogen complexes got underway in this country around 1930 at Du Pont's Belle, West Virginia, and Allied's Hopewell, Virginia, ammonia plants. Du Pont produced solid urea and urea-ammonia solutions. Allied made synthetic sodium nitrate and solutions based on ammonium nitrate (Chapter 6). Large-scale production of solid ammonium nitrate associated with ammonia plants did not come about until World War II.

Eighteen of the 56 ammonia plants operated by 16 companies and TVA in 1960 were producing solid ammonium nitrate as well. Around 700,000 tons of solid urea were produced at 13 ammonia plants in 1960. Five plants produced both ammonium nitrate and urea. Nitrogen solutions of various compositions also were produced. Ingredients were water, ammonia, and solutions of ammonium nitrate and urea in different combinations and concentrations. Pressure solutions, containing free ammonia, were used for ammoniation of superphosphates, and the non- or low-pressure solutions for direct application to the soil. NPK granulation plants often included sulfuric or phosphoric acid in formulations so they could use more nitrogen solutions containing ammonium nitrate and free ammonia; these solutions were the lowest cost source of nitrogen for granulation plants at that time. Anhydrous ammonia itself was being used increasingly during the 1950's for direct application (1,16,26).

Greater attention had to be given to anhydrous ammonia storage and transport as production of ammonia increased and its use for direct application mounted. Storage at the ammonia plants and at receiving and distribution points in the 1950's was in large spherical hortonspheres of moderately low pressure capabilities. These were equipped with a semi-refrigeration unit to guard against excessive pressures which permitted drawing off the ammonia vapor formed within the sphere as required. The vapor was compressed into a cold liquid and returned to the sphere. Insulated spheres were sometimes used to reduce the need for refrigeration. Aqua ammonia was stored in low-pressure, vertical tanks. Nitrogen solutions containing free ammonia usually were shipped out of the plant in special rail tank cars as fast as produced. When storage of the pressure solution was necessary, pressurized tanks of different sizes were used. Non- or low-pressure solutions were usually stored in non-pressure vertical tanks (1,24,46).

Most of the anhydrous ammonia in the 1950's was shipped out of the producing plants in 25-ton, high-pressure, insulated rail tank cars equipped with pressure relief valves. Truck shipments from the plant or storage tanks to nearby bulk distributor plants were made in 12- to 19-ton capacity high-pressure tanks equipped with pressure relief valves and mounted on tractor trailer trucks. The bulk distributor's tank usually was equipped with pressure relief valves, although a few had semi-refrigeration units. The product was moved to the farm in truck- or trailer-mounted tanks equipped with pressure relief valves. Transfer from one tank to another of all sizes was done with compressors and vaporizers, or by the vapor pressure of the ammonia itself (1,2,46).

The use of tank cars for ammonia transportation was pioneered by the U.S. Bureau of Explosives and the E. I. du Pont de Nemours and Company in 1926. The use of tank cars greatly reduced the cost of delivered anhydrous ammonia and consequently the cost of fertilizers and munitions (44). Allied Chemical shipped its first shipment by tank car in 1928 from its Hopewell plant to F. S. Royster Guano Company, apparently also in Virginia.

Big Single-Train, Centrifugal Compressor Plants

A giant step in ammonia production came in the early 1960's when the M. W. Kellogg Company, a division of Pullman, Inc., introduced the jumbo-size, single-train, centrifugal compressor ammonia plants. The innovation drastically cut capital and operating costs; ammonia could be produced in the big plants at one-half the cost in smaller plants equipped with conventional reciprocal compressors. The Kellogg Company, an engineering firm specializing in the petrochemical and petroleum fields, had started working in the ammonia field as early as 1944. The giant new ammonia plants were the result of Kellogg's knowledge of technology in these three fields, plus its decision to optimize the overall ammonia production process rather than go the usual route of concentrating on one or more of the individual steps involved (4,51,52).

Kellogg was the first to achieve significant savings by meeting all compression needs with a single centrifugal compressor driven by a steam turbine (replacing the conventional use of a number of small, electrically driven reciprocating compressors), and use of heat interchange throughout the plant. Sufficient energy was recovered not only to drive the compressor but also to provide the necessary heat input for endothermic processes requiring the addition of heat, for driving numerous pumps, and meeting various reheat needs. A number of other changes were made including reformer and synthesis pressures, and in the overall energy system in order to achieve the lowest manufacturing cost. Modifications also were made in the reformer, converter, and synthesis section designs (4,11,52).

The new plants proved more reliable with less downtime than the smaller reciprocal compressor plants. However, in contrast with reciprocals, the centrifugals could be throttled back only to about 70 percent of capacity. Thus, with the large plants, especially the 1,000- and 1,500-ton versions, it was much more difficult to retain a satisfactory supply-demand balance since a misjudgement leading to just a few too many plants could create serious overcapacity.

The new plants were an immediate success and engineering firms were kept busy. The first large plant to come into operation was a 600-tpd unit built for the American Oil Company at Texas City, Texas, in 1963. Three 1,000-ton plants came on stream in 1966. In 1971, Kellogg had 20 of its plants operating in the United States and 14 in other countries. Following Kellogg's introduction of the large centrifugal compressor plants, other engineering companies also designed and developed their own versions. Among those marketing the large plants in the United States were Chemico, the Haldor Topsoe Company of Denmark, and C. F. Braun and Company of California (52).

Table 9.3 summarizes the shift to large plants during the 1963-1980 period. By the end of the period they accounted for about 70 percent of the U.S. ammonia production capacity.

The trend toward concentrating ammonia production close to gas wells and water transport along the Gulf Coast and lower Mississippi River was further accelerated with the appearance of the new giant

The world's first 1,000-ton-per-day ammonia plant was designed and built for Coastal Chemical Company at Yazoo City, Mississippi. *(M.W. Kellogg Co.)*

plants. The building of the ammonia pipelines to the Midwest in the late 1960's encouraged still greater production by the large plants in Louisiana where the Gulf Central pipeline originated, and in the Texas Panhandle and, later, northern Oklahoma where ammonia was produced near gas wells and transported to the Midwest by the Mid-America pipeline. Kenai, Alaska, located near gas wells and ocean transportation, also became an important ammonia production center based on 1,500-tpd plants (13,28,30).

Table 9.3. Use of 600-1,500 ton per day centrifugal compressor ammonia plants in U.S. (20, 26, 27, 28, 30, 13).

Year	1964	1967	1969	1971	1976	1980
No. plants	1	10	28	38	39	43
No. companies	1	10	22	30	29	27
Total capacity, 1,000 t. NH_3/yr.	216	3,230	8,500	11,800	13,400	14,700
Percent of total U.S. ammonia capacity	3	27	50	69	61	71

In 1971, 11.8 million tons, or two-thirds of the U.S. ammonia production capacity was provided by 38 centrifugal compressor plants (Table 9.3) operated by 30 companies. The two leading states in use of the large plants were Louisiana with 10 plants having a capacity of 3.8 million tons of ammonia, and Texas with 7 plants and 2.3 million tons. Together these two states accounted for half of the total large plant capacity in the country. Donaldsonville, Louisiana, had become the leading center of production by jumbo plants with a capacity of 1.4 million tons. Other states at or within short distances from gas wells, and having water transport and/or ammonia pipelines included Mississippi, Arkansas, and Alaska. In 1971, these three states together had seven of the large plants with a capacity of 1.9 million tons (28).

The use of centrifugal rather than reciprocal compressor plants continued to increase during the 1971-1980 period but more slowly than during the 1960's—a net gain of five plants and 2.9 million tons of capacity. More of the 1,000- and 1,500-tpd plants appeared, not only replacing older reciprocal plants but also capturing the new plant market. Louisiana, the major ammonia producing state, appears to have used the jumbo plants exclusively. In 1980, it had 16 large plants with an annual capacity of 6.4 million tons, an increase of 2.6 million over 1971. Donaldsonville alone saw a doubling of capacity to 2.8 million. On the other hand, both production and plant capacities in Texas declined and several 600-tpd plants were closed. Oklahoma became a large ammonia producer, second only to Louisiana, as new, large centrifugal plants were built to provide ammonia for the Mid-America pipeline. Union Oil at Kenai, Alaska, added a second 1,500-ton plant to meet export demand (13).

Reshaping Ammonia Storage and Transport

Rapidly increasing concentration of ammonia production near gas wells and water transport, brought on by the introduction of the large centrifugal-compressor ammonia plants, required simultaneous changes in storage and transport. Equipment and systems in use prior to the large plants were incapable of handling the huge amounts of ammonia; both modifications and new technology were required.

Storage Tanks

Fully refrigerated storage for large-size tanks became dominant, replacing the old high-pressure and medium-pressure systems. Two types of tanks evolved: a single-wall tank insulated on the outside, and a double-wall tank with insulation between the walls. Both types have vertical walls, a flat bottom, and a domed roof. The tanks were designed to hold liquid ammonia at atmospheric pressure. The ammonia vapor that is generated continuously in the tank is collected in a closed system, and reliquefied; the cold liquid is returned to the tank where it is held at a temperature of about -33°C. Fully refrigerated tanks were used at terminals, barges, and oceangoing vessels. Semi-refrigerated ammonia storage, used earlier, continued to be used for smaller size storage tanks (46).

Jumbo Tank Cars

Jumbo tank cars with capacities of 70 to 80 tons (compared to 25-30 tons previously) were introduced. These have noninsulated tanks that are coated with a white reflective paint and designed for 400 psi. Most of the tank cars were purchased and leased from large tank car fabricating and leasing firms rather than being owned by the railroads. By 1968, approximately 16,000 of the small 25- to 30-ton cars and 7,000 jumbo cars were in use, the latter being used on the more distant shipments (2,24).

Barge Transport

Fully refrigerated barges dedicated solely to ammonia transport and having capacities of 2,000 to 3,000 tons came into use in the 1960's. Most of the barge shipments are on the Mississippi River and its navigable tributaries and the Gulf Coast coastal waterways, to large, fully refrigerated terminals. In 1968, some 85 barges were owned by or under long-term lease to major ammonia producers and petroleum companies, and a few to towing companies (2).

Ocean Shipment

Ocean shipment of ammonia also came into importance in the 1960's as ammonia exports increased. The first vessel specifically designed for ammonia (but also having LPG capabilities) was launched in 1964. The oceangoing vessels were equipped with insulated tanks or holds to contain the ammonia in liquid form at slightly above atmospheric pressure and at a temperature of −33°C, similar to that used in fully refrigerated storage. Transport was arranged by charter through owners or brokers. In 1979, 34 vessels with capacities ranging from 8,000 to 30,000 metric tons were available for ocean ammonia transport (2).

Long-Distance Ammonia Pipelines

The idea of building long-distance ammonia pipelines cropped up in several quarters during the 1960's. Piping ammonia, however, was not new; it had been done for short distances for years both in this country and Europe. An ammonia pipeline had been installed as early as the 1940's in Los Angeles to distribute ammonia for refrigeration purposes.

Commercial Solvents Corporation in the mid-1950's transported ammonia from its plant in Sterlington, Louisiana, 4 miles across farmlands to its ammonium nitrate plant. In the mid-1960's, the Humble Pipeline Company built a 19-mile pipeline connecting ammonia plants at Beaumont and Orange, Texas, transporting 220 tons per day (40). The first long-distance line was placed in operation by Petrolas Mexicanos (Pemex) in 1968; it ran 150 miles overland, linking Minatitlan, Mexico, on the Gulf Coast with a storage terminal at Salina Cruz on the Pacific coast from which the ammonia was transported by refrigerated tankers to the using areas of Rosarita and Guaymas to the north (5).

Although several long-distance pipelines were considered in this country, only two were constructed by 1980. Mid-America Pipeline Company (MAPCO) built a pipeline to carry ammonia from a 1000-tpd plant at Borger in the Texas Panhandle 850 miles through Oklahoma, Kansas, and Nebraska to northern Iowa. From Garner, Iowa, the original

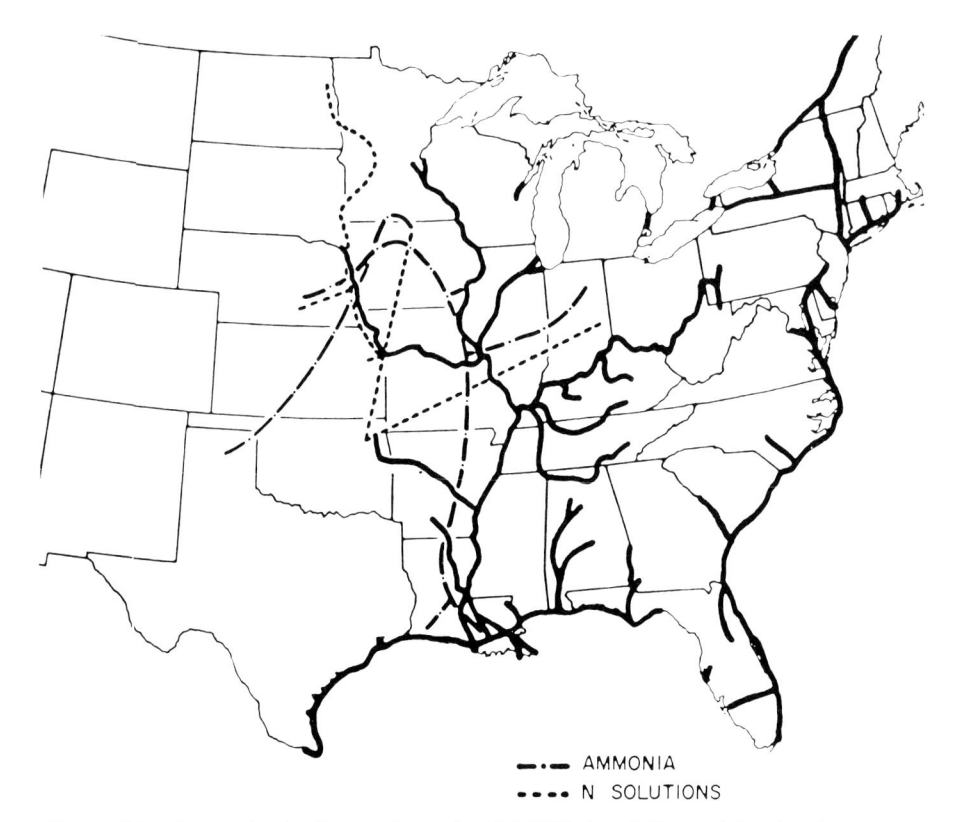

Figure 9.1. Ammonia pipeline system of mid-1970's in relation to inland waterways (solid lines).

line was extended to Mankato, Minnesota in 1968. Two additional 1,000-tpd ammonia plants were added to the system in 1975 through an extension to Enid and Verdigris in northern Oklahoma. The Gulf Central Pipeline completed a 2,000-mile pipeline in 1969 from southern Louisiana through Arkansas and Missouri to northern Iowa and then southwestward into Nebraska. A branch was extended from Hermann, Missouri, through Illinois into northeastern Indiana. Both pipeline companies shared a terminal at Garner, Iowa, whereby it was possible to transfer ammonia from one pipeline to the other (31,39,40,47).

Capacities of the pipelines initially were 1,300-tpd for MAPCO and 3,000 for Gulf Central; both about doubled their capacities by adding pumping stations. MAPCO used 8- and 6-inch pipe and Gulf Central 10-, 8-, and 6-inch. MAPCO had 15 storage terminals connected to the system with a total capacity of 300,000 tons; Gulf Central had 37 terminals at 28 locations, including storage facilities at ammonia plants totaling 1.5 million tons. Truck loading stations also were located along the pipelines. Gulf Central had several terminals that could be supplied by barge or ocean-going vessel (31,40).

All methods for transporting ammonia found a place in the overall system. Pipeline transport was less costly and preferred over rail shipment for distant points which could not be reached by barge. Barges held an advantage for terminals along the Mississippi and inland waterways, and along the Gulf Coast waterways, but ice usually closed the northern waterways during winter. Rail shipment filled in blank spots and also tapped barge and pipeline terminals for transfer to intermediate depots 100 to 250 miles distant. Trucks took care of the short runs from both ammonia plants and terminals (6).

The 1960's: New Companies, New Problems

The expansion of the ammonia-producing industry continued at an unprecedented pace in the 1960's. Consumption of nitrogen in fertilizers jumped from 2.7 million tons of N in 1960 to around 7 million in 1969 (16,28).

Giant corporations, largely from the oil, gas, and chemical industries, entered ammonia and fertilizer production in increasing numbers. The newcomers, with large capital resources, were purely interested in profits on their investments, of which ammonia and fertilizers represented only a portion of their widely diversified interests. By 1968, some 42 oil, gas, and chemical interests owned 73 percent of the total U.S. ammonia production capacity. Triggering their interest in ammonia and fertilizers was the much publicized world food problem along with the role fertilizers were expected to play in its solution (54).

Seventy-six companies were producing ammonia in 1969; of these, only 28 were operating in 1960, the remaining 48 being newcomers to the ammonia field. During the 1960-69 period, 10 companies had either dropped out or sold out, the largest being Spencer Chemical Company which was bought up by Gulf Oil. Also, by this time the large farmer cooperatives were becoming major ammonia producers. The five leading firms in terms of annual ammonia production capacities for 1962 and 1969 are given in Table 9.4.

The number of ammonia plants reached 110 in 1969 compared to 56 in 1960; annual production capacity reached 18.4 million tons as compared to 5.2 million in 1960 (Table 9.1). During the first half of the 1960's a steady market existed for 60- to 120-tpd plants located along natural gas pipelines, with 200- to 300-tpd single-train plants located in the larger market areas (53). Prior to the large centrifugal compressor plants, higher plant capacities were achieved by combining two or more single-train units. By 1967 and 1968 a number of the small, single-train units were being replaced by 600- and 1,000-tpd centrifugal-compressor plants.

Appreciable changes occurred in ammonia production capabilities among states and regions during the 1960's, following in part the pattern that began in the 1950's (Table 9.5). Most notable was the vast increase in the capacities of the South Central States (Louisiana, Texas, Mississippi, Arkansas), particularly Louisiana and Texas. This was the result of several factors: the swelling demand for nitrogen fertilizer especially in the Midwest, the introduction and construction of the jumbo centrifugal compressor plants, the existence of the inland and coastal waterways systems, the building of the ammonia pipelines into the Midwest, and the development of an ammonia and nitrogen materials export market. Another change of some magnitude apparent in the late 1960's was the increase in ammonia production capacity in several corn-growing states (Iowa, Nebraska, Illinois, Ohio, and Missouri) of the Midwest, and in the corn-wheat state of Kansas. In sharp contrast, New England, except for one short-lived plant, had no ammonia capacity, while the eight Mountain States had only three small plants. Of importance was the opening of a 1,500-tpd plant at Kenai, Alaska, near gas wells and a seaport (16,27).

Although consumption of ammonia and nitrogen fertilizers was increasing faster than at any time in the history of the industry, capacity and production were increasing much faster. Not only had the number of companies and ammonia plants almost doubled between 1960 and 1967, but production capacities also increased by 150 percent. Massive overproduction developed. By 1969, the wholesale price per ton of ammonia had fallen from $90 per ton level of the early 1960's to $20 per ton (16,26,41,54). Profits and returns on investment vanished.

Several factors were responsible for the unhappy situation: the ability of the new generation of centrifugal compressor plants to add capacity quickly (three 1,000-tpd or two 1,500-tpd added a million tons of ammonia per year); each company's disregard of what its competitors were doing; and over-optimism, based on the Green Revolution. These

Table 9.4. Annual Capacities of Five Leading Ammonia Producers (3, 27)

1962		1969	
	1,000 t. NH_3		1,000 t. NH_3
Allied Chemical	796	Allied Chemical	962
Phillips Chemical	500	Monsanto Chemical	830
Monsanto Chemical	408	E.I. du Pont de Nemours	800
E.I. du Pont de Nemours	336	Collier Carbon (Union Oil)	785
Spencer Chemical	334	Chevron Chemical	760
Percent of U.S. total	38	Percent of U.S. total	23

Table 9.5. Leading Ammonia Producing States (16, 27).

	1960			1969	
	Capacity 1,000 t.NH_3	Percent of U.S.		Capacity 1,000 t.NH_3	Percent of U.S.
Louisiana	586	12	Louisiana	3,745	21
Texas	557	11	Texas	3,553	19
California	551	11	Iowa	1,261	7
Ohio	428	8	Mississippi	1,131	6
Virginia	400	8	California	901	5
Kansas	284	5	Arkansas	840	5
West Virginia	281	5	Pennsylvania	633	3
Mississippi	229	4	Kansas	612	3
Arkansas	210	4	Nebraska	610	3
Pennsylvania	168	3	Illinois	527	3
Total	3,694	71		13,813	75
18 other states	1,506	29	22 other states	4,605	25
Total U.S.	5,200			18,400	

traits were prevalent throughout the industry, in the United States and worldwide. Decision-makers in most of the new companies had little experience or knowledge of the fertilizer field; some old-time ammonia producers, who should have benefited from experience, caught the expansion fever and added to the problem; and export markets never developed to the extent expected. The major problem facing the newcomers proved not to be finances or the mechanics of building and operating a plant but carving out a needed share of the market (54).

As the overproduction problem worsened, inefficient and poorly located plants were idled or cut back, resulting in a temporary drop in production in 1968. However, production increased again the next year but not at the pre-1968 rate. As profits continued to decline and returns on investment disappeared, the number of plants dropped from 109 in 1969 to 87 in 1971, and, although production continued to increase, the annual production capacity fell from 18.4 million tons to 17 million. During the same period the number of companies producing ammonia declined from 73 to 61 (26,27,28).

Highs and Lows of the Uncertain '70's

By 1973, the industry had come out of its depressed condition but construction of new ammonia plants had virtually come to a halt. At about the same time the government, which had held fertilizer prices at an abnormally low level, lifted price controls. World grain production dropped due to droughts and poor yields in certain regions, creating a sudden demand for U.S. grains which drove up domestic grain prices. The above, along with a sharp decline in fertilizer inventories at the end of 1973, spurred a flood of announcements of intentions to build new ammonia plants. By 1975, new plants were in production and the production capacity had climbed from the 1971 low of 17 million tons of ammonia to 18.5 million in 1975 (7,15,18).

Consumption increased substantially in 1974 but it declined abruptly in 1975. The drop resulted from high ammonia prices along with lower prices for crops. Ammonia, which had averaged $87 per ton in 1973 and $150 in 1974, jumped to $265 in 1975, reflecting mostly the lifting of the government price freeze on fertilizers and the rising natural gas prices (7,18,29,30). A major factor in the run-up in ammonia prices was the oil embargo of 1973 which created energy and feedstock shortages around the world.

In a sharp turnabout, consumption and production of nitrogen fertilizers reached a new, all-time high in 1976. Ammonia prices had fallen to $191, resulting in a more favorable price relationship between fertilizer nitrogen and farm crops. The unnerving two- and three-year up-and-down cycles experienced since 1968 were not over, however. In 1978, both nitrogen production and consumption again declined. This time, bad weather coupled with uncertainties as to the government's agricultural programs were held responsible. Both consumption and production recovered in 1979 and again reached new highs. Plant production capacities reached a new high of 22 million tons in 1978 then dropped into the 20-million-ton range in 1979 and stayed there in 1980. Since 1968, gloom and doom in the nitrogen and the fertilizer industry had alternated with brief periods of sunshine (12,13,30).

Adding to the many problems of the ammonia industry during the 1970's were curtailments and high prices of natural gas, starting in the early 1970's when it appeared that natural gas reserves were approaching exhaustion. Average costs to ammonia producers escalated from 30 cents per thousand cubic feet (mcf) in 1970 to 62 cents in 1975, and almost to $2.00 in 1980. (Gas prices between different ammonia producers varied considerably since some had long-term contracts made when gas was cheap.) As a result, many of the less efficient plants using high price gas and faced with curtailments either were closed or held idle. The ammonia industry, to counter the rising gas costs, found ways to use the gas more efficiently, reducing the average consumption from almost 40 mcf per ton of ammonia to around 36.5 mcf in 1980. Although this partially offset the energy costs, the cost per ton of ammonia still escalated from less than $13 in 1970 to $75 in 1980 (18).

Deep concern over declining domestic reserves of natural gas, and their effect upon fertilizer and food production and cost, resulted in a major effort to obtain an alternative ammonia feedstock. A program was launched in late 1975 by TVA's National Fertilizer Development Center with the support of The Fertilizer Institute, a leading industry trade association. The goal was to obtain hydrogen with advanced coal gasification technology. TVA selected a process developed by Texaco Development Corporation and tested in a small pilot plant. A scaled-up, semi-commercial plant was built at Muscle Shoals, Alabama, and connected to TVA's small ammonia plant. The major construction was completed in 1980; however, three years of additional work and modifications were required before the plant was brought into satisfactory operation (22).

Natural gas was not the only problem facing the ammonia industry in the 1970's; plant investment costs also were ballooning. In 1969, the investment costs for a 1,000-tpd plant were about $25 million. In 1976 the cost of a similar plant had reached around $70 million, and in 1980 it was approaching $100 million (17).

The amounts of nitrogen exported and imported, either as ammonia or other nitrogen fertilizer materials, changed considerably from 1965 on as shown in Figure 9.2. (The individual data plotted in the figure are the combined nitrogen contents of ammonia and other nitrogen-containing materials.) From 1966 through 1973 exports exceeded imports, and from 1974 until 1978 imports were greater than exports, with the situation again reversing in 1978. Since 1970, urea and diammonium phosphate together have dominated the export market, with ammonia providing from 20 to 40 percent of the total nitrogen exported. Imported nitrogen in the form of ammonia was less than 400,000 tons annually prior to 1975, but by 1980 it had mounted to 1.9 million tons or 70 percent of the total imports. Urea imports remained low until the early 1970's, about equaling urea exports. Urea imports exceeded exports through 1977, peaking at 640,000 tons of N, and then declining. Very little ammonium nitrate appeared either as imports or exports due to harbor restrictions following the Texas City disaster in 1947. Nitrogen solutions became an important export material in the 1970's (13,14).

Figure 9.2. Nitrogen fertilizer trade.

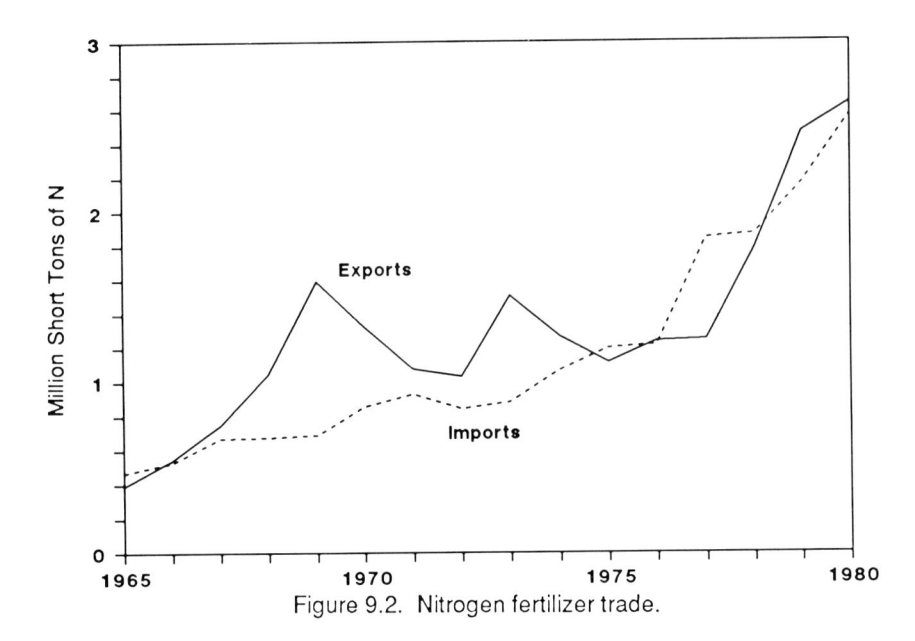

Ammonia producers from the 1960's onward continued to expand and broaden production of nitrogen-containing fertilizer materials. By 1980, only 25 plants and 16 companies out of a total of 89 plants and 54 companies limited production to ammonia only. Forty-two plants also produced ammonium nitrate; 41 produced urea; 36, nitrogen solutions; and 10, ammonium phosphates, mostly diammonium. Twenty-nine of the ammonia plants produced both ammonium nitrate and urea; 27, ammonium nitrate, urea, and nitrogen solutions; and 6, in addition to the latter three, also produced ammonium phosphates. Urea and nitrogen solutions were produced almost exclusively at the ammonia plants to utilize carbon dioxide produced in the shift-conversion step and necessary in urea manufacture. Ammonium nitrate was produced at 29 locations separate from ammonia plant sites. (Twenty-eight ammonium phosphate plants in 1980, in addition to the 10 located at ammonia plants, were mostly associated with sites where phosphatic fertilizer materials were manufactured, although a few were located at sites where by-product ammonia was produced.) (13).

Here One Year, Gone the Next

The 1970's contrasted sharply with the 1960's in the changes that occurred in numbers and location of the ammonia plants, ownership and numbers of companies, and production capacities. The number of ammonia plants declined from 109 in 1969 to 89 in 1980, and the number of companies from 73 to 54. Ammonia production capacities saw a general leveling off, peaking in 1978 at 22 million tons (up from

19.3 million in 1969) and then declining to the 20-million range in 1979 and 1980. Thirty-three companies operating in 1969 were gone by 1980; 10 were oil and gas companies and 18 were producers with small noncompetitive plants. The oil and gas dropouts were Arco Chemical, Continental Oil, Gulf Oil, Mobil Chemical, Reserve Oil and Gas, Shell Chemical, Sinclair Petrochemicals, Sun Oil, Tenneco Chemical, and Texaco, Inc. Also, Cities Service and Hill Chemical, both oil companies, entered production and dropped out between 1969 and 1980. Two new oil companies, Felmont Oil and Diamond-Shamrock, entered the field and were still operating in 1980 (13,27).

In 1980, the 54 companies and 89 plants had a total production capacity of 20.8 million tons. The number of large centrifugal plants had increased to 43 operated by 27 of the companies; they accounted for 70 percent of the total ammonia capacity. The 10 leading states in ammonia production capacity were Louisiana with 6.8 million tons and 19 plants; Oklahoma, 2.3 million and 7 plants; Texas, 1.8 with 8 plants; Mississippi, 1.2 and 4 plants; Iowa, 1.1 with 7; Alaska, 1.0 and 2; Arkansas, 0.6 and 2; Nebraska, 0.57 with 4; Kansas, 0.55 and 2; and Tennessee with 0.51 million and two plants. The 10 states accounted for 80 percent of the country's ammonia capacity. All of the leading states were close to either gas wells or natural gas pipelines. The Louisiana, Oklahoma, Texas, and Alaska ammonia plants were virtually on top of gas fields and all either had water transportation and/or fed into interstate ammonia pipelines. Donaldsonville, Louisiana, remained the ammonia and nitrogen capital of the Nation with seven large centrifugal compressor plants owned by four companies and a capacity of 2.8 million tons, or 13 percent of the Nation's total. CF Industries, the leading ammonia producer of the country, held over half of the location's production capacity (13).

Ownership of the 54 plants operating in 1980 was divided among companies of widely varying backgrounds and interests. Nine had predominantly oil backgrounds: Amoco, Chevron, Diamond-Shamrock, Felmont Oil, Hawkeye (Getty Oil), Occidental, Phillips Pacific, Phillips Petroleum, and Union Oil. Together the nine oil companies operated 14 plants with 16 percent of U.S. capacity. Fifteen companies had chemical backgrounds: Air Products; American Cyanamid; W. R. Grace; Grace-Oklahoma; Atlas Chemical; Allied Corp.; Dow Chemical; E. I. du Pont de Nemours; Hercules, Inc.; Monsanto; Olin; Borden; Reichold; Pennwalt; and Columbia Nitrogen. These 15 companies operated 21 ammonia plants having 27 percent of the total U.S. capacity. The three farm cooperatives, CF Industries, Farmland, and' Mississippi Chemical Corporation, operated 16 ammonia plants with 24 percent of the country's capacity (13).

Seven companies primarily interested in fertilizers operated 11 ammonia plants with 13 percent of the total capacity in 1980. These were Beker Industries, First Mississippi, J. R. Simplot Company,

In response to threatened shortage of natural gas in the 1970's, TVA built this coal gasification facility and demonstrated the technical feasibility of producing a syngas that could be used to make ammonia. Coal handling section is at right and gasification and gas purification at left. *(TVA)*

Unocal's nitrogen complex at Kenai, Alaska, is major supplier of West coast and export markets. *(Unocal Chemicals Division)*

Jupiter (Terra), TVA, and Agrico (Williams). Twenty other companies with various interests operated the remaining 27 plants and accounted for 20 percent of the country's ammonia capacity. Included in this category were Borden Chemical Company; Kaiser, Cominco and USS Agri-Chemicals (steel); FMC Corporation (machinery); Georgia Pacific (forest products); PPG (glass and chemical); and 13 others. Companies with the largest ammonia production capacities in 1980 were CF Industries, 2.2 million tons; Farmland, 2.2 million; Agrico Chemical-Williams, 1.7; Union Oil, 1.3; and Allied Corporation, 1.1. They accounted for 41 percent of the U.S. capacity (13).

Farmer cooperatives, most of which are exempt from Federal taxes, played an increasing role in ammonia production, starting in the summer of 1951 when the Mississippi Chemical Corporation completed a 1,000-tpd plant at Yazoo City. Mississippi Chemical was organized to provide farmer members in the Mississippi River Delta area with nitrogen for cotton (55). By 1964, cooperatives were operating five ammonia plants having about 7 percent of the U.S. capacity; 10 years later co-ops had about 20 percent of the capacity. In 1980, three cooperatives, CF Industries, Farmland, and Mississippi Chemical, operated 16 plants, 11 of which were of the large centrifugal compressor type; capacity totaled 4.9 million tons of ammonia, or 24 percent of the U.S. total (13,20,30). A major strength of the co-ops has been their built-in marketing system through some 7,000 local co-ops spread across the country.

Regardless of the vast number of changes among ammonia companies, a number have had long operating histories in the ammonia industry. Those operating in 1932 or before and still operating in 1980 were Allied Corporation, E. I. du Pont de Nemours, and the Olin Corporation, which traces back to the Mathieson Alkali Works. Hercules, Inc., Phillips Chemical, and TVA began operating during the World War II period. Ten other companies operating in 1960 were still producing ammonia in 1980. These were American Cyanamid, Chevron (originally Standard Oil of California), Dow Chemical, Diamond-Shamrock (then two separate companies), FMC, W. R. Grace & Co., Hawkeye Chemical, Monsanto, U.S. Steel, and Valley Nitrogen (13,16).

The U.S. ammonia industry for years has been one of the largest in the world. In 1980, the United States ranked first among nations in nitrogen production, followed closely in turn by China and the U.S.S.R. In consumption of nitrogen, the United States was second only to China with the U.S.S.R. in third position. The United States far outranked Canada and the U.S.S.R. in nitrogen exports; at the same time it led the nations in imports, with China and India in second and third positions (23).

REFERENCES

(To avoid confusion, the year indicated on the individual references for reports appearing in *Mineral Resources of the U.S.* and in *Minerals Yearbooks* is the year covered by the report and not the year of publication.)

1. Adams, J. R., M. S. Anderson, and W. C. Hurlburt. 1961. *Liquid nitrogen fertilizers for direct application.* U.S. Dept. of Agriculture, Agriculture Handbook No. 198.
2. Allen, C. B. 1979. Surface transport. In *Ammonia, Part IV.* Ed. by A. V. Slack and G. R. James, pp. 51-62. Marcel Dekker, Inc., New York and Basel.
3. Anon. 1962. *Fertilizer Trends.* Tenn. Valley Auth., Muscle Shoals, Alabama.
4. ____. 1967. Kellogg's single-train, large ammonia plants achieve lowest costs. *Chem. Eng.* 74(24):112-117.
5. ____. 1968. Mexico now operating new 150-mile anhydrous ammonia pipeline across isthmus. *Oil and Gas Jour.* 66(9):80-81.
6. ____. 1971. Midwest ammonia pipelines now in operation. *Chem. Eng. News* 49(1):17-18.
7. ____. 1974. Boom in agrichemicals. *Business Week,* pp. 53-59, June 8, 1974.
8. Atwood, K. and C. B. Knight. 1973. Reforming kinetics and catalysis l-A: Natural gas. In *Ammonia, Part I.* Ed. by A. V. Slack and G. R. James, pp. 145-174. Marcel Dekker, Inc., New York.
9. Axelrod, L. C. and T. E. O'Hare. 1964. Production of synthetic ammonia. In *Fertilizer Nitrogen.* Ed. by V. Sauchelli, pp. 58-88. Reinhold Publ. Corp, New York.
10. Blouin, G. M. 1979. Use of ammonia in agricultural and chemical industries. In *Ammonia, part IV.* Ed. by A. V. Slack and G. R. James, pp. 79- 183. Marcel Dekker, Inc., New York and Basel.
11. Bresler, S. A. and G. R. James. 1965. Questions and answers on today's ammonia plants. *Chem. Eng.* 72(13): 109-118.
12. Bridges, J. D. 1979. *Fertilizer Trends.* Tenn. Valley Auth., Muscle Shoals, Alabama.
13. ____. 1982. *Fertilizer Trends.* TVA, Muscle Shoals, Alabama.
14. British Sulphur Corporation. 1981. U.S. exports-the boom goes on. *Nitrogen* 133:21-25.
15. Cochrane, W. W. 1979. *The Development of American Agriculture.* Univ. of Minnesota Press, Minneapolis.
16. Douglas, J. R, 1960. *Fertilizer Trends.* Tenn. Valley Auth., Muscle Shoals, Alabama,
17. ____. 1980. *U.S. nitrogen industry at the crossroads 1980.* Presented at the Far West Fertilizer Assoc. Annual Convention, Spokane, Washington, Dec. 10-12, 1980.
18. ____. 1981. *Fertilizer costs, 1985.* Paper presented at The Fertilizer Institute's Sixth Annual World Fertilizer Conf., New York, Sept. 1981.
19. ____ and J. M. Ransom. 1958. *Fertilizer Trends.* TVA, Muscle Shoals, Alabama.
20. ____, E. A. Harre, and E. L. Johnston. 1964. *Fertilizer Trends.* TVA, Muscle Shoals, Alabama.
21. Edwards, C. S. 1945. Nitrogen, a history and future predictions. *Comm, Fert. 1945 Yearbook,* pp. 53-54, 56-57, 59.
22. Farm Chemicals. 1980. TVA unveils coal gasification plant. *Farm Chem.* 143(11):84-85.

23. Food and Agriculture Organization of the United Nations. 1980. *FAO Fertilizer Yearbook.*
24. Gillentine, F. and J. T. Huey. 1966. Handling ammonia. In *Agricultural Anhydrous Ammonia Technology and Use.* Ed. by M. H. McVickar, et al., pp. 143-168. Publ. by Agricultural Ammonia Inst. and Soil Science Soc. Amer., Madison, Wisconsin.
25. Harding, A. J. 1959. *Ammonia Manufacture and End Uses.* Oxford Univ. Press, New York.
26. Harre, E. A. 1967. *Fertilizer Trends.* Tenn. Valley Auth., Muscle Shoals, Alabama.
27. _____. 1969. *Fertilizer Trends.* TVA, Muscle Shoals, Alabama.
28. _____. 1971. *Fertilizer Trends.* TVA, Muscle Shoals, Alabama.
29. _____. 1973. *Fertilizer Trends.* TVA, Muscle Shoals, Alabama.
30. _____, M. N. Goodson, and J. D. Bridges. 1976. *Fertilizer Trends.* TVA, Muscle Shoals, Alabama.
31. International Fertilizer Development Center and UNIDO. 1978. *Fertilizer Manual.* T. P. Hignett, Editor. Publ. by International Fertilizer Development Center, Muscle Shoals, Alabama.
32. Johnson, B. L. 1944. Nitrogen compounds. *Min. Yearbook,* pp. 1525-1531.
33. _____. 1945. Nitrogen compounds. *Min. Yearbook,* pp. 1556-1564.
34. _____. 1946. Nitrogen compounds. *Min. Yearbook,* pp. 862-865.
35. _____. 1947. Nitrogen compounds. *Min. Yearbook,* pp. 857-860.
36. _____. 1948. Nitrogen compounds. *Min. Yearbook,* pp. 893-897.
37. _____. 1950. Nitrogen compounds. *Min. Yearbook.* pp. 863-868,
38. Leavitt, F. H. 1966. Agricultural ammonia equipment, development and history. In *Agricultural Anhydrous Ammonia, Technology and Use,* Ed, by M, H. McVickar, et al., pp. 125-142. Publ. by Agric. Ammonia Inst. and Soil Science Soc, of Amer,, Madison, Wisconsin.
39. Lee, J. J. 1968. Ammonia line has unusual features. *Oil and Gas Jour.* 66:103-108, Nov. 4, 1968.
40. _____ and W. A. Inkofer. 1979. Pipeline shipment. In *Ammonia, Part IV.* Ed. by A. V. Slack and G. R. James, pp. 63-67, Marcel Dekker, Inc., New York and Basel.
41. Lewis, J. R. 1968. Nitrogen compounds. *Min. Yearbook,* Vols. I-II, pp. 781-793.
42. Mahan, J. N., F. D. Lyon, and J. R. Douglas. 1956. *Fertilizer Trends,* Tenn. Valley Auth., Muscle Shoals, Alabama.
43. Mehring, A. L., J. R. Adams, and K. D. Jacob. 1957. *Statistics of fertilizer and liming materials.* U.S. Dept. of Agriculture Statistical Bull. No. 191.
44. Parker, F. W. and F. G. Keenan. 1932. Urea-ammonia liquor-a new fertilizer material. *Chem. & Met. Eng.* 39(10):540-541.
45. Pesek, J., G. Stanford, and N. L. Case. 1971. Nitrogen production and use. In *Fertilizer Technology and Use,* 2nd edition, pp. 217-267. Publ. by Soil Science Society of America, Madison, Wisconsin.
46. Reed, J. D. 1979. Storage and handling. In *Ammonia, Part IV.* Ed. by A. V. Slack and G. R. James, pp. 3-51, Marcel Dekker, Inc., New York.
47. Rohleder, G. V. 1968. First ammonia pipeline starts up. *Oil and Gas Jour.* 66(44):113-114, 116-117.
48. Ruhlman, E. R. 1956. Nitrogen compounds. *Min. Yearbook,* Vol. I, pp. 889-898.
49. Sharp, J. C. 1960. Nitrogen section 1: conversion of ammonia to fertilizer materials. In *Chemistry and Technology of Fertilizers.* Ed. by V. Sauchelli, pp. 10-36, Reinhold Publ. Corp., New York.

50. Skow, M. K. 1954. Nitrogen compounds. *Min. Yearbook,* Vol. I, pp. 875- 888.
51. Slack, A. V. 1973. *History and Status of Ammonia Production and Use. Part I.* Ed. by A. V. Slack and G. R. James, pp. 1-142, Marcel Dekker, Inc., New York.
52. ____. 1977. Commercial ammonia processes. In *Ammonia, Part III.* Ed. by A, V. Slack and G. R, James, pp. 291-369, Marcel Dekker, Inc., New York and Basel.
53. Snyder, J. L. and J. A. Burnett. 1966. Manufacturing processes for ammonia. In *Agricultural Anhydrous Ammonia Technology and Use.* Ed. by M. H. McVickar, et al., pp. 1-20, Agric. Ammonia Inst. and Soil Science Soc. Amer., Madison, Wisconsin.
54. Sweeney, G. C. 1970. The U.S. nitrogen industry. *Agr. Chem.* 25(2): 13-15.
55. Taylor, G. V. 1953. Nitrogen production facilities in relation to present and future demand. In *Fertilizer Technology and Resources.* Ed. by K. D. Jacob, pp. 15-61, publ. by Academic Press, Inc., New York.

10

A New Generation of Primary Nutrient Fertilizer Materials 1920-1980

A whole new generation of nitrogen, phosphorus, and potassium fertilizer materials emerged during the 1920-1980 period, replacing almost all of those that had been available. Most affected were the low-grade nitrogen materials which were largely replaced by those based upon synthetic ammonia. The old standby phosphate material, normal superphosphate, which had provided practically all of the phosphate in fertilizers since the 1850's, gave way to more concentrated materials made possible with the introduction of phosphoric acid as an intermediate. The conglomerate of low-analysis potash materials and grades existent in the 1920's rapidly gave way to higher grade potassium materials, primarily potassium chloride. The key position of potassium chloride was assured with the opening of the Carlsbad, New Mexico, underground deposits and, later, with imports of Canadian potassium chloride from Saskatchewan.

This chapter deals with the history of the more important fertilizer materials being consumed in the United States during the 60-year period, the last half of which witnessed a revolution in American agriculture. For the most part the chapter covers materials that were adopted commercially. Exceptions include a few that had reached the demonstration stage of development and had aroused considerable interest or debate in the fertilizer world but, for one reason or another, never achieved commercial production. Individual processes used in the commercial manufacture of major materials are discussed briefly inasmuch as the technology and design of a plant can determine whether a given material can be sold competitively with alternative materials.

Nitrogen Materials

Prior to the late 1920's, the U.S. fertilizer industry depended almost entirely upon nonsynthetic nitrogen. The only exceptions were calcium cyanamide shipped in from Niagara Falls, Ontario, since 1910 and small amounts of nitrogen-containing products imported from Europe during the 1920's. By the early 1930's, however, ammonia synthesis had advanced to the point in this country that Du Pont at its Belle, West Virginia, plant and Allied Chemical at its Hopewell, Virginia, plant seriously entered into production of synthetic nitrogen materials for use as fertilizers. This signaled a new era–one which eventually would free the U.S. fertilizer industry and the farmer from dependence upon natural organics, Chilean nitrate, by-product ammonium sulfate, and legume crops as major nitrogen sources.

This section deals with both the older and the newer nitrogen materials used during the 1920-1980 period. It does not include the highly important ammonium phosphates which, according to custom, will be presented under phosphatic materials.

Natural Organics

Natural organic materials that in 1910 accounted for 90 percent of the fertilizer nitrogen consumed in the United States declined to 34 percent in 1920 and 3.4 percent in 1950. Much of their decline after 1920 was due to the growing competition of chemical nitrogen materials derived from synthetic ammonia, and to the diversion of the higher grade organics to the more profitable livestock feed supplements market. The combined tonnages of cottonseed meal, dried blood, fish scrap, and animal tankage used for fertilizers dropped from 789,000 tons in 1920 to 79,000 in 1950. Tonnages of garbage tankage also declined, primarily due to its very low nitrogen content (2.5 to 3%), and the once popular bird and bat guanos became exhausted. However, two new natural organics, activated sewage sludge and digested sewage sludge, came on the scene (64, 90).

Activated sewage sludge, containing about 5 percent N and 3.5 percent P_2O_5 is produced from sewage freed from grit and coarse solids and aerated after inoculation with special microorganisms. The resulting flocculated organic matter is filtered, dried in rotary dryers, crushed, and screened. The city of Milwaukee began producing such a product in 1937, selling it under the trade name "Milorganite." About the same time the city of Pasadena, California, produced the product selling it under the name "Nitroganic." In the 1970's, 20 or more cities used the activated process but only a few heat-dried and sold it as a fertilizer. By 1950, about 120,000 tons of the activated sludge was produced (21,79).

Digested sewage sludge is produced by using the existing microorganisms to digest the solids in the sludge. It is air-dried and sold largely in bulk form to local mixers and farmers, or, in some cases, it is heat-dried and sold in bags. The air-dried material contains 3 to 6 percent primary nutrients and 10 to 30 percent water. Some 4,000 plants have produced the dried, digested sludge (21,32,79). About 300,000 tons of

Many cities are applying treated sewage to agricultural lands. Although the driving force is waste disposal, the sludge supplies significant quantities of plant nutrients to crops. (F.J. Myers--TVA)

natural organics were consumed in the United States in 1980, about two-thirds of it dried livestock manure sold mostly for nonfarm uses and the remainder largely sewage sludges (26).

Sodium Nitrate

Sodium nitrate imported from Chile remained a highly important fertilizer in the United States during the 1920's, amounting to about 600,000 tons annually, more than had been used at any time in the past. Over half went into mixed fertilizers and the remainder into direct application. By far the greatest amount was used in the South Atlantic and Middle Atlantic States (64). However, the specter of its replacement by synthetic nitrogen had been on the horizon since Germany successfully produced synthetic ammonia in large amounts during World War I. The Chilean Government, as a result, began to bolster the position of its sodium nitrate in the United States and in the world market.

Status of Chilean Nitrate—Most encouraging was a new process for extracting sodium nitrate from various grades of ore which, if perfected and placed in commercial production, would greatly improve the Chilean nitrate competitive situation. The new process was developed by the Guggenheim Bros., a firm engaged in developing a copper mine near the nitrate deposits in northern Chile. The Guggenheim process was placed in production in 1926. The new process was designed to replace the primitive Shanks process which was based upon extracting the nitrate-containing ore with a progressively more concentrated nitrate liquid held at the boiling point until the liquor was saturated.

The Guggenheim process involved extracting the ore with slightly warmed nitrate liquor until saturation was reached. This method increased the amount of nitrate recovered, lowered the energy and manpower requirements, and made possible the recovery of nitrates from low-grade ores (27,90,96). In practice, the process permitted using ore as low as 7 percent nitrate to as high as 75 percent, required only a quarter of the manpower, and produced 99 percent pure sodium nitrate. By 1930, the process accounted for two-thirds of the Chilean nitrate production and by 1950, 90 percent (96).

In addition to increasing mining and production efficiencies, an aggressive sales organization, the Chilean Sodium Nitrate Sales Company, was set up in the United States in 1926. The sales company avidly promoted the agronomic value of Chilean nitrate, claiming that the sodium contained in the product had value as a potassium supplement and stressing the value of micronutrients in the material. However, the all-out sales efforts along with the mining and production efficiencies did not make Chilean nitrate fully competitive with synthetic nitrogen materials. Its handicaps of low analysis (16.2 percent N) and remote location were just too great. Chilean nitrate received yet another blow when Allied Chemical began production of synthetic sodium nitrate at Hopewell, Virginia, in 1928.

Synthetic Sodium Nitrate—The first Allied sodium nitrate process involved two steps, oxidizing ammonia in the presence of an alkali sodium carbonate to form a solution of sodium nitrate and sodium nitrite, and then converting the nitrite to sodium nitrate by reacting with either nitric acid or nitrogen dioxide. The overall reaction is:

$$12NH_3 + 21O_2 + 4Na_2CO_3 \rightarrow 8NaNO_3 + 4NO + 4CO_2 + 18H_2O.$$

The nitrous oxide (NO) is returned to nitric acid or sodium nitrate production (23).

In 1943, Allied also began producing sodium nitrate by a two-step process in which sodium chloride is reacted with nitric acid and oxygen to form sodium nitrate and nitrosyl chloride (NOCl). The NOCl is then reacted with sodium carbonate, (Na_2CO_3) to yield additional sodium nitrate. The overall reaction is:

$$6NaCl + 8HNO_3 + O_2 \rightarrow 6NaNO_3 + 3Cl_2 + N_2O_4 + 4H_2O.$$

The dinitrogen tetroxide (N_2O_4) is used to manufacture nitric acid. The two processes together produced 907,000 tons of sodium nitrate during the peak year of 1945. The Olin-Mathieson Corp., using the first Allied process, began production at Lake Charles, Louisiana, in the early 1950's (23).

U.S. production of synthetic sodium nitrate amounted to 500,000 tons in 1935 and remained relatively high into the mid-1940's. By the 1970's, only modest tonnages were being produced, mostly as by-products of other manufacturing operations.

Consumption of sodium nitrate, synthetic and imported Chilean product, continued at modest levels. Total use was about equally divided between fertilizer and industrial sectors in the early 1960's. Fertilizer consumption amounted to about 580,000 tons of product in 1935, 730,000 tons in 1950, 450,000 tons in 1960, and 84,000 tons in 1980. Most current distribution is in the south Atlantic and Mid-Atlantic States, regions that have been the major users of sodium nitrate as a fertilizer for the past century (4,5,22,24,45).

Ammonium Sulfate

By-product ammonium sulfate (20.5 percent N), obtained from coke oven gases produced chiefly in the steel industry, was the most important fertilizer nitrogen source from the 1920's until 1944 when ammonium nitrate replaced it. Some 104 coke works in 18 states were producing the material in 1940. Small amounts of synthetic ammonium sulfate appeared in the 1920's apparently based on synthetic ammonia sometimes purchased by coke oven producers to supplement their by-product. Imports from Germany and Japan also supplied sizable amounts of ammonium sulfate during the 1930's (21,64).

Several methods were used to recover coke oven ammonia and to react it with sulfuric acid. The major production method in the 1940's was to pass the coke oven gases, after cooling and tar extraction, into a bubbler type saturator containing dilute sulfuric acid. Crystals were recovered by centrifuge or filter. A second method in use by 1960 involves cooling the gases by contact with a recirculating wash liquid, sending the liquid to an ammonia still to separate the ammonia from easily dissociated ammonia salts, and then passing the liquor through a "lime-leg" where the ammonia in more difficult-to-decompose ammonium salts is released and recovered by steam stripping and sent to a sulfuric acid washer. A third and most-used procedure, a compromise between the above two methods, results in high ammonia recoveries and a purer product (21,48,80).

Waste streams from various chemical and metallurgical processes also became a common source of by-product ammonium sulfate. Manufacturers of caprolactam, a synthetic fiber intermediate, produce by-product ammonium sulfate amounting to 4.5 tons for each ton of the main product. From about 1970 on, caprolactam production declined sharply (87).

Synthetic ammonium sulfate in the early 1940's was produced and marketed in this country under the trade name Arcadian. The process, similar to some by-product processes, involved vaporizing anhydrous ammonia and introducing it into dilute sulfuric acid through a distribution head located in the lower section of the saturator while the sulfuric acid was injected into the circulation system from above. The heat of reaction vaporized the water which was assisted by air introduced along with the ammonia vapor. The ammonium sulfate crystals were collected at the bottom of the saturator, withdrawn, centrifuged, dried, and the filtrate recycled. The synthetic product contained 21 percent N. Production of the synthetic product increased from 89,000 tons in 1945 to over 1 million in 1950 (21,35,64).

Later modifications of the synthetic process included vacuum evaporation, continuous operation, introduction of crystallizers, and production of large crystals. Large tonnages also were produced by reacting anhydrous ammonia with strong sulfuric acid. These plants usually employed continuous flow, use of evaporator crystallizer units operating at either atmospheric pressure or under vacuum, and continuous or automatic batch-type centrifuges (48).

Spent sulfuric acid from oil refineries, petrochemical plants, and various pickling operations is sometimes used in ammonium sulfate production. Not all spent acids can be used since some cause undue foaming or corrosion, or contain impurities that make the product undesirable as a fertilizer (48,71).

Ammonium sulfate, the last of the old-time fertilizer materials, continued throughout the 1920-1980 period as an important nitrogen material, although it was soon outdistanced by the newer nitrogen materials–ammonium nitrate, urea, ammonia, and nitrogen solutions. Ammonium sulfate (coke oven plus synthetic) nevertheless continued to increase in tonnage until 1965 when it leveled off at about 2.7 million tons of material, and retained this general level through 1980. The by-product material, however, peaked in 1955 at 981,000 tons and steadily declined thereafter. Synthetic, on the other hand, reached 1.2 million tons in 1955 and steadily improved its position with respect to the coke oven product. Synthetic's share of the total ammonium sulfate production climbed from 54 percent in 1954 to 84 percent in 1980. That year, 2.1 million tons of synthetic ammonium sulfate was produced and 398,000 tons of by-product (16,41).

As a fertilizer material, ammonium sulfate has many advantages: low hygroscopicity, good physical properties, no hazard problems, and no special precautions required for application to the soil. Further, its high sulfur content (24 percent S) makes it a premium material when applied in sulfur-deficient areas. Its main disadvantage is its low nitrogen content (21 percent N) which limits its use in areas distant from the point of manufacture (10). Since 1957, the Pacific States have accounted for about one-half of all the ammonium sulfate domestically consumed as a fertilizer (4,20,26,77).

Calcium Cyanamide

Calcium cyanamide (CaCN$_2$), the first fixed nitrogen material to be produced on a continuing basis from 1910 on in North America (Niagara Falls, Ontario), was marketed largely in the United States as a fertilizer. The fertilizer product contained 21-22 percent N, 15-20 percent free lime, and 11 percent free carbon. Initially, it was marketed in powder form which was disagreeable to handle and apply due to its dusty nature, corrosiveness, toxicity when inhaled, and irritating effect on the skin and eyes. Furthermore, the material was toxic to germinating seeds and seedlings unless planting was delayed for a week or 10 days following application Eventually, the dustiness problem was overcome by adding oil. Also, a suitable granular product was brought out in the late 1930's through use of a binding agent (21,90).

Cyanamide was used both as an ingredient of mixed fertilizers and for direct application. However, only 30 to 60 pounds of pulverized material could be added per ton of mixed fertilizer since larger amounts caused soluble phosphate in the mix to revert to less available forms (21,90). The major cyanamide-using areas, over the years, were the South Atlantic and East South Central States (5,20,64,77).

U.S. consumption of cyanamide as a fertilizer was never very great, running about 100,000 tons per year during the 1920's and 1930's, peaking at 131,000 tons in 1946, and declining thereafter, dropping to 71 tons in 1980 (5,25,26,64,77). The disappearance of cheap hydropower and low-cost electricity undoubtedly speeded its demise. Each ton of calcium cyanamide required 9,000 kilowatt hours to produce (12).

Improvements in Nitric Acid Production

Nitric acid produced from ammonia was in demand during World War I (Chapter 6), and afterward became an important intermediate in U.S. fertilizer production with the development of a domestic synthetic ammonia industry. Although the methods, construction and equipment for manufacture of nitric acid had changed greatly since the World War I era, the basic steps remained the same. These were the oxidation of ammonia to produce nitric oxide (NO), oxidation of the NO to produce nitrogen dioxide (NO$_2$), and the absorption of the NO$_2$ in water to form nitric acid (HNO$_3$).

One major improvement was the modification of the platinum catalyst used in the oxidation of ammonia by adding 2 to 10 percent rhodium. The addition of the rhodium increased the gauze strength of the catalyst, reduced catalyst losses, and increased the efficiency of the ammonia oxidation step (14,88).

Another area of substantial improvements is in the development of corrosion-resistant materials for construction and equipment. Stainless steel became the standard material for absorption towers and wherever corrosion might be severe. High-silicon cast iron is used in ammonia oxidation and NO oxidation steps where the gas, although hot, is dry. Aluminum often is used in storage tanks. Various fluorocarbon plastics came into use in piping, coatings, and gaskets (14,48,72). Such materials were essential for pressurized plants having improved coolers and special tower designs that greatly increased the efficiency of NO_2 absorption, permitted production of more concentrated acid (55 to 65 percent HNO_3), and decreased investment costs.

Energy efficiency was improved by recovering heat generated during ammonia oxidation (the temperatures reach 900°C) for use mostly in turbines that drive air compressors. This encouraged American firms to use high pressure (8-10 atmospheres) throughout the plants, including both ammonia oxidation and NO_2 absorption. (In contrast, European plants favor mid-pressures of three to five atmospheres although some use low pressure for ammonia oxidation and high pressure for NO_2 absorption.) (14,48,72).

Ammonium Nitrate

Ammonium nitrate apparently was first produced by Glauber of Germany in 1659 by reacting nitric acid and ammonium carbonate. It was considered to have medical value in the eighteenth century. Its value as an explosive was recognized in Sweden in 1867, where a patent was issued covering this use. Alfred Nobel in 1879 also was issued a patent on using ammonium nitrate as a partial replacement for nitroglycerin. Ammonium nitrate was first used in Europe as a fertilizer following World War I when large stocks unused for explosives became available. Following serious explosions in Germany in 1920 and 1921, the ammonium nitrate was dry-mixed with limestone, gypsum, chalk, or ammonium sulfate to eliminate dangers of explosions and to also serve as a conditioner to prevent caking. First use of ammonium nitrate in this country as a fertilizer was in 1926 when German imports of the nonexplosive product began arriving. The imported mixtures contained about 60 percent ammonium nitrate (21,47,64).

Ammonium nitrate is produced by reacting gaseous ammonia with nitric acid:

$$HNO_3 + NH_3 \rightarrow NH_4NO_3 + \text{heat}$$

Several processes have been developed using various modifications of different neutralization, evaporation, drying and finishing methods. Large tonnages of solid ammonium nitrate are produced in the forms of prills, crystals, and granules. Also, substantial amounts in solution form are produced for use in nitrogen solutions and in mixed fertilizers. The neutralization step can be carried out under atmospheric pressure or at pressures of four or five atmospheres. In plants where a crystalline product is produced, it is performed under vacuum. One common method involves preheating gaseous ammonia and nitric acid of 50 or 60 percent concentration. After heating, the two flow into a neutralizer tank where the heat of reaction further raises the temperature to about 160°C and evaporates most of the water as steam (72).

The concentration of the solution from the neutralizer is about 83 percent ammonium nitrate. The solution is evaporated further by using steam from the neutralizer to produce a solution containing 95 to 98 percent ammonium nitrate. Some plants produce a 99.5 to 99.8 percent solution. The less concentrated solutions, 94 to 98 percent, produce a low-density prill. Although used in fertilizers, its main use is in explosives. The newer, more concentrated solutions produce a high-density prill favored in fertilizers. Ammonium nitrate solutions used in nitrogen solutions contain 80 to 90 percent ammonium nitrate. A crystallization process uses a vacuum evaporator to produce ammonium nitrate crystals which are separated from the mother liquor by centrifuging (4,48,72).

All of the solid ammonium nitrate fertilizer is cooled and coated with clay. The finished product contains 33 to 34 percent N. Most of it is shipped and stored in bulk. Ammonium nitrate going into nitrogen solutions is shipped in the hot concentrated solution form to mixing plants and combined with other liquid materials, or the final solutions are prepared and mixed at the site of the ammonia plant (9,48,72).

U.S. capacities for producing ammonium nitrate were greatly expanded during World War II with the addition of government-owned munitions plants, including a remodeled World War I ammonium nitrate facility at Muscle Shoals, Alabama, operated by TVA. In 1943, needs for ammonium nitrate for munitions fell behind expectations and the outputs from TVA's plant, a Hercules Powder Co. plant in California, and three wartime Canadian plants were released for use as fertilizer (47,55).

Early Problems and Disasters—Soon after the explosives-grade ammonium nitrate became available to agriculture, it became apparent that it was unsatisfactory for use as a fertilizer. The fine, unprotected particles immediately absorbed moisture from the atmosphere and caked so badly in the bags that it could not be applied (according to farmers it "set-up like tombstones"). A crash program to remedy the situation was undertaken by the U.S. Department of Agriculture, TVA, Hercules Powder, and the Canadian producers. Research soon uncovered several leads that, taken together, would rectify the situation. These included (a) increasing the particle size of the grains or crystals; (b) conditioning the material by coating with kaolin, certain other clays, or kieselguhr; (c) coating with organic moisture repellents–petrolatum, paraffin, and rosin (these materials later were found to increase the explosion hazard); and (d) bagging in moisture-proof bags and avoiding storage temperatures above 38°C (later it was found that fluctuations through 32°C caused a crystal change that favored caking) (9,47). To increase the size of particles, TVA modified its graining technique to produce a coarser product. The Canadian producers adopted a prilling process in which highly concentrated, hot ammonium nitrate solution was sprayed from manifolds placed in the top of a cooling tower to form solidified droplets called prills (53).

Ammonium nitrate is subject to decomposition when heated, making it subject to burning. Fires once started in the ammonium nitrate are self-propagating and do not require oxygen from an outside source; once started, they can be stopped only by flooding with water. The fumes released during burning contain NO_2 and other oxides of nitrogen that are toxic. Chloride-catalyzed decomposition is a problem in some mixed fertilizers containing potassium chloride and ammonium nitrate. The resulting fires are slow-burning and referred to as "cigar-burning" (48,87).

Detonation of ammonium nitrate can occur from shock such as blasting with other explosives. It is particularly sensitive to detonation when mixed with organic materials (ammonium nitrate mixed with fuel oil is a common explosive used in mines). Some major disasters have occurred from detonation of fertilizer-grade ammonium nitrate (48,87).

A number of explosions and fires had occurred in ammonium nitrate or mixtures of ammonium nitrate and other materials prior to 1921 in Germany and the United States. In 1920, the steamer Hall Friend at Brooklyn, New York, containing ammonium nitrate, sodium nitrate, and other flammable materials burned, but no explosion took place. Also in 1920, explosions occurred in Kreiwold, Germany, when explosive charges were used to break up caked ammonium nitrate. Various causes were cited for the different events and some were considered accidents (28,58).

The first major disaster that focused real concern on the problem was the explosion at the famous Oppau plant of Badische Analin-und Soda Fabrik in September 1921. Some 9,900 short tons of Leunasaltpeter (the double salt of ammonium nitrate and ammonium sulfate) exploded, killing an estimated 585 people and injuring nearly 2,000. The practice in the plant was to blast caked fertilizer in storage using coal-mine safety explosives. It had been assumed up to that time that the product posed no explosive hazard (28,58).

The Texas City, Texas, disaster of April 16-17, 1947, resulted in the explosion of two ships loaded with cargoes containing large amounts of fertilizer-grade ammonium nitrate that virtually destroyed Texas City, killed 576 people and injured 3,000. The first ship to explode, the 10,000-ton Liberty-type freighter *Grandchamp* of French registry, had a cargo of 2,380 tons of bagged ammonium nitrate coated with petrolatum, rosin, and a small amount of kaolin as a conditioner. Fire was noted in one hold at 8:10 a.m. April 16, soon after loading operations of the previous day were continued. Attempts to extinguish the fire with water and steam failed, and the hatches of both holds were battened down. Combustion continued and the gases blew off the hatch covers. An hour later the ship exploded. The second Liberty-type freighter, the *High Flyer* of U.S. registration, in the slip adjacent to the *Grandchamp*, was loaded with 960 tons of the same type ammonium nitrate plus a cargo of 2,000 tons of sulfur. The explosion of the *Grandchamp* blew the *High Flyer* free of its hausers and drove it into another ship containing no nitrate. The two ships could not be separated and embers ignited the sulfur of the *High Flyer*. Efforts to salvage the ship were abandoned and the ammonium nitrate exploded at 1:10 a.m. April 17 (58).

Investigations indicated that conditions were right for detonation; namely, a large mass of melted ammonium nitrate resulting from the fires, the close confinement and pressure build-up in the ship holds, and the presence of the waxy material used in coating the ammonium nitrate prills made the nitrate ignitable at lower temperatures. The Texas City disaster triggered adoption of very tight domestic controls on ammonium nitrate storage, transport, and handling. However, the United States never went so far as to require that ammonium nitrate fertilizer be mixed with limestone or other materials that would render it nonexplosive. Within the United States, ammonium nitrate fertilizer is no longer considered to present undue hazards except from rail and other unpreventable accidents or intentional misuse (33,87).

Since World War II, ammonium nitrate use as a fertilizer accounted for about 90 percent of the total ammonium nitrate production from 1955 through 1965 before declining to about 83 percent in 1980. Production of solution and solid ammonium nitrate for fertilizer increased steadily from 383,000 tons of material in 1943 to 6.4 million tons in 1974, after which it went into a four-year slump before resuming its climb to 7.3 million in 1980. The solid product led the solution form in tonnage until 1978, after which the solution accounted for over half. Over the years, 80 to 85 percent of the solid ammonium nitrate was used for direct application. In 1955, this amounted to about one-third of all nitrogen materials being applied directly to the soil. The importance of direct application ammonium nitrate declined thereafter, dropping to 10 percent in 1980. It was exceeded by anhydrous ammonia in tonnage of directly applied N in 1960, by nitrogen solutions in 1970, and by urea in 1978 (16,41,64).

Anhydrous Ammonia

Anhydrous ammonia, which became the leading source of N for practically all nitrogen fertilizers as well as the leading direct application nitrogen material, presents both unusual advantages and problems. It contains 82.5 percent N, the highest nutrient content of any fertilizer material, permitting it to be shipped long distances at minimum cost. It can be injected directly into the soil or irrigation water with little or no losses if properly done.

Anhydrous ammonia, however, is a hazardous material. Direct contact with the skin or mucous tissues causes "ammonia burn" because of desiccation. In gaseous form, high contents of ammonia can cause severe irritation to the eyes and respiratory system. It is not a poison but can cause death from asphyxiation. Serious damage most commonly occurs when equipment fails, accidents occur, or it is mishandled. At atmospheric pressure, it immediately converts from liquid to gaseous form except when in contact with water for which it has an affinity. During shipping, handling, and storage, it must be kept under pressure and usually refrigerated to retain it in liquefied form. Tank car derailments and tank truck overturns are of particular concern. Safety regulations have been tightened considerably since the 1950's (3,48,81).

Use in Irrigation Water—The idea of using ammonia as a source of nitrogen to fertilize the soil is not new. Ammoniacal liquor from coal gas works had been variously tried as a fertilizer in England and Scotland by the 1840's. The first direct application of ammonia in the United States appears to have been made by injecting ammonia into irrigation water in California. The idea was developed by two brothers (Eugene and John Prizer) who had become concerned over the high labor cost involved in spreading soluble nitrogen fertilizers around each tree in large citrus groves. They also developed and patented an applicator that would dissolve solid nitrogen fertilizers and introduce them into irrigation water (3,59,103).

The Shell Chemical Co., considering producing synthetic ammonium sulfate at its Pittsburg, California, ammonia plant, began looking for ways to reduce production costs, especially by omitting the use of sulfuric acid. It was decided that it would be less costly and simpler just to introduce the ammonia itself into the irrigation water. The chief chemist at Shell, L. Rosenstein, contracted with the Citrus Growers' Association Laboratory to conduct experimental work for the project. The Citrus Growers' Laboratory began research in 1932 to determine if continued applications of ammonia would produce any deleterious effects upon the soil. When none was found, studies were initiated to define how best to use the new system in citrus groves under normal irrigation conditions. By 1934, enough practical information had been collected to permit setting up commercial distributors (59).

Injection Directly into the Soil—The Shell group soon concluded that to increase ammonia sales they would have to develop a market in areas where irrigation was not practiced. No one in the company had any ideas on how to do this until some of the Shell personnel observed a telephone company laying underground cable using a subsoiler with a tube in the back of the blade through which the cable passed. As a result of this observation, Shell engineers installed ammonia equipment on a cultivator and welded a tube to the back of a cultivator shank through which the anhydrous ammonia passed. The cultivator was equipped with a heavy drag to close the shank channel and reduce gaseous loss. Later, a rubber-tired tractor was equipped to replace the cultivator. Commercial application began in 1942 and the practice spread to include all three Pacific States (59).

The market for direct application of anhydrous ammonia amounted to 4,000 tons in 1939, presumably mostly being applied to irrigation water. By 1943, 7,000 tons was applied with most of the increase over 1939 being injected into the soil (3).

J. O. Smith of the Delta Branch Experiment Station, Mississippi, in 1930 adapted an ammonia applicator equipped with a small cylinder of compressed ammonia to a mule-drawn, one-row cultivator. However, other than a photograph no information on the rig is available (8,97). The photograph has been widely reproduced over the years in reputable publications.

The successful launching of anhydrous ammonia as a direct application material in the eastern half of the United States was left to W. B. Andrews and his coworkers of the Mississippi Agricultural Experiment Station. In 1943, Andrews with J. A. Neely and F. E. Edwards began experiments on direct application of aqua ammonia, and in 1944 on anhydrous ammonia. Their results and the principles governing injection of anhydrous ammonia were published in 1947 (8).

The equipment developed by the Andrews group for applying anhydrous ammonia consisted of the following mounted on a tractor: a flow meter which measured the rate of flow of the anhydrous ammonia out of the feeder tank; a knife-like applicator behind which an iron pipe was welded carrying a rubber tube for injecting the anhydrous ammonia 5 or 6 inches into the soil; and disc hillers or other covering equipment for immediately closing the applicator channel with soil to prevent gaseous losses of the ammonia. During 1944 and 1945, side-dressings of anhydrous ammonia were made with the equipment and compared with solid ammonium nitrate on cotton and corn using different times and rates of application. The overall project was supported in part by TVA from 1944 through 1948 (7,91).

As a result of a shortage of solid nitrogen sources in the winter of 1946-47, Mississippi Delta farmers became interested in the work with anhydrous ammonia. Investigations indicated that an adequate supply of anhydrous ammonia would be available along with enough steel to make the necessary ammonia tanks needed for transport and application. However, the flow meters were in short supply and had to be replaced with a different type of meter. Since there were no facilities for construction of the equipment, local Mississippi Delta machine shops rallied to produce and assemble the needed equipment (7).

Mississippi researchers used this home-made equipment for subsurface application of gaseous ammonia. *(Mississippi State University)*

Large tractor-drawn equipment is used for fast direct application of ammonia to large fields. *(F.J. Myers--TVA)*

Acceptance of anhydrous ammonia as a fertilizer material was immediate in the Delta. The large farms and level lands were well suited for anhydrous ammonia application. A farmer cooperative, the Mississippi Chemical Corporation, was set up at Yazoo City, Mississippi, to produce ammonia and other fertilizer materials needed in the area. The use of anhydrous ammonia spread rapidly northward into the Midwest and westward into the West South Central region (3).

Large-Scale Use for Direct Application—Growth in consumption of anhydrous ammonia for direct application and its spread into new areas was phenomenal. In 1945, some 14,000 tons N equivalent was consumed, most of it in the Pacific States for direct application in irrigation water and for injection into the soil. This accounted for 9 percent of all directly applied N and 3 percent of all fertilizer N used in the United States. Total use of anhydrous ammonia applied directly was 290,000 tons in 1955 accounting for 25 percent of all directly applied N and 15 percent of all the N consumed in the United States. During the 1955-1960 period about 50 percent of the consumption was in six states: California, Mississippi, Texas, Louisiana, Washington, and Arkansas. However, substantial movement also had gotten underway in the Midwest with seven of the midwestern states accounting for over 30 percent of the anhydrous ammonia applied (37,41).

In 1965, direct application of the material amounted to 1.3 million tons of N equivalent, which was 40 percent of all directly applied N and 28 percent of all fertilizer N consumed nationally. By 1980, consumption had grown to 4.5 million tons directly applied or 51 percent of all directly applied N and 39 percent of all fertilizer N used. During the overall 1965-1980 period, use in the Midwest continued to increase rapidly, amounting to 52 percent in 1965 and over 60 percent in 1980. Other leading states were Texas, Oklahoma, and California. None was applied in the New England States, Virginia, Alaska, and Hawaii (16,37).

Urea

Urea, $CO(NH_2)_2$, is a fertilizer material containing 46 percent N. Its chemical existence has been known since 1773 when Rouelle separated urea from urine by crystallization. Chemists continued to believe that only living processes could produce urea until Wohler of Germany announced in 1828 the synthesis of urea in a laboratory from ammonia and cyanuric acid. In 1868, Busarov produced urea from ammonium carbamate by heating under pressure. With the introduction of calcium cyanamide, some urea was produced commercially by hydrolysis of the calcium cyanamide. The present method, involving reaction of ammonia and carbon dioxide, was introduced by the I.G. Farbenindustrie of Germany in 1920. First commercial production in the United States was by Du Pont at Belle, West Virginia, in 1932 (19,46,48).

The use of urea, including calcium nitrate-urea, began in the United States during the early 1920's as a result of imports primarily from Germany. Du Pont's initial urea product in the early 1930's was a mixture of urea, ammonia, carbon dioxide, and water (a urea-ammonia liquor from the melt produced as the first step in urea synthesis). This was used commercially in the ammoniation of superphosphate. In 1935, Du Pont started production of crystal urea conditioned with an inert coating and containing 42 percent N, and sold under the trade name "Uramon" (68).

The commercial production of urea consists of reacting ammonia and carbon dioxide, both products of ammonia synthesis plants. The reaction takes place in two steps:

$$2NH_3 + CO_2 \rightarrow NH_2CO_2NH_4 \text{ (ammonium carbamate)}$$
$$NH_2CO_2NH_4 \rightarrow CO(NH_2)_2 \text{(Urea)} + H_2O.$$

The ammonia and carbon dioxide are reacted in a pressure reactor to form a melt containing urea, ammonium carbamate, and water along with some unreacted ammonia and carbon dioxide which are removed and recycled. The product is an aqueous solution containing about 75 percent urea which can be used either directly to produce nitrogen solutions or solidified by crystallizing, prilling, or granulating. Numerous variations in urea manufacture have evolved over the years; they differ in pressures, temperatures, solution recycle systems, and equipment arrangement (19,48).

Corrosion problems were the bottleneck in early urea manufacture. To prevent corrosion the reactor vessels were frequently lined with silver or lead. Du Pont, unable to find a desirable corrosion-resistant alloy for its first urea plant at Belle, West Virginia, in 1930-31 lined its 2-foot-diameter and 20-foot-long reaction vessel with silver (68).

Biuret ($NH_2CONHCONH_2$) formed by thermal decomposition of urea can be toxic to crops if it is present in urea fertilizer in large enough amounts. It is formed particularly when temperatures of the urea melts are raised to about 140°C for prilling and granulation. Damage to crops occurs when biuret exceeds about 2 to 3 percent in the fertilizer; however, in foliar sprays damage can be severe at much lower levels. For soil application, damage is most serious in application with or near seed. Biuret was often present in excess amounts in solid urea in the 1950's. However, careful control of temperatures in the concentration and evaporation steps minimized the problem (34,48).

Urea has both good and bad points as a fertilizer material. It has the highest nitrogen content of all solid nitrogen fertilizer materials, is very soluble in water and occupies an intermediate position relative to hygroscopicity. However, when either the solid or liquid forms are placed in contact with soil or plant material the urea hydrolyzes to ammonia and carbon dioxide due to reaction of the enzyme urease. Unless the urea is incorporated into the soil fairly soon after application by tillage, rainfall, or irrigation, loss of the free ammonia into the atmosphere can be appreciable (98).

Urea production for use in fertilizers increased rapidly during the 1948-1960 period, jumping from 47,000 tons to 549,000 tons of material. Production climbed relatively slowly from 1960 through 1975 when about the 3-million-ton level was reached. During this period, production in the liquid form for use in manufacture of nitrogen solutions and the solid form for use in direct application were about equal. After 1975, production again increased rapidly primarily as a result of a sharp increase in use of solid urea. In 1980, total production for fertilizer purposes amounted to 7.2 million tons, 60 percent of which went into the solid material. Of the total primary urea solutions produced at the ammonia plants, 75 percent went into fertilizers in 1960 and 92 percent in 1980. Major nonfertilizer uses were for livestock feed supplements and manufacture of plastics (16,41,64).

As a direct application material, solid urea was overshadowed by anhydrous ammonia, nitrogen solutions, and ammonium nitrate in tons of N consumed until 1978, after which it exceeded ammonium nitrate (16,41).

Nitrogen Solutions

Solutions of soluble nitrogen materials dissolved in water are used to manufacture liquid and dry mixed fertilizers and for direct application to the soil. These include aqueous ammonia, a low-pressure solution and solutions containing free ammonia plus ammonium nitrate or urea or both, classified either as low- or medium-pressure solutions depending upon the ingredients. Solutions with no free ammonia containing ammonium nitrate or urea or both, are classified as nonpressure solutions.

The first use of a nitrogen solution for direct application utilized ammoniacal liquor from illuminating gas works in England and Scotland. In 1843, T. Bishop of Scotland reported that ammoniacal water produced a 25-percent increase in grass yield but that the solution caused some scorching of the grass. J. F. W. Johnston in England in 1852 observed that application of diluted ammoniacal solutions by means of a watercart was profitable on wheat and other small grain crops (Chapter 1). In the early 1900's, reports of successful use were made by England and Germany, and a number of countries experimented with ammonia liquor for direct application following World War I. In this country, Andrews in Mississippi experimented with direct application of aqua ammonia. In 1947, Hanway and coworkers in Nebraska applied an ammonia-ammonium nitrate solution below the soil surface for winter wheat, and about the same time both Arizona and California received shipments of a similar type solution for application in irrigation water (2,3,86).

Ammoniating Superphosphate—The idea of ammoniating superphosphate with nitrogen solutions also is not new. In fact, ammoniation became the first use of nitrogen solutions in the United States. A U.S. patent on the use of superphosphate as an absorbent for ammonia from illuminating gas was issued to J. McDougal in 1873. Studies made on the ammoniation of superphosphate in France and Denmark about 1923 showed that the phosphorus reverted to less soluble compounds. The object of a U.S. patent granted to J. F. C. Hagen and coworkers in 1929 was to control the reversion of the phosphorus in superphosphate through limiting the addition of ammonia to a certain level. This patent was assigned to the Barrett Company, soon to become a division of Allied Chemical. Both Barrett and Du Pont conducted research on the subject and by 1932 sufficient information was available to permit commercial production (42).

Both Allied Chemical and Du Pont had large ammonia plants in operation, one in Virginia and the other in West Virginia, and were interested in developing the synthetic nitrogen fertilizer market. The two companies began marketing anhydrous ammonia for the ammoniation of superphosphate about 1928 but the material did not prove popular because of the special safety and equipment requirements. Aqua ammonia was the first alternative material, followed by solutions containing free ammonia and either ammonium nitrate or urea (21,42).

Allied Chemical, through its Barrett subdivision, began marketing a pressure solution in which 9.6 percent of the N was supplied from ammonium nitrate and 31.1 percent from ammonia. The company made its first tank car shipment in 1949 from Hopewell to Norfolk, Virginia. Later, Allied introduced a series of ammonium nitrate-ammonia solutions containing different proportions of ammonium nitrate to free ammonia. The first urea-ammonia solution was produced by Du Pont at its Belle, West Virginia, plant in 1932. It contained 15 percent urea N and 30 percent N from ammonia. A second urea-ammonia solution released by Du Pont in 1936 contained 20 percent N from the urea and 25 percent from ammonia (21,42,67).

Nitrogen Solutions for Direct Application—Ammoniation of superphosphate had become thoroughly established by 1936, and nitrogen solutions for direct application by the 1960's. Consumption of nitrogen solutions, including aqua ammonia for direct application, was mainly centered in the Pacific States with a market starting to develop in the West North Central States. In 1955, aqua ammonia production facilities were located at 17 of the ammonia synthesis plants, 13 of which had facilities for producing one or more other solutions. A listing in 1957 showed 53 different nitrogen solutions available commercially (3,54).

The last half of the 1950's and the early 1960's saw major changes in the demand for and relative importance of different types of nitrogen solution. Use of pressure solutions for ammoniation of superphosphates declined as the old batch processes were replaced by the continuous ammoniator-granulator for production of homogeneous NPK mixtures based largely on anhydrous ammonia (87).

Take-off of UAN—Starting about 1960, nonpressure, direct application solutions, particularly urea-ammonium nitrate (UAN), took off. UAN became available in three different mixtures of urea, ammonium nitrate, and water–28, 30, and 32 percent N–in order to provide a range of salting-out temperatures to meet storage requirements under different climatic conditions (106).

Besides the range in salting-out temperatures, UAN offers several advantages as a liquid nitrogen material. It contains more N than any other nonpressure solution. Furthermore, when in solution with water, the two materials together are much more soluble than either alone. UAN is easy to handle and apply, it does not need to be injected into the soil, and can be applied without volatilization losses in irrigation systems. It can be transported in petroleum pipelines, barges, and railroad tank cars without hazards, and it can be stored and handled in mild steel (87).

Manufacturing and Equipment—Very little information was published on facilities and equipment used in production of nitrogen solutions prior to about 1960; however, batch-type operations apparently were common practice (10). Nitrogen solution facilities by the 1960's had undergone changes, but still remained relatively simple.

Aqua ammonia is produced by mixing anhydrous ammonia with water and recycling cooled aqua ammonia in a pipe mixing chamber. The most popular mix contains 20 percent N and has a low pressure, permitting storage in 5-psig tanks. Production of the remaining nitrogen solutions hinges largely around the processes used in manufacture of the popular UAN (20,22).

Most nonpressure UAN solutions are produced at ammonia plant sites where concentrated ammonium nitrate and urea solutions are available. (This saves about 250,000 Btu/ton of N which is required to convert the concentrated solutions to solids.) Two types of production processes are used, batch and continuous. Both involve weighing the ammonium nitrate and urea solutions in the mix tank, and adding the desired amount of water and an inhibitor. After mixing, the product is cooled. The large producers use the continuous process and are located where transportation by barge or pipeline or both is available. (A network of pipelines is available in the United States for transport of petroleum products and can be used alternatively to transport UAN solutions.) Use of UAN is largely for direct application and in fluid fertilizers (20).

Pressure solutions made up in various combinations of free ammonia either with ammonium nitrate or urea or both, and water, are produced in the same batch plants used to produce the nonpressure UAN solutions. The batch tank usually is constructed to withstand 75 psig pressure; 75 psig anhydrous ammonia storage tank and piping systems also are added. The pressure solutions are used primarily as a nitrogen and ammonia source in continuous ammoniation-granulation NPK plants (20).

In 1980, 28 companies, practically all owners of synthetic ammonia plants, operated 46 nitrogen solutions plants located at ammonia plant sites. Of the 46 solution plants, 45 had their own ammonium nitrate base solutions and 26 produced urea solutions. Each of the latter also produced ammonium nitrate solutions. Annual production capacities of the nitrogen solution plants ranged from 10,000 tons of solution to one having 1 million tons operated by the Allied Corporation at Geismar, Louisiana (16).

U.S. production of nitrogen solutions (not including aqua ammonia) rose from 804,000 tons of N equivalent in 1960 to 2.1 million in 1975 and to 2.8 million in 1980, which was more than one-third of all the total N in fertilizers produced in this country. A major use of N solutions was for direct application to the soil, amounting to 195,000 tons of N in 1960, 1.2 million in 1975, and 1.9 million in 1980. As a direct application N source, N solutions were exceeded only by anhydrous ammonia, having overtaken ammonium nitrate in 1970 (16,41). UAN accounted for 60 percent of the N solutions production in 1975 and 77 percent in 1980 (106).

Slow-Release Nitrogen Fertilizer Materials

A number of slow-release nitrogen fertilizer materials based on urea have appeared over the years. They are aimed primarily at improving the recovery of nitrogen by crop plants through releasing the N at a rate more closely corresponding with the needs of the crop, reducing the number of fertilizer applications, and decreasing nitrogen losses through volatilization and leaching. In the United States attention has been focused mostly upon two products, urea-formaldehyde and sulfur-coated urea. Some isobutylidene diurea, a Japanese product, is marketed in the United States.

Urea-formaldehyde is prepared by reacting urea with formaldehyde under carefully controlled conditions to form a product that releases its nitrogen slowly. The commercial product is a mixture of unreacted urea and short-chain polymers with one, two, or three methylene (CH_2) linkages. More complex polymers having additional CH linkages make the product too unreactive for use as a fertilizer (6).

The slow-release effect of formaldehyde upon urea was first noted in the late 1930's when a fertilizer-ammoniation solution was developed which was capable of producing a slowly available, water insoluble urea-formaldehyde; however, the amount of the slowly soluble product obtained in the fertilizer upon ammoniation was quite small. U.S. Department of Agriculture scientists in 1946 found that it was possible to develop a product suitable for use as a slow-release fertilizer. It became commercially available in 1955. Marketed as "Ureaform," it found use primarily in the turf and ornamental markets; the product was too expensive for use on agronomic crops (19).

TVA in the 1950's began a search for compounds that might be used as a delayed-release fertilizer. Although a number were found, high costs of production ruled them out as a fertilizer. In 1961, TVA tried elemental sulfur as a coating material because of its low cost and its value as a plant nutrient. By 1968, after considerable laboratory and greenhouse research, enough encouraging information was gathered to permit building a small pilot plant. In 1976, a larger plant was built by the agency to supply materials for field testing and demonstration. The product contained between 36 and 38 percent N.

The process as developed by TVA involves spraying a coating of molten sulfur on urea granules in a rotating drum. The coated granules are discharged into a revolving drum where a wax-like sealant is sprayed on to provide a moisture barrier. After cooling, the material is conveyed into a drum where a clay conditioner is added to absorb excess sealant and impart good handling and storage characteristics. The product has been produced commercially in the United States, Canada, and Great Britain, but its use has been limited to fruits, some vegetables, turf, and ornamentals. Its high cost so far has prevented its use on agronomic crops (65,95).

Phosphatic Materials

Major changes took place in the production of phosphatic materials during the 1920-1980 period (Figure 10.1). Normal superphosphate, which had ruled supreme since the opening of the South Carolina phosphate deposits in 1870, peaked in 1952 and started a gradual decline. Concentrated superphosphate (after 1950 usually referred to as triple superphosphate) which had been produced in a small way since 1890, became increasingly important following World War II until about 1970 when it tended to level out. Ammonium phosphates soared from minor importance as late as 1960 to a world leadership position in the last third of the period; this class of fertilizer supplies major tonnages of both phosphate and nitrogen.

The shift from normal superphosphate to the higher grade phosphatic materials was made possible with the appearance of low-cost phosphoric acid that could be produced in large quantities. The acid, based on

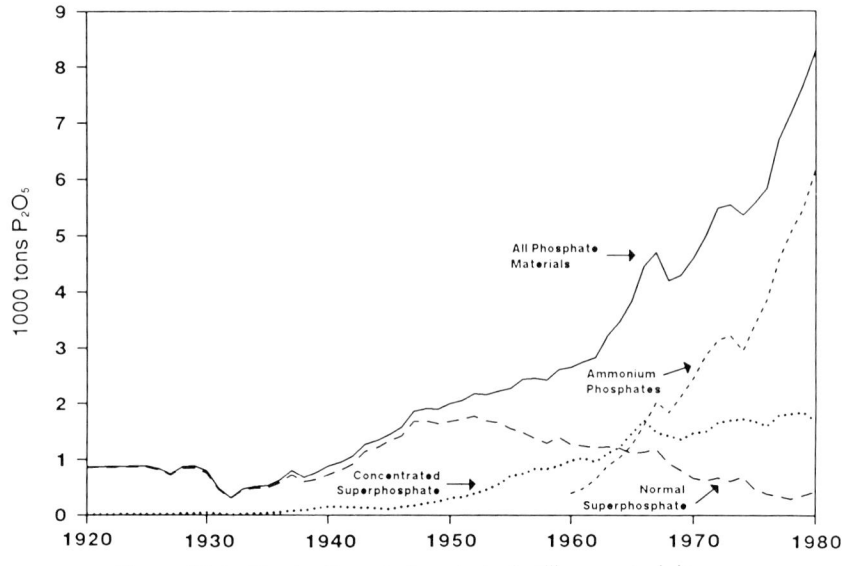

Figure 10.1. Production of phosphate fertilizer materials

sulfuric acid derived mostly from Frasch sufur, could be manufactured at or near phosphate mines and used at the site to manufacture high analysis phosphate materials. The finished materials could be shipped economically to the consuming areas. The lower grade normal superphosphate, on the other hand, depended mostly upon producing both the sulfuric acid and the low-grade superphosphate at sites in the market areas.

In addition to the superphosphates and ammonium phosphates, considerable attention was focused with varying success upon alternative phosphate products. Of major importance was the introduction of superphosphoric acid and ammonium polyphosphates which revolutionized the liquid fertilizer industry. Substitution of nitric acid for sulfuric acid in acidulating phosphate rock, although produced commercially by several organizations, never caught on in the United States as it did in Europe. Basic slag, also used extensively in Europe, was produced in small amounts domestically as a by-product by one company. (U.S. iron ores were too low in phosphorus to make their use as a fertilizer feasible.)

A great deal of effort was expended to perfect and introduce thermally-promoted processes that use heat to destroy the apatite structure of phosphate rock and release most of the fluorine. Also, TVA, the U.S. Department of Agriculture, and some members of private industry devoted considerable research and promotion effort toward developing a phosphate fertilizer industry based on elemental phosphorus produced by electric or blast furnaces. However, costs of energy and equipment were too high for most heat-based fertilizer materials to compete with the chemically-derived materials.

Wet-Process Phosphoric Acid

Wet-process phosphoric acid is used primarily as an intermediate in the production of concentrated and enriched superphosphates and ammonium phosphates. Also, to a limited extent, it is applied to the soil through irrigation water, particularly in the Western States. (The term "wet process" was adopted to distinguish it from phosphoric acid prepared from elemental phosphorus.)

The most-used method for producing phosphoric acid for fertilizers is the wet-process phosphoric acid method that converts the calcium from phosphate rock into calcium sulfate dihydrate (gypsum) as indicated by the following equation:

$$Ca_{10}F_2(PO_4)_6 + 10H_2SO_4 + 20H_2O \rightarrow 10CaSO_4 \cdot 2H_2O + 2HF + 6H_3PO_4$$

fluorapatite — sulfuric acid — water — calcium dihydrate — hydrofluoric acid — phosphoric acid

Alternative methods involve converting the calcium either to the anhydrite ($CaSO_4$) form or to the hemihydrate ($CaSO_4 \cdot 1/2H_2O$) form (70). The hemihydrate process is used in at least one major Florida facility.

The history of wet-process phosphoric acid production up until 1920 is reviewed in Chapter 4. Major advances have continued since then. An important advance was made in 1932 when the Dorr Company constructed the largest plant yet built, for the Consolidated Mining and Smelting Company at Trail, British Columbia. This plant consisted of three trains, each capable of processing 150 tons of phosphate rock daily. The plant was based on the Dorr process as developed by 1920 except that it included the Oliver continuous counter-current decantation process. The acid contained about 25 percent P_2O_5 equivalent. Since no one had done better up to this time, the system was known as the strong acid method. It was used into the early 1960's.

By 1960, capacities of phosphoric acid plants reached about 250 tons per day. By 1970, capacities of the more recent plants had grown to 1,000 tons daily (70,104).

The larger, more recent plants involve several technological advances. Incoming streams of pulverized phosphate rock and sulfuric acid are fed continuously into reaction tanks where they are mixed rapidly and thoroughly with the slurry. Weak phosphoric acid also is recycled to the reaction tanks to adjust the phosphoric acid content of the slurry. The composition of the slurry is carefully controlled to encourage formation of large gypsum crystals that are easily removed by filtering and that will wash free of phosphoric acid. To accomplish this the liquid phase of the slurry is adjusted to contain 1.5 percent of free sulfuric acid and a phosphoric acid content of about 30 percent P_2O_5. The solids content of the slurry is held to the 35 to 45 percent range. The phosphate rock in this type of slurry dissolves rapidly and the desired large gypsum crystals are formed. Nevertheless, producers tend to allow longer retention times of 1.5 to 12 hours to assure formation of the type of crystals that can be easily filtered and washed. Cooling of the slurry also is practiced (48,70,73).

The slurry from the reaction system is filtered to separate the acid from the gypsum using several methods, but the most popular are the tilting rotary pan filters and the continuous belt filter. The filter systems provide for two or three countercurrent washings. The concentration of the filtered acid is 28 to 30 percent P_2O_5 (48,70,73).

The filter acid is usually concentrated by evaporation to 40 to 54 percent P_2O_5. Concentration, which during the 1950's had been largely accomplished in steam heated spray towers by blowing hot air through the tower, was replaced in the 1970's by use of steam heated vacuum evaporation. In the phosphate complexes such as in central Florida, steam is produced by the heat generated by burning sulfur to produce sulfuric acid (70,73).

Pollution control in production of wet-process acid presents a substantial problem in this country. A principal product of the dihydrate process is an impure gypsum that has little value as a by-product. Four or five tons of gypsum is produced per ton of P_2O_5 in the acid. California uses some of the material to improve alkali soils, but in most of the country the dihydrate slurry containing the gypsum is pumped into waste ponds and the water reused. Dikes are built around the ponds and as the material settles and builds up; new dikes are built until eventually hugh mounds of gypsum are formed. This presents another problem–that of space and loss of valuable land.

Fluorine, originally discharged into the air and a serious problem, is removed by scrubbing and sold or discharged into the gypsum waste ponds where most of it converts to insoluble calcium fluoride (48,70).

Production of wet-process phosphoric acid grew rapidly as demand grew for triple superphosphate following World War II and for ammonium phosphates a few years later. Total production of the acid amounted to only about 130,000 tons of P_2O_5 equivalent in 1945, but by 1955 had jumped to 775,000 tons. Afterward, production doubled about every 10 years, reaching 10.2 million tons of P_2O_5 in 1980 (16,41,64).

Producers in the late 1950's began concentrating acid production at or near the Florida central pebble mining area which also was strategically located with respect to water transport of Frasch sulfur for production of sulfuric acid and anhydrous ammonia for production of ammonium phosphates. In 1976, 57 percent of all U.S. wet-process acid capacity, equivalent to 8.8 million tons of P_2O_5, was located in Florida at phosphate rock mine sites, and 22 percent was in the Gulf Coast area of Mississippi, Louisiana, and Texas, within close proximity to ammonia and Frasch sulfur production centers and where phosphate rock could be transported by water from Florida. Eight percent of the acid capacity was located at the Lee County, North Carolina, pebble mine; 5 percent near phosphate mines in Idaho and Utah; and the remaining 8 percent were mostly small plants in Illinois and California (16,41).

Considerable quantities of wet-process acid are shipped by rail from producers in Florida, North Carolina, and Louisiana to small fertilizer manufacturers at inland locations and to the large regional NPK ammoniation-granulation plants. Export of phosphoric acid increased from about 52,000 tons of P_2O_5 in 1969 to 783,000 in 1980 (16,107).

Phosphoric acid has been used to a limited extent as a direct-application material. Its first use in California and Arizona about 1940 involved direct application both to the soil and irrigation water. About 10,000 tons was applied directly in the Mountain and Pacific States in 1951 and 38,000 tons in 1965. Later data are not available (5,44,64).

Furnace-Grade Phosphoric Acid

Electric furnace phosphoric acid has been used extensively in the United States for industrial purposes but has found only minimal application to production of fertilizer materials. More important has been its catalytic effect upon bringing about technological advances in the fertilizer field that probably would not have come about otherwise, the most important being the discovery by TVA of the value of superphosphoric acid and polyphosphates in liquid fertilizer production.

Production of phosphoric acid using electric furnaces involves feeding a mixture of nodulized or lump phosphate rock, silica pebbles, and coke into the furnace and heating the mixture to a temperature of about 1,400°C by passing electric current into carbon or graphite electrodes. The following type of reaction occurs:

$$10CaF_2(PO_4)_6 + 15C + 6SiO_2 \rightarrow 1.5P_4 + 15CO + 3(CaO \bullet 2SiO_2) + CaF_2$$

| phosphate rock | coke | silica | mixture of phos. vapor and carbon monoxide gas | calcium silicate slag | calcium fluoride |

Iron, present as an impurity, reacts with phosphorus to form ferrophosphorus, a heavy material that settles to the bottom of the furnace where it is tapped separately from the silicate slag (16,41,64).

The carbon monoxide, phosphorus vapor, and entrained dust are fed from the furnace to electrostatic precipitators where the suspended particles are removed. The carbon monoxide and the phosphorus enter a condenser where the gases are cooled and phosphorus condenses to a heavy liquid and is discharged with the condenser water into a sump.

The carbon monoxide gas is used as a fuel or flared off. Phosphoric acid is produced by burning the phosphorus in a separate plant in the presence of air and hydrating to bring about the reaction (44,69,99):

$$\underset{\substack{\text{elemental}\\\text{phosphorus}}}{P_4} + \underset{\text{oxygen}}{5O_2} + \underset{\text{water}}{6H_2O} \rightarrow \underset{\substack{\text{phosphoric}\\\text{acid}}}{4H_3PO_4}$$

Phosphoric acid produced from elemental phosphorus is of high purity and, depending upon the degree of hydration, usually ranges from about 57 to 76 percent P_2O_5, the level used in superphosphoric acid. (Acids having P_2O_5 values above 80 percent are syrupy liquids.) Furnace-grade acid permits production of higher grade phosphate materials than is normally possible with wet-process acid.

Superphosphoric Acid and Polyphosphates

Superphosphoric acid is a mixture of phosphoric acids. It includes the common orthophosphoric acid (H_3PO_4) and the polyphosphoric acids: pyrophosphoric acid ($H_4P_2O_7$), tripolyphosphoric acid ($H_5P_3O_{10}$), and tetrapolyphosphoric acid ($H_6P_4O_{13}$). The mixtures, when made into acids containing about 75 percent P_2O_5, are fluid and contain about 50 percent by weight in the ortho form, 42 percent in the pyro, and the remainder in the higher polyphosphate forms. Superphosphoric acid is produced from electric furnace phosphorus by limiting the degree of hydration in the final step of its manufacture. Superphosphoric acid, also prepared by heating ordinary phosphoric acid, was long known as a laboratory product, first being prepared by Berzelius in 1816.

Striplin, McKnight, and Megar at TVA in 1956 demonstrated the possibility of using furnace-grade superphosphoric acid as a fertilizer intermediate in the preparation of ammonium polyphosphate (89). The first practical demonstration was made in 1957 when TVA shipped a tank car of the acid to the West Kentucky Liquid Fertilizer Company at Hopkinsville, where it was reacted with ammonia to form a 11-37-0 base solution for use in manufacture of liquid fertilizer. Substantial amounts of the furnace-grade superacid produced by industry moved into the liquid fertilizer industry during the 1960's and early 1970's, especially during periods of overproduction of furnace-grade orthophosphoric acid (93).

The production of ammonium polyphosphates using the furnace-grade superphosphoric acid opened the door to what proved to be a major technological advance in the liquid fertilizer field. The polyphosphate ions form stable, soluble complexes with iron, aluminum, and magnesium, all of which were serious contaminants in liquid fertilizers, and prevent them from precipitating and settling out or clogging application nozzles. The polyphosphate also was very effective in keeping the metallic micronutrients–copper, manganese, iron, and zinc–and certain pesticides in solution. Also, higher nutrient-content mixed fertilizer grades could be produced, especially those containing potash, thus reducing labor, transportation, and storage costs (108,109).

Unfortunately, it was more costly to make liquid fertilizers with furnace acid than with orthophosphate. As a result, both TVA and private industry sought ways to produce superphosphoric acid from orthophosphoric acid. Researchers found in 1961 that conventional phosphoric acid could be concentrated to superphosphoric acid through evaporation of water which brought about molecular dehydration. Wet-process acid containing 40 to 54 percent P_2O_5 could be concentrated to 68-72 percent P_2O_5 containing 40 to 50 percent of the phosphate in polyphosphate form. Concentration was obtained either by direct contact with combustion gases or by vacuum evaporation (70,93).

Another major advance came with the development of the simple pipe reactor by Meline, Lee, and Scott of TVA in early 1972. In this process, wet-process superphosphoric acid containing 68 to 70 percent P_2O_5, having 20 to 30 percent in the polyphosphate form, is ammoniated by introducing the acid into one arm of a 2-inch stainless steel pipe and gaseous ammonia into a second arm. The high temperature (340°-370°C) resulting from reaction of the two ingredients produces a melt of high polyphosphate content that, when dissolved in water, produces a 10-34-0 solution containing 60 to 75 percent of its P_2O_5 in the polyphosphate form.

The low-cost pipe-reactor process was immediately adopted by the clear liquid fertilizer producers; by 1980, at least 130 U.S. plants were using it. To produce as a superphosphoric acid intermediate having a lower polyphosphate content required only steam heating of the original wet-process acid, thus greatly reducing the energy requirement. Also, the lower polyphosphate acid was less viscous making it easier to handle and ship (94,109).

Production of superphosphoric acid grew fairly rapidly considering the modest size of the clear liquid fertilizer industry. By the early 1960's one large phosphate producer had begun commercial production of electric furnace phosphoric acid, and another of wet-process superacid. By 1970, production of furnace-grade superacid amounted to the equivalent of 549,000 tons of P_2O_5, a level that held through 1975 (the last year that data were available). Wet-process superacid production went from 312,000 tons of P_2O_5 in 1970 to 1.0 million tons in 1979. Occidental Petroleum Corporation in 1975 opened a second mine in northern Florida, part of the ore of which was to be used to produce superphosphoric acid for shipment to the USSR on a trade arrangement. However, a trade embargo issued by the U.S. Government discontinued shipments until 1981. In 1977, superphosphoric acid was being produced at 11 plants in the United States (16,31,41).

Superphosphates

Production of the superphosphates, normal, enriched, and concentrated, involves as a first step the reaction of sulfuric acid with domestic phosphate rock containing an impure fluorapatite. (The chemical formula of pure fluorapatite is $Ca_{10}F_2(PO_4)_6$ containing 42.2 percent P_2O_5 equivalent; however, U.S. phosphate rocks contain varying amounts of the carbonate ion, CO_3, which substitutes for the phosphate ion, PO_4, thus lowering the phosphorus content of the rock.) Normal superphosphate is produced by acidulating the rock with enough sulfuric acid to convert the fluorapatite to monocalcium phosphate and release the fluorine as indicated in the following equation:

$$Ca_{10}F_2(PO_4)_6 + 7H_2SO_4 + 3H_2O \rightarrow 3Ca(H_2PO_4)_2 \cdot H_2O + 7CaSO_4 + 2HF$$

fluorapatite — sulfuric acid — water — normal superphosphate — gypsum — hydrofluoric acid

The monocalcium phosphate and gypsum remain in the product which contains 16 to 22 percent available P_2O_5. Much of the fluorine is either recovered as a by-product or is absorbed in water and disposed of. The rest stays in the product as fluosilicates, fluorides, and other compounds. Concentrated superphosphate is prepared by reacting the phosphate rock with phosphoric acid, usually wet-process, from which the gypsum formed has been removed. The reaction is as follows.

$$Ca_{10}F_2(PO_4)_6 + 14H_3PO_4 + 10H_2O \rightarrow 10Ca(H_2PO_4)_2 \cdot H_2O + 2HF$$

fluorapatite — phosphoric acid — water — concentrated superphosphate — hydrofluoric acid

Thus, the main difference between normal and concentrated superphosphate is that the concentrated product does not contain gypsum and has a higher phosphorus content, 40 to 46 percent available P_2O_5, since it contains both the phosphate from the phosphate rock and from the phosphoric acid. Enriched superphosphate refers to all grades of superphosphate containing more than 22 percent and less than 40 percent available P_2O_5. Enriched superphosphate is mostly produced by acidulating phosphate rock with a mixture of sulfuric and phosphoric acids, although at times concentrated superphosphate is simply mixed with normal superphosphate (48,52,108)

Normal Superphosphate—The basic steps in manufacturing normal superphosphate changed little from the 1870's to the 1920's. The steps included the mixing of ground phosphate rock with sulfuric acid, solidifying the fluid mix in a den from 30 minutes to 4 hours, holding the solid material in a curing pile for 2 to 6 weeks, and pulverizing and bagging if marketed as a phosphatic material, or dry mixing with other fertilizer materials to form the desired various fertilizer grades.

Ammoniation of superphosphate, which started in this country in 1928, proved a way not only to add low-cost synthetic nitrogen to fertilizer but also to improve the physical and chemical properties of the product. This resulted in quicker curing, permitting bagging and shipping within a few days, neutralized acidity and prevented rapid bag deterioration. Some of the fine particles were agglomerated into weak granules, thus tending to reduce dusting. Too high ammoniation, however, reverted the monocalcium phosphate of the normal superphosphate into less soluble forms. More than 80 pounds of ammonia per ton of product was considered excessive; however, higher nitrogen contents were obtained through the addition of ammonium nitrate or urea in the ammoniating solution. Up until about 1950, most plants simply ammoniated the superphosphate by feeding a measured weight or volume of the ammoniating solution into a rotary batch mixer. Practically all superphosphate going into mixed fertilizers was ammoniated by 1950 (42).

Some 257 normal superphosphate plants were operating in 1920 and 217 in 1959. The plants were located in or near using areas inasmuch as it was more economical to ship phosphate rock containing 30 to 32 percent P_2O_5 to the using area than to manufacture the superphosphate containing 16 to 22 percent P_2O_5 at the mines and ship it to the using areas. From 1920 to 1941, 50 percent of the superphosphate plants had their own sulfuric acid production facilities, but the number declined to 40 percent by 1960 (49,51,52). The greatest concentration of plants was in the eastern seaboard states, the East North Central states, and the East South Central states (4,24).

Considerable progress was made in the manufacture of normal superphosphate during the 1920-1950 period. Of 200 normal superphosphate plants in operation in 1950, 111 had mechanical den systems of which 16 were continuous. Of the 89 plants having non-mechanical dens, 10 were still dug out by hand, 48 by draglines, 11 by overhead cranes, and the remainder by miscellaneous methods (49).

The use of mechanical dens became widespread in the 1920's. The popular Sturtevant den, developed in England, was first used in this country in the Armour Fertilizer Works at Columbus, Georgia, in 1922. This den, essentially a rectangular rail car with a concrete floor, could be moved on rails into a cutter. The ceiling of the den was the framework which supported a batch mixer and related equipment. The framework was equipped to remove fumes. It also supported two wooden sidewalls attached with hinges. The endwall was concrete and the other a vertical sliding door that could be raised or lowered. For filling, the two wooden walls and door were lowered in place forming a rectangular den. After the last batch had been dumped into the den and cured for 20 minutes, the door was raised, and the sidewalls loosened and allowed to swing free. The den with its solidified material moved forward on the rails into a cutting device made up of a series of revolving cutting knives that shaved off thin sections of the phosphate. In some plants the cutting device was moved into the den. The disintegrated phosphate fell onto a conveyor belt or into an elevator boot for transport to storage. Some 100 of the Sturtevant dens were in operation in the United States by the late 1950's (82,101).

Provision for continuous flow of material from the feeding devices through the mixers and den to curing piles was the next logical development. The first successful continuous system in this country was the Broadfield process patented in the United States by M. D. Broadfield in 1932, and first installed in 1929 at the plant of the Georgia Fertilizer Company at Valdosta, Georgia. By the 1950's, 12 of the plants were in operation. The process provided for the uninterrupted flow from the feeding devices into a type of pugmill through which a sulfuric acid-rock phosphate slurry was agitated for 2 or 3 minutes. The slurry discharged onto a continuous slat conveyor that served as the bottom of the den where it immediately solidified. The conveyor belt carried the material toward a revolving cutter from which the product was conveyed on a belt to the curing pile. Several other types of continuous systems also were developed (51,52,82).

In 1959, shortly after the decline in normal superphosphate began, the 217 plants were owned by 89 companies; 109 were in the hands of seven firms. The seven: Virginia-Carolina Chemical Corp., with 24 plants; American Agricultural Chemical Co., 25; International Minerals & Chemical Corp., 16; Armour Agricultural Chemical, 14; Swift & Co., 10; F. S. Royster Guano Co., 12; and Davison Chemical Co., 8. Also in 1959, 18 cooperatives produced normal superphosphate in 27 plants in 16 states (52).

Concentrated Superphosphate—Prior to 1920, five concentrated superphosphate plants had been brought into operation for varying periods. Only one of these survived to 1920, this being the Virginia-Carolina Chemical Corp. plant at Charleston, South Carolina. From 1920 through mid-1959, 22 additional plants came into operation, but half of these closed during the period. Of the 23 plants operating, 17 were based on wet-process phosphoric acid, four on electric furnace phosphoric acid, and one on blast furnace acid (61). Most wet-process-based plants were located near sources of phosphate rock in central Florida, Tennessee, or the Western States. Of the 11 plants active in 1959, five were in central Florida. (The high phosphate content of the concentrated superphosphate as contrasted with normal superphosphate made it more economical to ship the finished product to the using areas rather than the phosphate rock and sulfur.) (51).

Simplot's Don Plant for superphosphate manufacture at Pocatello, Idaho, early 1950's. *(J.R. Simplot Company)*

In 1976, all but 6 percent of the 17 U.S. concentrated superphosphate plants having a combined production capacity of 2.7 million tons of product were located near phosphate mining areas–78 percent in the Florida pebble areas, 10 percent in Idaho and Utah, and 6 percent in North Carolina at the Lee Creek mine. The remaining 6 percent was divided between Joplin, Missouri, and Pascagoula, Mississippi. Fifteen companies operated the 17 plants. Five of the plants had annual capacities ranging from 255,000 tons to 375,000 tons; five were in the 100,000-ton range; and the remaining seven ranged from 33,000 to 97,000 tons (41).

Until about 1950, manufacture of concentrated superphosphate was patterned after methods developed for production of normal superphosphate. Steps in common up to this time included (a) measuring a desired volume of phosphoric acid with a given weight of finely ground phosphate rock into a batch or pan mixer and stirring thoroughly; (b) denning (solidifying) the slurry from the mixer; (c) curing the material in large storage piles; and (d) crushing, sieving, and bagging for shipment. Each concentrated superphosphate plant produced its own phosphoric acid since merchant-grade product was not yet available (100,101).

Several concentrated superphosphate producers began using the Sturtevant den during the 1950's in conjunction with a batch-type mixer as used to make superphosphate. The phosphoric acid used, like that in most other concentrated superphosphate processes, contained 47 to 51 percent P_2O_5 (45,100).

An unusual process was developed and patented by H. H. Myers in 1923 in which the dilute phosphoric acid (25percent P_2O_5) as it came from the gypsum filtration step was used as the acidulant. The slurry following batch mixing was fed into a direct-fired rotary kiln and discharged as a thick slurry. This slurry was denned and cured as usual; however, before final storage and shipment the material required further drying in a rotary dryer (61). Armour built the first Myers plant near

Columbia, Tennessee, in 1929, and a second plant near Bartow, Florida, in 1949. The latter produced a granular product (36).

A continuous process was developed by TVA engineers G. L. Bridger, R. A. Wilson, and R. B. Burt in 1945 for mixing phosphate rock with phosphoric acid for the production of concentrated superphosphate (15). Known as a cone mixer, the process uses the kinetic energy (the energy associated with motion) generated by the reactants instead of mechanical energy to mix the phosphate rock with the phosphoric acid and to self-clean the unit. (The mixer has been variously described as a masterpiece of simplicity.) Although the process was developed using furnace-grade phosphoric acid, it found major use in the production of non-granular, wet-process concentrated superphosphate. The mixer also was used to make normal superphosphate (61,84).

The mixer consists of an inverted metal cone provided with a short stem at the bottom. The phosphate rock enters the cone from a vertical spout and impinges on a deflector. Four equally spaced pipes rest against the wall of the cone where the phosphoric acid flows under gravity through nozzles placed against the wall of the cone and imparts a swirling motion to the acid. The acid contacts the rock which enters the cone just below the acid. Water also is added through two nozzles. The high velocity of the swirling action permits the slurry to remain in the mixer for only a few seconds. The cone is 26 inches wide and 16 inches deep and the stem is 5 inches long. Forty-plus tons of product per hour is produced (15,61).

Two types of concentrated superphosphate were produced from about 1960 on–a nongranular form for use in the manufacture of granular, ammoniated NPK fertilizer, and a granulated form for use in direct application and in bulk blends. Most of the nongranular is produced using the TVA cone mixer with the slurry denned by feeding it directly onto a simple cup conveyor belt which moves slowly and retains the material until it solidifies. The solidified product is disintegrated as it comes off the belt. After curing, the nongranulated product is shipped in bulk to NPK homogeneous granulation plants (48).

Since about 1960, two general types of direct-granulation processes have been used to granulate concentrated superphosphate. One involves granulating the fresh product immediately following the denning step by moving it directly into a rotary drum where steam and sprayed water are added to promote granulation. It is then dried in a rotary dryer, screened, cooled and placed in storage. The second type produces most of the granular concentrated superphosphate in the United States. This utilizes slurry-type processes, the most popular being the Dorr-Oliver (now the Jacobs-Dorrco) process. In the process, ground phosphate rock and phosphoric acid (38 to 40 percent P_2O_5) are fed into the first of a series of two or three steam-heated reaction tanks and agitated. The thin slurry formed is fed to a blunger (paddle mixer) or to a rotary drum granulator along with a large amount of dried, recycled product (about a 10:1 ratio of recycle to product). The moist granules are dried, screened, cooled and sent to storage. An alternate method developed by TVA involved simultaneous acidulation and granulation. Preheated phosphoric acid, phosphate rock, and recycled fines are mixed and granulated in a rotary drum, and then dried and screened. The TVA process requires less recycling and produces a more porous product (48,70).

Production of concentrated superphosphate rose from about 700,000 tons of available P_2O_5 equivalent in 1955, to 1.7 million tons in 1966, and then leveled out within a relatively narrow range of 1.4 to 1.8 million tons (Figure 10.1). It was exceeded in tonnage of P_2O_5 by ammonium phosphates from 1967 on. Concentrated superphosphate became an important export material, starting in 1960 with 144,000 tons P_2O_5 equivalent and rising to 780,000 tons in 1980. As an export product, it was exceeded by ammonium phosphates in 1966 and thereafter and by phosphoric acid in 1979 and 1980 (16,41).

TVA produced concentrated superphosphate containing 46 to 48 percent available P_2O_5 using furnace-grade phosphoric acid from 1934 into the 1950's.

By 1950 the agency had produced 1.2 million tons of the high-analysis material which was distributed largely to cooperating test demonstration farmers at no cost except freight in the seven Tennessee Valley states and in 25 nonvalley states. The agency also sold appreciable amounts to the Agricultural Adjustment Administration for distribution to farmers. As a result of these activities, private industry strongly criticized TVA's fertilizer program on the basis that it replaced fertilizer that the industry would normally sell. Nevertheless, TVA's programs educated a large number of farmers and agricultural leaders to the value of fertilizers in increasing crop yields, reducing soil erosion, and improving farm life generally (64,91).

It is of interest that TVA chose this as its first demonstration fertilizer in view of the fact that the facilities it inherited from the World War I era had been designed to produce nitrogen materials. The reasoning, developed jointly with the agricultural colleges of the region, was to rely on legumes to supply the nitrogen. Phosphate and lime would be used to grow the legumes and support a general soil fertility improvement effort.

Ammonium Phosphates

Ammonium phosphates, first introduced in the United States in 1916 by the American Cyanamid Company at Warners, New Jersey, did not appear on the fertilizer market in substantial quantities until the early 1960's. By 1965, they had become the leading phosphate fertilizer used in the United States (Figure 10.1) and one of the most popular phosphate sources worldwide. The ammonium phosphates became important

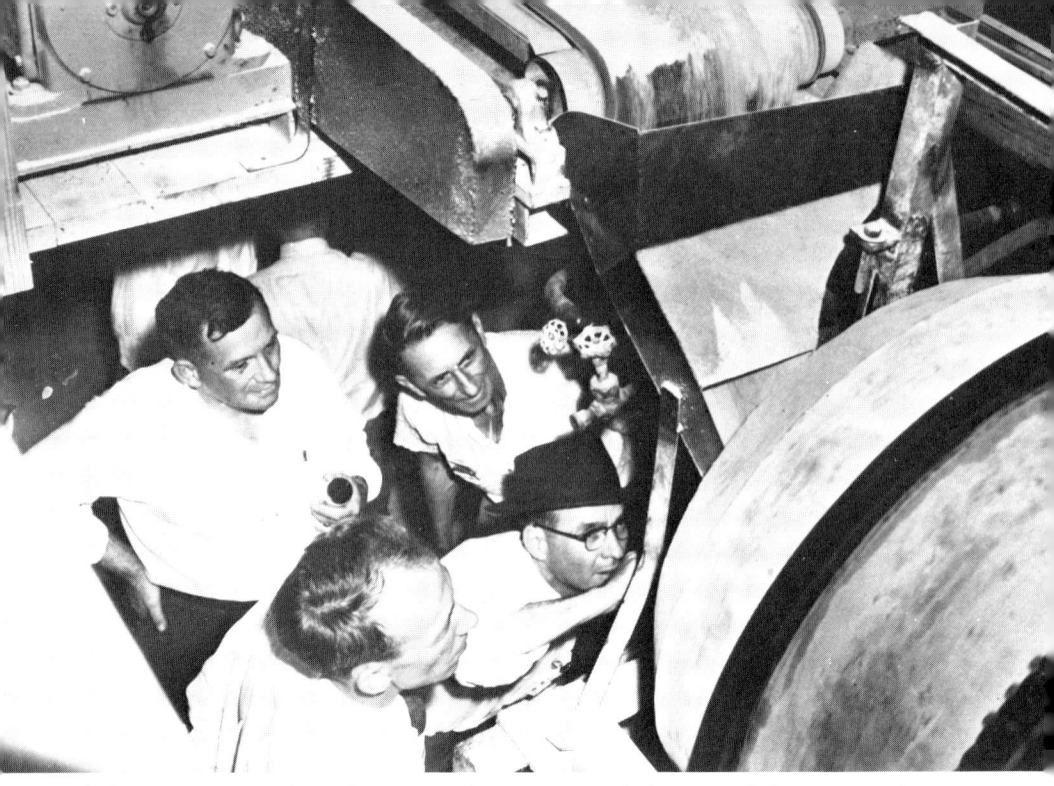

Industry representatives observe continuous ammoniation-granulation process in TVA pilot plant in 1953 (above). Below--some of the 461 representatives of 211 companies attending the 1964 TVA open house at Muscle Shoals show interest in new technology demonstrated in small pilot plant. *(TVA)*

fertilizer materials because of their high primary nutrient contents, due to the fact that they contain no calcium; most also contain no sulfate. They are produced from low-cost, wet-process phosphoric acid and anhydrous ammonia. Both granular and nongranular forms are produced. They have good physical properties and are water soluble. Main uses are for direct application and as an intermediate in the production of granular mixed fertilizers and bulk blends (70).

Ammonium phosphates are available in the monoammonium phosphate (MAP) and diammonium phosphate (DAP) forms. The basic reactions are as follows:

$$H_3PO_4 + NH_3 \rightarrow NH_4H_2PO_4$$
phosphoric acid + ammonia → monoammonium phosphate

and

$$H_3PO_4 + 2NH_3 \rightarrow (NH_4)_2HPO_4$$
phosphoric acid + ammonia → diammonium phosphate

By varying the conditions under which the reactions take place, different MAP:DAP ratios can be produced. Also, sulfuric acid can be mixed with the phosphoric acid to form MAP-ammonium sulfate mixtures, or nitric acid can be added to produce MAP-ammonium nitrate mixtures.

Many ammonium phosphate grades are produced commercially. Products predominately MAP include 11-55-0 and 11-48-0. A 16-48-0 grade is about one-third MAP and two-thirds DAP. The granular DAP, 18-46-0, became the most produced ammonium phosphate material. It is made with wet-process phosphoric acid. The DAP product 21-53-0 is based upon furnace-grade phosphoric acid and coke oven ammonia. Ammonium phosphate-nitrates, 25-25-0 and 30-10-0, are produced by reacting ammonia with nitric and phosphoric acids, or by neutralizing phosphoric acid with ammonia-ammonium nitrate solutions. Also, ammonium polyphosphate materials involving reaction of ammonia with superphosphoric acid are produced (discussed under liquid fertilizers) (16,41,70,72).

Monoammonium Phosphates—Ammonium phosphates prior to about 1955 had minimal impact upon U.S. fertilizer consumption. Production was limited to one plant at Trail, British Columbia, and three U.S. plants. In 1920, American Cyanamid launched production of two ammonium phosphate products, Ammo-Phos A, 11-48-0, and Ammo-Phos B, 16-20-0, at Warners, New Jersey. However, annual production never exceeded 60,000 tons, and the plant was discontinued in 1940. The Consolidated Mining and Smelting Co. at Trail, British Columbia, in western Canada began producing 11-48-0 and 16-20-0 using a process

IMC's operations at New Wales, Florida, include plants to make sulfuric acid, phosphoric acid, granular triple superphosphate, mono- and diammonium phosphate, animal feed supplement and uranium (yellowcake), along with facilities for handling and processing raw materials and storing finished products. *(IMC Fertilizers)*

developed by the Dorr Company. Phosphate rock was shipped to Trail from Montana and used with sulfuric acid recovered as a by-product of the smelting operations at Trail; production lasted through 1980. U.S. imports from Trail ranged from 11,000 tons of products in 1934 to 107,000 tons in 1950 (21,49,50,64).

Domestic production of ammonium phosphates resumed in 1946 when the Mathieson Chemical Corporation remodeled a World War II concentrated superphosphate plant at Pasadena, Texas, to produce ammonium phosphates, mostly 16-20-0 and some 11-48-0 and 13-39-0. Production by 1950 reached 200,000 tons of products (49,64). Production was still underway at Pasadena in 1976 by the Olin Corporation, a descendant of the Mathieson Corporation. The Missouri Farmers Association built a large-scale ammonium phosphate plant at Joplin, Missouri, in 1954 patterned after the Trail process and producing NP and NPK high-analysis fertilizers (62).

In the Dorr Company process used during the 1933-1950's period ammonia gas was passed into 50 percent P_2O_5 phosphoric acid or a mixture of phosphoric and sulfuric acids depending on the product being made. The reaction was carried out in a series of three agitator tanks lined with lead or acidproof brick. Most of the reaction is completed in the first tank. The considerable heat generated evaporated part of the water introduced with the acid. The slurry moved to a blunger (paddle mixer) and was mixed with a large amount of dry, previously-produced screenings and then passed through a hot air rotary dryer. After cooling, the product was screened to obtain a desired size range and the remainder recycled. By changing the ratio of phosphoric acid to sulfuric acid used, the nutrient contents can be varied. The process is continuous (35,42,69).

Two methods developed by TVA became available in about 1967 for producing granular MAP. One process involved lower ammoniation of the phosphoric acid in the preneutralizer step than in the DAP process with the ammoniation being finished to a desired mole ratio of 1.0 in the granulator. The second method involved higher ammoniation in the preneutralizer and then adding more phosphoric acid to the granulator to bring the $NH_3:PO_4$ mole ratio to 1.0–the desired value (108).

Several methods for producing nongranular MAP were developed about 1968. These are aimed at producing a simple low-cost method by elimination of the granulating, recycling, and drying steps, but still coming up with a product having good physical properties. Most of the processes were developed in Europe and Japan. One developed by Swift & Co. in the United States is similar in principle to the other processes but employs a unique two-fluid nozzle in which liquid ammonia is combined with wet-process phosphoric acid and discharged into a reactor pipe. The resulting slurry, containing finely-divided MAP, is sprayed into a cooling tower having a counter-current air stream which carries away the water vapor and cools the product. A strong demand developed for the nongranular product in the manufacture of homogeneous granulated mixed fertilizers (1,43,108).

Diammonium Phosphates (DAP)—During the early 1950's, electric furnace grade phosphoric acid came on the open market for the first time. As a result, several steel companies became interested in converting their ammonium sulfate recovery operations based on by-product ammonia from coke ovens to production of crystalline DAP of 21-53-0 grade. A changeover to DAP required no costly equipment changes other than providing evaporation equipment to remove the water introduced in the phosphoric acid. However, the plants could shift from one product to the other depending upon the market situation (62,74,87).

Four companies engaged in DAP production in the 1950's: the Ford Motor Company, Dearborn, Michigan; Colorado Fuel and Iron Company, Pueblo, Colorado; Kaiser Steel Company, Fontana, California; and Shell

Chemical Company, at Ventura, California. Both Ford and Kaiser were still producing DAP in 1980. TVA also began operating a DAP demonstration plant in 1955 using furnace-grade phosphoric acid and synthetic ammonia to make 21-53-0. The product was used for direct application and to make fluid and dry mixtures. Total production was 1,500 tons P_2O_5 equivalent in 1955; 24,000 during the peak year of 1971; and 10,000 in 1980 (16, 29, 40)

The move into 21-53-0 by TVA, which already had incurred considerable industry criticism because of the substantial tonnages of concentrated superphosphate and ammonium nitrate fertilizer distributed nationally, was attacked vigorously by some. The theme was that diammonium phosphate was too expensive to become a major fertilizer and that production by a Government agency was ridiculous and wasteful. As it turned out, history would see it differently following a major advance in the manufacture of granular DAP, 18-46-0, made by TVA in 1959 and 1960 that reshaped the phosphate industry. In the new process, wet-process phosphoric acid and acid from a scrubbing circuit is fed into a preneutralizer tank. The acid reacts with ammonia to the point where the molecular weight ratio of $NH_3:PO_4$ is controlled to about 1.4. The heat of the reaction evaporates part of the water in the preneutralizer slurry. The still hot slurry containing 16 to 20 percent water is pumped to a TVA-type ammoniator granulator where more ammonia is added to increase the $NH_3:PO_4$ mole ratio to about 2.0. Free ammonia from the granulator and the preneutralizer is acidulated with incoming phosphoric acid in a scrubbing circuit and returned to the process. The hot granules from the granulator are dried, sieved, and cooled in a rotary cooler. The final product contains only 2 percent moisture, needs no conditioner, and has superior handling and storage properties (108).

Following the introduction of the TVA DAP process, new plants based on the process sprang up rapidly. By 1962, 19 domestic plants had been installed having a combined capacity of 2 to 3 million tons of product annually. Two years later, 31 plants were in operation by 25 companies. The granular DAP plants tended to concentrate in the Florida pebble field (11, 30).

Phosphate Rock for Direct Application

Phosphate rock for direct application to the soil, a practice followed to varying extent since the opening of the first domestic phosphate rock mines, continued throughout the 1920-1980 period. Consumption amounted to 82,000 tons of material in 1920 and then dropped to 8,000 tons during the depths of the Great Depression. By 1939, consumption had recovered, reaching 107,000 tons, then climbed to a peak of 1.4 million tons in 1952. Once again, production declined, falling to 170,000 tons in 1970 and 24,000 tons in 1980 (24,26,64).

Basic ingredients for making finished fertilizers are produced in large plants, such as this phosphate complex of Farmland Industries at Bartow, Florida. *(F.J. Myers--TVA)*

Most phosphate rock during the early part of the period was finely ground Tennessee brown rock. By 1950, however, 71 percent came from Florida (soft rock, waste pond phosphate, and ground land pebble phosphate), 28.5 percent from Tennessee brown rock, and 0.2 percent from western rock (50).

All of the phosphate rock sold for direct application was finely ground at the source to pass 65 to 95 percent through a U.S. standard screen of 200 mesh. The total P_2O_5 content of the Tennessee brown rock and the Florida pebble ranged from 29 to 35 percent while that of the Florida soft rock and waste pond phosphate ranged from 18 to 25 percent (50).

Illinois was the major consuming state for many years as the result of C. G. Hopkins' early enthusiasm for raw rock (Chapter 4). During the 1930's the state consumed nearly one-half of all the phosphate rock directly applied, with most of the remainder going into the South Atlantic States. In 1952, Illinois still consumed 50 percent, and Missouri, which had only recently caught the phosphate rock fever, consumed 20 percent. Appreciable amounts were used in Indiana, Iowa, and Kentucky (64).

The use of phosphate rock as a direct application material declined as a result of the appearance of large amounts of concentrated superphosphate and DAP. These high-analysis materials could meet the farmer's phosphorus needs at a lower cost per acre and, being granular, were easier to apply. They also were much more chemically available for crop uptake than phosphate rock and could more easily supply the needs of modern-day farming systems and high yielding crops.

Basic Slag

Basic slag continued to be produced throughout the 1920-1980 period in small amounts by the Tennessee Coal, Iron, and Railroad Company in the Birmingham, Alabama, area where it was first produced in 1915. The material contains 8 percent total P_2O_5 and is used only for direct application, largely on pasture and forage crops. It serves both as a liming material and a source of phosphate. Alabama has been the largest consumer followed by Tennessee, the Carolinas, Georgia, and Louisiana. Annual consumption during the 1930's ran about 35,000 tons, peaked at around 400,000 tons in the 1950's, and leveled out at around 80,000 to 100,000 tons thereafter (4,24,25,26,49,64,76).

Calcium Metaphosphate

Calcium metaphosphate for use as a fertilizer was manufactured by TVA in demonstration-scale plants from 1938 to 1964. No commercial production of the material was ever made. The material contains 60 to 65 percent total P_2O_5 equivalent and is produced by reacting phosphate rock with phosphorus pentoxide according to the following equation.

$$\underset{\text{phosphate rock}}{Ca_{10}(PO_4)_6F_2} + \underset{\substack{\text{phosphorus}\\\text{pentoxide}}}{7P_2O_5 + H_2O} \rightarrow \underset{\substack{\text{calcium}\\\text{metaphosphate}}}{10Ca(PO_3)_2} + \underset{\substack{\text{hydro-}\\\text{fluoric}\\\text{acid}}}{2HF}$$

The phosphorus pentoxide is formed by burning elemental phosphorus from electric furnaces in a combustion chamber into which finely ground phosphate rock is injected. The melt is tapped, solidified, and crushed. Although it created a great deal of interest, it had limited usefulness as a fertilizer since it could not be ammoniated readily, contained no water-soluble phosphorus (although the phosphorus was available to plants grown on acid soils), could not be granulated economically and was not adapted for use in mixed fertilizers. Its value was primarily as a direct application material on humid region, acid soils (69).

Fused Phosphate Materials

Removal of fluorine from phosphate rock by heating the rock in the presence of silica is one way of making the phosphorus in the rock more available for plant uptake. Numerous investigations on the fusion method were carried out by the U.S. Department of Agriculture in the 1930's and TVA in the 1940's. Results appeared promising and, as a result, TVA constructed two oil-fired shaft furnaces at Godwin, Tennessee, in 1945 to produce a fused tricalcium phosphate containing about 24 percent P_2O_5 soluble in citric acid. The product was not sufficiently effective under enough soil and crop conditions to justify continued production. Production was discontinued in 1954. One company, however, adopted the process for commercial production of an animal feed supplement (92,102).

Calcium magnesium phosphate fertilizers produced by fusing olivine, $(Mg,Fe)SiO_4$, or serpentine, $Mg_3H_4SiO_2O_9$, with phosphate rock have been commercially manufactured in this country. The mixtures are fused in an electric furnace at 1,550°C. A calcium magnesium phosphate melt containing about 20 percent P_2O_5 (about 90 percent soluble in

2 percent citric acid) is formed which is quenched in water, dried, and finely ground.

Studies by TVA chemists in 1943 prompted a private laboratory to perfect the process. The process using serpentine was adopted by the Permanente Metals Corporation (later Kaiser Aluminum and Chemical Corporation) at Permanente, California, in 1945. Also, commercial production of the product using olivine was started in 1945 by Manganese Products, Inc. at Seattle, Washington. Apparently all domestic production was discontinued by the 1970's. Internationally, Japan, Korea, Taiwan, China, and Brazil produced calcium magnesium phosphates for use as fertilizer (48,49,105).

Nitric Phosphates

Fertilizers referred to as nitric phosphates in the United States or nitrophosphates in other countries use nitric acid to extract insoluble phosphate from phosphate rock. The basic reaction between nitric acid and phosphate rock to form phosphoric acid, calcium nitrate, and hydrofluoric acid is:

$$Ca_{10}F_2(PO_4)_6 + 20HNO_3 \rightarrow 6H_3PO_4 + 10Ca(NO_3)_2 + 2HF$$

phosphate rock / nitric acid / phosphoric acid / calcium nitrate / hydrofluoric acid

The calcium nitrate can be removed from the original slurry. If the calcium nitrate were left in the slurry, citrate-insoluble tricalcium phosphate in which the P_2O_5 is not available would be formed upon ammoniation. Also, the fertilizer would contain the highly hygroscopic calcium nitrate that would give the product unsatisfactory physical properties. As a result, processes have been developed to overcome these difficulties either by removing the calcium nitrate present or by preventing its formation (48,70).

The Odda process, patented in 1928 by Erling Johnson in Odda, Norway, crystallizes the calcium nitrate in the slurry and removes it by centrifuging. The recovered calcium nitrate is conditioned with wax and oil and sold. The slurry freed from most of the calcium nitrate is then ammoniated to form ammonium phosphate. Potash is added to the slurry if an NPK product is desired. Granular grades such as 20-20-0 and 15-15-15 are produced (70,85).

Methods that avoid formation of the troublesome calcium nitrate add soluble sulfate salts or sulfuric acid to the extracting solution. As a result, calcium sulfate is formed in the slurry and precipitates out leaving little calcium to form calcium nitrate. Phosphoric acid is commonly added to the extracting solution to increase the amount of ammonium phosphate formed during the ammoniation step and lessen the percentage of water-insoluble calcium phosphate in the final product. Use of mixed acids (nitric acid in various combinations with sulfuric or phosphoric acid or both) in extraction is the most common practice in the United States (48,60).

First commercial production of nitric phosphate was in Germany by Badische Analin und Soda Fabrik in 1933. New plants were limited until after World War II. By 1975, the estimated world production capacity was 23 million tons, 90 percent of which was in Europe (48,60).

In this country, TVA started investigating various processes about 1950 in response to a domestic sulfur shortage. Three plants were built starting in 1952: the Associated Cooperatives plant at Sheffield, Alabama (the plant closed about 1962); the Allied Chemical Plant at South Point, Ohio; and the operation of California Spray Chemical Company (later Chevron Chemical) at Richmond. All three used a mixed acid extractant, nitric acid with either sulfuric acid or phosphoric acid (85).

By 1967, the Allied Chemical plant had been closed and four new plants constructed. These were Chevron Chemical plants located at Kennewick, Washington, and Fort Madison, Iowa; a plant by Escambia Chemical at Pensacola, Florida; and a demonstration plant constructed in 1966 by TVA at Muscle Shoals, Alabama, and discontinued in 1975. All of these were based upon use of mixed acids. Three used the French PEC process in which either sulfuric acid or a sulfate salt was used to precipitate the calcium. TVA's plant also used a mixed acid process but utilized a preneutralizer and a rotary ammoniator. Farmers Chemical Association built a plant at Tunis, North Carolina, in 1969 using the Norsk Hydro process, a variation of the Odda process. The plant operated through 1972 (39,40).

Investments in new U.S. nitric phosphate plants ceased in 1970; DAP had become deeply entrenched and no severe sulfur shortages appeared imminent.

Potash Materials

The period 1920-1980 saw major shifts in use of potassium-bearing fertilizer materials. During the first 15 years of the period the country was heavily dependent upon potash imports from Germany. Domestic production was limited to production of potassium chloride from Searles Lake brines and to a number of small operations carried over from the potash-famine days of World War I based largely upon recovery of by-product potash and low-grade products from brines. The first two of the Carlsbad mines had come into operation, although they had not completed their refineries and were producing only run-of-mine manure salts (Chapter 5).

Sources: 1920-1938

A hodgepodge of different potash materials was being sold up until 1935, some of which had very low potash contents. Imports from Germany consisted of KCl, mostly a 50 percent K_2O grade; hardsalt, a natural mixture containing magnesium sulfate, halite, and sylvinite; kainite (KCl•$MgSO_4$•$2H_2O$); a mixture referred to as manure salts containing carnallite (KCl•$MgCl_2$•$6H_2O$), sylvinite, and sometimes potassium magnesium sulfate (K_2SO_4•$2MgSO_4$); potassium sulfate (K_2SO_4); and potassium magnesium sulfate. U.S. production consisted of a 60 percent K_2O grade of KCl from Searles Lake, and manure salts (run-of-mine, mostly sylvinite) from the two Carlsbad mines. Natural deposits contributing small amounts of potash during the period were the alkali lakes of western Nebraska and an alunite deposit near Marysville, Utah, both a carryover from the World War I period and soon abandoned. By-product sources, also of World War I vintage, were cement flue dust, distillery waste, wood ashes, tobacco stems, kelp, and cotton hull ashes. Total domestic production of potash (K_2O) in 1924 was 23,000 tons from 12 plants (in 1920, 49 plants were operating), and in 1935, 193,000 tons from 10 plants. Imports from Germany in 1920 were 198,000 tons and, in 1935, 229,000 tons (64).

A long-awaited national goal was achieved in 1938 when domestic production of naturally occurring potash sources exceeded German imports (Chapter 5). Four potash operations were responsible for most of the production: the two Carlsbad operations which by this time were producing mostly refined KCl, and the brine operations at Searles Lake and Bonneville Flats (Salduro Marsh), Utah, both producing KCl. Five other potash operations were producing potash, all by-product. Domestic production in 1938 had reached 317,000 tons of K_2O equivalent and imports had declined to 187,000 tons. Two years later the new International Minerals and Chemical Corporation (IMC) mine began operation at Carlsbad, producing large amounts of KCl and smaller amounts of potassium sulfate and langbeinite (potassium magnesium sulfate). Some renewal of European imports occurred after World War II but were insignificant compared to U.S. production (64).

Sources: 1939-1960

The opening of the vast, high-grade sylvinite deposits in Saskatchewan in 1962 followed by large exports assured that KCl would continue as the leading potash material consumed in the United States. By the mid-1970's, about 95 percent of this country's potash consumption was as KCl, the remaining 5 percent being largely potassium sulfate.

The companies that mine the potash or recover it from brines prepare their products in the forms sold to the purchasers. Up until the mid-1950's most of the potash was sold either for direct application or for use in the manufacture of pulverized, dry-mix fertilizers. However, by the early 1960's, dry-mix fertilizers were rapidly being replaced by bulk blends, granular homogeneous mixed fertilizers, and fluid fertilizers.

The major potash minerals used in this country for fertilizers, sylvinite and langbeinite, require no chemical modification to render the nutrient chemically available for plant uptake. Only physical separation is required to separate the minerals from sodium chloride, clays, and other unwanted impurities. The only chemical modifications of potash minerals before their use on farms are involved in the exchange of the chloride (Cl) ion in KCl for the sulfate (SO_4) or nitrate (NO_3) ion.

Since the 1950's, particle size ranges of potash materials have been modified physically by compaction and sieving. Froth flotation sometimes is used to separate the product into different size fractions. Coating of potash granules is not as necessary as is the case with more hygroscopic materials. Nevertheless, bulk potash often is coated with an organic conditioner to prevent caking.

Basic potash producers usually sell direct to the using companies or cooperatives on a contract basis, often of long duration. Regional offices may be maintained and warehouses established in different using areas. Potash shipments from the source or warehouse are made by rail or truck (83).

Potassium Chloride

Potassium chloride was by far the most important potash material produced in the United States or imported during the 1920-1980 period (Chapter 8). All domestic potash mining companies and brine producers except the Great Salt Lake Minerals and Chemical Corporation produced KCl, and the Saskatchewan potash mines produced only KCl. (The Canadian imports supplied 38 percent of all of the potash consumed in the United States by 1966 and 79 percent in 1980.) Potassium chloride accounted for 85 percent of the total U.S. potash consumption as early as 1937, 94 percent in 1960, and 95 percent in the 1970's. Worldwide, it accounts also for around 95 percent of the potash consumed as fertilizer (16,56,57,83).

In pure state KCl is a white, crystalline chemical containing 63.17 percent K_2O equivalent, all of which is water soluble. Commercial products during the 1920-1980 period ranged in K_2O equivalent from 50 to 63 percent. That obtained from flotation recovery processes has a pinkish to reddish color due to the presence of small quantities of colored impurities, particularly hematite. Products made from solution or recrystallization methods are white to off-white in color, the main impurity being sodium chloride (56).

Changes in technology and demand have led to considerable changes in physical properties of KCl materials in recent decades. In 1950, KCl was available in only two particle size grades: the standard form contained 60 percent K_2O and consisted of finely divided particles as they occurred after refining, and a granular form containing 50 percent K_2O was obtained mainly by preserving and separating the larger particles of sylvinite. Also during the 1950's, one company produced a 60 percent K_2O granular product by melting KCl and flaking it in a rotary cooler (38). By 1960, potash producers were marketing standard, coarse, and granular KCl products containing 60.0 to 62.5 percent K_2O. Approximate particle size ranges for the standard grade were 0.8 to 0.15 millimeters; coarse, 1.7 to 0.5 mm; and granular, 3.4 to 1.0 mm (57). By the mid-1970's, the maximum K_2O contents of the KCl products had increased slightly to 63 percent K_2O and the particle size ranges had tightened; the standard grade was 1.7-0.2 mm; the coarse, 2.4-0.6; and the granular, 3.4-0.8. In addition, a soluble or solution grade had been added using crystallized KCl containing 62-63 percent K_2O and having a particle size range of 0.4 to 0.15 mm (Chapter 8).

The tabulation below presents the North American (United States and Canada) sales by North American producers of potash by type and particle size grade (83). The data are only a slight inflation of U.S. use since Canada consumes very little fertilizer potash (267,000 tons in 1976).

Type	Size or grade	K_2O 1000 tons	Market %
KCl	Granular	1,664	26
KCl	Coarse	2,484	40
KCl	Standard	1,228	20
KCl	Soluble	494	8
KCl	Chemical	142	2
K_2SO_4	All	143	2
$2SO_4 \cdot MgSO_4$	All	123	2
Total sales		6,286	100

Granular and coarse grades are used primarily in bulk blends and for direct application, with the granular grade increasing in importance since its particle size range is more compatible with the other materials going into bulk blends. The standard grade, since about 1960, has been used mainly in the manufacture of granular homogeneous mixed fertilizers and in fluid fertilizers. In recent years, use of the soluble grade in fluid fertilizers has been increasing.

Potassium chloride has a number of desirable characteristics as a fertilizer material. It is high in primary nutrient content, has a low hygroscopicity, and is compatible with most other fertilizer materials. It

...oves the quality of a number of crops, and does 1 ...... from the soil. The presence of chlorine makes the material less desirable for certain chlorine-sensitive crops.

Potassium Magnesium Sulfate

Potassium magnesium sulfate ($K_2SO_4 \cdot 2MgSO_4$) occurs in mineable quantities in the Carlsbad area as the mineral langbeinite in association with halite and sylvite. Also, a German product imported into this country in the 1920's and 1930's was prepared by dissolving keiserite ($MgSO_4 \cdot H_2O$) in hot water until a desired concentration was reached and then cooled and KCl added until the double salt of potassium magnesium sulfate was formed (21).

Potassium magnesium sulfate (langbeinite) was first produced commercially in the United States by IMC's mine at Carlsbad in 1940. IMC remained the sole producer until the Duval Corporation began production in 1964. (Both were still producing in 1980.) Initially the langbeinite was separated by selective washing to dissolve away the chloride salts, leaving the less soluble langbeinite in solid form, which is separated from the wash waters by centrifuging. The dried product contained 96 to 98 percent langbeinite having about 22 percent K_2O, 11 percent Mg, and 22 percent S. Langbeinite was later separated from the chloride salts using a heavy media process developed by IMC, and by froth flotation. Potassium magnesium sulfate found continuing demand as a potassium fertilizer (13,48,56).

Potassium Sulfate

Potassium sulfate, a popular nonchloride fertilizer, does not occur naturally in free state but is produced chemically in the United States and elsewhere using a variety of processes. Its use as a general potash fertilizer is limited due to its higher production costs as compared to KCl.

IMC began producing potassium sulfate in the early 1940's by reacting KCl with langbeinite according to the following overall reaction:

$K_2SO_4 \cdot 2MgSO_4$	+	4KCl	→	$3K_2SO_4$	+	$2MgCl_2$
langbeinite		potassium chloride		potassium sulfate		magnesium chloride

The process involves a series of complex reactions of the liquid and solid phases of the salt pair system magnesium chloride, potassium sulfate, and water. The resulting crystalline K_2SO_4 is separated from the mother liquor by continuous centrifuging. The remaining slurry is concentrated using vacuum crystallizers to convert the leftover langbeinite and KCl mostly to leonite ($K_2SO_4 \cdot MgSO_4 \cdot 4H_2O$) and KCl. The mixed salts are removed and recycled. The separated K_2SO_4 is dried and sent to storage (57). IMC was still producing potassium sulfate from langbeinite in 1980, while the second producer, Duval Corporation, which had begun producing potassium from langbeinite in 1961, dropped the project in 1977, producing only langbeinite thereafter (Chapter 8).

The American Potash and Chemical Company (later Kerr-McGee) began producing potassium sulfate from Searles Lake brines in 1939. The process involved reacting burkeite [$Na_2CO_3(SO_4)_2$] with KCl to form glaserite ($Na_2SO_4 \cdot 3K_2SO_4$). The glaserite was separated and reacted with high-purity KCl brine to form solid K_2SO_4 which was removed from the resulting NaCl brine by filtering. The remaining brine was recycled (38,57).

A more recent method at Searles Lake permits recovery of potassium sulfate and boric acid remaining in end liquors of other processes containing potassium and sodium borates. The overall reaction, brought about by intermediate steps using chelates, follows.

$$K_2B_{10}O_{16} \cdot 8H_2O + 6H_2O + H_2SO_4 \rightarrow K_2SO_4 + 10H_3BO_3$$
potassium and   water   sulfuric   potassium   boric acid
borate mixtures   acid   sulfate

The Searles Lake complex of plants, besides producing KCl and K_2SO_4, also produces borax and other boron compounds, sodium sulfate, and calcined soda ash (66).

The Great Salt Lake Minerals and Chemical Corporation is the only company operating in the United States that produces potassium from kainite. The brine is obtained from an arm of the Great Salt Lake, Utah, that is 50 percent richer in potassium than the southern half of the lake as a result of restricted inflow of fresh water. The brine is further concentrated in evaporation ponds where kainite, schoenite, carnallite, and halite salts are separated. Potassium sulfate is obtained by converting kainite (KCl•$MgSO_4 \cdot 3H_2O$) to an intermediate salt schoenite ($K_2SO_4MgSO_4 \cdot 6H_2O$) which is later decomposed to potassium sulfate and magnesium sulfate. Also, fractions from certain plant streams that would normally be returned to the evaporation ponds are reacted with purchased KCl to form additional K_2SO_4. In 1975, a flotation circuit was added to concentrate the low-grade kainite and schoenite (48,83).

The Potash Company of America began producing potassium sulfate using KCl as a source of potassium in 1951. These plants were located in Texas near oil fields where the hydrochloric acid (HCl) by-product found a ready market for use in acidulating oil wells to increase oil recovery. One plant was located at Dumas, Texas, and another at Ft. Worth. Two processes were used: the Mannheim process which reacted sulfuric acid with the KCl to produce K_2SO_4 and HCl, and the Hargreaves process in which sulfur was burned in air to produce sulfur dioxide, which was reacted with the KCl in the presence of air and water vapor to form K_2SO_4 and HCl (63).

In 1980, four companies were producing potassium sulfate in the United States: IMC producing from langbeinite; Kerr-McGee from brines at Searles Lake; the Great Salt Lake Minerals and Chemical from the Great Salt Lake, Utah; and the PCA at Dumas, Texas.

Potassium sulfate is a white, crystalline compound containing in pure state 54.06 percent K_2O; the commercial product used as fertilizer contains 50 percent K_2O and 18 percent sulfur. It is the least hygroscopic of any of the primary fertilizer materials. It contains no more than 2.5 percent Cl, and is available in different particle size ranges. The low chlorine content assures the product of a ready market for use on crops, including tobacco and some potatoes, where quality may be adversely affected from the chlorine.

Potassium Nitrate

Potassium nitrate (KNO_3), although available on the U.S. market over most of the 1920-1980 period, was used only to a limited extent as a fertilizer material. During the early part of the 1920-1980 period, the material was imported in small amounts from Chile where it was a by-product of the Guggenheim process used to recover sodium nitrate from crude ores. KNO_3 also was produced until the 1950's by reacting sodium nitrate with KCl (17,57).

The Southwest Potash Company (later Amax Chemical Co.) began producing KNO_3 from KCl and nitric acid at Vicksburg, Mississippi, in 1963 using a novel process developed by the company. The process involved the following overall reaction.

$$4KCl + 4HNO_3 + O_2 \rightarrow 4KNO_3 + 2Cl_2 + 2H_2O$$

potassium chloride + nitric acid + oxygen → potassium nitrate + chlorine + water

However, to recover the desired products, several complex steps involving high-temperature distillation are required to complete the reaction and to separate out the chlorine coproduct. In the final step, KNO_3 crystals are recovered using vacuum crystallization followed by centrifuging and drying or melting and prilling. The chlorine is recovered and sold. The fertilizer-grade KNO_3 contained about 14 percent N and 46 percent K_2O equivalent. The Vicksburg operation, as a result of the highly corrosive intermediate steps, required costly construction materials. The Vicksburg operation was taken over by the Vertac Chemical Corporation (12,18,83).

Potassium nitrate also has been produced in the United States through the reaction of sodium nitrate with KCl in which a crystalline material was produced. However, high production costs limited its use to specialty fertilizers (56).

Plant Environmental Problems

In addition to the environmental problems associated with mining operations (Chapter 7), manufacturers of fertilizer intermediates and finished products also must cope with pollution problems. Several toxic substances are produced, transported, and stored in the fertilizer industry. Included are anhydrous ammonia, ammonium nitrate, fluorine, nitrogen oxide, nitric acid, sulfuric acid, sulfur dioxide (SO_2) and sulfur trioxide (SO_3), cadmium oxide, and various pesticide compounds often mixed with fertilizers.

This section outlines the main types of chemical gaseous and liquid or aqueous effluents that originate in fertilizer plants as they existed in the late 1970's. Most processes used to manufacture fertilizers discharge gaseous effluents. When gaseous ammonia is discharged from an operating plant it is usually due to spills and leaks from faulty equipment or is an operating problem. High concentrations of ammonia affect the mucous membranes of the nose, throat, eyes, and skin. Exhaust gases containing ammonia are usually scrubbed and the resulting scrubber liquors are recycled to the process.

Nitrogen oxides, mostly NO, NO_2, N_2O_4, are discharged from ammonia oxidation processes such as nitric acid plants or ammonium nitrate and NPK plants using the nitrophosphate route. Both NO and NO_2 can be harmful to people, plants, and animals.

The main source of sulfur dioxide or trioxide is as a gaseous effluent from fertilizer plants associated with manufacture of phosphoric acid. Most phosphate fertilizer complexes have one or more captive sulfuric acid plants. Hot gases of sulfur trioxide are absorbed in absorption towers to form 98 percent sulfuric acid. Sulfuric acid plants can cause widespread damage to vegetation and have serious pollution problems in areas near production plants.

Various fluorides are released in processing the phosphate rock, the most common being tetrafluoride (SiF_4) or hydrogen fluoride (HF). Wet-scrubbing is used to recover much of the fluorides which have a number of commercial uses. Gaseous fluoride compounds are also evolved in the production of nitrophosphates. Fluoride in the air can damage vegetation and animals.

Sulfuric acid plants produce pollution as mist and fumes. Fertilizer plants producing mixed granular fertilizers from feedstocks of phosphate rock, phosphoric acid and sulfuric acid produce gaseous effluents containing particulate matter mixed with vent gases from their reactors. Dust from fertilizer plants manufacturing superphosphate monoammonium phosphate, diammonium phosphate and NPK, and from solid materials handing equipment, is normally exhausted. If it is dry fine dust, it can be collected by a duct system and passed through bag filter equipment which will eliminate 99 percent of the particulate matter. High-efficiency cyclones are required to control dust from granulators,

TVA engineer checks level of emissions at Texas fertilizer plant. *(F.J. Myers--TVA)*

dryers, and coolers. Dust and fumes from prilling processes present a problem.

Emissions from ammonium nitrate plants originate during neutralization and evaporation, and from the prilling tower. Fumes are scrubbed in wet scrubbers. The major air pollution concern in urea plants is urea dust from prilling towers.

Aqueous effluents from single and triple superphosphate plants originate from gas scrubbers that are installed for the materials handling equipment and dens. The vent gases containing silicon tetrafluoride and phosphate dust are scrubbed with water or solutions of fluosilicic acid.

Safe disposal of solid wastes or byproducts from fertilizer plants is a major problem in a thickly populated area. Phosphogypsum is by far the largest byproduct in the manufacture of wet-phosphoric acid. Every ton of P_2O_5 produces five tons of phosphogypsum (Chapter 7).

Until the 1950's, fertilizer manufacturing facilities were relatively small and widely scattered. Only four million tons of primary nutrients were produced yearly. With the coming of the agricultural revolution, fertilizer production and use increased by leaps and bounds, topping 50 million tons of product in 1980. Larger and more efficient plants were built, but until fairly recently only minimal efforts were made to keep contaminants out of the air and water unless they were known to be harmful to man, livestock, or vegetation.

A new surge of public concern developed in the 1950's. The chief concern at this time were fluoride gas emissions from phosphoric acid plants and SO_2 emissions and sulfuric acid mists from associated sulfuric acid plants.

REFERENCES

1. Achorn, F. P. and D. G. Salladay. 1975. Production of monoammonium phosphates in a pipe-cross reactor. In *Proceedings of the 25th Annual Fertilizer Industry Round Table*. Washington, D.C.
2. Adams, J. R. 1964. Nitrogen solutions for direct application. In *Fertilizer Nitrogen*. Ed. by V. Sauchelli, pp. 344-364. Reinhold Publ. Corp., New York.
3. _____. M. S. Anderson, and W. O. Hulbert. 1961. *Liquid nitrogen fertilizer for direct application*. Agric. Handbook No. 198. Agric. Research Service, U.S. Dept. Agric., Washington, D.C.
4. Agricultural Research Service. 1961. *Consumption of commercial fertilizers and primary nutrients in the United States; year ending June 30, 1961*. U.S. Dept. Agr. Publ. No. ARS 41-19-5, Washington, D.C.
5. _____. 1965. *Consumption of commercial fertilizers and primary plant nutrients in the United States; year ending June 30, 1965*. U.S. Dept. Agric. Publ. No. SPCr 7(6-66), Washington, D.C.
6. Allen, S. E. 1984. Slow release nitrogen fertilizers. In *Nitrogen in Crop Production*. Ed. by R. D. Hauck, pp. 195-206. Publ. by American Soc. Agronomy, Crops Sci. Soc. Amer. and Soil Sci. Soc. Amer., Madison, Wis.
7. Andrews, W. B. 1956. Anhydrous ammonia as a nitrogenous fertilizer. In *Advances in Agronomy Vol. III*, pp. 61-125. Academic Press Inc., New York.
8. _____. J. A. Neely, and F. E. Edwards. 1951. *Anhydrous ammonia as a source of nitrogen*. Miss. Agr. Expt. Sta. Bull. 482.
9. Anon. 1943. The preparation of ammonium nitrate for use as a fertilizer. *Amer. Fert.* 99(7):5-8,22,24,26.
10. _____. 1955. Manufacture of liquid fertilizers. *Comm. Fert. Yearbook Sept. 1955*, pp. 103-104, 106-107.
11. _____. 1962. *Fertilizer Trends*. Tenn. Valley Auth., Muscle Shoals, Ala.
12. _____. 1967. Southwest potash: new route to KNO3. *Chem. Eng.*, Nov. 20, 1967, pp. 118-119.
13. Barber, S. A., R. D. Munson, and W. B. Dancy. 1971. Production, marketing and use of potassium fertilizers. In *Fertilizer Technology and Use*, 2nd edition, pp. 303-334. Soil Sci. Soc. Amer., Madison, Wis.
14. Bradley, J. K. and G. Drake. 1981. Nitric acid technology. *The Fertiliser Society Proc. No. 200*, Alembic House, London.
15. Bridger, G. L., R. A. Wilson, and R. B. Burt. 1947. Continuous mixing process for manufacture of concentrated superphosphate. *Ind. & Eng. Chem.* 39:1265-1272.
16. Bridges, J. D. 1982. *Fertilizer Trends*, Tenn. Valley Auth., Muscle Shoals, Ala.
17. British Sulphur Corp. 1971. Routes to potassium nitrate Part 1. *Phosphorus and Potassium* 51:50-53.
18. _____. 1971. Routes to potassium nitrate - Part 2. *Phosphorus and Potassium* 52:52-55.
19. Church, R. J. 1964. Chemistry and processing of urea and ureaform. In *Fertilizer Nitrogen*. Ed. by V. Sauchelli, pp. 247-279. Reinhold Publ. Corp., New York.
20. Cole, C. A. and D. G. Salladay. 1984. *Production and use of nitrogen solutions*. Prepared for National Fertilizer Assoc. Fluid Fertilizer Training Inst. 1984 Regional School at TVA.

21. Collings, G. H. 1941. *Commercial Fertilizers*, 3rd edition. The Blakiston Co., Philadelphia.
22. Crittendon, E. D. 1964. Chemistry and utilization of ammonia solutions in fertilizer manufacture. In *Fertilizer Nitrogen*. Ed. by V. Sauchelli, pp. 295-314. Reinhold Publ. Corp., New York.
23. ____. 1964. Synthetic sodium nitrate - production and use. In *Fertilizer Nitrogen*, pp. 331-342.
24. Crop Reporting Board. 1970. *Commercial fertilizers: consumption in the United States, f.y. ended June 30, 1970*. Statistical Reporting Service, U.S. Dept. Agric. SPCr 7(5-71), Washington, D.C.
25. ____. 1975. *Commercial fertilizers: consumption for year ended June 30, 1975*. SPCr (5-76).
26. ____. 1980. *Commercial fertilizers: consumption for year ended June 30, 1980*. SPCr (11-80).
27. Curtis, H. A. 1932. The Chilean nitrogen industry. In *Fixed Nitrogen*. Ed. by H. A. Curtis, pp. 54-70. Chemical Catalog Co., Inc. New York.
28. Davis, R. O. E. 1944. *The explosion and fire hazards in handling ammonium nitrate as a fertilizer*. Div. of Soil and Fertilizer, U.S. Dept. Agric. Released Jan. 1944.
29. Douglas, J. R. and J. M. Ransom, 1958. *Fertilizer Trends*. Tenn. Valley Auth., Muscle Shoals, Ala.
30. ____ and S. A. Cogswell. 1965. Past, present and future production and use of anhydrous ammonia. In *Agricultural Anhydrous Ammonia*. Ed. by M. H. McVikar, et al., pp. 73-99. Publ. by Agric. Ammonia Inst., Amer. Soc. Agron., Soil Sci. Soc. Amer., Madison, Wis.
31. Edminston, D. C. 1977. Phosphate supply-domestic. *Fert. Solutions*, Sept.-Oct. 1977, pp. 106-113.
32. Farm Chemicals. 1980. Dictionary of plant foods. In *Farm Chem. Handbook 1980*, Meister Publishing Co., Willoughby, Ohio.
33. Fire Prevention and Engineering Standards Comm. 1948. *The Texas City disaster, facts and lessons*. Publ. by National Board of Fire Underwriters, New York.
34. Goyal, S. S. and R. C. Huffaker. 1984. Nitrogen toxicity in plants. In *Nitrogen Production in Crop Production*. Ed. by R. D. Hauck, pp. 97-118. Publ. by Amer Soc. Agron., Soil Sci. Soc. Amer., Madison, Wis.
35. Gribbins, M. F. 1953. Conversion of ammonia to fertilizer materials. In *Fertilizer Technology and Resources*. Ed. by K. D. Jacob, pp. 63-84. Academic Press, Inc., New York.
36. Hardesty, J. O. 1964. Granulation. In *Superphosphate: its history, chemistry, and manufacture*. pp. 251-271. U.S. Dept. of Agric. and Tenn. Valley Auth. Supt. of Documents, Washington, D.C.
37. Hargett, N. L. and J. T. Berry. 1980. *Fertilizer Summary Data*. National Fert. Development Center, Tenn. Valley Auth., Muscle Shoals, Ala.
38. Harley, G. T. 1953. Production and processing of potassium materials. In *Fertilizer Technology and Resources*. Ed. by K. D. Jacob, pp. 287-322, Academic Press, Inc., New York.
39. Harre, E. A. 1969. *Fertilizer Trends*. Tenn. Valley Auth., Muscle Shoals, Ala.
40. ____. 1973. *Fertilizer Trends*. Tenn. Valley Auth., Muscle Shoals, Ala.
41. ____. M. N. Goodson, and J. D. Bridges. 1976. *Fertilizer Trends*, Tenn. Valley Auth., Muscle Shoals, Ala.
42. Harvey, E. W. and G. L. Frear. 1952. Ammonium phosphates and ammoniated superphosphates. In *Phosphoric Acid, Phosphorus, and Phosphatic Fertilizers*. Ed. by W. H. Waggaman, pp. 308-334, Reinhold Publ. Corp., New York.

43. Hicks, G. C. 1977. *Review of production of monoammonium phosphate.* National Fertilizer Development Center Bull. Y-119, Tenn. Valley Auth., Muscle Shoals, Ala.
44. Hill, W. L. 1952. Elemental phosphorus and phosphoric acid in the fertilizer industry. *Ind. & Eng. Chem.* 44(7):1526-1532.
45. ____. and W. A. Jackson. 1964. Concentrated superphosphate: manufacture. In *Superphosphate, its history, chemistry, and manufacture.* Ed. by K. D. Jacob, pp. 196-216. U.S. Dept. Agric. and Tenn. Valley Auth., Supt. of Documents, Washington, D. C.
46. Honti, G. D. 1976. Urea. In *The Nitrogen Industry.* Akademia Kiado, Budapest.
47. Horner, C. K. 1945. Ammonium nitrate from war to peace. *Comm. Fert.* 71(5):20-23, 43-45.
48. International Fertilizer Development Center, UNIDO. 1985. *Fertilizer Manual.* Ed. by T. P. Hignett. Publ. by Martinus Nijhoff/Dr. W. Junk. Dordrecht, Boston, Lancaster.
49. Jacob, K. D. 1951. Processes and facilities for manufacture of phosphate fertilizers in the United States. *Comm. Fert.* 82(2):20-31, 34.
50. ____. 1953. Phosphate resources and processing facilities. In *Fertilizer Technology and Resources in the United States.* Ed. by K. D. Jacob, pp. 117-165, Academic Press, Inc., New York.
51. ____. 1960. Fifty years of superphosphate in the United States. *Comm. Fert.* 101(3):24-30.
52. ____. 1964. History and status of the superphosphate industry. In *Superphosphate: its history, chemistry and manufacture.* Ed. by K. D. Jacob, pp. 19-94. Publ. by U.S. Dept. Agric. and Tenn. Valley Auth.
53. ____ and A. L. Mehring. 1947. Progress in the manufacture and use of fertilizers, *Agr. Chemicals* 2(12) 21-24, 61-65.
54. ____ and W. Scholl. 1955. Liquid fertilizers for direct application. *Comm. Fert. Yearbook,* 1955, pp. 94-97, 99-101.
55. Johnson, B. L. 1944. Nitrogen compounds. M*inerals Yearbook,* pp. 1525-1531.
56. Kapusta, E. C. 1968. Potassium fertilizer technology. In *The Role of Potassium in Agriculture.* Ed. by V. J. Kilmer, S. E. Younts, and N. C. Brady. Publ. by Amer. Soc. Agron., Crop Sci. Soc. Amer. and Soil Sci. Soc. Amer., Madison, Wis.
57. ____ and N. E. Wendt. 1963. Advances in fertilizer potash production. In *Fertilizer Technology and Use.* Ed. by M. H. McVikar, G. L. Bridger, and L. B. Nelson, pp. 189-229. Publ. by Soil Sci. Soc. Amer., Madison, Wis.
58. King, A. and A. Bauer. 1977. A *review of accidents with ammonium nitrate.* Dept, of Mining Engineering, Queen's Univ., Kingston,.Ontario.
59. Leavitt, F. H. 1966. Agricultural ammonia equipment-development and history. In *Agricultural Anhydrous Ammonia.* Ed. by M. H. McVikar, et al. Publ. by Agric. Ammonia Inst.i and Amer. Soc, Agronomy, Madison, Wis.
60. Lueth, G. 1967. 40 years Nitrophoska. In *Proc. 17th Ann. Mtg. Fertilizer Industry Round Table,* pp 114-117, Washington, D.C.
61. Lutz, W. A. and C. J. Pratt. 1960. Manufacture of triple superphosphate. In *Chemistry and Technology of Fertilizers.* Ed. by V. Sauchelli, pp. 167-196. Reinhold Publ. Corp., New York.
62. ____. 1960. Manufacture of concentrated water-soluble fertilizers based on ammonium phosphate. In *Chemistry and Technology of Fertilizers,* pp. 299-320.

63. MacDonald, R. A. 1960. Potash: occurrences, processes, production. In *Chemistry and Technology of Fertilizers*. Ed. by V. Sauchelli, pp. 367-402, Reinhold Publ. Corp., New York.
64. Mehring, A. L., J. R. Adams, and K. D. Jacob. 1957. *Statistics on fertilizers and liming materials in the United States*. Publ. by the Agric. Research Service, U.S. Dept. Agric. Bull No. 191. Supt. of Documents, Washington, D.C.
65. Myers, F., D. A. Russel, and R. D. Young. 1979. *Sulfur-coated urea, technical update*, Tenn, Valley Auth. Circ. Z-102. Muscle Shoals, Ala.
66. Noyes, R. 1966. *Potash and potash fertilizers*, Chem. Process Monograph No. 15, Noyes Development Corp., Park Ridge, N. J.
67. Parker, F. W. 1936. Urea-ammonia liquor-B. *Am. Fert.* 84(13) 26, 28.
68. ____. 1977. *The early history of urea in the United States*. 8 pp. unpublished. Tenn. Valley Auth., Muscle Shoals, Ala.
69. Phillips, A. B. and D. R. Boylan. 1963. Advances in phosphate manufacturing. In *Fertilizer Technology and Use*. Ed. by M. H. McVikar et al., pp 131-154. Publ. by Soil Sci. Soc. Amer., Madison, Wis.
70. ____ and J. R. Webb. 1971. Production, marketing and use of phosphorus fertilizers. In *Fertilizer Technology and Use*, 2nd ed. Ed. by R. A. Olson, et al., Soil Sci. Soc. Amer., Madison, Wis.
71. Pratt, C. J. 1964. Ammonium sulfate, nitrate, and chloride fertilizers. In *Fertilizer Nitrogen*. Ed. by V. Sauchelli, pp. 213-246. Reinhold Publ. Corp., New York.
72. ____ and R. Noyes. 1965. *Nitrogen fertilizer chemical processes*. Chem. Process Monograph No. 4, Noyes Development Corp., Pearl River, New York.
73. Robinson, N. 1980. Phosphoric acid technology. In *The Role of Phosphorus in Agriculture*. Ed. by F. E. Khasawneh et al., pp. 151-193. Publ. by Amer. Soc. Agron., Crop Sci. Soc. Amer., Soil Sci. Soc. Amer., Madison, Wis.
74. Rozian, I. W. 1960. Diammonium phosphate as produced at byproduct coke oven plants. In *Chemistry and Technology of Fertilizers*. Ed. by V. Sauchelli, pp. 251-268, Reinhold Publ. Corp., New York,
75. Ruhlman, E.R. 1956. Nitrogen Compounds. *Mineral Yearbook, Volume 1*, pp. 889-898.
76. Scholl, W. and H. M. Wallace. 1951. *Commercial fertilizers in the United States, 1950-51*, Bur. of Plant Industry, Soils, and Agric. Eng., U.S. Dept. Agric., Washington, D.C.
77. ____ et al. 1956. *Commercial fertilizer and primary plant nutrients, consumption in the United States year ended June 30, 1956*. Agric. Research Service, U.S. Dept. Agric., Washington, D.C.
78. ____, G. W. Schmidt, and C. A. Walker. 1961. *Consumption of commercial fertilizers and primary plant nutrients in the United States, year ended June 30, 1961*. Agric. Research Service ARS 41-19-5, Washington, D.C.
79. Schreiner, O., A. R. Merz and B. E. Brown. 1938. Fertilizer materials. In *Yearbook of Agriculture*, 1938. U.S. Dept. Agric., House Document No. 398, U.S. Gov't. Printing Office, Washington, D.C.
80. Sedlock, F. 1964. Chemistry and production of coke oven ammonium sulfate. In *Fertilizer Nitrogen*. Ed. by V. Sauchelli, pp. 128-138. Reinhold Publ. Corp., New York.
81. Sharp, J. C. 1966. Properties of ammonia. In *Agricultural Anhydrous Ammonia*. Ed. by M. McVikar, et al. Publ. by Agric. Ammonia Inst. and Amer. Soc. Agron., Madison,Wis.

82. Siems, H. B. 1953. Chemistry and manufacture of superphosphates and phosphoric acid. In *Fertilizer Technology and Usage*. Ed. by K. D. Jacob, Academic Press Inc., New York.
83. Singleton, R. H. 1978. *Potash*. Bureau of Mines, Mineral Commodity Profiles, MCP-ll. Washington, D.C.
84. Slack, A. V. 1964. Normal superphosphate manufacturing equipment. In *Superphosphate, its History, Chemistry and Manufacture*. Ed. by K. D. Jacob, pp. 131-164. Publ. by U.S. Dept. Agric. and Tenn. Valley Auth.
85. ____. 1967. It's time to consider nitric phosphates. Part I: Background and history. *Farm Chemicals* 130(4): 28-34.
86. ____ and J. O. Hardesty. 1964. Superphosphate in relation to other phosphates. In *Superphosphate, its History, Chemistry and Manufacture*, Ed. by K. D. Jacob, pp. 315-339. U.S. Dept. Agric, and Tenn. Valley Auth.
87. ____ and J. O. Hardesty. 1966. Fertilizers manufactured from ammonia. In *Agricultural Anhydrous Ammonia*. Ed. by M. H. McVikar, et al., pp. 32-72. Publ. by Agric. Ammonia Inst., Amer. Soc. Agron., and Soil Sci. Soc. Amer., Madison, Wis.
88. Sorgenti, H. A. and G. F. Sachsel. 1964. Chemistry and the manufacture of nitric acid. In *Fertilizer Nitrogen and Technology*. Ed. by V. Sauchelli, pp. 99-127. Reinhold Publ. Corp., New York.
89. Striplin, M. M., D. McKnight, and G. H. Megar. 1958. Phosphoric acid of high concentration. *Jr. Agr. and Food Chem.* 6: 298-303.
90. Taylor, G. V. 1953. Nitrogen production facilities in relation to present and future demand. In *Fertilizer Technology and Resources*. Ed. by K. D. Jacob, pp. 15-61, Academic Press, Inc., New York.
91. Tenn. Valley Auth. 1950. *TVA annual report*, Knoxville, Tenn.
92. ____. 1965. *The TVA fertilizer program - a statement of scope, impact, and future direction*. 57 pp. Unpublished, TVA, Muscle Shoals, Ala.
93. ____. 1978. *A review of TVA's fluid fertilizer introduction program*. Div. of Agric. Development, TVA, unpublished.
94. ____. 1978. *Trends in fertilizer technology — implications for global transfer*. National Fertilizer Development Center Bull. Y-133, Muscle Shoals, Ala.
95. ____. 1979. *Sulfur coated urea*. National Fertilizer Development Center Circ. Z-102, Muscle Shoals, Ala.
96. Tower, H. L. and H. C. Brewer. 1964. Natural Chilean nitrate of soda. In *Fertilizer Nitrogen*. Ed. by V. Sauchelli, pp. 315-330, Reinhold Publ. Corp, New York.
97. Vincent, G. 1977. Anhydrous ammonia, the miracle of crop production. *Successful Farming*, Oct. 1977, p. 36.
98. Voss, R. D. 1984. Potential use of urease inhibitors. In *Nitrogen and Crop Production*. Ed. by R. D. Hauck, pp. 571-577. Publ. by Amer. Soc. Agronomy, Crop Sci. Soc. Amer., Soil Sci. Soc. Amer., Madison, Wis.
99. Waggaman, W. H. 1952. Elemental phosphorus and its manufacture. In *Phosphoric Acid, Phosphates and Phosphatic Fertilizers*. Ed. by W. H. Waggaman, pp. 131-157, Reinhold Publ. Corp., New York.
100. ____. 1952. Concentrated or triple superphosphate. In *Phosphoric Acid, Phosphates, and Phosphatic Fertilizers*, pp. 290-307.
101. ____ and V. Sauchelli. 1952. Superphosphate, its manufacture and properties. In *Phosphoric Acid, Phosphates, and Phosphatic Fertilizers*, pp. 238-289.

102. Walthall, J. H. 1953. Chemistry and technology of new phosphate fertilizers. In *Fertilizer Technology and Use*. Ed. by K. D. Jacob, pp. 205- 255, Academic Press, Inc., New York.
103. Warnock, R. E. 1966. Ammonia application in irrigation water. In *Agricultural Anhydrous Ammonia*. Ed. by M. H. McVikar, et al., pp. 101-114, publ. by Agric. Ammonia Inst., Amer. Soc. Agron., and Soil Sci. Soc. Amer., Madison, Wis.
104 Weber, W. C. 1952. The manufacture of phosphoric acid by the wet process. In *Phosphoric Acid, Phosphates, and Phosphatic Fertilizers*, pp. 174-209., Reinhold Publ. Corp., New York.
105 Whitney, W. T. and C. A. Hollingsworth. 1952. Calcined, fused, and defluorinated phosphates. In *Phosphoric Acid, Phosphates, and Phosphatic Fertilizers*, pp. 376406, Reinhold Publ. Corp., New York.
106 Wright, E. B. and H. L. Kimbrough. 1984. *New materials for the fluid fertilizer industry*. Presented at the National Fertilizer Solutions Assoc. Fluid Fertilizer Training Inst. 1984 Regional Schools.
107 Young, R. D. and F. P. Achorn. 1977. *Trends in U.S. fertilizer technology for global transfer.* Tenn. Valley Auth. Bull. Y-133, Muscle Shoals, Ala.
108. ____ and C. H. Davis. 1980. Phosphate fertilizers and process technology. In *Role of Phosphorus in Agriculture*. Ed. by F. E. Khasawneh, et al., pp. 195-226.
109. ____ and N. L. Hargett. 1984. *Fluid fertilizers history, growth, and status*, pp. 5-13, TVA National Fertilizer Development Center Bull. Y-185, Muscle Shoals, Ala.

11

Secondary and Micronutrient Fertilizer Materials 1850's-1980

Deficiencies of secondary and micronutrients under field conditions are much less universal than are those of nitrogen (N), phosphorus (P), and potassium (K); but where they do occur they can be just as devastating to plant growth. Calcium (Ca), magnesium (Mg), and sulfur (S), traditionally referred to as secondary nutrients, are essential to plant growth–in somewhat smaller amounts than N, P, and K but in greater amounts than micronutrients. Application of Ca solely to overcome a Ca deficiency is very limited since most soils are well supplied with the element, either naturally or through liming. Magnesium and S deficiencies, on the other hand, occur frequently on a number of crops. Micronutrients, originally referred to as "minor" or "trace" elements, are required in small amounts for plant growth. Seven elements have been identified as micronutrients: boron (B), copper (Cu), iron (Fe), manganese (Mn), molybdenum (Mo), zinc (Zn), and chlorine (Cl). Chlorine, is of only limited concern as a plant nutrient since most agricultural soils are well endowed with the element. Chlorine, of course, is supplied with the addition of potash (KCl). Even so, a few Cl deficiencies have been reported. Each of the remaining six nutrients is important on certain kinds of soils, particularly in crops sensitive to a deficiency of a specific nutrient.

This chapter covers the discovery of secondary and micronutrients, sources and materials, extent of their deficiencies, consumption, and marketing. Chlorine is dealt with only from the standpoint of its discovery as an essential nutrient.

Secondary Nutrients

The importance of the secondary nutrients to plant growth was generally recognized by the late 1850's. Chemical analyses of plant ashes had consistently shown the presence of calcium, magnesium and sulfates. Also, pot culture experiments during the 1840's and 1850's indicated these elements were probably essential. Salm-Horstman of Germany in 1856 published the results of his carefully conducted pot experiments that apparently for the first time showed the essential nature of a number of elements, including the secondary nutrients. His procedure involved for the first time elimination of one or more elements from nutrient solutions and placing the solutions along with growing plants in wax-coated tin pots which contained a medium of sand, pulverized quartz, and acid-washed sugar charcoal whereby contamination was minimized. Starting in the 1860's, plant physiologists using water cultures (discussed later) proved beyond any doubt the essential nature of the three secondary nutrients (40,55).

Materials containing Ca, Mg, and S have been applied on soils for centuries to improve crops. The Greeks and Romans applied lime and marl to certain soils and crops (Chapter 1). Gypsum was being used as a soil amendment in Europe by the first half of the eighteenth century, and Pennsylvania farmers were applying gypsum imported from France about 1750 (Chapter 3).

Calcium

Large amounts of Ca from natural or applied sources are sufficient on most U.S. soils to meet crop needs. Calcium occurs naturally in various soil minerals, and some is held in exchangeable form on the surface of soil colloids and is readily available to plants. The Ca content of acid surface soils in humid regions ranges from about 0.1 percent to as high as 2.0 percent while calcareous soils in arid regions contain from about 5 to 25 percent. Deficiencies are most likely to be found in acid, sandy soils, and in peat and muck soils. The acid sandy soils are subject to leaching losses of Ca with the soil pH often falling to 4.5 or below (11).

The relative contributions from various applied sources in supplying Ca to agricultural lands were estimated during the 1940's. For the year 1945, liming materials provided an estimated 6.6 million tons of Ca on the acid soils of the United States; of this, limestone accounted for about 95 percent. Calcium applied through fertilizers in the continental United States amounted to 1.8 million tons. Normal superphosphate, the chief phosphorus source during the period, contained about 19 percent Ca in the forms of calcium sulfate (gypsum) and calcium phosphates. Mixed fertilizers contained about 12 percent Ca, with normal superphosphate in the mixture accounting for 70 to 85 percent and the remainder made up largely of limestone filler or of dolomitic limestone used to make the fertilizer nonacid-forming (35). Since these estimates were made, applications of lime to acid soils has continued to add large amounts of Ca. Use of normal superphosphate, however, has declined, being replaced with concentrated superphosphate, which contains no gypsum, and ammonium phosphate. Mixed fertilizers no longer contain added limestone.

Calcium deficiencies are seldom evident on field crops in this country. The most notable exception is peanuts grown on the very sandy, low-Ca soils of the southeastern coastal plain. Peanuts need large amounts of soluble Ca during the pegging period to ensure filling of the pods. Peanut growers normally apply about 500 pounds per acre of gypsum directly to the vines at the early bloom stage. Chelated Ca also has seen some use in foliar sprays to control blossom-end rot associated with tomatoes and peppers, both of which have high Ca requirements. Celery blackheart also can be controlled with Ca additions. Calcium deficiency has been noted in Illinois in heavily fertilized corn growing on very acid soils of pH 4.5 and below. Growth responses have been noted in alfalfa and potatoes grown on highly acid soils, but it is unclear whether these were due to the liming effect of the material applied or to the Ca as a nutrient (10,11,45,51,67).

Magnesium

Magnesium is usually present in plants in smaller amounts than Ca. Most soils are adequately supplied, with Mg content ranging from about 0.1 percent in certain leached humid region soils to about 4 percent in soils of semi-arid regions. Magnesium is more subject to leaching than Ca (46,51).

Magnesium deficiencies in the United States were first noted shortly after the turn of the century. Wheeler and Hartwell in 1904 found that crops grown on certain Rhode Island soils responded to applications of magnesium lime (MgO), and that a single application would remove the deficiency for a number of years. Garner and Brown of the U.S. Bureau of Plant Industry in 1919 showed that a characteristic chlorosis of tobacco, known as "sand drown," could be cured with an application of magnesium salts. Garner and other coworkers had observed by 1922 that the deficiency was most prevalent in deep, sandy soils during seasons of high rainfall and tended to occur late in the plants' maturity. Reed and Haas in 1924 observed that chlorosis of young citrus and walnut trees was due to Mg deficiencies. In the 1930's, various investigators reported that potato-producing areas along the Atlantic Coastal Plain extending as far north as Aroostock County, Maine, showed definite Mg deficiencies (27,28,37,42,46).

Minerals and inorganic compounds were used as sources of Mg during the 1920-1980 period. Magnesium, like Ca, is a constituent of limestone which has been a major source of the element in acid soils. Dolomite, $MgCO_3 + CaCO_3$, contains 13.1 percent Mg in true state while dolomitic limestones, which vary greatly in Ca:Mg ratios, average somewhat less. Limestone also was added to mixed fertilizers. During the 1920's large amounts of low-grade potash minerals, primarily the double salts of potassium and magnesium sulfates, were imported from Germany (Chapter 10). Although bought mainly for their K content, they also supplied Mg (35,51).

The addition of Mg as a nutrient element in mixed fertilizers eventually became fairly common in some parts of the country. The practice apparently got its start in 1921 when W. H. MacIntire of The University of Tennessee convinced the Knoxville Fertilizer Company to add dolomite to some of its mixed fertilizers. The practice was quite common by 1950 with the Mg materials being added solely or largely for their Mg content. Dolomite was the preferred material with about 450,000 tons used in mixed fertilizers in 1948 as compared with 26,000 tons of other Mg materials. The latter included potassium magnesium sulfate ($K_2SO_4 \cdot MgSO_4$), by then being produced at Carlsbad, New Mexico, and containing 11 percent Mg and 18 percent K. Other Mg-containing materials included Epsom salt, $MgSO_4 \cdot 7H_2O$ with 9.6 percent Mg; keiserite, $MgSO_4 \cdot H_2O$ with 18.3 percent Mg; and magnesium oxide, MgO, containing 55 percent Mg (35). Pierre (54) and Parker (53) were also early advocates of adding dolomitic limestone to mixed fertilizers not only for its value as a plant nutrient but also to render the fertilizer nonacid-forming when applied to the soil. (Most N fertilizer materials are acid-forming.) Considerable nonacid-forming fertilizers were produced in the 1940's and early 1950's. However, the practice was dropped as farmers began applying large amounts of high-analysis N fertilizers; it was easier to apply the limestone directly to the soil.

Data on the amounts of Mg applied to the Nation's soils are notably absent. The U.S. Department of Agriculture estimated that about 1 million tons of Mg was applied annually during the 1920's. Of this, about 5 percent was applied in fertilizers, mostly as dolomite; 11 percent in liming materials; 77 percent in animal manures, and the remainder in miscellaneous materials. Use was estimated at over of 2 million tons of Mg per year in the late 1940's, 7 percent in fertilizers, 63 percent in liming materials, and 27 percent in manures; dolomite provided nearly one-half of the total Mg (44). Data from about 1955 and later years are limited to the consumption of potassium magnesium sulfate and other Mg compounds used for direct application. Application of limestones for liming purposes, however, continued at around 25 million tons annually (51).

After many years of investigation and observation it is apparent that Mg deficiencies are most widespread on the acid, sandy soils of the East Coast, with some of the most severe problems in Florida. Low levels of available Mg have been noted in the Lake Central states and the Northwest. Deficiencies are most often found on citrus, tobacco, potatoes, cotton, and corn, but have been noted in many other species (7,51).

Sulfur

Sulfur has a long history as a plant nutrient or as a soil amendment. It was imported in gypsum in the 1770's, and its value as a soil amendment was recognized. This led to the discovery of gypsum deposits in New York and Ohio and opening of quarries about 1815 (Chapter 2). Responses of crops to S as a plant nutrient in this country were first observed in Oregon and Washington in the early 1900's. Increased tobacco yields from use of S were noted in Kentucky in 1914, and deficiencies were found in Minnesota in the 1920's. Since the 1950's, S deficiencies have increased as fertilizer manufacturers made more high-analysis grades containing little or no S, as sulfur oxides emissions to the atmosphere were reduced, and as per-acre crop yields increased. By 1972, deficiencies were known in 31 states (46,65).

Fertilizer compounds used to supply the primary nutrient materials (N,P,K) were substantial carriers of S–primarily in the sulfate (SO_4) form–during the 1920-1980 period. Normal superphosphate, containing about 12 percent S in the form of gypsum, was an important S source until its replacement by triple superphosphate and ammonium phosphates starting in the 1950's. Consumption of normal superphosphate peaked in 1952 at around 8 million tons of product containing nearly 1 million tons of S. Ammonium sulfate consumption as a fertilizer in 1920 amounted to about 273,000 tons of product containing 32,000 tons of S. It leveled out in 1965 at around 2.5 million tons of product containing about 300,000 tons of S. Ammonium sulfate in terms of S exceeded normal superphosphate by 1976 when S from normal superphosphate had fallen to 230,000 tons (12,29,31,44).

Several potash fertilizer materials were important sources of S. However, they were usually valued more as a chloride-free potash (the presence of Cl adversely affects the quality of certain crops such as tobacco and potatoes). Several K-containing materials also contained the salt $MgSO_4$ as a double salt, and thus were carriers of the three nutrients–K, Mg, and S. Several such materials were imported from Germany in the 1920's (Chapter 10) but were valued only for their K content. During the entire 1940-1980 period the most important potash material containing S was potassium magnesium sulfate containing 18 percent K, 11 percent Mg, and 22 percent S. The material was mined only at Carlsbad during the 40-year period. Potassium sulfate, containing 42 percent K, 18 percent S, and less than 2.5 percent Cl, was recovered from brines; it also was manufactured from langbeinite and KCl (Chapter 10). Data are not available on the tonnages of potassium magnesium sulfate and potassium sulfate either produced or consumed. Bureau of Mines sales data show that 143,000 tons of K_2O as potassium sulfate and 123,000 tons of K_2O as potassium magnesium sulfate were sold in the United States and Canada in 1975 (60).

Several other primary nutrient materials contain appreciable amounts of S. The ammonium phosphate-sulfates vary in S content depending on the amount of sulfuric acid added to the phosphoric acid during manufacture; a 16-20-0 grade contains 14 percent S and a 13-39-0 grade 20 percent S. Several methods have been used to add elemental S to primary fertilizer materials. Also, a granular triple superphosphate-elemental S material of 0-35-0-20S and 0-38-0-20S grades, and a urea-sulfur 40-0-0-10S grade have been produced by different methods. Sulfur-coated urea, a slow-release material, contains 13 to 16 percent S. The product, developed by TVA, has seen some commercial production. Sulfur also is incorporated in granular, homogeneous NPK fertilizers during manufacture by reacting sulfuric acid with ammonia to meet needs in S-deficient areas (6).

Sulfur is the only secondary nutrient used to any extent in clear liquid fertilizers. (Mg compounds are not used since they cause the phosphate to precipitate.) The three most popular S materials in use since about 1960 are ammonium thiosulfate $(NH_4)_2S_2O_3$, containing 26 percent S; ammonium bisulfite, NH_4HSO_3, with 17 percent S; and ammonium polysulfide, $(NH_4)_2S_x$, containing 40-45 percent S. Ammonium thiosulfate can be blended with nonacidic, fluid phosphate fertilizers and ammonium nitrate and/or urea nitrogen solutions. The material is not compatible with anhydrous ammonia. Ammonium bisulfite in combination with aqueous ammonia, urea, or UAN can be used to obtain almost any desired N to S ratio. It cannot be used in highly acid solutions. Ammonium bisulfite is a by-product of smelting operations and is primarily used on winter wheat in Oregon and Washington. Ammonium polysulfide can be blended with anhydrous ammonia or mixed with aqua ammonia and UAN solutions. Dual application of anhydrous ammonia and ammonium polysulfide is common in parts of the Pacific Northwest. Ammonium polysulfide was among the first sulfur materials to be used in fluid fertilizers. Fluid suspension fertilizers use a wide range of S materials including elemental S (6,8).

Several nonfertilizer sources of S, taken together, provide a large amount of S for crops. Soils in the arid regions of the United States naturally contain large amounts of sulfates. Crops residues and animal manures are important sources. Farmers near large feedlots particularly apply a great deal of manure to their soils. Certain river and well waters contain large amounts of S and, when used for irrigation, supply considerable S to the soil. Also, industrial activities release considerable SO_2 into the atmosphere which is brought down in rainfall as sulfuric acid.

Other sources of S include gypsum, an earlier fungicide, and certain micronutrient carriers. Gypsum ($CaSO_4 \cdot 2H_2O$) contains in pure form 18.6 percent S and is obtained from minable native deposits and a less pure by-product from wet-process phosphoric acid manufacture. The two sources are used in areas close to the mines and by-product production centers (6). Prior to 1950, before the introduction of modern fungicides, Bordeaux mixture, a mixture of hydrated lime and copper sulfate, was used extensively on grapes, fruits, and vegetables to control fungus diseases such as powdery mildew. It also added substantial amounts of S to the soils devoted to these crops (25). Micronutrient fertilizers containing sulfates of Cu, Fe, Mn and Zn add small amounts of S to the soil.

Discovery of the Essential Micronutrients

The micronutrients, with the exception of Fe, were much later than the primary and secondary nutrients in being recognized as essential for plant growth. This was due to the very low amounts required by plants, the infrequent occurrence of deficiencies on crops growing on most farmlands, and the difficulty in producing water and sand cultures of sufficient purity to permit determination of the essential nature of elements required by plants only in trace amounts. De Saussure, Liebig, Boussingault, and others by 1850 had established a fairly broad knowledge of the chemical elements that were present in appreciable amounts in plants. Nine elements–C, H, O, N, P, K, Ca, Mg, and S–were accepted as being necessary for plant growth. E. Gris of France in 1844, however, demonstrated experimentally that plants growing in an "iron-free" medium produced chlorotic leaves and made very little growth; adding a few drops of a solution of an iron salt to the medium caused the leaves to become green within a short time (46,55).

```
                13-13-13

GUARANTEED ANALYSIS:
Total Nitrogen (N) ....................... 13.0%
   Derived from Ammonium Nitrate, Ammoniated
   Phosphates, and Sulfate of Ammonia
Available Phosphoric Acid (P₂O₅) ......... 13.0%
   Derived from Superphosphate
   and Ammoniated Phosphates
Soluble Potash (K₂0) ..................... 13.0%
   Derived from Muriate of Potash
   and Sulfate of Potash Magnesia
Secondary and Micronutrients:
Magnesium (Mg) Water Soluble ........ 1.00%
Sulfur (S) ............................. 9.00%
Boron (B) .............................. .05%
Manganese (Mn) ........................ .20%
Zinc (Zn) .............................. .20%
SECONDARY AND
MICRONUTRIENT SOURCES:
Magnesium from Sulfate of Potash Magnesia;
Sulfur from Phosphates, Sulfate of Ammonia
and Sulfate of Potash Magnesia; Boron,
Manganese and Zinc from Oxides or Sulfates.
```

Salm-Horstmar of France from 1849-1851 used oats grown on a sand culture to identify elements taken up by the roots and thus essential for plant growth. His procedure was to eliminate in turn individual elements from a complete nutrient solution. Using this method, he established experimentally that N, P, K, S, Ca, Mg, and Fe were essential. He also was able to identify "gray speck" of oats as due to a Mn deficiency (32,63).

During 1859-1865, the plant physiologists Sachs, Knop, and Nobbe developed the general procedure in water cultures to the point where they could be used for establishment of the essentiality of micronutrients. Sachs published the first standard formula for a culture solution for plants in 1860, and Knop in 1865 proposed a solution that became one of the most widely used. Numerous other nutrient solutions also were developed, and the essentiality of N, P, K, Ca, Mg, S, and Fe was proven time after time. The other elements found in plants were attributed simply to their presence in the soil in soluble form and taken up by the roots, and it was generally believed that they served no physiological need in the plant. The inability to establish essentiality of other elements, as it was found out later, was due to use of impure chemicals, the presence of the elements in the seed, and inadequate precautions in avoiding contamination from other sources (46).

As culture techniques improved, renewed investigations began indicating that other elements might be essential. Bertrand of France in 1905 claimed that insufficient manganese in plants decreased growth and should be recognized as an essential element. Nagaoka in 1903 and Aso in 1907, both in Japan, noted the stimulating effect of Mn on rice. Agulhon of France in 1910 found that B increased production of dry matter of wheat, oats, and radish growing in sand culture, and of corn and turnips grown on field plots. Maze' in France from 1914 through 1919 using water cultures considered Zn, Si, Cl, Al, B, and possibly other elements as essential. McHargue in 1922 in Kentucky obtained convincing data that Mn and possibly other elements were essential to green plants. W. E. Brenchley in England published various studies on the essential nature of Cu, Mn, Zn, and B from 1910 through 1927. K. Warington in 1922 and later Brenchley and Warington published key studies on B as an essential element. A. L. Sommer and C. B. Lipman in this country published the results of an important investigation showing the need of Zn and B in plant nutrition in 1926. Lipman and G. McKinney in 1932 provided proof of the essential nature of Cu, although H. Bortels in Germany in 1927 using a culture medium of *Aspergillus niger* (common bread mold) had found evidence that the element was essential. It also had been noted that Bordeaux sprays (a mixture of lime and copper sulfate used as a fungicide) occasionally had stimulating effects on growth and yields on crops that were unrelated to control of diseases (46,56,57).

A major accomplishment was establishment of Mo as an essential element. It is needed by plants in very low amounts, and to establish it as being essential required providing an extremely pure culture solution and a contaminant-free environment. The first clue that the element might be of biological importance was obtained by H. Bortels of Germany in 1930 when he observed that the growth of microbial cultures of the bacteria *Azotobacter croococcum* (commonly present in soils) were improved by adding small amounts of the element. Other studies during the 1930's further verified that Mo was vital to life processes of microorganisms (5,64).

The major breakthrough showing without doubt that Mo was essential to growth of higher plants came out of studies at the University of California in a program to produce high degrees of purity in chemicals used to grow plants. D. I. Arnon and P. R. Stout, using highly pure water cultures, showed in 1939 that tomato plants could not complete their life cycle unless Mo was present; additions of 0.01 part per million to the culture solution permitted normal growth of the tomatoes. D. R. Hoagland of California in 1940 repeated the experiment using plum seedlings with similar results. C. S. Piper of Australia made similar studies using oats. A. J. Anderson of the Commonwealth Scientific and Industrial Organization in Australia laid out field experiments on pastures very low in productivity near Adelaide in 1942 and proved for the first time that Mo deficiencies could occur under field conditions (5,64).

Chlorine, the last micronutrient to be found essential, is needed by plants in larger amounts than any other micronutrient element except possibly Fe. However, Cl is so widely distributed in nature that deficiencies are not commonly found on agricultural soils, although some deficiencies have been reported in Africa. Chlorine was proved essential by T. C. Broyer at the University of California in 1954 during experiments to investigate cobalt (Co) as a possible essential element. Using the highly purified nutrient solutions in a specially-prepared contaminant-free environment, he found that healthy plant growth could not be supported without the addition of Cl (64). Since Broyer's work, no other elements have been proven essential, although two or three appear to be likely candidates.

Identification of Field Deficiencies, 1920-1950

The period from about 1925 to 1950 was a pioneering era in the United States for identification and correction of micronutrient deficiencies. It was a time of considerable accomplishment and excitement. Much of the activity centered in areas where the soils extremely deficient in one or more micronutrients were devoted to production of high-value-per-acre crops. Southern Florida, as a result of its high rainfall, the nature of its soils, and a preponderance of citrus and vegetable crops, received most of the early attention. The addition of certain micronutrients to diseased crops and unproductive soils miraculously cured them and, in the more dramatic instances, marginal agriculture was transformed almost overnight to a highly productive and profitable enterprise.

Some micronutrient deficiencies were observed for years before the true cause was identified. A striking example was that of a Cu deficiency of citrus in Florida known as "dieback." It was first described in 1875 by J. H. Fowler who believed it was due to a fungus disease. In 1913, dieback was controlled in tests by spraying trees with Bordeaux (lime-copper sulfate) solution. In 1916, it was found that a soil application of copper sulfate would control the disease. California also controlled a citrus deficiency with addition of Cu compounds, but neither the Florida nor California growers recognized that the problem was due to a micronutrient deficiency. It wasn't until 1927 that the problem was positively identified as a lack of sufficient Cu (14).

R. V. Allison and his associates in 1927 showed that the almost complete failure of many crops grown on the peat soils of the Florida Everglades could be corrected by applications of Cu, Mn, or Zn, or by combinations of the three. As a result of the predominance of sands, mucks, and marls which were subject to a range of micronutrient deficiencies, Florida became the first state to apply micronutrients routinely in mixed fertilizers. Without micronutrients, the state could not have developed a competitive agriculture (1,20).

Iron deficiency symptoms on citrus apparently were observed in California for many years before their cause was identified. C. B. Lipman and A. Gorden in 1925 and E. E. Thomas and A. R. C. Haas in 1928 conducted experiments for control of the problem and demonstrated the need for Fe. Deficiency of Fe in citrus in Arizona also was recognized by A. H. Finch, D. W. Albert, and A. F. Kennison in the early 1930's. Iron chlorosis of fruit trees grown on calcareous soils in Utah was identified as early as 1926. Several cases of Fe deficiency were identified in citrus in Florida growing on soils underlain by marl and in 1937 also on trees growing on acid sands. In Hawaii, M. O. Johnson worked from 1916 to 1928 on overcoming a chlorosis of pineapple induced by the presence of excessive Mn in a Mn-rich soil. Introduction of ferrous sulfate into a weekly spray program solved the problem (14,46).

Boron initially received a cool reception from the American farmer, compared to the other micronutrients. This was due to the unpleasant experiences many had during the World War I period and shortly thereafter due to the presence of large amounts of borax in certain potash fertilizers derived from brines in the western United States. Enough B was often present in some fertilizers to severely damage crops, particularly on sandy soils. Millions of dollars of damages were claimed, resulting in numerous lawsuits. As a result, the earlier field research with B from about 1917 into the early 1920's was concerned with the presence of excessive B in fertilizers and its bad effect upon plant growth. Although improved potash refinery methods solved the problem, farmers remained suspicious of B for many years (46,59).

G. H. Collings worked on B toxicity of soybeans in New Jersey in 1923 and apparently was the first to note that small amounts of boric acid or borax actually stimulated field-grown plants. However, it wasn't until the mid-1930's that research with B as a nutrient in field-grown crops actually got underway. J. E. McMurtrey in 1935 reported a field deficiency of B in tobacco. The same year, J. E. Kotila and G. H. Coons noted B deficiency on sugar beets in Michigan and Ohio. C. H. Dearborn and G. J. Raleigh obtained a response in field-grown celery in 1936, and E. R. Purvis and R. W. Ruprecht overcame cracked-stem of celery in 1937 in Florida. Responses to B were obtained by A. L. Cook in Michigan in alfalfa in 1937 and W. L. Powers the same year observed B deficiency in western Oregon soils. L. G. Willis and J. R. Piland in 1938 demonstrated B response of alfalfa in North Carolina and in 1939 K. C. Berger of

Several areas in this Nebraska corn field show iron deficiency. *(F.J. Myers---TVA)*

Wisconsin found the deficiency in Wisconsin. From then on, locations of B deficiencies became fairly well defined and high-B-requiring crops were identified (9,15,22,41,42,46).

Besides the identification of Cu deficiencies in citrus in Florida and California, R. V. Allison and his coworkers in 1927 found and reported extreme Cu deficiencies in vegetables in Florida. Deficiencies were reported on onions and lettuce in western New York by E. L. Felix in 1927 and J. E. Knott in 1932, and in Michigan by P. M. Harmer in 1932– all in peat or muck soils (1,46,61).

The marl soils of the Florida Everglades were found to be extremely deficient in Mn. On fields receiving a basic application of 2 tons per acre of NPK fertilizer, an additional 50 pounds of manganese sulfate increased tomato yields from almost total crop failures to as high as 450 crates per acre. Prior to the introduction of the manganese sulfate, tomato growers shipped in trainloads of barnyard manure from Mississippi and other nearby states. Use of the manure, applied each year in large amounts, was the only material at the time that permitted the tomatoes to be grown successfully in the Everglades. Analysis of the manure following the advent of manganese sulfate showed that the marked response was due mostly to its Mn content (58).

In addition to the reports of Allison and his coworkers on Mn deficiencies in Florida, O. Schreiner and P. R. Dawson in 1927 also reported the need for the element in tomatoes grown on the marl soils of the Everglades. The first reports on Mn deficiencies in citrus in Florida were made by J. J. Skinner and G. M. Bahrt in 1931 and by Skinner, Bahrt, and A. E. Hughes in 1934. E. R. Parker in California in 1934 also reported a deficiency in citrus. A deficiency in field-grown tobacco was reported by McMurtrey in 1938 (14,41).

Zinc deficiencies were observed in practically every citrus-growing area in field research programs in the 1930's. In California, W. H. Chandler, D. R. Hoagland, and P. L. Hibbard published a number of research papers on the control of little-leaf and rosette in citrus from 1932 through 1935, and A. Kozlowski reported on the same problem in 1936. E. R. Parker, also of California, reported on the use of Zn in 1934 and 1935 to control mottle-leaf in citrus. In Florida, Zn deficiency was related to bronzing of citrus in a number of reports released by A. F. Camp, G. M. Bahrt, and others from 1935 through 1937 (14,46).

Zinc deficiencies also were noted on other crops during the 1930's. W. H. Chandler, D. R. Hoagland, and P. L. Hibbard in 1933 found that spraying peaches and apricots with a zinc-lime mixture or injecting zinc sulfate in holes bored around the trunks controlled little-leaf and improved the quality of the fruit. H. Mowry and A. F. Camp in 1934 found that bronzing of tung trees in Florida could be overcome with either spray or soil applications of zinc sulfate. L. M. Barnette and J. A. Warner in 1935 and Barnette, Camp, Warner, and O. Gall in 1936 found that white bud of corn in Florida could be overcome with an application of zinc sulfate. They further found that peanuts, oats, velvet bean cowpeas, sugar cane and Napier grass responded to zinc sulfate. Rosette of pecans was found to result from Zn deficiency by A. O. Alben, J. R. Cole, and R. D. Lewis in 1932, and Alben and H. M. Boggs in 1936. Others noted that lack of Zn caused rosette in grapes and walnuts (15,21,33,46).

Interest in micronutrients broadened considerably in the 1940's. Use expanded into new areas and increased on lower per acre value agronomic crops. Up until this period, many nutrient deficiencies in agronomic crops were considered to be due to unfavorable moisture conditions or to damage from plant diseases or insects.

A major step in the late 1930's by the American Society of Agronomy brought together all of the available knowledge on plant nutrient deficiency symptoms. This project resulted in publication of *Hunger Signs in Crops* in 1941 by the Agronomy Society and the National Fertilizer Association. Most deficiency symptoms were illustrated with color photographs. This was followed in 1948 with the publication of *Diagnostic Techniques for Soils and Fertilizers* by the American Potash Institute. This book emphasized use of soil and plant analyses for determining nutrient deficiencies and updated information on the visual symptoms of malnutrition in plants. These two publications made it possible for nonexperts to identify the severe nutrient deficiencies, including micronutrients, that existed on farms at the time, or encouraged them to seek help from experts (3,4).

Estimates brought together by the U.S. Department of Agriculture during the 1920-1950 period gave a general picture of the use of micronutrients as fertilizer materials in the United States. They show that in 1920 only about 200 tons of copper sulfate ($CuSO_4 \cdot 5H_2O$) were used. The first use of manganese sulfate ($MnSO_4 \cdot 4H_2O$) was reported in 1925 with an estimated 100 tons applied. In 1939, an estimated that 7,000 tons of copper sulfate, 6,000 tons of manganese sulfate, and 1,200 tons of zinc sulfate were used (44).

The first attempt at making a micronutrient survey was made by the Production Marketing Administration in 1950. This showed that about 1,000 tons of B was consumed as fertilizer, 65 percent of it in states along the eastern coast; 5,900 tons of copper oxide (CuO) equivalent was used, 92 percent of it in Florida; 6,000 tons of manganese oxide (MnO) was used, 83 percent of it in Florida and 10 percent in Indiana; and 2,000 tons of zinc oxide (ZnO) was used, 64 percent in Florida, 18 percent in Georgia, and 11 percent in California. The PMA survey made in 1951 also showed that 260 tons of iron oxide (FeO) was consumed, half in Florida and practically all of the remainder in Arizona (40).

Until about the mid-1950's, the major micronutrient materials consumed were borax and the sulfates of Cu, Fe, Mn, and Zn, all of which were effective carriers for most soil and crop situations. No information was given on Mo.

The Changing Micronutrient Situation: 1955-1980

Considerable change took place in micronutrient needs, sales, types of materials, and end uses from about 1955 through 1980. Unfortunately no authentic data were published during the important transition period from 1951 through 1966 on sales, production, or consumption. In sharp contrast, considerable information was collected during the period on locations where micronutrient deficiencies existed and on the crops affected. Also, a vast literature developed on the role of micronutrients in plants and animals, on methods to diagnose deficiencies, and on the changes that micronutrient materials undergo upon application to the soil.

Deficiency Surveys—Several national surveys on the extent of micronutrient deficiencies were conducted from 1960 through 1966. The first, made in 1960, was conducted by the Trace Element Committee of the Council of Fertilizer Application. This was followed by a more complete survey in 1965 by the Soil Testing and Plant Analysis Committee of the Soil Science Society of America. The two Committee reports showed the same general distribution patterns of the individual nutrient deficiencies among the states although the second survey reported fewer deficiencies. The more comprehensive 1965 survey showed B deficiencies in 27 states, Cu in 5, Fe in 14, Mn in 10, Mo in 9, and Zn in 24. An independent survey by the Allied Chemical Corporation showed an even larger number of states reporting deficiencies than did the 1960 survey (9,20,62).

The surveys also yielded important information on the crops and soils where the deficiencies occurred. Boron was reported widely deficient, especially on alfalfa and sugar beets, and on crops grown on highly leached acid soils and on alkaline soils during periods of drought.

Table 11.1. Micronutrients Sold for Fertilizer in U.S. (16-19).

Element	1967-68	1969-70	1974-75	1979-80
	\multicolumn{4}{c}{Short tons of element}			
Copper	2,400	8	525	1,580
Iron	3,260	3,620	2,130	5,010
Manganese	10,670	13,510	11,330	15,060
Zinc	14,500	18,270	14,030	45,700
Molybdenum	80	70	143	140

Copper deficiencies, the least widespread, were found mainly in peat and muck soils. Iron deficiencies were found to be worst in the more arid regions on alkaline soils, and on the limited acreages of high-lime soils in humid regions. Manganese was most deficient in humid regions in plants growing on alkaline peat and muck soils, particularly those that were alkaline or heavily limed. Molybdenum deficiencies were greatest in legumes, citrus, and vegetables grown on highly leached acid soils. Zinc deficiencies occurred in a wide range of soils and crops.

Micronutrient Use—The U.S. Department of Agriculture in the 1967-1968 fertilizer year began publishing annual summaries of the use of Cu, Fe, Mn, Mo, and Zn as fertilizers. The data were obtained from all firms known to be primary producers of the five micronutrients for use in direct application or in mixed fertilizers (Table 11.1). Sales of B were not included.

Over the 12-year period ending June 30, 1980, Mn and Zn together accounted for over 80 percent of all micronutrient sales. Manganese sales during the period remained fairly constant from year to year. Zn use appeared to increase rapidly in 1977-78; however, this was related to a change in reporting which included use of industrial by-products as fertilizer. By far the greatest use of Mn throughout the period was in the South Atlantic, East North Central and West North Central regions. Zinc use, on the other hand, was fairly high in all regions except the New England, Mid-Atlantic, and East South Central regions. The large increase in Zn in the late 1970's was due mostly to substantial increases in the West North Central and Pacific regions.

Copper use throughout the 12-year period was consistently largest in the South Atlantic region, ranging from 53 to 77 percent of the all Cu used. The second largest user was the Mid-Atlantic region which ran from 7 to 21 percent of the total. Copper use in all regions except the Mountain region declined, reaching a low of 525 tons in the 1975 fertilizer year. However, by 1980 the tonnage had recovered. The decline apparently was due to lower recommendations for Cu use.

The regional data for Fe appear rather erratic between years with none of the regions standing out consistently as high consuming regions. About 80 percent of the Mo is used in the central part of the country–the East and West North Central regions and the East and West South Central regions (16,17,18,19). Although no official data on B use are available, B consumption in recent years is estimated at 3,000 to 5,000 tons of B per year (2). Deficiencies apparently are more extensive than for any of the other micronutrients (29).

Sales tonnage data can be misleading if used as an indicator of the comparative importance of a given micronutrient element because of the wide differences in per-acre application rates of the different nutrients. Application rates of Mo range from about 0.01 to 0.06 pounds per acre. Boron ranges from 0.5 to 4.0 pounds, and Fe and Zn from 3 to 10 pounds. The highest per-acre rates of application are for Cu and Mn which range from 5 to 20 pounds (36). The lower rate indicated for each element is associated with foliar application and the higher with broadcast application. Band application rates are usually intermediate. Too much B or Cu in the soil either from a large initial application or from residual accumulation can damage crops. Excessive use of Mo on forage and feed crops can cause toxicity problems in livestock. The small amounts of micronutrients applied per acre plus the difficulty in spreading the materials uniformly encouraged their incorporation with solid and liquid NPK fertilizers and in bulk blends (51).

Marketing—Prior to the 1950's, micronutrient fertilizers were marketed to farmers largely by the micronutrient producers who sold the materials directly or through dealers to farmers or to mixed fertilizer manufacturers either directly or through dealers or brokers. The farmers or commercial growers applied the materials or mixes directly to the soil, or applied the individual micronutrients in sprays to the crop. In California and some of the other Western States, small amounts of borax and sulfates of Cu, Mn, and Zn were applied to the soil through irrigation systems (43). U.S. Department of Agriculture data for the years 1944 through 1952 indicate that Mn and Zn were applied in much greater amounts from fertilizer mixture than from direct application of individual materials (data are not available for other micronutrients) (44). Most of the micronutrient-containing NPK mixtures were prepared for use on specific soil areas or on specific crops. Special mixtures containing Cu, Mn, and Zn especially were used on the peat and muck soils of the Florida Everglades, and along with B on organic soils in other states. Special citrus fertilizers also were marketed in Florida containing besides NPK, Cu, Mn, Zn and sometimes B and Fe (43).

Considerable change began in the mid-1950's in the marketing of micronutrients. Not only did the demand for Zn and Mn increase appreciably but numerous companies in addition to basic producers and brokers began marketing micronutrients. Most micronutrient

Table 11.2. Number of firms marketing micronutrients.

Nutrient	1970	1980
Boron	3	15
Copper	20	31
Iron	19	38
Manganese	20	38
Zinc	22	49
Molybdenum	1	9
Mixtures	20	46

sources are sold singly by manufacturers to wholesale distributors and to members of the fertilizer industry who produce fertilizers in final form for sale to farmers. Sellers listed in *Farm Chemicals Handbook* for 1970 and 1980 (23, 24) are shown in Table 11.2.

Changes in the marketing of NPK fertilizers in the mid-1950's brought about related changes in the marketing of micronutrients. The system for marketing micronutrient-containing NPK fertilizers shifted from one based mostly upon bagged-pulverized products to one based on bulk-granular and liquid-mixed products. Bulk blends, granulated-homogeneous NPK fertilizers, and fluid-mixed fertilizers dominated the field. Custom formulation to meet customers' specific nutrient needs along with custom application became common. All of this resulted in more uniform application of micronutrients, reduced costs of spreading, and broadened the use to include large-acreage field crops (30).

All of the changes occurring in the marketing of micronutrients have not proven beneficial. Chemical reactions can occur when micronutrients are mixed with certain other fertilizer components which can reduce the solubility of the micronutrient and reduce its availability for plant uptake. Segregation of micronutrient particles can occur in bulk blends, leading to non-uniform application. Also, some producers add micronutrients to NPK fertilizers on the premise that the addition serves as insurance against the occurrence of a deficiency or that the elements will serve as a maintenance program. Agronomists generally frown on this so-called "shotgun approach" inasmuch as the added nutrients are not likely to be needed, or, in cases of real deficiency, the rates applied may be inadequate (47).

Micronutrient Sources and Materials

Of the six micronutrients actually used in fertilizers, four—Cu, Fe, Mn, and Zn—are metal cations (metal elements that carry a positive charge).

Boron occurs always in combination with oxygen. Molybdenum occurs as molybdate anions with a negative charge. The amounts of these elements in nature vary greatly, ranging from Fe which is the fourth most abundant element in the earth's surface, to Mo which is very scarce.

The original sources of all six micronutrients were commercially mined ore or brine deposits which, with the exception of Mn, are located in the United States. Some of these require only refinement to make them satisfactory for use as a fertilizer material. Others are available as industrial by-products or are subjected to chemical changes that produce more desirable materials. The inorganic compounds may be incorporated into frits (glasses) formed by fusing with a silicate or phosphate matrix. Synthetic chelates and natural organic complexes are made into desirable carriers by reacting with metallic salts.

Table 11.3, which will be referred to throughout this section, lists the leading materials providing the different micronutrient elements.

Inorganic Salts

Depending on the micronutrient, inorganic salts include mined ores, manufactured oxides, and metallic salts of sulfates, carbonates, chlorides, and nitrates. Of the various micronutrient sources they usually are the least costly per unit of micronutrient, but they may not be the most effective.

Boron is obtained mostly as sodium borates extracted from old geological lake deposits in the Western States. The inorganic sources used in fertilizers are largely sodium borates of different degrees of hydration. The major materials are borax, $Na_2B_4O_7 \cdot 10H_2O$; sodium tetraborate (sold under the trade names "Fertilizer Borate" with numbers indicating the B_2O_3 content in percent) $Na_2B_4O_7 \cdot 5H_2O$ or Borate-46; $Na_2B_4O_7$ or Borate-65; and sodium pentaborate $Na_2B_{10}O_{16} \cdot 10H_2O$. Solubor, a trade name for a highly water-soluble mixture of finely ground, partially dehydrated sodium borates, is designed primarily for use in foliar and fluid fertilizers. Boric acid, H_3BO_3, finds use in small amounts in foliar application. In recent years, borates also have become available in fine, coarse, and granulated grades, the latter being designed for use in bulk blends (47,52).

Copper is derived from copper ores purified by flotation and roasted to form copper oxides. Reacting the oxides with sulfuric acid forms copper sulfates. Copper sulfate is highly soluble and is used both for soil and spray application. The copper oxides, CuO and Cu_2O, although less soluble than copper sulfate, are satisfactory for use on acid soils. Continued applications of Cu to soils can result in residual build-up and cause toxicity problems. Also, high concentrations of available Cu in soils can depress plant uptake of Fe, Zn, and Mo (47,52).

Table 11.3. Micronutrient sources and their nutrient contents (47, 2, 66, 12, 49, 50).

Source and chemical formula	Percent element
Borax, $Na_2B_4O_7 \cdot 10H_2O$	11
Borate 48, $Na_2B_4O_7 \cdot 5H_2O$	15
Borate 68, $Na_2B_4O_7$	21
Solubor, $Na_2B_4O_7$	17-20
Boric acid, H_3BO_3	17
Boron frits	10
Copper sulfate monohydrate, $CuSO_4 \cdot H_2O$	35
Copper sulfate pentahydrate, $CuSO_4 \cdot 5H_2O$	25
Cupric oxide, CuO	75
Cuprous oxide, Cu_2O	89
Copper frits	10-50
Natural organic complexes	5-6
Ferrous sulfate, $FeSO_4 \cdot 7H_2O$	20
Ferric sulfate, $Fe_2(SO_4)_3 \cdot 9H_2O$	20
Ferrous ammonium sulfate, $FeSO_4 \cdot 7H_2O \cdot (NH_4)_2SO_4$	14
Iron frits	10-40
FeHEDTA	5-12
FeEDDHA	6
Natural organic complexes	5-9
Manganese sulfate, $MnSO_4 \cdot 4H_2O$	23-28
Manganese oxide, MnO	41-68
Manganese frits	10-35
Natural organic complexes*	5-9
Ammonium molybdate $(NH_4)_6Mo_7O_{24} \cdot 2H_2O$	54
Sodium molybdate, $Na_2MoO_4 \cdot 2H_2O$	39
Molybdenum trioxide, MoO_3	66
Molybdenum frits	1-30
Zinc sulfate, $ZnSO_4 \cdot H_2O$	36
Zinc oxide, ZnO	50-80
Zinc carbonate, $ZnCO_3$	52-56
Zinc frits	10-30
Natural organic complexes	3-12

Inorganic Fe sources include both the ferric (Fe^{3+}) and ferrous (Fe^{2+}) forms. Ferrous sulfate ($FeSO_4 \cdot 7H_2O$) is the most common source and is most used in foliar sprays. Neither the ferric [$Fe_2(SO_4)_3 \cdot 9H_2O$] nor ferrous forms are very effective when soil applied since the ferrous form converts to insoluble compounds and the ferric form already is relatively insoluble. Ferric oxide is incorporated in homogeneous granular fertil-

This shows the approximate amounts needed to correct boron deficiency on 10 acres of corn and molybdenum deficiency on 10 acres of soybeans. (John Williams--TVA)

izers but its solubility is low. The iron sulfates are usually by-products of various industries including the paint industry (47,52).

The manganese ores consumed in the United States are imported and include pyrolusite (MnO_2), manganite $MnO(OH)$, and hausmannite (Mn_3O_4). The ores are ground and reduced to MnO or reacted with sulfuric acid to form manganese sulfate which is water soluble and widely used both for soil and foliar application. Manganese oxide is only slightly water soluble but compares favorably with the sulfate when applied on acid soils. Less-used carriers are $MnCO_3$ and MnO_2 (47,52).

The most abundant Mo mineral is molybdenum sulfide (MoS_2) which is associated with granitic rocks. It is mined in this country in Colorado. It also is a by-product of copper mining in Utah. The primary micronutrient materials produced from the mineral are sodium molybdate $Na_2MoO_4 \cdot 2H_2O$ and ammonium molybdate, $(NH_4)_6Mo_7O_{24} \cdot 2H_2O$, both of which are quite soluble. The molybdenum sulfide mineral is not used to any extent as a material since its solubility is low. In order to spread the small amounts of Mo required evenly it is desirable to mix the nutrient material with other fertilizer materials either in liquid or solid form. Molybdenum also is applied in foliar sprays and application on seed is a fairly common practice. Too much Mo on forage or feed crops can be toxic to livestock (38,47,52).

Zinc is mined chiefly as a mineral sphalerite (ZnS) which is roasted to form zinc oxide. Zinc sulfate is produced by reacting the zinc oxide with sulfuric acid (usually spent or by-product acid). Partially acidified products also are produced. Zinc as a by-product is recovered by various industries in flue and baghouse dusts and purified. Zinc sulfate is the most-used inorganic source followed by zinc oxide which, although somewhat less effective, also is less costly. Soil application is by far the most-used method for supplying the nutrient to the crop. Zinc deficiencies generally are intensified where large phosphate applications are made or by cold, wet weather during the early growing period. Zinc sulfate and other sulfate-bearing micronutrient materials contain appreciable amounts of impurities when spent or by-product sulfuric acid is used in their manufacture which makes them undesirable for foliar application (47,52).

Frits

Fritted micronutrient carriers are produced by incorporating one or more micronutrient-containing salts into a silicate or phosphate glass matrix to form a slow-release product. The process involves drying and mixing the micronutrient salt, usually oxides, with the matrix material, fusing the mix in a smelting furnace, and quenching the molten material, drying and grinding into a powder. The solubility of the salts in the frits is controlled by the particle-size distribution and the composition of the matrix. One or more micronutrients may be included in the same mix and the end product may be either compacted or granulated. Frits extend the time that a highly soluble or reactive micronutrient material will remain available in the soil for plant uptake. Phosphate glasses are more soluble than the more widely used silicate glasses (34,51).

Glass matrixes containing mineral substances were first investigated in the 1930's (34). The results indicated that the slowly soluble carriers would be superior to soluble forms, particularly in the case of B. Significant use of frits as a micronutrient carrier did not become important until after the mid-1950's when a demand developed for premium fertilizers containing both macro- and micronutrients and for custom-mixed fertilizers to meet needs of individual farms. Frits have been used as carriers for each of the six micronutrients (47,50;51).

Synthetic Chelates

An important advance in the field of micronutrients occurred in the early 1950's with the introduction of synthetic chelates as alternative carriers of the metallic cations Fe, Cu, Mn and Zn. Although their high cost per unit of micronutrient limits their use, they are usually much more effective than inorganic sources under some soil conditions, and are especially effective when applied in foliar sprays. The relative costs of chelates are many times higher per pound of element than inorganic sources, although much lower amounts per acre are required.

Synthetic chelates are complex organic compounds that hold a single metal cation tightly in a cyclic structure. They are formed by the reaction of metal chlorides or metal oxides with a sodium chelate. The chelates protect the metal cation against reactions with the soil but leave the element in a form that can be readily absorbed by the plant roots. Chelated elements are easily absorbed through the leaves from foliar sprays. The term "chelate" is derived from the Greek word "chela" or "claw." It first came into use to describe this kind of molecular structure in 1920. Iron chelate, the first chelate used as a fertilizer material, came into use in Florida in the early 1950's (13,39,47).

Several forms of chelating compounds are used as carriers for the four metallic micronutrients. These include EDTA, ethylene-diaminetetraacetic acid, the most-used chelating agent; EDDHA, ethylenediaminehydrophenylacetic acid; HEDTA, hydroxyethylene-diaminetetraacetic acid; and DTPA, diethylenetriaminepentaacetic acid. Certain of the chelating agents are more effective than others, depending upon the micronutrient element, the nature of the soil, the crop, whether or not it is incorporated in mixed fertilizers, and the kinds of NPK materials used. Chelates used as a source of Fe are FeEDTA, FeEDDHA, FeDTPA, and FeHEDTA. These can be used both in soil and foliar application. FeDTPA is effective only for soil application on acid soils. FeEDDHA is a good source over a wide range of soil pH's and on calcareous soils. FeHEDTA is intermediate in behavior between the two. The most frequently used Zn chelate is ZnEDTA, especially in liquid fertilizers. CuEDTA is somewhat more effective than inorganic sources and is frequently added to liquid fertilizers. MnEDTA is the most-used Mn chelate, although synthetic Mn chelates generally are not widely used (26,52). Most chelates are sold in liquid form since drying to form powder materials adds to the cost. The liquids are sold mainly for fluid fertilizers. Dry chelates are incorporated in granular fertilizers, but their use is greatest for specialty lawn and garden fertilizers (47).

Natural Organic Complexes

Natural organic complexes were introduced in the 1960's by reacting micronutrient metals (Cu, Fe, Mn, Zn) with lignosulfonates, phenols, and polyflavinoids–by-products of the wood pulp industry. Digest liquors from the wood processing in the calcium or sodium form are concentrated to about 40 percent solids. Soluble micronutrient sources, usually sulfates, and sometimes oxides, are added to form the complexes. Digest liquors used in the sulfide process produce lignosulfonates directly while those from the Kraft process must be sulfonated separately. Chelates also can be formed from wood pulp liquors. The most common complexes contain Zn or Fe. The organic complexes usually are not as effective as the synthetic chelates but cost less (47,50,51).

REFERENCES

1. Allison, R. V. 1932. The importance of the use of copper, manganese, and zinc salts in the agricultural development of the lowmoor soils in the Florida Everglades. In *The International Congress Soil Science*

Transactions, 2nd Moscow, 1930. Comm. VI. Subcomm. Peat Soils, pp. 257-275.
2. Allred, S. E. 1983. Micronutrient fertilizers in the United States. In *Fertilizers*, International Conf., London, Nov. 13-16, 1983. Proc. of the Conf., Vol. I preprints. Ed. by A. I. Moore.
3. American Potash Institute. 1948. *Diagnostic Techniques for Soils and Crops.* Ed. by H. M. Kitchen. Publ. by Amer. Potash Inst., Washington, D.C.
4. American Society of Agronomy and the National Fertilizer Assoc., 1941. *Hunger Signs in Crops.* Ed. by G. Hambridge. Publ. by Amer. Soc. Agron. and the National Fert. Assoc., Washington, D.C.
5. Anderson, A. J. 1956. Molybdenum as a fertilizer. In *Advances in Agronomy*, Vol. 8, pp. 163-202. Publ. by Academic Press Inc., New York.
6. Beaton, J. D. and R. L. Fox. 1971. Production, marketing, and use of sulfur products. In *Fertilizer Technology and Use*, pp. 335-374. Publ. by the Soil Sci. Soc. America, Madison, Wisc.
7. Beaton, J. D. and D. W. Bixby. 1974. Mixing techniques of secondary elements. *Fertilizer Solutions Magazine* May-June, 1974. 18(3):26-48.
8. Bixby, D. W., S. L. Tisdall and E. A. Krysl. 1975. Secondary nutrients in liquid fertilizers. Sulphur: Part 2 - Use and application. *Fertilizer Solutions Magazine* 19(1): 60,62,64,66.
9. Berger, K. C. 1962. Micronutrient deficiencies in the United States. *Jour. Agr. & Food Chem.* 10:178-181.
10. _____. 1965. *Introductory Soils*. Publ. by The MacMillan Co., New York.
11. _____ and P. F. Pratt. 1963. Advances in secondary and micro-nutrient fertilization. In *Fertilizer Technology and Use*. Ed. by M. H. McVickar, et al., pp. 287-340. Publ. by Soil Sci. Soc. Amer., Madison, Wisc.
12. Bridges, J. D. 1982. *Fertilizer Trends 1982.* TVA, Muscle Shoals, Ala.
13. Brown, J. C. and L. O. Tiffin. 1962. Properties of chelates and their use in crop production. *Jour. Agr. & Food Chem.* 10:192-195.
14. Camp, A. F., H. D. Chapman, G. M. Bahrt, and E. R. Parker. 1941. Symptoms of citrus malnutrition. In *Hunger Signs in Crops*. Ed. by G. Hambridge, pp. 267-299. Publ. by Amer. Soc. Agron. and the National Fert. Assoc., Washington, D.C.
15. Collings, G. H. 1941. *Commercial Fertilizers*, 3rd edition. The Blakiston Co., Philadelphia.
16. Crop Reporting Board. 1968. *Commercial fertilizer consumption in the United States,*. Statistical Reporting Service, U.S. Dept. Agric., Washington, D.C.
17. _____. 1970. *Commercial fertilizer consumption*.
18. _____. 1975. *Commercial fertilizer consumption*.
19. _____. 1980. *Commercial fertilizer consumption*.
20. Cunningham, H. G. 1972. Trends in the use of micronutrients. In *Micronutrients in Agriculture*. Ed. by J. J. Mortvedt, et al, pp. 419-430. Publ. by Soil Sci. Soc. Amer., Madison, Wisc.
21. Davidson, O. W. 1941. *Nutrient Deficiency Symptoms in Deciduous Fruits.* Ed. by G. Hambridge. Publ. by Amer. Soc. Agron. and National Fert. Assoc., Washington, D.C.
22. DeTurk, E. E. 1941. Plant nutrient deficiency symptoms in legumes. In *Hunger Signs in Crops.* Ed. by G. Hambridge, pp. 241-258. Publ. by Amer. Soc. Agronomy and the National Fertilizer Assoc., Washington, D.C.
23. Farm Chemicals. 1970. Who's selling micronutrients. *Farm Chemicals Handbook* 1970, pp. C121-C125. Meister Publishing Co., Willoughby, Ohio.

24. _____. 1980. Who's selling micronutrients. In *Farm Chemicals Handbook* 1980, pp. B46-B58.
25. _____. 1981. Pesticide dictionary. In *Farm Chemicals Handbook* 1981, pp. C3- C375.
26. Follett, R. H., L. S. Murphy, and R. L. Donahue. 1981. *Fertilizers and Soil Amendments,* Prentice-Hall, Inc., Englewood Cliffs, New Jersey.
27. Garner, W. W. and D. E. Brown. 1919. *Experiments with tobacco.* Maryland Expt. Sta. Bull. No. 255.
28. _____, J. E. McMurtrey, and E. G. Moss. 1922. Sand drown, a chlorosis of tobacco and other plants resulting from magnesium deficiency. *Science* 56:341-342.
29. Gupta, U. C. 1979. Boron nutrition of crops. In *Advances in Agronomy.* Ed. by N. C. Brady, pp. 273-307, Academic Press, N. Y., London, Toronto.
30. Hargett, N. L. and R. Pay. 1980. Retail marketing of fertilizers in the U.S. *Proc. 30th Annual Mtg. Fertilizer Industry Round Table,* pp. 82-95.
31. Harre, E. A., M. N. Goodson, and J. D. Bridges. 1976. *Fertilizer Trends 1976.* National Fertilizer Development Center, TVA, Muscle Shoals, Ala.
32. Hewitt, E. J. 1963. Mineral nutrition of plants in culture media. In *Plant Physiology, a Treatise, Vol. 3, Inorganic Nutrition of Plants.* Ed. by F. C. Stewart, pp. 97-133, Academic Press, Inc., New York, London.
33. Hoffer, G. N. 1941. Deficiency symptoms of corn and small grains. In *Hunger Signs in Crops.* Ed. by G. Hambridge, pp. 55-98, Publ. by Amer. Soc. Agron. and the National Fert. Assoc., Washington, D.C.
34. Holden, E. R., N. R. Page, and J. I. Wear. 1962. Micronutrient glasses in crop production. J. *Agr. and Food Chem.* 10:188-192.
35. Huschke, H. A. 1953. Resources and processing of materials containing calcium, magnesium, and sulfur. In *Fertilizer Technology and Resources in the United States.* Ed. by K. D. Jacob, pp. 323-353, Academic Press, Inc., New York, N.Y.
36. International Fertilizer Development Center. 1985. *Fertilizer Manual.* Ed. by T. P. Hignett. Publ. by Martinus Nijhoff/ Dr. W. Junk, Dordrecht, Boston, Lancaster.
37. Jones, H. A. and B. E. Brown. 1941. Plant nutrient deficiency symptoms in the potato. In *Hunger Signs in Crops.* Ed. by G. Hambridge, pp. 99-124. Publ. by Amer. Soc. Agron. and the National Fert. Assoc., Washington, D.C.
38. Krauskopf, K. B. 1972. Geochemistry of micronutrients. In *Micronutrients in Agriculture.* Ed. by J. J. Mortvedt, et al, pp. 2-40. Publ. by Soil Science Soc. Amer., Madison, Wisc.
39. Leonard, C. D. and I. Stewart. 1953. An available source of iron for plants. *Proc. Amer. Soc. Hort. Sci.* 62:103-110.
40. Lowe, J. N. 1953. Consumption of minor or trace elements as fertilizers. *National Fertilizer Review* 28(4):8-9.
41. McMurtrey, J. E. 1941. Plant nutrient deficiency in tobacco. In *Hunger Signs in Crops.* Ed. by G. Hambridge, pp. 15-54. Publ. by Amer. Soc. Agron. and the National Fert. Assoc.
42. _____. 1948, Visual symptoms of malnutrition in plants. In *Diagnostic Techniques for Soils and Crops.* Ed. by H. B. Kitchen, pp. 231-289, American Potash Institute, Washington, D.C.
43. Mehring, A. L. 1953. Special fertilizers, special uses for fertilizer and non-fertilizer sources of plant nutrients. In *Fertilizer Technology and Resources in the United States.* Ed. by K. D. Jacob, pp. 413-438, Academic Press Inc., New York.

44. ____, J. R. Adams, and K. D. Jacob. 1957. *Statistics in fertilizers and liming materials in the United States.* Agricultural Research Service, U.S. Dept. Agric. Bull. No. 191, Washington, D.C.
45. Melsted, S. W. 1953. Some observed calcium deficiencies in corn under field conditions. *Soil Sci. Soc. Amer. Proc.* 17:52-54.
46. Miller, E. C. 1938. *Plant Physiology*, 2nd ed., McGraw-Hill Book Co., Inc., New York, London.
47. Mortvedt, J. J. 1979. *Micronutrient fertilizer technology and use in the United States.* Paper presented at the India/FAO/Norway Seminar on Micronutrients in Agriculture, New Delhi, India, Sept. 1979.
48. ____. 1980. Do you really know your fertilizers zinc and copper. *Farm Chemicals* 143(11):56,58,60.
49. ____. 1980. Do you really know your fertilizers iron, manganese, molybdenum. *Farm Chemicals* 143(12):42-43,46-47.
50. ____. 1984. Focus on micronutrients. *Farm Chemicals* 147(12):115-116.
51. ____ and H. G. Cunningham. Production, marketing, and use of other secondary and micronutrient fertilizers. In *Fertilizer Technology and Use,* 2nd ed. Ed. by R, A. Olsen, et al., pp. 413-454. Publ. by Soil Sci. Soc. Amer,, Madison, Wisc.
52. Murphy, L. S. and L. M. Walsh. 1972. Correction of micronutrient deficiencies. In *Micronutrients in Agriculture.* Ed. by J. J. Mortvedt, et al. pp. 347-387. Publ. by Soil Sci. Soc. Amer., Madison, Wisc.
53. Parker, F. W. 1932. The importance of calcium and magnesium to the nitrogen fertilizer industry. *American Fertilizer* 76(2):13-15, 28-32.
54. Pierre, W. H. 1931. Effect of nitrogenous fertilizers on soil acidity. *Ind. Eng. Chem.* 23:1440-1443.
55. Reed, H. S. 1942. *A Short History of the Plant Sciences.* Chronica Botanica Co., Waltham, Mass.
56. Reuther, W. 1957. Copper and soil fertility. In *Soil, Yearbook of Agriculture 1957,* pp. 128-135. U.S. Dept. of Agric., Washington, D.C.
57. Sauchelli, V. 1969. *Trace Elements in Agriculture.* Publ. by Van Nostrum Reinhold Co., New York, Toronto, London.
58. Schreiner, O. 1928. Use of manganese in fertilizer. *Amer. Fert.* 69(11):40-42.
59. ____. 1930. New factors in fertilizer practices. *Comm. Fert.* 41(4):24-30.
60. Singleton, R. H. 1978. *Potash.* Bureau of Mines Mineral Commodity Profiles MCP-ll, Washington, D.C.
61. Skinner, J. J. 1941. Plant nutrient deficiencies in vegetable or truck-crop plants. In *Hunger Signs in Crops,.* Ed. by E. Hambridge, pp. 149-178. Publ. by Amer. Soc. Agron. amd the Nat. Fert. Assn.
62. Soil Testing and Plant Analyses Comm., Soil Sci. Soc. Amer. 1965. *A survey of micronutrient deficiencies in the USA and means for correcting them.* Publ. by Soil Sci. Soc. Amer., Madison, Wisc.
63. Stiles, W. 1946. *Trace Elements in Plants and Animals.* Cambridge at the University Press, New York, the MacMillan Co.
64. Stout, P. R. and C. M. Johnson. 1957. Trace elements. In *The Yearbook of Agriculture,* 1957, pp. 139 150. U.S. Dept. Agric., Washington, D.C.
65. Tisdale, S. L. 1974. Sulphur: Part I, and introduction. *Fertilizer Solutions Magazine,* 18(6):8-10, 16-18.
66. Turner, J. 1980. Boron: a major micronutrient. *Farm Chemicals* 143(2):36- 37,40.
67. Wofford, I. M. 1974. Secondary nutrients in liquid fertilizers: calcium. *Fertilizer Solutions Magazine,* 18(5):56-64.

12

Mixed Fertilizers 1920-1980

The production and marketing of mixed fertilizers changed entirely during the 1920-1980 period. The first change of importance occurred in the late 1920's and early 1930's when ammoniation of superphosphate was made feasible by the availability of domestically synthesized ammonia. The process involved neutralizing the acidity of the superphosphate with the low-cost ammonia to convert part of the phosphate to ammonium phosphates, ammonium sulfate, and dicalcium phosphate. The chemical reactions improved the physical condition of the product and the heat of reaction helped remove unwanted moisture from the product. Concurrently, the introduction of ammoniating solutions containing ammonium nitrate and urea in addition to ammonia permitted adding more low-cost nitrogen. By 1950, these new advances had virtually eliminated the old type mixes containing only solid materials (67).

Revolutionary changes came to the mixed fertilizer industry in the 1950's and early 1960's. During this short period homogeneous ammoniation-granulation NPK plants appeared along with bulk blend, clear liquid, and suspension fertilizer plants. The ammonia in the formulation cost less than solid nitrogen materials, and the heat evolved was used to granulate homogeneous NPK products. The same equipment with minor modifications could be used to produce ammonium phosphates and ammonium sulfate. Bulk blending, in contrast, was a dry-mixing operation which essentially replaced the old dry pulverized mixes with granular bulk materials. Blenders bought granular materials directly from primary producers. After blending to the desired grades, the blender sold the product directly to the farmer, mostly in bulk form (67).

Clear liquid mixed fertilizers gained market significance during the 1950's and 1960's. They have all of their plant nutrients in solution form, are excellent carriers of pesticides and certain micronutrients, and can be applied easily and accurately. Their major disadvantage was their inability to hold much K. Suspension fertilizers were developed to increase nutrient contents, including potassium, beyond those of clear liquids in order for fluids to compete better with solid mixes.

Suspensions achieved higher grades by using a suspending agent (usually attapulgite clay) to suspend finely divided crystals and reduce settling. Both fluid fertilizers were easy to produce in simple plants. Like bulk blenders, the fluid mixers purchased their fertilizer materials and marketed directly to farmers.

Production, marketing, and application of mixed fertilizers underwent tremendous change from 1920 through 1980. This is the subject of this chapter.

Mixed Fertilizers: 1920-1950

Nutrient Content

The average primary nutrient content of mixed fertilizers in the United States had not changed from 1890 through 1920. However, as shown in Table 12.1, the nutrient content gradually increased during the 1920-1950 period. The single material most responsible for the increase was high-grade potassium chloride (60-62% K_2O).

Nitrogen and P_2O_5 contents increased only moderately with most of the increase in the 1940's. During the 1920-1950 period, approximately two-thirds of all fertilizers consumed in the country were mixed fertilizers (the remainder was largely direct-application materials). Over 90 percent of the mixed fertilizers consumed were NPK mixtures. PK mixtures accounted for 4 to 6 percent of the total, and NP mixtures 2 to 3 percent (57).

The average nutrient content of mixed fertilizers varied among regions. U.S. Department of Agriculture data published in 1950 show that the older fertilizer-using areas–the South Atlantic States, the East South Central, the West South Central, and the Middle Atlantic States–averaged 21.7 percent in primary nutrients, while the newer fertilizer-using states averaged 28.15 percent. Greatest users of the NP grades were the Mountain, Pacific, and West North Central States where the soils are naturally high in available potassium. Highest users of PK grades were the East North Central States, the South Atlantic States, the East South Central States, and the Middle Atlantic States (66).

Materials Used in Manufacture

Materials used in the manufacture of mixed fertilizers underwent considerable change during the 1920-1950 period. Nitrogen materials changed from natural organics, Chilean nitrate, and certain by-products to materials derived from synthetic ammonia. Natural organics supplied 34 percent of the N in mixed fertilizers in 1920, but only one-tenth as much in 1950. Synthetic ammonium sulfate appeared and exceeded by-product ammonium sulfate by 1950 and ammoniating solutions and ammonium nitrate became important mixed fertilizer

Table 12.1. Consumption and Nutrient Content of Mixed Fertilizers (57).

Year	Consumption	Primary Nutrient Content			
		N	P_2O_5	K_2O	Total
	1,000 tons material	%	%	%	%
1880	350	2.40	9.10	2.00	13.50
1900	1,770	2.00	9.40	2.50	13.90
1920	4,062	2.30	9.20	2.40	13.90
1930	5,617	3.10	9.80	5.00	17.90
1940	5,513	3.80	9.63	6.49	19.92
1950	13,033	4.06	11.00	8.52	23.58

ingredients. Normal superphosphate, the principal supplier of P, increased in nutrient content from 16.7 percent P_2O_5 in 1920 to 20.1 percent in 1950. Potassium chloride containing 50 and 60 percent K_2O largely replaced low-grade potash materials, kainite and manure salts, which had been important in the 1920's. Potassium sulfate, containing about 50 percent K_2O, 18 percent sulfur, and practically no Cl, found use primarily in mixed fertilizers formulated for tobacco (24,50,57).

All in all, 50 or more materials were used in mixed fertilizers in the United States as late as 1947. Seven of these accounted for 85 percent of the 11.6 million tons of materials in mixed fertilizers (24).

Mixed Fertilizers Grades

Commercially mixed fertilizers were produced during this period in a multitude of low-nutrient grades. (A fertilizer grade is the respective percentages of N, P_2O_5 and K_2O.) Usually more than 800 different grades were sold annually in the continental United States with individual states offering from 20 to 50 each. However, about 80 grades accounted for about 90 percent with the leading seven grades alone accounting for nearly half (Table 12.2) (54,66).

A sizable portion of the weight of mixed fertilizers during the 1920-1950 period consisted of materials containing no primary nutrients. Adding inert, make-weight fillers such as sand, earth, cinders, and sawdust was a common practice. Other nonprimary nutrient materials included gypsum, dolomitic limestone and dolomite, and various organic materials to "improve the physical condition of the mixture." Use of inert fillers and secondary nutrient materials was greatest in the Southern States where farmers traditionally had applied low-grade mixtures. In 1934, fertilizers in Virginia, South Carolina, North Carolina, Georgia, Florida, Alabama, and Mississippi averaged 18 percent by weight of nonprimary nutrient materials (22,24,52,53).

Table 12.2. Seven Mixed Fertilizer Grades Used in Largest Tonnages (57).

1925		1939		1950	
Grade	Percent	Grade	Percent	Grade	Percent
3-8-3	20.8	3-8-5	9.0	3-12-12	10.2
4-8-4	5.7	2-12-6	8.6	5-10-5	9.3
2-8-2	4.6	4-8-4	8.2	2-12-6	7.3
2-10-2	3.4	3-8-3	7.4	3-12-6	6.7
3-10-3	3.4	6-8-4	3.1	3-9-6	.5
3-9-3	3.2	4-8-6	2.7	4-10-6	5.2
3-8-5	3.0	5-7-5	2.4	4-8-6	4.7
Total percent sold	44.1		41.4		49.9
Number of grades reported	886		982		838

Though not new in the United States, high-analysis mixed fertilizers were seldom used. The earliest high-analysis product was imported from Germany in 1895. In 1906, the Eastern Chemical Company of Boston apparently produced a 12.5-25-25 grade by mixing potassium nitrate and ammonium phosphate. In the early 1920's, the Synthetic Nitrogen Products Corporation in New York imported two grades of "Nitrophoska" from Europe having analyses of 15-11-26.5 and 16.5-16.5-20. A few manufacturers in New England began producing mixed fertilizers that were multiples of such grades as 3-12-3, 4-8-4, and 4-8-10. Included among the multiple-strength manufacturers was the International Agricultural Corporation at its plant in Woburn, Massachusetts. The Eastern States Farmers Exchange in 1924 began producing a 17 percent N-P_2O_5-K_2O mix which was eventually doubled to 34 percent. A. W. Higgins at Presque Isle, Maine, produced high-analysis mixtures for use on potatoes, and the Armour Fertilizer Works also began marketing concentrated mixtures. Unfortunately, high-analysis mixes were not well received, due to lack of secondary elements or to bad caking problems (50).

Attempts to Introduce High Analyses Mixes

It became apparent to the large fertilizer manufacturers and agronomists at the land-grant institutions by 1919 that it would be desirable to increase the nutrient content of mixed fertilizers and to decrease the number of grades. Marked savings could be made in freight and handling, and fewer bags would be needed. Supplying fertilizer to the

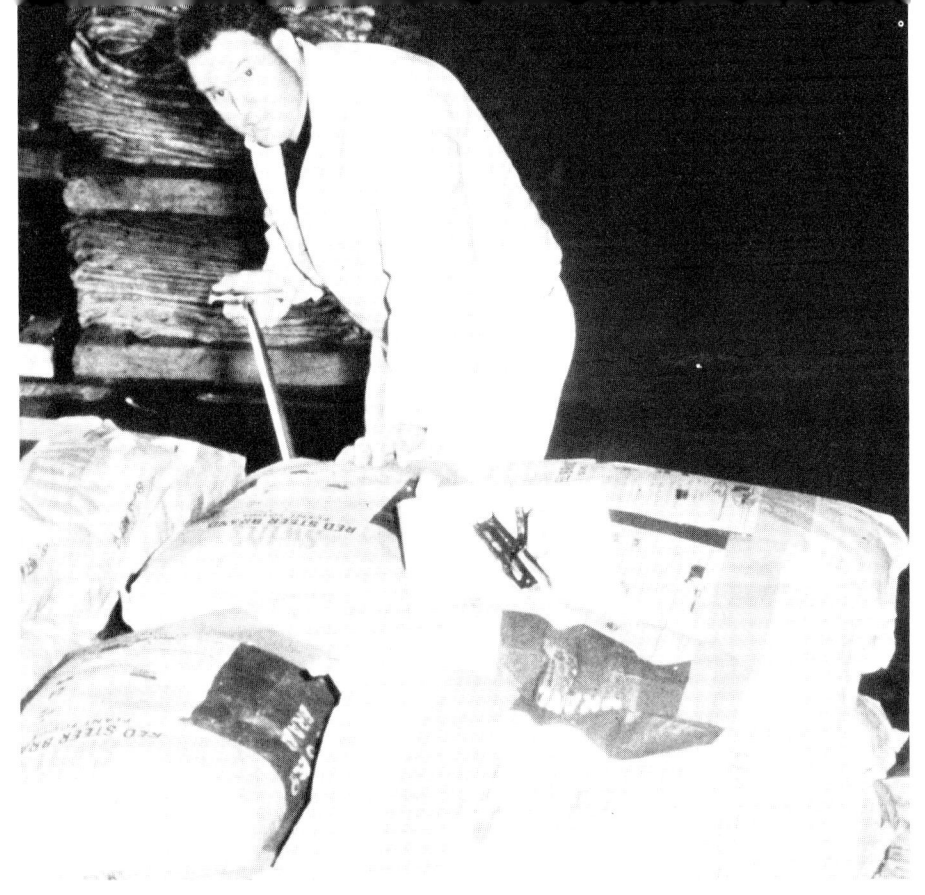

Buyer protection is assured by state officials who take samples of fertilizers to verify that they meet the claims of manufacturers. *(California Department of Agriculture)*

farmer at lower cost per unit of plant nutrient and in fewer grades would reduce confusion to farmers and make the job of agricultural specialists easier and more effective (10,26,63).

The National Fertilizer Association took action to remedy the situation. In 1919, its Soil Improvement Committee recommended certain mixed fertilizer grades as being more desirable than others. In 1922, the Association adopted a high-analysis resolution. As a result, a conference of agronomists representing the land-grant institutions in Ohio, Indiana, Michigan, Wisconsin, and Missouri met in Chicago with members of the Association the same year. The agronomists adopted a list of minimum grades which were believed best to meet the needs of the region. The general guiding principle was that complete NPK fertilizers should not contain less than a total of 14 percent NH_3, available P_2O_5, and K_2O (NH_3 at the time was the accepted equivalent for reporting N). NP and PK mixtures were to contain a minimum of 16 to 20 percent nutrients. Fifteen grades were adopted, 11 for use on mineral soils and 4 for organic soils (9).

New England agronomists and fertilizer manufacturers held a conference in Boston in 1923 to select and approve a list of preferred grades for their states. In a third conference in Baltimore, agronomists and manufacturers from the Middle Atlantic States approved a list of 15 grades for general use and four for special purposes (10).

Unfortunately, there was no great reduction in number of grades registered in most of the states; however, continuation of meetings led to a gradual increase in the nutrient content of the mixed fertilizers. Table 12.3 shows the average grades of mixed fertilizers consumed in the United States (57, table 95):

Table 12.3. Average Grades of Mixed Fertilizers Consumed in U.S. (57).

	N	P_2O_5	K_2O	Total
1920	2.30	9.20	2.40	13.90
1930	3.10	9.80	5.00	17.90
1940	3.80	9.63	6.49	19.92
1950	4.06	11.00	8.52	23.58

Types of Mix Plants in 1938

There were four types of commercial fertilizer plants producing mixed fertilizers by 1938: (1) a complete plant complex that manufactured its own sulfuric acid, bought or mined phosphate rock, produced ordinary superphosphate which the manufacturer used to produce his own mixed fertilizers, or sold a part of the sulfuric acid and/or superphosphate to other fertilizer mixers; (2) a plant that bought both sulfuric acid and ground phosphate rock, produced superphosphate, and made its own mixes; (3) a plant that ammoniated purchased ordinary superphosphate and dry mixed the ammoniated superphosphate with other materials; and (4) a dry mixer who bought all of the materials, ground them, and produced dry mixes. Plants that made their own superphosphate usually added the sulfuric acid to a mixture of phosphate rock and other materials going into the mixture. Of a total of 975 plants operating in 1938, 109 were of the first type, 101 of the second, 53 of the third, 703 were of the dry-mix type, and 9 were unclassified. States with the most plants were Georgia with 185; South Carolina, 90; North Carolina, 88; California, 62; Alabama, 57; and Florida, 55 (22).

Solid materials used in the manufacture of mixed fertilizers usually were shipped to the plants by rail in box cars. The materials were unloaded by hand or by a gasoline-powered lift-hopper truck. In the smaller plants the materials were still dumped into a "Georgia buggy," a two-wheeled cart equipped with large-diameter wheels and a wooden box. This permitted one man to move several hundred pounds of the material easily. Most larger plants by 1950 used gasoline-powered carts along with conveyors, bucket elevators, and hopper cars (22,73).

Dry, bagged fertilizers dominated the market well into the 1950's. *(J. B. Green--TVA)*

The dry-mixing operation consisted of weighing the desired proportions of the different materials, crushing, and then mechanically mixing them either in a rotary drum or passing them through a stationary gravity mixer where the dry materials were simply fed in at the top through a series of baffles. To decrease caking, the mixed materials were stored from 10 days to several weeks to permit chemical reactions among the ingredients. The caked, cured material was broken up and passed through a 6-mesh screen before bagging. The burlap bags (later cotton bags) came in several sizes to accommodate 100, 112, 167, and 200 pounds of product. The 200-pound capacity bags were most used, especially in the Southeastern States (22,73).

Granulation of Mixed Fertilizers

Interest in producing a homogeneous, granular mixed fertilizer developed in the 1920's and 1930's. The earliest process involved wetting the pulverized product with sufficient water to permit granulation in a rotating drum and then removing the water in a dryer. One process using the wet-dry technique was installed by the Davison Chemical Corporation about 1940 to granulate ordinary superphosphate or mixed fertilizers. Following fine grinding and mixing, the fertilizer was discharged into a large rotary cylinder where it was sprayed with sufficient water to permit agglomeration of particles. The moist mixture discharged from the conditioner was dried by passing through a rotary kiln where it was subjected to a co-current of hot air. In the 1930's and 1940's, ammoniation of superphosphate brought about some granulation. The ammoniation operation was carried out in stationary batch mixers (51,62,73).

The first of the advanced granulation plants appears to have been operated by the Iowa Plant Food Company at Des Moines in 1950. Ammoniation was combined with granulation to produce 10 to 15 tons per hour of grades such as 10-20-0, 5-20-10, and 4-16-16. The plant used batch mixers to mix the pulverized materials which were sent by a feeder to a weighing belt and then to a pugmill for ammoniation with nitrogen solutions. Water was added as necessary to complete the granulation in a rotating drum. The product was then sent to a rotary-cylinder dryer located below the granulator in which the granules were hardened (12).

Introduction of Pesticides into Fertilizers

Incorporation of pesticides with fertilizers was practiced only to a limited extent before World War II. Lead arsenate was incorporated by a few manufacturers in the Middle Atlantic States in a few hundred tons of various grades of mixed fertilizers in accordance with customers' specifications. It also was generally known that certain fertilizer materials were partially effective as fungicides. These included kainite, urea, ammonium sulfate, sulfur, and some micronutrient materials used to provide B, Mn, Zn, and Cu (55,56).

The 1940's saw the introduction of the first effective weed killer and a number of chlorinated hydrocarbons which proved to be very effective insecticides The herbicide 2,4-D and related forms were first applied in commercial mixed fertilizers in 1947. By 1950, 10 different fertilizer 2,4-D brands had been registered for sale in several states.

The first of a series of chlorinated hydrocarbon insecticides that included DDT, BHC (benzene hexachloride), chlordane, toxaphene, methoxychlor, aldrin and dieldrin was introduced in the 1940's. Except for toxaphene, none was easily decomposed in the soil; most retained their toxicity for several years. The hydrocarbons were generally compatible with mixed fertilizers and, being largely insoluble in water, they were added to the cured fertilizer as a dust containing 10 to 20 percent of the chemical. Sales of the mixed insecticide-fertilizer products were in the 5,000 to 7,000-ton range in South Carolina with several thousand more tons being sold among other states. Chlordane was the most-used material (14,55,56).

The insects that farmers most sought to control were corn root worms; wireworms in corn, potatoes, and other crops; and grubs and beetles. By the early 1950's, corn received more than half of the total pesticide fertilizer tonnage (14,55).

Mixed Fertilizers: 1950-1980

Mixtures dominated fertilizer consumption in the United States until late in the 1950-1980 period when direct-application materials forged ahead (Table 12.4). Although increasing in tonnage, dry mixes (bulk and bagged) declined in relative importance. In 1955, 15.2 million tons of the dry-mix products was consumed which amounted to 68 percent of the total U.S. fertilizer consumption. By 1980, the tonnage of dry-mixed fertilizers had increased only to 18.6 million tons with its percentage share of all fertilizers dropping to 35 percent. Mixed fluid fertilizer consumption, on the other hand, amounted to only 114,000 tons in 1955 but increased 40-fold to 4.6 million tons in 1980. However, in terms of total mixed fertilizer consumption, fluids accounted for only 1 percent of the total U.S. fertilizer consumption in 1955 and 20 percent of 1980 consumption (33).

Direct application materials consumed increased from 6.6 million tons in 1955 to 27.2 million tons in 1980. In terms of all fertilizers consumed, this amounted to 29 percent in 1955 and 52 percent in 1980. Leading direct application materials listed in descending order according to tonnages of material during the 1970-1980 period are nitrogen solutions, anhydrous ammonia, potassium chloride, ammonium nitrate, secondary and micronutrients, concentrated superphosphate, urea and ammonium sulfate. The two liquids, nitrogen solutions and anhydrous ammonia, together accounted for 39 percent of the tonnage of all direct application materials in 1970 and 45 percent in 1980 (33).

Primary Nutrient Contents

Table 12.5 shows the primary nutrient content of mixed fertilizers (solids and fluids together) over the 1950-1980 period. The total nutrient content of all mixes averaged 24.2 percent in 1950 and almost doubled by the 1979-1980 fiscal year. The N content of the mixes increased over 2.5-fold, available P_2O_5 increased 1.8-fold, and K_2O 1.4-fold. In general, the Mountain, the West North Central and East North Central States used higher grade mixes than the remainder of the country (28, 29,65,66).

Changing Marketing Systems

The traditional marketing system was still largely in force in the mid-1950's. In this system the prime producers provided the various N, P, and K materials in pulverized or semigranulated form and sold them to the wholesaler-mixer. The wholesaler-mixer dry-mixed the material and bagged, sold, and shipped it to retailers who sold to farmers, either directly off the rail car or from storage (30).

Not only did the prime producer obtain a reasonable price for his materials but he also added handling, storage, and his own shipping costs. The wholesaler-mixer added the cost of processing, paper bags, bagging, storage, shipping, costs to the retailer, and a reasonable return for his own investment. The retailer added costs for unloading, storage if any, and his own selling costs and profits. Because of the seasonal nature of the fertilizer sales, most of the retailers usually sold other agricultural products or engaged in other farm-related businesses. All told, the marketing system was a costly and cumbersome way to provide fertilizers to farmers (30).

Table 12.4. Consumption of Fertilizers by Classes (33).

	1955	1960	1970	1980
	\multicolumn{4}{c}{1,000 tons of material}
Dry bulk mixtures	859	2,831	8,974	13,535
Dry bagged mixtures	14,375	12,300	9,203	5,126
Dry bulk direct application materials	1,153	2,110	6,848	12,356
Dry bagged direct application materials	4,678	3,827	2,944	1,627
Fluid mixtures	114	519	2,540	4,609
Total all mixtures	15,348	15,650	20,961	23,270
Total direct application	6,587	7,850	17,331	27,220
Total fertilizer materials	22,724	24,877	39,589	52,787

Table 12.5. Primary Nutrient Content of Mixed Fertilizers (28,29,65,66).

	N	P_2O_5	K_2O	Total
	\multicolumn{4}{c}{Percent}
1950-51	4.18	11.03	8.98	24.19
1060-61	6.81	13.15	11.97	31.93
1970-71	9.59	18.33	13.00	40.92
1979-80	10.79	19.61	13.06	43.46

Developments of the 1950's and early 1960's changed the systems of mixing and marketing fertilizers in the United States. Ammoniation-granulation plants producing homogeneous NPK mixes, bulk blenders, and fluid mixers replaced the old type wholesale-mixers and the small local retailers who had dealt entirely with bagged products. Materials used by the mixers to formulate their products, however, continued to be provided by about 90 basic producers (30).

One of the most far-reaching advances during the period was the change from bagged to bulk fertilizers for both mixed and direct application materials. Use of the bulk materials eliminated the costs of bags and bagging, reduced labor costs in handling and application, and made use of the self-propelling, rapid application equipment feasible. Bagged fertilizers, however, did not disappear entirely since demand still existed on the small farm, home gardens, and certain horticultural markets (Table 12.4). Bagged mixes found their most enduring markets in the New England, Middle Atlantic, and East South Central regions.

Bagging declined the fastest in the Mountain, West North Central, and Pacific regions (33).

Granular, Homogeneous, Mixed Fertilizers

Granular, homogeneous, mixed fertilizers got their start in the early 1950's as a result of research and development conducted by TVA engineers and chemists to develop a continuous process to replace the batch process commonly used to ammoniate superphosphate. They observed that granulation often occurred during ammoniation and could be controlled by adding water or steam and adjusting the formulations to provide sufficient heat of reaction to increase the temperature to a range of 177° to 212°F. This permitted granulation with a minimum of moisture. When the heat of reaction was not sufficient, sulfuric or phosphoric acid could be added along with more ammonia. These observations led to a process for making a high-analysis, granular mixed fertilizer (43,79).

As originally demonstrated to the fertilizer industry in 1953, the TVA ammoniator-granulator consisted of a slightly inclined rotary cylinder with retaining rings at each end, and a scraper mounted inside the shell to keep the internal surface clean. Solid material was introduced continuously at the elevated end to maintain a rolling bed. Ammonia or ammoniating solutions were introduced under the bed through a horizontal, multiple outlet pipe set lengthwise beneath the surface of the rolling bed. Steam or sulfuric acid, if used, was introduced through a drilled pipe under the bed parallel to the ammonia distributor. Water was seldom added, but when used it was sprayed on the surface of the bed. In later work, phosphoric acid was used in some formulations by spraying on the surface. Air was blown through the ammoniator to remove the water vapor. The ammoniated material then passed continuously through a rotary granulator (later omitted) to an unfired dryer used as a cooler to roll the softly formed granules into firm, compact granules, and reduce the moisture content. The first two grades produced by TVA in the equipment were 6-12-12 and 10-20-20. Some of the commercial versions were modified to receive a slurry instead of the solid material by partially neutralizing ammonia or ammoniating solutions with sulfuric acid in a preneutralizing tank. The same equipment with the preneutralizer also was used to produce ammonium phosphates (5,37,79).

Most of the early work (1953-55) was spent identifying formulations that could be made without using a fuel-fired dryer, and several plants of this type were built and operated successfully. However, most companies included a dryer because they felt that lack of a dryer placed too much limitation on choice of raw materials or required too much skill of operators.

Later TVA work involved many changes in the pilot plant, including welding a fuel-fired dryer and equipping the granulator to receive slurries or melts from a pipe reactor, increasing its versatility.

Granules formed in the granulators had a moisture content of 2 to 4 percent by weight, which was reduced to 1 to 3 percent after cooling. The product from the cooler was screened to particles ranging from −6 to +16 mesh (3.4 to 1.0 mm). Oversize particles were crushed and recycled with the fines. The 6- to 16-mesh particles passed through a cooler where the product temperature was reduced from 220°F to 120°F. The final product was high-analysis homogeneous mixes in which grades as high as 8-24-24, 10-20-30, 12-24-24, 13-13-13, and 15-15-15 could be produced (5,61).

Over the years bulk handling stations in major using areas have marketed products from the large regional granular NPK plants. High-analysis, nonsegregating granules of fertilizer made it feasible to ship fairly long distances from the base plant. Each handling station was set up to store and market several grades used in the market area. Typical stations had about six storage bins with wooden walls and concrete floors, each with a capacity of 50 to 75 tons (5).

As described in 1971, the mixed grades were usually transported to the bulk handling stations by hopper-bottom railway cars or by specially designed trucks. Conveyors moved the product from under the car or truck to the desired storage bin. The fertilizer was removed from the bin by a front-end loader, weighed into an elevated scale-hopper, dumped onto another conveyor and emptied into the hopper of a bulk applicator truck. Another type of bulk handling station had elevated storage bins. Many of the bulk stations also marketed individual fertilizer materials to farmers in their area (5).

Homogeneous, granular NPK plants required a relatively large capital investment to build. In 1962, 250 granular plants of varying size were in operation. However, the number fell to 118 in 1973 and to 107 in 1980, the survivors being mostly the larger regional plants. The granulation plants produced 20-25 percent of the total fertilizer distributed in the United States in 1974, but by 1980 their market share had fallen to 16 percent.

Most of the plants were located in the East North Central and South Atlantic States followed by the Middle Atlantic and East South Central States. Very few plants were located west of the Mississippi River, and none in New England (34,35,36).

A typical plant in the 1970's produced about 70,000 tons annually. The larger plants aimed their products primarily at the farm market, distributing through bulk handling stations. However, about 40 percent was sold to bulk blenders for use in their blends or resale to the farmer. The smaller plants produced mostly for the nonfarm and specialty markets with most being bagged (5,36).

Ammoniation-granulation plant of Missouri Farmers Association, Palmyra. (F. J. Myers--TVA)

Granulation plants in the 1970's also were involved in other fertilizer production and sales activities and provided certain services for their own customers. Some included units with bulk blend fluid facilities; about three-fourths of the plants were equipped for adding micronutrients to the mixtures, and about 20 percent provided for addition of pesticides. Less than 10 percent, however, offered custom-application services, although about 20 percent rented application equipment to farmers. Over half offered soil testing and consultation services. Sixty percent or more had bagging facilities. Finished product storage was available for about 27 percent of the total annual production.

The Pipe-Cross Reactor

A second major advance in granulated mixed fertilizer technology was achieved by TVA in 1974 with the invention of the "pipe-cross" reactor. This reactor was designed to allow simultaneous feeding of phosphoric acid and sulfuric acid through separate, opposed feed pipes into a main pipe into which gaseous ammonia and water were fed. The chemical heat from the simultaneous reaction of the ammonia and the two acids resulted in a hot melt. The melt from the pipe-cross reactor, which fits into the granulator drum, was sprayed onto the rolling bed of solid materials. The melt causes granulation resulting in the final product containing less than 1 percent moisture. Further drying using outside sources of energy usually was minimal or unnecessary. Emission control also was easier since little or no small particles of ammonium chloride were present for release into plant environments (ammonium sulfate was formed instead but did not present a problem). The process, however, was not problem-free—the pipe in which the acid and ammonia react was subject to severe corrosion and required use of highly corrosion-resistant material. By 1980, some 22 ammoniation-granulation plants were equipped with pipe-cross reactors (8,34,61).

The invention of the pipe-cross reactor came about through the insights of TVA Engineer Frank P. Achorn, who was trouble-shooting a problem on how to use low-cost by-product sodium nitrate material in the conventional ammoniator-granulator plant of the Missouri Farmers Association near Palmyra, Missouri. A pipe reactor had previously been developed by TVA engineers and demonstrated to the industry; it was capable of producing an ammonium phosphate melt using ammonia and merchant grade phosphoric acid of the usual concentration (52-54 percent P_2O_5). The basic principles of the new reactor were conceived at the Missouri site by Achorn without the usual benefits of laboratories, a pilot plant, or assistance from fellow engineers (7).

The introduction of the pipe-cross reactor resulted in a change of the ingredients used to formulate the different mixed fertilizer grades. In addition to phosphoric acid (54% P_2O_5), sulfuric acid (76 to 98% H_2SO_4), and anhydrous ammonia, diammonium phosphate (18–46-0) became a popular source of both N and P. Standard-grade (fine) potassium chloride remained the major source of K. The plants with the new reactor proved an excellent way to use various by-product materials. Use of ammoniating solutions and normal superphosphate decreased in importance. Concentrated superphosphate and ammonium nitrate, however, remained important materials in conventional NPK granulation plants. The ammoniator-granulator remained a highly desirable way to incorporate micronutrient materials (34).

Bulk Blending

Bulk blending had its roots in Illinois as the outgrowth of a practice started by a few farmers who began dumping potash on ground phosphate rock in truck beds equipped with limestone spreaders in order to apply both materials in one trip across the field. The first company to produce and spread custom-made bulk blends commercially apparently was the Schofield Soil Service, a family-owned firm, at Paxton, Illinois, in 1944. The mixing operation was performed in a converted airplane hangar where the phosphate rock and potash were mixed using a screw auger. The company also provided a soil testing service for its customers. Another company began blending in Woodford County, Illinois, in 1947. By 1950, six bulk blend plants were operating in the state—five by private firms and one by a farmers cooperative. Three years later, 14 plants were operating in Illinois—nine by private firms and five by cooperatives. Most of the later plants mixed ammonium sulfate, phosphate rock, and potash. Granular bulk blends appeared in 1950 (15,16,17).

Bulk blending expanded in Illinois by leaps and bounds during the 1950's and the first half of the 1960's. By 1954, 33 bulk blend plants were being operated by 23 private companies and 10 cooperatives, and by 1957, the number of plants had increased to 92 operated by 44 companies and 48 cooperatives.

Bulk blending soon spread throughout the Corn Belt (all or parts of the East and West Central States). By 1959, 186 plants were operating and, in 1964, the number of plants had jumped to 1,536, most of which were still located in the Corn Belt. By 1970, 3,100 plants were in operation—one-third outside of the Corn Belt. In the 1970's the number exceeded

The pipe-cross reactor, which TVA introduced in 1970, is energy efficient and produces higher quality granules than conventional granulation. *(F. J. Myers--TVA)*

5,000, with at least some plants in all of the regions of the continental United States (6,16,35,36).

The rapid increase in importance of bulk blending was due to its being a good business venture both for the blender and the farmer. In contrast with the old dry-mix producer, the new blender retained both the mixers' and the dealers' profits. The farmer, in turn, could get the fertilizer applied on his land for about the same price as he would have paid for bagged mixes before spreading. Furthermore, fertilizer demand was expanding rapidly in the Corn Belt, opening the door for the influx of the aggressive bulk blenders (78).

Bulk blending provided the farmer with mixed fertilizer at lower cost per unit of plant nutrient and brought services that he needed. The blends were applied in bulk, no fillers were used, and the actual blending process was simple and did not require expensive equipment.

The rapid growth of the bulk blend industry during the earlier years was unusual. It grew without organized research input or promotion by state, Federal agencies, or by the basic fertilizer producers. The latter at first were skeptical of bulk blends, but their outlook soon changed as orders mounted for fertilizer materials (38).

Earlier blenders produced only bulk mixtures but, by the early 1960's, they had discovered a demand for bagged granular mixes and about 20 percent installed bagging equipment. The bagged products were used largely for application through grain drills, planters and cultivators equipped to band, hilldrop, or sidedress. Some bulk blenders expanded activities to market individual fertilizer materials for direct application and to produce their own fluid mixes (47).

Bulk blending plants underwent only minimal changes in design and equipment after the early 1960's. The main exceptions were the addition of corrosion-resistant equipment and modifications aimed at reducing segregation of granules. Typical plants produce from 2,000 to 5,000 tons of product annually with the plants operating mostly during the spring and fall seasons. The plants serve an area within a radius ranging from 25 to 50 miles. A major advantage of bulk blending is the low plant investment and operating costs (5).

A typical plant unloads the incoming material from bottom-unloading hopper cars (box cars were used earlier), moves it by screw conveyors to an elevator, and discharges it into storage bins which usually have wooden walls and concrete floors. A front-end loader removes the material from storage and dumps it into a batch-type retaining hopper equipped with weighing facilities. The desired amounts of the different materials flow into a batch mixer. These are often similar to those used on concrete ready-mix trucks in which the contents are mixed by rotating in one direction and discharged by reversing the direction. Rotary mixers also are commonly used in which the materials are loaded at one end and discharged at the other. A less popular mixer is the auger-screw, into which materials are continuously fed and mixed. Rates of mixing range from a few tons per hour up to about 50 tons. The mixed materials, regardless of type of mixing, are elevated to or moved by conveyor belts which discharge directly into trucks or holding storages (5,6,43).

Ingredients used in bulk blending include both single-nutrient component and two-component granular materials. The most used are monoammonium and diammonium phosphates, concentrated superphosphate, potassium chloride, ammonium nitrate, urea, and ammonium sulfate. Granular diammonium phosphate (18-46-0) was found particularly suited to bulk blending as a result of its high content of both nitrogen and phosphorus and a particle size distribution of its granules that is uniquely satisfactory for bulk blends. Also, it is chemically compatible with most of the other materials and its low delivered cost per unit of plant nutrient is a further advantage. Diammonium phosphate is generally considered responsible for the long-lasting success of bulk blends. It set the particle size distribution pattern that served as a model for the other materials used in the blends. Micronutrients and certain pesticides also are applied with the bulk blends, but it is difficult to distribute the small quantities uniformly throughout the mixture (5).

Segregation of large particles from small particles in bulk blends has been a major problem in bulk blends. The problem shows up as grade variations in official samples taken from truckloads and bags, which subjects the blender to penalties and results in nonuniform application, which causes uneven growth of crops (38).

In a bulk blending plant, ingredients typically are mixed in rotating equipment and discharged to a delivery vehicle. *(F. J. Myers--TVA)*

Blended fertilizer ingredients segregate by particle size during handling. Photo at right shows results when different sizes are mixed. *(C. U. Quillen--TVA)*

Studies by TVA showed that mismatch in particle sizes was most responsible for segregation and not variations in density or particle shapes as thought earlier. Segregation occurred most severely from three causes. These were from the rolling action of particles when dropped onto sloping piles of fertilizer—the larger particles rolling over the smaller toward the outside of the pile; from vibration and agitation during handling, transport, and in applicator hoppers during spreading which caused the smaller particles to sift down; and the ballistic action when blends are broadcast by fan-type spreaders that throw the larger farther than the smaller particles. Better particle size matching of the blend ingredients along with plant and equipment modifications greatly minimized but never fully overcame the segregation problem (38,40,41,42).

Estimates in 1976 indicated that about 5,600 bulk blend plants were in operation, producing about 19.6 million tons of mixed product which is equivalent to about 58 percent of all mixed fertilizers sold in the United States (6,35).

Surveys by the Association of American Plant Food Control Officials (AAPFCO) show that dry bulk blends rose from 33 percent of the total U.S. fertilizer distribution in 1973-74 to 36 percent in 1979-80. Bagged blends dropped from 9.2 percent to 5.7 percent over the same period. Applying these percentages to published U.S. fertilizer consumption data, tonnages of dry bulk blends increased from 15.7 million tons to 18.3 million tons as bagged blends decreased from 4.3 million tons to 2.9 million tons over the 6-year period.

Of the 4,000 bulk blend plants covered by the AAPFCO-TVA surveys, 41 percent were located in the West North Central States, 24 percent in the East North Central States, 11 percent in the West South Central, 8 percent in the South Atlantic, and 6 percent in the East South Central States. The remaining 10 percent were scattered over the other regions in the continental United States (34).

The leading bulk blend mixtures produced in 1979 were 9-23-30, 6–24-24, 10-10-10, 19-19-19, 17-17-17, 8-32-16, 10-20-20, 0-26-26, 6–15-40, and 10- 26-26. The average primary nutrient content of these 10 grades was 53.5 percent (34).

Blenders traditionally have provided other services to farmers. The 1979 AAPFCO-TVA survey showed that 44 percent of the fertilizer distributed by the blenders was custom applied by the blenders and 32 percent was spread by application equipment rented by the blenders. Twenty-two percent of the farmers applied blends with their own equipment, and 9 percent by custom operators other than the blenders. About two-thirds of the blenders were equipped to add micronutrients to the blends, 43 percent could add herbicides, and 29 percent insecticides. Forty-four percent could add seed, and 19 percent had bagging equipment. Soil testing service was offered by 85 percent of the blenders, and consultation services by 73 percent. About 14 percent of the blenders also had liquid and suspension fertilizer facilities. In addition to the blends, the blenders provided storage capacity for direct-application materials such as ammonium nitrate, diammonium phosphate, and often anhydrous ammonia and nitrogen solutions (34).

The AAPFCO-TVA 1979 survey showed 46 percent of bulk blend plants owned by corporations, 43 percent by cooperatives, 7 percent by sole proprietorships, and 3.7 percent by partnerships (34).

Fluid Mixed Fertilizers

The history of fluid fertilizers (liquid and suspensions) traces back for centuries. It was common practice in China, Japan, and Korea to collect

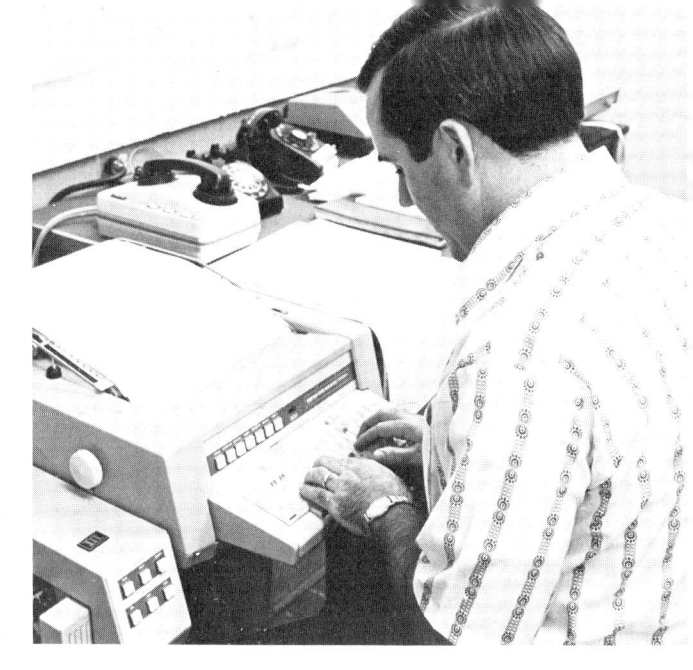

Electronic information systems introduced by TVA and others are used by thousands of mixers of fluid and dry fertilizers to compute formulations quickly and efficiently. *(F. J. Myers--TVA)*

human and domestic animal wastes from the cities, carry them to the fields in buckets, and apply with long-handled dippers (48). The Greeks transported sewage in canals from Athens to nearby vegetable gardens and olive groves and applied it to the land (Chapter 1). Sir Humphrey Davy in 1808 tested an inorganic liquid fertilizer that he had devised. James Murray in Ireland in 1841 began producing liquid fertilizer mixtures by pouring sulfuric acid over crushed bones and selling the liquid in 30-gallon casks (44). In the 1800's, numerous articles appeared in farm publications on use of liquid barnyard and sewage wastes on agricultural lands.

Domestic manufacture of liquid mixed fertilizers began in California in 1923 by G & M Fertilizer Company of Oakland (77). In 1928, Eugene and John Prizer, concerned over the large amount of labor required to hand-spread solid fertilizers in large citrus groves, built an applicator that would dissolve soluble fertilizer materials and introduce them into irrigation water. (A U.S. patent was granted on the applicator in 1932.) Application of anhydrous ammonia and nitrogen solutions in irrigation waters began in California in 1934 and of phosphoric acid in 1939 (49). NP liquid mixes, the next logical step, came into production in 1943 when some 900 tons was sold. Tonnages of liquid mixes escalated to 8,000 tons in 1948, due in part to the availability of surplus furnace-grade phosphoric acid. The early mixed fertilizers were highly acidic solutions made from phosphoric acid and dissolution of ammonium nitrate and potassium chloride. The mixtures, as a result, were highly corrosive and methods were sought to produce solutions that were essentially neutral in reaction (13,45,49,71).

During the 1950's, use of liquid mixes expanded rapidly, for use in irrigation waters and for direct application. From California and a few other Western States use of liquid mixes spread into the Midwest. In

1955, 76 plants were producing liquid mixes in the Pacific States and 25 in the East South Central States. Some 114 liquid grades were manufactured, half of which were NPK grades and most of the remainder the NP grades (27,36,45).

Cold Mix Plants—The process most used in the manufacture of liquid mixes in the 1950's involved dissolving in water solid ammonium nitrate or urea, ammonium phosphates, and potassium chloride, using mild steel or wooden tanks. The solids were introduced by dumping 80- or 100-pound bags of the materials into a feed hopper. The desired water was added to the fertilizer in the dissolution tank (usually 4,000-gallon capacity) using either a volume measure or a free-board on the tank. To speed dissolution, the mixture was kept at about 70°F by placing a hot water or steam heat exchanger in the tank. About 20 tons of liquid fertilizer could be produced in a 6- to 8-hour shift, or 80 tons per day by working around the clock. The liquid product was stored in mild steel or wooden tanks. This process had the advantage of low capital investment but suffered from the higher cost of the solid ammonium phosphates as compared with reacting ammonia with phosphoric acid (13).

Hot Mix Plants—The first commercial liquid-mix plant to neutralize phosphoric acid with ammonia and dissolve the potash to formulate a NPK liquid mixture was the Liquilizer Corporation plant at Vincennes, Indiana, in 1953. The first liquid grade produced was a 4-10-10; however, in the second year 9-9-9, 12-6-6, and 12-8-4 grades were produced by adding additional nitrogen in the forms of an ammoniating solution and solid urea (77). Other acid-neutralization, or hot mix, plants began to appear, varying considerably in size, details, and the supplemental raw materials used. All of the plants, however, depended on the heat generated during the neutralization to aid in the dissolution of the solid materials (70). In 1955, Barnard and Leas Manufacturing Company constructed its first commercial liquid fertilizer plant for sale (77).

Mixing equipment for the neutralization process was based on the batch system and was relatively simple. The mix tank where the reaction took place was of 5- to 20-ton capacity, made of stainless steel or rubber-lined mild steel, and equipped with an agitator. The mix tank was usually mounted on scales and the raw materials were either weighed or metered into it at the top. Ammonia was introduced through a perforated pipe at the bottom. During operation the liquid mix was recirculated through a cooler in order to prevent excessive boiling in the mix tank. (The earlier plants did not take this step and ran into considerable vibration.) Other equipment required for the hot-mix plants included suitable storage for the incoming materials, pumps and piping, and product storage (5,13,70).

Elevated view of small Kansas fluid fertilizer plant showing simple mixing equipment. *(F. J. Myers--TVA)*

Although liquid mixed fertilizers had made considerable progress during the 1950's, they had a number of shortcomings. High-grade NPK mixes and high potash-containing mixes could not be produced due to the low solubility of potassium chloride (potassium hydroxide and other more soluble potash materials were too costly). Overloading the solutions with fertilizer materials or impurities usually caused crystals to form and precipitate out during storage. Impurities introduced by wet-process phosphoric acid were particularly troublesome. (Furnace acid minimized precipitation but its cost was usually too high for use in fertilizers.) (39).

Polyphosphate Clear Liquid Fertilizers—Discovery of the value of superphosphoric acid (a mixture mostly of ortho-, pyro-, and tri-polyphosphoric acid referred to as polyphosphates; Chapter 10), proved to be a major breakthrough in preparation of high quality clear liquid fertilizers. Ammonium polyphosphate is made simply by ammoniating either furnace-grade or wet-process super-phosphoric acid. The polyphosphates hold aluminum, calcium, and magnesium in ammoniated wet-process phosphoric acid in solution. Also, they sequester the metallic micronutrients—copper, iron, manganese, and zinc—which normally would be insoluble in liquid fertilizers produced from wet-process phosphoric acid.

TVA engineers—M. M. Striplin, D. McKnight, and G. H. Megar—introduced furnace-grade superphosphoric acid in 1955, and TVA's work with ammonium polyphosphates using furnace acid led to production of a 11-37-0 polyphosphate-containing base solution (72,81).

TVA's original idea was to ship the superphosphoric acid to companies having hot-mix solution plants which could ammoniate the acid. Costs, however, proved too high, there was a shortage of stainless steel rail and storage tanks, and the nuisance of ammoniating the acid in plants not properly equipped resulted in abandoning the project. To avoid these problems, TVA in 1959 began ammoniating the acid at its Muscle Shoals facility and shipping the neutralized base solution to companies having cold-mix plants. The solution grades finally settled upon were a 10-34-0 and a high-polyphosphate 11-37-0. Typical grades of the final mixed liquids were 8-8-8, 8-26-8, and 7-21-7 (80).

A second advance of importance to the fluid industry occurred in 1961 when it was found that wet-process superphosphoric acid could be produced by concentrating regular wet-process acid (Chapter 10). This freed the industry from dependence upon the more costly furnace-grade acid to produce polyphosphates. Both private industry and TVA worked out methods and equipment for concentrating the wet-process acid. The most used base solution from the acid was 10–34-0 grade containing about 50 percent of the P_2O_5 as polyphosphate which had a salting-out temperature below freezing. Although the base solution kept most of the impurities in solution (sequestered), enough remained to precipitate and cause problems. The most troublesome were iron, magnesium, and aluminum crystalline precipitates of sufficient size to clog applicator nozzles. By 1968 at least six major companies were producing wet-process superphosphoric acid (39,75).

The third major advance was made in 1972 when TVA chemical engineers—R. S. Meline, R. G. Lee, and W. C. Scott—developed and introduced a simple pipe reactor which greatly reduced the cost of producing high-polyphosphate liquids (59). This reactor consisted of corrosion-resistant pipes welded together to form a tee (T) where vaporized ammonia passes through one arm of the tee and a low-polyphosphate (20 to 30%) wet-process superphosphoric acid was pumped through the second. The acid and the gaseous ammonia react to form a hot melt (600°F). The heat of reaction drove off water of hydration and raised the polyphosphate content of the P_2O_5 in the resulting ammonium phosphate to about 75 percent. The base solutions produced were 10-34-0 and 11-37-0 which contained about 75 percent of their P_2O_5 as polyphosphate. Supplemental piping and equipment provided for addition of water, cooling using a heat exchanger, vaporization of the incoming ammonia, and storage.

The low-polyphosphate, low-cost superphosphoric acid needed for the pipe reactor users soon became available commercially. Several companies—including Texasgulf, Inc., J. R. Simplot Co., and Stauffer Chemical Co.—produced the low-polyphosphate acid and shipped it directly to the pipe reactor plants. The high-polyphosphate 10-34-0 and 11-37-0 produced were shipped by rail or truck to the small cold-mix plants were they were usually mixed with urea-ammonium nitrate solution and dissolved potassium chloride to form grades such as 7-21-7, 8-8-8, and 21-7-0. Satellite cold-mix stations also were set up and serviced by central cold-mix plants to mix the high-polyphosphate solutions with urea-ammonium nitrate and high potash solutions such as 2-6-12 and 4-11-11. The pipe reactor proved to be an economical way to produce clear liquid mixes of high nutrient content not possible previously. By 1978, more than 100 U.S. plants were using the pipe reactor process (1,3,6).

Suspension Fertilizers

The need to increase the nutrient content of liquid fertilizers, especially potassium, led TVA in 1959 to explore suspension fertilizers in which finely divided solids were kept suspended by addition of a gelling-type clay. In suspensions, in contrast to clear liquids, solubility of materials is not a limiting factor. The first suspension produced on a demonstration scale by TVA in 1963 was a 12-40-0 base fluid made by suspending an ammonium polyphosphate produced using electric-furnace superphosphoric acid. A 12-40-0 base suspension apparently was first applied by the Chokee Fertilizer Company at De Soto, Georgia, in 1963 using an applicator equipped with an air sparger. International Minerals & Chemical Corp. also conducted pilot-plant tests that led to a field application of a 3-9-18 suspension using a jet-spray nozzle. Although progress was being made in the production and handling of suspensions, adoption was slow (68,74,75,77).

In addition to increasing the potash content, several other advantages of suspensions soon became apparent. Less pure and cheaper raw materials could be used, concentrations of materials were almost unlimited, less soluble micronutrients could be added, and pesticides were more often compatible. A major disadvantage of suspensions, however, not shared with clear liquid fertilizers is the need for frequent air sparging (introducing compressed air through a pipe) to prevent growth of large crystals during storage and transport that will settle out or clog nozzles (1,32).

Most suspensions made in the 1960's were produced from an ammonium polyphosphate base solution, 10-34-0 or 11-37-0 grade, produced either by electric-furnace or wet-process superphosphoric acid. The base solution was mixed with a nitrogen solution (28-32 percent N), solid potassium chloride (0-0-62), and usually attapulgite clay obtained in south Georgia and north Florida. By the 1970's, it had been found that solid materials such as granular monoammonium phosphate (MAP) and diammonium phosphate (DAP) could be converted to suspensions by recirculation using 5-inch-diameter pipes. In the case of MAP, solubility was increased by adding ammonia to the mix to generate chemical heat to help disintegrate the granules and aid formation of small crystals. About 1975, companies began producing suspensions directly from merchant-grade phosphoric acid. TVA also developed a 13-38-0 grade orthophosphate base suspension of excellent quality having stable small crystals (2).

Manufacture: Hot and Cold Mixes—Hot-mix and cold-mix plants usually can manufacture both clear liquid mix grades and suspensions. In order to produce suspensions in hot-mix plants, the clay usually is added while the solution is still hot, and solid potash is suspended after the mix is cooled. Cold-mix suspension ingredients include a 12-40-0 ammonium polyphosphate base suspension or, more recently, an ammonium orthophosphate 13–38-0 base suspension. Other ingredients include urea, ammonium nitrate (32-0-0), and solid potassium chloride (0-0-62), and water. Satellite stations also have been set up to provide cold-mix suspensions to nearby farmers. The satellites use the same NP base suspensions and urea ammonium solution as the main plant. However, the solid potash is replaced with a potash base suspension such as 5-15-30, 4-12-24, and 4-14-28. The materials are mixed in a small-scale mix tank. The storage tanks containing suspended materials are air sparged (5,32).

Status of Clear and Suspension Mixtures

Table 12.6 shows the status of liquid mixed fertilizers (clear liquids and suspensions) during the 1960-1980 period. The number of plants increased 8-fold, from 390 to 3,200. Consumption increased nearly 10-fold, rising from 480,000 tons to 4.6 million. Nevertheless, liquid mixes accounted for only 3 percent of the total consumption of all mixes (solid and fluid) in 1960 and only 16 percent in 1980, and only 2 percent of all fertilizers consumed in 1960 and 7 percent in 1980. However, by the late 1970's, suspensions were showing promise, advancing from about 25 percent of the total liquid-mix market in 1974, to 33 percent in 1976 and 40 percent in 1981 (81).

Table 12.6. Growth in fluid-mix (liquid and suspension) industry (81, 18, 19).

Year	No. Plants	Annual consumption 1,000 tons	Percentage of Mixtures	Percentage of All Fertilizers
1960	390	480	3	2
1970	2,750	2,540	10	5
1980	3,200	4,610	16	7

The liquid mixes also increased in total primary nutrient content during the period. The average nutrient content was about 28 percent in 1960 and, by 1981, averaged 35.2 percent. Most of the increase in analysis was due to increased use of suspensions (81).

The business side of the fluid-mix fertilizer industry was quite diversified. According to the 1979 AAPFCO-TVA survey, 64 percent of the fluid-mix plants were owned by corporations, 16 percent by cooperatives, 13 by sole proprietorships, and 7 by partnerships. Besides marketing fluid mixes of their own manufacture, they also marketed other fertilizer materials and mixes. The survey showed that a typical clear liquid-mix plant marketed 2,000 tons of its own product, 790 tons of anhydrous ammonia, 1,330 tons of nitrogen solutions of liquid direct-application materials such as 10-34-0 and 8-24-0. The liquid-mix plants also marketed bulk dry mixtures and materials such as ammonium nitrate and diammonium phosphate. Additions of pesticides to the mixes were offered by 37 percent of the clear mix-only plants and 80 percent of the suspension-only plants. Over half of the plants offered micronutrient additions and 80 percent also offered soil testing services of one kind or another. The liquid-mix plants had a storage capacity of around 45 percent of their total annual fertilizer distribution, and suspension plants 31 percent. About 40 percent of the liquid fertilizer tonnage was custom-applied—35 percent by the dealer and 5 percent by application contractors. The farmer applied 28 percent using his own equipment and 30 percent using rental equipment owned by the dealer (34,35).

The 10 leading grades of clear-liquid mixes consumed in 1979 were 20-10-0, 4-10-10, 7-21-7, 2-6-12, 7-22-5, 5-10-10, 6-18-6, 4-8-12, 10-34-0, and 16-20-0. The 10 leading suspensions were 3-10-30, 4-12-24, 3-9-27, 6-18-18, 13-13-13, 3-9-18, 10-30-0, 5-10-5, 20-5-10, and 5-15-30. During the last half of the 1970's, five states—Georgia, Illinois, Indiana, Iowa, and Texas—consumed almost half of the liquid-mixed fertilizers (34,35).

Fertilizer Application Methods and Machinery

Up until the 1950's, solid-mixed fertilizers were by far the major type of fertilizer consumed in the United States; as a result, application methods and machinery were developed around the existing mixes rather than direct-application materials. From 1920 to around 1950, the mixed fertilizers were largely nongranulated, available only in bags, and subject to caking. They were low in nitrogen and potash and high in phosphate. Application was by simple horse-drawn equipment that spread the fertilizer unevenly, and seldom achieved the desired rate.

Since the 1950's, new application methods and equipment have been developed to meet modern needs. Granular high-analysis mixes and direct-application materials have appeared along with clear liquid mixes and suspensions, and nitrogen solutions and ammonia for direct application. Rates of application and the acreage fertilized have increased markedly. Farmers farmed larger acreages and farm labor was in short supply, making time a premium during the spring and fall fertilizer seasons.

All of this did not go unnoticed by individual innovators and farm equipment companies. They designed new equipment and machines or modified older applicators to meet current application needs (initially some farmers built their own application equipment).

This section deals with all types of application equipment since the same equipment with little or no modification can be used to apply not only mixed fertilizers but also direct application materials. (Anhydrous ammonia is dealt with in Chapter 10.)

Methods and Machinery Prior to 1950

Early Methods Up Until 1920—Thousands of fertilizer application machines had been built in this country by the 1920's but most left much to be desired. The first U.S. patent on a fertilizer applicator was issued on Seymour's Broadcast Lime and Guano Sower in 1845, and the machines were sold to farmers from 1848 on. This broadcaster and those that came forth later consisted of an oblong hopper with an adjustable slit running the length of the bottom. The fertilizer was fed through the slit by a revolving roller or reciprocating agitator. Potato planters with fertilizer attachments appeared about 1880, and cotton and corn planters with fertilizer attachments were in use by the turn of the century. In the cotton-producing states the earliest fertilizer distributors were the "guano horns" used for banding fertilizer in furrows opened for the cottonseed. The horn consisted of a funnel attached to an elongated tube which was filled from a sack strapped to the laborer's back. Much of the cotton fertilizer, however, was broadcast by hand (46,58).

By far the most-used fertilizer applicator in the country prior to 1893 was a horse-drawn combination grain and fertilizer drill developed in Europe. Known as the Bickford and Hoffman drill, it was a favorite for many years. An important improvement in combination grain and fertilizer drills was the invention of the star-wheel in 1883. As the name implies, this was a starshaped wheel that revolved carrying a definite amount of fertilizer under a gate, the height of which determined the rate of application. (The first model was almost identical to those still used

Horse- and tractor-drawn drills were widely used in simultaneous planting and fertilizing operations. This drill was developed under specifications of conservation supervisors of the Washita River Valley in Oklahoma for seeding native and adapted grasses. *(Soil Conservation Service)*

in the 1930's and 1940's.) Fertilizer distributors that were separate and distinct from grain drills and planters were not used extensively until after 1900 (58).

A survey of the U.S. manufacturers of farm implements made in 1919 indicated the relative importance of the different types of fertilizer applicators. It showed that 27 percent of the corn planters sold, 35 percent of the potato planters, and 29 percent of the grain drills were equipped with fertilizer attachments. In 1928, 40 percent of the grain and beet drills and 4 percent of the cultivators were equipped for fertilizers. Practically all of the fertilizer applicators were designed for low-grade mixed fertilizers (58).

Dreaming up patentable ideas for fertilizer-distributing machines appears to have been a favorite pastime for inventors both in the United States and abroad. Several thousand patents were issued over the years by the United States Patent Office (58).

Prior to 1920, agronomists generally recommended broadcast application of fertilizer for most crops even though farmers were applying a considerable amount either in the hill or in the row. The agronomists argued that localized application would cause bunching of the plant roots and greater injury during periods of drought, and that hill or row application resulting in an irregular residual carry-over, causing uneven growth of the following crop (11,69).

Application Through the 1940's—In order to understand better the principles of fertilizer application and the relation of these principles to practical fertilizer use on corn, The National Fertilizer Association established its first research fellowship over a 5-year period at the University of Wisconsin in 1919 under the direction of Professor Emil Truog. Based upon these investigations, the Wisconsin workers came out strongly in favor of applying the fertilizer in a band above but not in contact with the seed. They also recommended a broadcast application mixed with the surface soil when relatively large applications were applied to build up the fertility of the soil. A little later a related fellowship was granted to the Iowa Agricultural Experiment Station with the results indicating that fertilizer for corn should be applied either at the sides of the seed or below the seed, but not in direct contact with the seed. Numerous other investigators in 20 fertilizer-using states also conducted placement experiments on different crops, soils, and locations (11,69,76).

In 1925, The National Fertilizer Association organized a National Joint Committee on Fertilizer Application to encourage development of special farm machinery which would apply fertilizer efficiently and without damage to the crop. The Joint Committee was composed of representatives of the American Society of Agronomy, the American Society of Agricultural Engineers, and The National Fertilizer Association. Truog was the first chairman (25,64).

An idea of the complexity of fertilizer application machinery available in 1930 on the farm machinery market is given in the following quotation by Mehring and Cumings in U.S. Department of Agriculture Technical Bulletin 182, page 42.

> Many types are in use, and according to the mechanical principles employed they may be classified as follows: Bottom-delivery distributors—guano horn, agitator, revolving plate, star-wheel, chain, paddle wheel, endless belt, roller, screw, and top delivery distributors—revolving cylinder, ascending hopper, and descending dispenser.
> The bottom-delivery distributors depend either partly or wholly upon gravity flow for the delivery of the fertilizer, whereas the top-delivery machines depend entirely upon positive mechanical action.
> Distributors may further be classified as broadcast and row machines. Broadcast distributors, while widely used in Europe, are not employed to any considerable extent in this country, except for spreading lime. Row distributors with closely spaced units are sometimes used as broadcast machines. Row distributors include guano horns and hand distributors, as well as single or multiple row horse-drawn machines and attachments. They may deposit the fertilizer in a continuous strip in or near the crop row or only at the hills. (58).

The variability of commercial fertilizer distribution machines for a single crop, cotton, was demonstrated in tests using 22 different machines in South Carolina in 1929. The machines tested included nine simple distributors (fertilizer only) and 13 combination planters and fertilizer distributors. Sixteen were of the walking type weighing with empty hoppers from 86 to 176 pounds, and six were of the riding type weighing approximately 500 pounds. Hopper capacities ranged from 16 to 100 pounds. Two fertilizers were tested, one a 4-8-4 and the other three times as concentrated (25).

The most noted defects were irregular distribution of fertilizer due to wheel slippage, lack of refinement of the distribution mechanism, changes in depth of the fertilizer, different depths of fertilizer in the hopper (rates increased as the depth of fertilizer decreased), tilting of the machine, and the inability of the fertilizer itself to flow uniformly. Segregation of the fertilizer components occurred to greater or lesser extent in all machines (25).

Methods of fertilizer application and application machinery changed considerably after World War II. Changes were made to accommodate the new, higher analysis fertilizer materials appearing in fertilizer mixes. Farmers with a good market for their products were increasing per-acre rates of application, hoppers and fertilizer boxes were made larger, and row planters became available with deep placement attachments. Also, better provisions were made for cleaning the equipment after use in order to decrease corrosion (23).

Farm tractors had largely replaced horses and mules for pulling fertilizer application machinery by 1950. (The number of tractors on farms increased from 246,000 in 1920 to 3.4 million in 1950.) Two- and

High flotation equipment was widely used by the 1970's to apply both fluid and granular fertilizers. At right, nurse truck is re-loading applicator.
(F. J. Myers--TVA)

Fluid fertilizers commonly are applied through boom applicators equipped with several nozzles. *(F. J. Myers--TVA)*

four-row machinery became common (21). Consumption of mixed fertilizers increased 2.4-fold between 1940 and 1950, from 5,500 to 13,000 tons (57).

Methods and Machinery: 1950-1980

The 1950-1980 period saw revolutionary changes not only in the amounts and kinds of fertilizer consumed but also in fertilizer application methods and machinery. The coming of bulk blends, bulk handling, fluid mixes (both clear liquids and suspensions), and the introduction of new direct application materials (both solid and liquid), impacted fertilizer application equipment and the ways fertilizers were applied. Unheard of in the past, custom application and rental of application machinery to farmers became common. With huge, self-propelled machines, fertilizers were applied to up to 2.5 acres per minute. Rates of nutrient application jumped to new highs. Granules replaced powdered mixtures, and broadcast applications largely replaced the old system of rationing small amounts of fertilizer placed near the seed.

Dealers began using flotation tires about 1960 to permit fertilizer application on fields too wet to support equipment without undue compaction. Ward Commons in the Willamette Valley in Oregon equipped a fertilizer rig with Goodyear super-wide tires in order to apply fertilizer on marshy turf-grass seed fields. The operation was successful and the next year the Ward Commons Manufacturing Company in Scio, Oregon, began manufacturing the "Wolverine Swamp Buggy" (77).

High-flotation equipment was in considerable demand by 1965. Rickel, Inc. of Niles, Kansas, introduced the "Big A," a three-wheel, self-propelled applicator, at The National Fertilizer Solutions Association's 1965 convention in St. Louis. The Walls Research Corporation of Indianapolis displayed a Dodge Power Wagon modified with Goodyear Terra tires. Also, the Modified Soil Equipment Company at Biglerville, Pennsylvania, began production of a flotation truck unit. From the mid-1960's on, practically all large self-propelled equipment used to broadcast solid and liquid fertilizers was equipped with high flotation tires (77).

Applying Solid Mixes—Solid bulk granular mixes or materials usually are broadcast from an open hopper mounted on a truck or specially developed machine with tilting sides from which the fertilizer is moved along the bottom to the rear with a continuous belt or chain conveyor. An adjustable gate controls the amount of fertilizer moving out of the hopper. The fertilizer drops onto either one or two spinners consisting of a flat disc upon which four or six blades are mounted. The blades rotate at an adjustable rate of about 500 rpm and throw the fertilizer in a swath behind the applicator (5). Unless great care is taken, the fertilizer is spread unevenly.

With the high-speed applicators applying fertilizer at rates of 1 to 2-1/2 acres per minute, the logistics of keeping the applicator supplied with fertilizer is of critical importance. Nurse trucks are kept in almost continuous operation. The fertilizer is transferred from the trucks to the applicator hopper either by screw augers or from 5-ton hoppers on the nurse truck which are raised and dumped hydraulically (4).

Applying Fluid Mixes—Fluid application methods fall into two general classes: broadcast and band application. Broadcasting usually precedes planting, although some crops are topdressed by broadcasting after the crop is established (5,60).

With fluid broadcast applicators, tanks, pipes, and pumps replace the hoppers, conveyors, and spinners associated with solid materials. Most clear liquid applicators in recent years have been equipped with a centrifugal pump to drive the liquid from the applicator tank to the nozzles. The desired pressure at the nozzles is obtained by bypassing part of the liquor going through the pump to the applicator tank. Smaller tractor-drawn broadcast-applicators use piston pumps driven off a drive wheel so that application is independent of applicator speed. Rates of application are governed by the length of the piston stroke (20).

Clear liquid fertilizers having no vapor pressure are distributed by spraying through nozzles attached to booms extending on each side of the applicator. (The booms are hinged to permit folding during road travel.) Flat fan nozzles which have a small opening are preferred where fine droplets are required such as when pesticides are introduced into the mixture. Under windy situations, flooding or hollow-cone nozzles with larger openings are used to increase droplet size and reduce drift. Ground speed of the applicator, the size of the nozzle orifices, and the pressure on the bypass line determine the application rate. Uneven broadcast application results unless there is a 100 percent overlap of the spray striking the ground. This is achieved when the width of a nozzle spray pattern striking the ground is double that of the nozzle spacing. The overlap is usually adjusted by changing the height of the boom (20).

Suspension fertilizers are transported and applied in much the same manner as clear liquids, except that they must be agitated to assure that the mixture remains in suspended form. Tank trucks and trailers are used to transport the suspensions from the plant to the field. Vibration within the transport tank weakens the clay gel, causing crystals to settle out. Crystals in suspensions in storage tanks also will settle out if left too long. Both settling problems are prevented by recirculating by air sparging. Transfer from the nurse vehicle to the applicator tank is accomplished with a pump capable of moving the fluid at a rate of 300 to 400 gallons per minute (1,2,32).

Suspensions usually are broadcast with the same type of equipment used for clear liquids; the major difference is in the type of nozzles. When applying high-potash grades, however, some applicators substitute a

University of Maryland researchers prepare to test specially designed "no-till" equipment for planting and applying starter fertilizer in unplowed field following small grain harvest. *(F. J. Myers--TVA)*

separate centrifugal pump for the piston pump in order to prevent clogging. Nozzles for applying suspensions are of the flooding type which provides uniform application if the overlap with adjacent nozzles is maintained. Nozzles mounted on booms can accommodate 100-foot-wide swaths. An earlier system for broadcast application of suspensions used an air sparger to minimize settling in the tank, and a single-flood nozzle, less subject to clogging, was used for distribution. The operator had to maintain a constant ground speed and proper pressure. The single nozzle gave a swath width of 40 feet (1,2,31,32).

Band applications were once made entirely by farmers using their own or rented equipment, but in the 1970's band application also was offered by custom operators. Band equipment built by farmers used a 55-gallon drum sealed from the atmosphere. Replacement air was drawn through a breather pipe which extended to 1 inch from the bottom of the drum. As the fertilizer was removed, a partial vacuum was maintained in the tank and a near-constant pressure was obtained at the orifice plate near the bottom of the drum. The orifice plate consisted of a flat disc with a hole drilled in its center. The application rate was controlled by the size of the orifice and the ground speed. Some equipment manufacturers made this type of applicator for attachment to planters and grain drills. Subsurface preplant applications of fluid fertilizers are made with tractor-drawn equipment usually having ground-driven piston or squeeze pumps. Knives or chisels are used to open the soil for injection of the fertilizer (5,20).

Aerial Application—Aerial application of fertilizer is limited largely to special situations. These include crops and areas which cannot accommodate ground application equipment such as steep lands, flooded rice, and forest trees. Also, aerial spraying of foliar sprays is used for correcting both micronutrient and primary nutrients in citrus. Both fixed-wing airplanes and helicopters are fitted with booms and closely spaced nozzles or venturi-type spreaders. Spray drift is a problem and various schemes are used to minimize it (5,20).

REFERENCES

1. Achorn, F. P. 1978. *Fluid fertilizers and their world-wide potential.* Presented at Second International Conference on Fertilizers, London, England, Dec. 4-6, 1978. Tenn. Valley Auth., Muscle Shoals, Ala.
2. ____. 1980. *Suspension fertilizers update 1980.* Presented at Iowa Fertilizer and Chemical Assoc., Ames, Iowa, Jan. 29, 1980. Tenn. Valley Auth., Muscle Shoals, Ala.
3. ____. H. L. Balay, and H. L. Kimbrough. 1973. Commercial uses of the pipe reactor process for production of highpolyphosphate liquids. *Fertilizer Solutions* 23(6):44-54.
4. ____ and M. F. Broder. 1982. What's ahead for application practices. In *Situation 82*. Bull. Y-174. Tenn. Valley Auth., Muscle Shoals, Ala.
5. ____ and T. R. Cox. 1971. Production, marketing, and use of solid solution and suspension fertilizers. In *Fertilizer Technology and Use*, 2nd ed. Ed.by R. A. Olson, et al. pp. 381-412. Publ. by Soil Sci. Soc. of Amer., Madison, Wisc.
6. ____ and H. L. Kimbrough. 1976. *Latest development in materials and equipment for bulk blending.* Presented at TVA Fertilizer Conference, Cincinnati, Ohio,. July 1976. Available from Tenn. Valley Auth., Muscle Shoals, Ala.
7. ____ and D. G. Salladay. 1975. Production of monoammonium phosphate in a pipe-cross reactor. *Proc. of the 25th Annual Meeting of the Fertilizer Round Table*, Washington, D.C., Nov. 4-6, 1975.
8. ____ and D. G. Salladay. 1976. Pipe-cross reactor eliminates drier. *Farm Chem.* 139(7):34-38.
9. Anon. 1922. High analysis campaign receives new impetus. *Amer. Fert.* 57(9):23-24.
10. ____. 1923. Better and fewer analyses. *Comm. Fert.* 26(3):27-29.
11. ____. 1926. The Wisconsin research fellowship. *Amer. Fert.* 64(2): 25-27.
12. ____. 1950. Granular fertilizers: new dream plant at Des Moines where Iowa Plant Food Company produces. *Agr. Chem.* 5(3):36-37, 93-94.
13. ____. 1955. Manufacture of liquid fertilizers. *Comm. Fert. Yearbook, 1955*, pp. 103-104, 106-107.
14. ____. 1955. Consumption of fertilizer pesticide mixtures jumps 71 percent in 1953, U.S.D.A says. *Croplife* 2(44):1, 20.
15. ____. 1963. 23 years of blending services. *Croplife*, Sept. 1963, pp. 6-8.
16. Bond, B. J. and E. R. Swanson. 1958. *A cost analysis of bulk blending.* Univ. of Illinois Agr. Expt. Sta. Bull. 632, pp. 1-2.
17. ____ and H. G. Walkup. 1958. *Bulk blending, an innovation in fertilizer marketing.* Univ. of Illinois and Tenn. Valley Auth. publ. F59AR2, pp. 1-2.
18. Bridges, J. D. 1979. *Fertilizer Trends 1979.* National Fertilizer Development Center, Tenn. Valley Auth., Muscle Shoals, Ala.
19. ____. 1982. *Fertilizer Trends 1982.* National Fertilizer Development Center, Tenn. Valley Auth., Muscle Shoals, Ala.
20. Broder, M. F. 1984. Application of liquids and suspensions. In *Fluid Fertilizers*. Ed. by J. M. Potts, pp. 110-119. Nat. Fert. Dev. Center Bull Y-185. Tenn. Valley Auth., Muscle Shoals, Ala.
21. Bureau of Census. 1975. *Historical Statistics of the United States.* Part I, pp. 469, 519-520. U.S. Dept. of Commerce, Washington, D.C.
22. Collings, G. H. 1941. *Commercial Fertilizers*, 3rd edition. The Blakiston Co., Philadelphia.

23. Cook, R. L. and W. C. Hulbert. 1957. *Applying fertilizer. Yearbook of Agriculture, 1957,* pp. 217-229. U.S. Dept. Agric., Washington, D.C.
24. Chucka, J. A. 1953. Physical and chemical problems in mixed fertilizer production. In *Fertilizer Technology and Resources.* Ed. by K. D. Jacob, pp. 375-392, Academic Press, Inc., New York, N. Y.
25. Cumings, G. A., A. L. Mehring, and W. H. Sachs. 1930. Field and laboratory studies of fertilizer distributions for cotton. *Agr. Engin.* 11: 149-160.
26. Cummings, R. W. 1953. Fertilizer technology in a changing world. In *Fertilizer Technology and Usage.* Ed. by K. D. Jacob, pp. 1-14, Academic Press, Inc., Washington, D.C.
27. Crop Reporting Service. 1967. *Consumption of liquid commercial fertilizers in the United States 1954-1965.* Statistical Reporting Service, U.S. Dept. Agric., Washington, D.C.
28. _____. 1971. *Commercial fertilizers: consumption in the United States, fiscal year ended June 30, 1971.* Statistical Reporting Service, U.S. Dept. Agric., Washington, D.C.
29. _____. 1980. *Commercial fertilizers: consumption for the year ended June 30, 1980.* Economics and Statistics Service, U.S. Dept. Agric., Washington, D.C.
30. Douglas, J. R. and R. D. Grisso. 1963. Potential value of bulk blending and distribution in southern agriculture. In *Southern Bulk Blending Fertilizer Conference,* pp. 145-152. Tenn. Valley Auth., Muscle Shoals, Ala.
31. Follett, R. H., L. S. Murphy, and R. L. Donahue. 1981. *Fertilizers and Soil Amendments.* Prentice-Hall, Inc., Englewood Cliffs, N.J.
32. Getsinger, J. G., F. P. Achorn, and G. Hoffmeister. 1984. Suspension fertilizers–production and use. In *Fluid Fertilizers.* Ed. by J. M. Potts. Bull. Y-195, pp. 86. 109. Tenn. Valley Auth., Muscle Shoals, Ala.
33. Hargett, N. L. and J. T. Berry. 1980. *1980 Fertilizer Summary Data.* Bul. Y-165. Tenn. Valley Auth., Muscle Shoals, Ala.
34. _____ and R. Pay. 1980. Retail marketing of fertilizers in the U.S. *Proc. of the 30th Annual Meeting of the Fertilizer Industry Round Table,* Atlanta, Ga., Oct. 1980.
35. _____ and L. G. Sills. 1977. Fertilizer distribution centers in the U.S. *Proc. of the 27th Annual Meeting of the Fertilizer Industry Round Table,* Washington, D.C., Oct. 1977.
36. _____ and R. H. Wehrmann. 1975. Fertilizer production and distribution centers in the U.S. *Proc. of the 25th Annual Meeting of the Fertilizer Industry Round Table,* Washington, D.C. Nov. 1975.
37. Hignett, T. P. 1956. Pilot plant studies of granulation of high analysis fertilizers. *Agric. Chem.* 11(3):34-37, 141-143.
38. _____. 1965. *Bulk blending of fertilizers: practices and problems.* The Fertiliser Society, Proceedings No. 87. The Fertiliser Society of London, England.
39. _____. 1972. Liquid fertilizers, production and distribution. *Chem. Tech.* 2:627-637.
40. Hoffmeister, G. 1965. How to avoid segregation in bulk blended fertilizer materials. *Agric. Chem.* 20:42,46,96,98.
41. _____. 1973. Quality control in a bulk blending plant. *Proc. Tenn. Valley Auth. Bulk Blending Conf., Aug. 1973.* Tenn. Valley Auth., Muscle Shoals, Ala.
42. _____, S. C. Watkins, and J. Silverberg. 1964. Bulk blending of fertilizer material: effect of size, shape, and density on segregation. *J. Agric. and Food Chem.* 12(1):64-69.

43. International Fertilizer Development Center. 1985. *Fertilizer Manual.* Ed. by T. P. Hignett. Publ. by Martinus Nijhoff/Dr. W. Junk, Dondrecht, Boston, Lancaster.
44. Jacob, K. D. 1964. History and status of the superphosphate industry. In *Superphosphate, Its History, Chemistry, and Manufacture.* U.S. Dept. of Agric. and Tenn. Valley Auth., Gov't. Printing Office, Washington, D.C.
45. _____ and W. Scholl. 1955. Liquid fertilizers for direct application. *Comm. Fert. Yearbook 1955,* pp. 94-97, 99-101.
46. Jensen, O. F. 1930. Methods and equipment for applying fertilizers. *Comm. Fert.* 40(4):50-54, 56-57.
47. Keim, M. M. 1963. Growth of bulk blending and distribution. *Proc. Southern Bulk Blending Conf.,* pp. 15-28. Tenn. Valley Auth., Muscle Shoals, Ala.
48. King, F. H. 1911. *Farmers of Forty Centuries.* Democrat Printing Co., Madison, Wisc.
49. Lemmon, A. B. 1949. Liquid fertilizers in California. *Comm. Fert.* 78(1): 48-52.
50. Lockwood, M. H. 1953. High-analysis mixed fertilizers. In *Fertilizer Technology and Resources.* Ed. by K. D. Jacob, pp. 393-412, Academic Press, Inc., New York, N.Y.
51. Mackall, J. N. and M. Shoeld. 1940. Granulating phosphate fertilizers. *Chem. and Met. Engin.* 47:102.
52. Mehring, A. L. 1934. The development of mixed fertilizers. *Comm. Fert. 1934 Yearbook,* pp. 33-44.
53. _____. 1947. The problem of filler in fertilizer. *Amer. Fert.* 106(10):7- 10, 26-30.
54. _____. 1949. *Higher analysis fertilizer grades.* Assoc. Amer. Fertilizer Control Officials Publ. 3:37-50.
55. _____. 1951. Combination fertilizers and pesticides. *Comm. Fert.* 82(1): 32-40.
56. _____. 1953. Special fertilizers. In *Fertilizer Technology and Resources.* Ed. by K. D. Jacob, pp. 413-438. Academic Press, Inc., New York, N.Y.
57. _____, J. R. Adams, and K. D. Jacob. 1957. *Statistics on fertilizers and liming materials in the United States.* Publ. by the Agric. Research Service, U.S. Dept. Agric. Bull. No. 191, Supt. of Documents, Washington, D.C.
58. _____ and G. A. Cumings. 1930. *Factors affecting the mechanical application of fertilizers to the soil.* U.S. Dept. Agric. Tech. Bull. 182, Washington, D.C.
59. Meline, R. S., R. G. Lee, and W. C. Scott. 1972. Use of the pipe reactor in production of liquid fertilizers with very high polyphosphate content. *Fertilizer Solutions* 16(2):32-45.
60. Nelson, W. L. and C. M. Hansen. 1968. Methods and frequency of fertilizer application. In *Changing Patterns of Fertilizer Use.* Ed. by L. B. Nelson, pp. 85-118. Publ. by Soil Sci. Soc. Amer., Madison, Wisc.
61. Office of Industrial Programs, 1982. *Energy efficient fertilizer production with the pipe-cross reactor.* U.S. Dept. Energy. DOE/NBM-1003. National Technical Information Service, Springfield, Va.
62. Ross, W. H. 1932. Granulation of fertilizers. *J. Assoc. Official Agric. Chem.* 15:632-635.
63. _____ and A. L. Mehring. 1938. Mixed fertilizers. In *Soils and Men, 1938 Yearbook of Agric.,* pp. 522-545. U.S. Dept. Agric., Washington, D.C.

64. Salter, R. M. 1938. Methods of applying fertilizer. In *Soils and Men, 1938 Yearbook of Agric.*, pp. 546-562. U.S. Dept. Agric., Washington, D.C.
65. Scholl, W., G. W. Schmidt, and C. A. Wilker. 1961. *Consumption of commercial fertilizers and primary plant nutrients in the United States, year ended June 30, 1961.* Publ. by Agric. Research Service, U.S. Dept. Agric., Washington, D.C.
66. ____ and H. M. Wallace. 1951. *Commercial fertilizer consumption in the United States, 1950-51.* Div. of Fertilizer and Agricultural Lime. Publ. by Agric. Research Service, U.S. Dept. Agric., Washington, D.C.
67. Slack, A. V. 1967. *Fertilizers. Chemistry and Technology, Vol. 9*, pp. 25-150. Publ. by John Wiley and Sons, New York, N. Y.
68. ____ and F. P. Achorn. 1973. *New developments in manufacture and use of liquid fertilizers.* Proc. No. 133, The Fertiliser Society, Alembic House, London, England.
69. Smalley, H. R. 1931. Progress in application of fertilizers. *Comm. Fert.* 32(1):30-33.
70. Smith, R. C. and B. Makower. 1963. Advances in manufacture of mixed fertilizers. In *Fertilizer Technology and Usage.* Ed. by M. H. McVickar, G. L. Bridger, and L. B. Nelson. Publ. by Soil Science Soc. Amer., Madison, Wisc.
71. Stanfield, Z. A. 1956. Economics of manufacture of liquid mixed fertilizers. *Comm. Fert. Yearbook, Sept. 1956.* 93(3A):101-109.
72. Striplin, M. M., D. McKnight, and G. H. Megar. 1958. Fertilizer materials: phosphoric acid of high concentration. *Agric. and Food Chem.* 6:298-303.
73. Taylor, R. P. 1953. Mechanics of mixed fertilizer production. In *Fertilizer Technology and Resources.* Ed. by K. D. Jacob, pp. 355-373, Academic Press, Inc., New York, N.Y.
74. Tenn. Valley Authority. 1965. *The TVA fertilizer program.* Unpublished review. Tenn. Valley Auth., Muscle Shoals, Ala.
75. ____. 1978. *A review of TVA's fluid fertilizer introduction program.* Unpublished review. Div. of Agric. Development, Test and Demonstration Branch, Tenn. Valley Auth., Muscle Shoals, Ala.
76. Truog, E. 1924. Method of applying fertilizers. *Amer. Fert.* 60(9):23-27.
77. van Buren, N. 1979. 25 years progress culminates in St. Louis. *Fertilizer Solutions* 23(6):8-18, 30-34.
78. Walkup, H. G. 1963. Potential value of bulk blending and distribution to southern agriculture. In *Proc. Southern Bulk Blending Fertilizer Conf., Jan. 21-23, 1963,* Knoxville, Tenn. Tenn. Valley Auth., Muscle Shoals, Ala.
79. Yates, L. D., F. T. Nielsson, and G. C. Hicks. 1954. TVA continuous ammoniator for superphosphate fertilizer mixtures. *Farm Chem.* 117(7):38-48 and 117(8):34-41.
80. Young, R. D. and F. P. Achorn. 1978. *Trends in U.S. fertilizer technology–implications for global transfer.* Nat. Fert. Devel. Center Bull. Y-133. Tenn. Valley Auth., Muscle Shoals, Ala.
81. ____ and N. L. Hargett. 1984. History, growth and status. In *Fluid Fertilizers.* Ed. by J. M. Potts, pp. 5-13, Nat. Fert. Devel. Center Bull Y-185. Tenn. Valley Auth., Muscle Shoals, Ala.

13

Fertilizer Consumption, Role, and Impacts 1920-1980

This chapter deals with the consumption and use of fertilizers and their impact during the 60-year period of 1920-1980. It can be divided into three 20-year periods. The first was a period of hard times and depression, stagnation of fertilizer consumption, and lack of innovation. The second was a period of transition and change–the period that saw the birth of the agricultural revolution. The third became a period of skyrocketing demand, with consumption jumping from 7.5 million tons of primary nutrients to an almost unbelievable 23 million tons, and with it came new problems. All three periods shared the common malady of overproduction of leading crops; it was a problem that would not go away, ate up billions of federal tax dollars, and made farmers dependent upon congressional handouts. To cap it off, in the 1970s fertilizers were charged as being a source of pollutants and a destroyer of the environment. Nevertheless, without fertilizers the United States and the world could not have provided the food required by the ever-increasing populations.

Primary Nutrient Consumption: 1920-1980

Tonnages of primary nutrients (N, P_2O_5, K_2O) consumed in the United States from 1920 through 1980 increased 20-fold (Table 13.1), from 1.2 million to 23.1 million short tons in 1980. Of this, nitrogen increased 50-fold from 228,000 tons to 11.4 million, phosphate 8-fold from 660,000 to 5.4 million, potash 24-fold from 257,000 to 6.3 million.

Regardless of the huge increase in fertilizer use, the 60-year period had its ups and downs. The first major blow occurred in the 1920's, followed by the Great Depression in the 1930's. Consumption in 1921 was the lowest in 12 years. This was followed by a small recovery, then a slump in 1927. The Great Depression hit in 1929 when the bottom fell out of the stock market. Prices of farm crops fell 70 percent between 1919 and 1932 when the depression bottomed out. By 1937, farm prices improved and fertilizer use increased to 1.6 million tons, double the 1930 level.

Chronic overproduction of farm commodities had been the rule from 1921 through the 1930's (9).

World War II initially created a strong need for U.S. food commodities among the allies. Post-war needs remained strong as the United States extended aid to needy countries. Prices received by farmers rose 138 percent from 1940 through 1946 and net farm incomes increased 236 percent. Demand for primary plant nutrients doubled from 1940 to 1950 (17).

Table 13.1. Consumption of Primary Nutrients for Selected Years, 1920-1980 (43,32,12,13,31).

Year	N	Available P_2O_5	K_2O	Total Nutrients
		1000 short tons		
1920	228	660	257	1,145
1921	159	433	189	791
1930	378	794	354	1,526
1932	214	413	192	819
1937	412	794	416	1,612
1940	419	912	435	1,766
1945	595	1,338	704	2,637
1950	956	1,930	1,070	3,956
1955	1,961	2,284	1,875	6,120
1960	2,738	2,572	2,153	7,464
1965	4,639	3,512	2,835	10,985
1970	7,459	4,574	4,036	16,068
1974	9,157	5,099	5,083	19,339
1975	8,601	4,505	4,453	17,561
1976	10,412	5,228	5,210	20,849
1977	10,647	5,630	5,834	22,111
1978	9,965	5,096	5,526	20,587
1979	10,715	5,606	6,245	22,565
1980	11,408	5,432	6,245	23,084

Demand for fertilizers continued to increase in the 1950-1960 period. Synthetic nitrogen was available in large amounts and its use nearly tripled; phosphate increased only 30 percent, and potash, now in great demand for the first time, doubled.

Consumption continued to accelerate during the 1960-1970 period. Total nutrient consumption increased from 7.5 million tons to 16 million, an average increase of 8 percent per year. Nitrogen, the most used primary nutrient, increased from 2.7 million tons to 7.5 million, an average annual increase of 10.5 percent per year. Phosphate increased from 2.2 million tons to 4 million, an average annual increase of 6.5 percent (30).

In contrast, the 1970-1980 period slowed down markedly. Total primary nutrient consumption moved from 16.1 million tons to 23.1 million, an average increase of only 3.6 percent per year. Nitrogen use during the same period increased from 7.5 million tons to 11.4 million, an average annual growth rate of 4.3 percent. Phosphate use increased from 4.6 million tons to 5.4 million, an average increase of only 1.7 percent. Potash consumption rose from 4 million in 1970 to 6.2 million in 1980 or an average increase of 4.3 percent (30).

Annual total primary nutrient consumption gained each year from 1940 through 1974, when a turnaround occurred. Fertilizer prices were doubling and tripling at the same time that market prices of wheat, corn, and other agricultural commodities were declining. This caused farmers to reduce fertilizer purchases by nearly 10 percent in 1975. By 1976, prices of commodities had improved and fertilizer prices had returned to normal (Table 13.1) (38).

Nutrient Consumption by Regions: 1934-1980

Each region has a section describing the primary nutrient consumption that affects the amount of fertilizer used and its effectiveness. This has been a common practice among agricultural publications since the 1950's. In the present text other factors affecting the amount of fertilizer consumed include the harvested crop acreage, the size of the cultivated farm land within the region, and the total nutrients applied per harvested acre. Other inclusions that help characterize a region are the more important crops, the approximate acreage, the nature of the soils, the climate, and the practice of irrigated or dryland farming.

The regions are shown in Figure 13.1. Because of similarity with respect to such factors as kinds of farming, crops, soils, climate, and others, the New England and the Middle Atlantic have been treated in this chapter as a single "Northeastern" region. East North Central and West North Central, both being in the corn belt, are treated as one.

The Northeastern States

New England consists of Maine, New Hampshire, Vermont, Massachusetts, Rhode Island, and Connecticut (Table 13.2). The Middle Atlantic States are New York, Pennsylvania, New Jersey, Delaware, Maryland, and West Virginia. The Northeast has a diversified agriculture of livestock farming, dairying, poultry, fruit, shade tobacco, potatoes in Maine, forages, and general or mixed farming. The better soils are on the Coastal Plain and are intensively farmed. Over the years New England agriculture has suffered from abandonment of poor farmlands. The two regions have a ready market for agriculture products (6, 11, 28, 30).

Figure 13.1. Major geographic subdivisions of the United States.

The northeast regions are modest users of chemical fertilizers as compared with other regions. New England's consumption of primary nutrients was 105,000 tons in 1950, 126,000 in 1970, and then slipped to 118,000 in 1980. Its share of the nation's total primary nutrient consumption amounted to only 5 percent in 1939 and less than 1 percent in 1980–the lowest in the nation. The Middle Atlantic region's consumption was 161,000 tons in 1934, 438,000 in 1950, 731,000 in 1970, and 840,000 in 1980. Its share of the U.S. total dropped from 15 percent in 1939 to 4 percent in 1980, the third lowest in the country. The pounds of primary nutrients applied per harvested acre in New England were 139 pounds in 1965, peaked at 175 pounds in 1970, and then dropped to 162 pounds in 1980. The Middle Atlantic states ranged from 102 pounds of primary nutrients in 1965 to around 137 in 1980 and 114 in 1980. Both regions were high users of phosphate until the 1950's and reached a 1-1-1 ratio of the three primary nutrients by 1960. The total harvested crop acreage in New England is only about 2 million acres while the Middle Atlantic averages 12 million (29, 30).

South Atlantic

The South Atlantic region consists of Virginia, North Carolina, South Carolina, Georgia, and Florida. By 1980, this region had become the nation's largest consumer of fertilizers. It led until 1950, at which time it was exceeded by the two north central regions. Application of total nutrients per harvested acre was the highest of the nine regions, averaging 220 pounds in 1965 and 217 in 1980. The harvested crop acreage for the five states was 15 million in 1965 and 20 million in 1980 (29, 30).

Phosphate was the most used nutrient from 1934 through 1950, with about equal amounts of nitrogen and potash. Phosphate became the least used after the mid-1960's with nitrogen and potash being consumed in equal quantities. The most productive croplands in the region are on the Coastal Plains, which accounts for 70 percent of primary nutrient use. The remainder is located largely upon the Piedmont and mountain areas having small cultivated fields. Florida, with its high per acre value crops and 310 to 365 frost-free days in the southern area, applies an average of 900 pounds of total primary nutrients. Nevertheless, the state's major crops are corn, soybeans, and cotton. Cotton is also grown in Georgia, North Carolina and South Carolina although acreages have declined sharply. Wheat is grown in all states except Florida. Tobacco is the region's most valuable crop. Forages and vegetables are common (29, 37).

East and West North Central

The East North Central region includes Ohio, Indiana, Illinois, Michigan, and Wisconsin. The West North Central states are Minnesota, Iowa, Missouri, North Dakota, South Dakota, Nebraska, and Kansas The East North Central region's harvested crop acreage in 1965 was 56 million and 65 million in 1980. The West North Central total ranged from 118 million acres in 1965 to 143 million in 1980. The two regions account for 60 percent of the harvested acreage of the United States.

Corn, soybeans, and wheat account for two-thirds of the harvested cropland in the two regions. In 1980, the acreage of corn amounted to 61 million acres, or 84 percent of the U.S. total. The corn acreage is about equally divided between the two regions. In 1965, soybeans were produced on 24 million acres, which was also about 80 percent of the nation's acreage. By 1980, the acreage had increased to 41 million acres but due to the crop's increase in popularity in other regions, its share of the U.S. total fell to 61 percent. Wheat is grown in both regions, but it is by far the most important crop in the West North Central region. Several other crops in the two regions are important. Grain sorghum is grown in South Dakota, Minnesota, Iowa, and Missouri; sunflowers and potatoes are grown in the two Dakotas and Minnesota; and hay, pasture, oats, barley, and potatoes are variously produced (30, 49, 64).

Both the East North Central and West North Central regions were slow starters in fertilizer consumption, especially the West North Central. In 1934, the East North Central used 102,000 tons of primary nutrients and the West North Central, 12,000. Both by 1960 were showing major gains and by 1980 the East North Central reached 6.3 million tons of

Table 13.2. Primary Nutrient Consumption by Regions (43,32,30,12,13,31).

	1934	1939	1950	1960	1970	1980
	\multicolumn{6}{c}{*1000 tons*}
	\multicolumn{6}{c}{New England}
N	15	16	24	32	41	42
Avail. P_2O_5	26	32	61	47	42	34
K_2O	24	27	46	43	43	37
Total	65	75	105	122	126	114
	\multicolumn{6}{c}{Middle Atlantic}
N	28	34	69	134	237	315
Avail. P_2O_5	86	135	246	227	259	244
K_2O	47	62	123	203	235	282
Total	161	231	438	565	731	840
	\multicolumn{6}{c}{South Atlantic}
N	121	166	275	463	806	944
Avail. P_2O_5	219	262	470	473	524	528
K_2O	110	169	331	574	751	954
Total	450	596	1,076	1,510	2,081	2,427
	\multicolumn{6}{c}{East North Central}
N	10	18	95	423	1,419	2,438
Avail. P_2O_5	66	102	396	641	1,174	1,480
K_2O	26	54	299	643	1,370	2,363
Total	102	174	790	1,707	3,963	6,281
	\multicolumn{6}{c}{West North Central}
N	1	2	60	495	2,338	4,032
Avail. P_2O_5	9	19	193	457	1,256	1,554
K_2O	2	4	60	224	854	1,501
Total	12	25	312	1,175	4,448	7,087
	\multicolumn{6}{c}{East South Central}
N	35	67	193	315	487	596
Avail. P_2O_5	62	89	289	280	348	420
K_2O	25	39	135	271	375	505
Total	122	195	617	867	1,210	1,521

	1934	1939	1950	1960	1970	1980
			1000 tons			
			West South Central			
N	11	22	95	315	1,060	1,348
Avail. P_2O_5	16	25	161	187	435	533
K_2O	6	12	50	102	253	318
Total	33	59	306	604	1,749	2,198
			Mountain			
N	0.20	1	22	127	375	605
Avail. P_2O_5	0.90	10	40	97	242	229
K_2O	0.01	0.1	2	5	18	33
Total	2.10	11.1	63	229	634	867
			Pacific			
N	19	29	123	382	646	1,036
Avail. P_2O_5	13	22	75	142	236	342
K_2O	5	8	23	47	94	136
Total	38	59	221	571	975	1,514
			Hawaii			
N	14	17	20	19	29	25
Avail. P_2O_5	11	7	8	8	19	19
K_2O	4	11	13	18	24	19
Total	29	35	41	45	72	63
			Alaska			
Total	–	–	0.2	1.8	2.3	3.5
			Puerto Rico			
N	14	16	29	33	22	17
Avail. P_2O_5	6	7	14	12	8	6
K_2O	10	12	22	22	17	13
Total	30	45	65	67	47	36
			United States			
N	270	384	1,370	2,738	7,459	11,407
Avail. P_2O_5	515	710	1,947	2,572	4,574	5,432
K_2O	259	399	1,104	2,153	4,036	6,245
Total	1,044	1,493	4,421	7,464	16,068	23,084

total primary nutrients and the West North Central, 7.1 million, making these two the nation's largest fertilizer using regions. The consumption patterns of the individual primary nutrients vary somewhat between the two regions. In the West North Central, nitrogen was by far the most used nutrient during the 1960-1980 period, starting with 495,000 tons and reaching 4 million in 1980; phosphate increased from 457,000 tons to 1.6 million and potash from 224,000 to 1.5 million. The East North Central consumed 423,000 tons of nitrogen in 1960 but reached only 2.4 million in 1980; phosphate increased from 541,000 to 1.5 million; and potash from 643,000 to 2.4 million.

Within the boundaries of the 10 states of the two regions is the so-called Corn Belt. The Corn Belt has an interesting history. Prior to the 1850's it was continuously cropped either to corn or wheat, and yields eventually declined. Farms then turned to alternating corn with wheat and then to wheat and clover. More complex rotations followed such as corn-wheat-clover, corn-oats-clover, and corn-corn-wheat seeded with clover or oats seeded with biennial sweet clover; the main purpose was to provide nitrogen, reduce plant disease, control weeds, and reduce insect damage. From about 1910 through 1950 improved rotations dominated the Corn Belt. After 1950 synthetic ammonia and nitrogen fertilizers derived from it became available in large amounts. As a result rotations gradually shortened or on more level lands corn-soybeans took over except for forages and hay for livestock farms (20, 22, 41). Several factors were responsible for the high natural productivity of the corn belt. These include friable, deep soils with a high water-holding capacity that shortens the growing season, and a level or rolling topography suited to use of large-scale machinery (50, 53).

East South Central

The East South Central region consists of Kentucky, Tennessee, Alabama, and Mississippi. As early as 1980, the region was an important fertilizer user, exceeded only by the South Atlantic and the Middle Atlantic regions, both seaboard states. Consumption of the three primary nutrients in the East South Central region increased from 122,000 tons in 1934 to 617,000 in 1950, and to 1.5 million in 1980. Nitrogen increased from 35,000 in 1934 to 193,000 in 1950, and to 596,000 in 1980. Phosphate use increased modestly from 62,000 in 1934 to 289,000 in 1950, and to 420,000 in 1980. Potash use was slow to take off, going from 25,000 in 1934 to 135,000 in 1980, and to 505,000 in 1980. Of the four states in the region, nitrogen consumption in 1980 was highest in Mississippi, where it accounted for about 55 percent of the three nutrients. Alabama, the second largest nitrogen user, consumed 37 percent. Kentucky and Tennessee consumed nearly equal amounts of the three nutrients (Table 13.2).

The harvested crop acres in the East South Central region increased from 15 million in 1965 to 21 million in 1980, with three crops–corn, cotton, and soybeans–making up about two-thirds of the total. Wheat was grown on limited acreage. Other crops accounted for the remaining one-quarter to one-half of the total cropland acreage. These include tobacco, peanuts, sugarcane, and a flourishing forest industry. Some 880,000 acres of pine are fertilized with phosphate (1, 10, 30, 61).

The region is divided into several subregions representing a range of climate, soils, and crops. The East Central Uplands is referred to as the Upper South. The area in Tennessee and Kentucky includes the limestone valley, the dissected plateaus, the Cumberland Plateau, and the mountains. Reddish, well drained soils derived from limestone occur in northern Alabama along with a gray, poorly drained, and less productive soil. Both have a low water-holding capacity making them subject to drought. The Coastal Plans and other subregions are described for the South Atlantic region. Soil erosion is a problems on slopes in Tennessee, Alabama, and Mississippi. The alluvial soils on the eastern side of the Mississippi are highly fertile for intensive cultivation (27, 47, 57, 62, 66).

West South Central

The West South Central states are Arkansas, Louisiana, Oklahoma, and Texas. The region includes both humid and arid climates. The sub-humid portion is subject to large variations in precipitation ranging from moist humid conditions to prolonged periods of drought. Soils in the western portions differ markedly from those found in the eastern portions, being less weathered, low in native nitrogen, and high in potash (7, 40, 61).

The West South Central region in 1934 used only 33,000 tons of primary nutrients; consumption was 306,000 tons in 1950, and 2.2 million in 1980. Nitrogen use accounted for 11,000 tons in 1934, 95,000 in 1950, and 1.4 million in 1980. During the 1970's nitrogen accounted for 60 percent of the region's total primary nutrient application. Phosphate reached about 500,000 tons or 25 percent of the total nutrients applied in the 1970's. Potash accounted for 15 percent (Table 13.2).

Soils of the South Great Plains region, much of which is west of the humid region, vary in acidity and alkalinity, texture, and depth. Much of the Ozark area of northern Arkansas and northeastern Oklahoma is mountainous. The Gulf Coastal Plains include parts of Louisiana and Texas. The Mississippi Delta area includes the fertile delta of the Mississippi River and the alluvium from the Arkansas and Red rivers. The Gulf Coastal Prairies in the southwestern Louisiana and southeastern Texas cover 8 million acres. Much of the area adjacent to the Gulf is marshland and drainage is a problem (27, 40, 61, 63).

Irrigation is practiced in the Texas Panhandle, in the lower Rio Grande Valley, and on alluvial lands along several rivers (27, 40, 61, 63). The region had 38 million harvested crop acres in 1965 and 46 million in 1980. Wheat, cotton, soybeans, and corn are the leading crops. Oklahoma and Texas accounted for 88 percent of the region's wheat in 1965 and nearly 93 percent in 1980. Cotton, the second most important crop, had a cropland acreage of 7.8 million in 1965 and 8.5 million in 1980. Soybeans were grown on 3.2 million acres in 1965 and 9.7 million in 1979, a peak year. Corn acreage in 1965 was 900,000, which doubled by 1980. Other crops of importance are irrigated rice, sugarcane and hay, improved pastures, and native hays (13, 30, 61).

Mountain

The Mountain States are Montana, Idaho, Wyoming, Colorado, Utah, Arizona, and New Mexico. Although the region has about one-fourth of the land acreage of the lower 48 states, harvested crop acreage is quite small, amounting to 23 million acres in 1965 and 27 million in 1980. The region varies greatly in elevations and annual precipitation, ranging from typical humid areas in northern Idaho to desert areas in Arizona and New Mexico. Temperatures, soils, and length of growing seasons also vary greatly. Except for dry-farmed wheat and humid areas, irrigation is essential for practically all crops in the region. Both surface and ground waters are used. The supply of irrigation water is sufficient for only a small part of the potential cropland (58, 65).

Use of chemical fertilizers in the region up until the late 1950's was negligible and that used was mostly phosphate mined and manufactured in Idaho, Utah, and Wyoming or shipped in from Trail, British Columbia. Consumption of the three primary nutrients amounted to only 2,000 tons in 1934, 63,000 in 1950, and 867,000 in 1980, or 4 percent of the U.S. total. Nitrogen use exceeded that of phosphate in 1960 and continued to increase; by 1980, it accounted for 70 percent of the region's primary nutrient consumption, while phosphate amounted to only 26 percent. Potash application was only 2,000 tons in 1950 and 33,000 tons in 1980 due to the high level of available natural soluble potassium. Of the many different crops grown in the region, wheat accounts for the largest harvested cropland acreage of about 10 million in the 1970's, or nearly 40 percent of the region's total cropland. Montana's wheat acreage made up nearly half, with Colorado and Idaho sharing the remainder, all of which is grown under dryland farming. Corn for grain is the second largest crop with about a million acres, all of which is irrigated and produced mostly in Colorado. Cotton accounts for about 800,000 acres in Arizona and New Mexico. Sugarbeets are grown in Wyoming, Colorado, Idaho, and Montana. Other crops are malting barley, oats, mountain meadows, alfalfa, peas, beans, lentils and potatoes. The region also has a wide range of fruits and vegetables in adapted areas. Citrus fruits are produced in Arizona (30, 65).

Pacific

The Pacific region consists of California, Washington, and Oregon. It is an area with a wide range of climatic conditions, varying from the cooler, humid north portion to the hot, dry desert conditions of the Imperial Valley in southern California where crops can be produced all year under irrigation.

Harvested acreage of the three states amounted to 14 million in 1980. Approximately 5 million is in Washington, 3 million in Oregon and 6 million in California. A humid, cool summer exists west of the Cascade Mountains in Washington, Oregon, and the northeastern corner of California. The area east of the Cascades in Washington and Oregon extends to near the border of Idaho. This huge area has precipitation ranging from 6 to 12 inches close to the eastern side of the Cascades and east of this to 16 to 32 inches. California, except for the eastern mountains and along the Coastal range, is hot in the summers. Precipitation runs from 20 inches in the northern valleys to less than 5 inches in the southern areas (2, 16, 38, 52).

Most of California's irrigated agriculture is in the Sacramento Valley in the northern part of the state and the San Joaquin Valley in the south. These two valleys account for three-fourths of California's cropland. Other major agricultural areas are in the coastal valleys and foothills, the Salinas Valley and the Imperial Valley, which together account for another 20 percent of the the state's cropland (2, 52).

Consumption of primary nutrients in the Pacific region was only 38,000 tons in 1934 and 221,000 in 1950; it then rose rapidly to 1.5 million in 1980. Nitrogen has been the dominant nutrient, accounting for half of the nutrients applied in the 1934-1950 period and over three-fourths thereafter. Phosphate accounted for about one-third during the earlier period and one-quarter for the 1950-1980 period. Potash, the least used, accounted for 13 percent in 1934 and 10 percent after 1950. Each of the states followed the same pattern of primary nutrients consumption. California was the highest per-acre user of the primary nutrients with 160 pounds in 1965 and 286 by 1980. Washington and Oregon together averaged 76 pounds in 1965 and 148 in 1980.

The region's climatic diversity permits production of an estimated 200 commercial crops. Wheat is grown on the largest acreage with 3 million in 1965 and 5.7 million in 1980. Other large acreage crops are corn, rice, and fertilized Douglas fir (2, 16, 38). Irrigation is essential on much of the region's cropland. Washington and Oregon irrigate 20 percent of their cropland and California, 80 percent.

Hawaii, Puerto Rico, Alaska

Hawaii with only 105,000 harvested acres is one of the highest primary nutrient users in the world, averaging about 1,300 pounds per acre over the 1970-1980 period. Nitrogen is the most consumed primary nutrient with the state using 25,000 tons in 1965 and 23,000 tons in 1980. Phosphate consumption in 1965 amounted to 11,000 tons and in 1980, 19,000 tons. The use of potash about paralleled that of phosphate. The major crops are sugarcane, pineapples, and other tropical crops. The island of Hawaii's main agriculture activity is livestock grazing (30).

Puerto Rico consumed 72,000 tons of total plant nutrients in 1965 but declined steadily to 37,000 in 1980. Between 1965 and 1980, nitrogen use fell from 33,000 to 17,000 tons, phosphate from 13,000 to 6,200, and potash from 25,000 to 13,000. The declines were due to lessening interest in agriculture as other industries increased on the island.

Alaska has 365 million acres of actual land area, practically all of which is non-agricultural land and forest. What farming is practiced involves general farming, livestock grazing, and dairying. Two areas where commercial farming is practiced are the Fairbanks area and the Matanuska Valley. About 3,000 tons of primary nutrients were consumed in the 1975-1980 period about equally divided among the three nutrients (30).

Highest Fertilizer-Using States

The relative importance of the leading fertilizer-using states changes over the years. Table 13.3 lists the seven highest primary nutrient-using states in 1939 and by 10-year intervals from 1950 through 1980, in declining order according to their percentage of the U.S. total consumption. This is a function of both a state's total harvested cropland acreage and the total primary nutrients applied in pounds per acre harvested (30).

As shown in Table 13.3, five of the top seven nutrient-using states in 1939 were in the South, with North Carolina and Georgia heading the list. The seven states accounted for over half of the U.S. total. Use shifted westward, and by 1970, six of the top seven were located in the Midwest, Texas being the exception (30, 43).

The percentage share of the U.S. total primary nutrient consumption also changes with the years both for the seven-state totals and the consumption of the individual states. In 1939, the seven leaders accounted for 51 percent of the U.S. total, with North Carolina consuming about 13 percent. By 1950, use in the seven states had dropped to 30 percent with North Carolina dropping to 9 percent. By 1960, the total consumption of the seven states had leveled out while the leading state, Indiana, dropped to about 6 percent. The seven-state total increased to 43 percent in 1970 and Illinois, the leading state, to 9.5 percent. In 1980,

Table 13.3. Share of U.S. Nutrients Used by Seven Leading States (53,36).

	1939		1950		1960		1970		1980	
Rank	State	%	State	%	State	%	State	%	State	%
1	NC	12.6	NC	8.7	Ind.	6.4	Ill.	9.5	Ill.	10.6
2	Ga.	8.7	Ohio	5.6	Ill.	5.6	Iowa	8.8	Iowa	9.4
3	SC	7.6	Ga.	5.4	Calif.	5.5	Tex.	6.2	Minn.	5.8
4	Ala.	6.3	Ala.	5.4	Ga.	5.3	Ind.	5.6	Ind.	5.7
5	Fla.	6.2	Ind.	5.1	NC	5.1	Minn.	4.5	Tex.	5.0
6	Ohio	5.0	Calif.	4.3	Ohio	5.1	Ohio	4.2	Ohio	4.6
7	Pa.	4.8	Fla.	4.1	Fla.	4.5	Nebr.	4.2	Nebr.	4.6
Total		51.2		38.6		37.5		43.0		45.7

both the seven-state total and the leading state continued to increase, reaching nearly 46 percent and 11, respectively, with Illinois remaining the leading state (30, 43).

The amounts of primary nutrients applied per harvested acre varied greatly among the states. The highest users during the 1970's were Hawaii with 1,200 pounds, Florida with 846, and Rhode Island with 508. The lowest per acre users were South Dakota with 24 pounds, Montana with 28, and Wyoming with 36. Of the remaining states, several ranged between 50 and 100 pounds, about 20 states between 100 and 200 pounds, and 10 states between 200 and 300. The U.S. average was 135 pounds per acre. Application rates in Europe and a number of countries greatly exceed those in the United States in terms of pounds applied per harvested acre. For example, the Netherlands applies around 700 pounds per acre, Ireland 600, France 260, Denmark about 230, Mainland China 160, and the two Koreas 300 (23, 30).

Crop Yield Breakthroughs

Although mankind strived to increase crop yields as early as 2500 B.C., it wasn't until chemical fertilizers and supporting practices appeared that per-acre yields of crops began to increase in much of the world.

Per-acre yields of major crops in the United States remained unchanged from about 1800 until the 1940's when chemical fertilizers, including synthetic nitrogen, appeared in large amounts and improved crop varieties such as hybrid corn were available. During the first half of the 19th century, an increasing number of innovative farmers and plantation owners began to amend their soils with lime, gypsum, rich bottomland, Peruvian guano, and to experiment with Chilean nitrate. From 1850 to the turn of the century, the country's expanding crop needs were met by bringing new lands, primarily to the west, under

Fertilizers replace nutrients removed from the soil by crop harvests and by other losses. The use of fertilizers has been one of the keys in America's increasingly efficient production of food and fiber.
(F.J. Myers--TVA)

483

cultivation. Although commercial fertilizers were becoming available, they were either not used at all or applied in such small amounts that their impact was minimal. From 1900 to about 1939, fertilizer production and consumption were held back, first with the coming of World War I, and then the depressions of the 1920's and the 1930's. These events and the overproduction of most agricultural commodities limited any interest in increasing crop yields (Chapter 4).

The 20-year period starting in 1940 was marked by increased demands for food products not only in the United States, but also by our allies. A widespread interest in improving crop yields and quality brought to the forefront earlier scientific and other advances that had lain unused and the introduction of several improved practices and their integration into optimum combinations (Table 13.1).

Crop yields per harvested acre began to increase about 1935 in the United States. Average corn yields did not exceed 30 bushels (56 pounds per bu.) per acre until 1935. Following 1935, average yields increased to 57 bushels in 1960, 72 in 1970, and 110 in 1979. Wheat yields averaged only 11 bushels (60 pounds per bu.) per harvested acre in 1866 and did not reach 15 bushels until 1940, but reached 24 in 1960, 31 in 1975, and 34 in 1980. (Yield increases for wheat are less spectacular than the other crops because much of it is grown under dryland farming). Cotton yields averaged 122 pounds per acre (1 bale = 500 pounds) in 1866. From 1870 through 1949 yields ranged from a low of 157 pounds per acre in 1930 to a high of around 250 pounds in the 1940's. During the 1970's yields roughly doubled with a top of 548 pounds in 1979. Irish potato yields per harvested acre from 1866 through 1910 ranged from 75 to 101 hundredweight (cwt.) depending on the year. From 1920 through 1940, yields ranged from 112 to 132 cwt. and increased steadily to 262 cwt. in 1980 (1, 16, 21). The take-off in yields resulted from the bringing together of a number of production practices. These include improved crop varieties, increased use of chemical fertilizers, use of chemical herbicides and insecticides, plant disease control, adjustments in plant populations, improved soil tillage practices and use of modern mechanization in order to achieve more timely planting and harvesting, and, under irrigation, proper water management (8, 59).

Selection of good production factors and their integration was primarily the contribution of a large number of agronomists and, on the mechanical side, engineers. The integration process was perfected largely in the United States and became known as the agricultural revolution, the basic principles of which were exported to developing countries. The appearance of high-yielding hybrid corn and short-stem, non-lodging wheat were the result of discoveries in plant breeding and genetics from 1900 to about 1940. The introduction of effective chemical insecticides and herbicides in 1939 and the early 1940's was the result of screening innumerable chemicals in Europe and the United States that were thought might be of biological importance during wartime.

Both insecticides and herbicides found agricultural use within five years of their discovery and became the forerunners for dozens of complex chemical compounds including those that controlled certain plant diseases. Chemical fertilizers which were produced a century earlier had become less costly and more effective (42, 74).

More timely planting, harvesting, and other farm operations were made possible through improved farm mechanization brought about by the introduction and perfecting of the internal combustion engine for powering tractors, trucks, and other equipment such as combines. The new engine as early as 1920 began replacing horses and mules, which dropped in number from 15 million in 1920 to 7.6 million in 1950, while tractors on farms increased from 246,000 to 3.4 million (14, 17).

A number of other factors played important roles in making the breakthrough in crop yields possible. Seven of the more important are listed below: (a) the establishment of agriculturally oriented land-grant colleges and agricultural experiment stations and the state agricultural extension services; (b) the entrance of TVA into fertilizer research and development and the creation of the Soil Conservation Service; (c) the development of a cadre of well-trained and experienced agricultural scientists and other professionals who were in a position to help establish the agricultural revolution during its formative years; (d) the understanding through research of the reactions that each of the primary nutrients undergoes upon application to the soil and its effect upon plant uptake; (e) the role of the different plant nutrients in plant nutrition; (f) the development of a process for fixing the inert nitrogen in the atmosphere into a usable form through synthesis of hydrogen and nitrogen to form ammonia, and (g) the development of statistical methods for designing and laying out sound field experiments and analyzing the validity and significance of the results as governed by mathematical laws of probability (54).

Various estimates have been made of the contribution of each of the various inputs, especially fertilizers, upon the yield of grain crops. Two approaches have been made. One involves estimating how much of the increased grain production over a given period of time is due to fertilizer use, while the second attempts to ascribe a percentage distribution among two or more inputs.

The Council of Agricultural Science and Technology in 1974 estimated that about 33 percent of the U.S. grain production was due to fertilizer. Christensen and coworkers in 1964 estimated that 55 percent of the U.S. grain yield during the period of 1940-1955 was due to fertilizer. Auer and Heady, using the 1939-1961 yields of corn in the Midwest, estimated that 31 percent of the total per acre increase came from use of fertilizers. Shaw and Durost attributed 25 percent of the yield increase of corn from 1929 through 1962 to fertilizer (3, 18, 19, 53).

The proportionate shares of different inputs during the 1939 to 1961 period on corn was calculated by Auer, Heady, and Conklin. These showed that fertilizer accounted for 31.4 percent of the total yield increase, with 35.7 percent due to variety improvement, 17.8 percent due to production location, and 15.1 percent to other factors. Perrin and Heady showed that in the late 1960's and early 1970's nitrogen fertilizer was about equal in importance to hybrid seed for grain sorghum. TVA in 1976 estimated that the contribution of fertilizer to the total U.S. crop was 37 percent. Another study made by Auer, Heady, and Conklin on the yield increases in the Midwest during the 1940-1960 period showed an estimated average increase due to fertilizers was 31.4 percent, crop variety improvement 35.7 percent, production location 17.8 percent, and other factors 15.1 percent (4, 24, 48).

International Assistance

Helping developing countries caught the enthusiasm of agronomists, scientists, and the U.S. fertilizer industry in the 1960's. It became so popular that it was termed the "Green Revolution." The fertilizer industry looked upon the food needs of the developing countries as an opportunity to tap an unlimited market for fertilizer and to build new fertilizer plants both in the United States and in the developing countries. The dreams failed to materialize and profits disappeared. The oil companies jumped onto the fertilizer bandwagon in the mid-1960's, and a few years later were among the first to jump off (33, 46).

Although the developing countries consumed considerably less fertilizer than the developed, their consumption grew from about 1 million short tons of primary nutrients in 1950 to 66 million in 1980. During the same period the developed countries increased from about 14 million to 86 million short tons. Nitrogen was by far the most needed and used nutrient in the developing countries, reaching about 38 million tons in 1980, or about 40 percent of the world's fertilizer nitrogen. Phosphate was second with about 10 million, or 30 percent of the world's phosphate consumption. Potash amounted to only 4.4 million or 16 percent. During the same 30-year period the population of the developing countries increased from 1,700 millions to 3,700 millions. Six out of every seven people added to the world population from 1960 through 1980 were in the developing countries. The average consumption of primary nutrients per inhabitant was about 24 pounds in developing countries as compared with 140 pounds in the developed countries in 1980 (23).

The developing countries by the late 1970's had made considerable progress; 75 out of 112 showed that food supplies were increasing faster than the population. The regions making the most notable improvement per capita are the Far East and the Middle East. On the negative side, the poorer countries, mostly in Africa, where unable to keep food production abreast of the rapidly growing population (34, 42).

United States cooperation in assisting developing countries in improving food crop production began in 1943 when the Rockefeller Foundation assigned a small staff to Mexico at the request of Mexico's Minister of Agriculture. Emphasis was mostly on corn and wheat improvement. So successful were these projects in Mexico that in the 1950's several Central American republics requested assistance in agricultural research. This led to the establishment of a series of international agricultural institutes. The International Rice Research Institute was established in the Phillippines in 1960. The Mexican corn and wheat programs, along with their staffs, were reorganized in 1966 as international institutes and funded by the Rockefeller and Ford Foundations. These were followed in the 1960's by two other institutions suppported by the two foundations, one in Nigeria and the other in Colombia (54).

In 1971, a Consultive Group on International Agricultural Research (CGIAR) was established. Its main purpose was to establish and coordinate funding and provide general guidance. Other initial sponsors included the World Bank, the United Nations Development Program, and the Food and Agricultural Organization of the United Nations. By 1980, there were 13 international centers and programs involving a wide range of activities supported by 33 donor members from 20 countries, 4 foundations, 3 international organizations, and 6 regional organizations. (The United States was represented by the Agency for International Development). The esteem in which the programs were held was evidenced by the selection of Norman Borlaug, the agronomist for the wheat program in Mexico, as recipient of the 1970 Nobel Prize for Peace. Fertilizers were included in all or most of the international agricultural research programs as a yield-producing input (21). Numerous developing countries in the 1960's expressed their need and desire to build fertilizer industries of their own. Many turned to TVA's National Fertilizer Development Center (NFDC), which had a world-wide reputation in fertilizer technology and development, to help them in solving their problems. TVA's experts assisted them with matters such as determining the best kinds of fertilizer, investigating best sources of raw materials, locating plants, deciding what kinds of fertilizers to produce, developing most effective marketing systems, and keeping manufacturing facilities in operation. Numerous TVA fertilizer teams were dispatched to developing countries. Most of these nations eventually became self-sufficient in fertilizer production. TVA offered training courses at its own headquarters at Muscle Shoals, where trainees could work first hand with TVA employees in plant upkeep and operations.

By 1975, demand for assistance from TVA's NFDC by the developing countries exceeded the agency's capability to meet both the growing international load and the domestic programs as spelled out in the TVA Act. TVA's role with the developing countries was turned over to the newly-formed International Fertilizer Development Center (IFDC), a non-profit organization incorporated under the state laws of Alabama. In March,1977, IFDC was designated as a public international organization by executive order of the President of the United States. The purpose of the organization is to improve fertilizers and knowledge of fertilizer use in developing countries through research and development, technical assistance, training, and communications. The organization is funded by the United States, other governments and a wide range of national and international agencies for performing special services. IFDC is under the general direction of a 12-member Board of Directors. The organization's headquarters, major laboratories, and pilot plants are on the TVA reservation at Muscle Shoals, adjacent to the NFDC. This permits the two organizations to complement each other in technical manpower, facilities, and special services, and also gives IFDC easy access to NFDC's staff and national fertilizer library. IFDC's staff is recruited from 20 countries. Most of of the staff is stationed at Muscle Shoals, although an increasing number are being located in Africa, Asia, and Latin America. Training programs for fertilizer specialists from developing countries are offered both at Muscle Shoals and at various developing countries. Since its organization, IFDC has played an increasing role in all aspects of fertilizer production, marketing, and use. It has become an important factor in helping developing countries become self-sufficient in food (39).

Changes in Farm Production and Efficiency

The agricultural revolution brought about major changes in farming. Before 1940, the farmer and his family provided most of the farm labor. Machinery and mechanical power were limited largely to 2-plow tractors, 1-row corn pickers, and 2-row planters. Capital requirements were minimal and the per acre return from his crops was limited. The amount of purchased feed, seed, and livestock was low, and cropland acreage farmed remained stable and relatively low. Use of fertilizers was low and lime was sparingly applied (17, 36).

From 1940 to 1960, the volume of purchased off-farm inputs roughly doubled and continued to increase thereafter. The farm labor input declined drastically, falling nearly 80 percent from 1940 through 1980. The total input from land remained about the same over the entire 1920-1980 period, not surprising since the United States has only about 340 million acres of harvested cropland without bringing less desirable land under cultivation. Fertilizers increased a huge 1,240 percent, followed by farm machinery with a 200-percent increase, and feed, seed, and livestock by 180 percent. Fertilizers proved to be one of the most effective substitutes for land since it usually boosted crop yields appreciably at a relatively low cost (17, 36).

Table 13.4. Changes in Farm Population and Number of Farms (1).

Year	U.S. Total Population	Farm Population	Farm Share of Total	No. of Farms
	1,000			1,000
1920	106,089	31,556	0.7	6,448
1930	122,775	30,529	24.9	6,288
1940	131,820	39,547	23.2	6,097
1950	151,132	25,058	16.6	5,382
1959	176,264	21,172	12.3	Est. 3,400
1970	204, 401	9,712	4.8	2,949
1980	227,020	7,241	3.2	2,428

Table 13.4 shows the changes that have occurred in farm population and the number of of farms at 10-year intervals from 1920 through 1980. The farm population in 1920 was 31.5 million or 29.7 percent of the U.S. total population. During the next 20 years it increased to 39.5 million, an all time high, which amounted to 23 percent of the nation's total population. From 1940 on the farm population declined to 7.2 million or 3.2 percent of the total of the nation in 1980. During the same period, the number of farms fell steadily from 6.4 to 2.4 million (1).

Farming became big business in areas with a favorable climate, good soils, and a level topography that would accommodate large machinery. Leading examples include the Corn Belt, the wheat and sorghum-producing areas of the Great Plains, and certain irrigated areas in the western states. Large family-operated commercial farms in 1979 utilized capital resources of about $500,000, with some running to $2 to $3 million. These large farmers face investment decisions and cash flow problems equal to those encountered in non-farm businesses. To be successful, the large farmer has to keep abreast of technological advances and achieve input balances that will assure him maximum economic crop yields. Furthermore, he faces the risks and uncertainties over which he has no control: droughts, hailstorms, new strains of plant diseases, insect invasions, and unexpected fluctuations of the prices paid for his crops. Not all farmers have the capability, desire, or knowledge to compete, and some lose their farms to their more aggressive and capable neighbors (56).

A second category of farmers is the intentional small farmer who farms in areas having small fields supplemented with additional pasture and grazing lands on steep or irregular slopes. Such farms are common in Appalachia and the Ozarks. Small farms also are operated by part-time farmers who depend upon high per-acre returns by growing crops such

TVA and university researchers jointly conducted many studies during the 1960's and 1970's to find out exactly what happens to fertilizer nutrients, especially nitrogen, after application to the soil. Shown are monitoring of North Carolina watershed and fertilizer tagged with a nitrogen isotope prepared for Illinois investigations.
(F.J. Myers--TVA)

as tobacco or by engaging in high-return enterprises such as poultry- and dairy-farming. Another group is made up of those who prefer farm life for themselves and their families, even at a sacrifice of income. Then there is an unfortunate group, the rural poor, dependent largely upon welfare programs (6, 83).

A breakdown of the approximate percentages of U.S. farms by income classes (farm products marketed) in the last half of the 1970's is as follows: Less than $1,999–6; $2,000 to $6,999–20; $7,000 to $14,999–32; $15,000 to $24,999–25; $25,000 and over–1.

As a result of increasing agricultural productivity, the United States has been able to provide abundant food supplies for its increasing population at decreasing real prices. In 1890, consumers paid about 40 percent of their income for food. In the 1930-1960 period, the percentage ranged from 20 to 24 percent, and from 1971 through 1980, from 16 to 17 percent. Nevertheless, a part of our population must obtain its food through food stamp programs, surplus give-away programs and some from handouts through charity organizations (56).

Environmental Impacts

Throughout the period of rapid growth in fertilizer use farmers faced little restraint in how or the extent to which they applied fertilizer materials. Nevertheless, by the 1960's and 1970's, many scientists could see problems down the road. Researchers at TVA and elsewhere conducted fairly extensive studies, for example, to identify the pathways of fertilizer nitrogen–what happens to it physically and chemically after application to the soil. They were concerned with the potential pollution of groundwater by nitrogen fertilizer, as well as the economic impact of lost nitrogen. Most researchers fully expected a heightening of public concerns and foresaw the possibility of restrictions in fertilizer use (65) (Chapters 7, 10).

Limited research also was done to check for any problems that might be associated with heavy metals found in phosphate rock, some of which end up in fertilizers. In general, problems appeared minimal.

REFERENCES

1. *Agricultural Statistics*, 1936, 1939, 1940, 1943, 1946, 1950, 1952, 1959, 1963, 1970, 1973, 1980, 1982. U.S. Dept. Agric. Gov't. Printing Office, Washington, D.C.
2. Aldrich, D.G. 1957. The dry mild-winter region, *Yearbook of Agric.*, 1957, pp. 467-474. U.S. Dept. of Agric., Washington, D. C.
3. Auer, L.. and E.O. Heady. 1965. The contribution of weather and yield technology to changes in U. S. corn production, 1939 to 1961. In *Weather and Our Food Supply.* CAED Rpt. 20. Center for Agricultural and Economic Development. Iowa State Univ., Ames, Iowa.
4. ____, E. O. Heady, and F. Conklin. 1966. Influence of crop technology on yields. *Iowa Farm Science* 20:13-16.
5. Bachman, K.L. and J.V. McElveen. 1958. Trends in kinds and sizes of farms. In *Land the Yearbook of Agric.*, 1958. pp. 302-309. U.S. Dept. of Agric. Washington, D. C.
6. Bandel, V.A., and R.H. Fox. 1984. Management of nitrogen in New England and Middle Atlantic States. In *Nitrogen in Crop Production.* pp. 677-689. The Amer. Soc. Agron., Crop Sci. Soc. Amer.,and the the Soil Sci. Amer. Madison, Wisc.
7. Barnes, C. P. and F. J. Marscher. 1958. Our wealth of land resources. In *Land the Yearbook of Agric.* 1958. pp. 10-17. U.S. Dept. Agric., Washington, D. C.
8. Barton, T. B. 1958. How our pr;oduction has expanded. In *Land the Yearbook of Agric.* 1958. pp. 460-465, U.S. Dept. Agric., Washington, D. C.

9. Bean, L. H., J. P. Cavin, and G. C. Means. 1938. The causes: price relations and economic instability. In *Soils & Men Yearbook of Agric.*, 1938. pp. 171-197. U.S. Dept. Agric., Washington, D. C.
10. Bengtson, G. W. 1979. Forest fertilization in the United States: progress and outlook. *J. of Forestry*, 78 (4): 222-229.
11. Brady, N.C., R. A. Stuchmeyer, and R. H. Musgrove. 1957. The northeast. In *Soil the Yearbook of Agric.* 1957. pp. 598-619. U.S. Dept. Agric., Washington, D. C.
12. Bridges, J. D. 1983. *Fertilizer trends, 1982.* Bull. Y-176 National Fertilizer Development Center, Tenn. Valley Auth., Muscle Shoals, Ala.
13. _____, 1986. *Fertilizer trends 1986.* Bull. Y-195, Nat. Fert. Dev. Center, Tenn. Valley Auth., Muscle Shoals, Ala.
14. Bureau of Census. 1975. *Historical statistics of the United States. Colonial times to 1970. Part I,* U. S. Dept. of Commerce, Washington, D. C.
15. Cathcart, J. B. 1980. The phosphate industry of the United States. In *Role of Phosphorus in Agriculture.* pp. 19-42. Amer. Soc. Agron., Crop Sci. Soc. Amer., Soil Sci. Soc. Amer. Madison, Wisc.
16. Cheney, H. B. 1957. The North Pacific valleys. *Soil the Yearbook of Agric. 1957.* pp.456-457. U.S. Dept. Agric., Washington, D. C.
17. Cochrane, W.W. 1979. *The development of American agriculture: a historical analysis.* Univ. of Minnesota Press, Minneapolis, Minn.
18. Council for Agricultural Science and Technology. 1974. *The U.S. Fertilizer situation and outlook.* Iowa State Univ. Press, Ames, Iowa.
19. Christensen, R., W. Hendrix, and R. Stevens. 1934. *How the U.S. improved its agriculture.* U.S. Dept. Agric. Foreign Agric. Economics Rpt. No 76. Washingt;on, D. C.
20. Crickman, C.W. 1958. The use of land in the corn belt. *Land the Yearbook of Agric.* 1958. pp. 122-128. U.S. Dept. Agric. Washington, D. C.
21. Dalrymple, D. G. !981. Global research wins a cigar (CGIAR). Will there be enough food? *Yearbook of Agric.* 1981. pp. 259-266. U.S. Dept. Agric., Washington, D.C.
22. Danhof, C. H. 1969. *Change in agriculture: the northern states, 1820-1870.* Harvard Univ. Press, Cambridge, Mass.
23. Food and Agriculture Organization. Various volumes of the fertilizer yearbook. Food and Agric. Org. of the United Nations. Rome, Italy.
24. Free, W. J., B. J. Bond, and J. L. Nevins. 1976. Changing patterns in agriculture and their effect on fertilizer use. *Fertilizer Conference, July 27-28.* Bull. Y-106. Nat. Fert. Dev. Center, Tenn. Valley Auth., Muscle Shoals, Ala.
25. Gilliam, J. W. and F. Boswell. 1984. Management of nitrogen in the South Atlantic states. In *Nitrogen in Crop Production.* pp. 691-705. Amer. Soc. Agron., Crop Sci. Soc. Amer., Soil Sci. Soc. Amer., Madison, Wisc.
26. Glick, P. M. 1938. The soil and the law. *Soils & Men Yearbook of Agric.* 1938. pp. 296-318. U.S. Dept. Agric., Washington, D. C.
27. Grissom, P. 1957. The Mississippi Delta region. *Soil the Yearbook of Agric.* pp. 524-530. U. S. Dept. Agric., Washington, D. C.
28. Hamstead, L. and G. C. Fite. 1955. *Agricultural regions of the United States.* Univ. of Oklahoma Press. Norman, Okla.
29. Hargett, N. L. 1972. *Fertilizer summary data. 1972.* Bull. Y-53. Nat. Fert. Dev. Center, Tenn. Valley Auth., Muscle Shoals, Ala.
30. _____, and J. T. Berry. 1980. *Fertilizer summary data, 1980.* Bull. Y-165. Nat. Fert. Dev. Center, Tenn. VAlley Auth., Muscle Shoals, Ala.

31. ____, and J. T. Berry. 1986. *Commercial fertilizers*. Bull. Y-196. Nat. Fert. Dev. Center, Tenn. Valley Auth., Muscle Shoals, Ala.
32. Harre, E. A., M. N. Goodson, and J. D. Bridges. 1977. *Fertilizer trends 1976*. Bull. Y-111. Nat. Fert. Dev. Center, Tenn. Valley Auth., Muscle Shoals, Ala.
33. ____, O. W. Livingston, and J. T. Shields. 1974. *World fertilizer review and outlook*. Bull. Y-70. Nat. Fert. Dev. Center, Tenn. Valley Auth., Muscle Shoals, Ala.
34. Harris, G. T. And E. A. Harre. 1979. *World fertilizer situation - 1978-85*. Int. Fert. Dev. Center and Nat. Fert. Dev. Center. Tenn. Valley Auth., Muscle Shoals, Ala.
35. Hayes, H. K. 1951. A half century of crop breeding research. *Agron. J.* 49: 626-631.
36. Heady, E. O., E. O. Haroldson, L. V. Mayer and L. G. Tweeton. 1965. In *Roots of the Farm Problem*. Iowa State Center for Agricultural and Economic Development. Iowa State Univ. Press, Ames, Iowa.
37. Henderson, J. R. and F. B. Smith. 1957. Florida and flatwoods. In *Soil the Yearbook of Agric*. 1957. pp. 595-598. U.S. Dept. Agric., Washington, D. C.
38. Horner, G. M., W. A. Star, and J. K. Patterson. 1957. The Pacific Northwest wheat region. In *Soil the Yearbook of Agric*. 1957. pp. 475-481. U. S. Dept. Agric., Washington, D. C.
39. International Fertilizer Development Center. 1985. *The IFDC story*. General Publ. IFDC-G-5. Int. Fert. Dev. Center, Muscle Shoals, Ala.
40. Johnson, J. R. 1957. The Southern Plains. In *Soil the Yearbook of Agric*. 1957. pp. 516-523. U. S. Dept. Agric. Washington, D. C.
41. Kurtz, L. I., L. V. Boone, T. R. Peck, and R. G. Hoedt. 1984. Crop rotations for efficient nitrogen use. In *Nitrogen in Crop Production*. Ed. by R. D. Hauck. pp. 295-306. Amer. Soc. Agron., Madison, Wisc.
42. McCune, D. L. and P. J. Stangel. Int. Fert. Dev. Center. Personal interviews.
43. Mehring, A. L., J. R. Adams, and K. D. Jacob. 1957. *Statistics of fertilizer and liming materials in the United States*. U. S. Dept.Agric. Statistical Bull. 191. Washington, D. C.
44. Muckenhirn, R. J. and K. C. Berger. 1957. The Northern Lake states. In *Soil the Yearbook of Agric*. 1957. pp. 547-556. U. S. Dept. Agric. Washington, D. C.
45. Nelson, L. B. 1975. Fertilizers for all-out food production. In *All-out Food Production: Strategy and Resource Implication*. Ed. by W. P. Martin. ASA Special Publ. No 23. Amer. Soc. Agron. Madison, Wisc.
46. O'Hanlan, J. M. 1968. All that fertilizer and no place to go. In *Fortune* 77 (6): 90-95, 128. Time, Inc., Chicago, Ill.
47. Pearson, R. W. and L. E. Ensminger. 1957. Southeastern Uplands. In *Soil the Yearbook of Agric*. 1957. pp. 379-598. U. S. Dept. Agric. Washington, D. C.
48. Perrin, R.K. and E. O. Heady. 1975. *Relative contributions to major technological factors and moisture stress to increased grain yields in the midwest: 1930-1971*. Card Rpt. 55. Center for Agricultural and Rural Development. Iowa State Univ., Ames, Iowa.
49. Peterson, G. A. and R. D. Voss. 1984. Management of nitrogen in the West Central states. In *Nitrogen in Crop Production*. Ed. by R. D. Hauck. pp. 721-733. Amer. Soc. Agron., Madison, Wisc.
50. Pierre, W. H., and F. F. Reicken. 1957. The midland region. In *Soil the Yearbook of Agric*. 1957. pp. 535-547. U. S. Dept. Agric., Washington, D.C.

51. Rasmussen, W. D. editor. 1975. *Agriculture in the United States: a Documentary History.* Vol. 3: 1991-2907; Vol. 4: 2915-2245. National Economics Analysis Div. U. S. Dept. Agric. Random House, New York, N. Y.
52. Rauschkolb, R. S. , T. L. Jackson, and A. I. Dow. 1984. Management of nitrogen in the Pacific states. In *Nitrogen in Crop Production.* Ed. by R. D. Hauck. pp. 765-777. Amer. Soc. Agron., Crop Sci. Soc. Amer., and Soil Sci. Soc. Amer. Madison, Wisc.
53. Shaw, L. H. and D. D. Durost. 1965. *The effect of weather and technology on corn yields in the corn belt: 1929-1962.* Agric. Economics Rpt. No. 80. U. S. Dept. Agric., Washington, D. C.
54. Stakman, E. C., R. Bradfield, and P. C. Mangelsdorf. 1967. In *Campaigns against Hunger.* The Belknap Press of Harvard Univ. Press. Cambridge, Mass.
55. Stanford, G. and J. O. Legg. 1984. Nitrogen and yield potential. In *Nitrogen in Crop Production.* Ed. by R. D. Hauck. pp. 264-272. Amer. Soc. Agron., Crop Sci. Soc. Amer., and Soil Sci. Soc. Amer. Madison, Wisc.
56. Sundquist, W. B. 1981. Farming and U. S. well-being through the years. Will There Be Enough Food? In *The Yearbook of Agric.* 1981. pp. 10-21. U. S. Dept. Agric. Washington, D. C.
57. Tharp, M. M. and E. L. Langsford. 1958. Where our cotton comes from. In *Land the Yearbook of Agric.* 1958. pp. 129-135. U. S. Dept. Agric. Washington, D. C.
58. Thorne, W. 1957. The grazing-irrigated region. In *Soil the Yearbook of Agric.* 1957. pp. 481-483. U. S. Dept. Agric., Washington, D. C.
59. ____. 1977. *Agronomists and food contributions and challenges.* Ed. by M. D. Thorne. pp. 9-25. ASA Special Publ. No. 30. Amer. Soc. Agron. Madison, Wisc.
60. Tisdale, S. L. and W. L. Nelson. 1975. *Soil fertility and fertilizers.* 3rd ed. Macmillan Co. Inc., New York and Collier Macmillan Publishers, London.
61. Tucker, B. B. and L. W. Murdock. 1984. Nitrogen use in the South Central states. In *Nitrogen in Crop Production.* Ed. by R. D. Hauck. pp. 735-749. Amer. Soc. Agron., Crop Sci. Soc. Amer., and Soil Sci. Soc. Amer. Madison, Wisc.
62. U. S. Dept. of Agriculture. 1941. Climates of the states. In *Climate and Man the Yearbook of Agric.* 1941. pp. 749-1221. U. S. Dept. Agric. Washington, D. C.
63. Walker, R. K. and R. J. Miers. 1957. The Coastal Prairies. In *Soil the Yearbook of Agric.* 1967. pp. 531-534. U. S. Dept. Agric. Washington, D. C.
64. Welch, L. F. 1984. Nitrogen management for the East North Central states. In *Nitrogen in Crop Production.* Ed. by R. D. Hauck. pp. 707-719. Amer. Soc. Agron., Crop Sci. Soc. Amer., and Soil Sci. Soc. Amer. Madison, Wisc.
65. Westfall, D. G. 1984. Management of nitrogen in the Mountain states. In *Nitrogen in Crop Production.* Ed. by R. D. Hauck. pp. 752-762. Amer. Soc. Agron., Crop Sci. Soc. Amer., and Soil Sci. Soc. Amer. Madison, Wisc.
66. Winters, E. 1957. The east-central uplands. In *Soil the Yearbook of Agric.* 1957. pp. 553-577. U. S. Dept. Agric. Washington, D. C.

14

Fertilizer Trade Associations

The first trade associations, then called "exchanges," began operating in the 1860's and 1870's, mainly in East Coast port cities where shipments of guano and Chilean nitrate entered the U.S. market. Their primary purpose was to stabilize prices and protect members from fraud (16)(Chapter 4).

There are thousands of trade associations in the United States. However, only a few hundred are involved in professional organizations, the American Medical Association being the largest and fertilizer associations among the smaller. Some associations are strong and others weak. Some overlap in membership. Associations may operate on a national basis, be limited to regions or have branch organizations in individual states. Several factors other than the number of members influence the effectiveness of a professional-type association. Loyalty, stability, morale, and experience are of higher importance than is financial remuneration. However large an association, it will not amount to much if the group is divided internally and the members fail to work together (15).

The management and staffs of U.S. fertilizer trade associations have changed over the years. The management of the first, the National Fertilizer Association (NFA), formed in 1883, was simple. It consisted of a president, a vice-president, and a combined secretary-treasurer. Committees were appointed to coordinate matters of mutual interest such as transportation, trade rules, state laws, and chemical analysis. Yearly reports were issued. The NFA after five years ceased to exist (16).

Twelve manufacturers from the Midwest and Northeast formed "The Fertilizer Manufacturers Association in the West" in 1893. This association had a president, a first vice-president, a vice-president from each state represented by the membership, a secretary-treasurer, and an Executive Committee of five members.

From this time on the United States has not had a shortage of fertilizer associations replete with presidents, vice-presidents, some type of executive boards, and people to serve as treasurers and secretaries. However, association objectives have varied according to the current concerns of members.

This chapter deals only with fertilizer trade associations of national importance in the United States. and not with State and regional affiliates of the national organizations. Also, it deals only with associations in which fertilizers are the prime concern.

The National Fertilizer Association and the Southern Fertilizer Association: 1920-1925

By 1920, two associations were active—the National Fertilizer Association which had been formed in 1901 and the Southern Fertilizer Association, formed in 1906. These two strong fertilizer associations had considerable duplication of membership, having more or less parallel interests and activities. Both held annual meetings at the same time and place. One of their major activities was the work of the soil improvement committees aimed at increasing fertilizer consumption in a way that would assure farmers good returns. The first was in the Midwest followed by a southern improvement committee within a few years (16) (Chapter 4).

National Fertilizer Association, Inc.

The two trade associations merged in 1925 to become the National Fertilizer Association, Inc. Spencer L. Carter of the Virginia-Carolina Chemical Company in Richmond was elected as president, and the widely known Charles J. Brand was employed as its full-time secretary-treasurer. In 1925, the NFA, Inc. had 161 active members and 76 associate members. The association's principal objectives were to discourage the U.S. Government from operating the wartime nitrate plants at Muscle Shoals, Ala., lower freight rates, gather fertilizer statistics, eliminate unnecessary fertilizer grades, and support agronomic educational programs. The NFA, Inc. held its annual July meeting at the Greenbrier in White Sulphur Springs, W. Va., and a fall convention at Atlanta. The two soil improvement commmittees merged in 1929. (A major part of the national association's programs from 1911 to 1969 included an emphasis on agronomic education to increase fertilizer consumption.) (16).

Under Brand's leadership, the agronomic activities of NFA were expanded. However, at its lowest point during the Depression, membership dropped to 132 and associates to 51. Activities were curtailed, and other research, educational and public relations programs were crippled. During the mid-1930's, troubles began to gather for the association. The Tennessee Valley Authority started to produce high-analysis phosphate fertilizer and to distribute it to farmers in the Valley at little or no cost in order to help improve the welfare of the destitute farmers (16). By 1940, the picture was improving for the association and the active membership jumped to 307 although the associate members dropped to 60 (13,16).

Starting as early as 1936, however, the trade practices of the fertilizer industry came under investigation by the Department of Justice. By 1939, the investigation became nationwide. In the spring of 1941, the association and its members were charged with anti-trust violations by the U.S. Government. The fertilizer industry was in a state of turmoil. However, the case was essentially settled before the United States entered World War II (12,16).

During the war years, NFA activities were dominated by government regulations. Fertilizer materials needed for the war effort were allocated, causing frequent shortages and disruptions in the domestic fertilizer market. NFA served primarily as a liaison between the government and the industry. Annual meetings of the members were restricted or prohibited by the government; members of the industry were eager to belong to NFA and to support its programs. Associate membership numbered 300 companies in 1941 (13,16).

In 1944, the long-considered threat of the government's competition finally was realized. Senator Hill of Alabama introduced legislation in the Congress to establish a "National Fertilizer Policy and Program," under which the government would produce and distribute fertilizer in direct competition with the industry. The initial purpose was to build one phosphate plant in Mobile, Ala., under TVA's jurisdiction. However, the bill was modified to allow for two plants in the West—one to produce phosphate and the other, potash. The entire membership of NFA, Inc. opposed this threat, but could not agree on a plan to stop it. Some members, smarting from the antitrust settlement, were still unhappy with the NFA management. Discord increased with the threat of government competition. One group of members resigned and formed the American Plant Food Council (APFC) whose principal purpose was to defeat the "Hill Bill." The bill was narrowly defeated in 1946; it was introduced again in 1947, but was never seriously considered thereafter (4,16).

The turmoil of the "Hill Bill" took its toll: after 20 years with NFA, Charles J. Brand was forced to resign April 1, 1945. Daniel S. Murphy, a former judge who had worked on the NFA's staff for many years, was elected executive secretary and treasurer for two years. In April 1947, M. H. Lockwood of Eastern States Cooperative was employed as president of NFA. He served until June, 1948. In November 1948, Russell Coleman, director of the Mississippi Agricultural Experiment Station, was elected president. Under Coleman's leadership, the NFA strengthened its research and educational programs with the Land-Grant Colleges and the U.S. Department of Agriculture, and established a cooperative program between the NFA industry members and TVA. Industry was beginning to recognize the value of TVA's research, that it was here to stay and also that the agency's test-demonstration programs could be an asset rather than a liability (16).

American Plant Food Council

Clifton A. Woodrum, a member of the U.S. House of Representatives, was named President of the American Plant Food Council in August 1945. Woodrum simultaneously announced that he would not seek re-election to the House the next year. A period of friendly cooperation developed between APFC and NFA and when Woodrum died in 1950, a serious attempt was made to bring the two associations together again. Discord still existed and APFC selected Paul T. Truitt who had been highly successful as president of the National Association of Margarine Manufacturers. From 1950 to 1955, the APFC continued to emphasize government relations while NFA continued to stress research and development (5,16).

National Plant Food Institute

In 1955, NFA and APFC merged into the National Plant Food Institute (NPFI) with both Coleman and Truitt serving as executive vice-presidents reporting to an elected chief executive. E.A. Geoghegar of Southern Cotton Oil Co. was NPFI's first chairman and J.A. Howell of Virginia-Carolina Chemical Co. was its first president. The Middle West Soil Improvement Committee merged into NPFI where it was an effective force in stimulating fertilizer consumption. Other regional offices were established in the North, Southeast, Southwest, and West. New personnel were employed in these regions to work closely with Land-Grant Colleges, bankers, and farmer organizations in key states. The NPFI continued strong agronomic programs and published the *Plant Food Review* (16).

Coleman resigned from NPFI in 1960 to become president of the newly-formed Sulphur Institute. Truitt was elected president of NPFI and held this position until he retired in 1968. The united association functioned effectively (16).

American Potash Institute and Successors: 1935-80

On July 1, 1935, three American producers and importers of potash–the American Potash and Chemical Corp; United States Potash Co. of America; and Potash Company of America–joined with the N.V. Potash Export My., Inc. to form the American Potash Institute (API) "to promote the use of potash through collective action." Thus the new

Institute brought together in a single organization all the important domestic producers and the German-Frasch cartel's exclusive agency. Collectively they accounted for virtually all of the potash sales in the United States (22). In 1935, 192,000 tons were produced, imports were 229,000 and U.S. consumption 307,000 tons (23).

The new Institute was established at Washington, D.C. to carry on scientific and agricultural investigations to promote the efficient and profitable use of potash in crop production. It was to cooperate as opportunity afforded with State and Federal institutions in carrying on research and experimental work in the United States, Canada, and Cuba along with the work sponsored by the National Fertilizer Association and other other trade organizations (7).

Dr. J.W. Turrentine was President. For years he had been in charge of potash research for USDA's Bureau of Chemistry and Soils, and was well known in America and Europe. He had been connected with USDA since 1911 (Chapter 5); in fact, Turrentine had been associated with every organization in the United States that had anything to do with potash. G.J. Callister was Vice-President and Secretary; he had been connected with N.V. Potash Export My., Inc. for 24 years (3).

In 1955, the API remained a unique organization supported by five U.S. producers who continued to promote greater use of potash. Potash was no longer imported and some two million tons of K_2O was consumed as fertilizer. API undoubtedly helped increase potash consumption but the extent is unknown. API's headquarters was still at Washington, D.C. Major functions were in four categories: agronomic, economic, informational, and reference, with a library that dealt with almost anything related to potash. Turrentine served as API President Emeritus; Dr. H.B. Mann became president in 1948. Mann had long been associated with API as southern manager and also as API Vice-President (7).

The five potash producers in 1955 were the American Potash and Chemical Corp.; Potash Company of America; United States Potash Co; Southwest Potash Corp.; and Duval Sulphur and Potash Co. The governing body of the Institute consisted of two representatives from each of the five producers and the API President. The board appointed officers, set the budget, and determined matters of policy. Thirty-one people comprised the API staff. These included 16 agronomists, 2 editors, 2 librarians, and 11 secretarial and clerical employees. A recent API publication was "Better Crops" which was distributed widely to agricultural workers, fertilizer dealers, and others (7,27).

Dr. J. Fielding Reed succeeded Mann as president in 1964. Reed had a long career as an agronomist in southern universities. He had been API's southern director from 1949-to1962, and was vice-president in 1963-1964. He also was chairman of the Board of the Foundation of International Research in 1964.

Dr. Robert E. Wagner became president of the Potash Institute in 1975 upon Reed's retirement. Wagner, like his predecessors, was especially qualified for his new job. He was first employed as a forage crops specialist, and became a research agronomist and project leader at the USDA Plant Industry Station at Beltsville, Md. From Beltsville, he moved to the nearby University of Maryland to become head of the Agronomy Department. In 1959, he joined API, serving first as eastern director, then as vice-president. After eight years with the Institute he was named director of the Cooperative Extension Service at the University of Maryland, where he served until 1975 (24).

The Institute in 1977 was enlarged to become the Potash & Phosphate Institute (PPI). Existing members of the Institute included Amax, International Minerals and Chemical, Cominco American, Duval, Great Salt Lake Minerals and Chemicals, Mississippi Chemical, PCA, Potash Company of Canada, Potash Company of Saskatchewan, Texasgulf, and U.S. Borax. The new members include IMC's phosphate operations, Agrico, Mobil, Occidental, Royster, Smith-Douglas, Borden, and Texasgulf Phosphates (9).

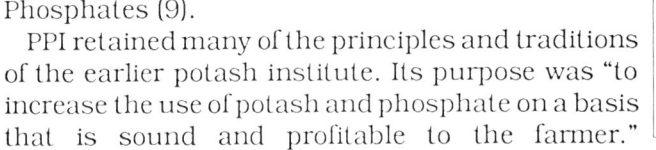

PPI retained many of the principles and traditions of the earlier potash institute. Its purpose was "to increase the use of potash and phosphate on a basis that is sound and profitable to the farmer." Basically, it is the research and education arm of the potash and phosphate industries. It is international in scope, including not only the United States and Canada, but also Latin America, Japan, South Korea, and Southeast Asia. Its programs are agronomic in nature and conducted by a staff of highly trained and experienced agronomists. Under Wagner's leadership the Institute has greatly expanded the size and diversity of its programs. Dissemination of informational material increased and new publications were added to help meet dealers' needs. Over 100 research grants are made to 145 universities and other research institutions (24).

The Instititute in 1980 launched a Foundation for Agronomic Research to permit other industries and groups to invest in research to improve crop production. High on its list of priorites is the encouragement of maximum crop yield research whereby high yield components are combined in a way to bring maximum economic returns to the farmer (24). Publications of the PPI include *Better Crops with Plant Food*, a quarterly, and newsletters, article reprints and technical reference booklets. Conventions are always in October.

Agricultural Ammonia Institute

The Agricultural Ammonia Institute (AAI) appeared in 1951–an expedient time. In 1949, the direct application of anhydrous ammonia had started spreading rapidly from the Delta areas of Mississippi, Arkansas, Missouri, and Tennessee into the Midwest. Several developments made this possible. Injection into irrigation water and into soils had been used commercially in California. This was pioneered by the Shell Chemical Company (Chapter 10).

The location of a number of Government-owned World War II ammonia synthesis plants east of the Rocky Mountains assured a large supply of low cost ammonia (Chapter 9). In 1947, W.B. Andrews, agronomist, and F.E. Edwards, engineer of the Mississippi Agricultural Experiment Station, introduced anhydrous ammonia to the Mississippi Delta. The spread of direct application of anhydrous ammonia began in the Mississippi Delta in March 1947, at a time of critical nitrogen shortage. The shortage assured the interest of the farmers. During the rest of the year that followed, two or three educational meetings per week were conducted by P.H. Grissom of the Mississippi Agricultural Experiment Station's Delta Branch, with attendance ranging from 25 to 500. During 1947, most of the interest was restricted to the Delta area of Mississippi; but by fall and winter of 1947-48, the interest had spread to other states. Application amounted to 57,000 short tons of nitrogen equivalent in 1950; 290,000 tons in 1960, 582,000 in 1965, and 4.5 million tons in 1980 (14,18,19).

The trade association dealing with anhydrous ammonia got underway in December 1950 in Memphis with 29 charter members. The new organization began operating in January 1951. Ed Gill was the first president. The organization had no home and limited funds. The secretary, Mono Jennings, set up office in her dining room. Other early presidents were Virgil Rule, Jeff I. Davis, E.W. Thomas, and Mark Kraft. The first executive vice-president was Jack F. Crisswell; he was named in 1955 when Thomas was president (6).

The *Agricultural Ammonia News*, the official publication of AAI, was started in 1951. It was initially published in January, April, July, and October; a November issue was added later. The *News* tended not to focus primarily on anhydrous ammonia but promoted nitrogen overall. The association encouraged research and frequently made research grants. The first research grant in 1955 was for long needed research on anhydrous ammonia equipment and tank failure. Other grants were for research on safely handling ammonia and safety measures to protect people working with anhydrous ammonia.

The best known information on anhydrous ammonia and its use in agriculture was brought together in the mid-1960's in a symposium and published in the book *Agricultural Anhydrous Ammonia: Technology and Use*. The publication was sponsored by the Agricultural Ammonia Institute, the American Society of Agronomy, and the Soil Science Society of America. Its aim was to bring together the available facts and principles relating to effective use of anhydrous ammonia. The participants were recognized authorities in their respective subject matter areas, and the book was highly successful.

The Institute engaged in a number of other activities, including a group life insurance program for its members. It also had encouraged formation of state associations. An Agricultural Ammonia Handbook prepared by the Agronomy Committee was enthusiastically received and within six weeks it was sold out and a second edition was required. Jack F. Crisswell had nine successful years as Executive Vice-President. He was succeeded in 1984 by Zenas H. Beers.

In addition to declining interest in the state AAI associations, the parent AAI also was weak. Nelson D. Abell, a highly respected leader in the U.S. fertilizer field, and Zenas Beers as Executive Vice-President tried to turn the situation around. A summer meeting of the Board of Directors was called. Items discussed included the possibility of attracting more members by lowering membership dues and by a drive to solicit new members. The Board also heard a review of the 1965 activities of AAI and an update of the statement of objectives and installed a long-range planning committee. The Board also was asked to develop a new editorial policy for *Agricultural Ammonia News* which would direct the publication more toward industry people than toward consumers. The *News* was to give more attention to ammonia. Abell pointed out that the objective of a trade association was to protect and further the interest of the members. Regardless of the difficulties, an outstanding convention and trade show was held at Dallas in January 1967 with more than 1,200 paid registrations (1).

Traditionally, the general purpose of the AAI was to advance the cause of agriculture through the accumulation and dissemination of information and knowledge on the use of anhydrous ammonia for direct application. This changed in February 1967, when the membership voted unanimously to change the name of AAI to Agricultural Nitrogen Institute (ANI) so that the Institute might broaden its function to extend services to cover all nitrogen materials. The name of the journal was changed from *Agricultural Ammonia News* to *Agricultural Nitrogen News*.

The final issue of the *Agricultural Nitrogen News* occurred with Volume 20 issued in January-February in 1970. J.F. Sloan, the outgoing president of ANI, issued a message stating there had been a change in the thinking of the ANI members about the future course of action. By overwhelming vote, ANI members merged with the National Plant Food Institute into the Fertilizer Institute, a larger, stronger organization better equipped to serve the needs of the membership (28).

The National Fertilizer Solutions Association

The National Fertilizer Solutions Association (NFSA) is the main trade association for the fluid fertilizer industry, with member companies in the United States and a few other countries. It is dedicated to advancement of all aspects of fluid fertilizers. Its roots trace back to 1954, a time when bulk nitrogen liquids and liquid mix fertilizers were a struggling industry. The earlier U.S. history of fluid fertilizers, however, had dated back to the early 1920's. One of the first plants for producing liquid fertilizer was G&M Liquid Fertilizer Company at Oakland, California, which was operating in 1923. In 1928, the Prizer Brothers developed an applicator, a machine for dissolving a soluble fertilizer and metering the solution into irrigation water. In 1932, the Shell Oil Company, which had an ammonia plant in California began research on introduction of ammonia into irrigation water (32).

Before 1955, manufacturers of liquid-mixed fertilizers were attempting to break away from an established, conservative industry with a drastically different product and marketing system. Additional services were needed and improved application equipment was essential. The early pioneers had both technical and economic problems, and some companies failed. About 147 companies were operating in 1955 but only 72 were making mixes for farm use. Only 25 producers were east of the Rocky Mountains. U.S. production in 1954 was 27,500 tons. Application was by weed sprayers. A fluid marketing system had not emerged and quality of the mixed product was low (35).

Fluid fertilizer enthusiasts soon became interested in forming a trade association dealing only with liquids. An outdoor show was held near Shenandoah, Iowa, in 1954 in to spur interest in liquid-mix fertilizers and lay the groundwork for a trade association. Twelve exhibitors participated. According to Wayne Johnson, who was to be NFSA's first president, "The problem back then was how to merchandise the product. So we held the trade show and attracted about 250 people who were associated with our then rather obscure fluid industry." (32, p. 8).

That September a trade association was officially formed as the National Nitrogen Solutions Association. It was chartered as a not-for-profit corporation in Nebraska. According to Johnson, "The association grew like topsy and I can't tell you why." (32, p.8).

In l956, the name of the organization was changed to the National Fertilizer Solutions Association (NFSA). Quoting Johnson, "There was a purpose in changing the name: We wanted to include all the fluid fertilizer industry, not just nitrogen solutions." (32, p.8).

Early presidents following Johnson were Richard Cecil, 1958; O.L. Ohnstad, 1959; and Hugh S. Surles, Jr. 1960. There were no executive vice-presidents to manage the association until Harold Schelm became vice-president in 1961. Instead of managing its own organization the NFSA Board of Directors opted to contract management responsibilities to outside firms. A Chicago firm, Storms and Westcott, was selected to manage the association per directives of the Board. The firm had responsibilities for all activities including solicitation of new members.

All trade show arrangements for NFSA were handled by the Freeman Decorating Company (32).

In 1958, the association elected to purchase an existing publication named *Nitrogen Solutions* from its publisher, Wayne Johnson. Johnson had published 10 editions between 1955 and 1958, absorbing all expenses and income from the operation. Upon its take-over by NFSA, complete management responsibilities for the magazine, with assistance from the association's Editorial Committee, also were given to Storms and Westcott to publish the magazine bimonthly. The name of the magazine was changed to *Fertilizer Solution* and in 1979 to *Solutions* (32).

Under the prodding of Edward O'Man, NFSA's seventh president, the Board decided in 1961 to employ its own management when the fees of the outside organizations became unreasonable. An early board member, Harold Schelm, was selected to manage the association as executive secretary, a position he held through 1973, with offices in Peoria, Illinois. Quoting Schelm, "I had to keep the wolf from the door for three years" (32, p.12).

Up until 1954 it appeared that fluid-mix fertilizers could compete with solid fertilizers only when they were introduced into irrigation waters. The first breakthrough occurred in 1953 when the Liquilizer Corporation neutralized electric furnace-phosphoric acid with ammonia and dissolved potash in the resulting hot solution to produce a 4-10-10 liquid mix. As a result, a number of new companies were formed. Unfortunately, the furnace-grade acid was too costly for use in fertilizer (32,35).

Other breakthroughs occurred when TVA chemical engineers and chemists, including some of the world's leading fertilizer technologists, made basic discoveries without which fluid fertilizers could not have competed with solid fertilizers (Chapter 10) (35).

TVA introduced superphosphoric acid, which contains polyphosphates, in 1956. Polyphosphates, the backbone of clear liquid fertilizers, are formed by removing chemically combined water from the common orthophosphoric acid. Polyphosphates keep salts in the clear liquid fertilizer from forming solids and settling out. In the 1960's, TVA scientists and several in private industry found how to make superphosphoric acid by heating and dehydrating. The super-acid was then ammoniated to produce ammonium polyphosphate (Chapters 10 and 12) (35).

In 1972, TVA developed the pipe reactor process for making high-polyphosphate liquids for preparation of a 10-34-0 ammonium polyyphosphate solution. Using wet-process superphosphoric acid with only 20% to 30% of the P_2O_5 as polyphosphate, ammoniation in the pipe produces a melt of high polyphosphate content that is dissolved in water to produce 10-34-0 containing 60 to 75% of the P_2O_5 as polyphosphate. Their simple pipe-reactor process caught on in the industry like wildfire; by 1980 over 130 commercial plants were using it (35).

In the late 1950's and early 1960's considerable efforts were expended to increase the nutrient content of liquid-mix fertilizers, particularly of potassium. The main effort centered around suspending finely divided solids. TVA developed and demonstrated suspension fertilizers which have substantial portions of small crystalline plant nutrient materials suspended in the fluid by using about 2% of gelling clay. Suspensions allow production of high analysis grades that are twice the concentration of clear liquid grades. They also permit suspending some micronutrients (35). Suspensions never caught on until the 1970's when they underwent a continuing vigorous growth. By 1980, about 1,500 fluid fertilizer mix plants were producing suspensions (17,35)

While TVA and the private industries were laying the major technological foundation for a sound fluid fertilizer technology base, the NFSA was actively promoting all aspects of fluid fertilizers as dynamically as in its formative years. Use of fluid-mixed fertilizers increased dramatically. In 1955, there were 147 liquid fertilizer plants in the United States; in 1967 about 1,500 liquid and suspension plants; and by 1980, 3,200 fluid plants (17,35).

NFSA took a big step in the educational arena in 1967 when it launched its first Round-Up in St. Louis, which attracted more than 800 industry members. The purpose of the Round-Up was to help close a widening gap between the basic research areas and the applied aspects of fluid fertilizer use. Consumption and membership skyrocketed the NFSA's responsibilities; member services were broadened and its physical accommodations and staff were increased. A full component of sales and marketing aids was developed for members, including brochures promoting fluid fertilizers. These included, in addition to the magazine, a Fertilizer Manual, newsetters, dealer training schools, insurance programs for members and their employees, and grant-in-aid programs for agronomic research to colleges and universities. In 1974, Richard L. Gilliland became Executive Vice-President, replacing Harold Schelm, who had retired. Gilliland held the position until 1979 when David K. Murray, a long time NFSA employee, took over. In 1974 and again in 1979, NFSA had to move to larger quarters. Its staff increased to 17 people (32).

The strength of NFSA and the loyalty of its members was demonstrated in 1969-70 when the Agricultural Nitrogen Institute and the National Plant Food Institute formed the strong Fertilizer Institute. NFSA was expected also to join the merger but the NFSA Board voted to retain its own association (8,21).

NFSA experienced an era of outstanding progress during the 1970's. Member services were further strengthened and membership continued to grow. Membership totaled 445 companies in January 1973; 1,000 by mid-1975; and 1,400 in 1979 (32).

The Fertilizer Institute

Following the resignation of Paul Truitt, Edwin M. Wheeler was selected as NPFI's president in September 1968. Wheeler, a successful lawyer, had been assistant to the president of the Santa Fe Railroad. He was resolved to change NPFI's emphasis and improve its image. In 1970, the Agricultural Nitrogen Institute merged with NPFI to form The Fertilizer Institute (16).

Wheeler wasted no time in searching out the weaknesses and strong points of the NPFI. Meetings were held with fertilizer leaders to examine the responsibilities of the fertilizer industry and its needs. Most of those interviewed favored the formation of a single, strong association–one that would also play an active role (33).

Wheeler with Gary D. Myers, Executive Vice-President, set up a logical system of voting membership representation. A 36-member Board of Directors would be elected as follows: Class A, made up of 15 producers of primary, secondary, and micronutrient plant food elements; Class B representing 6 fertilizer manufacturers; Class C, 9 members representing fertilizer distributors and retail dealers; Class D, 4 from manufacturers or jobbers of fertilizer equipment, manufacturers of additives except pesticides, and engineering compounds servicing the fertilizer industry; and 2 elected at large. In 1976, the Board was increased to 39. W.J. Turbeville, Jr. was the first chairman of the TFI Board, and Nelson D. Abell, the first Vice-President (34).

The TFI expanded its staff and activities during the 1970's, especially in public relations and government affairs. The old regional and state offices of NPFI were eliminated, and agricultural research and educational programs were de-emphasized. Instead of functional TFI regional and state offices, the organization established affiliations and working relationships with those state associations supported and controlled by the local industry (16).

Fertilizer Progress, the official magazine of TFI, appeared out of the merger of NPFI and ANI in 1970. The new publication appeared bimonthly–January, March, May, July, September, and November. It published articles of current interest or concern to the industry.

TFI also initiated a new financial data service for its members–Fertilizer Financial Facts. It was described as "How is your company doing as compared with the rest of the fertilizer industry" (34).

TFI wasted no time in broadening the knowledge of the association. The first annual TFI convention was held at White Sulphur Springs, West Virginia, in June 1970. Almost 1,000 people representing all segments of the fertilizer industry attended, including 32 TFI state and regional affiliates in the United States and five in Canada. TFI also initiated industry trade fairs featuring exhibits, educational sessions and field demonstrations of application equipment. The first trade fair was held at Overland Park in Kansas City, Kansas, in August 1971.

In addition to trade fairs, the TFI staff also provides members services, arranges meetings and conferences, and maintains liaison with legislative bodies, regulating agencies, and other organizations and groups. The Institute is recognized by the U.S. Congress as the single voice of the plant food industry (25). In 1980, with its 39-member Board, the member companies participated actively on 10 "action" committees covering key areas of concern or of interest to the industry and agriculture. The Washington headquarters staff numbered 34 in 1980.

During Wheeler's tenure as President of TFI, the association became more powerful and innovative. At the same time it has been flexible and responsive to its members' changing needs (16).

The Sulphur Institute

The Sulphur Institute (TSI) was organized in 1959 by basic producers of sulfur. The mandate was to increase sulfur consumption in industry and agriculture on a world-wide basis by developing new uses, and products and new processes through technical research. Financial support was to be obtained by assessing sulfur producers on a per ton basis. Offices were to be established at Washington, D.C. and London, England. The TSI was patterned after the American Petroleum Institute (20).

TSI selected Dr. Russell Coleman, an agronomist, as president in 1960. Coleman, a nationally known leader in fertilizers and agriculture, most recently had been vice-president of the NPFI.

Sulfuric acid is a key material in manufacturing soluble phosphate fertilizers necessary to increase crop yields and quality. Sulfur and some of its acid-forming compounds are used to improve water-penetration and soil conditions in arid irrigated areas. These conditions occur not only in the United States and Canada but also in many other parts of the world.

Also associated with TSI in the 1960's was another agronomist, Dr. Samuel L. Tisdale. Tisdale was a former regional director of the National Plant Food Institute. He served TSI as Director of Agricultural Research and was promoted to Vice-President in 1965 and later to Executive Vice-President (24, 29, 31).

Since 1960, TSI sponsored and supported research and development programs on uses of sulfur in agriculture. TSI has no research facilitites of its own. Its agricultural programs were carried out through grants or research centers. By 1977, such grants had supported work in Western Europe, Africa, Australia, South America, Canada, and the United States. Sulfur deficiencies and responses have been noted in all of these areas. Sulfur deficiencies have been observed in 35 states, including Alaska and Hawaii, and from Ontario westward in Canada (30).

TSI published a series of technical bulletins on various aspects of sulfur in agriculture of interest to both research and extension workers and the fertilizer industry (9). By 1980, interest in sulfur as a plant nutrient had increased to the point where many professional people consider it the "fourth major nutrient" (10, 26, 30).

Some of the more effective fertilizer activities of TSI have been the Phosphate-Sulphur Symposia–eight of which had been held by 1980. Other fertilizer activities of TSI have included identifying new locations where there is a need for sulfur as a plant nutrient. In the arid-irrigated soils of the western United States, which are highly alkaline and calcareous, sulfur and its compounds are used to keep them productive (29). In addition to agriculture, TSI is charged with carrying out a variety of new or existing industrial uses supported by appropriate information and promotion activities. These include corrosion-resistant sulfur concrete, sulfur-asphalt paving, pigments, and use of sulfur in recycling conventional asphalt pavements. Sulfur asphalt is established commercial technology. Use of sulfur in agriculture has increased dramatically, partly due to the rapid increase most years of ammonium phosphates in both U. S. consumption and export (14).

By 1981, considerable changes had taken place in membership. Dr. Tisdale had replaced Coleman, who retired in 1979 and established his own consulting firm. The members and voting representatives had reached 24: 10 from the United States, 7 from Canada, 2 from Mexico, 3 from Japan, 2 from Spain, and 1 each from Italy, Finland, France, Norway, Saudi Arabia, Sweden, and West Germany. In addition, there were associate members and two honorary members. The Board of Directors had 30 members (11, 26). Seven members served on the Executive Committee with C.F. Fogarty, Chairman. Four committees in addition to the Executive were set up: Finance/Audit, Advisory Committee on Program Development, European Advisory, and the Advisory Committee on Agricultural Research (11).

In 1980-81, the TSI staff involved only eight people. There were Tisdale, President; H.L. Fike, Vice-President; Secretary and Treasurer A. Carpenter, Vice-President-Europe, located in Paris; H.L. Fike, also Director of Industrial Research; Vacant Director of Agricultural Research; J.S. Plateau, Director of Information; D.W. Bixby, Director of Fertilizer Technology; and C.A.. McCord, Director of Administration. The Institute's programs are not carried out through a large staff but by grants-in-aid to public and private research. Research projects in 1980-81 were in 23 countries, and the organization worked with professionals in over 150 research and educational institutions (11).

Summary

Nine different fertilizer associations operated at one time or another during the 1920-1980 period. All dealt primarily with fertilizers and were replete with officers and staffs–serving one overriding objective, that of selling fertilizer and fertilizer equipment. At the same time, most helped the farmers make more money and in turn buy even more fertilizers the following year. Some associations were more innovative and did this better than others. While some people in the associations were motivated only by sales, others looked upon their role as an opportunity to help farmers use fertilizers more effectively.

During the 60-year period covered in this chapter, some associations spent a good share of their time battling U.S. Government fertilizer policies and responding to anti-trust violations while others served as a liaison between the government and the fertilizer industry. Discord within associations sometimes resulted in splits of membership that led to formation of new associations or merging of several. The longevity of an association varied greatly, ranging from a few years to half a century. Leadership capabilities within an association also varied considerably.

Overall, the fertilizer trade association filled a necessary function, without which the fertilizer industry could not have prospered. During the 1960's and 1970's, TVA's National Fertilizer Development Center worked closely with the major associations in sponsoring joint conferences and workshops and determining priority fertilizer research needs.

REFERENCES

1. Abell, N.D. 1965. The president's message. *Agric. Ammonia News.* 15 (14): 2.
2. Anon. 1893. Associated Fertilizer Manufacturers. *The Amer. Fertilizer* 1 (4): 228-230.
3. _____. 1935. American Potash Institute is incorporated. *Comm. Fert.* 51 (1): 24-26.
4. _____. 1944. Secretary Wickard criticizes Hill fertilizer bill. *Amer. Fert.* 101 (12): 11-12.
5. _____. 1945. Formation of the American Plant Food Council. *Amer. Fert.* 102 (12): 11 and Amer. Fert. 103 (2): 13.
6. _____. 1954. Editorial Section entitled "Mono Jenkins" *Agric. Ammonia News.* 4 (1): 9
7. _____. 1955. American Potash Institute observes 20th birthday. *Croplife* 2 (40): 1, 8.
8. _____. 1970. ANI votes for merger into the Fertilizer Institute. *Croplife.* Jan. 1970: P.18.
9. _____. 1977. Potash Institute adopts phosphate program. *Green Markets* 1 (26): 7-8.
10. _____. 1977. News and notes—technical bulletins available. In *Sulphur in Agric.* Vol. 1 p. 18.
11. *Annual Report 1980/81.* The Sulphur Institute. 16 pp. Washington, D.C.

12. Brand, C.J. 1939. Current problems of the fertilizer industry. *Comm. Fert.* 59 (3): 10,12, 14-21).
13. _____. 1940. A brief history of the National Fertilizer Association. *Comm. Fert.* 61 (1): 12, 14-16.
14. Bridges, J.D. 1982. *Fertilizer Trends.* Bull.Y-176. National Fertilizer Development Center, TVA, Muscle Shoals, Ala.
15. Burns, J.M. and J.W. Peltuson. 1966. Government by the people. Sixth Ed. In 11, *The Dynamic Role of Interest Groups.* pp. 278-305. Publ. by Prentice-Hall Inc. Englewood Cliffs, New Jersey.
16. Coleman, R. and L.B. Nelson. 1983. Your fertilizer association: a century of progress. *Fert. Progress.* 14 (3): 12-13, 24-25,32.
17. Getsinger, J.G., F.P. Achorn, and G. Hoffmeister. 1984. *Suspension fertilizers - production and use.* Bull. Y-185. National Fertilizer Development Center, TVA. Muscle Shoals, Ala.
18. Grissom, F.H. 1957. 10 years of anhydrous ammonia in the Mississippi Delta. *Agricultural Ammonia News.* 7 (2): 13-14, 58-59.
19. Harre, E. A., M.N. Goodson, and J.D. Bridges. 1976. *Fertilizer Trends.* Bull. Y-111. National Fertilizer Development Center, TVA, Muscle Shoals, Ala.
20. Larson, L.P. and J.M. Poley. 1959. Sulfur and pyrites. In *1959 Mineral Yearbook Vol. 1. Metals and Minerals* pp. 1035-1058. U.S. Bureau of Mines.
21. Long, L. 1969. Unification of three fertilizer groups moves nearer as NPFI Board ratifies merger. *Croplife.* Nov. 1969. p. 7.
22. Markham, J.W. 1958. *The Fertilizer Industry, a Study of an Imperfect Market.* p.90. Vanderbilt University Press, Nashville, Tenn.
23. Mehring, A.L., J.R. Adams, and K.D. Jacob. 1957. *Statistics of fertilizer and liming materials in the United States.* U.S. Dept. Agric. Statistical Bull. 191. Washington, D. C.
24. Nelson, L.B. 1981. Bob Wagner: man with a mission. *Farm Chemicals.* 144 (4): 23, 26.
25. _____. 1982. Ed Wheeler of TFI. *Farm Chemicals.* 145 (2): 23-26.
26. _____. 1982. Mr. Dealer, meet Mr. Sulfur. *Farm Chemicals.* 145 (4): 42-44.
27. Romaine, J.D. 1955. American Potash Institute, what it does and how it does. *Comm. Fert.* 91 (3): 48-49, 51-52.
28. Sloan, J.F. 1970. A message from the outgoing president. *Agric. Ammonia News.* 20 (1): 4.
29. Stromberg, L.K. and S. L. Tisdale. 1979. *Treating irrigated arid land with acid-forming sulphur compounds.* The Sulphur Institute Tech. Bull. 24. Washington, D. C.
30. Tisdale, S. L. 1977. Sulphur in agriculture - 17 years of research. In *Sulphur in Agriculture.* Vol. 1. pp. 2-3, 17. Publ. by The Sulphur Inst. Washington, D.C.
31. _____. 1982. *Sam Tisdale interview: the Sulphur Institute.* Biographical Information. Typed. Prepared at request of L.B. Nelson.
32. van Buren, N. 1979. 25 years of progress culminates in St. Louis. *Fertilizer Solutions.* 23 (6): 8, 10, 12, 16, 18, 30, 32.
33. Wheeler, E. M. 1969. NPFI to remain flexible enough to accommodate industry changes. *Croplife.* March, 1969. pp. 26-28.
34. _____. 1970. A new and expanded Institute serves the entire industry. *Fertilizer Progress.* 1 (1): 15-16.
35. Young, R.D. and N.L. Hargett. 1984. History, growth, and status. In *Fluid Fertilizers,* J.M. Potts, Ed. Chapt. l, History, Growth, and Status.Bull. Y-185. pp.5-13. National Fertilizer Development Center. TVA. Muscle Shoals, Ala.

SELECTED READINGS

Blakey, A. F. 1973. *The Florida Phosphate Industry: A History of Development and Use of a Vital Mineral.* Harvard University Press, Cambridge, Mass.

Carrier, L. 1923. *The Beginnings of Agriculture in America.* McGraw-Hill Book Co., Inc. New York.

Chazal, P. E. 1904. *The Century in Phosphates and Fertilizers--A Sketch of the South Carolina Phosphate Industry.* Lucas-Richardson, Charleston, SC.

Clarke, M. 1977. "The Federal Government and the fixed nitrogen industry. 1915-1926." Oregon State University Ph.D. thesis; copies available through University Microfilms International, Ann Arbor, Michigan.

Cochrane, W. W. 1979. *The Development of American Agriculture.* University of Minnesota Press, Minneapolis.

Collings, G. W. 1941. *Commercial Fertilizers.* The Blakiston Co., Philadelphia.

Eddy, E. D., Jr. 1956. *Colleges for Our Land and Time.* Harper and Brothers, New York.

Fussel, G. E. 1965. *Farming Technique from Prehistoric to Modern Times.* Pergamon Press Ltd., London.

_____. 1971. *Crop Nutrition: Science and Practice before Liebig.* Coronado Press, Lawrence, Kansas.

Gray, L. C. 1933. *History of Agriculture in the Southern United States to 1860.* Carnegie Institute, Washington, D.C.

Hubbard, P. J. 1961. *Origins of TVA, the Muscle Shoals Controversy. 1920-1932.* Vanderbilt University Press, Nashville, TN.

Jacob, K. D. 1964. *Superphosphate: Its History, Chemistry, and Manufacture.* U.S. Dept. Agr. and Tennessee Valley Authority. U.S. Government Printing Office, Washington, D.C.

Johnson, S. W. 1968. *How Crops Grow: A Treatise on the Chemical Composition, Structure, and Life of the Plant.* Orange Judd & C., New York.

_____. 1870. *How Crops Feed: A Treatise on the Atmosphere and the Soil as Related to the Nutrition of Agricultural Plants.* Orange Judd & Co.

Liebig, J. 1940. *Organic Chemistry and its Application to Agriculture and Physiology.* Ed. by L. Playfair. Taylor and Walton, London.

Markham, J. W. 1958. *The Fertilizer Industry: A Study of an Imperfect Market.* Vanderbilt University Press, Nashivlle, TN.

Noyes, R. 1966. *Potash and Potassium Fertilizers.* Chemical process monograph No. 15. Noyes Development Corp. Park Ridge, NJ.

Reed, H. S. 1942. *A Short History of Plant Sciences.* Chronica Botannicca co., Waltham, MA.

Rossiter, M. W. 1975. *The Emergence of Agricultural Science: Justice Liebig and the Americans. 1840-1880.* Yale University Press, New Haven and London.

Ruffin, E. 1832. *An Essay on Calcareous Manure.* Published by J. W. Campbell. Petersburg, VA.

Slack, A. V. 1973. "History and status of ammonia production and use." In *Ammonia*, ed., by A. V. Slack and G. R. James. pp. 5-142. Marcel Dekker, Inc., New York.

Stocking, G. W. 1931. *The Potash Industry, A Study of State Control.* Richard R. Smith, Inc., New York.

Tisdale, S. T. and W. L. Nelson. 1975. "Soil fertility--past and present." In *Soil Fertility and Fertilizers*, third edition, published by MacMillan Publishing Co., Inc.

True, A. C. 1894. "Education and research in agriculture in the United States." U.S. Department of Agriculture. *Yearbook*, pp. 81-116. U.S. Government Printing Office, Washington, D.C.

_____. 1929. "A history of agricultural education in the United States--1785-1925." U.S. Department of Agriculture, Misc. Pub. No. 36, U.S. Government Printing Office, Washington D.C.

_____. 1937. "A history of agricultural experimentation and research in the United States--1607-1925." U.S. Department of Agriculture, Misc. Pub. No. 251. U.S. Government Printing Office, Washington, D.C.

INDEX

Agricultural Ammonia Institute, 500-502 (see Agricultural Nitrogen Institute)
Agricultural Institutions
   State Agricultural Colleges, 97, 130, 131
   State Agricultural Experiment Stations, 97, 131, 134
   State Extension Services, 134-135
   U.S. Department of Agriculture, 34, 97, 135-136
Agricultural Nitrogen Institute, 502, 505, 506 (see Agricultural Ammonia Institute, Fertilizer Institute)
Agricultural training
   colleges, 31-34
   Grange movement, 134
   Morrill Act, 130, 133
   Smith-Lever Act, 135
   vocational schools, 33
Agrico Chemical Company, 245, 347 (see Williams Bros., American Agricultural Chemical Co., Continental Oil Co., Spencer Chemical Co., Palmetto Phosphate Co., Peace River Co., Pierce Phos. Co.)
Allied Chemical and Dye
   ammonia production, 226, 229, 323, 325, 326-7, 329, 332-333, 341, 345, 347
   ammoniation of superphosphate, 368
   nitrogen solutions, 370
   nitric phosphate production, 392
   micronutrient survey, 419
   sodium nitrate process, 354
Amalgamated Phosphate Company, 71, 243 (see American Cyanamid Co.)
Amax Chemical Corporation, 311, 398 (see Southwest Potash)

American Agricultural Chemical Company (see Agrico)
   Chilean nitrate, 108
   phosphate rock mining (71, 79, 106, 243, 244, 253
   superphosphate production 103, 380
American Cyanamid Company (see Kerr-McGee, Brewster Phosphates)
   ammonium phosphates, 383, 385
   ammonia synthesis, 345, 347
   calcium cyanamide, 111, 197, 205, 211-213, 217, 219-220
   Muscle Shoals facilities, 224-225
   phosphate rock mining, 244, 247
American Phosphate and Chemical Company, 117, 118
American Plant Food Council, 498 (see National Plant Food Institute)
American Potash Company, 186, 187 (see United States Potash Co.)
American Potash and Chemical Company, 498, 499 (see American Trona Corp.)
American Potash Institute, 498-500 (see Potash and Phosphate Institute)
American Trona Corporation, 184 (see American Potash and Chemical Co.)
Ammonia
   feedstock, 329-332
   large plant development, 333-336
   production capacities, 325-327, 331, 332, 335-336, 340-342, 344-348
   storage and transport, 336-339
   synthesis, 198-202, 208-211, 323-347
Ammoniation-granulator, 388
Ammonium chloride, 13

Ammonium nitrate, 217, 324, 325, 327, 332, 344
  conditioners, 359
  explosion hazard, 360-361
  manufacturing, 358-359
  production and use, 361
Ammonium phosphates, 107, 119, 217, 238, 260, 372
  ammonium polyphosphate, 372, 376-377, 452
  diammonium phosphate, 260, 387-388
  exports, 237
  monoammonium phosphate, 385-387
  process reactions, 385
Ammonium sulfate, 6, 13, 44, 107, 110-111, 217
  manufacturing process, 355-356
  soil acidity effects, 138
Anhydrous ammonia, 324, 333, 362-365
  consumption, 365
  direct application to soil, 362-365
  hazards, 362
  use in irrigation water, 362
Anaconda Copper Mining Company, 255, 256, 257 (see J. R. Simplot Co.)
Andrews, W. B., 363, 367
Armour Fertilizer Works (see Armour Agricultural Chemical Co., U.S. Steel, USS Agrichemicals)
  ammonia synthesis, 332
  mixed fertilizer, 434
  phosphate rock mining, 71, 79, 253, 254
  superphosphate, 103, 106, 117, 379
Armour Agricultural Chemical Company, 380 (see Armour Fertilizer Works)
Association of American Plant Food Control Officials (AAPFCO), 448, 455

Association of Official Agricultural Chemists (AOAC), 122
Atlantic Richfield Company, 264, 268, 271
Atmospheric Nitrogen Corporation, 226
Atwater, W. O., 132, 136
Badische Analin-und Soda Fabrik (BASF)
  ammonia synthesis, 199, 200, 201, 202, 203, 210, 229, 330
  nitrogen fixation, 195
  nitric phosphate, 392
  sulfuric acid, 128, 261
Baker (H. J.) and Bro., 108
Basic slag, 16, 118, 389-390
Baugh and Sons Company, 39, 40, 103, 106
Beker Industries, 259, 260, 345
Best Fertilizer Company, 246 (see Occidental Agricultural Chemical Co.)
Bones, 43
  acidulated, 13, 14, 15
  bone meal, 116, 120
Borden Company, 244, 245, 345, 347 (see Smith-Douglas, Inc.)
Boussingault, J. B., 19, 21
Brewster Phosphates, 244-245 (see American Cyanamid Co.)
Bulk blending, 315, 316, 431, 440, 444-448
  dealer services, 448
  leading grades, 448
  materials used, 446
  segregation, 315, 446-448
Bureau of Soils, USDA
  ammonia synthesis, 202, 209, 215
  byproducts as potash sources, 184
  kelp as potash source, 159-160, 165, 181, 190
Buttenbach (J.) and Company, 67, 69
Calcium as plant nutrient, 408-409
Calcium cyanamide, 107, 111-112, 351-352
  characterization and use, 357

Muscle Shoals plant, 211-214, 217, 218
process, 196-197
Calcium nitrate, 217, 218, 391
Calcium metaphosphate, 258, 390
Camp (C and J) Phosphate Company, 67
Carnallite, 121, 156, 288, 393
Central Canada Potash, 302, 303, 304 (see CF Industries)
Central Farmers Fertilizer Company (see CF Industries)
   ammonia synthesis, 345, 347
   phosphate rock mining, 245, 258
   potash mining, 318
Central Phosphate Company, 78 (see CF Industries)
CF Industries, 318
Charleston Mining and Manufacturing Company, 57, 71, 78, 79, 253 (see Virginia-Carolina Chemical Co., Mobil Chemical Co.)
Chevron Chemical Company
   ammonia synthesis, 341, 347
   nitric phosphate, 392
Chilean nitrate, 107, 193, 204, 352, 353, 354, (see sodium nitrate)
Cities Service Oil Company (see Tennessee Corp., Gardinier)
   ammonia synthesis, 345
   phosphate rock mining, 244
   recovered sulfur, 270
Collier Carbon, 341
Columbian Phosphate Company, 77
Concentrated superphosphate, 107, 117, 237-238, 244, 260, 371, 380
   cone mixer, 382
   process reaction, 378
   rotary drum granulator, 382-383
Consolidated Mining and Smelting Company (COMINCO)
   ammonia synthesis, 347
   monoammonium phosphate, 385
   phosphate rock mining, 256
   phosphoric acid production, 373

Continental Oil Company, 244 (see Agrico)
Coronet Phosphate Company, 71, 243
Cottonseed meal, 45, 113
Crookes, Sir William, 194
Crop yield increases, 481-486
   effect of fertilizer inputs, 485
   other production practices, 484-486
Davison Chemical Corporation, 244, 380, 437 (see W. R. Grace, Southern Phosphate Co.)
Davy, Sir Humphrey, 10, 30
DeSaussure, Theodore, 10
Dickson, David, 46-47
Dorr Company, 118, 386-387
Dow Chemical, 345, 347
Duck River Phosphate Company, 74
Ducktown Sulphur, Copper and Iron Company, Ltd., 87-88
Dunnellon Phosphate, 66, 67
DuPont, E. I., de Nemours and Company, 345, 347
   ammoniating superphosphate, 368
   ammonia synthesis, 227, 323, 325, 329, 332
   capacity, 341
   transportation, 333
   sulfur pyrite mining, 87
   urea production, 365, 366
Duval Corporation (see Duval Texas Sulfur Co.)
   Frasch sulfur mining, 263, 264, 265, 267, 268, 269
   potash mining, 307, 308, 311
   potassium magnesium sulfate production, 396
   potassium sulfate production, 397
Duval Sulphur and Potash Company, 499
Duval Texas Sulphur Company, 262, 263 (see Duval Corp.)
Early agriculture
   Arabs, 3
   American colonists, 24-26
   American Indians, 23-24
   Greeks, 1

improvement efforts, 28-29
Romans, 2
Electric phosphorus furnaces, 252-254
Enriched superphosphate, 378
Environmental problems
    mining and manufacturing, 247-249, 399-400
    on farms, 491
FMC Corporation, 347
Farmer cooperatives, 347
Farmland Industries, 245, 389
    ammonia production, 345, 347
    Frasch sulfur mining, 265
Federal Chemical Company, 75, 79, 253, 254
Fertilizer application methods, 456-463
Fertilizer consumption
    1870-1920, 99-105
    1920-1980, 469-491
    by geographic regions, 471-480
Fertilizer control laws, 49, 128, 129
    Association of Official Agricultural Chemists (AOAC), 129
Fertilizer evaluation
    early tests, 49
    field experiments, 136-140
Fertilizer grades, 433-434, 442
Fertilizer industry (early development)
    company consolidation, 102-107
    expansion, 45
    frauds, 48
    geographic shifts, 46, 99
    inspection, control laws, 49, 97
Fertilizer Institute, The, 506-507 (see The Agricultural Nitrogen Institute, The National Plant Food Institute, Middle West Soil Improvement Committee)
Fertilizer journals, 148
Fertilizer testing (see fertilizer evaluation)
Fertilizer trade associations
    fertilizer associations, 145, 146
    fertilizer exchanges, 145
    institute formation, 498-508
    soil improvement committees, 146
Fertilizer use
    shifts in use, 99, 480-481
    substitute for land, 488
Fish scrap, 41-42
Fixed Nitrogen Research Laboratory, 215-217, 227, 229
Florida Mining Company, 71 (see International Agricultural Corp.)
Florida Phosphate Council, 247, 248
Florida Phosphate Mining Company, 71, 243 (see Royster Guano Co.)
Florida phosphate rock deposits
    hard rock, 63-64, 65, 66, 235, 241
    land pebble, 63, 69, 70, 71, 243
    river pebble, 63, 67, 68, 69
    soft rock, 64, 67, 235, 242
Franklin, Benjamin, 27
Fluid fertilizers
    liquid mixes, 376, 377, 431, 449-452
    suspension mixes, 431-432, 453-456
Frasch, Herman, 91
Frasch process, 262-269
Freeport Sulphur Company, 92, 262, 264, 265, 266 (see National Potash Co.)
Fused phosphates, 390-391
Gardinier, 245 (see Cities Service)
Gilbert, Joseph Henry, 17
Glauber, Johann, 8, 358
Goessman, Charles A., 50, 51
Grace (W. R.) and Company (see Davison Chemical Co.)
    ammonia production, 345, 347
    Chilean nitrate, 108
    phosphate rock mining, 245
    normal superphosphate production, 40
Great Salt Lakes Minerals and Chemicals Corporation, 307, 308, 313, 397

Green Revolution, 486
Grange (The), 134
Guano (see natural organic nitrogen materials), 11, 34-36, 114
　bat guano, 113
　Peruvian, 23, 34-35
　phospho-guano, 35, 39
Gypsum
　early soil application, 26, 27
　in normal superphosphate, 378
　removed from wet process phosphoric acid, 373-374
　source of sulfur, 411, 412
Hall, A. D., 19
Harsh Phosphate Company, 253, 254
Hatch Act, 130, 133, 134, 136
Hellriegel and Wilfarth, 21
Hercules Powder Company, 325-327, 329, 345
Hooker Chemical Company, 254 (see Occidental Agricultural Chemical Corporation)
Hoover and Mason Phosphate Company, 253, 254
Hopkins, C. G., 119, 131, 147, 389
Humbolt, Alexander, Von, 11
Humus theory, 2, 16
International assistance, 486-488
International Fertilizer Development Center (IFDC), 488
International Ore and Fertilizer Corporation (Interore), 246
International Phosphate Company, 71
Interstate Chemical Company, 71
International Agricultural Corporation (see International Minerals and Chemical Corp., Florida Mining Co.)
　mixed fertilizer production, 103, 106
　phosphate rock mining, 71, 78, 79, 254
　sulfuric acid production, 88
International Minerals and Chemical Corporation (see International Agricultural Corporation)
　normal superphosphate production, 380
　phosphate rock mining, 71, 243-244, 245, 254
　potash mining in U.S., 286-287, 289, 307, 308, 310, 316, 318, 393
　potash mining in Canada, 281, 297, 302, 310
　potassium magnesium sulfate production (langbeinite), 396, 397, 398
　suspension fertilizers, 454
Jefferson, Thomas, 29
Johnson, S.W., 48, 51, 129, 131, 132
Jones, Charles C., 80
Kainite, 122, 393, 397
Kaiser Aluminum and Chemical Corporation, 308, 312, 347, 391
Kalium Chemicals, 298, 300, 301, 303, 318
Kellogg (M. W.) Company, 333
Kelp, 159-160, 165, 181, 190
Kermac Potash Company, 291-292, 308-309, 310
Kerr-McGee, 244, 309 (see American Cyanamid Co.)
Land-grant colleges, 130-131
Langbeinite (see potassium magnesium sulfate)
Law of Minimum, 17
Lavoisier, Antoine-Laurent, 19
Lawes, Sir John, 13, 14, 15, 17, 18, 36
Legumes, 21, 352
Liebig, Justus von, 11, 13, 14, 16, 31, 32
Lion Oil, 326, 332 (see Monsanto Chemical Co.)
Liquid fertilizers (see fluid fertilizers)
Manure salts, 122, 392
Mapes, James J., 36-37
Mathieson and Hegler Zinc Company, 87

Mathieson Alkali Works, 227, 325, 326
Mathieson Chemical Corporation, 386
    (see Olin-Mathicson)
Meadows (T. C.) and Company, 77
Micronutrients
    deficiency surveys, 419-420
    deficiency symptoms, 415-519
    essential for plant growth, 413-415
    marketing, 421-422
    sources and materials, 422-427
    use (consumption), 420
Middle West Soil Improvement Committee, 146, 147, 498 (see National Plant Food Institute)
Mississippi Chemical Corporation, 309, 318, 345, 347, 365
Missouri Farmers Association, 386, 443
Mixed fertilizers, 36, 106, 107, 123-126, 431-464
    1920-1950, 432-438
    1950-1980, 438-455
    bulk blends, 431, 440, 444-448
    consumption, 440
    fluid mixtures, 440, 448-456
        liquid mixes, 376, 377, 431, 449-452
        suspension mixes, 431-432, 453-456
    granular, homogeneous mixtures, 431, 440, 441-443
    marketing system, 438
Mobil Chemical Company, 244, 445, 254, 345 (see Virginia-Carolina Chemical Corp.)
Monocalcium phosphate, 378
Monsanto Chemical Company (see Lion Oil)
    ammonia production, 341, 345, 347
    phosphate rock mining, 254, 258, 259, 260
    sulfuric acid production, 261
Montana Phosphate Products Company, 256, 257
Muscle Shoals controversy, 218-226
Nashville Fertilizer Company, 74

National Fertilizer Association, Inc. 146, 147, 226, 435, 458, 495-497 (see The Southern Fertilizer Association, National Plant Food Institute)
National Fertilizer Development Center, 487 (see The Tennessee Valley Authority)
National Fertilizer Solutions Association, 461, 503, 505
National Plant Food Institute, 498, 505 (see Fertilizer Institute)
National Potash Company, 307, 308, 309, 311 (see Freeport Sulphur Co.)
Natural organic nitrogen materials
    animal tankage, 112
    cottonseed meal, 45, 113
    fish scrap, 41-42, 114
    guano, 11, 34-36, 113, 114
    poudrette (human waste), 45, 113
New Jersey Zinc Company, 87, 128
Niagara Ammonia Company, 227
Nitrate of soda, 11, 12, 13 (see sodium nitrate)
Nitric acid, 7, 202, 332, 372
    production improvements, 357-358
Nitric phosphates, 391-392
Nitrification, 20
Nitrobacter, 20
Nitrogen, 18
    consumption, 324-325, 339, 342
    export and import, 343-344
    in fertilizer, 323, 324, 325
Nitrogen industry, 193-220, 323-347
Nitrogen fixation processes
    ammonia, 198-202
    arc, 194-196
    cyanamide, 196-197
    cyanide, 197
Nitrogen solutions, 324, 332, 367-370
    aqua ammonia, 367
    manufacturing and equipment, 369-370
    production and use, 370

solutions for direct application, 368-369
urea-ammonium nitrate solutions, 369
use in irrigation water, 362, 449
Nitrophosphates (see nitric phosphates)
Nitrosomonas, 20
Normal superphosphate (see superphosphate)
North Carolina phosphate deposits, 249
Occidental Agricultural Chemical Corporation, 245, 246 (see Hooker Chemical Co., Best Fertilizer Co.)
Olin Corporation, 347
Olin-Mathieson, 326, 354 (see Mathieson Chemical Co.)
Ordinary superphosphate (see superphosphate)
Owens Agricultural Phosphate Corporation, 254
Pacific Guano Company, 57
Palmetto Phosphate Company, 71 (see Agrico)
Peace River Company, 68, 69 (see American Agricultural Co.)
Phillips Chemical, 326, 332, 341, 347
Pierce Phosphate Company, 71 (see Agrico)
Pipe-cross reactor, 443, 444
Pipe reactor, 377
Pharr Phosphate Company, 69
Phosphate Export Association, 241, 245
Phosphate rock deposits, 16, 233
  beneficiation, 239-241
  direct application, 119, 138, 147, 237, 254, 388-389
  discovery and development, 55-85
    Florida, 63-72
    North Carolina, 249-250
    South Carolina, 55-63
    Tennessee, 72-79, 250-254
    Western, 79-84, 255-260
  exports, 233, 236
  mining, 238-239
  production by states, 234
  reserves, 236
  thermal treatment, 372
Phosphate Rock Export Association (PHOSROCK), 250
Phosphogypsum, 248, 400 (see gypsum)
Phosphoric acid, 260-261
  furnace-grade acid, 375-376, 377, 383
  superphosphoric acid, 372, 376-377, 452, 504
  wet-process acid, 118, 351, 371, 373-375, 385
  exports, 237, 375
  process, 373
  production, 374
  use in irrigation water, 449
Plant nutrients, 140
  composition in crops, 141
  determining soil fertilizer levels, 141-145
  fate of applied nutrients in soils, 140
Plant nutrition, 8-21
Potash and Phosphate Institute, 500 (see American Potash Institute)
Potash beneficiation, 285-287, 292-295
Potash Company of America
  mining in Canada, 297, 303
  mining at Carlsbad, 189, 283, 285-286, 293, 308, 309-310
  potassium sulfate production, 397
Potash consumption, 122, 123, 282
Potash mines
  Carlsbad, 186-190, 281-295
  Canadian, 295-304, 317
Potash mining
  in Canada, 281, 297, 302
  in U.S., 286-287, 289, 307, 308
Potash particle size grades, 314-315, 395
Potash production
  Canada, 295-304
  Carlsbad, 281-283, 285, 288, 304, 307, 308-309, 317

Searles Lake, 281, 283, 284, 304, 308
Potash reserves, 318 (U.S. Bureau of Mines)
Potash sources examined before Carlsbad discovery, 155-186
Potassium chloride, 394-396, 433
Potassium magnesium sulfate (langbeinite), 122, 287, 293, 396, 397, 410, 411
Potassium nitrate, 18, 398
Potassium sulfate, 122, 283, 315, 316, 393, 396-398, 398, 411
Presnell Phosphate Company, 254
Priestly, Joseph, 9
Rhizobia, 21, 140
Rothamsted Experiment Station, 14, 15, 17, 18, 19
Royster (F. S.) Guano Company, 71, 103, 106, 244, 380 (see Florida Phosphate Mining Co.)
Ruffin, Edmund, 30, 46, 56
Russell, E. John, 17
Saltpeter, 6 (see potassium nitrate)
San Francisco Chemical Company, 81, 84, 255, 256, 257
Scott's Fertilizer Company, 69
Secondary nutrients
    calcium, 408-409
    magnesium, 409-410
    sulfur, 411-413
Sewage sludge, 352-353
Shell Chemical Company
    adding ammonia to irrigation water, 362
    ammonia synthesis, 229, 323, 325, 326, 329-330, 345
    diammonium phosphate production, 387, 388
    injection of ammonia into soil, 362-363
Simplot (J. R.), 256, 257, 259, 260, 345 (see Anaconda Copper and Mining Co.)
Slaughterhouse wastes, 42-43

Slow-release nitrogen materials
    sulfur-coated urea, 370
    urea-formaldehyde, 370
Smith-Douglas, Inc., 244 (see Borden Company)
Sodium nitrate, 13, 44, 107, 109, 138, 353 (see Chilean nitrate)
    consumption, 355
    manufacturing process, 354
Soil acidity
    liming needs, 138, 141
Soil fertility
    fate of added plant nutrients in soils, 140-141
    nutrient exhaustion, 27, 46, 47, 48, 101, 144
    soil analyses, 141-142
    soil testing, 142
Soil Improvement Committees, 146-147
Southern Fertilizer Association, 146, 496 (see National Fertilizer Association)
Southern Phosphate Company, 243 (see Davison Chemical Corp.)
Southwest Phosphate Company, 74
Southwest Potash Corporation, 290, 308, 315 (see Amax Chemical Corp.)
Spencer Chemical Co., 326, 329, 332, 341 (see Agrico Chemical Co.)
Standard Phosphate and Chemical Company, 79
State Phosphate Company, 71 (see Swift and Co.)
Stauffer Chemical Company
    electric phosphorus furnaces, 259
    mining of phosphate rock, 254, 258, 260
    mining of sulfur pyrites, 87
    recovered sulfur, 270
Stockbridge, Levi, 60
Sulfur, 6
    discovery and development, 85-93
    elemental sulfur, 88, 269
    Frasch mining, 91, 262-269

pyrites, 86-87, 262, 263, 274-275
smelter gases, 87-88
transportation, 272
Sulfuric acid, 13, 126
  manufacture, 127-128, 261
  use in phosphate fertilizer production, 260, 372-374, 378
Sulphur Institute,The, 507-508
Sulphuric and Superphosphate Manufacturing Company, 99
Superphosphates
  ammoniated superphosphates, 217, 333, 368, 369, 379, 431
  concentrated superphosphate, 107, 117, 237-238, 244, 260, 371, 380
    cone mixer, 382
    export, 383
    process reaction, 378
    production and use, 383
    rotary-drum granulator, 382-383
  crop response, 138
    early development, 13, 15, 36-41, 99
  enriched superphosphate, 378
  early producers, 103, 107
  exports, 237
  manufacturing process, 115-117, 378-380
  mixed fertilizers, 433
  normal superphosphate (also called ordinary superphosphate)
  shifts to higher analysis materials, 351, 371, 372
  source of calcium, 408
  uses, 237-238, 260
Swift and Company (see State Phosphate Co.)
  consolidation, 103
  entry into commercial fertilizers, 106
  monoammonium phosphate production, 387
  phosphate rock mining, 71, 243, 244
  superphosphate production, 380

Swift Chemical Company, 245 (ESMARK)
Swift Fertilizer Company, 79
Sylvite, 156, 186, 188, 282, 294, 295 (see potassium chloride)
Sylvinite ore, 186, 189, 282, 283, 287, 290, 291, 294, 296, 318
T-A Minerals Corporation, 245
TFI (see Fertilizer Institute)
Tennessee Chemical and Fertilizer Company, 88
Tennessee Corporation, 244 (see Cities Service Oil Co.)
Tennessee Phosphate Company, 74, 77
Tennessee phosphate field, 72-79, 250-254
  blue rock, 73, 76, 78, 235, 251
  brown rock, 72-73, 76, 77, 78, 251-254, 389
  white rock, 73, 74, 78
Tennessee Valley Authority (TVA) (see National Fertilizer Development Center)
  ammonia production, 326, 328, 332, 347
  ammonium nitrate, 327, 332, 359, 360
  ammonium polyphosphate, 452, 504
  bulk blends, 447-448
  calcium metaphosphate, 258, 390
  concentrated superphosphate, 382, 383
  continuous ammoniator-granulator, 384, 388
  diammonium phosphate, 388
  electric furnace treatment of phosphate rock, 242, 253, 372
  feedstock from coal, 343
  fertilizer effect on crop yield, 485
  fertilizer introduction, 383
  fused phosphates, 390-391
  granular, homogeneous mixed fertilizers, 441-442
  liquid mixed fertilizers, 449-453

monoammonium phosphate, 387
nitric phosphates, 391-392
phosphate rock mining, 242, 251, 252, 254
pipe-cross reactor, 443, 444
pipe reactor, 377, 453, 504
soil injection of ammonia, 363
sulfur-coated urea, 371
superphosphoric acid, 376, 377, 452, 504
suspension mixed fertilizers, 453-456, 505
Texas Gulf Sulphur Company (see Texasgulf, Inc.)
   phosphate rock mining, 249, 250
   potash mining, 290-291, 294, 308, 312, 318
   shipping elemental sulfur, 272
   sulfur mining, 92, 262, 264, 266, 267, 269
Texasgulf, Inc. (see Texas Gulf Sulphur Co.)
   mining of sulfur, 264, 265, 266, 268
   potash mining, 308, 312
The Fertilizer Institute (TFI) (see Fertilizer Institute, The)
Union Oil Company, 347
Union Phosphate Company, 81, 84
Union Sulphur Company, 93
United Phosphate and Chemical Company, 85
United Phosphate Company, 71
United States Department of Agriculture, 34
   Bureau of Soils, 135-136, 181
   early research and extension, 97
   electric furnace treatment of phosphate rock, 372
   fused phosphates, 390

United States Potash Company (see American Potash Co., U.S. Borax Co.)
   potash granulation, 316
   potash mining, Carlsbad, 186, 188, 283, 308, 309
Unocal Chemicals Division, 346 (see Union Oil Co.)
Urea, 7, 217
   production, 324, 332, 344, 365-367
   sulfur coating, 370
   use in fertilizer, 367
U. S. Borax Company, 285, 309 (see U. S. Potash)
U. S. Geological Survey
   search for potash deposits, 156-161, 163, 180-181, 185
U. S. Steel, 244, 347
USS Agrichemicals, 245, 347 (see U.S. Steel)
Valley Nitrogen Producers, Inc., 347
Von Helmont, Jan Baptiste, 7, 8
Ville, Georges, 19
Virginia-Carolina Chemical Company (see Mobil Chemicals Co.)
   ammonium phosphate, 120
   concentrated superphosphate, 117, 380
   consolidation, 103
   phosphate rock mining, 62, 71, 79, 106, 244, 254
Wando Fertilizer Company, 57, 99
Warington, Robert, 18, 19, 20
Washington, George, 27
Way, J. Thomas, 20
Western Phosphate Company, 82, 84
Western phosphate field, 79-84
Williams Bros., 245, 347 (see Agrico Chemical Co.)
Winogrodsky, S. N., 20
Wood ashes, 43